NAVIGATING THE MISSOURI

NAVIGATING THE MISSOURI

Steamboating on Nature's Highway, 1819–1935

WILLIAM E. LASS

THE ARTHUR H. CLARK COMPANY

An imprint of the University of Oklahoma Press

Norman, Oklahoma

2008

Also by William E. Lass

(with Wesley R. Hurt) *Frontier Photographer: Stanley J. Morrow's Dakota Years*
(Vermillion, S.Dak., 1956)
A History of Steamboating on the Upper Missouri (Lincoln, Nebr., 1962)
From the Missouri to the Great Salt Lake: An Account of Overland Freighting
(Lincoln, Nebr., 1972)
Minnesota: A Bicentennial History (New York, 1977)
Minnesota's Boundary with Canada: Its Evolution since 1783 (St. Paul, 1980)
Minnesota: A History, 2nd ed. (New York, 1998)

Library of Congress Cataloging-in-Publication Data

Lass, William E.
  Navigating the Missouri : steamboating on nature's highway, 1819–1935 / William
E. Lass.
     p. cm.
  Includes bibliographical references and index.
  ISBN 978-0-87062-355-4 (hardcover : alk. paper)
  1. Steam-navigation—Missouri River—History. 2. Missouri River—Navigation—
History. 3. River steamers—Missouri River—History. 4. Steamboats—Missouri
River—History. 5. Railroads—West (U.S.)—History. 6. Missouri River—Descrip-
tion and travel. 7. West (U.S.)—Commerce—History. 8. Missouri River Region—
Commerce—History. 9. Frontier and pioneer life—West (U.S.) 10. Steam-navi-
gation—Political aspects—United States—History. I. Title.
  HE630.M63L37 2008
  386'.3097809034—dc22

                              2007037519

                        1 2 3 4 5 6 7 8 9 10

To
BARBARA AND WADE
and
BILL AND VICKIE

Contents

ILLUSTRATIONS

MAPS

TABLES

PREFACE

Missouri River steamboating has been one of my long-standing interests. I was first attracted to the topic while researching and writing my master's thesis on a frontier photographer at the University of South Dakota in 1953–54. The photographer, Stanley J. Morrow of Yankton, Dakota Territory, often traveled great distances by steamboat. At Vermillion, home of the University of South Dakota, the Missouri's influence was pervasive. Originally, Vermillion was a Missouri River town, but during the great flood of 1881, the river suddenly rerouted itself to a new channel several miles to the south. Nonetheless, the Missouri's influence on the area's geology and history and on the psyche of its residents was evident. With a little imagination, one could stand alongside the great river and visualize its impact on the parade of people who had navigated it for hundreds of years.

I first had the opportunity to systematically study Missouri River steamboating while writing my doctoral dissertation at the University of Wisconsin–Madison. Because I wanted a manageable topic that could be completed within a relatively short time, I confined myself to the upper Missouri. My book titled *The History of Steamboating on the Upper Missouri River* (1962) was an outgrowth of the dissertation. Then, I was quite willing to leave the history of steamboating for the entire Missouri to someone else.

Subsequently, I moved on to other scholarly interests but revisited steamboating from time to time because of requests to write articles, present talks, participate in symposia, referee manuscripts, and respond to inquiries. As I approached retirement from a forty-five-year teaching career, it occurred to me that there was still no history of Missouri River steamboating that covered the whole river and its major navigable tributaries. So I decided to write one.

In researching and writing this book, my primary objective was to emphasize the economic history of Missouri River steamboating. Any transportation mode is sustained for an economic reason. When steamboating or any other method reaches the point where it is unprofitable, it dies. Nostalgia never covered a boat's operating costs. I found that most steamboatmen were very practical business-men who knew when to cut their losses and shift to other ventures. Of course, there were some who had difficulty distinguishing between an end and a decline. Their hopes for a trade revival constitute an interesting facet of the steamboat story.

By stressing economic history, I do not mean to imply that steamboating was a business and nothing else. Especially when it was the best way of moving peo-ple and freight, steamboating affected all aspects of life. In the political arena, such matters as river improvement, government regulation, and boat safety were major public policy issues.

Likewise, steamboating made a deep impression on the society and culture of river communities. In the popular mind, steamboats were far more than mere transporters. As the mechanical marvels of their day, they symbolized progress and modernity. To the many people who were at least semi-isolated over winters, their arrival was greeted as a reawakening of life. It is understandable that many Amer-icans continue to be fascinated by the romance of steamboats. Even during their heyday, they always drew spectators to the levees, and their passing left people with a sense of loss about what must have seemed their good old days.

I have endeavored to place Missouri River steamboating in the context of national and regional transportation developments. Although some steamers were used primarily on the Missouri, they typically spent part of their careers on the Mis-sissippi and the Ohio and such other Mississippi system rivers as the Illinois, Wabash, Cumberland, Tennessee, and Arkansas. St. Louis, the longest-lasting base of Missouri River steamboating, was also an important hub for the routes lead-ing up to St. Paul, down to New Orleans and east to Pittsburgh.

Since steamboating was only one aspect of the nation's transportation system, I also considered its interrelationships with the various modes of overland move-ment. By the standards of the early twenty-first century, it is absolutely amazing how much time and effort people expended during the steamboat era in simply getting around. In many situations, people and goods had to be delivered by a com-bination of steamboats, wagons, and stagecoaches. Consequently, roads and trails emanating from steamboat ports have great significance in steamboat history.

In the long-range view, one could say that steamboating succumbed to railroad-ing, which was both speedier and more efficient. But until railroads developed sys-tems that connected all major markets, there was a period of railroad-steamboat cooperation. In some instances, railroads worked with steamboat companies, but in other cases, they operated their own boats.

Aside from being affected by other transportation modes, steamboating was changed by communication advances. The advent and dissemination of the tele-graph were especially important in changing the nature of the steamboat business.

Missouri River steamboating has to be considered as part of the Industrial Rev-olution that rapidly transformed the United States. It was both a progeny and a victim of technological advances. But for a time, it played a vital role in the set-tlement and development of the Trans-Mississippi West.

ACKNOWLEDGMENTS

I appreciate the assistance and support I received during the preparation of this history. Research grants from the Richard S. Brownlee Fund of the State Historical Society of Missouri and the Faculty Research Council of Minnesota State University, Mankato, facilitated travel during the early research stages. James W. Goodrich, former director of the State Historical Society of Missouri, not only encouraged me to undertake the study but gladly helped me gain a better understanding of Missouri's history and society. Lynn Wolf Gentzler, the associate editor of *Missouri Historical Review*, assisted during my preparation of an article that enhanced my understanding of the steamboat business.

Bette Gorden, curator of the Herman T. Pott National Inland Waterways Library in the Mercantile Library at the University of Missouri–St. Louis, graciously located sources and discussed aspects of the topic with me.

Nancy Tystad Koupal and Jeanne Kilen Ode of the South Dakota State Historical Society were very helpful. Because of their interest and assistance, I received the opportunity to write an article associated with a ledger about wood sales to steamboats. It gave me a better understanding of both the fuel problem and the changing environment of the upper Missouri region. Ken Stewart, reference librarian of the historical society, helped locate some elusive sources and otherwise enthusiastically responded to my questions about South Dakota history.

Several regional historians gladly shared their expertise with me. Michael M. Casler of the Fort Union Trading Post National Historic Site read and commented on the entire manuscript and provided information about the fur trade and aspects of steamboat navigation on the upper Missouri. Paul L. Hedren, an authority on frontier military history, made a number of helpful comments. Harold H. Schuler shared his research materials about the Pierre–Fort Pierre area with me. Frank E. Vyzralek of Bismarck, a walking encyclopedia of North Dakota history, answered numerous questions and critiqued a portion of the manuscript.

Peter Jarnstrom and Kristen Hobday of the Memorial Library at Minnesota State University, Mankato, filled my numerous interlibrary loan requests, and

Mark McCullough, the library's reference coordinator, was especially helpful in locating federal government document sources.

I am also grateful to Yvonne Schmeling of Minnesota State University, Mankato, for helping to improve my computer skills.

James Worm, who prepared the maps, was efficient and timely. The following individuals helped locate and supply photographs—Henry Armstrong, Joel F. Overholser Historical Research Center, Fort Benton; Terry Coulson, Yankton, South Dakota; Katie Curey, Montana Historical Society; Doug Haar, Yankton, South Dakota; Linda Hein, Nebraska Historical Society; Diane Mallstrom, Public Library of Cincinnati and Hamilton County; Kathleen Moenster, Jefferson National Expansion Memorial; Christine Montgomery, State Historical Society of Missouri; Marshall Owens, DeSoto National Wildlife Refuge; Ken Robison, Joel F. Overholser Historical Research Center; Sharon A. Silengo, State Historical Society of North Dakota; Ellen B. Thomasson, Missouri Historical Society; and Denise Vondran, National Mississippi River Museum and Aquarium.

Lastly, I thank my children, Barbara and Bill, for their moral support. Since the death of my wife, Marilyn, in 1994, they have been my confidants.

NAVIGATING THE MISSOURI

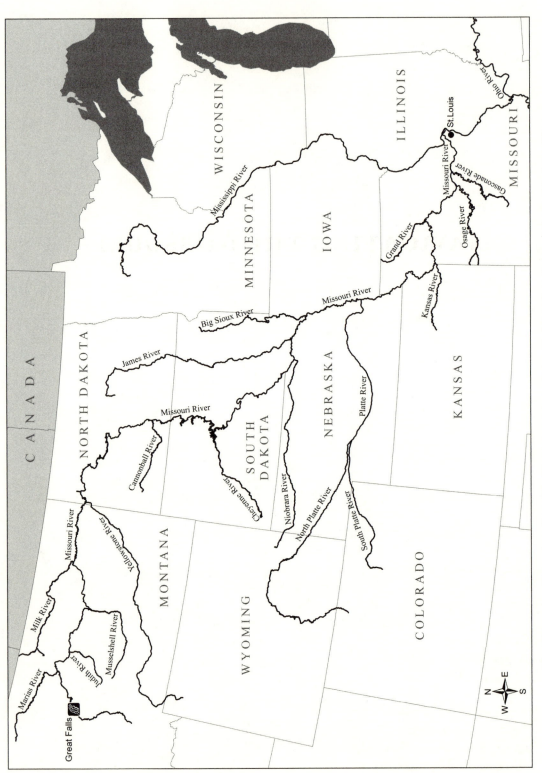

The Missouri and its major tributaries. (Current state boundaries are shown for reference.) *Prepared by James Worm.*

I

NATURE'S HIGHWAY

Before railroads were built in the United States, rivers and lakes offered the easiest and fastest transportation. Faced with the need to travel great distances to reach remote frontiers, Americans and the preceding French and British used waterways whenever possible. The nation's only continuous water route from an eastern state to the Rocky Mountain region was the combination of the Ohio, Mississippi, and Missouri rivers from Pittsburgh, Pennsylvania, to Fort Benton, Montana.

By the time Pittsburgh's first steamboat was launched in 1811, St. Louis, on the Mississippi about eighteen miles below the Missouri's mouth, was the base for western exploration and Indian trading. Over the ensuing years, when the city became famous as the "Gateway to the West," the Missouri was the main entry to the great movements that rapidly transformed the Trans-Mississippi West. The Santa Fe trade, the first settlement of Oregon, and the gold rushes to California, Colorado, and Montana all had links to St. Louis and the Missouri River.

The value of the Missouri as a highway was first made apparent to most Americans by the celebrated expedition of Meriwether Lewis and William Clark (1804-1806), who navigated from St. Louis to its source on their way to the Pacific Ocean. The explorers detailed the river's essential features. It was long, shallow, and rapid, and most of it was broad, muddy, and meandering, with numerous islands and sandbars.

Having established that their "Three Forks"—the merging of the Jefferson, Madison, and Gallatin rivers near present-day Three Forks, Montana—was the start of the Missouri, Lewis and Clark calculated the distance from the mouth as 2,465 miles. They determined that such important landmarks as the mouth of the Platte, the mouth of the Yellowstone, and the Great Falls were respectively 630, 1,850, and 2,240 miles upriver.[1]

But steamboatmen, who usually made only rough estimates, concluded that the stream was considerably longer. When Fort Benton, 37 miles below the Great Falls, became the practical head of navigation, boatmen commonly claimed it was

3,000 miles from St. Louis. Using information from steamboat operators during the Montana gold rush, the editor of *Trade and Commerce of the City of St. Louis for 1865* published a table of distances showing the Yellowstone and Fort Benton mileages from St. Louis as 2,270 and 3,175, respectively.[2]

The report left the impression that the distances were fixed, but the precise length of steamboat voyages depended on channel levels and courses. Boats could cut across flooded points that were unnavigable during low water, and furthermore, the best channel was continually altered as the river's coursing shaped bends and, during flood stages, cut across oxbow necks.[3]

But steamboatmen also tended to overestimate distances. Since their standard unit for setting freight rates was 100 pounds per 100 miles, they recognized that carefully surveyed distances would be disadvantageous. If they had been so inclined, they could have improved on estimating. When the U.S. Army was reconnoitering the Yellowstone in 1873, Captain Grant Marsh, perhaps at the instigation of accompanying army officers, measured distances by counting the number of boat lengths his *Key West* went from point to point. He stationed three men on the top deck, whose length was known. With one acting as the calculator, the other two would alternately pace from bow to stern while keeping abreast of some object onshore. For each walk to the stern, the boat had obviously advanced the length of the deck.[4]

Official distances were not established until army engineers and the Missouri River Commission surveyed the river in 1879–91. Interestingly, their conclusions were much closer to Lewis and Clark's distances than to those used by steamboatmen. They determined that Fort Benton and the confluence with the Yellowstone were respectively 2,285 and 1,760 miles from the Missouri's mouth.[5]

Because of the Missouri's great length, its navigators spoke of it as having two sections, lower and upper. But before 1882, when the Army Corps of Engineers designated Sioux City, Iowa, as their demarcation, the terms were imprecise. Boatmen and travelers obviously thought Jefferson City, Missouri, was on the lower Missouri and such places as Fort Benton and the mouth of the Yellowstone were on the upper Missouri, but they did not use a boundary. The most meaningful demarcation to them was the ever-shifting point where settlement ended and they entered "uncivilized" country. Among other things, this meant they would have to obtain their own wood rather than purchase it at commercial woodyards.[6]

This shifting concept of lower and upper is well illustrated by comparing the observations of Maximilian, Prince of Wied-Neuwied, who traveled up the river on the steamer *Yellow Stone* in 1833, with those of army engineer Major Charles W. Howell thirty-four years later. To Maximilian the most meaningful demarcation was the mouth of the Kansas River, then the boundary between ceded land and the "free Indian" region. After passing it, he wrote that he was on the "upper Missouri." But Howell thought the division occurred at Fort Randall, the utmost point where "civilization adds its changes to the general features of the country," 170 miles above Sioux City.[7]

Nonetheless, some historians regarded Council Bluffs, Iowa, as the dividing point.[8] They were probably influenced by early fur trade usage. Some of the first Indian traders thought the mouth of the Platte separated the lower and upper river. Henry Marie Brackenridge, who ascended the river on Manuel Lisa's 1811 trading expedition, observed: "The river Platte is regarded by the navigators of the Missouri as a point of as much importance, as the equinoctial line amongst mariners. All those who had not passed it before, were required to be shaved, unless they could compromise the matter by a treat. Much merriment was indulged on the occasion." This practice did not last very long. The American Fur Company, which succeeded Lisa's Missouri Fur Company, divided the lower and upper sections at the mouth of the Big Sioux, three miles above later Sioux City.[9]

As steamboating evolved, neither the Platte's mouth nor Council Bluffs, 25 miles above it, had particular distinction. The town was the final destination for some St. Louis steamers, but it was never a base for upstream navigation. A much stronger case can be made for Sioux City, which was near the American Fur Company demarcation and succeeded St. Louis as the mistress of the steamboat trade to Fort Benton and waypoints. However, the Corps of Engineers selected Sioux City as the juncture of the sections as a matter of administrative convenience, not for a historic reason.[10]

Army engineers also made a distinction between the physically different "Rocky River" and "Sandy River." The Rocky River defined the 172-mile section from Fort Benton downstream to Carroll, nearly 40 miles above the Musselshell. The Rocky River resembled a mountain stream. Its waters were quite clear, because it flowed through rock and gravel. Its narrow bed curved some, but its banks were stable and it was much straighter than the Sandy River. Its steep gradient, averaging 2.07 feet per mile, and its boulder-strewn rapids and shallow chutes over rock ledges made the Rocky the greatest challenge to navigators. In the 85-mile course upstream from the rapids around Two Calf Island, there were seventeen rapids. Some bore names derived from nature, such as Snake Point, Bird, Magpie, Lone Pine, and Bear. Dauphin Rapids and the ominously named Drowned Man's Rapids were among the most difficult.[11]

The valley of the Rocky River contained the Missouri's most picturesque scenery. Great spires and other formations of severely eroded sandstone towered above the narrow, mostly timberless bottoms. The sight inspired William Clark to write: "The Hills and river Clifts of this day exhibit a most romantick appearance on each Side of the river is a white Soft Sand Stone bluff which rises to about half the hight of the hills, on the top of this Clift is a black earth on points, in maney places this Sand Stone appears like ancient ruins some like elegant buildings at a distance, Some like Towers."[12] Later observers, who had a similar reaction, named such places as Castle Rock, Citadel Bluff, and Cathedral Rock.[13]

The 152-mile stretch from Carroll down to Big Dry Fork was a transition zone from the Rocky River to the Sandy. In this segment the banks were less stable, some winding occurred, and the bottomlands widened.[14] From Big Dry Fork to the mouth, the Sandy River flowed through a generally broad valley flanked by bluffs. Even the most casual observers discerned that the valley had been shaped by former channels of the ever-wandering stream. Bottoms, the valley's lowest, flattest portions near the stream, were regularly flooded during high water.

Most of the Sandy River valley was two to three miles wide. But portions between the Cannonball downstream to the Niobrara were often no more than a mile across. The broadest section was from the Niobrara downstream to Sioux City. Near Yankton the bottomlands ranged from four to ten miles across, and just above Sioux City the widest spot, seventeen miles across, occurred. The normal width of the stream itself was generally 800 to 1,000 feet. But below the mouth of the Kansas it was 1,200 feet, with a range from 500 feet to a mile. Usually the navigable depth in pools was three feet at low water and nine feet at high water. But during low water, the channel would divide, sandbars would form, and the river would become a series of pools with intervening sandbars. The current's average velocity was about three miles an hour. But in chutes and other narrow places, that doubled during flood stages.[15]

During the navigation season, from ice breakup to freeze-up, the stream ordinarily had high- and low-water periods. As a general rule, spring and early summer was the high-water period, and midsummer to late fall the low-water period. The ice blockade usually gave way downstream from the Kansas River in late February to mid-March and reformed in the first half of December. Farther upstream the ice-free period ordinarily lasted from late March or early April to mid-November. Because of the prevalence of warming Chinook winds in the westernmost plains, ice sometimes went out at Fort Benton before such downstream points as Bismarck or Yankton. But this did not benefit navigation, because Fort Benton was a destination, not a wintering site for steamboats. In some years when wintertime thaws opened the river, steamboats navigated the river's lowest 200 to 300 miles every month. In some instances, these were boats that had been frozen in at such places as Glasgow and Boonville.[16]

Once the ice went out, navigators counted on the Missouri River phenomenon of two annual rises. The first rise, which usually started in late March, was caused by the melting of snow on the plains and early spring rains. It ordinarily abated somewhat before the June rise carried the meltwater from the Rocky Mountains. Throughout the plains, rain amounts declined after June. During especially dry late summers and falls, the icing-over date was simply an idle statistic, because low water stopped boating much earlier. Even below Kansas City, the wettest portion of the entire valley, steamboats sometimes had to be withdrawn in late summer because of low water.[17]

The Sandy River featured muddy water, unstable banks, and long loops. As it undercut the banks, the channel, loaded with sand and soil, ricocheted from side to side. Like a giant separator, the current dumped thick sediment to form sandbars downstream and opposite the cut banks. As meanders aged and shifted somewhat downstream, they also became longer as opposite banks eroded.[18]

The raging water's greatest force was at meander ends. Consequently, the necks of the turns narrowed and became more vulnerable over time. The sheer force of floodwaters often forged new channels across them. The immediate effect was to shorten the river at that point, which increased the gradient through the newly formed chutes. After being abandoned by the new channel, the deepest portions of old meanders sometimes endured as lakes with the telltale curvature of the parent river. Although meanders greatly lengthened the river, they benefited ascending vessels. Switchbacking like mountain climbers, boats could easily cope with the Sandy River's average gradient of only 8.5 inches per mile.

Most of the Sandy was a succession of bends that looped around points. By the time army engineers surveyed the river, most of the bends and points had proper names. Great Bend below present-day Pierre, South Dakota, was one of the best-known. This impressive landmark was 25 miles around but only 1.75 miles across. Boat-weary passengers would sometimes hike across to await the ascending steamer. Captain Joseph A. Sire, who commanded steamboats for Pierre Chouteau, Jr., and Company, was customarily irked by time-consuming stops to cut wood. But at Great Bend he would send a party overland to get an early start on preparing fuel.[19]

As settlement and steamboating increased along the Missouri, the names of many bends reflected those activities. Naming bends for communities such as Glasgow, Liberty, Marthasville, and Miami was a common pattern, but others were more colorfully dubbed Bushwhackers and Jackass. Wrecked steamboats were the most likely to have their names perpetuated. Thus, between Sioux City and Yankton two of the prominent bends became known as Kate Sweeney and North Alabama. Points, which sometimes resembled small peninsulas, were often named for some physical feature, such as Black, Dry, Oak, Stony, and Willow.[20]

As the Sandy River surged toward the Mississippi, the current carried boulders and hundreds of trees from collapsing banks into the water. The timber debris formed sawyers, snags, driftwood, and rafts.

Sawyers—entire trees with soil still enclosing their roots—bobbed up and down near the bank. While aggravating to boats, they did not cause wrecks. But sometimes they blocked the most navigable channel and forced boats into shallow waters. Over time, water action and the annual ice-outs transformed some of the sawyers into snags. Released from a collapsed bank and stripped of smaller branches, the base of a tree would become embedded in the streambed. All snags came from large trees, because only they had sufficient weight to cause their roots to become firmly fixed in the bottom. Snags stood alone or in clusters below timbered points. New snags often retained some large branches and, as the wood was bleached by sun and water, resembled an array of ghost trees.[21]

As they aged, snags became more dangerous. Everything above or slightly below the waterline was broken off, and the sharpened ends of the remnant trunks were often undetectable in the murky water. Pilots had to be constantly on the alert for small ripples, a telltale sign of snags just under the water.

Prior to the use of federal government snagboats, navigators sometimes had to clear a channel by reaching the snags with a rowboat and cutting them off. But there was no assurance the passage would last. Even during moderate water stages, the channel could shift several hundreds yards in a few weeks. As it did, the current cut away new timbered banks and washed away sandbars, exposing buried snags.

Smaller trees and parts of larger trees broken off from snags floated downstream. This driftwood, prized by steamboatmen because it was usually well dried and relatively easy to gather, often collected on sandbars and bottoms. But if it lodged on the head of an island or some other obstruction such as the hull of a wrecked boat, it would continually snare enough floating timber to form a raft, so-called because, like the man-made craft, they floated on the water. French-Canadian voyageurs aptly named them *embarras* (troubles). Rafts sometimes grew so large that they blocked the head of a channel around an island. Although not fatal, they slowed boat movement. Navigators could be forced to use a shallower channel, or if they were unaware of the raft beforehand, had to back their vessel down to the foot of the island before trying another approach.[22]

The number, size, and variety of trees growing along the Missouri varied considerably throughout its course and throughout the history of steamboating. From the mouth to the Grand River (present-day Brunswick, Missouri), the first boatmen found the river flowing through a dense forest, which was a sort of mixed blessing. There was always plenty of steamboat fuel, but there were also more sawyers, snags, and rafts. Cottonwood and sycamore were the largest trees and the most likely to become snags. But there was a considerable variety of hardwoods, including ash, oak, hickory, and mulberry. From the Grand up to the Platte, timber stands that extended up the bluffs and prairies were interspersed.[23]

Above the Platte, there was much less timber. Trees were ordinarily found only in the bottoms lying between the water and the grassy bluffs. After proceeding westward from the bend at later Sioux City, navigators noted that trees were both sparser and smaller—a harbinger for their entry into the least timbered area, from about the Niobrara to the Cannonball. In this section, where the narrowest bottoms occurred, the best stands of the main indigenous trees—cottonwood and cedar—were on islands. But driftwood from far upstream helped allay the timber shortage. From the Cannonball to the Yellowstone, because the bottoms became broader, more timber was available. Above the Yellowstone to the Rocky River there was a good supply of cottonwood in the bottoms. Willow thickets grew on newly formed sandbars and bottoms, but the reedlike growth hardly qualified as timber.

Timber was scarce in the Rocky River. There were isolated cottonwood stands in the narrow bottoms, with the best concentrations at the mouth of such tributaries as the Judith and Marias. Pine, the largest growth on the steep bluffs, was widely dispersed. Nonetheless, when woodhawks, who sold wood to passing steamers, went into business there during the Montana gold rush, some pine, which was vastly superior to cottonwood, became available for fuel.[24]

The amount of timber along the Missouri was never static. Weather cycles, prairie fires, and floods all affected timber growth. Native people, who had used the valley's timber for thousands of years, certainly affected timber patterns. But the most dramatic changes occurred with the invasion of white farmers, who tended to clear forests and encourage tree growth in prairie environments.

The timber supply was of great concern to steamboatmen, who usually needed to refuel at least once a day. With their inefficient high-pressure engines, steamboats usually consumed about 1.25 cords of wood per hour. Oftentimes, because of cargo and passenger needs, they had a limited amount of space for wood, and more weight increased the boat's draft. A cord of cottonwood, for example, ranged from 2,160 pounds for very dry and 4,400 pounds for green cut during the growing season. So the common practice was to maintain a small reserve and replenish at short intervals.[25]

The steamboats' demand for wood rapidly diminished the supply in some places.[26] Captain Sire, who apparently did not appreciate trees as a renewable resource, seemed to think that once the wood was gone, it was gone forever. In 1841 while refueling near present-day Chamberlain, South Dakota, he complained that the crew had to go about a quarter mile to find wood. Then he observed: "During the ten years that the boats have been coming to this country all the wood near at hand has been depleted and, unless one takes measures to replenish in advance, I would not be surprised if, in the future, the boats will fail at their trip."[27]

Sire's comment was made when only about a dozen steamboat voyages had been made to the upper river. Yet, during the Montana gold rush, when nearly sixty steamers were on the upper river each year, there seemed to be no shortage of wood. Part of the reason for the change was the advent of woodhawks. Since these professional cutters had wood available at a landing, boatmen were not delayed in gathering their own fuel. Going a quarter mile or more to cut wood was no particular inconvenience for a woodhawk.

But a more fundamental change was in the nature of the countryside itself. While navigating the *Trapper* between the Big Sioux and Niobrara rivers in 1841, Sire noted that wood was becoming "rarer and rarer." Evidently, the terrain had not changed appreciably since Lewis and Clark ascended through the same section in 1804. On that occasion, Clark noted that the only woods were on the Missouri's points. Yet, when Major Howell traveled through the area in 1867, he found that "cottonwood groves continue to hold their places on the lower grounds, but the hillsides gradually exchanged their nakedness for a valuable covering of oak, hickory and walnut." In 1893, army engineers described the same section as having a "dense growth of timber" in the bottomlands.[28]

Why did the amount of timber increase? A partial answer lies in the passing of big game such as buffalo and elk. The grazing of the original thousands and thousands of buffalo, especially, helped maintain the prairie and deterred the spread of trees. Additionally, as the local Indians had to range farther west to hunt, their use of the valley and its resources diminished. Travelers reported that Indian ponies especially curtailed timber growth, because their usual wintertime subsistence was bark stripped from small trees. Their masters sometimes accelerated destruction by chopping down large trees so the ponies could feed on the smaller branches. And when the Yankton Sioux were placed on a reservation in 1858, some of the valley was without human habitation for a short time. The movement of whites into the area apparently helped the spread of trees. It is true that settlers used the valley's wood for fuel and construction, but by tilling the land, they prevented prairie fires, probably the greatest timber destroyer.[29]

The nature of the timber itself contributed to rapid changes. The main tree—the plains cottonwood—was easily propagated by wind- or waterborne seeds, and it was fast-growing. From sprouting, it could reach a height of seventy feet in twenty years. Thus Howell could have seen trees that had not even sprouted until six years after Sire's 1841 voyage.[30]

As the major stream between the Rockies and the Mississippi, the Missouri had numerous tributaries in its vast drainage area. Most of its basin was on its right side. As the river flowed eastward and southward, its left-side basin, because of its relative proximity to the Hudson's Bay and Mississippi drainages, was comparatively narrow. Consequently, the Missouri's main tributaries all flowed into its right side. Four of them—the Yellowstone, Kansas, Osage, and Gasconade—proved to be navigable by steamboats.

The Platte, whose sources lay in the Colorado Rockies, was both the most impressive and the most useless to navigators of large boats. Some might contend that the common derision that it was a mile wide and an inch deep was only a slight exaggeration. Rather than cut deep channels, it spread out over a broad, sandbar-choked valley. Its very name, variants of "Nebraska" to the Omaha and Otoe Indians and "Platte" to French explorers, described its appearance as flat.[31]

Observers were impressed by its breadth, speed, shallowness, and sand-laden waters. Meriwether Lewis found its mouth to be 600 yards wide, but the current—flowing at least eight miles an hour, about 25 percent faster than the Missouri at that point—had a maximum depth of only five feet. He learned that upstream were numerous small islands and sandbars and noted: "The banks of this river are very low, yet it is said, that it very seldom overflows them, or rises more than about 6 feet perpendicular above its lowest tide."[32] Edwin James, the chronicler of Stephen H. Long's expedition, reported that in mid-September 1819 the water at the mouth of the Platte flowed "almost unseen through a number of small channels," which had "a great extent of naked sand-bars."[33]

By the time steamboating was introduced to the Missouri in 1819, it had been an important artery since the advent of the first people. The three main craft used by Missouri River Indians— dugout canoe, hide canoe, and circular bullboat—persisted into the steamboat era.

Dugouts were fashioned from a large log (usually cottonwood on the Missouri) by fire and adz. The thickness of the shell ranged from about two inches on the bottom to one on the rim. Within the shell some crosswise wood was left in place to provide rigidity. Lengths ranged from about 8 to 25 feet and widths from 2 to

3 feet. The smallest dugouts could be navigated by one man. But two paddlers were needed for those 12 to 16 feet long. Dugouts slightly less or slightly more than 20 feet long required a crew of three men—one on each side and the third in the stern. Although they lacked the graceful lines and striking appearance of the birchbark canoes used throughout the Great Lakes region, dugouts were a practical adaptation to the Missouri. They were tough enough to survive glancing blows from snags and driftwood or scraping in very shallow places.[34]

Where large logs were unavailable, Natives covered canoes with tough bull buffalo hides whose hair had been removed. Once the canoe sides and bottom were made with lengthwise stout willow poles, the framework was completed with smaller willow branches. To prevent spreading, several cross poles were lashed to the sides. All parts were tied together with buffalo sinew. The covering, made by stitching large squares of hides together with sinew, was soaked in water before being stretched over the frame. Shrinking while it dried, it fit snugly. The vessels were partially waterproofed by treating the seams with a mixture of ashes and buffalo tallow. But even if they did not leak at the seams, they absorbed water. On longer voyages they would have to be unloaded at the nightly stops and inverted to dry. Periodically, the seams had to be resealed. Contemporary travelers such as Henry Marie Brackenridge referred to them as skin canoes, and historians Phil. E. Chappell and Hiram Martin Chittenden retrospectively called them bullboats.[35]

But that latter designation was also given to small, shallow tublike craft usually made by stretching a single bull buffalo hide over a willow-branch framework. These circular bullboats accommodated only one person—the paddler. Many times, they were used by women for crossings and other short trips related to such household tasks as transporting meat or wood. The sight of fleets of them impressed travelers as one of the great curiosities of the upper river region. Brackenridge, who called them circular canoes, observed: "There was but one woman in each canoe, who kneeled down, and instead of paddling sideways, places the paddle before. . . . The water being a little rough these canoes almost disappeared between the waves, which produced a curious effect; the squaws with the help of a little fancy, might be supposed, mermaids sporting on the billows; the canoe rising and sinking with them, while the women were visible from the waist upwards."[36]

St. Louis traders, who by the mid-1790s had pushed up the Missouri as high as the Mandan villages, used both dugouts and hide canoes for long voyages. But like their Ohio and Mississippi River brethren, they found their business required larger boats. Their first alternative was the pirogue, a craft used throughout the Mississippi River system. Basically, the pirogue was an oversized dugout canoe with a square stern. It was commanded by a *patron* (boss), who steered it with a stern tiller and rudder. Pirogues were sometimes equipped with masts and sails. Because pirogues, like canoes, were easily capsized and had limited cargo space, traders developed variants. One form was two parallel dugouts connected at least several feet apart with boards lashed or nailed to the inside edge of each. A catamaran-like enhancement was made by placing a connecting platform over part of both dugouts, providing some dry storage area in the shells under two sections of the platform. Interestingly, the various forms of pirogues did not have discrete designations. So when eyewitnesses mentioned only the general name, the specific type can only be conjectured from other comments in the account.[37]

Pirogues were the main vessels of the Spanish licensed traders on the upper Missouri a decade before Lewis and Clark. In the summer of 1794, Jean Baptiste Truteau traveled upstream from St. Louis with eight men in a pirogue. The next year James Mackay led a party of thirty-three men in four pirogues.[38]

Lewis and Clark, well aware of their predecessors, used two pirogues to supplement their keelboat. Both of the vessels, which were acquired on the upper Ohio, were dugouts. The larger one, which they generally called the "white pirogue," was equipped with a mast, two sails, and a stern rudder. The smaller, "red pirogue," which was usually rowed and sometimes towed, also had a stern rudder. The most fragile parts were the iron rudder mountings, which were prone to break or be wrenched loose. After sending their keelboat back to St. Louis from the Mandan village in the spring of 1805, the explorers proceeded to the Great Falls with the pirogues as their main vessels. They cached both below the falls and went ahead by portaging the dugout canoes around the falls.[39]

Navigators who needed more than pirogue capacity sometimes used bateaux, a generic name for a variety of flat-bottomed, open, keelless vessels made of thick boards. Some were pointed on both ends like a canoe, some had squared, raked ends, and yet others had a pointed prow and a squared stern. The largest, which were 40 to 75 feet long with a 10- to 12-foot beam, required eighteen to twenty rowers. Other than rowing, bateaux were propelled by poling, towing, and sailing.[40]

The French, who developed the bateau, started using it on the upper reaches of the Ohio shortly before the outbreak of the French and Indian War in 1755. With a capacity of up to 40 tons, bateaux were the principal cargo vessels on the Ohio until keelboats succeeded them. British and Americans, the successors of the French in the Trans-Allegheny region, generally called the smallest bateaux "skiffs," although they sometimes used that name for all bateaux.

On the Missouri, pirogues and bateaux were generally replaced by keelboats and mackinaw boats in the first two decades of the nineteenth century. In 1811, when rival traders Manuel Lisa and William P. Hunt engaged in their famous keelboat race, they used mackinaws as their complementary vessels. But at that time some pirogues and bateaux were still in use. Trader John C. Luttig, while ascending the Missouri in 1812 with a keelboat and a mackinaw, met four bateaux and several pirogues in the Fort Osage vicinity below the mouth of the Kansas. When steamboats were introduced in 1819, keelboats were the main alternative two-way commercial vessel.[41]

Both keelboats and mackinaws originated in the Trans-Allegheny. The first keelboats were adaptations of bateaux. It occurred to someone that bateaux would be easier to keep in the channel if a long, heavy timber was nailed lengthwise to the outside center of the bottom. Once this proved to be true, builders began fashioning boats with internal keels soon after the Revolutionary War.[42]

The Keelboat, drawing by Paul Rockwood.
Keelboats were the principal commercial watercraft prior to steamboats.
Courtesy of the Jefferson National Expansion Memorial/National Park Service.

As developed in the Pittsburgh area by professional boatbuilders, the keelboat, made of lumber, was usually 40 to 80 feet long and 7 to 10 feet wide, with a 20- to 40-ton capacity. Its ends were tapered. Most of the deck was enclosed by a six-foot-high box, which accommodated freight and sometimes passengers. Because of their light construction, even fully loaded keelboats drew only two feet.

Keelboats were managed by a helmsman (the patroon to Americans) manning a long-handled rudder. Some were designed to be propelled by every conceivable means. They were rigged with a mast and sails so wind could be used whenever possible. When sailing was impossible during calms and headwinds or gales that threatened to tip the vessel, the crew resorted to more strenuous methods—rowing, poling, towing, warping, and even bushwhacking. Although some models, especially those used on narrow streams, lacked sails, they seemed to a popular feature on Missouri River keelboats. They were used on the Lisa and Hunt keelboats as well as those of the 1825 Atkinson-O'Fallon Expedition.[43]

On any given upstream voyage or sometimes even during a day, the crew used all types of propulsion. Four to twelve rowers, seated in the bow, powered the boat when it could not be sailed, the water was too deep for poling, and heavily timbered banks precluded towing. Poling, which was sometimes done simultane-

The Mackinaw, drawing by Paul Rockwood.
This type of mackinaw, which featured tapered ends, was used by Missouri River fur traders.
Courtesy of the Jefferson National Expansion Memorial/National Park Service.

ously with rowing, was performed by men who walked on narrow, cleated passage-ways (*passe avants*) above the gunwales. When rowing and poling did not generate sufficient power, as many as several dozen men towed the vessel with a cordelle—a stout hawser. Cordelles, which were sometimes a thousand feet long, could be used only when the banks were stable and relatively free of overhanging trees and brush. In rapid places with many chutes, only warping would suffice: the cordelle was snubbed to some rigid object such as a tree or large snag and then taken up. A combination of towing, poling, and warping was not uncommon in particularly difficult spots. Bushwhacking, advancing the vessel by grasping brush and tree branches, was sometimes substituted for cordelling.[44]

While the keelboat was an advancement over its predecessors, its navigation was slow and difficult. Sometimes only a few upstream miles could be accomplished in a day. Accustomed to slow progress, keelboaters were amazed at Lisa's 1811 trip from St. Louis to Great Bend when he averaged eighteen miles a day.[45]

Mackinaws, introduced about the same time as keelboats, proved to be more popular and long-lasting on the Missouri. Like bateaux, they were open, flat-bottomed, and keelless and were made with lumber nailed or pegged to crosspieces.

Generally, they were smaller than either bateaux or keelboats, usually 25 to 40 feet long and 6 to 8 feet wide. Their gunwales were supported by wooden knees connecting them to the floorboards. Generally, the pilot commanded the mackinaw and worked the stern rudder, while four to eight men rowed, though some mackinaws were equipped with a mast and sail. Sometimes the gunwales were modified to improve security from possible Indian gunfire. One method was to lash extra boards above them to shield the crew and passengers. Another, used during the Montana gold rush, was not only to increase their height but also to double-board them. The oars were then passed through portholes, and the pilot worked in a fortified box built over the tiller.[46]

Like bateaux, there were several types of mackinaws. One had a tapered bow and stern, another had a canoelike bow and a squared stern, and a third model was rectangular, with squared bow and stern raked at about forty-five degrees. Historians such as Hiram Martin Chittenden, who categorically stated that mackinaws had sharp ends, seemed to assume that models never changed during the century-long history of the craft. James H. Bradley, an army officer who saw mackinaws at Fort Benton, reported that their sterns were square. But a Montana Historical Society photograph taken a few years after Bradley's observations shows a mackinaw with squared, raked ends.[47]

Deck configurations also varied. Fur traders, primarily moving buffalo robes and pelts, built shallow decks fore and aft for storing personal possessions and stacked their packs of robes and pelts near the enclosures. But the decks of gold rush mackinaws, whose loads were mostly passengers, were generally covered with board seats.

Mackinaws were mainly downstream craft. By taking advantage of the current, they could often navigate a hundred miles a day. Throughout most of the steamboat era, they were a vital transportation component. Fur traders, whose exports exceeded their imports, complemented their steamers with mackinaw shipments. Mackinaws were particularly popular during the Montana gold rush for miners who wanted to work late into the fall before going downstream. Because of their light draft, mackinaws could operate long after the river had become too low for steamboats.

Mackinaws had uses other than downstream navigation. Prior to steamboating, fur traders moved them upstream along with keelboats. Even after the advent of steamboats, some traders, who found them relatively easy to construct, used them for local two-way trade. Most were sold for lumber at their downstream destinations, but sometimes they were towed back upstream by steamboats to serve as lighters in shallow places.[48]

The steamboat was the outcome of long experimentation to find bigger, faster two-way vessels. But especially in comparison with its main predecessor—the keelboat—the steamboat was revolutionary. It was a child of the Industrial Revolution, when labor-saving machinery stimulated material progress.

The shortcomings of its predecessors added to the appeal of the steamboat, which offered unprecedented speed and efficiency. Nevertheless, steamboating was often difficult. Throughout the Mississippi River system ("the West" for much of the nineteenth century), voyages were plagued by low water, sandbars, snags, rafts, and rapids. Commercial boatmen realized that their vessels had to be adapted to nature's rivers, but they also wanted the rivers to be unnaturally adapted to them. Consequently, modifying the boats and modifying the rivers were interrelated concerns.

Western steamboats have to be defined within the context of their times. There was no such thing as a standard model that lasted from beginning to end of the era. Designs evolved through trial and error. The earliest steamboatmen needed high-pressure engines to generate enough power for rapid currents, but their boats were poorly designed to deal with shallowness and sandbars. The first-generation steamers were usually heavily constructed, with deep holds and relatively narrow hulls.[49]

In their quest to lessen draft, boatbuilders gradually changed to broader hulls with more bearing surface, which caused them to float higher. Freight and passenger capacity was increased by adding decks to achieve a tiered structure. Ironically, these changes were facilitated by the relatively short lives of western steamboats. Since they were usually wrecked or worn out in about five to six years, builders always had opportunities to innovate. Nonetheless, some old habits died hard. The predominance of side-wheelers, which were prone to damage from floating debris, persisted in the antebellum period. But by the 1870s they had generally been replaced with stern-wheelers.

Varying trade demands also affected boat sizes. To compensate for the heavy construction of the first steamboats, builders generally limited their freight capacity to 150 tons or less. But as Missouri River trade increased sharply in the 1840s, the tendency was to enlarge some boats to a 400- to 500-ton capacity. By 1880 several 1200-ton behemoths were being used on the Missouri. But in the post-railroad era, when most long-haul river freighting was devastated, there was a marked reversion to smaller steamers, many with less than a 100-ton capacity.

Other than hull structure, steamers were adapted to river conditions by the development of special equipment. Judging by frequent references in steamboat logs, grounding on sandbars was probably the chief reason for steamboat delays. Extrication methods including offloading cargo or waiting for a rise. But in many instances sparring worked.[50]

Sparring a boat over a sandbar involved using two long, stout spars, which were dropped over the bow to the bar at about a forty-five degree angle. Once the spars were set, looped lines which ran through pulleys on their tips, were wound onto a capstan, firmly mounted on deck. As the lines were shortened, the boat was lifted enough for water action to remove some of the sand. Relaxing the lines would cause the elevated vessel to fall forward a few feet. This time-consuming process, which often entailed numerous repetitions, was sometimes called "walking" a boat or, because the set spars resembled the hind legs of a squatted grasshopper, "grasshoppering."[51]

Until the widespread use of the steam-driven capstan in the 1850s, sparring was done by manually winding up the ropes. It was a hazardous undertaking, because

With its squared, raked bow and stern, the mackinaw *Montana*, shown at Fort Benton
in 1878, was typical of those used during the Montana gold rush.
Courtesy of the Montana Historical Society, Helena.

a breaking rope or a shattering handle could injure or kill the massed crew members who powered the capstan. The advent of the steam capstan not only reduced
risk but also provided much more power. Its operation, of course, added to the
already noisy boat operation.

Sometimes even the most powerful steamers could not ascend chutes or rapids.
Then it was necessary to warp forward by taking up a line. Like sparring, warping became much easier with the steam capstan. Normally, the rapids portion of
the Rocky River required the most warping. In some situations, the channel in the
rapids was so narrow and swift that even descending boats were warped through
as a way of controlling them.[52]

Sparring and warping helped in many situations, but Missouri River steamboatmen never had effective ways of coping with the wind and snags. If anything,
these dangers became more aggravated as the development of taller and more
lightly constructed hulls, made them increasingly vulnerable to both wind and
snags. Wind was more of a problem on the upper river, where the gales that swept

over the open prairies made it impossible to control boats. Faced with the likelihood of being blown onto a sandbar or crashed into a bank, captains had only one choice—anchor until the wind subsided. Throughout steamboating, however, snags were the greatest hazard. Because of their bulk and speed, steamboats were much more likely to be snagged than smaller, slower vessels. The heaviest snag concentrations were naturally in the densely forested portion of the lower river, but with the spread of cottonwoods in the bottoms of the upper river, snags became a menace on the Sandy River as well.

Snag removal was the first and longest-lasting river improvement method. Reasoning that nothing was more vital to the prosperity of the people than a river free for the using, boatmen and everyone else whose livelihood depended on river commerce contended that the federal government was obliged to improve rivers. Funding snag removal was a persistent political issue because there was no permanent solution. An area freed of snags could easily have a new crop within a few weeks. Therefore, demands for snag removal were just as likely to occur in 1910 as in 1830.

Removal of snags was kept in the public eye because they were the leading cause of steamboat wrecks. Throughout the history of Missouri River steamboating, approximately four hundred vessels were sunk or disabled. Snagging alone accounted for more losses than all other causes—such as ice, fire, bridges, and explosions—combined. But losses were only part of the story. Compilations of the number of wrecks did not consider the numerous snag-related accidents such as damaged hulls, wheels, and rudders that required repair stoppages and increased operating costs.[53]

The removal of snags by the thousands never altered the fundamental nature of the Missouri. However, near the end of the nineteenth century, river improvement took on a new meaning when the federal government began channelizing the Missouri from the mouth to Kansas. By damming chutes, erecting wing dams, and revetting banks, army engineers began the process of taming the wild river. By the end of commercial steamboating, the channelization project from the mouth to Kansas City was complete.

Anyone traveling on or along the Missouri today can only imagine the river's appearance at the start of the steamboat era. The onetime free-running stream is channelized to Sioux City, and a system of gigantic earthen dams and artificial lakes control upper river flow. Nature's river, along with steamboats, can be seen only through history.[54]

2

THE LURE OF TECHNOLOGY

The introduction of steamboats on the Missouri River in 1819 occurred during a surge of American nationalism. The United States emerged from the War of 1812 in an Anglophobic mood, determined to wrest physical control of its vast northwestern lands from Great Britain. America had acquired its massive westernmost region by the Louisiana Purchase from France in 1803. But despite this legal claim, British fur traders continued to operate in the upper Mississippi and upper Missouri regions. Frustration with British occupancy aggravated the warlike mood in such western states as Tennessee, Kentucky, and Ohio.[1]

The War Hawks, whose most extreme aim was the acquisition of Canada, failed to add any land to the United States. Nonetheless, the War of 1812 was decisive. The rising power of America and preoccupation with European affairs caused British statesmen to acknowledge at war's end that firm boundaries should separate the United States and Canada. Under the Treaty of Ghent, signed on Christmas Eve 1814, the countries agreed to jointly survey the controversial international boundary from upstate New York westward to the northwesternmost point of Lake of the Woods. In 1817 they agreed to demilitarize the Great Lakes and the next year fixed the northern boundary of the Louisiana Purchase at the forty-ninth parallel across the Great Plains.[2]

Although these were significant diplomatic achievements, they did not dispel public and governmental distrust of either British motives or British traders. American expansionists insisted that the United States had to protect its interests by establishing army posts on the upper Mississippi and upper Missouri. This policing of the frontier was intended to safeguard American traders, force British traders to withdraw to Canada, and cause the indigenous Indian tribes to cease their traditional cooperation with the British and become subjects of the United States.[3]

At war's end the nation's most remote frontier posts were obviously inadequate to accomplish these goals. On the Missouri, the army manned Fort Bellefontaine and Fort Osage. Bellefontaine, founded in 1805 on the south side of the river four miles above its mouth, was on the edge of the frontier during the War of 1812. Fort

Osage, started by William Clark in 1808 on the south side of the river near present-day Sibley, Missouri, about forty miles below the mouth of the Kansas River, was abandoned during the war because pro-British Sauk and Fox Indians isolated it by ravaging central Missouri. The fort had been founded in response to a recommendation by Clark, who during his famed expedition with Meriwether Lewis, observed that occupation of the hill overlooking the Missouri, with a good navigable channel at its base, would serve as a well-placed bastion.[4]

The reoccupation of Fort Osage in 1816 would obviously not affect British traders hundreds of miles to the north. Therefore Clark, while serving as governor of Missouri Territory, suggested the creation of a post near the mouth of the Platte, which emptied into the Missouri about six hundred miles above Fort Bellefontaine. His idea was in keeping with the aims of James Monroe, who in January 1815, while serving as both secretary of state and secretary of war in the James Madison administration, proposed army posts on the upper Mississippi.[5]

Monroe first intended to fortify the trading village of Prairie du Chien on the Mississippi about four miles above the mouth of the Wisconsin River. Despite the presence of an American militia post there, British forces had seized the village in the summer of 1814. Not only was this loss a great embarrassment to the United States, but it also underscored American inability to control the area all the way north to the Canadian boundary. Moving decisively, the U.S. Army started Fort Crawford at Prairie du Chien in the summer of 1816.[6]

Monroe naturally carried thoughts of additional upper Mississippi fortifications into his presidential administration, which opened on March 4, 1817. During the summer, topographical engineer Stephen H. Long reconnoitered the strategically important Falls of St. Anthony area (present-day Twin Cities) and recommended high ground overlooking the juncture of the Mississippi and Minnesota rivers as the site of future Fort Snelling. Planning for the fort's establishment was left to the nationalistic John C. Calhoun, who became secretary of war on October 8, 1817. Within months, Calhoun, a congressional leader of the War Hawks during the late war, developed a grand strategy for fortifying the northern plains.[7]

This strategy was to be accomplished by erecting a sister fort approximately 650 miles northwest of the Falls of St. Anthony. On March 16, 1818, Calhoun wrote to Brigadier General Thomas A. Smith of Fort Bellefontaine that "it has been determined to establish a permanent military post at the mouth of the Yellow Stone river." Smith was ordered to "take immediate and efficient measures to carry it into effect."[8] Calhoun was content to deal only with broad strategy. He left planning details such as means of transportation and provisions for the troops to Smith's discretion.

Calhoun was obviously familiar with the experiences of Lewis and Clark. He knew that in their first year they had ascended the Missouri only to the Mandan village about eighty miles upstream from present-day Bismarck, North Dakota. Consequently, he cautioned Smith: "It is probable that the lateness of the season will prevent the detachment from reaching the post contemplated this summer, and in that event, as intermediate posts will probably be required, it will take post at the Mandan village."[9]

But with the ultimate goal of the Yellowstone in mind, Calhoun explained his vision for the mission. The commander, to be named later, was "to use every means to conciliate the Indians, and impress on them the belief that our intention is friendly towards them." Moreover, Calhoun saw the expedition as a symbol of the nation's might, observing that "the glory of planting the American flag at a point so distant on so noble a river, will not be unfelt. The world will behold in it, the mighty growth of our republic, which but a few years since, was limited by the Allegany, but now is ready to push its civilization and laws to the western confines of the continent."[10]

Unfortunately, only the most dramatic aspects of Calhoun's orders were publicized. Within two months of his missive to Smith, the nationally distributed *Niles' Weekly Register* of Baltimore reported "that a military post is about to be established at the mouth of the Yellow Stone river, which empties into the Missouri about 1800 miles from the mouth of the latter."[11] This was the first step in promoting what was soon labeled the "Yellowstone Expedition" as the elixir for the country's northwestern frontier security problem.

New information about the upper Missouri region, obtained by Calhoun in the spring and summer of 1818, caused him to consider an alternative to the Yellowstone fort. On August 18, he wrote to Andrew Jackson, the commander of the army's Southern Division, which then included the Missouri, that "I am inclined to think the principal post ought to be at the Mandan Village." That place, he thought, was "the point on the Missouri nearest to the British post on the Red River, and the best calculated to counteract their hostilities against us or influence with the Indians." A Mandan village post, he believed, would also facilitate communication with the fort to be built at the juncture of the Mississippi and Minnesota rivers. This combination of new Missouri and Mississippi posts, he reiterated to Jackson, would help fulfill his strong desire "to break British control over the Northern Indians." He felt obligated to explain to Jackson that this concern would justify his shifting a much greater proportion of the army to the northern sector.[12]

Calhoun's revised thinking was privately conveyed to Jackson. Since he did not publicize his decision to forsake the Yellowstone post, it is quite understandable that journalists, army officers, and civilian contractors continued thinking, talking, and writing about the "Yellowstone Expedition."

In authorizing the upper Missouri post, Calhoun was influenced by Stephen H. Long, a topographical engineer assigned to Brevet Brigadier General Thomas A. Smith's command at Fort Bellefontaine. After graduating from Dartmouth College in 1809, Long served as principal of a New Hampshire academy and a Pennsylvania public school. His talents in mathematics and engineering and his co-invention and patenting of a hydrostatic engine caused the army's chief of engineers, Brevet Brigadier General Joseph G. Swift, to recruit Long for the Corps of Engineers in 1814. Long's first assignment was teaching mathematics in the U.S.

Military Academy at West Point, New York. In 1816, after obtaining a commission of brevet major in the topographical engineers unit, he was assigned to Smith's command.[13] By the end of 1817, he had established an excellent reputation within the War Department for his assessment of fortifications in Illinois and explorations of the upper Mississippi and lower Arkansas river areas. In praising Long to Calhoun, Smith wrote that his "character for science, industry, and perseverance is not surpassed by any topographer of the American army."[14]

After his first season's work as a surveyor and explorer, Long was convinced that the great distances of the western frontier could best be negotiated by steamboats. While visiting Washington, D.C., in January 1817, he proposed to President-Elect James Monroe that the Great Lakes and major western rivers be explored and charted by steamboat. Monroe did not respond, but a year later the determined Long approached Smith about purchasing a steamboat for use in mapping the Mississippi and its tributaries. On that occasion, Long, in responding to Smith's questions, recommended the mouths of the Kansas, Platte, and Yellowstone rivers and the Mandan village as possible new fort sites on the Missouri.[15]

On February 16, 1818, Smith relayed Long's steamboat exploration proposal and his opinions on fort sites to Calhoun. Historians Roger L. Nichols and Patrick L. Halley concluded that "it is difficult to prove whether Stephen Long's ideas and information on frontier military matters provided the basis for War Department decisions or merely reflected known interests within the army."[16] But they reasoned that even if Calhoun did not directly follow Long's recommendations, it is clear that the two thought in the same vein about extending American authority on the frontier and counteracting British influence.

Long's proposal for mapping by steamboat was the genesis of a Missouri River scientific expedition that was to be distinct from the military expedition. In suggesting the revival of activities that had been dormant since the Jefferson administration, Long expressed his belief that obtaining information about flora, fauna, geography, and geology was a natural and necessary corollary of military expansion. Calhoun agreed and showed his strong support by usually working directly with Long rather than through the military chain of command. The two regularly shared details about obtaining a steamboat and scientific instruments and elaborating the Scientific Expedition's goals.[17]

When Calhoun approved of Long's steamboat use on September 1, 1818, the two were planning on purchasing a boat. Recognizing that the Missouri was a difficult stream that had never been navigated by steamboat, they calculated that a relatively small, light-draft craft was necessary. But with due regard to the next military appropriations bill, it also had to be inexpensive. They wanted to spend no more than $5,000 for a vessel that would draw only eighteen inches. As they soon found out, no such boat existed. The solution was to persuade Congress to allot $5,000 for the construction of such a steamer. As the appropriations bill was pending in Congress, Calhoun asked Long for a detailed steamboat exploration plan.

Long's response bristled with optimism and enthusiasm. He thought the steamboat would be ready by March 1, which would enable him to navigate it from Pittsburgh to the Missouri during a high-water stage. Intending to take advantage of the rising Missouri, he would ascend it to the Platte and steam up and down it before following the Missouri to the Yellowstone. Obviously unaware of Calhoun's revised thinking about the military expedition's destination, he planned "to arrive at the Yellow Stone at or before the arrival of the Troops destined for that place." Next he would "ascend the Yellow Stone which would then be swollen by the Spring tide, after which our course should be directed up the Missouri to the falls, and up as many of its tributaries below that point as the season would allow us to ascend."[18] Their belief that all this could be accomplished in one navigation season helps explain Long's and Calhoun's faith in steamboat navigation. Neither seems to have had any reservations about the capability of steamboats, even if using them in new places was strictly experimental.

Calhoun's fascination with equipping the Scientific Expedition with a steamboat carried over into his plans for transporting and supplying the hundreds of troops on the Missouri Expedition. He must have been pleased with the plaudits from western newspapers. For example, the editor of the *Missouri Gazette and Public Advertiser* of St. Louis exulted that steamboat transportation would enable troops to reach the Yellowstone "in sixty days, whereas by the common mode, they would not reach there before July or August, 1819." The editor believed that "a steam boat, with 2 or 3 pieces of cannon and 500 men on board, would make a more lasting impression upon the minds of the sons of the forest, than would an army of 10,000 men marched by land."[19]

In keeping with well-established War Department practices, Calhoun intended to use a civilian contractor. Not surprisingly, both the subsistence and transportation contracts were awarded to James Johnson of Great Crossings, Scott County, Kentucky. Johnson had qualifications no aspiring competitor could match. He was experienced, wealthy, patriotic, and politically well-connected. Johnson held contracts during the War of 1812 and after the war was granted a number of contracts, including transportation to New Orleans, delivering stores to various frontier posts, and supplying the army with gunpowder. In combination with his brothers, Johnson was reputed to be worth millions, which would logically infer that he had the wherewithal to finance supply and boat purchases and employ men while fulfilling contracts.[20]

Johnson's supporters, who invariably extolled his patriotism, usually cited his war record. In October 1813, while serving as a Kentucky militia officer under the command of his brother Richard Mentor Johnson, he fought in the Battle of the Thames. During this smashing American victory on the Canadian side of Lake Erie, the famous Shawnee Indian chief Tecumseh was killed. The battle proved to be very decisive. Tecumseh's death, along with the obvious British inability to bolster their Indian allies, caused the rapid breakup of the Indian confederation in the Great Lakes region. Richard Mentor Johnson claimed to have personally killed the chief, and James Johnson benefited from reflected glory. Both brothers were acclaimed to be war heroes and great patriots, which were potent labels in the tense postwar years.

Their combat experience boosted the Johnson brothers' political stock. In 1818 Richard, while serving in the House of Representatives, was chairman of its Military Appropriations Committee. In that key position, he made no pretext of being neutral relative to brother's contracting business. Instead, he acted like a partner by openly representing James and, under a power of attorney, signing military contracts for him. There is good reason to believe that Richard also orchestrated a letter-writing campaign to Calhoun in the drive to make James the subsistence and transportation contractor of the Missouri Expedition. Ringing endorsements from important political allies, including Henry Clay, a fellow Kentuckian and the speaker of the House, and Armistead Thomson Mason, a former senator from Virginia, emphasized James Johnson's heroism, enterprise, zeal, and devotion to his country.[21]

James Johnson's status, prestige, and support certainly helped him win the transportation contract without facing the challenge of competitive bidding, although Quartermaster General Thomas S. Jesup later tried to explain that he chose not to call for bids for fear the process would delay troop movements.[22] The contract Jesup signed at Washington on December 2, 1818, with Richard Mentor Johnson, as the legal representative of James Johnson, specified that the contractor had to have two steamboats ready for duty by March 1. These boats were to carry troops and their equipment and provisions to destinations on the Arkansas, upper Mississippi, and Missouri rivers, including the mouth of the Yellowstone. If two steamboats proved to be insufficient, Johnson was to supply one or two more. In the event the steamboats failed, he was obligated to fulfill his commitments by using keelboats. Since steamboat use was unprecedented, Johnson and Jesup decided to defer establishing rates. But they agreed that Johnson "shall be allowed a reasonable compensation, taking into consideration the hazard attending the navigation of waters at points so distant and heretofore unexplored by such mode of navigation."[23] Johnson was also to be paid "such reasonable and further allowance, as may be equitable and just" if his boats were detained because of the government's fault. The contract wording, seemingly judicious when it was written, laid the basis for later legal quibbling between the government and the contractor.

A unique aspect of the contract was that it required Johnson to use steamboats. Calhoun later explained the presumed advantages of steamboats. They would, he thought, "give much more interest and éclat to the expedition and would probably impress the Indians and the British with our means of supporting and holding intercourse with the remote posts on the Missouri."[24]

Calhoun was obviously satisfied that steamboats had proven themselves during their short history. The *New Orleans,* the first to navigate western rivers, was launched at Pittsburgh in March 1811. Planned by Robert Fulton and financed by his wealthy New York associates, including Robert R. Livingston and Dewitt Clinton, it was named for its intended home port. Soon after he demonstrated the practicability of steamboating by trial-running the *Clermont* on the Hudson River in 1807, Fulton turned his attention to the West. At his behest, Nicholas Roosevelt made a flatboat reconnaissance in 1809 from Pittsburgh to New Orleans. Roosevelt's observations of the heavy flatboat trade on the Ohio and the lower Mississippi showed there was enough commerce for a lively steamboat business.[25]

When the *New Orleans* was built, Pittsburgh boatbuilders were still influenced by their experience in making oceangoing ships. In the late eighteenth century, some ships that were later used on Atlantic coastal waters sailed from the head of the Ohio to the Gulf of Mexico. The *New Orleans* and most first-generation steamboats bore striking resemblances to them. The 138-foot-long *New Orleans* had a bowsprit, portholes, and a deep hold, which housed the machinery and cabin.

Roosevelt captained the *New Orleans* on her maiden run, started in the late fall of 1811. He was delayed by low water over the troublesome Falls of the Ohio at Louisville. The falls were a twenty-five-foot drop over the course of two miles. Caused by a geological fault, the rock-strewn rapids were the Ohio's greatest navigation hazard. They could be negotiated by small boats, but steamboats could pass through only during high river stages.[26]

After the Ohio rose, Roosevelt was able to descend the falls and reach New Orleans in January 1812. The boat subsequently showed a profit in nearly two years of running between New Orleans and Natchez. Its initial success caused the Fulton group to add a second boat, the *Vesuvius*, in 1813.

The Fulton interests, which aspired to monopolize western steamboating, were challenged by several independents in 1814. Of these, the most significant was Henry M. Shreve, who navigated the *Enterprise* from Pittsburgh to New Orleans. While working for the army, he helped move troops and supplies for Andrew Jackson's New Orleans campaign and once daringly ran the British blockade. These feats led Jackson and other army officers to see great military potential in steamboats.[27]

After the war, Shreve demonstrated that steamboats could move effectively upstream as well as downstream on the Mississippi and Ohio above Natchez. Taking advantage of the 1815 flood, he steamed the *Enterprise* from New Orleans to Louisville in twenty-five days. To skeptics this proved only that a steamboat could ascend the Ohio and its falls during extraordinarily high water. But in 1817, Shreve, using his *Washington*, made the same trip during a normal river stage. This landmark achievement was acclaimed to have "removed doubt as to the future of upstream navigation."[28]

Meanwhile, other operators, including David Prentiss, entered western steamboating. After building the *Zebulon M. Pike* at Henderson, Kentucky,[29] Prentiss had it navigated to Pittsburgh and then to St. Louis, where it gained the distinction of being the first steamboat to reach that place. Its arrival at St. Louis on August 2, 1817, where it was greeted with "great rejoicing" by a crowd on the levee, was symbolically important.[30] The voyage demonstrated the extension of the new technology to the very edge of the frontier. To isolated St. Louisians, it seemed to diminish the time and space separating them from the more economically and culturally advanced East.

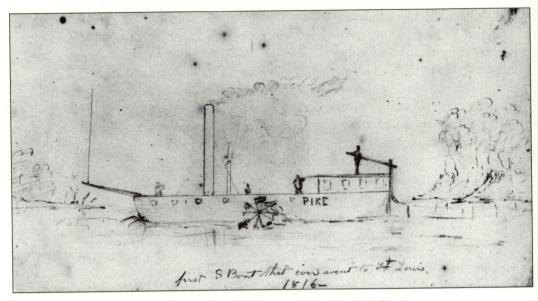

The *Zebulon M. Pike*, the first steamboat to reach St. Louis.
It was said to be "sort of a cross between the keelboat and the steamboat."
Drawing by Henry Lewis. *Courtesy of the Missouri Historical Society, St. Louis.*

But the *Pike*, described as "sort of a cross between the keelboat and the steamboat," also exemplified steamboating's limitations.[31] The craft's low-pressure engine and paddle wheels were augmented by keelboat-like *passe avants* so it could also be poled. With a capacity of only 31 tons, less than that of many keelboats, it was smaller than any previous western steamboat. However, its diminutiveness did not compensate for its lack of power. During the *Pike*'s tortuously slow six-week trip from Louisville, Captain Jacob Reed had to resort to poling to struggle up the Mississippi while a helmsman guided the boat with a stern rudder. Later in the season, the *Constitution* also reached St. Louis, which until 1819 remained the utmost point above the Ohio's mouth visited by a steamboat.[32]

In the meantime, steamboats were becoming more popular on the Ohio and lower Mississippi. In the spring of 1819 the *Niles' Weekly Register* reported that "since the year 1812, forty steam boats have been built upon the western waters—7 have been wrecked, burnt or abandoned, 33 are plying from place to place, and 28 more are building."[33] But steamboats were still quite a novelty among hundreds of flatboats. In 1818 an upbound steamboat passenger counted 643 flatboats descending the Mississippi and the Ohio.[34]

In December 1818, when Johnson secured his transportation contract and Congress authorized the construction of the Scientific Expedition's steamboat, the goal of reaching the Mandan village the next season seemed realistic. The initial

movement of troops in the fall had gone well. This contingent of about 350 officers and men led by Captain Wyly Martin, reached Cow Island, near later Atchison, Kansas, about October 20. Martin used ten keelboats during his fifty-day
ascent from Fort Bellefontaine. On Cow Island he supervised the erection of Martin Cantonment, temporarily the nation's westernmost army post.[35] Martin's wintering troops were to proceed upriver with the main force in 1819. The *Niles' Weekly
Register* publicized that Martin's final goal was "to ascend the Missouri river to the
mouth of the *Yellow Stone.*"[36]

The movement of Martin's advance party was the only aspect of the military
and scientific expeditions done in a timely fashion. Delays in readying steamboats
helped ruin any chance of launching the expeditions early in the spring of 1819.

In late December 1818, Long moved to Pittsburgh to supervise the construction
of the Scientific Expedition's steamboat. The boat, named the *Western Engineer*
for its regional destination and the Corps of Engineers, was hurriedly built at the
nearby federal arsenal on the Allegheny River. Long's greatest problem was procuring seasoned wood. He later complained that he even had to use green wood in the
hull portion housing the boilers, furnace, and engine. Subsequent warping and leaking made it impossible to keep the machinery, cargo, and cabin passengers dry.[37]

Long's basic construction principles were obviously influenced by previous
steamboat design. Since he did not have to transport great numbers of personnel
and provisions, the boat was to be small. To stem the Missouri's obstruction-
laden channel, Long intended to make it light-draft. However, even before construction was started, he decided to both lengthen and broaden the hull by three
feet. The resulting craft was 75 feet long and 13 feet wide. The *Western Engineer*
was the forty-fourth steamboat built on western waters and one of the first stern-
wheelers.[38] Long thought a stern-wheeler would be less likely to be damaged by
snags and floating logs in the Missouri than a side-wheeler.

Other than the stern wheel novelty, the *Western Engineer* was conventionally
built. Its machinery and cargo storage space were placed below deck. Despite portholes, which provided some ventilation, one can well imagine the miserable working conditions for its confined firebox stokers on hot, humid, Missouri days.
Because its engine power was suspect, the boat was equipped with a mast, so it
could, if necessary, be sailed or cordelled like a keelboat. With a limited capacity
of only 30 tons, the *Western Engineer* drew more water than Long initially planned.
After the addition of machinery, supplies, and personnel, it had a draft of 2.5 feet.[39]

The most distinctive feature of the *Western Engineer* was that it appeared to be
riding on the back of a giant serpent. During construction, Long and his associates evidently talked at length about whether their boat would really awe Indians.
Their conclusion was that an ordinary looking vessel with a standard vertical chimney would not. Consequently, they agreed to add a dramatic touch. The origina-
tor of the serpent apparition is not known. Richard Thorp credited an unnamed
stoker. But Long was the key decision maker; without his approval it would not
have been added. A serpent image probably seemed particularly apt because of

widespread fascination with mythical dragons, whose images were etched in butt and trigger plates of the army's muskets and rifles.[40]

The *Western Engineer's* serpent was artfully done. At the bow, its giant head with gaping jaws, red mouth, and protruding tongue appeared to be belching fire and smoke because the chimney was channeled into it. To add to the illusion, small mirrors inside the mouth reflected the light of a whale oil lamp. The body of the scaly beast, which appeared to be swimming, lay along the water line on both sides. Its upraised tail extended over the stern wheel.[41]

The serpent decoration was probably not worth the extra work and cost. Those most impressed included sightseers and newspapermen who assumed that the sham beast would terrify Indians, but they seem to have been much more dazzled by the boat's size and weaponry. One writer commented that

> taken all through, and without intelligence of her composition and design, it would require a daring savage to approach and accost her with Hamlet's speech.

> > Be thou a spirit of health, or goblin damned,
> > Bring with thee airs from heaven, or blasts from hell,
> > Be thy intents wicked, or charitable,
> > Thou com'st in such a questionable shape
> > That I will speak with thee.[42]

Hoping to begin descending the Ohio by mid-April, Long had the *Western Engineer* trial-launched on March 26. However, its paddle wheel did not work well because the boat rode too low in the water. Long had miscalculated the effect that an enlarged crew and the machinery would have on increasing the boat's draft. Following some redesigning and reconstruction, the boat left the arsenal on May 3 and two days later, after loading more provisions at Pittsburgh, started for St. Louis.[43]

Even with this delayed start, Long evidently believed he could still carry out the mission ordered by Calhoun on March 8. Calhoun instructed Long to "first explore the Missouri and its principle branches and then in succession Red river, Arkansas and Mississippi above the mouth of the Missouri." Since the "object of the expedition is to acquire as thorough and accurate knowledge as may be practicable of a portion of our country which is daily becoming more interesting, but is as yet but imperfectly known," Long was to "permit nothing worthy of notice to escape" his attention. Calhoun singled out the "extreme bend of the Missouri to the north" as a "very interesting point." He did not specifically describe it but was obviously thinking of a site within striking distance of the forty-ninth parallel, which he wanted Long to ascertain at some point. Such a determination of the international boundary, he thought, "will tend to prevent collision" between American and British traders. Since Calhoun was most concerned about trade conflicts in the Missouri-Red rivers area, he probably wanted Long to at least reach the point where the Missouri turned west above the Mandan village. Such a goal would have been consistent with his aim of establishing a military post at the village.[44]

Otherwise, Calhoun was concerned with the region's "productions whether

The *Western Engineer* was the first steamboat to reach present-day Omaha–Council Bluffs.
Courtesy of the National Mississippi River Museum and Aquarium, Dubuque, Iowa.

animal, vegetable or mineral" and the "number and character of the various tribes with the extent of country claimed by each." With the long shadow of Meriwether Lewis and William Clark in mind, Calhoun thought Long should also study Thomas Jefferson's instructions to them for further guidance.

During their preliminary negotiations, Calhoun and Long agreed that the scientists on the expedition would be unpaid volunteers. They assumed correctly that qualified men would be interested in venturing into mainly unexplored lands. They were well aware that the popularity of the first published journal of Lewis and Clark and expansionist sentiment had created much popular interest in the West's land and life. This fascination with a new region coincided with the emergence of scientific specialization, which in the United States was led by two Philadelphia organizations—the American Philosophical Society, founded by Benjamin Franklin in 1743, and the Academy of Natural Sciences of Philadelphia, which was started in 1812. Long obtained the assistance of these organizations when he solicited applications.[45]

By early April, Long's small staff, including three scientists, had assembled in Pittsburgh. The scientists were Dr. William Baldwin, Thomas Say, and Augustus Edward Jessup. Baldwin had begun studying botany before earning his medical degree in 1807. While practicing and sometimes serving as a surgeon for both the army and the navy, he collected botanical specimens in the Philadelphia area,

Georgia, and parts of South America. Some of his studies on flora were published in the American Philosophical Society's *Transactions*. These qualifications enabled Long to appoint Baldwin the expedition's botanist, doctor, and surgeon. Other than providing an opportunity for new botanical discoveries, Baldwin hoped the western trip would benefit his health. He had been afflicted with consumption for over a decade, and prevailing medical belief held that certain climates had curative effects. Thomas Say, an eminent entomologist, was one of the founders of the Academy of Natural Sciences of Philadelphia. In part because of his work on the Long expeditions of 1819–1820 and 1823, he discovered more insect species than any of his predecessors. His classics—*American Entomology* and *American Conchology*—helped earn him the designation "father of American descriptive zoology." Jessup, a Philadelphia businessman and a member of the Philadelphia Academy of Natural Sciences, was the expedition's geologist. His inclusion showed Long's interest in such practical geological applications as the determination of soil types and mineral prospecting.[46]

To complete his staff, Long chose army officer Major John Biddle as the expedition's scribe; Titian Ramsey Peale, the son of the famous Philadelphia painter Charles Wilson Peale, as assistant naturalist and sketcher of animal specimens and geological formations; and Samuel Seymour as landscapist. Lieutenant James D. Graham and West Point cadet William H. Swift were to assist Long in making astronomical and barometric calculations. The twenty-year-old Graham, who had graduated from West Point in 1817, proved to be a fortuitous choice, because of his mechanical aptitude. During the expedition from St. Louis he became the principal operator of the *Western Engineer*. The pilot and mechanic that Long employed at Pittsburgh went no farther than St. Louis. Long failed to replace them there, because he would not pay the wages demanded by qualified men.

Part of the boat's crew, consisting of a sergeant and eight privates, doubled as security guards. They were augmented by civilian workers, including a mechanic, a pilot, a clerk, a carpenter, and two cabin boys, which brought the boat's total Pittsburgh complement to twenty-four.[47]

Although Long's Scientific Expedition was discrete from the military or Missouri Expedition, Calhoun assumed they would move in concert. This meant that the movements of the *Western Engineer,* James Johnson's steamboats, and the troops had to be coordinated. Logically thinking in stages, the first obvious goal was to assemble all three at St. Louis.

Like Long, Johnson was unable to meet an early spring deadline. When he obtained the transportation contract, his only steamboat—the *Johnson*—was aground with broken machinery near the mouth of the Ohio. The 140-ton sidewheeler, built in 1818 at Wheeling, Virginia, was first based at New Orleans. As the winter passed quickly, Johnson scrambled to assembly his fleet. By mid-February, facing his obligation to deliver 430,000 daily rations to Fort Bellefontaine, he had decided he needed four steamboats. But he soon changed his mind again and made arrangements to lease or charter a fifth.[48]

Besides the *Johnson*, the contractor-owned boats were the *Expedition*, the *Jefferson*, and the *Calhoun*. At 175 tons each, the *Expedition* and the *Jefferson* were designed to trade on the Ohio and lower Mississippi. Even Johnson conceded that they were larger than his desired capacity of 100 to 150 tons for the Missouri's untested waters. The *Calhoun*, so-named as part of the Johnson brothers' campaign to flatter the secretary of war, was launched at a Kentucky River boatyard near Frankfort on March 20. Richard Mentor Johnson proudly reported to Calhoun that it was "the first in the bosom of the State & christened amidst the acclamations of a numerous and intelligent audience." With only a 100-ton capacity, it seemed to be the best suited for the Missouri. Lastly, Johnson made arrangements to use the *Exchange*, a 212-ton side-wheeler completed at Louisville in the spring.[49]

Even before the size of these boats was known, army officers questioned Johnson's capability of fulfilling his contract. They were deeply influenced by Wyly Martin, who was introduced to the difficult Missouri during his keelboat passage to Cow Island. While professing ignorance of steamboat technology, Martin believed that only "small steam boats of 50 tons and under would do well upon this river." Citing hazards that baffled "the art of the best pilots," Martin preferred keelboats.[50]

Another source of concern was Johnson's indebtedness to the Bank of St. Louis. By February this had created enough of a stir in St. Louis to cause Lieutenant Colonel Talbot Chambers, the first commander of the 1818 advance party, to inform Calhoun that the bank was planning to get civil authorities to seize Johnson's steamboats.[51] Such an action, which would have imperiled the entire military expedition, was strongly supported by a number of St. Louisians, whose views were reflected in the *St. Louis Enquirer*, one of the town's newspapers.

Like the *Enquirer*, army officers who were associated with the expedition excoriated Johnson for his tardiness. But they conveniently overlooked the army's own shortcomings. To staff the expedition, some troops had to be moved from as far away as Plattsburgh on Lake Champlain in northeastern New York. Colonel Henry Atkinson, who had been named to command the military expedition, did not leave Plattsburgh with a force until March 29. Proceeding slowly to St. Louis by way of New York City, Philadelphia, and Pittsburgh, he started his army down the Ohio in a fleet of ten armored keelboats on May 8. When Atkinson reached St. Louis on June 1, he found Johnson had been there for two weeks, but Long and the *Western Engineer* did not arrive until June 9.[52]

Meanwhile, as soon as Calhoun realized that Atkinson and Johnson could not possibly start moving up the Missouri in early spring, he questioned the advisability of trying to reach the Mandan village in 1819. He thought the establishment of an intermediate post at either the Council Bluff[53] or farther upstream at the Great Bend would be more attainable. But he concluded that Atkinson, who would be best acquainted with day-to-day conditions, should select the first year's destination.[54]

Despite the delays, Calhoun, Long, Johnson, and other steamboat boosters assumed that the federal government would pioneer Missouri River steamboating. Much to their surprise, they were upstaged by a civilian promotion. On May

28, 1819, the *Missouri Intelligencer and Boon's Lick Advertiser* of Franklin, Missouri Territory, announced that the steamboat *Independence,* captained by John Nelson of Louisville, Kentucky, had reached Franklin in thirteen days from St. Louis. This feat caused Nathaniel Patten, the paper's editor, to proclaim "the grand desideratum, the important fact is now ascertained, that Steam Boats can safely navigate the Missouri river."

The ascent of the *Independence* inspired another round of promoting the Boon's Lick country and Franklin, its main town. The region began attracting settlers before the War of 1812, when Missouri was still part of Louisiana Territory. In 1806 or thereabouts, Nathan and Daniel Morgan Boone, sons of the celebrated Kentucky frontiersman, went up the Missouri some 250 miles to make salt. Near present-day Boonesboro in western Howard County, they boiled water from natural salt licks to produce a marketable product. They exported some salt by dugout canoes made from sycamore logs, but soon abandoned the business. Nonetheless, their venture advertised the area and, because of their famous surname, gave it an identity.[55]

The Boon's Lick area did not have formal boundaries, but emigrants who went there generally thought it was the belt of land on both sides of the Missouri between the mouths of the Osage and Chariton rivers. Those who define things in terms of present-day cities would say approximately between Jefferson City and Glasgow.

Boon's Lick attracted settlers before most of Missouri to the east of it. When the first land seekers arrived in 1808, the only settlements between them and St. Charles, which was about twenty-five miles above the mouth of the Missouri, were Loutre Island, bordering Montgomery County, and Côte sans Dessein in Callaway County. The Boon's Lickers were drawn by the acclaimed fertility of the region's rich black soil, proximity to the Missouri, a presumed salubrious climate, and proximity to both woods and prairies. Boon's Lick lay in the transition zone between the forests to the east and grassland to the west. Wooded hills and valleys beyond the forested river bottoms were interspersed with fertile patches of prairie.[56] To aspiring farmers this varied terrain represented the best of both worlds. An early traveler noted, "This is probably the easiest unsettled country in the world to commence farming in. The emigrant has only to locate himself on the edge of a prairie, and he has the one-half of his farm a heavy forest and the other half a fertile plain or meadow, he has then only to fence in his ground and put in his crop."[57]

For a time Boon's Lick emigration was stalled by legal and Indian problems. Benjamin Cooper's and several other families tried to settle near later Boonville and Franklin in 1808. Their attempt to occupy Osage Indian lands provoked Meriwether Lewis, governor of Louisiana Territory, to order their evacuation. But circumstances favored the settlers. On November 10, 1808, Pierre Chouteau, a well-known St. Louis trader, signed a cession treaty with the Great and Little Osage at Fort Osage. By this agreement the Indians sold all of their remaining lands in Missouri and Arkansas north of the Arkansas River and east of a longitudinal line running through Fort Osage. The treaty's ratification on April 28, 1810, added the Boon's Lick country to the nation's public domain.[58]

The exiled squatters who returned in 1810 were soon joined by some slavehold-ing emigrants from Kentucky, Tennessee, and Virginia. By the outbreak of the War of 1812 an estimated eighty families lived in the region. They marked claims, but had to await the establishment of a local federal land office before they could acquire legal titles.[59] Their hopes for rapid development were dashed by pro-British Indians during the war. The Osage remained loyal to the United States, but roving bands of Sauks, Foxes, Iowas, and Potawatomis raided the isolated settlements. Throughout the war, Boon's Lickers, who were beyond any organ-ized county, hunkered down in hastily constructed log stockades and formed vol-unteer ranger units to battle the hostile Indians.[60]

As elsewhere in the American West, the end of the War of 1812 precipitated a sharp revival of settlement on the Missouri River frontier. If nothing else, the war forced many Indian tribes to abandon their alliances with the British and accept their new roles as subjects of the United States. They, like the land itself, were soon engulfed by American expansion.

Postwar movement into the Boon's Lick country was championed by Joseph Charless, editor of the *Missouri Gazette* of St. Louis. Charless was a master at cre-ating images of fertile wildernesses that needed only the hand of American civi-lization to become another promised land. His widely circulated portrayals of Boon's Lick as a latter-day Garden of Eden helped lure emigrants from Kentucky, Tennessee, and Virginia.[61]

By 1816 there were enough Boon's Lick settlers to cause the legislature of the four-year-old Territory of Missouri to provide them with county government. Howard County, like many frontier counties in American history, was initially made extraordinarily large to extend civil jurisdiction over widely scattered but sparse settlements. Territorial commissioners chose a squatter's claim, which was soon named Franklin after its Tennessee namesake, as the county seat. Located on Missouri River bottomland, Franklin got a post office and circuit court in 1817. However, its most significant prize was a U.S. land office, which opened in 1818.[62]

Because of their need to legalize claims, squatters had to visit Franklin, which was quickly recognized as the main community in the Boon's Lick country. The town's estimated population was four to five hundred by the end of 1818 and some-what over one thousand a year later.[63] A member of Long's Scientific Expedition, which stopped there in July 1819, observed that Franklin "contained about one hundred and twenty log houses of one story, several framed dwellings of two sto-ries, and two of brick, thirteen shops for the sale of merchandize, four taverns, two smiths' shops, two large steam-mills, two billiard-rooms, a court-house, a log prison of two stories, a post-office, and a printing press issuing a weekly paper."[64]

Franklin in the late teens was unrivaled as the political, economic, and cultural capital of the Boon's Lick country. The next-largest community, Chariton, lay some thirty miles by river to the northwest. Chariton, started in 1817 on the Chari-ton River about seven hundred yards above its merger with the Missouri, devel-oped quickly. By mid-1819 it had about fifty houses and nearly five hundred inhabitants. Because of its commercial potential, Chariton was visited by Captain Nelson during the maiden run of the *Independence*.[65]

Members of Long's party liked the prospects of a third place—Boonville, which was begun in 1819 on high ground south across the Missouri from Franklin. They noticed that aspiring developers had started other places as well, which were naturally boomed as the next great cities. At various sites below Franklin, claims consisting of sometimes nothing more than a single cabin, were designated by such names as Nashville, Smithton, and Rectorsville.[66]

Franklin's promotion of a steamboat voyage reflected the ambitions of its leaders, who envisioned a rapid transition from subsistence to commercial economy. The hopes of this rather atypical community were influenced by the composition of its first settlers. Dominated by propertied slave owners from the upper South, Franklinites emphasized land speculation and a desire to raise and market cash crops. Relatively well-off when they arrived, they expected to become richer. With land as the most obvious source of wealth, speculation was rife during the boom of 1818. Half-acre lots fronting Franklin's town square sold for $400 by February, or about double the price of the previous year. In December the lot price was a record $1,350.[67]

Rising land values, which created the illusion of wealth and the prospect of rapid growth, stimulated the desire of Franklinites to develop commercial ties with St. Louis and points east and south of it. Their remoteness from major markets and feelings of isolation led them to dramatically jolt their town into the emerging machine age. What little trade they had in 1819 could easily have been handled by keelboats and flatboats, but the use of either would not have attracted much attention. However, a steamboat arrival, especially of the first one to ascend the Missouri, could be promoted as the epochal event in their young history. The boat, which would represent the extension of technology to the backwoods, could be touted as part of the image-making of Franklin as the future metropolis of central Missouri.

Colonel Elias Rector of St. Louis, who speculated in lands in the Boon's Lick area, led the way in Franklin's community effort to recruit Captain Nelson and the *Independence*. Like all steamboat operators, Nelson, a middle-aged Louisville captain–boat proprietor, was a businessman. He could not have been convinced to steam to Franklin only to aid a local publicity stunt. Consequently, Rector arranged a paying trip by chartering the boat. The 98-ton side-wheel *Independence,* which had been launched earlier in the year at Shippingport, Kentucky, was loaded with flour, whiskey, sugar, iron, and other merchandise for Franklin and Chariton merchants. Editor Nathaniel Patten was kept informed of developments so he could help arrange a boisterous reception.[68]

When the *Independence* docked at Franklin on May 28 with Elias and Stephen Rector among its passengers it, was greeted by the "acclamations of an admiring crowd" who fired thirteen cannon shots. This so-called "federal salute" (for the thirteen original states) was returned by the *Independence*. In publicizing this dawn of a new age, Patten extolled the *Independence's* speed. Nelson had made it from St. Louis in seven running days during a thirteen-day span.[69]

As presented in the pages of the *Missouri Intelligencer and Boon's Lick Advertiser,* the voyage proved the "practicability of Steam Boat navigation" on the Missouri. Because of the precedent set by the *Independence,* Boon's Lick "shall be brought nearer to the Atlantic, West India, and European markets, and the abundant resources of our extensive and fertile region will be quickly developed."[70] Patten prophesied that steamboats would enable Americans to expand quickly up the Missouri. "At no distant period," he wrote, "may we see the industrious cultivator making his way as high as the Yellow Stone, and offering to the enterprising merchant and trader a surplus . . . yielding wealth to industry and enterprise."[71]

Patten's fellow townsmen celebrated the arrival of the *Independence* the next day with a sumptuous public banquet presided over by President Asa Morgan. Franklin banquets, which reflected the town's upper South heritage, were formal affairs replete with an elected president and vice president and a battery of toasts. Indeed, drinking another round in honor of some person, thing, or achievement epitomized Franklin sociability. Many diners were given a chance to make a toast; thirty-one accepted the honor at the first steamboat recognition banquet. They toasted such diverse subjects as the Missouri River, the memory of Robert Fulton, Captain Nelson, internal improvements, the purchase of Florida, Andrew Jackson, and the citizens of Franklin and Chariton.[72] One historian concluded that such excessive imbibition "must have taxed even frontier capacity. Perhaps the editor's frequent assurance that the utmost harmony and decorum prevailed was not entirely supererogatory."[73]

After toasting that he would "ever bear in grateful remembrance the liberality and hospitality of the citizens of Franklin"[74] Nelson moved his boat upstream to Chariton. There on May 31 the *Independence* "was welcomed by the cheering acclamations of hundreds of our citizens."[75] To show Nelson "some mark of their respect for his enterprise, skill, and perseverance," town leaders hosted him and his crew at a public banquet. Again the obligatory round of toasts honored things dear to the nation and area, including "the memory of the illustrious Washington" and the Missouri River.

The return of the *Independence* to St. Louis was perfunctory and anticlimactic. Its ascent to Franklin and Chariton raised false hopes that the Boon's Lick area was about to begin a booming cash business in exporting agricultural produce. Further, its reported incident-free voyage belied the difficulty of navigating the Missouri. Whether Nelson was skillful or just lucky is not known, but the *Independence* avoided a major disaster and had enough power to proceed against the Missouri's current. Nelson and the *Independence's* promoters certainly benefited from sympathetic newspaper coverage. It is quite likely that the ascent of the *Independence* was not as smooth as the public was led to believe. The boat was idled for nearly half of the days on its way to Franklin, far longer than the time required for refuelings. These long stoppages suggest there may have been groundings or mechanical problems. But given the promotional value of the voyage, there was probably a conspiracy of silence regarding any such complications.

Nelson returned to St. Louis as the town was absorbed with the pending launchings of the military and scientific expeditions. His voyage made it appear that the Missouri could be navigated easily by steamboats. Unfortunately for Johnson and Long, the *Independence's* accomplishment became the standard by which their steamboats would be measured.

When Colonel Atkinson began organizing his expedition at St. Louis and Fort Bellefontaine, he had to have been concerned about its dependence on steamboats. He was aware of the slow movement of Johnson's boats down the Ohio and was influenced by St. Louis–area army officers, who were very critical of the steamboat plan. Nonetheless, he felt obliged to tell Calhoun, "I have not the least doubt of the practicability of navigating the Missouri with steam power, notwithstanding the almost universal opinion to the contrary."[76]

But within several weeks, Atkinson was a keelboat advocate. Of Johnson's five boats, only three—the *Expedition,* the *Jefferson,* and the *Johnson*—were able to reach St. Louis. The *Calhoun* and the *Exchange* were stalled well downstream on the Mississippi, and their cargoes had to be forwarded by keelboats sent from St. Louis. This delay caused frustrated quartermaster officers to step up their criticism of Johnson. In their zeal to fault Johnson, the officers never acknowledged that some of his steamboat delays were caused by a severe drought that greatly lowered the Ohio.[77]

Atkinson also was influenced by the shortcomings of the *Western Engineer,* although it was not part of his command. His trip from Pittsburgh coincided with Long's movement, and the two met at Louisville, where the *Western Engineer* was being repaired for a second time. Atkinson reported that its "faults are not known to me, but I understand that the power which her boilers are capable of generating has not been properly applied to her propel[l]ing machinery."[78]

Long frankly admitted the boat's deficiencies. Writing to Calhoun before turning up the Mississippi, he noted that " our progress has been much retarded by occurrences beyond my control or foresight."[79] "Defects in the constitution of the Boat and engine" were aggravating, Long stated, but after making repairs at Cincinnati and Louisville, he was "inclined to think that our boat has now sufficient speed to stem the most rapid current of the navigable waters of this country." He must have had doubts after bucking the Mississippi's current. Lack of power forced him to use an auxiliary sail and lighten the boat's load by having some members of his party walk onshore alongside the boat. Interestingly, the pedestrians easily kept abreast of the boat.[80]

When Long's men arrived in St. Louis on June 9, they found great excitement about the impending expeditions. Atkinson was on hand with hundreds of troops. Johnson was frantically trying to forward military supplies to Fort Bellefontaine, and the quartermaster general of the U.S. Army, Thomas S. Jesup, was on hand to supervise outfitting the expedition. This largest peacetime movement of troops in the nation's history caught St. Louisians up in the spirit of the great adventure.

At the time, the fifty-five-year-old community had about four thousand inhabitants. When explorer Henry Rowe Schoolcraft visited St. Louis in 1818, he observed that many of its 550 buildings were made of stone and that the community featured forty stores, a post office, a land office, three banks, a brewery, two distilleries, and four flour mills. He thought its "situation in point of beauty, health, and convenience, is rarely equalled, and no place in the world, situated so far from the ocean, can at all compare with it, for commercial advantages."[81]

To the local press, St. Louis's destiny lay in its river commerce. In the spring of 1819, it had the "aspect of a seaport town," one editor observed: "Barges and keel boats with masts, sails and rigging, almost constantly line the shore for a mile and a half in front of the town. Steam boats are frequently seen anchored in the river." The town itself "presents the crowd, activity and bustle of a city while every branch and department of business exhibits a daily and striking increase."[82]

Long, Atkinson, and Jesup appreciated St. Louis hospitality, but Johnson had no reason to fondly remember the place. During his two-month stay in the area, he was harangued by civil authorities and vilified by army officers. His problem with local authorities stemmed from his alleged indebtedness to the recently closed Bank of St. Louis. The bank, beset by stockholder lawsuits and other litigation, convinced a St. Louis judge that Johnson had failed to repay a $50,000 loan. The judge, in turn, ordered the county sheriff to seize Johnson's steamboats as a way of satisfying the debt. But when the sheriff appeared at Bellefontaine to execute the writ, Captain Silas Craig of the *Expedition* threatened him by drawing a pistol. The sheriff pulled back but promised to return with more force. Colonel Talbot Chambers, commandant of Fort Bellefontaine, said he would not get involved in the spat by protecting Johnson with troops. Fearing the loss of his steamboats and other property, Johnson escaped Missouri's jurisdiction by removing to the Illinois side of the Mississippi opposite the mouth of the Missouri.[83]

This ploy further provoked army officers. By relocating to the Illinois shore, Johnson complicated the transference of goods to the military expedition. Chambers and Brevet Brigadier General Daniel Bissell, commander of troops in the St. Louis district, insisted that all subsistence rations and other goods brought by Johnson from Kentucky be unloaded on shore, unpacked, inspected, and repacked. These actions were justified, they contended, to assure that both quality and quantity stipulations had been met. Naturally, they preferred to handle the process at Fort Bellefontaine.[84]

James Johnson reacted in typical fashion. He complained to his brother Richard, at home in Great Crossings, Kentucky, who relayed his concerns to Calhoun. The Johnsons implied that the bank debt had been repaid, but that the bank's cashier absconded with the funds and failed to credit James Johnson's account. To complicate matters, Richard Johnson suggested to Calhoun that Chambers and Bissell be court-martialed for their roles in delaying the expedition.[85] With an arrogance honed by their penchant for dealing only with the highest authorities, the Johnsons presumed that Quartermaster General Jesup would agree with them.

However, within a matter of days after his arrival at Bellefontaine, Jesup was openly allied with Chambers, Bissell, and the quartermaster officers who were to outfit the expedition. Complaining about Johnson's steamboats, Jesup wrote that "they are badly managed and their crews are entirely without discipline."[86] Other Johnson critics thought the contractor was particularly vulnerable on the steamboat issue. Chambers was appalled that the *Expedition* took five days to cover the twenty-five miles from St. Louis to Fort Bellefontaine. With its seven-foot draft and "feeble" machinery, he thought, "there exists but little doubt but that she can never reach her destined station" on the Missouri.[87]

On the civilian front, the *St. Louis Enquirer* led the attacks on Johnson and his steamboats. When the *Calhoun* failed to reach St. Louis, the paper stated, "she is below in the river, and from a defect in her machinery, or in her management, makes a wretched progress against the current of the Mississippi."[88] Under the guise of reporting the news, the *Enquirer,* like most newspapers of its day, intermingled factual information and editorializing. Some St. Louisians probably discounted its attacks on Johnson because they thought that Thomas Hart Benton, the *Enquirer*'s editor and also a stockholder in the Bank of St. Louis, disguised his real motive for ridiculing Johnson.[89]

By the time Atkinson and the three Johnson steamboats started up the Missouri from Fort Bellefontaine on July 5, army officers and the contractor were thoroughly disillusioned with each other. Atkinson, Jesup, Bissell, and their subordinates charged that the failure to get under way sooner was Johnson's fault. The nonarrival of the *Calhoun* and the *Exchange* caused Atkinson to announce a modest season's goal of establishing his main post at the Council Bluff. But he also thought if the expedition moved fast enough, he would send some troops to the Mandan village. Anticipating a heavy reliance on keelboats, Atkinson began experimenting with propelling them by man-powered side wheels.[90]

Other than contending that Johnson's steamboats were unsuitable, Jesup and Bissell charged that he shortchanged the army in measuring barreled pork, that some of the meat was of inferior quality, and that he did not deliver as much goods as he had agreed to do. Because of these alleged shortcomings, Jesup authorized purchases of flour and some other foodstuffs at St. Louis and engaged independent St. Louis keelboat operators to transport them.[91] Johnson challenged all of these contentions and actions. He insisted his boats would do well on the Missouri, that he had honored his government contracts, and that Jesup violated the contract by employing other freighters.[92]

Long was aware of Atkinson's decision to stop at the Council Bluff before the Scientific Expedition left St. Louis on June 21 aboard the *Western Engineer*.[93] "This undertaking," commented the *Missouri Gazette and Public Advertiser* of St. Louis, "is worthy of an enlightened and patriotic government, and its success will confer deserved renown both on its projectors and its executors."[94] After the experience of the *Independence,* the editor, like most of the public, thought the *Western Engineer* would proceed rapidly up the Missouri.

But Long and his men soon found out otherwise. When they entered the Missouri on June 22, the raging river was at an unusually high flood stage, but sandbars were still exposed. The *Western Engineer* grounded twice on the same bar within two miles of the mouth. Frequent groundings throughout the trip were compounded by rapid currents in chutes, which the boat could not stem under its own power. The usual supplemental power was achieved by running out a line, which was either towed by men walking on the bank or tied to a large tree and taken up by a man-powered windlass.[95]

Other delays were caused by the river's silt-laden water. The boilers were often clogged by baked mud. Sometimes they had to be cleaned more than once a day. Cleaning required stopping long enough for the boilers to cool down before a man could crawl inside them and scrap off the residue. Plagued by these delays, the inventive Long adopted the expedient of blowing the boilers out with a tube. More serious problems were caused by the abrasive action of sand in the water, which damaged the engine valves. This difficulty forced Long to stop six days at Franklin to make repairs.[96]

Beyond Chariton, the last place where wood could be obtained from settlers, the *Western Engineer*'s crew had to spend hours onshore gathering deadwood and cutting trees. Deadwood from two of the largest and softest trees—cottonwood and basswood—did not burn well, because it had absorbed too much moisture. After considerable experimentation, Long determined that the best fuel, when it could be found, was dry mulberry wood.[97]

On the way to Franklin, Long's complement was enlarged at St. Charles when Benjamin O'Fallon, the recently appointed agent for Indian Affairs on the Missouri, and his interpreter, John Dougherty, came on board. At that community, Say, Jessup, Peale, and Seymour left the boat to proceed overland apace with the *Western Engineer*. By then, Baldwin, who had been very ill since the expedition left Pittsburgh, was confined to the boat. The overlanders, who rejoined the boat at Loutre Island, had no difficulty keeping up. The methodical Long kept records of the expedition's ascent. From St. Charles to Franklin, which was reached on July 13, he ran the *Western Engineer* for ninety-seven hours during eighteen and a half days.[98]

Long and his men were treated like visiting dignitaries at Franklin. The town's newspaper lauded the scientific purpose of their expedition but was unimpressed with their use of a steamboat. Editor Patten thought a steamboat was too large and cumbersome to make the frequent stops required for scientific observations. Long's revelation to Franklinites that he intended to go only to the Council Bluff was their first information that the "Yellowstone Expedition" had been canceled. A pall was cast over the enthusiastic greeting of the expedition by Dr. Baldwin's worsening lung failure. He was left behind with some townspeople in the desperate hope that he would recover, but he died on September 1 of a "pulmonary complaint."[99]

During his Franklin stop, Long reflected on his disappointing progress. The *Western Engineer* had averaged slightly over two miles an hour from St. Charles, considerably less than his expectation of three. Calhoun and Long hoped that faster movement above Franklin would validate their faith in steamboats. Calhoun encouragingly noted that "the navigation of the Missouri is said to be much better above than below Franklin."[100]

But instead of speeding up, the *Western Engineer* slowed somewhat to just under two miles an hour over the remaining distance to the Council Bluff. With the boat averaging only eleven miles per day of operation, the Scientific Expedition did not reach its Council Bluff destination until September 17. Long stopped briefly near Fort Lisa, the post of St. Louis trader Manuel Lisa's Missouri Fur Company. Two days later his men started building their winter camp, Engineer Cantonment, on the west side of the river about a half mile above the fort and five miles below the Council Bluff. There they awaited the arrival of Atkinson's expedition.[101]

The movement of Atkinson's 1,100-man expedition was a logistical nightmare. The men who had wintered at Martin Cantonment were reduced to hunting and scavenging while they awaited being resupplied by Johnson's steamboats. Others who were sent from Fort Bellefontaine before the steamboats were inadequately supplied by their keelboat escorts. Because the poor-performing *Jefferson* was delayed in reaching Fort Bellefontaine, Atkinson did not start moving his command and the three steamboats until July 5. He intended that they would overtake all advance units, resupply the troops, and move on to the Council Bluff as a unified force.[102]

While Atkinson had misgivings about the steamboats, he could hardly have anticipated their dismal performances. With appropriate regard for military orderliness, Atkinson supervised a grand send-off. Precisely at noon on July 5, the three steamboats moved out in "military array," with the *Johnson*, Atkinson's headquarters boat, leading the *Expedition* and *Jefferson* upstream. Three days later, after numerous groundings and using towlines to overcome the strong current, they had only reached St. Charles, twenty-five miles from their start. In disgust, Atkinson left the *Johnson* and announced that he would take men overland to Fort Osage and that each boat was on its own.[103]

Steamboat problems on the way to St. Charles proved to be prophetic. None of the boats reached their destination and generally, while they were operating, moved slower than keelboats. The *Expedition* performed the best by managing to reach Martin Cantonment, where it was grounded and forced to spend the winter because of low water. The *Johnson*, whose major mechanical problems included a two-week halt because of a hole burned in a boiler, was crippled a short distance above Fort Osage when a cylinder head burst into pieces. The *Jefferson*, which gained only twenty-seven miles in a two-week period, was snagged near Côte sans Dessein.[104]

Thomas Hart Benton of the *Enquirer* proclaimed the boat to be "a whimsical affair": "It is credibly said that she draws seven feet water when empty, five when loaded—is hog backed—and spends much of her time aground in a river half a mile wide and thirty feet deep."[105] Benton was somewhat hyperbolic, but William

David Hubbell, the *Johnson*'s twenty-one-year-old clerk, confirmed that none of the boats had an even draft. Declaring them to be as "totally unfit for the trip as could be," Hubbell recalled that, when empty, they drew 6.5 feet aft and 2 feet in the bow and when loaded 6 feet in the stern and 4.5 in the bow. His own boat, Hubbell wrote, "was aground every day and frequently, at nights, we could look back and see the place we started from in the morning."[106]

Cargoes of the steamboats were forwarded by keelboats to the Council Bluff. This work fell to Silas Craig, master of the *Expedition,* and Uriel Sebree, Johnson's field supervisor. Johnson himself returned to his Kentucky home soon after the boats left Fort Bellefontaine. Jesup, who went as far as Fort Osage, and Atkinson regularly reported the steamboat fiasco to Calhoun. News of the steamboat failure was widely distributed throughout the country after being reported by St. Louis newspapers.[107]

The *Expedition* and the *Johnson* were retrieved the following spring, but the *Jefferson* was a total loss. The spring rise made it possible for some of Johnson's men to take the *Expedition* back to St. Louis, and the *Johnson* was repaired and navigated downstream after a replacement cylinder head was obtained in Louisville, Kentucky. Sebree simply abandoned the badly damaged *Jefferson* after removing its cargo in late August 1819. It thus became the Missouri's first steamboat casualty.[108]

Within days after Atkinson reached the Council Bluff vicinity on September 29, he started building winter quarters. Camp Missouri was placed on wooded bottomland on the west bank about a mile and a half above the famed bluff where Lewis and Clark had met with Otoe and Missouri Indians. Although Atkinson did not attempt to send any men to the Mandan village, having reaching the Council Bluff was a considerable achievement. Atkinson and the troops who had started from Plattsburgh had traveled 2,628 miles—a new record for the longest movement of a U.S. Army command.[109]

Atkinson and Long assumed their stops at Council Bluff completed only the first phase of their movements to the Mandan village. So did Calhoun. As fall melded into winter, Atkinson and Long dealt separately with Calhoun about plans for 1820. Long proposed that he would reach the Mandan village from the east by way of Lake Superior and the new fort on the upper Mississippi. Then he would descend the Missouri to Engineer Cantonment before exploring westward along the Platte River.[110]

As Calhoun contemplated advancing the military expedition to the Mandan village, he believed the 1819 system, with some improvements, should be continued. He ruled that Johnson's existing contract applied to 1820, and he still insisted that steamboats were the best way of impressing Indians and British traders with America's ability to maintain remote forts. But he was also attentive to Jesup's admonishment that any steamer should be no larger than about 100 tons and have a draft of no more than four and a half feet.[111]

For their part, the Johnsons not only thought they were entitled to the 1820 business but also wanted a reconstituted expedition to go all the way to the Yellowstone. Richard Mentor Johnson in particular championed a Yellowstone fort to help realize America's expansionist destiny. He also linked Missouri River exploration with the economic distress of Kentucky and nearby states and territories. The Panic of 1819 had severely depressed the regional economy. Johnson believed federal expenditures for military supplies and transportation would provide some relief from bank foreclosures and lagging sales. To prove the economic benefits of the military expedition, James Johnson pointed out that he had employed some 350 men in 1819 to procure and forward military supplies.[112]

The political influence of the Johnsons was not easily ignored. It was common knowledge that during the summer of 1819, President Monroe had personally authorized an advance of $107,500 on the Johnson transportation contract. He took this action after going out of his way on his Southern tour to visit Richard Mentor Johnson at Great Crossings, Kentucky.[113]

As events transpired, the fate of the two suspended expeditions was decided by Congress rather than Calhoun. Since one of the congressional reactions to the panic was to reduce federal expenditures, the expeditions were obvious targets. On December 21, 1819, the House of Representatives passed a resolution requesting information on "the expenditures which have been, and are likely to be, incurred in fitting out and prosecuting the expedition ordered to the mouth of the Yellow Stone."[114]

Calhoun's response of February 23, 1820, shocked some House members. It showed that Johnson, who had drawn $229,762 in warrants from the Quartermaster Department, claimed the government still owed him $256,818.05. The House was so outraged by the expenses of the costliest peacetime expedition in the country's history that it ordered a complete investigation of Johnson.[115]

Meanwhile, the War Department and Johnson had agreed to submit their respective cases to a panel of three arbitrators. Significantly, the House and the arbitrators reached different conclusions. The House investigating committee reported that Johnson had been allowed $47,249.51 for undocumented claims and $14,969.28 for the transportation of articles not carried on his boats. But the arbitrators agreed with Johnson that Jesup and other quartermaster officers should have given him more time to rectify problems before arranging transportation with St. Louis keelboatmen. Their judgment was that the government still owed him $275,215.[116]

Once the alleged excessive cost of the expeditions became public, they were a political liability to the Monroe administration. In March 1820, after it was obvious that Congress would not fund any further military move up the Missouri, Calhoun ended the military expedition and revised Long's mission. From Engineer Cantonment, Long and a small party of scientists explored westward along the Platte River and returned to the Mississippi by following the Arkansas River. Lieutenant Graham navigated the *Western Engineer* downstream to St. Louis in June 1820.[117]

When it reconvened in 1821, Congress not only rejected the arbitration award but also sought to recover some funds from Johnson. The ensuing government suit against Johnson was denied by a federal court in Frankfort, Kentucky.[118]

Despite the furor over his steamboats and his contract, neither James Johnson nor his de facto partner Richard Johnson suffered politically. James was elected to the House of Representatives from a Kentucky congressional district in 1824 but died during his first term. Richard had been chosen as a U.S. senator from Kentucky in 1819. After ten years in the Senate, he served four terms in the House. His political career was capped by four years as vice president of the United States during the Martin Van Buren administration, 1837–41.[119]

The steamboat experiences of 1819 provoked a realistic appraisal of their effectiveness. The army, which was left with a new fort and a partially completed mission, still faced the problem of effectively supplying the post and bringing the Indians of the distant upper Missouri country under American control. Henry Atkinson was convinced that the use of steamboats was premature. For troop movement, he preferred using keelboats or overland routes paralleling the river. The Quartermaster Department did not categorically rule out steamboats but decided they should be used only when they could be run during high river stages.

The Boon's Lick settlers had no reason to be disappointed with the performance of the *Independence*. But the depressed conditions caused by the Panic of 1819 forced them to recognize that regular steamboat traffic would be possible only if and when their area had enough trade to justify a relatively large two-way commerce. Promotion made headlines, but a new costlier transportation system could be achieved only when everyone involved could make money.

3

ESTABLISHMENT OF THE
STEAMBOAT TRADE, 1820–1836

Steamboat commerce on the Missouri did not develop nearly as rapidly as Franklin's boosters had assumed. Their hopes for a rapid transition to commercial agriculture were first stalled by the Panic of 1819 and then by the stubborn persistence of a subsistence economy in the Boon's Lick region. Furthermore, the poor performance of the Johnson boats on the Missouri Expedition raised serious doubts about the likelihood of efficient and profitable steamboating. However, increased migration, economic improvement, and more powerful steamboats led to the start of a regular packet trade—vessels carrying both freight and passengers—in 1829. Three years later a St. Louis–based steamboat reached the mouth of the Yellowstone.

Steamboating was based on population growth, which caused the rapid formation of counties and towns. In 1820, Missouri Territory's last full year, its 66,586 inhabitants, including 10,222 slaves and 376 free blacks, lived mainly along the Mississippi from about Cape Girardeau upstream to approximately forty miles above St. Louis and along the Missouri westward to Chariton. The two greatest concentrations were in St. Louis County and the Boon's Lick area. St. Louis, with 4,598 residents, far surpassed any other municipality in size, but Franklin, with about a thousand people and a central location, aspired to become Missouri's metropolis. Franklin's hopes sprung from the rapid pace of Boon's Lick growth. Howard County, with 13,426 residents, and neighboring Cooper County, with 6,959, were home to more than a third of all Missourians.[1]

But Franklin's dreams of becoming the next great place were dashed by a series of misfortunes. Its ebullience had been thwarted by the expanding financial panic, which had struck the region east of Missouri in 1819. After a heavy influx of settlers in 1819 and the spring of 1820, hard times reached the Boon's Lick country. Its fragile economy was especially vulnerable because of excessive land claims. Many first setters were also land speculators who had claimed far more land than they actually needed by making only down payments. As money was drained off by Eastern creditors, many who had bought on the margin tried to sell, without success, and became land-poor. As the value of farmland and town lots plummeted, foreclosures became commonplace.[2]

The panic was compounded by Missouri's lack of banks. The Bank of St. Louis, Missouri's first, closed in the spring of 1819. The second bank—the Bank of Missouri—failed four years after its founding in St. Louis in 1817. Without a banking system, the panic worsened. Bartering was widespread, and no capital was available to stimulate transportation, manufacturing, and internal improvements.

When President James Monroe declared Missouri a state on August 10, 1821, panic conditions were rampant. As a partial solution, the first state legislature approved a two-and-a-half-year moratorium on land debts. The legislators also established a system of state loan offices to act as a type of state bank. This scheme failed. Its underfunding alone probably would have killed it, but the coup de grâce was a state supreme court decision that it was unconstitutional.

Without effective state aid, Boon's Lick merchants and farmers increased production and processing of hemp and tobacco for local and export markets. The area was well suited for both crops. The climate was favorable, many of the settlers who had moved from Kentucky, Tennessee, and Virginia had experience with them, and slaves satisfied their labor-intensive requirements. Boon's Lick farmers also started raising some cotton.[3]

In October, 1821, Isaac N. Bernard opened a Franklin rope walk to make hemp products. Rope walks were long, low buildings in which spinners paced back and forth to twist strands of hemp fiber into various kinds of light and heavy cordage, ranging from fishlines to keelboat cordelles. After fastening fibers to a hook on a revolving wheel, the rope maker walked backwards while releasing hemp fiber from a supply carried on his waist. After strands were made in this way, several of them were twisted to make rope. Bernard hoped his venture would make the Boon's Lick economy more self-sufficient. He vowed to undersell all imported cordage to help keep more dollars at home. To supply his need for hemp, he offered to negotiate multiyear contracts with area farmers.[4]

Tobacco, likewise, lent itself to local processing. After being harvested in the fall, it was aged in farm storage sheds over the winter and marketed the next summer. Franklin's pioneer buyers were merchants Henry V. Bingham and William Lamme. Early in the spring of 1822 they started advertising that their "tobacco manufactory" was selling "a variety of Chewing Tobacco and Cigars" as well as "Good Leaf Tobacco."[5]

During the panic years especially, "selling" was the Boon's Lick euphemism for bartering. Franklin's general merchants accepted such products as beef, pork, tobacco, hemp, tallow, lard, salt, "country linen," beeswax, and honey for imported goods and to settle debts. Dollars and cents provided a value system, but with only scant cash on hand, business was stymied. Imported goods sold very slowly.[6] Consequently, there was no need to import large quantities of merchandise from the two principal supply points—New Orleans and Philadelphia. The modest shipments did not require steamboat capacities. In 1821 Henry Shreve navigated his steamboat *Washington* to the Council Bluff with supplies for the army post. But Franklin's spring imports were shipped by the keelboats *Domestic* and *Missouri*. The *Domestic,* owned by a Pittsburgh company, made the voyage from St. Louis in an unprecedented ten days—only a third to a half of normal keelboat speed. Since the *Domestic* moved as rapidly as the steamer *Independence* had, keelboating seemed adequate for Franklin's importing.[7]

To export hemp, tobacco, and other produce, Franklinites used relatively inexpensive flatboats. These craft were easy to make from locally cut wood. In the fall of 1821 several Boon's Lick flatboats laden with produce for New Orleans passed St. Louis. The boats were reported to "compose the van of a much greater number that are on their way down."[8]

Franklin's leaders hoped to stimulate business by organizing the Boon's Lick Exporting Company, intended to provide "prosperity of the farmer, and through him prosperity of the whole community."[9] The company's sponsors proposed to raise at least $50,000, but not more than $500,000, by selling $50 shares in an enterprise that would buy, store, and ship produce by flatboats. In the depressed economy, raising that amount in cash was impossible. So the organizers invited subscribers to obtain shares by granting the company a lien on any clear-title property. Any such purchasers were required to pay at least 2 percent in cash. Lack of funding doomed the ambitious scheme. After its initial publicity, the company was not newsworthy. So Franklin merchants independent of the company continued buying, storing, and shipping.

Like all river ports, Franklin developed a storage and commission business. In the spring of 1822 Giles M. Samuel advertised that he would accept produce "on storage or for disposition as the owners may direct" at his two warehouses.[10] Storage was necessitated by the nature of boating. Since farmers brought their products to a landing in wagons over a period of time and boats ran only when there was a full or nearly full cargo, secure storage had to be available at the landing. Agents such as Samuel charged monthly storage fees and sales commissions. Transactions, including payments to farmers, could not be completed until the products were sold at a distant market.

Boating was vital to Boon's Lick development because it was the fastest and most efficient way of making large shipments. But the Missouri was usually closed by ice during the winter and oftentimes too low during the navigation season. So certain activities, such as moving mail and light freight and facilitating the movement of emigrants who had wagons and livestock, led to demands for good roads. Boon's Lickers, on the western edge of the nation's farming frontier, wanted state roads connecting them with the Mississippi and the extension of the Cumberland Road into Missouri.

The Cumberland Road, commonly called the National Road, had its genesis in an 1806 congressional act authorizing a federal road connecting the Potomac

River and the state of Ohio. The start of construction west of Cumberland, Maryland, was delayed until 1811, but by 1818, stagecoach traffic was opened from Washington, D.C., to Wheeling, Virginia, on the Ohio River. In 1820, roused by the increasing political clout of western states, Congress approved the extension of the road from Wheeling to the mouth of the Illinois River on the Mississippi.[11]

The original Boon's Lick trail connecting St. Charles and Franklin was only a trace through timbered bottomland along the Missouri River. Its frequent muddiness stalled movement. Mail delivery time by stages over its some 200 miles ran from eight to fifteen days. In 1822 a new higher, drier, and straighter road was opened well north of the river. Paralleling present-day I-70, it followed ridgetops whenever possible. Franklinites were enthused by a June 1822 report that mail stages using the new road would reach them in only three days from St. Charles. But editor Nathaniel Patten wanted weekly or, better yet, semiweekly mail instead of the planned biweekly deliveries.[12]

A "new arrangement" of a weekly service from St. Louis was publicized in late 1823. But within six weeks it was discontinued "sine die," having never been conducted for more than a third of the route. Finally, in June 1824 a line of mail stages from Louisville, Kentucky, to Franklin was "in full operation."[13] Difficulties in delivering mail, passengers, and some freight were blamed on unsafe bridges and holes in the road. Through his newspaper, Patten campaigned for road improvement and lamented the "neglected condition of our highways, which every where admonish us that barbarism still lingers in a country pretty well peopled by christians."[14]

Despite bad roads and infrequent river trade, the Boon's Lick economy gradually improved after 1822. The start of some new towns, which stimulated the need for skilled laborers, helped. Immigration, reported to have "gained considerable impetus" in 1824 swelled as much as tenfold the next year. These new Missourians accelerated settlement both inland from the Missouri and westward along it.[15]

Franklin's leaders were encouraged about revived trade prospects when the steamboat *Pittsburgh and St. Louis Packet,* captained by William Scott, arrived with "full freight" in early spring 1823. The St. Louis–based 131-ton side-wheeler was the first steamboat after the *Independence* to have Franklin as its final destination, and its record time of 77 hours over slightly less than six days was promising. But movement northward in Howard County left Franklin on its southern edge. The would-be metropolis suffered a heavy blow when the county seat was moved to the centrally located new town of Fayette in the fall of 1823.[16]

Meanwhile, other towns—Boonville, Columbia, Jefferson City, and Rocheport—were becoming regionally important. Boonville, south across the Missouri River from Franklin, developed a trade to the south. Its hilltop location not only was flood-proof but was also alleged to be healthier than humid bottomland. Columbia was platted in 1821 as the seat of Boone County, which had been separated from Howard the year before. Jefferson City was a child of Missouri's decision to have a centrally located state capital. The state constitution provided that commissioners would choose a permanent capital site to succeed St. Charles. In

1821 they selected the location, which the legislature approved. In 1826, four years after the "City of Jefferson" was platted, the legislature began meeting there. As the city grew, it took on added significance as a major port, the seat of Cole County, and the home of the state penitentiary. Rocheport, at the mouth of Moniteau Creek, probably had the best natural harbor on the Missouri. Deep water below a rocky bluff assured a stable landing that was quite immune to changes in the erratic stream. By 1820, five years before the town's founding, a warehouse had been built at the mouth of the creek, which was a launching point for flatboats.[17]

Upstream from Chariton, settlement followed the Missouri across the state, whose western boundary was a due north-south line running through the middle of the mouth of the Kansas River. The first cabin at what became Liberty Landing was erected in the spring of 1820. Two years later Clay County was organized, with Liberty, about six miles north of the Missouri, as its seat. South of the river, settlement in westernmost Missouri was temporarily blocked by a twenty-four-mile-wide strip of unceded Indian land running from the Missouri River to the state's southern boundary. The United States acquired the tract in 1825 by two treaties William Clark negotiated with Indian representatives at St. Louis. As part of much larger cessions, the Great and Little Osage and the Kansas Indians relinquished all their land claims in Missouri. The next year, the state legislature formed Jackson County, and soon thereafter state commissioners designated the site of Independence as its seat. The first lots in Independence, several miles from the Missouri, were sold in 1827. Between Chariton and Independence, the main river town was Lexington, started in 1822.[18]

During the immigration resurgence, Franklin's future was decided by the cantankerous Missouri. The great flood of 1826 started the downfall. By mid-May the river was said to be "higher than has been known in thirty years."[19] All the bottomlands downstream from the Council Bluff were flooded, and part of Franklin washed away when its unstable riverbank crumbled. Some Franklinites decided it was time to leave permanently. Among them was Nathaniel Patten, who moved his *Missouri Intelligencer* fourteen miles north to Fayette.[20] Observing that Franklin had risen fast "with fictitious splendor," Patten sold his property "(which had cost us a fortune) for a mere song" because he thought the town could not survive.[21] Those who stayed were devastated by another flood in 1828. Many responded by moving two and a half miles inland and starting "New Franklin," which was well advertised by the fall of 1829.[22] They took their braggadocio along. When New Franklin was barely three years old, it reportedly had " increased in so rapid a manner as to astonish the original proprietors; and augurs fair to be, at no remote period, in population and wealth, second only to the great metropolis of the state."[23] As neither a port nor a county seat, New Franklin was destined to remain small, but its planners had big dreams. They hoped to engage in Missouri River commerce by a railroad connection. Town meetings in 1832 led to a plan for holding a railroad lottery to raise some $15,000 to build the short line. But the scheme never got beyond the promotional stage.[24]

Meanwhile, a remnant of Old Franklin lingered until yet another flood, in June 1835. After a sudden sharp rise, caused by snowmelt from the distant Rockies, carried away the last buildings, Old Franklin was reduced to a memory of its brief glory days. Its smallness belied its impact. As the main community in central Missouri, it was both the end of the Boon's Lick Trail and the beginning of the Santa Fe Trail. Its ambitious promoters stimulated settlement and steamboating. An amazing number of its citizens became famous during or after their Franklin years. Four members of the community—Lillburn W. Boggs, Hamilton R. Gamble, Claiborne F. Jackson, and John Miller—became Missouri governors. Gamble and three other onetime Franklin lawyers—Abiel Leonard, John F. Ryland, and George Tompkins—served as state supreme court justices. William Becknell, "the Father of the Santa Fe Trade," was a Franklinite. Another of its famous sons was artist George Caleb Bingham, whose father was an early promoter of tobacco processing.[25] Unfortunately, Old Franklin's genius did not include river geology. Members of Long's Scientific Expedition noted that the town stood on alluvium recently deposited by the meandering river. They observed that the steam "which appears to be at this time encroaching on its bank" would probably reclaim the Franklin site.[26]

Despite surging population, the Boon's Lick trade required no more than one steamboat a year until 1828. In 1826 only the *Muskingum* from Pittsburgh delivered general merchandise at Franklin. Importing and exporting were increased in 1828 by single voyages of the *Bolivar,* the *Illinois, La Grange,* the *Liberator,* and the *Maryland.* Dealer Jesse Spence used *La Grange* to ship Chariton and Franklin tobacco to New Orleans, and all five boats carried general merchandise to Boon's Lick ports. Shipments on *La Grange* and the *Liberator* included dry goods, hardware, groceries, and queensware. For one Franklin merchant, the *Illinois* delivered five hogsheads of sugar, seven barrels of mackerel, and four tons of assorted iron. Lamme and Brothers of Franklin and David S. Lamme and Company of Columbia had "a large and extensive assortment of fancy spring goods" transported by the *Bolivar.*[27]

This unprecedented steamboat commerce was due, in part, to the Santa Fe trade and federal government activities. Missouri's trade with Santa Fe, New Mexico, some eight hundred miles southwest of the mouth of the Kansas River, began by happenstance. In the fall of 1821 William Becknell and several companions left Franklin with pack animals to trade with Comanche Indians. On the distant western plains Becknell chanced to meet some Mexican troops who invited him to take his goods to Santa Fe. There Becknell was cordially greeted by the governor, who encouraged further trade. When New Mexico was part of Spain's North American claims, American traders had not been not welcome. But when Mexico achieved its independence in 1821, its officials saw benefits from dealing with American traders. New Mexico, which could be supplied easier from Missouri than from points in Mexico, was chronically short of dry goods, hardware, and other household goods but had a surplus of specie, mules, and horses. On their return trip, Santa Fe traders often acquired beaver and other furs from American Rocky Mountain trappers and traders.[28]

Becknell dramatically publicized his success in late January 1823, when he returned to Franklin. Reportedly, he dumped "heaps of dollars" on Franklin's sidewalks and paid one townsman a $900 return on a $60 investment.[29] In the panic-stricken Boon's Lick economy Becknell found eager investors for another Santa Fe expedition. With twenty-one men, three farm wagons, and a number of pack animals, he led the way from Franklin westward to the Arrow Rock ferry and past the site of Fort Osage. His second profitable expedition and his pioneer use of wagons, earned Becknell the "Father of the Santa Fe trade" designation.[30]

From its beginnings the Santa Fe trade was a community venture. Unlike the Missouri River fur trade, which was dominated by an elite St. Louis group, the Santa Fe business lent itself to widespread local participation. Organizers got their men, animals, vehicles, and investors in the Franklin vicinity without forming major companies or having the backing of distant capitalists. In 1822 a second Franklin-based expedition, led by Benjamin Cooper, also traded with Santa Fe. By 1824 newspapers reported that nearly everyone in Franklin was directly or indirectly involved in the Santa Fe trade.[31]

That year the Santa Fe expedition, led by Meredith M. Marmaduke, had eighty-one men with an assortment of twenty-five dearborns, carts, and freight wagons. With returns of $180,000 in gold and silver and $10,000 in furs, its economic benefits to Missouri were enormous. Anticipating expanding business, traders were apprehensive about passing through unceded Indian lands west of Missouri. They wanted the federal government to survey and mark the trail and obtain a right-of-way through Indian country. They found a willing ally in the expansionistic Senator Thomas Hart Benton, who introduced appropriate legislation.[32] Congress approved Benton's proposal on March 3, 1825. During the following summer, three federal commissioners surveyed and marked the road. While thus engaged, they obtained rights-of-way from the Osage and Kansas Indians in exchange for modest $500 payments in either goods or money.[33]

By 1828, Franklin's last major trading year, the Santa Fe trade continued to expand. That May, Fayette as well as Franklin presented "to the eye of the beholder a busy, bustling and commercial scene"[34] replete with buying, selling, and packing goods and training mules. The *Missouri Intelligencer* estimated that the number of traders from Howard and nearby counties would probably exceed 150. The entire wagon train consisted of a number of economic subparts, which banded together for security. In some instances men were employees of investors, but some independent operators, including local merchants, carried their own goods.

Since most of the goods bound for Santa Fe originated in Philadelphia, prices were based on wholesale costs there. Outfitters bought merchandise from Franklin and other Boon's Lick area merchants at 20 to 30 percent above the Philadelphia prices. Their expected return on these purchases was 40 to 60 percent. So the value of the trade had to be reckoned on both the cost at the Missouri starting point and the worth of Santa Fe receipts. Total purchases to ready the 1828 train reportedly approached $100,000.[35]

Old Franklin's demise did not bring a sudden end to Howard County's Santa Fe trade. A caravan including Franklin merchant Samuel C. Lamme, who was killed by Indians on the trip out, traded from the county in 1829.[36] In conventional thinking, the Santa Fe Trail was an overland route. But considering the origin of its merchandise, it was really a combined water-land route. Water transportation was invariably cheaper and faster than overland freighting. Even if the Missouri had not destroyed Franklin, the town would have lost its dominance in the Santa Fe business as soon as some upstream community near the mouth of the Kansas had adequate outfitting facilities. By 1830, Independence had enough merchants, steamboat connections, and population to become the new mistress of the Santa Fe trade.

As the Santa Fe business was being developed, some Missouri River boating resulted from the frontier activities of the army and the federal Indian service. After the Missouri Expedition of 1819, the army had to supply its new fort near the Council Bluff. The scurvy-ridden troops suffered through their first winter and, the next spring, were forced by the flooding river to relocate Camp Missouri on nearby higher ground. In January 1821 the post was renamed Fort Atkinson by order of Secretary of War John C. Calhoun.[37]

Post commander Henry Atkinson and his successor, Henry Leavenworth, supplied Fort Atkinson by both river and overland. In 1820, when the post was most dependent on imports, the *Expedition* delivered provisions. After some of James Johnson's men repaired the *Johnson*, it and the companion *Expedition* reached St. Louis in early April 1820. The *Johnson* was taken out of Missouri River service, but the *Expedition*, the most successful Johnson steamboat in 1819, was sent to the Council Bluff fort. Captain Silas Craig navigated to Franklin in only eight days but then struggled for over a month to reach the fort, where the boat was stranded by low water. The crew returned to St. Louis by keelboat. After wintering over for the second consecutive year, the *Expedition*, commanded by a Captain McGuire, did not return to St. Louis until early June 1821. In 1820 another steamboat, the *Missouri*, at least got part of the way to the fort. Carrying flour and other provisions, it hit a snag and sank near Franklin. Since it had settled in shallow water near shore, it was expected that the cargo would be salvaged and the boat repaired.[38]

Despite their complaints about steamboats being too large and deep-drafted for the Missouri, quartermaster officers contracted with Henry Shreve to deliver provisions in 1821. Shreve's five-year old steamboat *Washington* was massive by the standards of its day. With a 403-ton capacity, the 148-foot-long craft was heavy-drafted like the Johnson boats.[39] Amazingly, Shreve, succeeded. He navigated the *Washington* from St. Louis to Franklin in only sixty-six running hours, prompting the *Missouri Intelligencer* to proclaim that "the practicability of navigating the Missouri, with safety and facility, may be considered as established beyond the possibility of doubt."[40] But after passing Fort Osage, the boat slowed considerably. Shreve's total round-trip of nearly two months did little to convince skeptical army officers that they could depend entirely on steamboats for their river transportation.[41]

In 1822 Fort Atkinson's supplies were shipped by several keelboats from St. Louis. While stopping in Franklin, some fifty of the keelboatmen, although unprovoked, attacked the empty town jail with "various weapons." Only the intervention of some townsmen saved the jail from being destroyed. Seventeen of the hooligans were apprehended and jailed overnight. The town newspaper's judgment was that "indeed we have seldom seen a more villainous set of fellows."[42]

Even before reaching the Council Bluff in 1819, Atkinson concluded that it was foolhardy for the army to have all of its provisions carried from St. Louis. He thought that such products as cattle and hogs, either on the hoof or processed, should be bought in the Boon's Lick area and moved overland. One of his first actions at the Council Bluff was to order Lieutenant Gabriel Field to lay out a road from Camp Missouri to Chariton. In September and October 1819, Field and his party of thirty men located a 257.5-mile direct-line road to Chariton. Moving quickly, they marked the road by wooden stakes in open ground and blazing trees in timbered sections. Evidently, later that fall Field drove some milk cows and hogs to the fort. In the fall of 1820 Field and a work party bridged about sixty streams on the Chariton trail and returned to the fort with 70 milk cows. This addition, reportedly increased the garrison's herds to 120 milk cows and 700 hogs.[43]

Meanwhile, Atkinson, endeavoring to make the troops healthier and more self-sufficient, started farming. In their first year the men produced about 13,000 bushels of corn and 10,000 bushels of potatoes and turnips.[44] Corn production increased to 15,000 bushels in 1821, when forty acres of potatoes and a dozen or so large vegetable gardens were also cultivated. During the summer a grist and saw mill was erected, "which will enable the troops to manufacture their own bread-stuffs and relieve them from the fatigues of sawing plank etc. by hand."[45]

With the settlement of Clay County, Fort Atkinson could obtain cattle and hogs closer than Boon's Lick. In the fall of 1822 a detachment of troops marked a new route from Liberty. During the following January and February, Captain James S. Gray with twenty-four men improved the road by building nineteen log bridges and grading fords over the five largest streams. The Liberty road was subsequently used by troops and civilian contractors. For 1823, quartermaster officers let a contract for 90,000 pounds of beef "to be delivered by estimation on the hoof" and also for quantities of butchered beef.[46]

For river navigation, Fort Atkinson was more dependent on keelboats than steamboats. However, in 1824 the steamboats *General Neville* and *Mandan* made round-trips from St. Louis during the early-season high-water stage. Apparently, the army had decided that steamboats could be used selectively but were unsuitable throughout the open-water period.[47] Keelboats were used exclusively for the two largest troop movements involving Fort Atkinson—the Leavenworth Expedition of 1823 and the Atkinson-O'Fallon Expedition of 1825.

The Leavenworth Expedition to Grand River, near later Mobridge, South Dakota, was prompted by an Arikara Indian attack on traders who were led by William H. Ashley. Moving upstream by keelboats from St. Louis, Ashley's men stopped to parlay and trade with the Arikaras. But their hosts, with a history of opposing American traders, suddenly turned on them. Two dozen of Ashley's men were killed or wounded, and the Arikaras seized quantities of goods. Once apprised of the affair by survivors, Colonel Henry Leavenworth, then commanding Fort Atkinson, responded by leading a 220-man force against the Arikaras. Leavenworth's supplies and some of his troops were moved by keelboats, but other troops marched overland. Joined by a loose coalition of traders—headed by Joshua Pilcher, president of the Missouri Fur Company—and Teton Sioux warriors, Leavenworth participated in a desultory attack on the Arikara villages.[48]

Since these erstwhile allies had never agreed on their goal, it is not surprising that the outcome satisfied no one. Pilcher wanted to safeguard the Missouri for American traders, the Sioux wanted to raid their traditional enemies, and Leavenworth wanted Ashley's property restored. So the Sioux and Pilcher's men did most of the fighting and Leavenworth negotiated an agreement with the Arikaras that they would return the goods and cease harassing traders. The muddled outcome was that the Arikaras sneaked away during the night, the Sioux ransacked their villages, some of Pilcher's men burned the abandoned villages and Leavenworth condemned the traders' conduct. Nonetheless, the expedition had long-range significance. The Arikaras never threatened traders again, and Ashley ordered his traders to leave the Missouri below Grand River and trek overland to the Rockies. Some of them moved from the Great Bend, and others pioneered the Platte River valley route.

The Arikara incident raised concern over the chaotic state of Indian relations on the upper Missouri, the presumed continuing threat of Hudson's Bay Company traders, and the inability of the American army, as demonstrated by Leavenworth, to control the region. Congress, goaded by Senator Thomas Hart Benton, moved to pacify the Indians and protect American fur traders from illicit British competition.

In 1824 the War Department started organizing the Atkinson-O'Fallon Expedition at St. Louis. Brevet Brigadier General Henry Atkinson was then commanding the Right Wing of the army's Western Department, and Benjamin O'Fallon was the head of the Upper Missouri Indian Agency. Atkinson again faced the challenge of moving a large force up the Missouri, but this time, unlike his situation in 1819, he was not fettered by a War Department command to use steamboats. He did not want to use steamboats on this new mission but was displeased with the performance of conventional keelboats. Believing that keelboats could be made speedier by adding side-wheels, he resumed his experiments of 1819.

In conceiving of some type of propelling devices on deck that would be connected by gears to an axle on which the side-wheels were mounted, Atkinson was probably inspired by team boats. Often called horse ferries, team boats first appeared in the eastern United States in the 1790s. They were propelled by side-wheels that were powered by horses on deck, pulling a capstan in a circle.

But Atkinson wanted to use only manpower. With the assistance of a St. Louis craftsman, he devised a system of having men seated on benches slide mounted crossbars forth and back. Power generated by thirty-two to forty men was transferred to the side-wheels by a succession of geared wheels and pitmans. In the fall of 1824 Atkinson sent Captain Stephen Watts Kearny and about 150 troops to Fort Atkinson on four wheelboats.

After Atkinson joined Kearny with four more wheelboats and more troops the next spring, the expedition was launched. With about 475 troops, Atkinson and O'Fallon moved up the Missouri to the mouth of the Yellowstone. Part of the force proceeded beyond there to reach a point near later Poplar, Montana, about a hundred miles above the Yellowstone. During the summer, Atkinson and O'Fallon concluded twelve treaties with upper Missouri tribes. Negotiations, replete with full-dress military parades to impress the Indians with American power, led to the signing of formal documents. By these "friendship treaties," the Indians recognized the authority of the United States and pledged to deal only with American traders. The government, for its part, was obliged to give the Indians presents on an unspecified schedule.

Atkinson was pleased with the wheelboat performance. Oftentimes his men were able to power the boats with their sliding crosspieces. But they sailed whenever there was sufficient wind, and they cordelled to navigate rapids and to avoid sandbars and snags. Atkinson's innovation was not imitated. Following the Atkinson-O'Fallon Expedition, fur traders continued to move their keelboats by customary means.[49]

Significantly, the Atkinson-O'Fallon Expedition had repercussions on the army's Missouri River presence. Atkinson believed that British traders were not a threat and that no new military post was needed. His conclusion about the lack of a British menace buttressed the judgment of Brevet Major Stephen H. Long, who had explored the Red River valley in 1823. Their observations led army commander Major General Jacob Brown to question the need to maintain Fort Atkinson. Without an apparent military purpose, Fort Atkinson came under intense scrutiny. Colonel George Croghan, the army's inspector general, had visited the fort in 1826 and both lauded and condemned its large farming operations. The farms were marvelous, he thought, but did nothing to enhance the army's raison d'être.[50]

Criticism of Fort Atkinson coincided with Brown's reorganization of the Western Department and a congressional call to provide military protection for the Santa Fe Trail. Desirous of improving training facilities and logistics, in 1826 Brown ordered the replacement of Fort Bellefontaine with a new facility—Jefferson Barracks—on the Mississippi a few miles south of St. Louis. As Jefferson Barracks was being started, Thomas Hart Benton sponsored a congressional resolution calling for a military post at a point where the Santa Fe Trail crossed the Arkansas River. Brown countered that the site should be "on or near" the Arkansas, which he later interpreted to mean a Missouri River site.[51]

On March 7, 1827, Brown ordered Colonel Henry Leavenworth to select a fort site on the left bank of the Missouri within ten miles of the mouth of the Platte

River. This Platte, not to be confused with the large stream that flowed eastward from the Rockies, entered the Missouri south of present-day Platte City, Missouri. During his reconnaissance, Leavenworth found only undesirable bottomland on the left bank. Seeking a high-ground and purportedly salubrious location, he chose a right-bank bluff-top site 150 feet above the Missouri. Within weeks the army sent four companies of troops by keelboats from Jefferson Barracks to start a permanent fortification. Other troops were moved from abandoned Fort Atkinson. Post returns of October 31, 1827, showed a garrison of 14 officers and 174 enlisted men. The War Department named the place Cantonment Leavenworth initially and elevated it to fort status in 1832.[52]

As steamboats became more common on the Missouri, the army began using them to transport troops and their dependents. In April 1828 the steamer *Missouri* carried Leavenworth and four infantry companies from Jefferson Barracks to Cantonment Leavenworth. The next year, the men who were assigned to provide a military escort for the annual Santa Fe caravan were moved on the *Diana*.[53] According to Lieutenant Philip St. George Cooke, this was quite an experience. He found it "remarkable how large the proportion of married men were among those selected to fill our companies. . . . The boat swarmed with their wives and children; the deck was barricaded with beds and bedding; infants squalled, and chickens cackled."[54]

For supplies, Fort Leavenworth relied in part on nearby Missouri farmers. During the summer of 1828, soldiers and settlers cut a straight twenty-foot-wide road from the fort to the town of Barry, near Liberty. Ferries were used to cross the Missouri and Platte rivers. Some Clay County farm products, including beef, pork, bacon, lard, and vegetables, were delivered to the fort on flatboats. Some of the garrison's needs were indicated in a September 1828 public advertisement calling for proposals to supply the garrison with nearly 400 barrels of pork, 40,000 pounds of "fresh beef on the hoof" by December 1, and another 6,000 pounds of fresh beef for each of the next six months.[55]

When it was the army's only Missouri River post, Fort Leavenworth was a major Indian affairs center. Federal government relations with Indians were administered by regional superintendents and tribal agents. One effect of the Missouri and Scientific expeditions of 1819 was the extension of the Indian service up the Missouri. Only weeks before the expeditions left St. Louis, Congress authorized the Upper Missouri Agency. Benjamin O'Fallon, nephew of William Clark, was named to direct it. O'Fallon was not assigned to a specific tribe, and the agency's boundaries were not delineated. There seems to have been a general assumption that O'Fallon would work to draw Indians all along the Missouri who were beyond ceded lands into alliances with the United States. O'Fallon traveled to the Council Bluff with Long on the *Western Engineer* and established his first headquarters at Fort Atkinson. In the summer of 1820 O'Fallon held a grand conclave with nearby tribes at the fort. After that he was generally content to stay home in St. Louis and leave the fieldwork to subagents.[56]

Probably because he was the Upper Missouri Indian agent and had experience in dealing with tribes, O'Fallon was named co-commissioner of the 1825 expedition. When he resigned the next year, he was soon succeeded by John Dougherty, who had served as the subagent at Fort Atkinson. When Fort Atkinson was evacuated, Dougherty chose to move with troops to Fort Leavenworth. He kept the Upper Missouri Agency there until 1832, when it was shifted upriver to Lucien Fontenelle's trading post of Bellevue, near later Omaha. As Upper Missouri agent, Dougherty was responsible for distributing the annuities promised to Indians by the 1825 and other amity treaties.[57]

Meanwhile, the government had started removing Indians indigenous from the Old Northwest to the Fort Leavenworth region. The wholesale relocation of tribes was prompted by a major change in federal Indian policy. Shortly before leaving office in 1825, President James Monroe announced a plan to move Indians from the Old Northwest and the Southeast to "permanent homes" west of Missouri and Arkansas Territory. The policy seemed reasonable to its proponents, but it was based on the false assumptions that American settlers had reached their natural western limits in the Mississippi Valley and that lands west of Missouri and Arkansas were a Great American Desert unfit for white habitation.[58]

To relocate tribes from the east, the government had to obtain land cessions from Plains tribes. William Clark's 1825 treaties with the Osage and Kansas Indians opened vast tracts west of Missouri. Clark's immediate objective was to remove Indians from Missouri. During the late eighteenth century some Shawnees and Delawares from Ohio voluntarily moved westward. After crossing the Mississippi, they were granted land near Cape Girardeau, Missouri, by Spanish officials. Later, some Foxes, Sauks, and Kickapoos from Illinois moved into Missouri. After achieving statehood, Missourians intensified their efforts to force these Indians out. The Shawnees were placed on a reservation southwest of Fort Leavenworth. In short order, the Delawares and Kickapoos were moved to nearby reservations.

The United States also started moving other Indians directly from states of the Old Northwest. Since the area of the proposed "Permanent Indian Frontier" lay west of Missouri, it included a tract east of the Missouri River. The United States obtained the Platte River country, as this area came to be known, from various Indian claimants by an 1830 treaty negotiated at Prairie du Chien, Wisconsin. Then, three years later, the government began moving some Potawatomis, Chippewas, and Ottawas onto it. All that separated them from Missouri settlers was the boundary running due north from the mouth of the Kansas River.[59]

Under the terms of removal treaties, the United States was obligated to make annual payments (i.e., annuities) in goods and money to the tribes. Delivering annuities through a system of civilian contractors became a big business for St. Louis merchants, traders and steamboatmen. The initial removal of Indians, along with the intensifying farming and the Santa Fe trade, provided the economic impulse for increased steamboating.

In 1829, for the first time, a single steamboat made more than one Missouri River trip. The *William D. Duncan,* commanded by a Captain Crooks, reached Franklin several times from St. Louis. The small 97-ton side-wheeler, built at Pittsburgh, was advertised in St. Louis newspapers as a "regular packet between this city and Franklin." The *Diana* and the *Native* each voyaged to Franklin that season. In 1830 the *William D. Duncan* was navigated to a trading post near the mouth of the Kansas River, and the *Globe* and the *Liberator* were steamed to Franklin, whose remnant continued as the landing for interior markets until the place was completely abandoned. In 1831 nine steamboats—*Chieftain, Don Juan, Globe, Huntsman, Liberty, Missouri, Talisman, Union,* and *Whig*—were used in a trade extending to Fort Leavenworth, and the *Yellow Stone* was taken to the upper Missouri.[60]

This degree of steamboating reflected the growing economies of St. Louis and its Missouri River hinterland. The census of 1830 showed that Missouri had 140,455 inhabitants, almost half of whom lived in counties bordering the Missouri River. Howard, the most populous on the river, had 10,854 persons—only about 3,200 less than St. Louis County, the state's leader.[61]

Missouri River steamboating was becoming important to St. Louis by the late 1820s, but nonetheless it lagged far behind trade on the city's three other water routes. With their advantageous location near the great crossroads of the north-south Mississippi and the east-west Ohio-Missouri routes, St. Louisians traded in all four cardinal directions. The Ohio linked them with Pittsburgh, the most important source of new steamboats and iron products and the transshipment point for many products originating in Philadelphia and other East Coast cities. The lower Mississippi path to New Orleans was their access to seagoing trade. North of St. Louis, the 1823 voyage of the *Virginia* marked the extension of upper Mississippi steamboating to Fort Snelling. But the major upper Mississippi destinations were along the tributary Illinois and Fever rivers. By 1830 the lead-producing region of northwest Illinois and southwest Wisconsin had attracted more than 10,000 miners. Lead had been mined and processed there by Indians and traders, but the rush of American miners was inspired by former army contractor James A. Johnson, who arrived in 1822 with 150 slaves. Galena, Illinois, the principal lead-producing community and the Fever's head of navigation, was the main port of call for St. Louis steamboatmen.[62]

As the metropolis for the Missouri River, St. Louis, like the rest of the region west of Pittsburgh, depended on manufactured goods shipped from either East Coast cities or New Orleans. Western buyers wanted their southern and eastern supply routes to be competitive in order to lower shipping costs. But New Orleans, once it became a steamboat center after the War of 1812, could deliver freight to St. Louis and Ohio River towns cheaper than either Philadelphia or New York could. Unlike its eastern rivals, New Orleans had an unobstructed waterway upstream to the Falls of the Ohio. While nature favored New Orleans, it frustrated Philadelphia and New York, which lacked navigable river access to the West.

Eastern sellers and western buyers realized that only man-made improvements would enable the eastern route to become competitive with New Orleans. New

York, led by canal commissioner and later governor DeWitt Clinton, acted first by constructing a 363-mile canal from Albany on the Hudson River to Buffalo on Lake Erie. Completed in 1825, the Erie Canal became a great pathway to the West. A continuous water route from New York City to the Ohio River was accomplished with the completion of the Ohio and Erie Canal in 1833. The State of Ohio expended almost $8 million to construct the 300-mile waterway linking Cleveland on Lake Erie to Portsmouth on the Ohio.[63]

In the meantime, Philadelphia responded to New York's initiative by persuading Pennsylvania to link it with Pittsburgh by a system of railroads, canals, and inclined planes. The 400-mile route, opened in 1834, was about 600 miles shorter than the one from New York City to Portsmouth. Although it was hailed as a major breakthrough, the Pennsylvania System proved to be slow. Its major defect was the use of ten inclined planes in a mountainous 38-mile section. Cable cars carrying canal boats were drawn up and let down steep inclines by stationary steam engines.[64]

While the Pennsylvania System and the Ohio and Erie Canal were being constructed, the Ohio River was improved by a short canal bypassing the Falls of the Ohio. The Louisville and Portland Canal Company, with the federal government as its major stockholder, built a waterway with three locks on the Kentucky side. The federal government's financial interest resulted from the strategic consideration that the canal was vital to national interests. In the event a foreign power gained control of the mouth of the Mississippi, the Ohio would remain as the only water route linking the East and West. Completed in 1830, the canal, whose small locks could accommodate nearly all steamboats of that time, was hailed by western shippers.[65] Increased trade showed the canal's impact. In 1825 only 42 steamboats made a total of 240 trips in the trade downstream from Louisville. The business of 1834 used 165 steamboats, and 430 of their 1,104 trips were to St. Louis. After collecting tolls of $64,848.17 in that year alone, the Louisville and Portland Canal Company paid a 6 percent dividend on its stock.[66]

Missourians welcomed anything that reduced shipping times from their major supply points. The impact of the Pennsylvania System was noted in the marketing of coffee. New Orleans had traditionally supplied the coffee for St. Louis and the Ohio River valley cities as far east at Pittsburgh. But in 1834, for the first time, Philadelphia coffee was marketed in the West. This development led the *Missouri Republican* to proclaim that "the order of trade seems now about to be reversed."[67]

To compete with Eastern suppliers, New Orleans strived for faster steamboat service. Steamboatmen, like the public at large, were always in a hurry. They loved to set new speed records, and newspapers loved to report them. Under the headline extraordinary speed, the *Missouri Republican* hailed the steamboat *Siam*, which broke previous records by making the trip from St. Louis to New Orleans in five days and two hours and returning in seven days and ten hours.[68]

In their four-way trade, St. Louis steamboatmen depended on a complex of allied services. They needed agents, insurance brokers, warehouses, harbor facilities, mechanics, carpenters, blacksmiths, draymen, food suppliers, and other specialists such as makers of steamboat furniture and bedding. Their movements were coordinated by forwarding and commission agents, who usually owned wharf-side warehouses. During a season, any given steamboat might be used on all St. Louis routes. Typically, a boat that carried freight to the Missouri started from an Ohio River town and after its Missouri River trip might be sent to either the upper or lower Mississippi.

Until the late 1830s when the Missouri River trade could support a number of regularly scheduled boats, agents sent craft to particular destinations whenever they could get a paying load. Most shippers sending anything from St. Louis, be it a single package or a consignment of groceries, would have it stored by an agent until the next boat departed. As freight was stockpiled, agents would make judgments about the prospects for a paying load. Typically, they would advertise that such and such a boat was on its way to St. Louis from the Mississippi or Ohio and was to be sent to a Missouri River destination. If their warehouses held a full load, the boat would be advertised to leave "immediately upon arrival." However, if only partial loads were on hand, they would continue advertising until they had more freight.

Captain Joseph Brown recalled deceptive practices by agents and captains to get boats loaded. Boats would "have steam up for a week, telling people and shippers that the boat was going to leave in an hour, and even have their planks taken in, all but one and then launch their planks out again. All this was done to decoy people on board."[69] Anyone who used steamboats quickly learned that announced departure dates were oftentimes only expressions of hope. It was not uncommon for the same ad, with appropriate date changes, to appear again and again over the course of several weeks. Meanwhile, those who deposited freight in the stone and brick warehouses on Water Street, facing the boat landing, were charged monthly storage fees.

St. Louis's commission and forwarding agents were among its leading businessmen. During the 1830s the most active agencies were Hill, McGunnegle, and Way; E. and A. Tracy; and Vairin and Reel. Hill, McGunnegle, and Way was started by William Hill in the late 1820s. When George K. McGunnegle became Hill's partner, the firm became Hill and McGunnegle and—several years later with the addition of James C. Way—Hill, McGunnegle, and Way. With Hill's withdrawal in 1835, the partnership was renamed McGunnegle and Way. E. and A. Tracy's partners were Edward Tracy and his nephew Alfred. Julius Vairin and John W. Reel formed the partnership of Vairin and Reel. Other agents were Henry Von Phul and John H. Gay.[70]

To coordinate steamboating and marketing, St. Louis agents either had to establish branch offices in other cities or make cooperative arrangements with other agents in major terminal markets and Missouri River ports. Vairin and Reel opened a New Orleans house in 1831 to work in conjunction with their St. Louis business. In 1829 Hill and McGunnegle began sending lead, hemp, pork, beef, tobacco, and "other produce of our country" to James G. Stevenson of New Orleans. In turn, they received and administered the distribution of Stevenson's shipments to St. Louis.[71]

Until 1836 the charges of St. Louis agents were determined only by competition. Steamboatmen and any shippers usually "shopped around" for the best deals on the multiplicity of services offered by agents. This system, which provided some bargains, also led to such frauds as kickbacks and false weighing. Agents, who generally deplored the lack of regulations, saw the advantages of a system using uniform charges. With that end in mind, on July 15, 1836, "the merchants and traders of the city of St. Louis" formed a chamber of commerce and chose Edward Tracy as its president, Henry Von Phul as vice president, and George K. McGunnegle as a member of its Appeals Committee.[72] The organization was modeled after the New Orleans Chamber of Commerce, started two years earlier. The New Orleans body published a detailed listing of commission, storage, and shipping charges and, significantly, established standards for determining tonnage equivalencies.

Before steamboats were put in service, they had to be registered with the federal Customs Service, an agency in the Treasury Department. The registration entailed a calculation of the boat's tonnage, or capacity, as well as its length, breadth, depth, and draft. One hundred cubic feet equaled a ton. Boats, because of their somewhat tapered bow and stern, were measured in a series of cross sections.[73]

Customs agents were required by federal law to determine tonnage to the nearest fraction expressed in 95ths. For example, they would record a boat tonnage as 172 and 57/95ths. Boats had to display at all times a registration form showing their tonnage and assigned number. Contemporary newspapers and steamboat historians invariably rounded the tonnage to the nearest whole number. Any remodeling that changed tonnage had to be reported to the Customs Service.

The record of tonnage was used in other ways as well. Wharfage, the daily docking fees collected by municipal harbormasters, was based on the size of each boat. On the principle that larger boats took up more space, the fee was usually a flat charge per ton for use of the city's levee facilities.

In their charges for loading and dispatching boats, agents made price distinctions between various-sized craft. The St. Louis Chamber of Commerce decided that the charge per trip for steamboats under 150 tons would be $10. Boats of 150 and less than 300 tons, 300 and less than 400, and over 400 respectively were to be billed $20, $25, and $30.[74]

When setting freight rates, agents and steamboatmen worked with the concept of the ton-mile—the charge for transporting a ton one mile. Charges to a specific destination could then be calculated from any subdivision of a ton or any multiple of miles. For public consumption, they usually reported to newspapers that their charges were so much for a hundredweight for a hundred miles. Since they tended to report only the average rate, many people then and later thought there was a uniform rate for all types of goods. But rates varied by commodity, depending on how much actual weight was needed to constitute 100 cubic feet.

Steamboat agents faced the age-old problem of marine shippers. They had to establish the relationship of tons as space and tons as weight. Steamboatmen inherited the system, which was probably originally determined from observations that 100 cubic feet on average would hold about 2,000 pounds. However, everyone realized that lightweight materials could take up 100 cubic feet but weigh less than 2,000 pounds, and 100 cubic feet of dense items would weigh more than 2,000 pounds. Their challenge then was to agree on appropriate equivalencies. The New Orleans Chamber of Commerce developed widely imitated standards. For example, a ton of pimento in casks had an actual weight of 950 pounds. In bags, which could be packed tighter, it weighed 1,100, about the same as dry hides. Coffee beans in casks weighed 1,568 pounds and in bags 1,830. Eight 196-pound barrels of flour were a ton. On the other hand, it took 2,240 pounds of pig and bar iron, lead, and other metals or ore to make up a ton. Therefore, a standard charge per ton-mile meant that the rate per pound on bagged pimento was about twice as high as that on iron and lead.[75]

The highest rates were always levied on such hazardous materials as gunpowder, which required special handling. To cut costs, some merchants who bought and packed their own goods in St. Louis disguised gunpowder shipments. In deploring "the practice" of shipping gunpowder under "deceptive markings," the editor of the *Missouri Republican* told of a Franklin merchant who, when shipping goods on the steamboat *Iowa*, hid six kegs of powder in a cask labeled "LaGuayra Coffee." Although he covered the powder with coffee beans, the fraud was discovered because the cask seemed to be too heavy for just coffee.[76]

The "tariff of charges" issued by the St. Louis Chamber of commerce specified commissions for various services of agents as well as forwarding and storage rates. Acting as bankers, the agents charged 2.5 percent interest on making cash advances, negotiating drafts, and selling or buying stock and 10.0 percent per annum on all overdue debts. Their commission on sales of merchandise or produce was 5.0 percent, and they charged 2.5 percent to ship goods to another market. For selling and purchasing boats and for chartering them, their commission was 2.5 percent. These commissions were in addition to charges for receiving and storing goods. The agents assumed no liability caused by fire and theft. Shippers' only security was to buy cargo insurance, which agents would willingly sell them for a commission, of course.[77]

Monthly storage rates were calculated on the amount of warehouse space any given commodity required. The charge for storing 100 pounds of iron, steel, lead, and shot was 5 cents—half that of bagged coffee, pepper, and pimento. All rates were halved for the second and succeeding months.

The rates for receiving and forwarding goods took into account their weight, bulkiness, and the work required to handle them. The charge for 100-pound sacks of wheat, corn, and salt was 4 cents, but the rate for the same amount of assorted merchandise was 10 cents. Agents collected 25 cents for a keg of gunpowder, but only 10 cents for a barrel of beef, pork, or whiskey. Space-consuming carriages and gigs would be received and forwarded for $3 each.

Merchants in Missouri River towns worked closely with commission and forwarding agencies of St. Louis and other major steamboat ports. The experience of the Aull brothers offers insight into their modus operandi. James and Robert Aull, who began merchandising in Lexington in 1825, added stores at Richmond, Liberty, and Independence six years later. As buyer for the firm, James regularly made an annual wintertime trip to Philadelphia to buy dry goods, clothing, books, writing supplies, medical remedies such as castor oil and Epsom salts, and amusement items, including playing cards and parts for musical instruments. He shipped his heavier merchandise by Atlantic-coast sailing vessel to New Orleans, where he used an agent to forward it by steamboat. His lighter freight was hauled across Pennsylvania to Pittsburgh and carried from there by steamboat. On his return trip, Aull bought hardware in Pittsburgh and sometimes flour in Pittsburgh and Cincinnati. Although the Aulls never visited New Orleans, it was their main source of sugar, molasses, coffee, and other groceries. They supplemented these spring supplies during the navigation season with orders handled by St. Louis agents.[78]

Because of the Santa Fe trade, some rather unique items were sold by Missouri River merchants. In 1831, J. Coleman Boggs of Columbia advertised both "Swain's Celebrated Panacea" and "Potter's Vegetable Catholicon with directions (printed in the Spanish language) and packed in cases expressly for the Mexican Market."[79]

Merchants found steamboating to be both costly and unreliable. For goods originating at Pittsburgh and points west, the Aulls reckoned that freight charges, transfer commissions, and insurance averaged about one-fourth of the purchase cost. In 1832 they paid $1.95½ per hundredweight on general freight from Pittsburgh to Lexington, and three years earlier had paid a premium of $769.97 to insure $10,000 worth of goods on an Ohio River steamboat. They always bought cargo insurance. Steamboat wrecks were an occupational hazard. In 1831 the *Trenton*, carrying their consignment from Pittsburgh, was wrecked about twelve miles up the Missouri. In 1834 and 1835 their business was disrupted by the loss of the *Halcyon* and the *Iowa*.[80]

The Aulls and other shippers had no choice other than to live with the perils of steamboating. Boats were short-lived and relatively expensive to build, maintain, and operate. During the period 1820–36, at least 59 different steamboats made one or more Missouri River trips. The fate of 57 of them has been determined. Their average longevity was only four years, which means that annual depreciation was 25 percent of the boat's construction cost. Thirty-five of the 57 were lost, and 22 were abandoned. Other than snagging, which claimed 18 boats, 5 were burned, 4 were stranded, 2 exploded, 2 were wrecked in collisions, 1 was crushed by ice, and 3 were lost from indeterminable causes.[81] Boats were abandoned when it was no longer feasible to maintain them by repairing the hull and machinery. Abandonment sometimes occurred in as little as two years. Boat carpenters could handle minor remodeling, wind and water damage, and even holes poked in the hull, but they were unable to cope with widespread rotting and warping.

Boat owners tried to protect their investments by shared ownership, hull insurance, and pleas to the federal government to improve rivers. Shared ownership was really a type of self-insurance. Even if an individual could afford to buy his own boat, he was more likely to cooperate with other parties and obtain a fractional interest in several boats, thereby spreading the risk. Marine insurance policies were sold by most of the companies that insured residential and commercial buildings. In St. Louis the insurance business was dominated by the commission and forwarding agencies, who represented various eastern companies. In 1828 both the Protection Insurance Company of Hartford, Connecticut, and the Traders' Insurance Company of New York City, operating through St. Louis agents, sold policies on steamboats, keelboats, flatboats, and their cargoes. In 1836 the eastern companies were challenged by the formation of the Missouri Insurance Company, which was probably the brainchild of the St. Louis agencies. George K. McGunnegle, Edward Tracy, and Henry Von Phul were all members of its original board of directors.[82]

Marine insurance was expensive. One study concluded that the average annual premium on steamboats in the Louisville–New Orleans trade during the 1830s was $4,092. On average, these boats had a tonnage of 310 and a construction cost of slightly over $34,000. So even an annual policy on a new boat would have cost about 12 percent of the boat's value. The gap between the premium and the boat's value would narrow sharply as the boat aged. The same study found that the average longevity of the Louisville–New Orleans boats during the decade was six years. Thus the original value of $34,000 figure would have decreased by one-sixth with each passing year.[83]

Data on the Louisville–New Orleans boats offer insight into the costs of Missouri River boats. Louis C. Hunter determined that the construction costs per ton of all western steamboats in the 1830s ranged from $80 to $100.[84] The fifty-nine boats that were on the Missouri in 1820–36 averaged only 125 tons, indicating that only the smallest western steamboats were deemed suitable for that stream. At $90 per ton, their average construction costs would have been $11,250. In all likelihood, insurance rates on them were higher than for the Louisville–New Orleans boats, because of the greater risk of snagging on the Missouri and thus a considerably shorter anticipated longevity. But even if the rates were the same, the annual premium on Missouri River boats would have been about $1,500. Under the circumstances, it is not surprising that many steamboatmen limited their coverage to something less than the boat's full value or did not obtain insurance at all. According to one estimate, approximately a third of the total value of all St. Louis steamboats and cargoes in the 1830s was uninsured.[85]

Dependent on steamboat commerce, most Westerners saw river improvement as an economic stimulant. They fervently believed that the federal government, for the public good, had an obligation to remove obstructions to navigation. They were strongly supported by the army, whose troop movements during the War of 1812 had been frustrated by river hazards. After army engineers urged improvement of the Ohio and Mississippi, Henry Clay, a strong advocate of internal improvements, led the 1824 congressional drive for appropriations. By that time the West, with ten states bordering the Ohio and the Mississippi, had considerable political clout amid the nation's total of twenty-four states. In approving the country's first inland navigation act, Congress earmarked $75,000 for improvement of the two rivers.[86]

Some Missourians tried to get funding for Missouri River improvement in the act. The editor of the *St. Louis Enquirer* insisted that "Missouri too has claims which require their [Congress's] attention, and which it is in the interest of the nation to grant. We mean an appropriation to remove obstructions to the navigation of the Missouri River."[87] The case for the Missouri could hardly be justified on the basis of its feeble commerce, but advocates of river improvement always had the unexpressed motive of getting federal dollars spent in their area.

One of the significant outcomes of federally sponsored river improvement was the development of the snagboat. Steamboatmen and army engineers agreed that snags, the single greatest impediment to navigation, should be removed. To prompt development of special snag removal equipment, the chief of the army's Corps of Engineers offered a $1,000 prize for the best device. John W. Bruce of Kentucky won by submitting plans for a "machine boat." Patterned after horse ferries, Bruce's craft consisted of twin-hulled flatboats moved by the traditional methods of flat-boat navigation. The boat would be maneuvered to place a snag between the hulls. The snag was then hooked by an iron claw at the end of a stout rope attached to a windlass, which was turned by four men. Theoretically, they would be able to lift snags and cut them up. But the apparatus was not powerful enough to handle most snags. Bruce, with some political assistance from Henry Clay, was awarded a contract to remove snags from the Ohio and Mississippi in 1824. But he was soon dismissed after his device proved to be ineffective.[88]

After Congress continued to appropriate river improvement funds, the Corps of Engineers in 1826 named the veteran steamboat designer, builder, and captain Henry Shreve to supervise river improvement on the Ohio and the Mississippi below the mouth of the Missouri. While working manually to remove snags, Shreve convinced his superiors to fund the construction of a steam-powered snag-boat, which would use a steam winch to lift snags and steam saws to cut them up.[89]

His first snagboat, the *Heliopolis,* was put into service in the summer of 1829. Its double hulls were connected at the bow by a heavy eight- to twelve-foot-long beam. In operation, the beam was rammed into a snag, which was either broken off or loosened. The snag would then be lifted and sawed into pieces small enough to be carried away by the current.

With the *Heliopolis,* Shreve removed so many snags in 1830 and 1831 that he considered working in waters beyond his original jurisdiction. Advocates of Missouri River improvement thought the snagboat was the answer to their needs. With snag removal as his principal aim, Congressman William H. Ashley campaigned to get an appropriation for the river in the Rivers and Harbors Act of 1832. Ashley, who had served as Missouri's first lieutenant governor and had formed a fur trade company, was then serving his first term in the House of Representatives. He was instrumental in getting $50,000 added to the bill for removing snags from the Missouri upstream to the mouth of the Kansas. Considering the river's light commerce, that was a great accomplishment. In 1832 only 9 of the estimated 220 western steamboats operated on the Missouri.[90]

When it became evident that Ashley had congressional support, Shreve, apparently trying to get a sense of a likely Missouri River assignment, attacked some snags in an eight-mile stretch above the river's mouth. In one instance he was challenged by a sycamore snag seven feet in diameter. The *Heliopolis* raised it about forty feet, but it was still embedded in the sandy bottom below twelve feet of water. After Shreve had the portion above water cut off, he found that the remainder was hollow. He had it packed with fifty pounds of gunpowder, whose explosion loosened the snag enough to permit its easy removal. Shreve thought that with congressional authorization he could effect Missouri improvement "so as to render the navigation as safe for every description of boats as the Mississippi now is."[91]

Shreve must have been pleased with the first news from Washington. On July 1, 1832, Ashley wrote to the editor of the *Missouri Intelligencer* that the rivers and harbors bill, including an appropriation for the Missouri, "was finally passed yesterday." He continued, "As soon as it receives the signature of the President, instructions will be given to Capt. Shreve to commence operations on the Missouri."[92]

Ashley seems to have assumed that Andrew Jackson would routinely sign the bill. But instead the president refused to support appropriations for improving rivers above customhouses. Citing constitutional grounds, he insisted that only navigation routes to customhouses qualified as interstate commerce. Since St. Louis had a customhouse, improving the lower Mississippi was permissible, but no work could be done on the upper Mississippi or the Missouri. The anti-Jacksonian press lambasted Jackson and made an issue of his action in the 1832 presidential campaign. But his decision stood. Shreve was ordered to begin removing the great raft in the Red River of the South, and Missouri River steamboatmen had to continue plying snag-infested waters.[93]

Missouri newspapers kept the Missouri River improvement issue alive by publicizing steamboat disasters. The *Trenton* was snagged and sunk near St. Charles in April 1833. The following year the *Halcyon* was lost by snagging in the same vicinity. The boat settled in only eight to ten feet of water. Most of its cargo was salvaged, but the hull, filled with mud, could not be raised. Five of the thirteen boats on the Missouri in 1836 were lost. The *St. Charles* was burned at Richmond Landing. Only a fourth of its estimated $12,000 value was insured. The *Chariton, Chian, Diana,* and *John Hancock* were all snagged. Whenever possible, owners and insurance underwriters salvaged cargo and boat parts. In late 1836 the St. Louis auction house of Savage and Austin advertised a public sale of engines, tackle. and furniture from the *Chariton, Diana* and *John Hancock.*[94]

Meanwhile, the most dramatic development in the 1830s was the extension of steamboating by the American Fur Company to the mouth of the Yellowstone. Using steamboats in the upper Missouri fur trade was first recommended by Kenneth McKenzie, the bourgeois of Fort Union near the mouth of the Yellowstone. McKenzie had been one of the key men in the Columbia Fur Company, which merged with the American Fur Company in 1827. Under the merger agreement, the Columbia Fur Company became the Upper Missouri Outfit of the American Fur Company. John Jacob Astor, head of the American Fur Company headquartered in New York City, conducted his Missouri River business through a working arrangement with the St. Louis firm of Bernard Pratte and Company. McKenzie urged the partners of the Upper Missouri Outfit, including the influential Pierre Chouteau, Jr., to build a new, large post to assure its dominance on the upper Missouri. Once authorization was received, McKenzie supervised the construction of Fort Union in 1828–30. When completed, it was staffed by 120 of the 258 men in the Upper Missouri Outfit.[95]

McKenzie thought the company's transportation would be made faster, cheaper, and more efficient by using steamboats instead of keelboats from St. Louis to Fort Union. He was aware that steamboats had been improved during the 1820s and was evidently impressed by the establishment of the steamboat trade to Fort Leavenworth. McKenzie convinced Chouteau, who in turn persuaded Astor to authorize the building of a steamboat at Louisville during the winter of 1830–31.[96]

Christened the *Yellow Stone* for its destination, the steamer reached St. Louis on April 10, 1831. With a length of 120 feet, a width of 20 feet, a 6-foot hold, and a capacity of 144 tons, the side-wheeler typified steamboats then being used on the lower Missouri.[97] All of the heavy- drafted boats retained features of oceangoing ships. McKenzie and Chouteau could only hope that the river would be high enough to accommodate the *Yellow Stone*. Its arrival excited St. Louisians. The *St. Louis Beacon* enthused that if the boat succeeded in reaching Fort Union, "we shall have the pleasure of beholding what, it was thought the other day, was reserved for the next generation."[98]

Captained by Bernard Young, the *Yellow Stone* left for Fort Union only six days after arriving from Louisville. Pierre Chouteau, Jr., went along to see for himself how well the boat worked and to inspect company posts. The *Yellow Stone* was crammed with supplies and 97 men, including Young, Chouteau, a crew of nearly two dozen, and a number of employees being sent to various trading posts.[99]

Beyond the Fort Leavenworth vicinity, Young had to stop occasionally to cut wood. With ten cords needed for each full dawn-to-dusk running day, wooding stoppages were the main reason for delays below the Niobrara. But in late May, near the mouth of the Niobrara, shallow water halted the boat. The impatient Chouteau ordered relief from Fort Tecumseh, some two hundred miles upstream. Daniel Lamont, the post's bourgeois, sent two keelboats to lighten the *Yellow Stone*. After much of its cargo was off-loaded on the keels, Young managed to navigate the *Yellow Stone* to Fort Tecumseh, near present-day Fort Pierre, South Dakota. In slightly over two months, the *Yellow Stone* got only about two-thirds of the way to Fort Union. With no prospect of a rise, Chouteau had the boat turned about. She was returned to St. Louis with "a full cargo of buffalo robes, furs and peltries, besides 10,000 pounds of buffalo tongues."[100]

Although the *Yellow Stone* failed to reach Fort Union, Chouteau was convinced

The *Yellow Stone*, painting by Karl Bodmer.
Typical of side-wheelers of the early 1830s, the vessel was the first steamboat
navigated to the upper Missouri. *Courtesy of the State Historical Society of North Dakota.*

that the company should continue steamboating. In 1832, with the aim of capital-
izing on both the April and June rises, the boat, commanded by Andrew Bennett,
was dispatched for Fort Union on March 26.[101] Once again Chouteau made the
voyage. He was joined by the well-known Indian portraitist George Catlin. Dedicated to "rescuing from oblivion the looks and customs of the vanishing races of
native man in America,"[102] Catlin welcomed the opportunity to visit the upper Missouri tribes. Other than helping the artist, Chouteau and his associates apparently
thought their hospitality would lead to favorable publicity. The company had to
obtain trading licenses from government officials and wanted to win federal contracts for delivering annuities to Missouri River tribes.

On the way to Fort Union, the *Yellow Stone* was stopped for nearly a week at
the new post that was replacing the abandoned Fort Tecumseh. In Chouteau's
honor, the place was named Fort Pierre. After leaving Fort Pierre on June 5, Bennett covered the approximately six hundred miles to Fort Union in only twelve days.

Finding the water level at the mouth of the Yellowstone to be as high as that at the mouth of the Missouri, he believed the boat could be taken yet higher. But the company had no reason to proceed farther. So after taking on robes and furs, Bennett averaged one hundred miles a day for most of the return trip to St. Louis.[103]

The voyage was hailed for demonstrating the "entire practicability of steam navigation in that upper region."[104] Reaching the mouth of the Yellowstone by steamboat had been a goal since 1819, and to Nathaniel Patten, editor of the *Missouri Intelligencer*, the *Yellow Stone* was fulfilling America's destiny. He thought "this enterprise will no doubt greatly add to our trade and intercourse with the Indians and subtract from that of the British trader."[105] Chouteau, said to be in "high spirits" because of the trip, helped publicize the voyage. Writing from France, Astor informed Chouteau that the *Yellow Stone* had "attracted much attention in Europe, and has been noted in all the papers here."[106]

The American Fur Company had a second steamboat built for its 1833 upper Missouri trade. The 149-ton side-wheel *Assiniboin*, at 120 feet long and 20 feet wide, with a hold 6 feet deep, was comparable to the *Yellow Stone*. Built at Cincinnati, it was delivered to St. Louis on March 13, 1833.[107]

The *Assiniboin*, captained by Bernard Pratte, Jr., and the *Yellow Stone* traveled together to Fort Pierre. Once again the company had a distinguished guest—the German nobleman Maximilian, prince of Wied-Neuwied, who was accompanied by his servant David Dreidoppel and the twenty-eight-year-old Swiss artist Karl Bodmer. Maximilian, an accomplished naturalist, had studied Amazonian flora during a two-year expedition to Brazil. His interest in the Missouri River region was whetted by his correspondence with Thomas Say. Originally, he planned to travel overland, but Chouteau and William Clark convinced him that a river expedition would be more fruitful. Maximilian and his companions and nearly a hundred fur company employees were passengers on the *Yellow Stone* to Fort Pierre.[108]

On June 2, nearly two months after leaving St. Louis, the *Yellow Stone* was loaded with seven thousand buffalo robes and other furs at Fort Pierre and ordered to return to St. Louis. Maximilian's party transferred to the *Assiniboin* for the remainder of the trip to Fort Union.[109] The *Assiniboin*, with a "full cargo of furs, skins, etc.," arrived in St. Louis on July 11.[110] Maximilian wintered at Fort Clark and returned to St. Louis by mackinaw in 1834.

The American Fur Company's use of steamboats attracted the attention of Campbell and Sublette—its principal competitor. Formed by Robert Campbell and William Sublette in late 1832, the new firm decided to start rival posts, including one near Fort Union. To outfit their stations, Campbell and Sublette chartered the 163-ton side-wheel *Otto*, which had been built at Evansville, Indiana, in 1832. With Sublette on board, the boat was steamed to Fort Pierre in 1833. Unable to proceed higher, Sublette had his goods forwarded by keelboats to a site only three miles below Fort Union, where he established Fort William.[111]

The American Fur Company took the *Yellow Stone* out of Missouri River service in 1834 but again sent the *Assiniboin* to Fort Union. It never returned to St. Louis.

Commanded by Captain John Carlisle, the boat reached Fort Union on June 26. It was then sent upstream about a hundred miles to supply a satellite post the company had started the year before to challenge rival traders. While at this place, near the mouth of the Poplar River, it was stranded by low water sometime before July 26. Carlisle, his "mulatto woman," who had accompanied him from St. Louis, and his crew lived near the boat in stockaded Fort Assinniboine until early April 1835.[112]

Once under way for St. Louis, Carlisle took on robes and furs at Fort Union and was detained by low water on the way to Fort Clark, which was not reached until May 26. Below Fort Clark, low water continued to be a problem. Soon after passing the mouth of the Heart River at present-day Mandan, North Dakota, the *Assiniboin* was grounded. As the crew was struggling to free it on June 1, a fire was ignited by a stovepipe in one of the cabins. Tinder-dry steamboat hulls were notoriously combustible. The *Assiniboin* burned so rapidly that the men only had time to cut loose four live buffalo, which swam to shore. Everything else, including several cases of Maximilian's bird and animal specimens, was lost. A contemporary newspaper article placed the value of the uninsured boat and cargo at an estimated $70,000–$80,000. McKenzie reported to Maximilian that the cargo alone was worth $60,000–$80,000.[113]

While the *Assiniboin* was on the upper Missouri, seventy-year-old John Jacob Astor retired from the fur trade. On June 1, 1834, he sold the Western Department of the American Fur Company to Pratte, Chouteau, and Company, which became Pierre Chouteau, Jr., and Company four years later.[114]

Among other things, Pratte, Chouteau, and Company acquired the *Assiniboin* and the recently completed steamboat *Diana*. The 103-ton side-wheel *Diana*, built at Louisville, had a short history. In 1834 it was used to supply a post near the Council Bluff. The company intended to send it to Fort Union in 1835, but for some reason its captain did not steam beyond Fort Pierre. While upbound in March 1836, the boat was snagged near Lexington. Its cargo was placed onshore, only to be carried away by the rising river. The company managed to have the boat raised and returned to St. Louis, where it was repaired. After its Fort Union trip, the *Diana* was being used on the lower river, where it was destroyed by a snag near Rocheport.[115]

Despite the loss of the *Diana* and four other steamboats in 1836, Missouri River steamboating was at a new high. This set the stage for a booming trade caused by a 50 percent increase in Missouri's population during the preceding four years, the beginning of Brunswick and Glasgow, the expanding Santa Fe trade, the extension of steamboating to the upper Missouri, the creation of Indian reservations west of Missouri, specialized crop farming in the Boon's Lick area, and congressional action to enlarge Missouri by adding the Platte River country.

4

THE BOOMING TRADE,
1837–1845

Heavy Missouri River steamboat commerce by the late 1830s reflected Missouri's expanding economy. Thousands of farmers made the transition to commercial agriculture by raising and exporting tobacco, hemp, wheat, corn, and various meat products. The demand for farm produce stimulated further settlement and the creation of new communities in the Missouri River region. The most dramatic development in the state's expansion was the addition of the Platte Purchase lands on its northwestern frontier. The enlargement of the Santa Fe trade, the business of supplying Indians west of Missouri, and the upper Missouri fur trade created demands for more steamboating. Missouri and Missouri River commerce also benefited from American interest in the Oregon country. As settlers began the long overland trek from the Missouri River to the Columbia River region, Missouri's westernmost towns became the outfitting centers for all trail needs, including wagons, animals, groceries, hardware, and other supplies.

State censuses of 1836 and 1844 showed Missouri's population surged from 244,208 to 511,937.[1] Part of the increase was caused by the addition of the Platte Purchase west of the original state boundary north of the Missouri River. The area of approximately two million acres between the longitudinal line and the Missouri River became very controversial after the federal government decided to make it part of the "Permanent Indian Frontier." By the 1830 Treaty of Prairie du Chien, Wisconsin, the government acquired the right from the Sauk, Fox, Iowa, and Eastern Dakota Indians to use present-day Platte, Buchanan, Andrew, Holt, Nodaway, and Atchison counties as part of its Indian frontier.[2]

But Missourians reacted strongly to this arrangement. As Potawatomi Indians from Indiana were being relocated on some of the Platte Country lands, Liberty, the seat of Clay County, became the focal point of Missouri expansionists. The longitudinal line seemed reasonable to many Missourians before white settlement, but incoming farmers saw the Missouri River as their natural boundary. With aspirations of exporting farm produce by river, they thought their livelihood depended on access to westward-flowing tributaries such as the Platte, Nodaway, and Tarkio rivers. But their path was blocked by the federal government and its Indian wards. Some law-abiding settlers adjusted by moving north from Clay County, where Clinton County was organized in 1833. However, others ignored the state boundary and illegally began settling on Indian land. For a time it appeared that the trespassers, who complained about Potawatomi thievery, would soon be warring with their Indian neighbors.[3]

The obvious solution for western Missourians was to exile the Indians by extending the state to the Missouri River. They were supported by the state legislature and by Missouri's congressional delegation, led by Senators Thomas Hart Benton and Lewis F. Linn. Clay Countians forced the issue by holding a meeting in Liberty during the winter of 1834-35. They called for the boundary adjustment and named a committee to represent their views to their congressional delegation and President Jackson. In a not too subtle threat, they contended that the notion of placing Indians in the Platte country was not only bad for Missouri but bad for the Indians themselves, because it would prove to be "the speediest means which could have been devised to exterminate them."[4] Thus the prospect of bloodshed became another argument for granting Missouri its proclaimed natural boundary.

The initial federal response deepened the tension. On July 1, 1835, Indian agent Richard W. Cummings reported that he had received instructions from his superiors to inform the estimated 250 to 300 trespassing families that they had to remove themselves immediately. Subsequently, they were evicted by militiamen. But many soon returned, in the belief that sympathetic politicians would resolve the matter. The crisis stimulated Missouri's campaign to win congressional approval for enlarging the state.[5]

By an act signed by President Andrew Jackson on June 7, 1836, Congress agreed to extend Missouri's western boundary to the Missouri River. But it stipulated that "this act shall not take effect until the President shall by proclamation, declare that the Indian title to said lands has been extinguished; nor shall it take effect until the State of Missouri, shall have assented to the provisions."[6] During the summer and early fall federal commissioners negotiated several treaties with the Indian signatories of the 1830 Prairie du Chien treaty. Collectively, they made up the "Platte Purchase." In exchange for modest payments, the tribesmen ceded any claims they may have retained and freed the United States from its obligation to preserve the tract for Indian use. Soon thereafter the Missouri legislature approved the boundary adjustment act, and President Martin Van Buren on March 28, 1837, proclaimed it to be in effect.[7]

The Sauk, Fox, and Iowa Indians in the northern part of the purchase soon left for reservations west of the Missouri River. But the more recalcitrant Potawatomis, in the southern part of the area, balked. The government responded by sending Brevet Brigadier General Henry Atkinson from Jefferson Barracks to supervise their removal to lands near later Council Bluffs, Iowa.[8]

Thousands of settlers moved to the extension of Missouri's agricultural frontier. By the end of 1845, all six Platte Purchase counties had been created by the legislature. The 1844 census reported the total population of its four southernmost counties was approximately thirty-seven thousand.[9]

Of the Missouri River towns established in the Platte Purchase, St. Joseph, started in 1843, became the most important. Its founder, Joseph Robidoux, had been trading with Indians in the Blacksnake Hills since the early 1830s. After Buchanan County was formed in 1839, he expanded his interests to include supplying settlers, flour milling, and townsite speculation. As settlers approached his riverside land claim, Robidoux had St. Joseph, named for himself, platted. Brisk sales of lots soon made the town a major steamboat port.[10]

Below St. Joseph a former Fort Leavenworth soldier chose a riverside townsite in Platte County, which was platted as Weston in 1839. Within a year it had three hundred residents and was the major steamboat port in that vicinity of the Platte Purchase.[11]

Mainly because of the expanding Santa Fe and Indian trades, new communities were platted near the mouth of the Kansas River. The first white occupant of the later Kansas City, Missouri, site was Francois Chouteau, a half-brother of Pierre Chouteau, Jr. Francois moved from St. Louis in 1821 to begin trading with Indians. In association with his half-brother and his father-in-law, Pierre Menard, his trade increased as Indians were relocated in Kansas. His trading post was the main inducement for steamboats to proceed above the landings that served Independence.[12]

Chouteau's reliance on steamboats was probably the inspiration for Joseph C. McCoy to establish a Santa Fe outfitting base west of Independence. For overland freighters, whose ox- or mule-drawn wagons moved at only two or two and half miles an hour respectively, even saving a relatively short distance was significant. Also, freighters were easily lured to locations that had more public grazing lands than older communities. In 1833 McCoy opened a store on the Santa Fe Trail about four miles south of the Missouri. Since it promised to be the new gateway to the Southwest, he dubbed his claim Westport. To supply Westport, he started Westport Landing, a short distance above Chouteau's post. By routing his imports through the new levee, McCoy saved eighteen miles of overland travel relative to the most popular of Independence's several landings.[13]

In 1838 McCoy and thirteen associates started a town just south of Westport Landing. After purchasing the claim of one of the pioneer French settlers, the group platted the "Town of Kansas," which had five hundred residents by 1840. It retained that designation until it was chartered as the "City of Kansas" in 1853. Thirty-six years later its name was officially changed to Kansas City.

Downstream from Westport Landing, Brunswick and Glasgow, both started in 1836, became the two leading tobacco-exporting river towns. Brunswick was a project of the enterprising James Keyte, an English-born Methodist minister who began serving a Chariton congregation in 1821. After Chariton, which had a reputation as a malarial bottomland, was affected by the 1826 flood, Keyte recognized

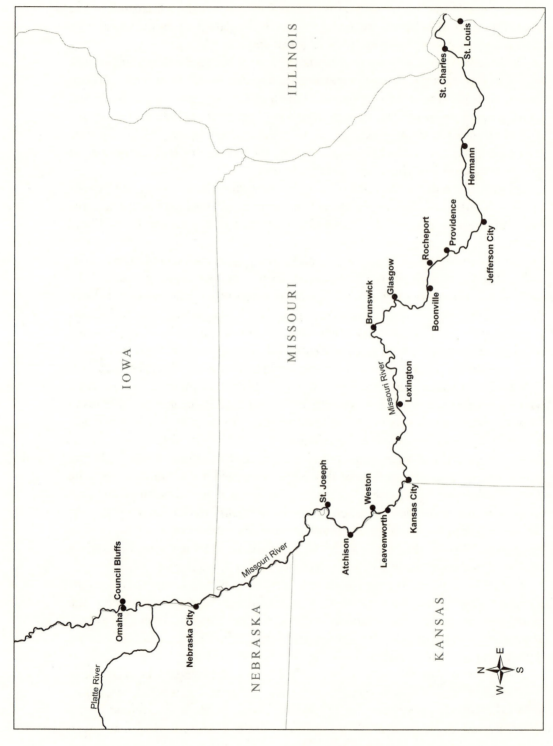

Major ports on the lower Missouri. (Current state boundaries are shown for reference.) *Prepared by James Worm.*

the attractiveness of an inland site. Soon after platting Keytesville in 1832, he donated some of its land to Chariton County, which led to the transfer of the county seat from Chariton in 1833.[14]

Keytesville's central location made it a desirable county seat, but area residents needed a good Missouri River port. Keyte platted Brunswick, about twelve miles west of Keytesville, on the northernmost bend of the Missouri River within the state. Originally located on the Missouri's left bank about a mile below the Grand River, Brunswick was ideally situated to tap the trade of a rich agricultural hinterland to the north.

Glasgow, in westernmost Howard County, grew in part because of the demise of nearby Chariton, which, like Old Franklin, declined sharply after the 1826 flood and the loss of its county seat. In his 1837 gazetteer, Alphonso Wetmore proclaimed Chariton was a "deserted village." Interestingly, St. Louis steamboat agents continued to advertise it as one of their destinations, and in 1839 a local booster pointed out that it had three tobacco processing establishments, a warehouse, a steam sawmill, a steam flour mill, a grocery store, a post office, and two blacksmiths, as well as a doctor, a tailor, a hatter, a shoemaker, a wagonmaker, a gunsmith, a cooper, a carpenter, and a milliner. Wetmore's premature claim was nonetheless prophetic. Soon after the 1839 assertion that Chariton was alive and well, it was abandoned.[15]

During the late 1830s, settlers claimed lands along the Missouri that had been bypassed during the initial rush to the Boon's Lick country. Hermann, which became the seat of Gasconade County, was established in 1836 by immigrants sponsored by the German Settlement Association of Philadelphia. The same year, the town of Bassora was started just upstream from the southernmost bend of the Missouri. Subsequently, it was absorbed by Washington, platted in 1839.[16]

As the demand for steamboats rose, Missouri River operators extended their navigation seasons whenever nature allowed. Normally, by mid- to late December the river was closed by either low water or ice. Sometimes droughts closed the river much earlier. By August 20, 1842, the largest boats were forced to withdraw because of extremely low water.[17] That fall a Jefferson City newspaper reported, "There is less depth of channel now in the Missouri, than has been known in many years."[18] In November 1845, another dry time, only one boat of twenty advertised in a St. Louis newspaper was destined for the Missouri.[19]

The opening of "spring navigation" varied considerably. In most years, the ice had melted sufficiently by mid-February to early March to permit navigation. But during the exceptionally warm winters of 1838–39 and 1839–40, there was some steamboat navigation during every winter month because the river alternately thawed and refroze, even in January. Before mid-January 1840 the *Rhine* steamed to Jefferson City and the *Bedford* to Boonville. But by January 20, masses of floating ice at St. Louis stopped navigation for a few days, and on February 1 the Missouri at St. Charles had refrozen to such an extent that teams and wagons were crossing on it. Again, in January 1844, the *Monona* ascended to Jefferson City in the face of some floating ice.[20]

Steamboat customers always yearned for faster service. Newspapermen in Missouri River towns depended on the steamboat delivery of St. Louis and eastern newspapers for their latest information. This service was usually performed by steamboat clerks, who in return would get some free publicity for their boat from grateful editors. Any improvement in delivery times enabled Missouri readers to get somewhat closer to the actual happening. As an example of news lag, in 1841 word of President William Henry Harrison's death on April 4 was first publicized in Jefferson City thirteen days later.[21]

Increasingly speedier delivery times were achieved during the boom that started in 1837, made possible in part by the construction of more powerful and shallower-drafted boats. In 1839 the editor of the *Jeffersonian Republican* marveled at the great progress since 1826, when only one steamboat reached Jefferson City. Pronouncing that "our river is now enlivened with boats of the finest class propelled by steam, bidding defiance to the mighty flood of the Missouri," he reported that any of his fellow citizens could make an approximate 300-mile round-trip to St. Louis in less than four days.[22]

In 1841 the customary 40- to 48-hour ascent from St. Louis was reduced to 36 hours. The next year, the *Mary Tompkins* cut the time to only 23 hours "and some minutes." But the new standard was smashed within days by the *Emilie*, which steamed up in 22 hours and 15 minutes. Another fast boat, the *Lewis F. Linn*, made an 1844 trip from St. Louis to Jefferson City in 23 hours and 15 minutes, which, for some reason, prompted its officers to think that 19 hours was achievable.[23]

Like some other boats, the *Emilie* and the *Mary Tompkins* ran around the clock. The advent of nighttime navigation was facilitated by better knowledge of the river and the removal of snags in some of the most troublesome bends. The narrowness and crookedness of the Missouri generally precluded boats running against each other, but captains realized the value of having newspapers publicize their boat as the fastest in a type of time trial. Invariably, speed records were set by new boats, which were in better condition than older competitors. Hence, travelers tended to think that a fast boat was also safer and more commodious than older, slower craft.

Some of the haphazardness of timing steamboat arrivals and departures was removed by the introduction of scheduled packet service in 1841. Because he believed the quantities of freight and numbers of passengers assured weekly cargoes, Captain N. J. Eaton of the *Iatan* began offering weekly trips that left St. Louis and the Missouri River turnabout town at times advertised well in advance. Eaton assured customers that his boat would leave St. Louis for Glasgow every Saturday at 4:00 P.M. and would start down from Glasgow every Tuesday at 3:00 P.M. The ascent was scheduled for something less than three days, but the return would be completed by early on Thursday. He did not attempt to set precise arrival times for intermediate points. Anyone leaving Arrow Rock, Rocheport, or Boonville for St. Louis was given the time of "Tuesday evening," and such downstream shippers and passengers as those at Jefferson City, Hermann, and Washington were told to expect a Wednesday arrival and departure.[24]

During the season, the *Iatan* made twenty-four regular weekly trips to Glasgow and several more to points above.[25] The *Jeffersonian Republican* praised Eaton's experiment by noting that "this packet during the summer has never failed of arriving at the appointed hour." According to the editor, this reliability assured Eaton's boat "a very liberal portion of the business of the river."[26]

Others soon emulated Eaton. In 1842 Captain John W. Keiser of the *Emilie* and a Captain Walter, master of the *Mary Tompkins,* began offering scheduled packet service from St. Louis to Glasgow. They and the *Iatan* were the leaders in Glasgow's lively tobacco trade. Thereafter, scheduled packets dominated the business. Eaton replaced the *Iatan* with the *Wapello* in 1843, and the next year Captain William Miller of the *Huntsville* and Captain M. Kennett of the *Lewis F. Linn* ran regularly scheduled trips from St. Louis to Jefferson City.[27]

During the rapid expansion of steamboating, the balance of trade became favorable for Missouri River towns. The passage from subsistence to commercial farming not only decreased the need to import such things as flour and tobacco products but also resulted in the exportation of massive quantities of tobacco, hemp, cordage, corn, bacon, and ham. In the spring of 1841 the editor of the *Jeffersonian Republican* observed that "this is the first year that has borne any appearance of the balance of trade being in our favor." Farm exports were said to have increased tenfold while imports of Missouri River town merchants "have greatly diminished."[28]

Upriver shipments starting from St. Louis included such essential grocery items as sugar, coffee, and salt. Salt, usually obtained from mines along the Kanawha River in western Virginia (now West Virginia) and islands in the West Indies was in great demand for home-curing meat. Ordinarily, ten pounds were needed to prepare the brine for curing a hundred pounds of meat. In early 1841 two Jefferson City merchants advertised that goods they had received by the steamers *Colonel Wood* and *Thames* included silk, muslin, calico, painted lawns (a type of fabric), shawls, soap, seven barrels of American and French brandy, and an assortment of boots and shoes. General merchandisers also routinely had bar iron, books, drugs, gunpowder, raw cotton, nails, and a variety of hardware brought from St. Louis.[29]

Some freight originating in St. Louis was bound for the fur trade of the upper Missouri, the Santa Fe trade, and the Indian reservations west of Missouri. The nature of some of the goods for the tribes recently moved to the Permanent Indian Frontier showed the government's determination to assimilate them into a white lifestyle. In the fall of 1839 a Captain Cleveland, commanding the *Pizarro,* took a cargo of 20 spinning wheels, 20 looms, 300 axes, 100 plows, and $10,000 in specie from St. Louis to Westport Landing. The Indian reservations also provided Missouri farmers and merchants the opportunity to ship to the West as well as downstream to St. Louis and New Orleans. Government contracts for supplying reservations with bacon, ham, livestock, flour, corn, and wheat were generally filled in the Missouri River valley.[30]

There was also a certain amount of steamboat trading between Missouri River towns. The principal source of pine lumber was sawmills along the Gasconade

River. Lumber was routinely rafted down that stream to its mouth near Hermann and carried on the Missouri by steamboats. Until Jefferson City got its own flour mill in 1842, wheat raised nearby was shipped upstream to Boonville to be ground with some of the flour being carried back to Jefferson City. This arrangement benefited steamboatmen but obviously drove up the price of flour in Jefferson City.[31]

Tobacco was the leading steamboat export. Its culture was concentrated in Little Dixie—seven of the counties abutting the Missouri River upstream from near the mouth of the Osage. These counties—Callaway, Boone, Howard, Cooper, Saline, Lafayette, and Clay—had the state's highest proportion of slaves. Their slave tradition began with the first movement of upper South emigrants to the Boon's Lick country and was perpetuated by the commercial significance of labor-intensive crops. Some tobacco was also raised in the Mississippi River counties above and below St. Louis.[32]

Tobacco leaf—"strips" in the parlance of the business—was shipped the year after it was raised. Tobacco was partially cured in the field before the stalks were aged over the winter in sheds. The next spring the leaves were stripped by hand from their stems, usually in specially constructed tobacco stemmeries, which resembled warehouses. All of the leading tobacco towns such as Rocheport, Glasgow, Brunswick, and Lexington had stemmeries. Some leaf was sold locally to manufacturers of smoking and chewing tobacco and cigars. But most was packed and pressed into large hogsheads destined for markets in St. Louis, New Orleans, eastern cities, and Europe.[33]

Production was measured in pounds and hogsheads, with each hogshead weighing three-fourths of a ton. An 1839 newspaper correspondent reported that, for the preceding several years, Missouri's annual exports had ranged from 3,000 to 5,000 hogsheads. Production increased during the next decade. Missouri's exports for 1841 were said to be about 4,000 hogsheads, and the 1844 yield, despite flood losses, approached 10,000.[34]

With numerous hogsheads crammed on the main deck of steamers, individual shipments were newsworthy. In an 1841 trip from Glasgow and nearby points, the *Iatan* was loaded with 200 hogsheads. The next year, boats returning to St. Louis were reported to be heavily laden with tobacco, with the expectation that shipments of tobacco and other farm produce would double or triple within a year.[35]

Hemp, which became more popular in the early 1840s, was the Missouri River's second-ranking steamboat export. Several of the original Boon's Lickers raised and processed some hemp, but changing economic and political conditions led them to increase production. The expansion of the cotton industry in southern states greatly increased the need to bale and ship cotton, which in turn created a demand for more baling rope and bagging. Missourians also benefited from the protective tariff of 1841, which increased duties on imported hemp and bagging. Because of the act, shipments from Russia, the traditional foreign supplier, were sharply reduced, and Kentucky, the leading hemp-producing state, could not meet domestic needs. Some began raising hemp because Congress determined that the Navy

Department should be supplied with domestic hemp. Hemp cultivation was also a natural outgrowth of the advent of "scientific agriculture." Through agricultural societies and fairs, farmers were encouraged to diversify in order to adjust to ever-changing national and international markets.[36]

As with tobacco, most of Missouri's hemp was produced in Little Dixie and nearby counties. Throughout the hemp-producing period, Platte County, with Weston as its main port, and Buchanan County, home of St. Joseph, ranked among the leading producers. Processing was laborious. After the tall stalks were cut with cradle scythes, they were aged for several months, including a period of lying on the ground. This "dew-rotting" phase enabled laborers to remove the usable fibers from the partially decayed stalks. After further clarifying, the fibers were pressed into bales. Some were sold to local rope walks for cordage production, but most were stored in levee warehouses until they could be loaded on steamboats.[37]

A good sense of the nature and amount of Missouri River steamboating can be derived from various contemporary newspaper reports. Glasgow, with 158 arrivals in 1838, had 312 in 1841. In the years 1839–42, Jefferson City had 264, 325, 365, and 380 arrivals respectively. Eighteen boats, making a total of 108 trips participated in the 1838 trade, led by the *St. Peters*, which made 18 trips. Others that made ten or more were the *Dart*, 15; the *Astoria*, 13; the *Howard* and the *Pirate*, 11 each; and the *Kansas*, 10. The *Platte* completed 8 voyages, and the *Little Red* 4. Five of the boats made only one trip. The estimated total of the up and down freight combined was 20,000 tons. The 1841 business of 46,000 tons for all up and down freight used twenty-five different boats.[38]

As this heavy traffic developed, it was becoming increasingly apparent that the Missouri River towns were nothing more than a part of St. Louis's hinterland. The old dream of a Boon's Lick metropolis had faded, and those living along the Missouri came to feel like country cousins vis-à-vis the rapidly expanding St. Louis. Since they depended on St. Louis as both their supplier and their market, Missouri River merchants were wary of being exploited by steamboatmen.

An 1838 report indicated that steamboat freight rates were considerably higher for the Missouri than for any other route. The charge per hundredweight to Missouri River destinations from St. Louis ranged from 75 cents to $1.50, whereas shipments to Galena, Illinois, cost 37.5 to 75 cents, about the same as those to the head of navigation on the Illinois River. The charges from Pittsburgh to St. Louis, a route about seven times longer than that from St. Louis to Jefferson City, were 50 to 75 cents per hundredweight.[39]

Some western Missourians asserted that they were being victimized by St. Louis interests. The editor of Liberty's *Western Star* alleged that the rates were disproportionately high because of collusion between St. Louis forwarding merchants and steamboatmen. He charged that the St. Louis rate to Liberty Landing had run as high as $3.00 per hundredweight for some early spring shipments. Western Missourians, he believed, were being assessed an "'odious tariff.'" Defending St. Louis, the *Missouri Republican* responded that there was no collusion, because forwarding merchants and steamboatmen were not distinct groups. He claimed that many boats were partially owned by St. Louis forwarding agencies and, for that matter, by Missouri River merchants. The main reason for the high Missouri River rates, he insisted, was that the stream was uniquely risky. Steamboatmen and insurers thought that losses and detentions by such things as low water were at least 100 percent higher on the Missouri than on other routes.[40]

Theoretically, competition between boats should have had a moderating effect on rates. But in the spring of 1845 the steamboat captains and owners of all regular Missouri River boats agreed on season-long prices for both freight and passengers. Their compact had the general effect of raising charges but at least assured shippers uniform rates. The only possible challenge to this arrangement was "transient boats," whose captains traded randomly on any route where they could get a cargo. But the regular packets, the darlings of Missouri town newspapers, were hard to challenge because of their local reputations.[41]

As Missouri's economy matured and more people moved upriver as the first leg of their treks to distant frontiers, steamboatmen emphasized the passenger trade as an essential part of their business. The new wealth and opportunities created by the commercialization of agriculture increased business travel between St. Louis and Missouri River towns. Traveling salesmen, peddling everything from elixirs to books, newspapers, and insurance became a regular fixture on steamboats. The combination of St. Louis's growth as a minor metropolis and the expanding Missouri River valley populace stimulated leisure travel. Invariably, passengers wanted to move speedily, safely, and comfortably.

Steamboat owners and builders responded by catering to passenger desires. New boats were regularly advertised as fast, light-draft, and commodious. Passage was of two types—cabin and deck. Cabin passengers, oftentimes the economic and social elite, were quartered in private or semiprivate staterooms featuring good beds and linens, as well as maid service. The staterooms, so-called because each bore the name of a state in the Union, were adjacent to separate ladies' and men's cabins, or lounging rooms. Cabin passage included meals served in the dining saloon. Most captains realized the benefit of gaining a reputation for having good fare, so meals usually featured fresh meat and vegetables and fine liquors, including imported wines and brandy.[42]

Deck passage, which ordinarily cost about half as much as cabin passage, simply meant the individual got nothing more than a ride. Deck passengers had to carry their own food and bedding. At night, like the deckhands, they found a convenient spot to sleep. Unlike cabin passengers, whose ranks were limited by the number of staterooms, deck passengers were crammed onto boats with little concern for their comfort.

This passenger trade was augmented by the continuing Santa Fe business, the start of overland movement to Oregon, the Mormon disturbance in western Missouri, political conventions, and pleasure cruises. Santa Fe traders were usually newsworthy when they amassed large returns. In the fall of 1839 the steamboat

Pizarro delivered passengers from Independence to St. Louis who had $60,000 in specie for the season's Santa Fe business.[43]

Many Missourians, including longtime senator Thomas Hart Benton, were deeply interested in American expansion into Oregon. They were certainly motivated in part by patriotic fervor to win the contest with the hated British. In 1818, when the United States and Great Britain set the forty-ninth parallel boundary across the northern Great Plains, they had agreed to leave the Oregon country— the area west of the Continental Divide—free and open to nationals of both countries. American expansionists realized that the United States could solidify its claims by settling the land.[44]

But Missourians also knew that their state would benefit from any movement to Oregon. The only practical overland route for New Englanders and other easterners lured to Oregon was through Missouri by way of St. Louis and the Missouri River. At or near Westport Landing, emigrants would embark on the overland trail. Thus various Missouri River towns could become involved in the business of outfitting emigrants. In 1841 the first emigrant party, accompanied by Roman Catholic missionaries Pierre-Jean De Smet and Nicholas Point and Methodist minister Joseph Williams, made its way from Westport Landing to Oregon. It was but a harbinger of the so-called Great Migration of 1843, when about a thousand emigrants moved. This unprecedented migration led to expanded movements from western Missouri to Oregon and California as well. Until they crossed South Pass in present-day southwestern Wyoming, the Oregon and California emigrants used the same route.[45]

In the spring of 1839, steamboats were used to move some of the thousands of evicted Mormons from Clay and several nearby counties to their new Zion of Nauvoo, Illinois. The Mormon religion, officially the Church of Jesus Christ of Latter-day Saints, was formed by prophet Joseph Smith in upstate New York in 1830. Based on the angel Moroni's revelations to Smith, the religion stressed the need to minister to Indians, to convert Gentiles (i.e., non-Mormons) to the true faith, and to organize a society based on theocratic communal principles that challenged the traditional private enterprise system. Faced with intolerance, Smith soon led his followers to the "promised land" of Kirtland, Ohio. From there some of the faithful were soon sent to Independence, Missouri, near the eastern edge of the Indian frontier. In 1833, clashes with other Missourians, who abhorred Mormon doctrines, forced the Saints to move across the Missouri River into less populous Clay County, where they established the community of Far West.[46]

As the numbers of both Mormons and Gentiles increased, the pattern of the Jackson County hostilities was repeated. When destruction of Mormon property intensified, militants on both sides urged a bloody conflict. Governor Lilburn Boggs, rather than act as a peacemaker, proclaimed that the Mormons should be driven out or exterminated. Boggs ordered several hundred militiamen to oust them. After the militia occupied Far West in October 1839, hundreds of irregular anti-Mormons readied for a decisive battle. But rather than ending in an

Armageddon-like showdown, the disturbance featured several bloody skirmishes, which forced the Mormons to forsake their Missouri colonization project.

Following the Mormon exodus, the passenger business was given another boost by the Whig Party's decision to hold its 1840 state convention in Rocheport. The small town was chosen for the three-day conclave because it was a steamboat-accessible site near the center of the state. Rather than select representatives, the Whigs in the various counties and towns decided that anyone who attended would be a "delegate." As a result, the St. Louis delegation comprised about three hundred men, and the entire convention about three thousand. Special arrangements were made with booking agents and captains weeks in advance.[47] The St. Louis group traveled on the *Platte* and the *Rienzi*—two of the largest Missouri River boats, which were lashed together during loading. Preceded by two bands, the delegation made a showy march from the courthouse to the landing. To advertise presidential candidate William Henry Harrison's "Log Cabin Campaign," the boats also carried two log cabins, which had been shipped to St. Louis from Rockport, Illinois, and Clarksville, Tennessee. The *Rhine* was used to transport the Glasgow delegation and organizers, though another three or four boats were needed to carry passengers from towns above there.

In July 1844 the Democrats held their state convention in Boonville. The *Iatan* and other boats provided transportation to the "immense multitude," which was treated to a four-hour speech by Senator Benton.[48]

Emulating Ohio and Mississippi river steamboatmen, Missouri River operators began offering special excursions, usually billed as "pleasure cruises." The role of the steamboat in enlivening river town social life was especially evident during Independence Day observances. On the evening of July 3, 1839, a group of some two hundred St. Louisians—including various ladies and gentlemen, a unit of the city's militia, and two bands—boarded the *Naomi* to observe the Fourth in St. Charles. The editor of the *Missouri Republican,* one of the celebrants, was thrilled when the captain of the *Shawnee* decided to race the *Naomi.* The contest was close for ten to twelve miles, but he gleefully reported that by the time the *Naomi* reached the mouth of the Missouri, she "had left her competitor some distance in the rear." In St. Charles the excursionists were greeted by thirteen rounds from the town's cannon, and during their "sumptuous" Fourth of July dinner, they and their hosts symbolically made thirteen champagne toasts to commemorate the formation of the original Union.[49]

In 1843 a number of Jefferson Citians observed the Fourth by taking the *Osage Packet* to the farm of their host thirteen miles up the Osage. Playing such songs as the famous "Hail Columbia" and "Yankee Doodle" and a local favorite—"Going up the Osage"—an accompanying band provided entertainment. Their dinner, featuring pit-barbecued venison, was closed with only one toast: "Our GOD, *first—* and then our COUNTRY."[50]

Other captains found that they did not need a special occasion to undertake a pleasure cruise. In April 1842 a "large company of young gentlemen and ladies" from

Jefferson City made a one-day round-trip on the *Mary Tompkins* to Glasgow. Then, following a common practice, they published a card of thanks, which included a recommendation of the boat, in one of the town's newspapers. Later in the season the *Rowena* made an excursion from St. Louis to the Blacksnake Hills. Among its many stops was one at Jefferson City to enable the tourists to see the state capitol.[51]

Pleasure seekers on short trips were usually exhilarated by the scenery and the novelty of a boat ride, but those who traveled with some regularity found boat life tedious. Consequently, they sought various social diversions to help break up the days. For cabin passengers, mealtimes were usually the highlights of the day. Most male passengers resorted to drinking alcohol and gambling. Charles Augustus Murray, an English tourist, was openly amazed at western egalitarianism. He thought a "true republican equality" existed, because of the lack of tradition-bound social classes. To illustrate his point, he observed that he had "seen the clerk of a steam-boat, and a grocer in a small village on the Missouri, sit down to take grog or play at cards with a member of Congress and an officer in the army; laughing together, swearing together, and the names of Bill, Dick, and Harry, passing familiarly between them!"[52]

Since politics and especially disputes over presidential candidates were common conversational items, passengers sometimes settled their differences by taking a presidential poll. In an 1839 voyage from Fort Leavenworth to St. Louis, Henry Clay, the presumed Whig candidate for 1840, outpolled Democratic president Martin Van Buren seventeen to four. St. Louis's Whig newspaper opined that the vote was "about the relative popularity of the two men with that portion of the community who travel about."[53] The next year, William Henry Harrison, the Whig candidate, bested Van Buren fifty-six to ten in a steamboat poll.[54]

In noting that Whig candidates always won in steamboat polls, the editor of the *Jefferson City Inquirer*, a Democratic organ, ridiculed the "steamboat presidents." The polls, he charged, were nothing more than a sham effort to influence public opinion. He noted that if the election of presidents had been left to steamboat passengers, John Quincy Adams would have defeated Andrew Jackson in 1828 and Henry Clay would have come out ahead of Jackson in 1832. Steamboat passengers, he contended, did not represent a cross section of society. The majority were "merchants and their clerks," he maintained, adding, "not one in ten a farmer or mechanic."[55] His observation was apt. It was well known that the Whigs got much of their support from businessmen, while the Democrats' greatest appeal was to the farmers and laborers

On other occasions, passengers organized meetings to thank boat officers. On a St. Louis to Weston trip, 104 passengers signed a resolution recommending the *Admiral* as a "safe and commodious" boat. The resolution was the outcome of a formal meeting in which "Charles Neal, Esq. was called to the chair and Wm. McCoy, Esq. appointed Secretary."[56] Such resolutions, which interestingly were published in friendly newspapers, were obviously intended to boost a boat's stock. In some instances, the expression may have been a sincere thought initiated by happy passengers, but there was also a possibility of collusion between captains and certain passengers, who may have had a vested interest in the boat.

The rapid increase of steamboating did not extend beyond St. Joseph. To many St. Louisians, the lands beyond Missouri's western boundary were "Indian country," where the only business was the fur trade. As St. Louis became older and larger, its people acted more and more like urbanites fascinated by a "Wild West." Such destinations as Fort Union and the Rockies were remote and somewhat mysterious. Reaching them seemed to require Herculean efforts, so the steamboatmen and traders were often seen as conquering heroes.

Upstream from Fort Leavenworth, the first noteworthy steamboat destination was Bellevue. As the agency for regional Indians expelled from the Platte Purchase, including the Potawatomis, Bellevue attracted traders and missionaries. After Pierre Chouteau, Jr., and Company opened a new post there in 1840, Bellevue became yet more important as a rendezvous for those proceeding up the Missouri or westward along the Platte.[57]

In both 1838 and 1839 the *Wilmington* delivered Indian annuities at Bellevue. On the 1838 trip, Father Pierre-Jean De Smet, then in the early phase of his celebrated missionary career, traveled on the boat in late May from near Fort Leavenworth. De Smet was on his way from St. Louis to establish a mission among the Potawatomis at the site of later Council Bluffs, Iowa. De Smet was awed by the forests of snags, the time-consuming task of warping off sandbars, and the persistent threat of a boiler explosion. As for creature comforts, he found "the weather was excessively hot; the warm, muddy water of the Missouri was our only drink, and myriads of mosquitos, fleas, and other insects were our traveling companions."[58] He was puzzled by the comments of some of his boat mates about the "beautiful" voyage. As a veteran Atlantic Ocean traveler, De Smet compared that experience to the Missouri trip: "I fear the sea, I will admit, but all the storms and other unpleasant things I experienced in four different voyages did not inspire so much terror in me as the navigation of the somber, treacherous and muddy Missouri."[59]

On the 1839 voyage, the *Wilmington*'s captain saw the wreck of the *Pirate*, about seven miles below Bellevue. It sank in less than five minutes after the current and a strong wind pushed it back against a snag. The *Pirate* was carrying flour, bacon, and corn loaded at Liberty Landing for the Potawatomis and Otos and some supplies for the Bellevue trading post. Since the boat settled in very deep water, it was presumed that no effort would be made to raise it or salvage the cargo.[60]

Above the Bellevue area, the only steamboating was done by Astor's successors, who continued to be popularly known as the American Fur Company, and the competing Union Fur Company. In attempting to better adapt to the characteristically shallow upper river, Pierre Chouteau, Jr., and his associates experimented with many side-wheelers (table 1). The *St. Peters*, the 1837 boat, was replaced with the *Antelope*, which was used for the next three years. To lessen the boat's draft, Chouteau had the *Antelope* extensively remodeled over the winter of 1840–41. When the altered boat had to be reregistered to comply with federal law, it was

TABLE I

DIMENSIONS AND TONNAGE OF CHOUTEAU'S SIDE-WHEELERS

Name	Length	Width	Depth of hold	Tonnage
General Brooke	144 '	20 '	5 '	143
Huntsville	—	—	—	138
Nimrod	156 '	25 ' 10 "	5.7 '	210
Omega	142 ' 10 "	21 ' 6 "	—	144
St. Peters	139 '	18 ' 8 "	5.9 '	119
Trapper (née *Antelope*)	132 '	19 '	—	132

Source: See note 61 of chapter 4.

renamed to *Trapper*, which was steamed to the upper river in 1841 and 1842. Because of the challenge from the Union Fur Company, Chouteau sent a second boat, the *Huntsville*, to Fort Union in 1842. The two-voyage pattern was repeated the next year, when Chouteau used the *Omega* as well as the *Huntsville*. The 1844 boat, *Nimrod*, was succeeded by the *General Brooke* in 1845.[61]

Fort Union was the utmost destination for Chouteau's boats. With the exception of low-water 1839, when the *Antelope* could ascend no higher than Fort Clark, they reached it. But in 1842 the descending *Trapper* was stranded by low water near Fort Pierre in late July. Captain Joseph A. Sire returned to St. Louis by mackinaw. His 1843 *Omega* passengers included an extra crew led by Captain John Durack, who returned the *Trapper* to St. Louis.[62]

From Sire's journals, Mark H. Bettis calculated that the average St. Louis–Fort Union round-trip for 1841–46 voyages, with the exception of those by the *Huntsville*, was 83 days. Ascending, they averaged 30 miles a day, and descending, 77. Sire's laconic record emphasized the usual aggravations of coping with fuel and water shortages. Above Bellevue, wood sellers were rare, so his men usually had to catch driftwood or stop to cut wood. Oftentimes a yawl was sent in advance to take soundings to determine if there was a navigable channel. When the channel was too shallow, the boat would be wholly or partially off-loaded and the cargo advanced by lighters, which were carried or towed by the steamboat. When Sire was forced to abandon the *Trapper* in 1842, he had reached a point where there was no continuous channel deep enough for the boat.

Chouteau's upbound boats were loaded with an assortment of trade goods and provisions for Fort Union and the principal posts below it—Fort Clark, Fort Pierre, Fort Vermillion, and Bellevue. The nature of the freight is well illustrated by the 1841 Fort Union consignment transported on the *Trapper*. Among its entire range of general merchandise were about 600 blankets, 2,000 yards of cloth, 700 shirts of various types, groceries, hardware, tobacco, dishes, and rifle flints.[63]

Upon arriving at Fort Union, the boats were hurriedly unloaded and reloaded

The *Trapper* was used by Pierre Chouteau, Jr., and Company on 1841 and 1842 voyages from St. Louis to Fort Union. *Courtesy of the Nebraska State Historical Society.*

with return cargoes of buffalo robes and other animal pelts and hides, including deer, mink, muskrat, otter, raccoon, wildcat, and wolf. Because Chouteau's company was leery of loading its steamboats too heavily, some of its downstream shipments were made with mackinaws, which were built at boatyards near its upriver posts. The degree of reliance on mackinaws was dictated by water conditions. In 1837 the returning *St. Peters* transported about 2,000 packs of buffalo robes and a "considerable amount" of other furs. But the company also used a fleet of twelve to fifteen mackinaws. When the river was unusually low in 1838, the *Antelope* was loaded with only 1,000 packs of buffalo robes, and the company sent its "more valuable furs" to St. Louis by mackinaws. In 1839 eight mackinaws transported 2,400 packs of buffalo robes, about two and half times as many as the *Antelope* carried that year.[64]

Most of the passengers on the company's steamboats were its employees, but Pierre Chouteau, Jr., continued his practice of hosting famous guests, including Joseph N. Nicollet in 1839 and John James Audubon four years later. Nicollet, a French astronomer-cartographer, established a reputation as an explorer soon after moving to the United States. In 1835–36 he ascended the Mississippi by steamboat from St. Louis to Fort Snelling. From the vicinity of the fort, he undertook private explorations of the Mississippi's source at Lake Itasca and a canoe route leading from the Mississippi to Lake Superior. His skill as a mapmaker was brought to the attention of the War Department, which was interested in detailed, accurate mapping of the lands between the upper Mississippi and the upper Missouri.

While employed by the government, Nicollet in 1838 explored from the Mississippi westward to the Coteau des Prairies—the ridge separating the Mississippi and Missouri watersheds.[65]

In 1839 he was authorized to traverse the land from west to east by proceeding from Fort Pierre to the Mississippi via the James River, Devils Lake, and the coteau. With seven other men, including John Frémont as his principal assistant, Nicollet left St. Louis on the *Antelope* in early April. Because of low water, the trip was tortuously slow—63 days to Fort Pierre. The boat was often grounded on sandbars and sometimes had to be negotiated through snags. Nicollet thought the snags appeared "like a forest of monsters armed with pikes and pitchforks rising 10 or 15 feet above the water."[66] To get through, the crew had to clear a channel by sawing and chopping.

The *Omega*'s 1843 voyage to Fort Union was well documented by the naturalist and painter John James Audubon; one of his four companions, Richard Harris; and Captain Joseph A. Sire. Nearly fifty-nine years old when he undertook the trip, Audubon had gained fame with the publication of his *Birds of North America* in 1838, which included over four hundred of his bird paintings. In collaboration with the Scottish naturalist William MacGillivray, he completed a five-volume companion work, *The Ornithological Biography*, in 1839. Audubon continued his bird studies on the Fort Union trip, but his main purpose was to research mammals. His Missouri River travel contributed to the posthumous publication of his coauthored *Viviparous Quadrupeds of North America* (1854).[67]

Audubon and his small party left St. Louis on April 25. They shared the *Omega* with its officers and crew, several Iowa Indians, and "a hundred and one trappers of all descriptions and nearly a dozen different nationalities, though the greater number were French Canadians, or Creoles of this State."[68] Leaving St. Louis for a wilderness outpost was a decisive moment in the lives of the engagés. Audubon observed that "some were drunk, and many in that stupid mood which follows a state of nervousness produced by drinking and over-excitement."[69] As the *Omega* pushed away from the levee, they crowded on the upper deck and fired their guns in the air—a type of salute they repeated at all of the river towns.

High water on the lower river enabled Sire and his young pilot, Joseph La Barge, to steam the *Omega* to Fort Union in a record 49 days. Audubon and Harris were preoccupied with collecting animal and bird specimens. But some of the boat's cargo impressed Audubon. He noted that it started out carrying 500 dozen eggs, as well as "15 dozen of Claret, some Brandy and Whiskey."[70] Sire dropped Audubon and his companions off at Fort Union and turned the *Omega* about for St. Louis within two days. Audubon's party spent approximately two months at Fort Union before returning to St. Louis in a mackinaw piloted by Etienne Provost, one of the company's best-known guides.[71]

When Audubon was on the upper river, Pierre Chouteau, Jr., and Company was being challenged by the Union Fur Company. This new opposition firm was also known as Bolton, Fox, Livingston, and Company, for Curtis Bolton, Samuel

M. Fox, and Mortimer Livingston, its New York City financial backers, or as Ebbetts and Cutting for its two principal field agents, John A. Ebbetts and Fulton Cutting. During its four-year history, the company established two upper Missouri posts—Fort George, twenty miles below Fort Pierre, and Fort Mortimer, near the site of the deserted Fort William, only three miles from Fort Union.[72]

To service these posts, the company twice leased steamboats in St. Louis. In 1843 the 86-ton side-wheeler *New Haven* reached Fort Mortimer, and the next year the 126-ton *Frolic*, a stern-wheeler, was sent to the Yellowstone post. But low water stopped the boat at Fort George, where it had to be wintered. By the time the *Frolic* was returned to St. Louis in the spring of 1845, its high leasing fee contributed to the collapse of the Union Fur Company, which had been engaged in a price war with Chouteau's company. Like Chouteau, the Union Fur Company used mackinaws to send buffalo robes and furs to St. Louis. In 1844 three of the craft transported 550 packs of robes and furs from Fort Mortimer to St. Louis.

Despite continual experimentation with new boats, Pierre Chouteau, Jr., was apparently satisfied that steamboating improved the efficiency of the upper river trade. As willing participants in the fur trade, the indigenous tribes welcomed traders and their goods. But these contacts also brought them less desirable features of white society, including diseases to which they had no natural immunity.

The 1837 smallpox epidemic in the upper Missouri region ranks as one of the greatest disasters in the entire history of the American frontier. The disease was carried upstream by the *St. Peters*, commanded by Bernard Pratte, Jr. Ignoring the affliction of several passengers, Pratte was intent on reaching the upriver posts. Unwittingly, the pox was spread when the boat stopped at Fort Pierre, Fort Clark, and Fort Union. From the posts it was disseminated by traders and roving Indians to bands far from the river.[73]

Within several weeks, Indian deaths started to mount. By late August, Francis A. Chardon, Fort Clark's bourgeois, reported that as many as fifty Mandan men were dying daily. About a month later, he placed the total number of smallpox deaths among the Three Tribes— Mandans, Hidatsas, and Arikaras—at approximately eight hundred. However, by the time the disease had run its course, the Mandans were reduced to thirty survivors, only a remnant of their preepidemic population of about seven hundred to a thousand. Estimates of Hidatsa deaths ranged as high as three-fourths of the tribe. At Fort Union, ten of every twelve Indians were reported to have died. A resident trader estimated the pox was fatal to over half of the Assiniboins and two-thirds of the Blackfeet.[74]

Pratte returned the *St. Peters* to St. Louis, blissfully ignorant of the havoc wrought by his voyage. Reports of the epidemic circulated in St. Louis after the *Antelope's* return in 1838. Relying on information from one of the company's agents, a St. Louis newspaper reported that "the Assiniboines are said to be extinct, and most of the Blackfeet have fallen victims. It is believed more than 25,000 died of the disease."[75] The epidemic made some Indians angry with the traders. But seeing no alternative, the tribes continued working as partners in a business destined to be short-lived.

Meanwhile, steamboating was extending from the Missouri to the Osage River, the first tributary to have significant commerce. The waters of the Osage, which entered the Missouri about ten miles downstream from Jefferson City, rose in eastern Kansas. Its two upper branches—the Marais des Cygnes and the Little Osage—merged some twenty miles inside Missouri. From that point to its mouth, the stream was called the Osage. It received the waters of the tributary Sac about two miles above the town of Osceola, and downstream, those of the Niangua near Linn Creek. During dry seasons the Niangua, which entered from the south, provided over half of the Osage's flow.[76]

The sinuous Osage was a characteristic plains stream with numerous oxbows and sharply fluctuating levels from year to year and within any given navigation season. Along its upper portion, the land was rolling prairie, but from Osceola downstream it ran through wooded and oftentimes hilly terrain. As on the Missouri, snags were hazardous, but stranding on the numerous shoals was the major impediment to Osage steamboating.

By 1830 there was enough settlement along the Osage above Cole and Osage counties, which bordered both the Osage and the Missouri, to spur the opening of a few country stores. As population increased, the legislature created Miller County, south of Cole, in 1837. Its seat, Tuscumbia, became the most important steamboat destination on the lower river. Within four years all of the Osage valley in Missouri was organized into counties. Upstream from Tuscumbia were Warsaw, the seat of Benton County, and Osceola, the seat of St. Clair County. As the leading trading centers in the area, they became the goals of steamboatmen.[77]

The first steamboat trip up the Osage was organized by the St. Louis forwarding and commission firm of Crow and Tevis. In early March 1837 they proposed to charter a steamboat "of light draught" to ascend the Osage. After several weeks the company succeeded in engaging the *American,* a 128-ton side-wheeler built in Cincinnati two years earlier. In April the boat, commanded by a Captain Lusk, ascended the Osage for "about 100 miles." This was less than Crow and Tevis hoped and probably was somewhat short of Tuscumbia.[78]

The *American*'s voyage and the opportunity for Osage River business soon caught the attention of the owners of the *North St. Louis,* which, as the first steamboat built in St. Louis, had been recently launched with considerable fanfare. With a capacity of only 88 tons, the small side-wheeler seemed to be ideally suited for shallow water. Optimistically, its managers planned to reach Osceola, which would certainly have proven the Osage's navigability. But rather than triumph, the *North St. Louis* became lodged "high and dry" on the head of an island about 75 miles up the Osage. Only a rise could free it.[79]

Apparently frustrated by the limited performances of the *American* and the *North St. Louis,* St. Louis steamboatmen concluded that the Osage would accommodate only boats that were yet smaller. The forwarding agency of McGunnegle and Way in 1838 arranged to send the 49-ton *Adventure* up the Osage. The three-year-old Pittsburgh-built stern-wheeler, commanded by a Captain Ball, ascended the river for 160 miles.[80] But within days its record voyage was surpassed by the *Relief*, a 78-ton side-wheeler, which reached the community of Argus, 200 miles above the river's mouth. The *Daily Missouri Republican* reported: "We learn that the Osage is very high and the boat experienced no difficulty in reaching her destination. She could have gone to Osceola. This settles the question of the navigation of this river."[81] Evidently, boatmen thought the river was navigable only during high water. In 1839, when the lower Missouri and the Osage were extremely low, no one attempted to take a steamboat up the Osage.

From the start, steamboatmen recognized that generally only the smallest steamboats should be used on the Osage. But in 1840 the owners of the *Osage Packet* made an important change. Rather than run their boat all the way from St. Louis, they kept it at Osage City, the town at the mouth of the Osage. As freight was delivered from St. Louis, it was transferred to the *Osage Packet*, which offered a shuttle service to Osage River towns. The *Osage Packet* was the first steamboat advertised as "fitted up expressly for the Osage waters."[82]

A good stage of water in the spring of 1841 enabled St. Louis suppliers to send the fully loaded *Leander*, a 137-ton side-wheeler, to Osceola and waypoints. The next year, the 63-ton side-wheeler *Maid of Osage* was built at Osage City. Owned and operated by Captain Nansen Bennett, it was designed for the Osage River. From his Osage City base, Bennett ran the boat in connection with the Missouri River steamer *James H. Lucas*. But on occasion the *Maid of Osage* was used on the Missouri to, among other things, transport pine lumber from the mouth of the Gasconade to Jefferson City.[83]

In 1844 the *Maid of Osage* was challenged by the *Agatha*, *Huntsville*, and *Warsaw*. The 65-ton *Warsaw*, a side-wheeler, was built at Boonville in 1842. It was the first Osage River boat to run on a schedule. Captain J. F. Ware offered a regular weekly packet service from Osage City, which it left every Monday at 10:00 A.M. for Warsaw and Osceola. The *Agatha*'s tonnage was almost identical to that of the *Warsaw* and the *Maid of Osage*, but less than half that of the *Huntsville*. The use of the *Huntsville* was facilitated by the great flood of 1844.[84]

Because of the deluge, Captain Nansen Bennett of Côte sans Dessein was able to navigate his *Maid of Osage* into new waters. He steamed her up to the abandoned Harmony Mission several miles above Papinsville. Then the seat of Bates County, Papinsville, about forty miles above Osceola, was on the left bank of the Marais des Cygnes a few miles above its juncture with the Little Osage. Bennett may have been enticed by a land reward offered by Bates County. County officials were so determined to end their isolation that they proffered town lots and a quarter section of land to the first person to land a steamer at Papinsville.

Meanwhile, those interested in developing the Osage River valley wanted to be freed from the vagaries of nature. The growth of their region, they contended, required the improvement of the Osage. Turning to the state for aid, they influenced the 1839 legislature, which sought to establish "a general system of internal improvements" throughout Missouri. By two February acts, the lawmakers first

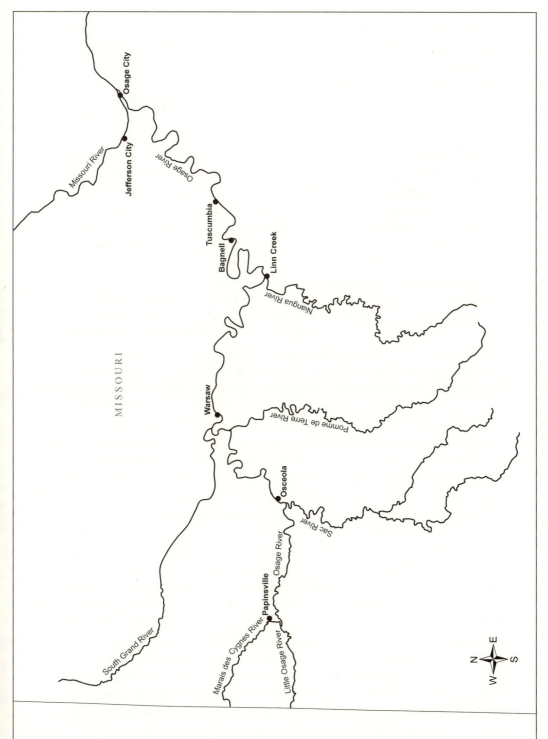

Osage River. (Current state boundaries are shown for reference.) *Prepared by James Worm.*

created a Board of Internal Improvements, whose five members were to appointed by the governor "with the advice and consent of the Senate." A supplementary act specified that the board had to arrange reconnaissances of the Osage, Grand, Meramec, and Salt rivers and submit a detailed report to the next legislature about the feasibility of navigating those streams.[85]

By late summer the board, with George C. Sibley of St. Charles as its chairman, began meeting and organizing surveys. The Osage survey was done by William E. Morrell, the board's engineer. Morrell, in turn, had a geological reconnaissance of the Osage valley conducted by Henry King. In 1840 Morrell reported that he had surveyed the Osage 230.5 miles from its mouth. He recommended a state expenditure of $204,600 to improve the stream by removing snags, trees, and rocks, stabilizing some banks with rocks, and constructing wing dams to achieve a four-foot channel. With shallow-draft steamboats built expressly for the Osage, Morrell thought the improvements would assure four- to seven-month annual navigation seasons and help stimulate the region's economy. Improving the river, he claimed, would save valley residents $329,000 in shipping costs each year, or nearly $125,000 more than the entire improvement cost.[86]

However, legislators looked at the cost to the state rather than the saving to Osage valley shippers. They were unwilling to add to the state's indebtedness to improve the Osage or any other river. But Osage River improvement advocates were encouraged by an 1841 federal law, which granted Missouri and eight other states 500,000 acres of land each "for purposes of internal improvement."[87] They thought the state should use proceeds from the sale of those lands to improve the Osage. They did convince Governor Thomas Reynolds. In his annual message to the legislature of November 22, 1842, Reynolds recommended the improvement of the Osage and Grand rivers with funds raised by selling the internal improvement lands. He reasoned: "While the greater number of our citizens are supplied with ample water communication by means of the Missouri and Mississippi rivers, nearly the whole of the southwestern portion of the State is dependent upon the navigation of the Osage, which, while unimproved, can only be available, to any considerable extent, for a small portion of the year."[88]

Despite the governor's endorsement, a bill to apply some of the money obtained from the land sale to Osage River improvement, failed in the next legislature. Reacting to this rejection, pro-improvement forces intensified their drive. A gathering of valley leaders at Warsaw in September 1843 unanimously accepted a call for an improvement convention to be held in their town. The ensuing "Osage Convention" of December 18–19 attracted delegates from thirteen counties. They passed resolutions urging the legislature to improve the Osage by a system of locks and dams and asking the state's congressional delegation to seek federal funding. In an effort to gain further support, they also resolved to oppose any state executive or legislative candidates who did not support Osage River improvement.[89]

The convention was well publicized. The sympathetic *Jefferson City Inquirer* and other state newspapers carried lengthy articles replete with the verbatim text of the resolutions about the convention. Additionally, the delegates, at their own expense, had a Warsaw newspaper, the *Osage Yeoman,* print and distribute five thousand copies of the proceedings. Calvin Gunn, editor of the *Jeffersonian Republican,* was a particularly strong pro-improvement voice. Seeing improvement as vital to southwestern Missouri, he not only editorialized but also published promotional articles written by "Osage," an anonymous spokesman.

Sentiment to improve the Osage from the sale of the internal improvement lands was not strong outside of the Osage valley. Most legislators thought that the paramount need of the areas they represented was road improvement. So with their own districts in mind, the lawmakers decided that the proceeds from the sale should be equally distributed to all of the state's counties. This solution so offended Osage improvement advocates that they tried to mount a drive to have it repealed.[90]

Like everyone concerned with steamboating, those who agitated to improve the Osage hoped to make the business more stable and less expensive. Rapid flux characterized the trade. Many steamboats were lost from various navigation hazards. But even those that were not destroyed were destined for short lives, because their hulls succumbed to the incessant pounding of battling the current, grounding, and striking obstructions. Of the seventeen steamboats used on the Missouri in 1838, only four were still active two years later.[91]

An analysis of twenty-four of the twenty-five steamboats on the Missouri in 1841 shows their nature and fate. All were side-wheelers, whose average and median tonnage was 165. The average was 40 more than that of steamboats used on the Missouri from 1821 to 1836 inclusive. The *Amazon,* 231 tons, was the largest, and the *Warsaw,* 65 tons, was the smallest. Eleven of the boats were built in Pittsburgh and two in nearby Brownsville, Pennsylvania. The only other construction sites with more than one were Cincinnati, Ohio, with five, and Wheeling, Virginia, with two. One each was built at Smithland and Louisville, Kentucky; Jeffersonville, Indiana; and Boonville, Missouri. This construction record was in keeping with earlier steamboat building, which was virtually monopolized by ports of the Ohio and its tributaries.[92]

The average achieved age of twenty-three of the boats was 4.16 years. Of these, eleven were destroyed and twelve abandoned when no longer functional. Eight of the destroyed craft were snagged and three stranded. The destroyed boats had an average longevity of only 2.91 years, whereas the abandoned ones averaged 5.33 years. Sometimes, the engines and boilers of abandoned boats were salvaged and installed in other boats. Because the boats were routinely used on the Mississippi, Ohio, and Illinois rivers as well as the Missouri, it is not possible to attribute their duration to a specific stream. Abandoned boats were generally left in some home port such as St. Louis. Of the eleven destroyed boats, five each were lost on the Missouri and the Mississippi and one on the Ohio.

Recognizing the limitations of their craft, steamboat operators influenced builders to regularly modify previous designs. To help avoid snags, shoals, and sandbars, they gradually lessened drafts. This was achieved by using lighter materials, decreasing the depth of holds, and widening the hull to add floating surface. Somewhat wider hulls also had the effect of increasing tonnage. A comparison of the 119-ton *St. Peters* and the 210-ton *Nimrod,* constructed in 1836 and 1844 respectively, is insightful. With a breadth of 18 feet 8 inches and a length of 139 feet, the *St. Peters* tonnage per linear foot was only 0.85, whereas the *Nimrod,* 156 feet long and 25 feet 10 inches wide, had a tonnage of nearly 1.4 per foot.[93]

By 1837 the new steamboats delivered to St. Louis were regularly advertised as being built in the "newest fashion" or "modern style." Both labels were translated as "strong and fast-running" and "splendid." Their increased power and speed came from the innovation of adding a second engine so that each side-wheel operated independently. The *Platte,* which reached St. Louis from Pittsburgh in May 1838, was the first double-engine steamboat to enter the Missouri River trade. The somewhat overused adjective "splendid" invariably referred to the cabin accommodations. Individual staterooms equipped with good beds and linen became a regular feature of the new boats.[94]

As new steamboats were brought to St. Louis from the east, its business community became increasingly resentful of their dependence on Pittsburgh and Ohio River construction sites. The importation of boats was another aggravating reminder that St. Louis had a type of colonial status relative to Pittsburgh and Cincinnati. Because St. Louis was one of the country's leading steamboat ports, its boosters thought it should also be a major construction location.

St. Louis's first venture in steamboat building came from the partnership of W. M. Thomas and M. Glenn, formed in early 1837. Thomas and Glenn planned to construct "steamboats or any size or description," which they vowed would be the equal of any on "the western waters."[95] The launching of their first steamboat—the *North St. Louis*—on March 29, 1837, became a matter of community pride. An estimated one thousand people were present, and a leading city newspaper not only lauded the builders but also used the occasion to editorialize: "Why is it that we annually send away half a million dollars to give employment to the boat builders of Cincinnati and Pittsburgh?"[96] The message was clear. St. Louis should strive to retain its boatbuilders and induce others to join them. However, the completion of the *North St. Louis* proved to be an isolated event rather than a catalyst for widespread boatbuilding. Thomas and Glenn ceased their St. Louis operation, but in 1842 a "Messr. Glenn," who may have been one of the former partners, built the *Maid of Osage* at the mouth of its namesake stream.[97]

Undeterred by the demise of Thomas and Glenn, the *Missouri Republican* intensified its effort to make St. Louis a boatbuilding center. To demonstrate the potential worth of the business, it publicized the construction costs of twelve steamboats in the St. Louis trade that had been recently built at Pittsburgh or other Ohio River ports (table 2).[98] Editor Adam Black Chambers contended that the boats could have been built as cheaply in St. Louis. But he was challenged by an unidentified writer who pointed out that costs in St. Louis were higher than in Pittsburgh. Iron was at least a cent per pound more, labor 83.33 percent more, and pine, the lum-

TABLE 2

CONSTRUCTION COSTS (1839) OF

TWELVE STEAMBOATS USED IN THE ST. LOUIS TRADE

Name	Cost ($)	Tonnage
Corsican	25,000	224
General Brady	25,000	177
Glaucus	23,000	191
General Leavenworth	24,000	160
Maid of Orleans	30,000	276
Monsoon	25,000	171
Naomi	23,000	165
Osceola	16,000	93
Pizarro	16,000	107
Platte	22,000	158
Rosalie	18,000	145
Shawnee	25,000	164

Source: See note 98 of chapter 4.

ber used in steamboat finishing, cost twice as much. Nonetheless, he believed that boatbuilders in St. Louis could profit in the long run.[99]

Judging by the continuing lull in St. Louis boatbuilding, the anonymous writer's economic assessment apparently was better than Chambers's. But even if costs were higher, Chambers thought St. Louis had a future in boatbuilding. To illustrate the scope of steamboat construction, he noted that up to April 20, 1839, a total of 378 steamboats had been built for the western rivers since the beginning of steamboating. Of them, 130 were built at Pittsburgh, 83 at Cincinnati, 22 at Wheeling, and the rest at other Ohio River ports. Using an average construction cost of $25,000, he calculated that the entire business amounted to $9,450,000. Chambers rhetorically asked: "With such an income is it surprising that the manufacturers of the Ohio have grown rich?" Observing that much of the construction money came from St. Louis, he thought it placed a drain on the local economy.[100]

Evidently there were enough changes in the St. Louis economy by 1842 to induce its boatbuilders to renew the business. Four steamboats—*Chicago, Inda, Potosi,* and *St. Louis Oak*—were produced that year. The *Chicago* and *Potosi* were built at the Case boatyard, and the *St. Louis Oak* at the Coonse yard. With the city's continuing rapid growth, St. Louis had an unprecedented supply of skilled laborers. The population increase and the effects of the Panic of 1837, which did not reach Missouri until the early 1840s, lowered labor costs. Further, pine lumber was becoming more plentiful because of the continuing development of the Gasconade River forests and the opening of pineries along the St. Croix River, a tributary of the upper Mississippi.[101]

TABLE 3

STEAMBOATS LAUNCHED

BY ST. LOUIS BUILDERS IN 1845

Name	Cost ($)	Tonnage
Convoy	39,000	750
Dial	7,000	140
Governor Briggs	9,000	91
Helen	8,000	61
Iowa	22,000	249
Laclede	20,000	239
Little Dove	5,500	77
Missouri	45,000	887
Ocean Wave	17,000	205
Prairie Bird	17,000	213
Total	189,500	2,912

Source: See note 102 of chapter 4.

The Emerson boatyard opened in 1843 with the construction of the *Henry Bry.* The next year, Emerson completed the *Nimrod* for Pierre Chouteau, Jr., and Company and the *Die Vernon.* In 1845, St. Louis builders launched 10 steamboats (table 3).[102] This local construction accounted for a third of the steamboats and nearly half of the tonnage added to the St. Louis commercial fleet that year. Eight other steamboats were built elsewhere for the St. Louis trade, and St. Louisians also purchased 12 boats from other places.

By St. Louis standards, steamboat construction in 1845 was impressive. But the city lagged far behind Pittsburgh and Cincinnati, which respectively had 25 and 17 steamboat completions. The demand for new boats was indicated by a federal government report for 1842, which showed that 132 steamboats were built nationwide and 30 were worn out or destroyed. Four-fifths of those constructed were for the Mississippi and its tributaries.[103]

Building steamboats better adapted to western rivers was done by private ventures. Steamboatmen believed they could, to a degree, change their craft to mitigate losses. But they continued to maintain that the federal government should improve rivers and harbors to make navigation safer and hence less expensive.

In Missouri the paramount improvement issues were removing snags on the Missouri River and assuring a good navigable channel for the St. Louis harbor. President Martin Van Buren abandoned Andrew Jackson's position that snag removal should not be undertaken above customhouses. In 1838 he approved a congressional rivers and harbors bill that included an appropriation of $20,000 to improve the upper Mississippi and the Missouri. The money was welcome, but some Missourians were miffed that it was less than half that granted for Arkansas River improvement.[104]

Political consideration of harbor and river improvement was generally divisive. The quest for funding pitted section against section and, within any given region, city against city. Missourians and other residents of the Mississippi River drainage basin wanted improvement of rivers and selected harbors, but representatives from eastern states and those engaged in the commerce of the Great Lakes insisted on harbor improvements for their own ports. The result was polyglot legislation replete with compromising trade-offs that gave everyone something, but did not really satisfy anyone.

The 1838 Missouri River allowance was used by army engineers the next year to remove snags between the mouth and a point eight miles below Liberty, near the state's western border. Combined, the crews of the snagboats *Archimedes* and *Helipolis* destroyed 2,100 snags and cut 2,311 trees from banks that were likely to collapse. The *Helipolis* removed nearly 100 snags in Camden Bend, above Lexington.[105] The season's work caused one editor to proclaim that the "obstructions and dangers to [Missouri River navigation] are fast becoming overcome."[106]

But any snag removal was not a permanent solution. As the Missouri's current sliced away at the alluvial soil and toppled trees into the river, the birth of snags, like the change of seasons, was a continuing natural process. Therefore, effective snag removal could be achieved only by a regular, systematic program.

Missouri's Senator Lewis F. Linn tried to revive Missouri River improvement in January 1843. He presented Congress with memorials from citizens of St. Louis and the St. Louis Chamber of Commerce, requesting appropriations for the Missouri and other western rivers. Late that summer a federal snagboat was used on the twenty-mile stretch of the Missouri from its mouth to St. Charles.[107] But then, for lack of funding, snag removal lapsed again. The *Jefferson City Inquirer* of September 25, 1845, used the snagging of the steamboat *Lexington* to call for federal help. The editor hoped that "our delegation in Congress will take the matter in hand, and press upon the authorities at Washington the necessity of having two or more snag boats built expressly for, and to be kept constantly at work in, the Missouri River. A fearful sacrifice of life and property would thus be averted."

St. Louis's harbor problem started developing about the time of the first steamboat arrival in 1817, when the Mississippi began forming a sandbar between the levee and Bloody Island. Over the years, the river enlarged the bar as its deepest channel ran on the Illinois side of the island. By 1833, when steamboat access from upstream was nearly blocked, city officials tried a novel experiment. With funds donated by fur trader Bernard Pratte, Sr., and other citizens, they hired a man to plow the sandbar with oxteams in the hope that the loosened sand would be washed away by high water. Other than provide employment for the plowman, the work accomplished nothing.[108]

Faced with the prospect of losing their landing, the city turned to the federal government. Backed by congressional funding, Lieutenant Robert E. Lee of the Army Corps of Engineers began surveying the situation in August 1837. Lee soon devised a radical solution. At an estimated cost of $158,554, he proposed diverting the deep channel to the St. Louis shore by building a dam at the head of Bloody Island and running a dike down its west side.[109] After receiving authorization from his superiors, he started working on the dam and dike within a year. By late summer 1838, Lee's project was proclaimed as promising "to be eminently successful," because his partially completed dam and dike had already raised the water level over the sandbar.[110]

But there was no quick solution to the harbor problem. When the federal government failed to complete Lee's work quickly, the city continued the project. By 1854, with an expenditure of about $250,000, city engineers had managed to compress the channel to only about 600 yards between the levee and Bloody Island. This, in turn, created a channel deep enough for even the largest steamers along the nearly five-mile steamboat front. Although the work was pronounced a success, the city had to continue working on the dam and dike as the levee expanded.[111]

Many citizens thought that in addition to improving rivers and harbors, the federal government should take measures to improve steamboat safety. Their particular concern was boiler explosions, which were always dramatic and often tragic. Snagging, the leading cause of western steamboat losses, generally failed to arouse emotions.[112] Most of its loss was to property, and passengers and crews were usually evacuated as the boat settled in the stream. But emerging unscathed from a boiler explosion was another matter. The explosions came with little or no warning, and many who were not scalded to death were blown into the river. The greatest accidents, replete with details of human suffering, were often the leading newspaper stories of their day. In contrast to snagging, which was often attributed to a natural cause, explosions of a man-made device were generally blamed on either its maker or its user. Since someone was thought to be responsible, it seemed to many that laws regulating boiler construction and operation would enhance the public good.

Steamboat explosions were particularly rife on the western rivers because its steamboatmen invariably used boats with high-pressure engines. The original Fulton-type eastern steamboats were equipped with low-pressure engines, which generated only about 7 to 10 pounds of pressure per square inch. When western boatmen found that such engines did not have enough power to cope with their currents, they turned to high-pressure engines, which by 1824 were producing up to 150 pounds of pressure per square inch. The engines brought the desired result of more power and speed but also a much higher risk of boiler explosions. But steamboatmen knew that high-pressure engines had other advantages. They were more compact and lighter, which helped lessen a boat's draft, and they were cheaper to build and easier to operate and maintain.[113]

Originally, those concerned with improving steamboat safety turned to the states. Alabama, in 1826, became the first state to legislate a safety measure. Its act required annual boat inspections and provided a procedure for filing damage suits. A Louisiana law of 1834, which mandated quarterly boiler hydrostatic pressure tests by a state inspector, was yet more rigorous. But the effectiveness of both the

Alabama and Louisiana statutes was severely limited, because they could be enforced only on steamboats operating in intrastate commerce. The vast majority of western steamboats were interstate carriers. Clearly, only the federal government could claim jurisdiction over them.[114]

Public demands for federal regulation were spurred by some sensational and highly publicized explosions and fires. Three of the greatest steamboat disasters shocked the nation. At about 1:00 A.M. on May 8, 1837, the *Ben Sherrod*, while racing another steamer up the lower Mississippi, was destroyed by fire and explosions. The next spring, the *Oronoko* exploded about a hundred miles above Vicksburg, Mississippi, and only four days later, on April 25, 1838, the *Moselle* was devastated by a boiler explosion after steaming down the Ohio for about a mile from the Cincinnati levee. The disasters bore striking similarities. All of the boats were heavily loaded with passengers, the loss of life was unprecedented for steamboat accidents, and the calamities were caused by negligence of the officers and crews or by faulty equipment.[115]

In the case of the *Ben Sherrod*, drunken firemen added pine knots and rosin to the firebox to generate more heat and pressure. Then the red-hot boilers set fire to some sixty cords of wood. During the ensuing blaze, the boat was racked by exploding boilers, gunpowder, and barrels of liquor. The captain's attempt to shore the vessel was thwarted by loss of steering, because the fire destroyed her hemp tiller ropes. Mainly because of the *Ben Sherrod* disaster, safety advocates urged that tiller ropes should be replaced with metal cables.[116]

Negligence was not a factor with the *Oronoko*, whose explosion was caused by a collapsed boiler flue. But the *Moselle* catastrophe was blamed on a speed-hungry captain and an intoxicated engineer. Its explosion killed the captain, whose body was thrown high on the river's bank, and perhaps as many as one-third of its estimated three hundred passengers. The tragedy so affected Cincinnati that within days a specially composed "Dirge for the Dead of the Moselle" was sung at a city orchestra concert.[117]

Some critics thought that only the banning of high-pressure engines would make steamboats safe. The editor of the *Missouri Argus*, contending that high-pressure engines were preferred to low-pressure because they were cheaper to build, thought that "thousands upon thousands must yet be immolated at the shrine of avarice, ambition, and vanity—thousands must be crushed under the wheels of these floating Juggernauts before a favorable change will be wrought in the public mind." The "evil," he insisted, would not be solved by such measures as boiler inspection, which was then being considered by Congress.[118]

Congress was persuaded to act because steamboats, the nation's leading interstate carriers, affected millions of people. Two 1840 reports showed the enormity of the trade. The country's seven hundred steamboats had a total tonnage of slightly below 200,000, of which 108,923 were employed on the western rivers.[119] When Congress passed the first steamboat inspection act in 1838, it was mostly concerned with exploding boilers and hemp tiller ropes. The law, approved on July

7, required all steamboat owners to have their boats newly enrolled and licensed by a customs collector by October 1, 1838. The stipulated annual inspection of hulls, boilers, and machinery was to be done by an inspector appointed by a district judge. The inspector was to issue a certificate attesting that the boat passed inspection, which had to be displayed in the boat at all times. Significantly, the inspectors were not federal employees. Their only compensation was the $5 fee they collected from boat owners for each inspection.[120] Other provisions of the law mandated that steamboats be equipped with lifeboats, signal lights, a fire engine with accompanying hoses, and iron rods or chains rather than tiller ropes. Violators of the law were subject to fines, suits brought by the federal government, and manslaughter charges for officers whose alleged misconduct led to fatal accidents.

Newspapers, which obligingly published verbatim copies, helped customs agents circulate news of the act. Congress was satisfied with its work, but by late September, when Fontain M. Dunnica was appointed inspector for the port of St. Louis, steamboatmen were complaining about it.[121] The *Missouri Republican* reported that "considerable dissatisfaction is expressed by those who have been fitting up their boats under this law. Many of its provisions will be found useless and some impracticable."[122]

The strongest opposition came from Cincinnati's steamboat officers and owners. In their formal meeting of October 6, they drafted resolutions about the law's deficiencies. While commending Congress for having good motives, they asserted that the lawmakers, because of their ignorance of steamboating, had passed a measure that threatened to be regarded "as a mass of absurdity, unworthy of notice or respect."[123] The Cincinnati group's strongest objection was about the required metal steering lines. They insisted that such technology was not proven to be workable and would actually make steamboating more hazardous. They made a valid point. Metal tiller lines were then only in an experimental mode. But by late November 1838 a Cincinnati maker of "wire tiller ropes" was reported to have outfitted fifteen steamboats with lines that were just as pliable as hemp ropes and had the advantages of being cheaper than rope as well as fireproof.[124] Despite this announced breakthrough, many steamboatmen continued to complain about the tiller requirement. Ultimately, they prevailed to a degree. In 1843, Congress amended the 1838 statute by permitting the use of hemp tiller ropes, provided that metal lines also be installed as a backup steering system.[125]

In retrospect, the 1838 steamboat inspection law was an inadequate first attempt. It did not have the desired effect of lowering steamboat losses. The method of appointing inspectors was fraught with the usual hazards of a good-old-boy system. Anytime inspectors were dependent on the inspected for their compensation, they were in a compromising position. Some customs collectors later reported that even boiler examinations were nothing more than perfunctory scans of the exterior.[126]

Public dissatisfaction with the law was aggravated by continuing steamboat accidents. Calvin Case, a St. Louis salvager employed by various insurance companies, reported that thirteen steamboats were lost on the Missouri during 1840–42. He placed the total value of the boats and cargoes at $274,500, which was $63,500 more than the losses for the Mississippi above the mouth of the Missouri. Below the Missouri, the Mississippi's losses amounted to $2,046,578.[127]

The heaviest loss of life was caused by the boiler explosion of the *Edna* on July 4, 1842, near the mouth of the Missouri. Fifty-five German immigrants bound for Hermann were killed by scalding water, and a number of others were burned severely.[128]

Though always inconvenient and costly and sometimes fatal, steamboat accidents did not diminish the overall trade. Other carriers, unimpeded by the occupational hazards of the business, soon filled the void.

During the ever-increasing steamboating of the 1840s, the Missouri River trade was temporarily disrupted by raging floodwaters. The great flood of 1844, which affected the Missouri downstream from the Council Bluff as well as all of the Mississippi and its tributary Ohio, Illinois, and Arkansas rivers, was caused by torrential rains. The downfalls, which started in the early spring, became more intense in June, with rainfall on twenty-two days in the western part of Missouri.

At the flood's peak in late June, the Missouri at Lexington was reported to be five or six miles wide, thirty feet above the low-water mark, and ten feet higher than the flood of 1826. With all of the bottomlands flooded, those people who could, fled to nearby bluff tops. Drowning victims were reported on the Missouri and the Osage, and crops, stored grain, buildings, livestock, and sometimes people were swept downstream. Officers of the steamer *Mary Tompkins* reported seeing houses floating downstream, sometimes with people, chickens, hogs, dogs, and cats on the roofs. Sudden rises caused some people to cut holes in the tops of their houses to get onto the roofs.[129]

The disaster brought out people's best impulses. Townspeople helped flood victims with food, housing, clothing, and money. Abandoning their normal business, steamboat captains used their boats to evacuate hundreds of imperiled residents. Since the river was out of its banks, they were able to navigate far from the normal channel. With all of the riverside woodyards washed away, driftwood was their main fuel source.

As the waters receded in July, steamboating and other routine activities were resumed. But the effects of human and property losses lingered. The small riverside town of Nashville near Jefferson City had been swept away by the flood. But quirkily, Jefferson City actually benefited from the deluge, which replaced a sandbar that had been forming in front of the city's levee with a deep channel.

For a time, it appeared that Platte City on the Platte River also gained from the flood. Because of extraordinarily high water, three steamers—*American, Colonel Woods,* and *Lexington*—were navigated about five miles from the Missouri to the town. Their landings spurred town promoters to dream that by constructing a lock and dam on the Platte River, Platte City could become an important port. They not only reserved town land for a wharf but also formed a company that bought the steamer *Haidee*. With Anderson Martin as her captain, the *Haidee* was run on the Missouri for a few years. But Martin never managed to get the boat to Platte City.[130]

Midway in the 1840s, Missouri River steamboating reached new heights. In 1845, Weston had 118 arrivals from below. Thirty-one of the boats, mostly bound for St. Joseph, went on upstream. That year St. Louis had 249 steamboat arrivals from the Missouri, about a 100 more than in 1840. While regionally important, Missouri River steamboating amounted to only about a tenth of the aggregate St. Louis trade. St. Louis in 1840 and 1845 had 1,721 and 2,050 steamboat arrivals respectively.[131]

5

THE EXPANDING FRONTIER, 1846–1854

During the late 1840s and early 1850s an explosive burst of national expansion benefited St. Louis and all places along and beyond its western outlet—the Missouri River. For the first time in its short history, the United States became a transcontinental power. With the end of the Mexican-American War, the nation affirmed its recent annexation of Texas and gained California and the Southwest. During the war, the lingering contention with Great Britain over the Oregon country was resolved by the boundary treaty of 1846, which extended the forty-ninth parallel demarcation westward from the Continental Divide to Puget Sound. Another wartime happening, the beginning of the Mormon movement to the Great Basin, developed settlement in the interior West. Recognizing the compelling need to link the far West with the rest of the nation, the federal government fortified both the Oregon-California and Santa Fe trails.

The California gold rush, which started in 1849, accelerated the popular drive for the construction of a transcontinental railroad. As thousands of argonauts made their way to the new El Dorado, the federal government, heeding the calls of states and cities, responded by ordering transcontinental railroad surveys. When it appeared that the Indian frontier west of Missouri would impede railroad plans, Congress responded with the Kansas-Nebraska Act. The formation of Kansas and Nebraska territories in 1854 not only opened large portions of the Great Plains to settlement but also signaled America's determination to abandon the altruistic notion of a "Permanent Indian Frontier."

Missouri River steamboating figured prominently in the rush to these new frontiers. As Americans thronged to the West, the demands to supply outfitting towns on Missouri's western border and Council Bluffs, Iowa, intensified. Although it was remote from the large overland treks, the upper Missouri region was also affected by the unprecedented westward movement. The government's aims of determining a route for a northern transcontinental railroad and pacifying Indians along its likely path began changing the region's traditional fur trade economy.

The outbreak of war with Mexico was welcome news to an overwhelming majority of Missourians. With a vested interest in the Santa Fe trade, a desire to annex California and a hatred of Mexico that dated at least to the 1836 Battle of the Alamo, Missourians enthusiastically supported hawkish President James K. Polk. By the time he sent an American army commanded by General Zachary Taylor to disputed ground on the north bank of the Rio Grande in January 1846, Polk was intent on war. With American and Mexican armies facing each other, conflict was inevitable. A Mexican raid across the Rio Grande gave Polk all the pretext he needed. Asserting that Mexican troops "invaded our territory and shed American blood upon the American soil,"[1] Polk asked Congress to authorize a declaration of war.

Approved by Congress on May 11–12, 1846, the declaration was accompanied by an authorization to raise 50,000 volunteer troops. Once Missouri had its assigned quota, Governor John C. Edwards issued a call for volunteers. The greatest need was to rush men to Fort Leavenworth, where Colonel Stephen Watts Kearny, assigned to conquer New Mexico, was organizing his Army of the West.[2]

By the second week of June, approximately 1,350 Missouri volunteers had reached Fort Leavenworth.[3] Most of those from the central and eastern parts of the state followed the Missouri River route—either by riding steamboats or marching on nearby roads. The 104-man mounted Laclede Rangers of St. Louis ascended on the steamboat *Pride of the West*. At Jefferson City, "they were saluted on their arrival by the discharge of artillery and the cheers of . . . citizens."[4]

Kearny's 1,658-man army left Fort Leavenworth for Santa Fe in a series of segments throughout June. Most of the Missouri volunteers were placed in the First Missouri Volunteer Regiment, commanded by Alexander William Doniphan, a thirty-seven-year old lawyer from Liberty. Doniphan, who proved to be popular and capable, had enlisted as a private but was elected to the rank of colonel by the regiment's men. Other Missourians in the Army of the West included the Laclede Rangers and four other St. Louis companies.[5]

Following the mountain branch of the Santa Fe Trail, Kearny's forces moved rapidly toward Santa Fe, New Mexico's capital. Before Kearny entered the city on August 18, the Mexican governor fled southward toward El Paso. After a five-week occupation in which he organized a provisional government and left instructions for Doniphan's next movement, Kearny, with about 300 men, struck southwestward toward his ultimate goal of southern California.[6]

Doniphan was ordered to lead his regiment down the Rio Grande through El Paso before invading the Mexican province of Chihuahua. The Chihuahua campaign was intended to protect the western flank of two American forces that had invaded northeastern Mexico. Before Doniphan moved out of Santa Fe on October 26, his regiment had been relieved by other Missourians, led by Sterling Price.[7]

Price's regiment had been rendezvoused at Fort Leavenworth after the Army of the West was strung out along the Santa Fe Trail. Like Doniphan's men, some of Price's troops took steamboats to Fort Leavenworth and others went overland. The steamboats *Lewis F. Linn* and *Little Missouri* were used by infantry companies from Gasconade and Osage counties, but the De Kalb Rangers of St. Louis and volunteer companies from Cole and Franklin counties marched to the fort. As Price's force was marching west, about 150 other Missouri volunteers were discharged at Fort Leavenworth preparatory to returning to their homes downstream from Jefferson City on the steamboat *Amelia*.[8]

Doniphan led his regiment, bolstered to nearly 1,000 men, on the war's longest campaign. As the force approached El Paso, it was engaged by a numerically superior Mexican army. But in the Battle of El Brazito, fought on Christmas Day 1846, the Missourians smashed their enemy. After the ensuing occupation of El Paso, Doniphan's force began marching toward Chihuahua City, the capital of the province, about 250 miles south of the west Texas town. On February 28, 1847, a short distance north of Chihuahua City, the Missouri volunteers overwhelmed a much larger Mexican force in the Battle of Sacramento.[9]

While occupying Chihuahua City, Doniphan received orders from General Zachary Taylor to join General John E. Wool's army at Saltillo, more than 600 miles southeastward across a desert. From Saltillo, the Missourians briefly rendezvoused with Taylor's army at Monterrey before heading homeward by way of the lower Rio Grande. Doniphan arranged ship transportation from Matamoros to New Orleans, where the regiment was discharged in late June 1847.

Although ostensibly on their own, many of the former troops kept some semblance of military organization. Generally, they rode steamboats up the Mississippi to St. Louis, where Doniphan paraded 300 of them on July 2. For those like Doniphan, who came from the western part of the state, they moved from St. Louis to their homes by steamboats, stagecoaches, or hiking. Well known for their exploits in the popular war, Doniphan's men were hailed as conquering heroes on their homeward trek. Volunteers on the steamers *Amelia*, *Rowena*, and *Whirlwind* were welcomed at Jefferson City "with the cheers of . . . citizens and the firing of cannon."[10] A week later Doniphan and part of his command steamed past Jefferson City on the *Little Missouri*.[11]

As the First Missouri Volunteer Regiment was ending its active duty, other Missouri volunteers were being moved from St. Louis to Fort Leavenworth. During the 1847 navigation season, other troops were boated downstream from Fort Leavenworth to either St. Louis or Jefferson Barracks. All troop steamboat transportation was arranged by quartermaster officers, who negotiated contracts with either captains or clerks. Since there were no organized boat lines, all of the contracts were for single voyages by individual boats.

In May 1847, quartermaster officers signed two contracts with Captain H. T. Beer of the *Mandan* and one with Captain R. Wright of the *Little Missouri*. Each pact specified that the boats were to transport one company of Missouri volunteers from St. Louis to Fort Leavenworth at $7 for each officer and $2.50 for each man, including all personal baggage.[12]

Probably because their bargaining was limited by a shortage of steamers, quartermaster officers at Fort Leavenworth had to pay more. On May 30, 1847, First Lieutenant William E. Prince, assistant quartermaster, agreed to compensate J. T. Douglass of the *John J. Hardin* $4.60 for each of 87 privates to be carried from the fort to St. Louis. The sole officer received free passage. In late October, when the river was low, Quartermaster Captain Langdon C. Easton signed agreements with W. G. Monroe of the *Archer* and Thomas Miller of the *Amelia* to transport personnel and horses from Fort Leavenworth to Jefferson Barracks. Rather than using unit rates, these contracts called for sum payments. Monroe was to be paid $402 for carrying 1 officer, 34 men, 1 woman (probably a laundress), and 36 horses. For $375, Miller agreed to transport 1 officer, 30 men, and 35 horses with their stores and baggage.[13]

As the demands of the Mexican-American War stimulated St. Louis–Fort Leavenworth steamboating, packet service to the upstream Council Bluffs vicinity also increased. The expanded trade north of the Platte was stimulated first by the westward trek of the Mormons.

The Mormons' decision to leave Nauvoo, Illinois, was prompted by the greatest crisis in their brief history. Under the leadership of prophet Joseph Smith, Nauvoo prospered in its first five years. With an 1844 population of 15,000, it was Illinois's largest city. But the Mormons found that their new Gentile neighbors were no more tolerant than those of Ohio and Missouri. Anti-Mormonism peaked with the assassination of Smith and his brother Hyrum by a Carthage mob on June 27, 1844.[14]

Brigham Young, president of the Council of Twelve Apostles, became the new prophet. He was able to effect a truce with Illinois officials by agreeing to abandon Nauvoo in 1846. With his church's recent history in mind, Young realized that Mormons would never be welcomed among Gentiles. Hence he decided to lead his people west to a new frontier where they would be isolated from American society.

As the Mormons straggled across Iowa to near the Council Bluff, Young evidently had not decided on the precise site of the next Zion. His main goal in 1846 was to assemble thousands of his followers on the Missouri River preparatory to moving farther west the next year. Near the Council Bluff, at a point where trader Peter Sarpy operated a ferry, some 3,000 of Young's followers crossed the Missouri. At present Florence, Nebraska, just north of Omaha, they built the community of Winter Quarters.[15]

Many others remained on the Iowa side of the river, where they started building a log cabin village. The place was named Kanesville in 1848 to honor Thomas L. Kane, a Philadelphia lawyer who had befriended the Mormons in 1846 when they were camped at the Missouri. Four miles from the river, where the bottomland met the base of the bluffs, Kanesville became the area's most important community. It was first dominated by Mormons, but with the California gold rush and settlement of western Iowa, non-Mormons flooded in. Gentile control was obvious by 1853, when city leaders, spurning the Mormon heritage, had the place renamed to Council Bluffs when it was chartered by the state legislature.[16]

Until the opening of Nebraska Territory in 1854, Kanesville was the main outfitting point north of the Platte for Mormons and other western emigrants. Before leaving Winter Quarters in the spring of 1847, Brigham Young had decided to locate his followers near Great Salt Lake, then in land claimed by Mexico. Proceeding on the north side of the Platte, he led a pioneer band to the ground where Salt Lake City was established. In the next few years, thousands of the faithful moved there by following the Mormon Trail. When Utah Territory was created by Congress in 1850, it had a population of 11,380. In the next decade the number of Utahans increased to 40,273. Over a fifth of them lived in Salt Lake City, the territorial capital and headquarters of the Mormon faith.[17]

Kanesville's fragile pioneer economy was characteristic of isolated frontier towns. At the upper end of the St. Louis supply route, it had a highly unfavorable balance of trade. Its merchants had to import groceries, hardware, clothing, drugs, bar iron, and virtually all other manufactured goods. Some wheat, fresh meat, and eggs were locally produced for the town's market. The community's meager industry was geared to its overland trade. Blacksmiths and wheelwrights were in demand, and the emigrants' needs for great quantities of rope to control animals and secure loads prompted the opening of a rope walk. In 1849 Reuben W. Allred, who probably imported hemp from Missouri, advertised that his new rope walk could supply "all kinds of rope and cordage, from a fish line to a cable."[18]

Because of seasonal steamboating and the heavy demand for provisions during the height of the spring migration, shortages of goods and accordingly higher prices typified Kanesville business. In mid-May 1849 the *Frontier Guardian* noted articles that "constitute the bone and sinew of life in the West, and are mostly needed for a mountain expedition; such as flour and bacon, are becoming scarce and dear in this section of the country." While he deplored the "extravagant" prices, the editor observed that costs of all goods reflected the need to replace them from Missouri by steamboats.[19]

Normally, steamboats that reached Kanesville from below started at St. Louis. But in 1851 Captain John Corby thought there might be enough business for his *Utah* in a regular packet trade from St. Joseph. Corby made his first run from St. Joseph to Kanesville in his "neat and light draught craft" in about five days. He believed, however, that the trip could be accomplished in as little as three. Corby's plan was heartily endorsed by the editor of the *Frontier Guardian*, who obviously hoped that St. Joseph would become a commercial rival of St. Louis. Despite considerable fanfare, Corby could not develop a regular trade with his small 89-ton side-wheeler.[20]

The St. Louis–based steamboats that dominated Kanesville's trade were particularly active in 1852, a record emigration year. They carried all the bulky freight and passengers who chose to reach Kanesville by water rather than use overland routes across Iowa or the road from St. Joseph. The *Kansas*, a 276-ton side-wheeler built at St. Louis in 1847, was the most active boat. Captain John McCloy ran it as a regular St. Louis, St. Joseph, and Kanesville packet throughout the season. Making round-trips in 20 days, the boat became Kanesville's most dependable connection with St. Louis. As such, it was praised by the Kanesville newspaper, whom McCloy obviously cultivated by delivering St. Louis papers.[21]

Despite their good newspaper reputations, McCloy and his boat were lambasted by some disgruntled passengers. Sixteen male grievants signed a letter replete with preamble and eight resolutions. They found the boat to be "INTOLERABLY SLOW" and its table fare "niggardly" and overpriced. As for the boat's officers, McCloy and all but the second clerk were denounced as uncouth, vulgar, and dogmatic. Captain McCloy, they insisted, "was entirely unfit for his situation" and was better suited to be nothing more than a deckhand.[22] Perhaps their threat to circulate their complaints among friends "far or near" prompted the newspaper editor to publish their letter to create a basis for refuting it. The *Western Bugle*'s editor related his pleasant experiences in traveling on the Kansas and printed a refutation by six men, who not only praised McCloy and other officers but also contended that the complainers had launched "a lying, slanderous, and vicious attack—and an unprovoked assault upon the property and character of their betters."[23]

The *Western Bugle*'s defense of McCloy and the *Kansas* was in keeping with the standard practice of river town editors, who routinely lauded their regular packets. Captains who had a particularly close identity with a community were invariably portrayed as chivalrous gentlemen, and news articles about them were often nothing more than thinly disguised commercials. Coverage of other 1852 Kanesville steamboats—*El Paso, Delaware, Honduras, Robert Campbell,* and *Saranac*—was more dispassionate.

Steamboat travelers to Kanesville were subjected to the usual delays—wooding stoppages and strandings on sandbars—and sometimes disaster. Twenty-four-year-old Lucy Rutledge Cooke, bound for California from Dubuque, Iowa, left an interesting memoir of her adventures on the *Pontiac No. 2.* After booking cabin passage at St. Louis for $20 each, she and other members of her party proceeded slowly up the Missouri. In the first four days, the boat covered only 200 miles because of frequent groundings. Cooke noted: "The river abounds with sand bars on which we often stick a long time, last night we were on one most of the night."[24] Cooke's tedious voyage ended abruptly a short distance above Weston when one of the boat's bottom planks was broken by a log embedded in a sandbar. The crew desperately tried to plug the leak with blankets and comforters, but water soon engulfed the boiler deck. Passengers walked planks to board yawls, which hauled them to shore. Later the crew removed baggage and after a day-long chilly wait, the passengers were taken to St. Joseph on the steamer *Midas.* Since the *Midas* was not navigated above St. Joseph, Cooke and her companions had to continue to Kanesville on another boat.[25]

Other emigrants to Kanesville from Missouri chose to take the road from St. Joseph. Many used their own wagons, but some commercial transportation was available. In August 1850 Henry Mower began preparing to run stagecoaches on the route. Beginning the next March, he offered a weekly stage service by four-horse teams. In addition to passengers and mail, his stages transported packages and other lightweight freight. As emigration increased, the route attracted some businesses, including a rope ferry across the Nodaway River and a rope walk near Fillmore, Andrew County, Missouri.[26]

An important adjunct of Missouri River steamboating at Kanesville was ferrying emigrants across the Missouri, which was not fordable. During the 1850 migration at least three ferries were in operation along a stretch of about twenty-six miles from the Old Mormon Crossing on the north to just upstream from the mouth of the Platte on the south. Other than provide decent boats, ferry operators were careful to locate at points where there were good roads on firm ground on both sides of the river. Additionally, they had to control enough ground to provide wood, water, and pasturage for thousands of animals as emigrants waited for their crossing times. In 1852 Thomas Clark advertised that at his Old Mormon Crossing ferry he also had facilities to corral as many as a thousand head of cattle at one time.[27]

Kanesville's first ferries were propelled by taking up rope, but in late March 1852, P. L. McLaughlin and Reuben Middleton began using the steam ferry *Eagle*. Steam ferries, which had earlier come into vogue at downstream crossings, were specially built with a hull wider than that of ordinary steamboats. More deck space for passengers, livestock, and wagons was also achieved by consolidating the placement of the boat's machine and not having to store quantities of wood. McLaughlin and Middleton advertised that the *Eagle* had a capacity of 60 to 100 head of cattle.[28]

Getting across the Missouri was a stressful time for emigrants. As they waited their turns to take a ferry, those bound for California or Oregon worried about reaching their destinations before winter. Because the grass was usually not high enough for grazing until at least May 1, they could not leave before then. But the longer they waited, the greater the threats of drought on the plains and snow-blocked mountains in the fall became. Consequently, the best time for crossing the Missouri was from late April to early June. Emigration through Kanesville in 1852 was reported to be about double the number of teams and treble the number of persons of any previous migration. By late May, nearby ferries and two packets had moved five to six thousand teams across the river and "many thousands more" were reported to be in the vicinity awaiting crossing.[29]

The opportunity to make money by ferrying the season's unprecedented migration attracted the captains of the steam packets *El Paso* and *Robert Campbell*. Rather than quickly head downstream after making deliveries, they turned to ferrying because the regular ferryboats could not handle the waiting crowds. Captain Andrew Wineland of the *El Paso* reported that during a four- to five-day period his boat earned over $5,000 for ferrying more than 2,000 people, 500 wagons, and 4,215 head of livestock.[30]

As Kanesville was being developed, the United States fortified the Oregon-California and Santa Fe trails. The need to protect American emigrants on the long overland routes that connected the new western frontiers with Missouri and the rest of the nation was apparent to President James A. Polk even before the start of the Mexican-American War. In his annual message to Congress on December 2, 1845, Polk recommended the building of suitable forts manned by mounted riflemen on the Oregon Trail. Authorization and funding were approved by Congress on May 19, 1846.[31]

Stephen Watts Kearny took the first action before he was aware of the declaration of war against Mexico. In late May 1846 he traveled about 100 miles above Fort Leavenworth to revisit a likely fort site at the mouth of Table Creek (present Nebraska City, Nebraska). He had first recommended constructing a fort there in 1838. Subsequently, because some Oregon-bound emigrants crossed the Missouri there, the location seemed to be even more important. On May 23 Kearny selected the specific site and left a small contingent of troops there. The fort, which came to be known retrospectively as Kearny I, had a very brief history. A blockhouse, the only building of note, was completed before the place was temporarily vacated in the summer of 1846. It was reoccupied by Missouri volunteers the next summer and then finally abandoned in May 1848, preparatory to the start of Kearny II on the south side of the Platte near the head of Grand Island.[32]

The site of the Grand Island post, close to the convergence of various feeder routes leading west from the Missouri, was selected by First Lieutenant Daniel P. Woodbury in the fall of 1847. The following spring, troops were transferred from Table Creek. By year's end, after the construction of three temporary buildings, the new fort, 310 miles from Fort Leavenworth, was officially named Fort Kearny. As the post was being outfitted with permanent buildings in 1849, the army started another fort about 330 miles to its west. Rather than build a new place, the government purchased the old fur trading post of Fort Laramie, an adobe quadrangle that stood on the left bank of the Laramie River about a mile above its confluence with the North Platte. The army soon changed the appearance of Fort Laramie, which dated to 1834, by constructing new buildings.[33]

Until difficulties with Indians during the Civil War, Kearny and Laramie were the army's only strongpoints on the Oregon-California route between Fort Leavenworth and the Continental Divide. Both were relatively small, one-company posts with a usual annual complement of eighty troops each.

The Santa Fe Trail and New Mexico were more heavily fortified. On his westward march in 1848, Kearny established Fort Mann on the Arkansas River in southwestern Kansas. It was replaced by nearby Fort Atkinson two years later. Once his forces occupied Santa Fe, Kearny started Fort Marcy there. After the Treaty of Guadalupe Hidalgo ended the war in February 1848, the United States, partly because of threatening Navaho and Apache Indians, bolstered its forces in the New Mexico region. Forts Conrad, Defiance, Fillmore, and Union were started in 1851, and the next year, Fort Massachusetts, the first American army post in present Colorado, and Cantonment Burgwin, near Fort Union, were added. In his 1851 report to Congress, Secretary of War Charles M. Conrad noted that the United States had somewhat more than 1,300 troops assigned to installations in New Mexico Territory.[34]

Supplying the overland trail forts was challenging. Because the installations were far removed from navigable waters and were generally in unproductive agricultural districts, they had to depend on freight wagon deliveries. Rather than operate its own supply trains, the army contracted with civilian freighters based at Fort Leavenworth, the transfer point from river to overland trade. As St. Louis–based quartermaster officers negotiated numerous contracts for steamboats to carry men and supplies from St. Louis, Jefferson Barracks, and Alton, Illinois, Fort Leavenworth assumed its new role as the supply point for the remote posts. Brevet Major Edmund A. Ogden, Fort Leavenworth's quartermaster, reported that, in the spring of 1851, steamboats delivered freight "equal in bulk to at least 18,000 barrels."[35]

Fort Leavenworth initially did not have adequate storage facilities for this staggering amount of goods.. Ogden resorted to storing provisions in stables, barracks, a ninepin alley, and two leaky blockhouses until he could have new warehouses erected. His main project was to complete a three-story stone warehouse, 40 × 100 feet. Split level, it fronted on the levee, which was graded to the river and had a dirt bank at its rear. Steamboat imports were received at the lowest level and picked up by wagons at the top story on the other side.[36]

During the period 1848–54, quartermaster officers signed dozens of contracts with St. Louis steamboatmen to deliver officers, troops, horses, and supplies to Fort Leavenworth. Since the dollar's value was very stable. the rates did not fluctuate appreciably from year to year. The greatest variations were seasonal, with higher rates being charged for early spring and late fall shipments.[37]

Most of the contracts specified a precise charge for each officer, man, or horse, but sometimes the boatmen agreed to a lump fee, which was no doubt calculated from the rate for each unit. From April through midsummer, when the Missouri was normally the most navigable, contractors transported officers for $8 to $10 each, enlisted men and laundresses for $2 to $4 each, and horses for $7 to $10 each. When navigation was poor, the rate for officers was sometimes as high as $15 and that for enlisted men and laundresses $6. The difference between officers and men was the normal variation between cabin and deck passage. Sometimes when quartermaster officers booked cabins for sick troops, they agreed to pay the officer rate for each cabin.

All freight other than personal baggage and weapons, which were covered by passenger fares, was transported at the rate of a hundredweight for the 420-mile route from St. Louis to Fort Leavenworth. The author's review of approximately one hundred contracts shows this charge ranged from $0.20 to $0.75. Hauling lumber, the only item distinguished from general freight, cost $5.00 per 1,000 board feet.

Available statistics are suggestive, not definitive. But the shipments were impressive. In 1848, for example, when ten contracts were signed at St. Louis and Fort Leavenworth combined, 916 troops, 39 officers, and 274 horses were carried up or down the river. That amount of trade was at least matched in each of the next two years.

The high cost and slowness of overland wagon freighting gave the army and other shippers an increased appreciation of steamboats. Although reviled because they were accident-prone and often delayed, steamboats afforded much cheaper transportation than wagon trains. Adjusted to rates for carrying 100 pounds 100 miles, the St. Louis–Fort Leavenworth steamboat charges were from slightly less than a nickel to approximately 19 cents. By contrast, wagon freighters from Fort Leavenworth to posts on the Oregon-California and Santa Fe trails were paid at least $1.20 per hundredweight for 100 miles and sometimes about $2.00. In 1849, for example, freighter John Dougherty agreed to carry stores from Fort Leavenworth to Fort Kearny for $6.00 a hundred, with an additional charge of 5 percent for all bacon. In 1850 Ogden signed separate contracts with Brown, Russell, and Company and David Waldo. Combined, the agreements called for the delivery at least 750,000 pounds of stores at Santa Fe, 821 miles distant, for $14.50 per hundredweight.[38]

Primarily because of overland freighting, the costs of maintaining the frontier army increased dramatically. For the fiscal year ending June 30, 1851, Ogden disbursed $528,569.22 at Fort Leavenworth. His largest expenditure was $321,825.92 for sending 626 wagons with 3,131,175 pounds of freight to forts on the Oregon-California and Santa Fe trails.[39]

Coincident with its increased Fort Leavenworth trade, steamboating was expanded because of heavy overland migration to California, Oregon, and Utah. Most emigrants were lured west by the California gold rush, which opened in 1849. The California hysteria was a delayed reaction to the discovery of gold in January 1848 at John A. Sutter's sawmill in the foothills of the Sierra Nevada. Soon thereafter, local workers turned to mining, and news of their finds reached San Francisco in May. Throughout the summer and fall, hundreds of Californians, as well as some Oregonians, Mexicans, and Hawaiians moved into the gold region.[40]

As letters from California were carried to the East, newspapers started publicizing the discoveries. The first such notice appeared in the New York *Herald* of August 19. Later, persons returning from California brought gold with them. The *St. Joseph Gazette* of November 23 announced the arrival of a small gold-bearing party from California at the Missouri River. News of these "large quantities" of dust was publicized by other Missouri newspapers.[41]

People were generally not convinced by the first newspaper articles. The dubious public was obviously looking for something more believable. Seeming confirmation of rich strikes came from no less an authority than the president of the United States. On December 5, James K. Polk, in his annual message to Congress, briefly mentioned the abundance of gold in California. Polk may have been seeking only to allay criticism of the recent costly war with Mexico.[42]

Whatever his motives, Polk's message tripped off a media frenzy. Newspaper editors nationwide ballyhooed the acclaimed riches of the new El Dorado. Within days, as gold fever swept the land, aspiring argonauts began planning to move to California. Those who intended to move overland realized they could not leave the Missouri River until pasturage was available. Consequently, the first to leave were seafarers. Many of them traveled from Atlantic Coast ports or New Orleans by voyaging to Panama, crossing the isthmus, and then resuming their trip on another ship. Others took the way by Cape Horn, the southernmost tip of South America. In 1849 alone, as many as 25,000 Americans may have embarked for California by ships.[43]

This aspect of the rush did not affect Missouri greatly. However, a number of western Missourians began moving to New York City and other ocean ports by taking steamboats down the Missouri. Conversely, some who later returned to their Missouri homes from California went by ship to New Orleans before completing their trip on Mississippi and Missouri river steamboats. Traveling by water was considerably faster than going overland. Sometimes the time saved was dramatic. For instance, several men returning to central Missouri from San Francisco by way of the Isthmus of Panama reached Glasgow in a month, including a daylong stop in New Orleans and another of two days in St. Louis.[44]

Despite the expectation of needing as much as six months to reach California on the 2,200-mile route from the Missouri River, thousands of gold rushers preferred to follow the oxbowlike trail running through the Platte River valley and South Pass. These overlanders reached various Missouri River outfitting towns by land and river. Those who crossed Iowa usually went to Kanesville, but some of them veered south to ferry landings at Table Creek and even northwest Missouri. The most popular wagon routes in Missouri ran from Hannibal to St. Joseph and from St. Louis to towns near the mouth of the Kansas.[45]

Whether they traveled by wagon or steamboat, many emigrants reached the Missouri well before they could set off across the plains. Other than allowing adequate travel time, they were understandably anxious about outfitting at the Missouri and organizing wagon trains and arranging ferriage. On March 31, 1849, the *Jefferson Inquirer* reported that "several boats have passed up the river the past week, crowded with immigrants for California." By mid-April a number of steamboats full of "golden pioneers" had passed Jefferson City. The *St. Louis Republican* estimated that 30,000 headed for the promised land would leave western Missouri that spring. The more cautious editor of the *Liberty Tribune* thought there were about 10,000 emigrants waiting to cross the Missouri at Independence and St. Joseph. Because the spring was chilly and late, they had to camp near the Missouri for several weeks until the plains grass grew more.[46]

The California gold rush and the simultaneous movements of Oregonians and Mormons were of incalculable benefit to the Missouri River region. Most provisions—other than locally produced meat, flour, eggs, cordage, and tobacco—had to be shipped by steamboats from St. Louis. Among other things, the overlanders created an unprecedented demand for wagons, which were often carried upstream by steamboats. The sheer number of emigrants suggests something of their economic impact. In 1849 the overland movement was 25,000 to California, 1,500 to Utah, and 450 to Oregon. The total migration exceeded that of all previous years combined. Overland migration nearly doubled the next year, declined sharply in 1851, and then reached an all-time high of 70,000 in 1852.[47]

The massive 1852 migration caused the *St. Louis Republican* to observe its impact on steamboat traffic: "Boats from the Ohio, Illinois and other rivers, come in crowded to excess, and every boat for the Missouri has more than she can accommodate."[48] The number of emigrants told only part of the story. For the period May 1–June 6, 1852, the movement from Independence and St. Joseph combined consisted of 16,302 men, 3,242 women, 4,266 children, 6,538 horses, 4,686 mules, 59,392 cattle, 10,523 sheep, 150 turkeys, 6 guinea fowl, 4 ducks, and 1 hog.[49]

Not surprisingly, the economy of western Missouri's steamboat ports was based heavily on outfitting emigrants. During the gold rush, Westport, the Town of Kansas, Weston, St. Joseph, and Savannah all became richer. Westport and the Town of Kansas grew somewhat at the expense of nearby Independence. Both had good reputations as starting points, although the wagon routes from them were the longest. Weston, the only town in the vicinity of Fort Leavenworth, had excellent ferry service and merchants who specialized in outfitting emigrants. St. Joseph, which had a population of slightly over 1,500 in late 1848, was attractive for those who wanted to shorten the overland route somewhat. At the opening of navigation in 1849, seven steamboats—*Alton, Boreas No. 3, Kansas, Mary Blane, St. Ange, St. Joseph,* and *Timour*—were advertised to run in the St. Louis–St. Joseph trade. Upstream from St. Joseph, Savannah, the seat of Andrew County, became a significant supply and ferry site. Its rise was attributable in part to the inability of the downstream ports to accommodate the massive numbers of people, animals, and wagons.[50]

All of the towns featured muddy or dusty streets, lots of manure, crowds, and bawdiness, but Weston had the nastiest reputation. An itinerant temperance advocate found it to be a "hard place." He reported that the level of imbibition was unparalleled: "We had supposed that the business men of St. Louis were honestly entitled to the unenviable notoriety of being the greatest traffickers in Rum in the Western country. But Weston, in this respect, is far ahead of St. Louis." He found drinking in Weston to be so rampant that even dry goods merchants kept liquor in their back rooms for free use by their customers. He also condemned the town's violence. During his weeklong stay, there were seven shooting or stabbing cases.[51]

Overland emigration provided the foremost impetus for Missouri River ports from Westport and the Town of Kansas upstream to Kanesville. But below Independence the steamboat business of Lexington, Brunswick, Glasgow, Jefferson City, Boonville, Rocheport, and other stops continued to be dominated by the importation of groceries, clothing, cloth, iron, hardware, and other manufactured goods and the exportation of agricultural produce.

The magnitude of steamboating can be seen from various statistical reports. To determine the commerce of St. Louis, its harbormaster routinely calculated the number of steamboat arrivals from the rivers in the city's trade area. The reported arrivals from the Missouri River for the years 1846–52 were respectively 258, 314, 327, 355, 390, 301 and 317. Another perspective was provided by a report on the number of arrivals at Weston for 1845–50 (table 4). The considerably higher propor-

St. Louis levee, 1852.
Some travelers thought the crowded levee looked like
a forest of steamboat chimneys. Daguerreotype by Thomas M. Easterly.
Courtesy of the Missouri Historical Society, St. Louis.

tion of boats going upstream from Weston in 1849 and 1850 apparently reflects the importance of outfitting emigrants in that sector.[52]

To form an estimate of his future railroad's business, James P. Kirkwood, chief engineer of the Missouri Pacific, examined freight books of 1850 Missouri River steamboats. Knowing that the line's route would be located south of the Missouri River when it was constructed westward from St. Louis, Kirkwood was first interested in population growth. He determined that the population of the counties bordering the river to the state's western boundary, including the next southern tier, increased from 191,095 in 1848 to 236,100 in 1850. Further, he concluded that the Missouri River trade was increasing about 10 percent annually. In 1850 the two-way steamboat business amounted to 83,000 tons and 107,000 passengers, with total receipts respectively of $450,000 and $368,000.[53] Kirkwood did not attempt to quantify upriver and downriver freights and passengers. But he did note that the total upstream shipments were much less than exports from the Missouri River. However, because steamboatmen charged more for upbound goods, the receipts of the two were about the same.

The nature of upbound steamboat cargoes is evident from reports about the busi-

TABLE 4

STEAMBOAT ARRIVALS IN

WESTON, MISSOURI, IN 1845–1850

	1845	1846	1847	1848	1849	1850
Total arrivals	118	132	182	193	216	226
Arrivals that went to places upriver	31	36	47	68	146	160

Source: See note 52 of chapter 5.

ness of certain towns. In 1852, Glasgow was serviced from St. Louis by three regular packets. One of them, the *Martha Jewett*, made twenty-four round-trips. Its clerk, W. C. Nanson, reported that the principal items carried up for the season were 5,574 barrels of liquor, 319 tons of iron, 1,516 barrels of salt, 26,473 sacks of salt (100 pounds each), and 343,000 board feet of lumber. A more detailed report showed the worth of Lexington's 1854 imports as dry goods, $314,556; groceries, $107,737; lumber and shingles, $36,911; clothing, $35,000; drugs, medicines, oils, and paints, $26,500; carriages and carriage materials, $23,800; tin, sheet iron, copper, and stoves, $18,500; saddlery, and harness materials, $13,300; hardware, iron, and cutlery, $12,500; boots, shoes, hats, and caps, $12,000; furniture, $12,000; books and stationery, $10,000; queensware, $10,000; millinery and trimmings, $7,500; tobacco and cigars, $7,500; and confectioneries, $4,500.[54]

With the exception of lumber, most of the upbound shipments originated in St. Louis or were routed through it. Hermann, near the mouth of the Gasconade River, was the commonest source of pine lumber. Logs and lumber from the yellow pine stands along the upper Gasconade were floated down the stream and then sent either upstream or to St. Louis. In 1847 the steamer *Rowena* carried more than 50,000 board feet of pine planks from Hermann to Jefferson City and other towns. Although river town sawmills made lumber from local hardwoods, the need to import pine, which was best for framing and siding buildings, was a continuing problem for such growing towns as Glasgow, Brunswick, Jefferson City, and Lexington.[55]

Tobacco, hemp, and hemp products were the principal exports. By 1847 Glasgow was recognized as Missouri's leading tobacco center. Its main rival was nearby Brunswick. Both communities were important regional centers, with hinterlands stretching northward from the Missouri. Tobacco buyers from Glasgow and Brunswick toured the farmlands to make arrangements for buying, packing, and, if need be, storing tobacco preparatory to the opening of navigation. Tobacco was usually hauled to the river by wagons, but some of it was floated down the Grand River on rafts and flatboats when the water was high enough. Naturally, merchandising of other products occurred during the tobacco trade. Brunswick espe-

St. Louis levee scene, 1853, showing stockpiled freight and drayage vehicles.
Daguerreotype by Thomas M. Easterly. *Courtesy of the Missouri Historical Society, St. Louis.*

cially, because of its location on the northernmost bend of the Missouri, was able to tap an extensive hinterland stretching as much as sixty miles from the river. Its merchants were the middlemen for storekeepers in such places as Chillicothe, Trenton, and Milan. Goods were usually delivered to Chillicothe by a professional hauler who offered a regular weekly service with a two-horse hack.[56]

In 1852 the St. Louis Chamber of Commerce reported that tobacco "has within a comparatively few years past, become one of the chief sources of agricultural wealth in our State."[57] The increased cultivation of Missouri tobacco, which was called "Western Tobacco" in London and Liverpool markets, was attributed to the movement of experienced planters from such tobacco-producing states as Virginia, Kentucky, and Tennessee. Its popularity in domestic and foreign markets was partly due to the willingness of planters to agree to quality specifications regarding color and length in their contracts with agents of eastern dealers.

Tobacco shipments from Glasgow were of two types. Tobacco leaf was packed in 1,500-pound hogsheads. But "manufactured," or ready-to-use, tobacco was shipped in boxes. On average, seven boxes were produced from a hogshead. Unlike most agricultural commodities, the tobacco box did not have a statewide standard. The Glasgow box averaged 135 pounds, 5 more than that of all other points. For the years 1847–51, St. Louis tobacco receipts in hogsheads from all Missouri points were respectively 11,015, 9,044, 12,846, 9,216, and 11,038. Nearly half of them were shipped from Glasgow. St. Louis received 14,023 hogsheads in 1852 and 10,102 the next year. About three-fourths of these amounts came from Glasgow and other Missouri River ports.[58]

In 1847, Glasgow had four manufacturing plants and St. Louis two. Before that, Missouri's tobacco manufacturing was reported to be "but in its infancy."[59] For the years 1847–51, Glasgow produced over half of all tobacco manufactured in Missouri. Its box production was respectively 3,682, 4,834, 4,047, 4,316, and 5,218. By late 1852, when the population of Glasgow was only about 1,000, processing tobacco dominated its economy. There were thirteen tobacco establishments—stemmeries and manufactories—in the town and its immediate vicinity. One of them was an 80-by-160-foot building with an annual processing capacity of 500 hogsheads. In 1854 one of Glasgow's manufactories was the largest in the state. It employed about 100 hands and manufactured about 6,000 boxes during the year. By comparison, St. Louis's main tobacco processing plant used 40 to 50 men and boys to produce 2,189 boxes.[60]

Glasgow and Brunswick also exported hemp and hemp products, but the bulk of those shipments was from Lexington and points upstream to St. Joseph. About 95 percent of all hemp and hemp products received in St. Louis was from the Missouri River. Baled hemp was one of the commonest steamboat cargoes. For the period 1846–53 an annual average of about 55,000 bales was marketed in St. Louis. In 1846 and 1847 seven bales were the equivalent of a ton, but thereafter it was six. Boatloads of hemp were impressive sights, with bales sometimes stacked as high as the upper deck. To prevent chimney sparks from starting the bales ablaze, deckhands stood by with pails of water.[61]

St. Louis was also the principal market for rope coils and bagging pieces manufactured at numerous rope walks in the hemp-producing region. From 1846 through 1853, St. Louis received an annual average of 27,000 coils and 2,100 bagging pieces. In 1846 twenty coils equaled a ton, but subsequently coils were enlarged. The equivalency was nineteen in 1847 and 1848 and eighteen thereafter. Twelve bagging pieces equaled a ton.

The impact of hemp is evident from export statistics of specific towns. In 1854, Lexington shipped 20,799 hemp coils worth $263,620 and 6,697 bales valued at $205,780. During that navigation season, Weston exported 22,000 bales and 450 coils, and one firm in Liberty manufactured 7,991 coils.[62]

The exportation of other agricultural produce also contributed to steamboating. Meatpacking, especially of hogs, was an important industry in all river towns. Sacked corn, wheat, and other grains were major exports. Grain shipments were the most significant outside of the prime tobacco- and hemp-producing areas. For example, St. Charles in 1854 shipped more than 100,000 bushels of wheat and 15,000 bushels of flour to St. Louis. Corn, the main crop around St. Charles, was used locally to fatten cattle acquired in the Southwest. Ordinarily, they were subsequently driven from St. Charles to the St. Louis market.

The considerable variety of exports is evident from the business of various towns. Other than rope and hemp, Lexington in 1854 shipped out bacon, lard, flour, whiskey, coal, cattle, hogs, wheat, corn, barley, hempseed, hides, grass seed, feathers, tallow, hair and bristles, pecans, dried fruit, flaxseed, peltries, honey, and butter. The same year, John H. Grover, a forwarding merchant of Cambridge, Saline County, exported 174 tons of hemp, 2,000 bushels of wheat, 296 hogsheads of tobacco leaf, 40 boxes of manufactured tobacco, 262 barrels of green apples, 97 sacks of dried apples, and 32 sacks of dried peaches, as well as some corn, oats, hempseed, bacon, lard, livestock hides, deer skins, and beeswax.

While important to steamboating and the economies of river communities, Missouri River shipments of produce other than hemp and tobacco commanded only a small portion of the St. Louis market. In 1853 approximately 10 percent of the 2,077,427 bushels of wheat, 5 percent of the 200,000 barrels of flour, and 4 to 5 percent of the 113,000 barrels of pork and lard received in St. Louis were from the Missouri River.[63]

Steamboat rates were of utmost concern to all shippers and passengers. Indeed, the wildly fluctuating rate structure was one of the main reasons for dissatisfaction with steamboating. Anyone who planned a budget realized there was no such thing as a standard rate throughout the navigation season. The rate reports published in newspapers usually gave only an average or a range of charges for all commodities at any given time. What shippers actually paid was determined by river conditions, supply and demand of boats, and the nature and quantity of each item. As a general rule rates were the highest during the winter months of January, February, and December, and the lowest in June, July, and August, when trade tended to decline after the spring rush.[64]

James P. Kirkwood researched 1849 freight rates for the 232-mile river distance from St. Louis to Boonville. First he found from steamboat officers that shipping upstream cost about a third more than downstream. He was able to compile a season-long average. For example, he determined that the year's average for hauling a hogshead of tobacco was $2.52, with monthly ranges from $10.05 for February and $2.00 for June, July, and August. The average charge for a ton of hemp was $4.27. But in November and December the rate was $8.00 and in July and August $3.00. The varying ton-to-weight equivalences were also evident in his report. The lowest rates were for bulky commodities sent in large consignments that could be packed efficiently, including hemp bales, sacked grain, and sacked salt. Individuals who sent boxes and packages paid slightly more than twice as much for each hundredweight than grain shippers. Handling such items was considerably more work. Steamboat clerks had to make out separate bills of lading for every shipper and had to arrange the boxes and packages to facilitate unloading at various destinations.

For cabin passengers, Kirkwood ascertained that the average annual fare was $5.50, or about 2.4 cents per mile. Generally, passenger charges had dropped since the advent of steamboating. On the Ohio and lower Mississippi in 1819, cabin passengers paid as much as 10 to 12.5 cents per mile for upstream passage. By 1840, rates on the upper Mississippi were sometimes as low as 3 cents a mile.[65]

Steamboatmen ran their craft on the Missouri whenever there was a navigable channel. The stream was usually frozen throughout January. The rare voyages that month were often limited to downstream trips of steamboats that had been iced in or stranded by low water late in the fall. Upstream deliveries of spring goods, which ordinarily commenced in February, were affected by ice breakups. Since the ice first cleared out on the lower part of the river, boatmen would ascend until stopped by an ice jam. Ordinarily, some of the first boats sent to St. Joseph or Kanesville had to wait at some way port such as Glasgow or Lexington until ice upstream thawed enough to be cleared out by the current.[66]

Once the river was completely open in late February or early March, boat owners would begin regular packet service to the various river towns. The St. Louis forwarding agencies that dominated the trade consistently advertised boat itineraries as well as a list of their cooperating agencies at various towns and landings. Agents would arrange for scheduled packet service to selected towns. Often, the utmost seasonal destination was determined before the opening of navigation. Some boats would be navigated no higher than Glasgow, and others would have Weston, St. Joseph, or Kanesville as their terminal. Regardless of their goal, all boats made scheduled stops at waypoints.

Starting in the early 1850s, steamboat lines began operating on the Missouri. "Line" had an imprecise meaning. Some lines were legal entities incorporated by a state. Ordinarily, each of the owners, who typically included forwarding agents, captains, and merchants, had a part interest in all of the line's boats. But others were simply working arrangements of several boats. The line arrangement enabled agencies to assign designated boats to certain river sectors. As a general rule, the heaviest-drafted boats would operate only below the mouth of the Kansas and the lightest-drafted ones above there. Since boatbuilders tended to reduce drafts slightly over time, new boats were usually used the farthest upstream. The acclaimed light-draft El Paso, an 180-foot-long side-wheeler built at St. Louis in 1850, was often used as a forwarder for goods carried to Westport or the City of Kansas by cooperating boats.[67]

Normally navigation was closed by ice in the first half of December. But often it would be suspended temporarily months beforehand because of low water. Especially as rainfall diminished after mid-August, boats were reduced to carrying fractional loads or were stopped until the water rose. A compilation of steamboat arrivals at St. Louis from the Missouri River for 1846–49 shows that on average there were eight in December and two in January, whereas March, the peak month, had forty-eight.[68]

Realizing that steamboat service was vital for their economies, river towns provided landing facilities for boatmen. Following the well-established practices of St. Louis and other major steamboat ports, Missouri River towns improved landings with municipal funds. Towns partially recouped construction costs by assessing a wharfage fee for each boat landing. Wharfage was collected by municipally appointed wharfmasters, whose only reimbursement was a portion of the fees. Specific fees and the wharfmaster's share were established by town ordinances. Typically, the towns also dictated a schedule of drayage charges for the hackmen who moved freight to and from the levee.

In 1847 Jefferson City authorized the construction of a 228-foot wharf, starting in front of the city's main waterside warehouse. E. B. Cordell, who contracted to build the wharf, was also named wharfmaster. He was authorized to collect $2 for every regular packet landing, a dollar more for every landing by a transient boat, 50 cents for flatboats, and a nickel for each wood cord. The distinction between regular boatmen and transients is interesting. Captains and other officers of the regular packets tended to be well known in river towns and quite likely influenced the Jefferson City council to give them a reduced rate. Transients were the river's vagabonds. Their captains, with a lone-wolf mentality, did not join lines and usually did not work through agencies or advertise in newspapers. Their practice was to make unscheduled runs throughout the Mississippi River system and pick up cargoes and passengers whenever they could. Consequently, transients were seen as outsiders by town newspaper editors and business leaders.[69]

In St. Joseph the town-owned land reserved for a steamboat wharf could not be used by flatboats and other makeshift craft. The municipal ordinance authorized fining of trespassers. In 1850, after initiating action by the town council, St. Joseph's voters authorized a $10,000 bond issue for paving the levee and building a stone wharf. The council appointed a wharfmaster and established a wharfage fee of $3 for each steamboat landing.[70]

As with any other transportation method, the economics of steamboating was vital to owners, employees, and customers. But to river town residents, steamboats were far more than just commercial haulers. Every river town's society and culture were affected by the boats and their crews. The first boat of the season was the harbinger of spring, when the isolated towns sprang to life after the winter doldrums. The arrival of the long-anticipated first boat brought throngs of people to the levee to excitedly watch the passengers exit and the crew and locally hired stevedores unload the freight. While first landings were especially important symbolically, the novelty of watching landings persisted throughout the season. There was always something worthy of notice, be it the mate directing the crew or a drayman maneuvering his hack on the crowded levee.

The boats themselves were objects of much interest. Their massiveness tended to overawe spectators, and their machinery was seen as a technological marvel. To people accustomed to working with hand tools, the very idea of a steam engine, let alone an actual one in view, inspired wonderment.

Since steamboat captains were men of action competing in a rather perilous business, townspeople tended to glorify them. Perhaps these men, who commanded massive vessels that loomed above town landings, were reminiscent of characters in a romantic novel. The seemingly heroic captains of regular packets were treated like celebrities. They hobnobbed with town elites and basked in the praise of fawning newspaper editors.

The most newsworthy captains during the late 1840s and early 1850s were Thomas H. Brierly, William David Hubbell, William C. Jewett, John McCloy, Ambrose Reeder, Henry W. Smith, and Andrew Wineland. Brierly was the master of the *El Paso* for part of 1850, but he is better remembered for commanding the *Polar Star* in 1852 and 1853. The *Polar Star*, a large 309-ton side-wheeler completed at St. Louis in 1852, was designed to cater to the passenger trade. Its cabins and dining saloon were elaborately furnished with Brussels carpets, ottomans, sofas, and chandeliers. A natural American scene was painted on each stateroom door. The ornateness of the *Polar Star* attracted attention, but it became yet more famed because of its speed.[71]

In 1853 Brierly took the *Polar Star* on the 565-mile run from St. Louis to St. Joseph in an amazing 68 hours of actual operating time. St. Joseph's citizens, like all river town residents, claimed bragging rights whenever a new speed record was set. They honored Brierly and the *Polar Star* by presenting the captain with a set of polished elk horns whose mounting was inscribed: "Saint Joseph TO CAPT. BRIERLY. The fleetest Elk has shed them from his brow. Fit emblem 'Polar Star' to deck thy prow."[72] Although the honor was new to the Missouri, the presentation of horns to the captain of the fastest boat was a well-established custom on the Ohio and Mississippi. Responding to a round of toasts by town dignitaries, including the militia company's commander, Brierly vowed to best any challengers for the horns. Subsequently, elk horns became the most prized trophy of Missouri River boatmen. At any given time, there were several sets of horn awards, each recognizing the record time for a particular route.[73]

William David Hubbell, captain of the *Tamerlane*, was one of Liberty's prominent businessmen. He had first engaged in steamboating as the clerk for James Johnson's ill-fated *Johnson* in 1819.[74]

William C. Jewett, who successively captained the *Rowena*, the *Kansas*, and the *Martha Jewett*, was an icon in steamboating to Glasgow and Brunswick. When he entered Missouri River steamboating in 1842, he promised merchants that if he stayed in the business ten years, he would build the "champion steamer." True to his word, he financed the construction of the 230-foot *Martha Jewett* at Hannibal, Missouri, in 1852. In completing all the painting, gilding, and furnishing at St. Louis, Jewett had the boat outfitted with a luxurious carpeted ladies' saloon replete with elegant furniture, piano, and mirrors. As added touches, the *Martha Jewett* featured a bridal chamber named Columbia, and a sign over the door to the main cabin bore the motto "Be kind to the loved ones at home."[75]

With a capacity of 408 tons, the side-wheeler *Martha Jewett* was one of the largest Missouri River steamers. But it was also one of the fastest. The cylinders of its two engines were 22⅝ inches in diameter and had a 7-foot stroke, and the three boilers were each 28 feet long and 40 inches in diameter.

To amuse spectators, who routinely wagered on the outcome, Jewett eagerly competed to have the fastest time in leaving the Glasgow levee. Departing boats were timed for the nine miles downstream in which they were visible. In June 1853 the *Martha Jewett*'s best time was 21 minutes and 30 seconds, half a minute better than the *Polar Star* but a minute and a half slower than the *Bluff City*, another fast boat. But within weeks Captain Jewett established a new standard when the *Martha Jewett* disappeared from view in 17 minutes and 20 seconds. By this feat "the boatmen relieved . . . town friends of sundry boots, hats, and other articles of clothing, to say nothing of actual cash." Some of the boat's boosters immediately started preparing to present Jewett with a set of elk horns.[76]

John McCloy was best known in Kanesville. After captaining the *Kansas*, the first regular packet in the trade, he commanded the *Bluff City*, which was put into operation about the time Council Bluffs was chartered.[77]

Part of the reason Ambrose Reeder attracted so much attention was that his steamer, the *F. X. Aubrey*, was named for the legendary horseman Felix X. Aubrey. In 1853 Aubrey, using a relay of horses, sped the 775 miles from Santa Fe to Westport in only 5 days and 13 hours. Some believe that this celebrated ride was the inspiration for William H. Russell to launch the Pony Express in 1860. Aubrey's image as a folk hero was perpetuated by Reeder, who had the carved figure of a man astride a galloping steed prominently mounted between the chimneys of the *Aubrey*.[78]

Captain Henry W. Smith entered a partnership with merchants from Glasgow and Boonville. Their most prized boat was the *J. M. Clendenin*, built at Louisville in 1852 for $26,000. With a capacity of 276 tons and a length of 200 feet, it was one of the most impressive boats on the Missouri. Smith demonstrated its power and speed when he made a record 35-mile upstream run from Glasgow to Brunswick in 4 hours and 24 minutes.[79]

Smith, who later became a founder of the Anchor Line, one of the largest firms in the history of Mississippi River steamboating, epitomized the gracious, generous, gentlemanly captain. On a voyage from St. Louis to Brunswick in 1853 he provided, at his own expense, a cabin on the *Clendenin* for a German emigrant woman about to give birth. The grateful parents decided to christen their imminent newborn Clendenin Smith. But when the baby proved to be a girl, they imaginatively switched to Clendena Missouri, which was certainly novel with the surname of Azberg. Smith reciprocated by buying the child a half dozen dresses in Brunswick.

Some of Andrew Wineland's reputation rested on his longevity. He began his career as a Missouri River steamboat captain in 1836. At midcentury he was commanding the *Fayaway*, a weekly packet from St. Louis to Jefferson City. He succeeded Brierly as captain of the *El Paso*, which became reputed as a "splendid, fine, fast running, light-draught" steamer.[80]

Other than captains, clerks were the most publicized steamboat officers. As the business managers of boats, first clerks were acquainted with the editors of river town newspapers. It was the clerks who normally presented editors with newspapers from St. Louis and other cities. Thankful editors invariably acknowledged these gestures by printing flattering notices about the clerks and their boats. Often clerks were part owners of boats and thus had a financial stake in getting free advertising.

The role of steamboats as carriers of the latest news was diminished somewhat by the introduction of telegraph service. After its practical invention by Samuel F. B. Morse in 1837, the magnetic telegraph soon attracted public interest. In 1843, Congress funded the construction of an experimental line between Washington, D.C., and Baltimore. Its success stimulated rapid expansion throughout the speed-conscious nation. The completion of the St. Louis connection with Louisville and points east on December 20, 1847, was hailed for bringing Missouri's main city within minutes of economic developments in the country's financial centers.[81]

Businessmen in Missouri River towns eagerly sought the new "lightning" communication. By early November 1850, poles were installed for a line from St. Louis to Jefferson City, which began operating the following year. To extend service westward from the capital city, several partners, including E. B. Cordell of Jefferson City, Robert Aull of Lexington, and William McCoy of Independence, organized the St. Louis and Missouri Telegraph Company on December 11, 1851. By February 1853 the company was offering service to Glasgow. Within several months the line was extended to Brunswick, whose newspaper editor started using it to send reports to St. Louis and points east.[82]

Steamboating, like all businesses, was affected by the telegraph. Telegrams enabled forwarding agents of St. Louis and Missouri River towns to readily communicate with each other and with boat officers. For the first time in history, they could share instantaneous information about arrivals, departures, schedule changes, cargoes, and mishaps. Prior to the telegraph, news of steamboat accidents was usually unknown in St. Louis until they were reported by the officers of another returning boat.

One unintended consequence of telegraph service was the advent of truly accurate measurement of steamboat speeds. In some instances the starting time of boats running between Brunswick and Glasgow was sent to the destination town by telegraph. Using this method, the *Polar Star* was timed at 1 hour and 32 minutes in traveling the 35 miles downstream from Brunswick to Glasgow.[83]

Unprecedented steamboat speeds and telegraph service pleased Missouri River businessmen. But despite the beneficial effects of technology, they suffered from an inadequate road system that deterred the economic development of their hinterlands. Ever since the first settlers started branching out from the Missouri River, they wanted dependable road connections with steamboat ports. The oftentimes muddy, impassable trails were sharp reminders of a more primitive age. Modernization of business and society required improved ways of getting to and from the Missouri. The problem became more aggravating with each passing decade as settlers moved farther inland.

The most promising solution for dirt roads seemed to be plank roads, which became somewhat of a rage in midcentury Missouri. Pioneered in Russia in 1834, plank roads were introduced into upper New York State by way of Canada. Good publicity from the successful construction and operation of a plank road near Syracuse, New York, led to the introduction of plank roads into Ohio, Michigan, and Wisconsin.[84]

Part of the appeal of plank roads in Missouri was the ready local supply of hardwoods. The oak sills and planks needed to construct the seemingly cheap, durable roads could always be obtained and cut by water- or steam-powered mills near the routes. The first plank road was chartered by the state in 1849, two years before the legislature passed an act specifying the legal requirements for plank roads. Missouri's general plank road act of 1851 stipulated that any plank roads chartered by the state were to be granted the right of eminent domain, the authority to hold land for the road and the necessary tollhouses, and the power to collect tolls. The specific conditions for each road were stipulated in its charter, which had to conform with the broad outlines of the general act.[85]

Enthusiasm for plank roads led to the chartering of forty-nine companies, which aspired to build roads ranging in length from 1.75 to 165 miles. Only seventeen of the companies completed their roads. The two most ambitious projects—from St. Louis to Glasgow and from Boonville to Warsaw—were never built. Much of the likely support for the St. Louis–Glasgow road was undercut by the construction start of the Missouri Pacific Railroad westward from St. Louis toward Jefferson City.[86]

Roads running from the river ports of Glasgow and Providence were heavily promoted but proved to be financial disasters. In late 1852 the construction firm of English, Dohany, and Company used about one hundred men to operate three steam sawmills and begin grading a 24-mile plank road from Glasgow northward to Huntsville. The owners of this road completed it in 1854 as a cost of $84,000. Their plans to extend it beyond Huntsville were frustrated by the construction of the Northern Missouri Railroad through Macon County. Like other similar businesses, the Glasgow and Huntsville Plank Road Company found that maintenance was costly because of the continuing need to replace broken and crooked planks. The owners abandoned the scheme in 1860 when the legislature authorized them to replace the planks with gravel.[87]

The Columbia and Missouri River Plank Road Company, which built and operated the 9-mile road connecting Providence and Columbia, was the brainchild of John Parker. After Nashville was washed away by the great flood of 1844, Parker founded Providence, which he named for God's blessings. The town's economy depended on the transshipment of freight to and from Columbia, the seat of Boone County and home of the University of Missouri.[88]

The Providence Plank Road, as it was usually called, was completed in the spring of 1856 at a cost of $33,000. Both Boone County and the City of Columbia helped defray its construction costs. Despite its name, the mile-and-a-half segment closest to Columbia was surfaced with gravel and rocks rather than planks. High maintenance costs, difficulty in collecting tolls, and setbacks in other business ventures forced Parker to sell his plank road company at a sharp loss after only about a year and a half of operation. Although some semblance of the company lingered until 1866, it was never a paying venture.

During the plank road craze, some shippers built experimental short-line railroads. On May 3, 1850, the *Liberty Tribune* announced that "the first railroad ever built in Missouri," from Independence to the Missouri River, was in operation. The Independence railroad, which was intended to meet the challenge of the Santa Fe trade defections to Westport and the Town of Kansas, consisted of cars pulled by mules on wooden rails faced with iron. The line, which William Larkin Webb concluded was "the first railroad ever built west of the Mississippi," proved to be only a novelty. It was rendered useless when the Missouri formed a sandbar in front of the Independence landing.[89]

At approximately the same time the Independence line was built, another mule-powered railroad was completed in Ray County. The four-and-a-half-mile line, which ran from Farmville, then a village a half mile north of present-day Henrietta, to a point directly across the river from Lexington, was privately built by James R. Allen, a well-to-do brick manufacturer, flour miller, and storekeeper. Allen, who was primarily interested in servicing his own businesses, also hauled goods for others. In addition to freight cars, the railroad, which ran on a daily schedule, had a passenger car. Whether this was Missouri's first railroad, as R. B. Oliver asserted, is open to question. Oliver, apparently unaware of the Independence railroad, concluded that Allen's line was built sometime between 1849 and 1851.[90]

In Warsaw, Tuscumbia, Osceola, and other communities in the Osage valley, rivers continued to be the most important target of internal improvements. Merchants of the river towns, steamboatmen, and Jefferson City promoters, who thought the capital city would become the major supplier for the valley, insisted that improving the Osage was vital to economic growth in southwestern Missouri. After the legislature rejected their bid to use proceeds from the sale of federally granted internal improvement lands, they vented their frustration during the Osage Convention held in Warsaw in December 1843. When their call for radical improvement of the Osage by a system of locks and dams was ignored by both the state and federal governments, they changed tactics.

With the goal of improving the Osage by voluntary donations of labor and financial support from adjoining counties, they persuaded the legislature to charter the Osage River Association in February 1847. After electing officers, the association reviewed the survey by William E. Morrell before adopting a course of action. The group's directors determined that their main aim should be to make the Osage navigable from its mouth to Papinsville in Bates County. They knew that the steamer *Maid of Osage* had reached Papinsville during the 1844 flood, but they also recognized that Osceola was the practical head of navigation.[91]

Given their meager finances, the directors had to seek modest improvements. Without support from the state and federal governments, they could not entertain any thoughts of constructing locks and dams. The Morrell survey identified the lack of a continuous navigable channel as the main deterrent to Osage navigation. The river, which was generally about two hundred yards wide downstream from Osceola, featured alternating pools and shoals. Water in the pools was often seven to fifteen feet deep, but nearby shoals sometimes had no more than eight inches. The main task then was to increase the water level over the numerous shoals. In the 220 miles from Osceola to the river's mouth, Morrell identified 98 shoals with an aggregate length of about 25 miles. The association proposed to raise the water level over them by erecting a series of wing dams and dredging.[92]

In order to encourage local participation in all river segments from the mouth upstream to Papinsville, the association created five improvement districts. The first ran from the mouth to Tuscumbia in Miller County, the second from Tuscumbia to Erie (soon thereafter renamed to Linn Creek), the third from Erie to Warsaw, the fourth from Warsaw to Osceola, and the last from Osceola to Papinsville.[93] During the fall of 1847, Osceola citizens and other Osage River residents were reported to "have turned out in numbers and are prosecuting the work of improvement with zeal and industry."[94] They made four shoals navigable. On the basis of this opening work, the association estimated that the entire project would cost no more than $50,000 to $60,000.

The primary method of improving shoals was to construct wing dams just below them. Extending diagonally into the stream, the dams had a brush base with the butt ends pointed downstream. A rock wall up to four feet thick and as much as two feet higher than the low-water mark was built on top of the brush. The effect of these barriers was to back water up over the shoals, with the aim of making them navigable for shallow draft steamers and flatboats. To complement the dams, workers sometimes dredged selected spots in the riverbed. Additionally, some trees were removed in particularly hazardous bends to prevent the continuing accumulation of snags and preclude chimney collisions with overhanging trees.[95]

The association's spokesmen tended to be long on hyperbole. An anonymous improvement promoter known only as "B." wrote a series of reports for the *Jefferson City Inquirer*. James Lusk, the *Inquirer*'s editor, enthusiastically endorsed B.'s claims. Lusk thought that Jefferson City would benefit more than any other place by Osage River improvement. It was, he insisted, poised to become the emporium of southwestern Missouri, which would mean it would "compare with any town on the Missouri River as a shipping and commercial point."[96] Echoing similar sentiments, B. predicted that because of improvement, in twenty years steamboat commerce from St. Louis would boom industry in the Osage valley to the point where the "now obscure frontier towns" of Warsaw and Osceola "will become the Birminghams of the west." In lauding the potential of Osage River steamboating, B. thought "the genius of Fulton has redeemed this western country from a wilderness, in which nothing previous was heard but the howling of the wolf and the careening war whoops of the wild Indian."[97]

Despite its well-organized publicity campaign, the Osage River Association could not raise enough funds to complete its improvement project. Consequently it was forced to concentrate on selected spots. The directors decided that the greatest need was shoal improvement in the Erie-to-Warsaw district. By the fall of 1849, they had spent $4,504.91, slightly over half of their total expenditures on this section. They devoted only $893.47 to the stretch from the river's mouth upstream to Tuscumbia and $406.18 to the area from Osceola to Papinsville. In the other two sectors—Tuscumbia to Erie and Warsaw to Osceola—they spent $1,746.33 and $1,431.74 respectively. Their single greatest achievement was to raise the water level over the Linn Creek shoal, said to be the worst on the river, from 8 inches to 18 to 20 inches. Obviously, even with this type of modification, steamboatmen would have to continue to rely on small, light-draft vessels that sometimes towed flatboats.[98]

Partially to service their own businesses, some Osage valley merchants became involved in steamboating. In the spring of 1848 William Waldo of Osceola purchased the four-year-old side-wheeler *Wave* to make regular runs from the river's mouth to Osceola. The 78-ton boat, which had been built in Louisville, drew only sixteen inches "light." Obviously, there would be no point in running a boat light, which is to say without cargo. However, even when loaded to capacity, the *Wave* probably drew no more than about two and a half feet. Before it sank in the fall of 1849, the *Wave* dominated the Osceola trade.[99]

Joseph Washington McClurg, a Linn Creek merchant, became the most important Osage River steamboatman. After attending Oxford College in Ohio, he was admitted to the bar while living in Columbus, Texas, from 1839 to 1841. But instead of practicing law, he started merchandising in Hazelwood near present-day Seymour, Webster County, Missouri. In 1849, at the age of thirty-one, he moved to California and operated a store for the first two years of the gold rush. He moved to Linn Creek in February 1851, in partnership with his son-in-law John Jones and W. D. Murphy. Under the firm name of McClurg, Murphy, and Jones, they acted as commission and forwarding agents, conducted retail and wholesale merchandising, operated a pork slaughterhouse, and owned and managed several steamboats. Their annual steamboat exports to St. Louis included over 300,000 pounds of dressed pork.[100]

Whenever water levels permitted, some of the shallowest-drafted Missouri River steamers were used on the Osage, such as the *El Paso*, the *Financier*, the *Mary Blane*, and the *St. Ange*. Because no large cities developed along the river and the distances to be covered were relatively short, Osage steamboating never required many boats. During the high water in 1851, eight steamers ran as far up as Osceola, but the next year the trade was handled by only three. Under the best conditions, upstream-bound boats could make 5 miles an hour and could move almost twice as fast going downstream. In 1851 the *Financier* was steamed from Warsaw to St. Louis in only 22 hours.[101]

As with Missouri River towns, the main imports to the Osage valley were iron, salt, groceries, hardware, and cloth. Exports from the valley reflected the nature of its agriculture. Its farmers emphasized pork production, some tobacco cultivation, and a variety of grains, fruits, and diary products. The 1854 steamboat exports from Warsaw are revealing. From the town of about five hundred people, which had eight dry goods and grocery stores, boats transported 11,994 pieces of bacon, 200 barrels of salted pork, and 363 casks of hams and shoulders. The numerous hogs in the valley were free-ranging creatures whose main diet was oak mast. The season's tobacco shipment amounted to 60 hogsheads, and the 5,500 bushels of wheat led the grain shipments. Evidently, raising fruit was an important activity. An amazing 3,606 bushels of dried peaches were shipped out. The significance of hunting and trapping was apparent from the exportation of 144 bales of deer skins and 2,230 animal pelts. Miscellaneous exports included 21 barrels of butter, 108 bushels of castor beans, 33 barrels of beeswax, and 15 bales of feathers.[102]

During the Mexican-American War and its aftermath, the upper Missouri region was the least affected by the migration tides sweeping the Trans-Mississippi West. The fur trade conducted by Pierre Chouteau, Jr., and Company and the new opposition firm of Harvey, Primeau, and Company remained the main economic activity upstream from the Council Bluffs area to the Rocky Mountains.

To supply his upriver posts, Chouteau aimed to have at least one steamer a year navigated to Fort Union and, if conditions permitted, beyond it. Generally, his company chartered or leased new boats from various St. Louis owners. The newest boats, likely to have more power and less draft, were most desired for the upper Missouri. In 1846 Chouteau used the company-owned *General Brooke*, commanded by Captain Joseph A. Sire, for the Fort Union trip. But Sire's retirement from the business forced the company to make new arrangements.

Chouteau turned to Joseph La Barge to transport his company's goods and men in both 1847 and 1848. La Barge, a native St. Louisian whose father had migrated from Quebec, first went to work for the American Fur Company in 1832, when he was just sixteen years old. As an engagé assigned to the Bellevue post, he was a passenger on the *Yellow Stone*'s second trip up the Missouri. After later serving on various steamboats, he worked as one of Sire's pilots on the 1843 and 1844 voyages of the *Omega* and *Nimrod* to Fort Union.[103]

La Barge bought the *General Brooke* from the company in the fall of 1846 but soon sold it so he could build a boat better suited for the upper Missouri. His new steamer, *Martha*, a 180-ton side-wheeler with two engines, four-inch-thick bottom planks, and a light draft of only two feet, was dispatched from St. Louis for Fort Union on May 15, 1847. La Barge's wife, Pelagie, accompanied him, thus gaining the distinction of being the first white woman to visit Fort Union. In 1848 La Barge captained the *Martha* on the round-trip from St. Louis to Fort Union in only 65 days. His downstream cargo was 1,700 bales of buffalo robes, 260 packs of miscellaneous furs, quantities of salted buffalo tongues, and a veritable menagerie of native animals, including buffalo, bear, antelope, elk, and beaver. Apparently, the larger beasts were tethered or penned on the main deck, but La Barge kept the beaver in a large water tank.

Although his biographer Hiram Martin Chittenden is silent on the point, La Barge must have become financially obligated to the Chouteau company when he

Fort Union, 1853.
Until the 1850s, Fort Union, near the confluence of the Missouri and the Yellowstone,
was the Missouri's head of navigation. *Courtesy of the State Historical Society of North Dakota.*

had the *Martha* built. He was forced to sell his interest in the vessel to the company after the 1848 trip. Chouteau apparently intended to use the *Martha* for a third consecutive year, but when it was destroyed in the great St. Louis fire of May 17, 1849, he had to scramble to find a replacement. He managed to lease the *Amelia* for a run to Fort Union, down to the Council Bluff, up to Fort Pierre, and the return to St. Louis.

La Barge meanwhile had a new boat, the *St. Ange,* built at St. Louis. The 254-ton side-wheeler was 170 feet long and 28 feet wide. During its first year, La Barge used the *St. Ange* primarily to transport men and supplies for the army in the St. Louis to Fort Leavenworth trade. But Chouteau also hired him to carry men and provisions to Fort Pierre and, in both 1850 and 1851, to Fort Union. During the high water of 1850 La Barge navigated the boat to Fort Union in a record 28 days.[104]

However, La Barge's feat paled in comparison to the voyage of the *El Paso,* which became one of the most famous steamboats in upper Missouri navigation. Despite its rather imposing size, the 260-ton side-wheeler, which was 180 feet long and 28 feet wide, was reputed to be one of the shallowest-drafted steamboats on the Missouri. After it was built at St. Louis, Chouteau paid $1,200 monthly to charter it for a voyage to the upper river. Commanded by Captain John Durack, an experienced boatman who had once served in the British navy and had made at least one trip to the upper Missouri on Chouteau's behalf, the *El Paso* set out from St. Louis on May 6, 1850.

Chouteau apparently ordered Durack to steam the boat as far as possible above Fort Union. Since Chouteau had long since determined that steamboats were more efficient and faster than either keelboats or mackinaws, it made economic sense to push them farther and farther up the Missouri. By 1850 the vast region above Fort Union had become extremely important. In 1847 the company established Fort Clay on the left bank of the Missouri, only thirty-seven miles below the Great Falls. The new base promised to be the future practical head of steamboat navigation. Company employees called it Fort Benton as early as 1848, but after it was rebuilt as an adobe enclosure in 1850, it was formally rechristened Fort Benton in a Christmas Day ceremony in honor of Senator Thomas Hart Benton, longtime supporter of Chouteau's company and western expansion.[105]

Departing St. Louis, the *El Paso* carried about 200 tons of provisions, a hundred company employees, and Dr. John Evans, a medical doctor and geologist who had been sent by David Dale Owen of the U.S. Geological Survey to continue his study of Badlands geology. Evans performed his survey over three seasons. In 1849 he ascended to Fort Pierre on the *Amelia,* and in 1851 he was a fellow passenger of De Smet's on the *St. Ange.* While surveying the rugged Badlands terrain, Evans collected mammalian fossils that dated to the Tertiary period. His finds, which were analyzed by Dr. Joseph Leidy of Philadelphia, contributed significantly to the emerging field of vertebrate paleontology.[106]

After dropping Evans off at Fort Pierre, Durack moved the *El Paso* upstream, only to encounter ice floes on June 11 below Fort Clark. A week later the mackinaw Durack had in tow was sunk, but with a good current he ordered the *El Paso* beyond Fort Union. Once he reached the point where the *Assiniboin* had been wintered in 1834–35, Durack knew he was setting a record with each passing mile. But low water forced him to turn around at a point 8 miles above the mouth of the Milk River, or about 185 miles from Fort Union. To mark his achievement, Durack had a wooden sign erected on the riverbank with the inscription: "The Steamer El Paso landed at this point on the 20th June, 1850—thirty-five days from St. Louis, John Durack, Captain."[107] El Paso Point, which stood as the Missouri's steamboat head of navigation for nine years, became the target destination for later steamboatmen.

Descending rapidly, Durack completed the round-trip from St. Louis in 56 days. Besides carrying buffalo robes and other furs down, he brought quantities of elk horns gathered in the Fort Pierre vicinity by company employees. He also provided passage for Thaddeus A. Culbertson from Fort Pierre to St. Louis. Culbertson, the half-brother of company trader Alexander Culbertson, had gone overland from Fort Leavenworth to the Badlands. His *Journal of an Expedition to the Mauvaises Terres and the Upper Missouri in 1850,* which was partially published by the Smithsonian Institution in 1850, was the first scientific study of Badlands flora and fauna.[108]

Providing transportation for such scientists as Evans and Culbertson was characteristic of Chouteau, who was always conscious of the goodwill engendered by such gestures. Chouteau also befriended missionaries, whom he saw as important figures in familiarizing Indians with Euro-American culture. In 1851 he provided free passage for the Jesuits Pierre-Jean De Smet and Christian Hoecken. Once again Chouteau used the services of Joseph La Barge and the *St. Ange*, but the trip to Fort Union was fraught with problems. A number of passengers were stricken by cholera, and about a dozen died. After De Smet became seriously ill, the burden of caring for the afflicted fell to Hoecken. While ministering to the sick, Hoecken was smitten with the disease and expired suddenly near the mouth of the Little Sioux River above the Council Bluff. La Barge had a coffin built, and de Smet presided over a burial service. Keeping a promise he made to de Smet that Hoecken be reburied in a Jesuit cemetery near St. Louis, La Barge disinterred the remains on his return trip.[109]

As the only regular steamboat transporter on the upper river, the Chouteau company was routinely used by the federal government. Most of this business, done under annually negotiated contracts, called for the delivery of annuities from St. Louis to various subagencies of the Upper Missouri Agency. The government payments, which were first mandated by the Atkinson-O'Fallon treaties of 1825 were ostensibly distributed by Indian agents, who were government employees. But the agents, who tended to have very short tenures, usually found upriver accommodations at trading posts to be miserable. Consequently, they limited their actual time in the field and prevailed on company employees to dole out government property. The opportunities for confusion of private and public property, to say nothing of outright fraud, were rife. Nonetheless, the government year after year persisted in using private contractors to deliver and oftentimes distribute annuities.

In the spring of 1853, Pierre Chouteau, Jr., and Company was given the opportunity to bid on a new type of government contract. Although more bound by the traditional way of life than regions to its south, the upper Missouri area was not immune to the effects of westward expansion. Responding to widespread calls for transcontinental railroads, the administration of President Franklin Pierce authorized reconnaissances of several prospective lines. Planning the expeditions was left to Secretary of War Jefferson Davis. The northernmost transcontinental line was projected to run from St. Paul, the capital of young Minnesota Territory, to Puget Sound. Such a road was deemed vital to connect St. Paul, the practical head of navigation on the upper Mississippi, with deep-water ports for oceangoing ships on Puget Sound. The northern transcontinental railroad was of great interest to those who wanted to develop the Pacific Northwest and trade with China and other Asian countries.[110]

The Pierce administration named Isaac Ingalls Stevens of Massachusetts to head the northern survey. A West Point graduate who had served as an engineer on General Winfield Scott's staff during the Mexican-American War, Stevens actively campaigned for Franklin Pierce, who was elected president in 1852. Thinking he should be rewarded for his efforts, Stevens personally applied to Pierce for various positions. Pierce responded by selecting him to fill three positions—director of the northern railroad survey, governor of the newly formed Washington Territory, and ex officio superintendent of Indian affairs for the territory.[111]

In preparing for the survey, Stevens decided to lead his main party northwestward from St. Paul and to send a small support group and some supplies up the Missouri by steamboat. While passing through St. Louis on his way to St. Paul, Stevens arranged for quartermaster officers to contract with the Chouteau company for the transportation of some men and supplies to Fort Union. The party carried on the *Robert Campbell*, then under charter to Chouteau, consisted of Second Lieutenant Andrew Jackson Donelson, Second Lieutenant John Mullan, and six enlisted men. Chouteau agreed to provide cabin passage for Mullan and Donelson from St. Louis to Fort Union for $100 each. His charge for the six men, who had deck passage, was $50 each.[112]

The four-year-old *Robert Campbell*, a 268-ton side-wheeler, was owned and named for Chouteau's longtime rival. Apparently the differences between Campbell and Chouteau were not severe enough to preclude an occasional business accommodation. Donelson, Mullan, and their men were delivered to Fort Union before Stevens arrived with his overland party of 120 men, several hundred horses and mules, and numerous wagons and other vehicles. At Fort Union, Stevens assigned different segments of his command to proceed overland to Fort Benton, their next base. Stevens apparently had some of his provisions forwarded on the *Robert Campbell* with the intention of going as far as possible. But the boat's progress was blocked by sandbars about seventy miles above Fort Union.[113]

The failure of the *Robert Campbell* to challenge the *El Paso*'s record did not diminish Stevens's optimism about steamboating prospects above Fort Union. On the basis of his examination of the river and conversations he had with Alexander Culbertson and other Chouteau company officials, he was convinced that modified steamboats would prevail. Contending that previous steamboats on the upper Missouri "had not been of a good class," he believed that "first-class" boats with lighter drafts and more powerful engines should be used. Such vessels, drawing eighteen to twenty inches, he thought, could be navigated even past Fort Benton to Highwood Creek, only fifteen miles below the Great Falls.[114]

While the Chouteau company was extending steamboating on the upper Missouri and expanding its government business, it was sharply challenged by Harvey, Primeau, and Company. The new opposition firm had been created by Alexander Harvey and Charles Primeau and several of their associates in 1846. Harvey, who had spent years on the upper Missouri as a Chouteau trader and bourgeois, had a notorious reputation. During periodic fits of rage he killed Indians and even a rival trader to avenge perceived wrongs. But the role of a violent thug was only one aspect of his personality. To some sedate St. Louisians he appeared to be a larger-than-life folk hero who personified the harshness of the fur trade. Around Christmas 1839 he had set out walking alone from a post above Fort Union for St. Louis, which he reached in early March. This feat so impressed Pierre Chouteau,

Jr., that rather than follow through on his decision to fire Harvey for his inability or unwillingness to work harmoniously with other traders, he rehired him. Apparently Harvey had considerable ability. Trader Charles Larpenteur, who knew him well, claimed he was "undoubtedly the boldest man that was ever on the Missouri—I mean in the Indian country." He seemed to attribute some of Harvey's unseemly nature to alcohol, with the judgment that Harvey was "inclined to do right when sober."[115]

But another quarrel with company leadership caused Chouteau to dismiss Harvey. The vengeful Harvey responded by persuading Primeau and several others, including Joseph Picotte and A. R. Bouis, to leave the Chouteau company and form Harvey, Primeau, and Company. Throughout its eight-year history, Harvey, Primeau, and Company was often backed financially by Robert Campbell, one of St. Louis's wealthiest men. Of Scotch-Irish ancestry, Campbell first entered the fur trade in 1825 as an employee of William H. Ashley. For about a decade he worked in the Rockies in association with such famous traders as Jedidiah S. Smith and William Sublette. About 1835, when he was thirty-one years old, Campbell began his St. Louis business career, which came to include wholesaling, banking, operating a forwarding agency for Indian traders, investing in real estate, and steamboating. Over the years, he was one of the strongest and most persistent opponents of the American Fur Company and its successor, Pierre Chouteau, Jr., and Company.

Harvey and his associates decided their best tactic was to erect rival posts near Chouteau's main installations. Consequently, they started Fort Defiance (also called Fort Bouis) near Fort Pierre, Fort Primeau near Fort Clark, Fort William near Fort Union, and Fort Campbell near Fort Benton. To conduct their trade, they used Chouteau's standard method of chartering steamboats and supplementing them with mackinaws. For the delivery of emergency supplies when the river was unnavigable, they used pack trains from the vicinity of St. Joseph. The overland trail paralleling the Missouri, which had been pioneered by the American Fur Company, was also used by couriers who sometimes delivered wintertime messages from the upriver posts to St. Louis.

Normally, Harvey, Primeau, and Company used a single annual steamboat. In 1846 the 132-ton side-wheeler *Clermont* made a routine run to Fort William. But the next year, Harvey had a great adventure with the small 86-ton side-wheeler *Lake of the Woods*. Near the mouth of the Cheyenne River the boat was disabled by bursting steam pipes. Somehow the crew managed to get it back to St. Louis. But the impatient Harvey hastily built a sawpit, hand-cut timber, and built a mackinaw. His men managed to tow it upstream until their passage was blocked by ice on November 6. Abandoning the river, Harvey and his companions rode horses to Fort Campbell. During the winter Harvey and several companions made their way from the fort, first by dogsled and then by mules, to the Mormons' Winter Quarters near the Council Bluff. The entire affair, which enhanced Harvey's reputation as an adventurer, must have been a financial disaster.[116]

Like Chouteau, Harvey saw an advantage in navigating steamboats above the mouth of the Yellowstone. His 1848 boat, the *Bertrand*, was steamed about fifty miles above Fort William. Continuing his reliance on Campbell, in 1849 Harvey chartered the 132-ton *Tamerlane*, owned by Robert Campbell and his son William. During 1854, Harvey, Primeau, and Company used the *Genoa*, a 170-foot, 226-ton side-wheeler partially owned by both Robert Campbell and Captain Joseph Throckmorton, a veteran steamboatman of the Missouri and Mississippi. The *Genoa*'s trip to Fort William was the last major activity of Harvey, Primeau. and Company. Harvey's death at Fort William on July 20, 1854, left the firm in disarray. His partners, with some encouragement from Campbell, gave Chouteau some feeble opposition for only another two years.[117]

During the period 1846–54, the Chouteau and Harvey companies used a total of fourteen different steamboats on the upper Missouri, all of them side-wheelers. The smallest were the *Lake of the Woods*, the *Bertrand*, and the *Clermont*. The largest by a considerable margin was the *Sonora*, owned by Joseph La Barge. The 363-ton boat, built at St. Louis in 1851, was 220 feet long and 32 feet wide. While working for Chouteau, La Barge navigated the *Sonora* to Fort Union in both 1852 and 1854. The second-largest steamer in terms of tonnage was the *Kate Swinney*, whose 280-ton capacity made it 12 tons larger than the *Robert Campbell*. Chouteau used the *Kate Swinney* for an 1854 trip to Fort Pierre. The boat had been built at Jeffersonville, Indiana, in 1852 for W. D. Swinney, a Glasgow tobacco merchant who named it for his daughter.[118]

Although the Chouteau-Harvey rivalry increased upper river steamboating, both companies continued to use mackinaws for downstream shipments. The mackinaw trade was changed somewhat after the founding of Kanesville. Some mackinaw cargoes were transshipped from there by steamboats. Since Kanesville, like most new frontier towns, was chronically short of lumber, the companies had no difficulty selling their mackinaws there.

American expansion during the Mexican-American War era boomed St. Louis, whose commercial empire was linked by steamboating. In 1848 the city had almost 56,000 inhabitants, nearly double the population five years earlier. As St. Louis grew, it became more important as a manufacturing, wholesaling, and retailing center. These developments enabled its merchants to increase their business in the city's expanding hinterland and thus lessen the region's dependence on eastern suppliers.[119]

As the nation's westernmost major port, St. Louis was the home of 122 steamboats in 1848. Some of them had been built expressly for either the Missouri or the Osage, but all were used sometimes on various segments of the Mississippi River system. On occasion nearly half of the steamers registered at the St. Louis customhouse were tied up at the Front Street levee.[120] One St. Louis observer thought that, to any visitor who arrived by boat, "the town seems covered and defended by a fleet of steamboats, exhibiting a front of chimneys."[121]

An analysis of the 1848 St. Louis fleet provides good insight into western steamboating. The 122 boats had an aggregate tonnage of 35,578. Records of 120 of the boats show that 106 were side-wheelers and only 14 were stern-wheelers. Slightly more than a third of the boats had been built in St. Louis, and nearly a third in Pittsburgh and nearby Pennsylvania towns. Most of the remainder had been made in Cincinnati, Louisville, and other Ohio River ports.[122]

On average, the boats lasted 5.7 years. But the longevity of the 76 that were destroyed was only 4.38 years. Other studies of western steamboating invariably show snagging as the principal cause of steamboat losses. However, the 1848 St. Louis fleet, which lost 35 steamers to burning, proved to be an exception, mainly because of the devastating levee fire of May 17, 1849.

The Great Fire, as it came to be known in St. Louis, started about 10:00 P.M. on the steamer *White Cloud* and spread quickly to the neighboring *Edward Bates.* Both vessels ignited other boats and some freight on the levee as they drifted downstream. By the time it was done, the blaze had consumed 23 steamboats, 3 barges, and a canal boat. After a strong wind blew the flames across the levee, some 500 buildings in a fifteen-square-block area were destroyed. Most of them were burned, but some were deliberately destroyed by the city's volunteer fire department, which exploded kegs of gunpowder to check the fire's spread. The worth of the burned boats and their cargoes was estimated to be about half a million dollars, but insurance covered about 50 percent of the loss. The value of the destroyed buildings and their contents was placed at approximately $2.1 million, but after insurance payments the total loss of boats, buildings, and merchandise was reportedly under $1,000,000.[123]

Although they were dismayed by the losses due to the Great Fire, steamboatmen accepted high risk as a normal part of doing business. None of them expected steamboats to be long-range investments. An 1850 report stated that on western rivers "the life of a steamboat does not average more than five years."[124] In 1848, of the 208 steamers built nationwide, 155 were constructed in the Mississippi River system. Rapid construction was required to expand steamboating, which had an estimated 800 boats on western waters in 1850, and to replace destroyed and worn-out boats. In 1848 alone, 67 western steamboats were destroyed.[125]

St. Louis steamboating recovered rapidly from the Great Fire. In 1853, steamers based in the city had an aggregate 37,000 tons. The estimated value of St. Louis commerce was $100 million, which was twenty times more than that of 1833.[126]

The allied effects of steamboating permeated all aspects of the community's economy. An 1854 business directory listed eight steamboat agencies engaged in the commission and forwarding business. Providing storage was an essential service and an important source of their income. Agencies typically advertised a schedule of monthly storage charges. For example, in 1847 the agency of Wayman Crow charged 50 cents for a hogshead of tobacco and 40 cents for a one-hundred-pound box of bacon. George W. Jenks, who operated a hemp warehouse, charged $3 for each bale.[127]

The influence of the agencies permeated the marine insurance business. Agents routinely sold policies on hulls and cargoes. With their intimate knowledge of steamboat trade, they were uniquely positioned to assess risks. Apparently acting on the advice of forwarding and commission agents, the Board of Underwriters of the City of St. Louis on January 1, 1850, adopted a schedule of minimum cargo insurance premiums. For the various segments of the Mississippi River system, the premiums ranged from 0.5 to 4.5 percent of a cargo's value. The following Missouri River charges show the correlation between increased risk and longer ascensions of the Missouri.

> To points not above St. Charles: 50 cents
> To points not above Lexington: $1.00
> To points not above Westport: $1.25
> To points not above Council Bluffs: $2.00

Although the rates to Council Bluffs were twice as high as those to St. Paul, the Mississippi's practical head of navigation, they were only about half of those to the highest navigable section of the Arkansas River.[128]

Because boat captains were businessmen, it behooved them to keep accurate financial records. This need was apparent to Jonathan Jones, whose Jones' Commercial College of St. Louis was incorporated by the Missouri legislature on January 24, 1849. Among other courses, Jones offered "Steamboat Bookkeeping," which he admonished boat owners was vital "to protect their interests from the incompetent, the careless and the designing."[129] Jones's institution trained steamboat clerks with an introductory bookkeeping course followed by practical training in compiling balance sheets and other records unique to steamboating, such as portage books and fuel books. He proudly advertised that his graduates included steamboat captain and agent Nicholas Wall and Thomas W. Scott, captain of the *St. Ange*.

Despite the dominance of steamboats, some rivermen persisted in using keelboats and flatboats. During the year ending June 30, 1847, keelboats built in St. Louis numbered 43.[130] In May 1847 the St. Louis harbormaster recorded the arrival of 453 steamboats and barges, which were towed by steamers, and 77 flatboats and keelboats. In 1848 there were 349 flatboat and keelboat arrivals in the city. Their annual tonnage of 13,960, or 40 tons per landing, was nearly triple that delivered by barges. Flatboats and keelboats, described as "another important branch to the carrying trade of this city," were sometimes mentioned in statistical reports but generally ignored by newspapers.[131]

Before 1849 was over, the Great Fire proved to be St. Louis's second-ranking disaster. By mid-May a cholera epidemic was raging. An Asiatic disease that spread westward through Eurasia, cholera was first introduced into the United States by ship passengers in 1832. It abated, but a second outbreak was caused by afflicted immigrants moving into American ports. The disease, which appeared in New Orleans in December 1848, was quickly carried up the Mississippi by steamboat passengers. In January 1849 about 30 St. Louisians died from it. Although St. Louis had experienced cholera in 1832, the initial response in 1849 was to pretend it did not exist. The city's government officials, business community, and newspapers feared that publicizing the disease would impair trade. They continued this disastrous course until late June, by which time the awfulness of the epidemic could not be ignored. In May there were about 500 cholera deaths and in June a staggering 1,259.[132]

The citizenry was shocked not only by the high incidence of deaths but also by the number of people who died within several days or sometimes only several hours after getting sick. Living thirty-five years before the cholera germ was identified by Robert Koch, a pioneering German doctor, St. Louisians could not explain the cause of the epidemic. But they recognized that the highest incidence of deaths occurred in those parts of the city where stagnant ponds contained human waste. Since the city did not have a sewer system, the contents of its cesspools, which included ponds and underground caverns, became intermingled with its water supply. As human waste was carried into the Mississippi, the source of the city's cooking and drinking water, the disease spread rapidly. No one at the time knew that the cholera germ was carried from human intestinal systems into waste repositories, which in turn polluted drinking water, but some astute observers, including many doctors, recognized that cholera was at its worst in the most unsanitary areas, which usually were the poorest slums.

The scientific response to this observation was to encourage people to leave filthy cities in favor of country sites free of accumulated waste. Generally, those who moved to rural areas were spared. In St. Louis an estimated two-fifths of the population, including the entire city council, left town. The effects of this mass migration were profound. The city's government could not function, and nothing was done to deal with the epidemic until a group of citizens organized a Committee of Public Health in late June. Commerce was sometimes stalled because there were not enough laborers and draymen to unload steamboats. The levee was atypically dull because the customary crowds of gawkers did not form.

Although the Committee of Public Health encouraged sanitation, its members were also influenced by the unfortunate widespread assumption that cholera victims had incurred God's wrath. In St. Louis and other American cities the epidemic's greatest toll was on the poorest people living in vice-ridden slums. To some prosperous churchgoers who lived in clean neighborhoods and were not affected by the disease, it seemed that cholera was divine punishment of sinners. Thus those believers in an anthropomorphic God who actively intervened in human affairs saw prayer as a solution. Local groups, including the St. Louis Committee on Public Health, designated a day of prayer and fasting. This and similar actions in other cities influenced President Zachary Taylor to name Friday, August 3, 1849, as a national day of "fasting, humiliation and prayer." Taylor implored "the Almighty to lift the pestilence from the land."[133]

St. Louis' cholera epidemic peaked in mid-July, when 639 victims were interred in one week. It slackened in August, and by September there were only some incidental cases. For the entire year the city's cholera deaths amounted to 4,285.[134]

Diseased steamboat passengers rapidly carried cholera to Missouri River towns. Five passengers on the *Monroe* died en route to Jefferson City, where the boat arrived on May 10, 1849. After several more died the first day the boat was tied up at the wharf, the mayor and aldermen forced the boat and its passengers to relocate below the city. There the sick were placed in "a comfortable building." As fear gripped the community, ten to fifteen of the passengers died within a week. Within days, cholera was reported to be "making terrible havoc among the population of Arrow Rock and the Bottoms" above it. Many slaves died, including nine on a single farm. Cholera deaths around Kanesville were first recorded by mid-May. Among the first to succumb was an English immigrant who ascended the river on the steamer *Dahcotah*. The disease was said to be particularly calamitous among the Potawatomis. And as ailing steamboat passengers transmitted the disease up the Missouri, overland emigrants carried it with them on the trail to California and Oregon.[135]

After the shock of 1849, there were incidences of cholera in Missouri River towns for three more years. In a five-day period in late August 1851, ten victims died in Jefferson City. Within days the disease also claimed William W. Robards, Missouri's attorney general.[136] In June 1852, Mayor Jason Harrison complained that Jefferson City had been "severely scourged by that awful pestilence, the cholera." since 1849.[137] The disease was reported to be "prevailing to some extent in some of the river towns" above Jefferson City.[138] The editor of Kanesville's *Western Bugle* exhorted residents to resort to such preventive measures as removing offal, opening drains to free stagnant water, and strewing "lime about and around the most offensive places."[139]

Despite cholera's disruptive effects on Missouri River towns, steamboating expanded. Heavy overland migration, troop movements, and a lively trade in agricultural commodities all contributed to the increase in river commerce.

Although their business rose during the Mexican-American War era, steamboatmen were generally displeased with their treatment by the federal government. They wanted continued and expanded river improvement, but it was denied. They opposed added safety measures, but Congress nonetheless dictated more stringent measures.

Despite widespread concern about its constitutionality, Congress appropriated about $2.5 million to improve western rivers in 1824–44. Most was spent on the Ohio and the Mississippi below St. Louis, but some modest expenditures were made on the Missouri.[140] Given this history, steamboat interests assumed that the government was committed to river improvement, so they were taken aback by President James K. Polk's veto of a congressional appropriation of $1,378,450 for more than forty river and harbor improvement projects nationwide. In his veto message of August 3, 1846, Polk concluded: "The Constitution has not, in my judgment, conferred upon the Federal Government the power to construct works of internal improvement within the States, or to appropriate money from the Treasury for that purpose."[141] In addition to invoking his narrow constructionist view of the constitution, Polk argued that the expense could not be justified when the nation was borrowing to fight the war with Mexico.

Westerners, especially, launched a vigorous, prolonged counterattack. Finally, they agreed to convene a national protest convention in Chicago on July 5, 1847. Expressly for this meeting, the St. Louis committee—dominated by Adam Black Chambers, editor of the *Missouri Republican*, and Edward Tracy, a veteran forwarding and commission merchant—prepared a strong statement on the importance of steamboating to the economy of the West and to the nation's welfare and security. In their thirty-two-page pamphlet laced with trade statistics, the St. Louis delegates reported that in 1846 there were 1,190 steamboats on the western waters. Figuring at $65 per ton, they concluded the boats had an aggregate value of $16,188, 561. The total annual cost of operating the boats, calculated at $125 for each of 220 navigation days, was $32,725,000. Other expenses were insurance, interest, and depreciation. They placed annual hull insurance at $1,942,627—12 percent of the total value of all 1,190 boats. They chose to assume that the entire value of all boats was borrowed capital on which owners were paying 6 percent interest, which added $971,313. Claiming that annual depreciation, which they described as "wear and tear," was 24 percent, they added another $3,885,254. To illustrate the widespread effects of steamboating on the economy, they estimated that 41,650 persons were employed on all the boats on the Mississippi and its tributaries. In addition to this steamboat workforce, they reported there were about 20,000 persons working on some 4,000 keelboats and flatboats.[142] The committee insisted that the government should improve rivers to safeguard not only this massive private investment but also its own interests, by reducing the loss of steamboats that carried mail and government supplies and personnel.

Organizers of the Chicago convention, including Chambers and Tracy, tried to get prominent politicians involved. They invited former Democratic president Martin Van Buren, Senator Thomas Hart Benton, and 1884 Whig presidential candidate Henry Clay. All declined.[143]

Deeply influenced by the St. Louis report, which was published verbatim in the *Niles' National Register* of July 31, 1847, the Chicago Convention approved a lengthy memorial to Congress. Polk's decision not only stood, however, but also dominated federal river improvement policy until the end of the Civil War. The government appropriated improvement funds only once during that score of years. The River and Harbors Act of 1852, approved by Whig president Millard Fillmore, granted nearly $2.1 million for projects nationwide. The appropriation for the Missouri was $40,000, and its navigators may have also benefited from the provision that $150,000 be used to construct and repair snagboats and dredges to be used throughout the Mississippi River system.[144]

As steamboat explosions continued to highlight the news, public disenchantment with the 1838 steamboat inspection act grew. Many believed that the best solution was to require steamboat inspections by federal employees. A stronger regulatory measure was introduced in the Senate in 1840 but could not attract majority support. As senators and representatives continued to contemplate the issue of steamboat safety, their interest turned to such notions as licensing engineers and testing boilers. But proposals for both ideas failed in Congress in the mid-1840s.[145]

Congressmen decided they needed more information about steamboat accidents before further considering new regulations. By the time they began drafting the act of 1852, they had been influenced by three major reports. The first was a special study of steam boiler explosions by Edmund Burke, the U.S. commissioner of patents. The second was documents presented by Senator John Davis (Whig, Massachusetts), the leading advocate of tighter regulations, and the third was a report from Secretary of the Treasury Thomas Corwin.[146]

To determine steamboat losses caused by faulty boilers for 1830–47 inclusive, Burke had surveyed customs collectors nationwide. Besides compiling an extensive list of steamboat losses, Burke asked the collectors for comments. Their narratives were the most damning part of the report. Time and time again they ridiculed the ineffectiveness of the 1838 law in preventing explosions. They thought the required inspections were usually nothing more than cursory scannings.[147]

In addition to reporting on the nation's steam marine commerce for the year ending June 30, 1851, Corwin included lists of 736 steamers that had been destroyed on the western rivers from the beginning of navigation through 1848. Sinking by striking snags and other obstructions accounted for 419 of the losses. Of the remainder, 104 burned, 82 exploded, 67 had collapsed flues, 45 collided, and 19 had burst pipes.[148]

Despite Corwin's information that sinking by striking snags and other obstructions was the principal reason for steamboat losses, much of the public support for increased regulation was caused by intense, dramatic newspaper coverage of steamboat explosions. Burke observed that heavily reported boiler explosions left the erroneous impression that steamboats on inland waters were uniquely dangerous. Navigation at sea resulted in far more losses, he noted, but those disasters often occurred in remote places with few witnesses and often were never mentioned in newspapers.[149]

Burke's point was well illustrated by the newspaper coverage of the explosion of the *Saluda* at Lexington, Missouri, on April 9, 1852. The boat's two boilers exploded just as Captain Francis T. Belt was about to head the craft upstream from the levee. The blast, which blew away everything above the main deck, threw boat fragments into downtown Lexington, about a quarter mile away. The bodies of Belt, other officers, and some passengers were hurled about a hundred yards onto bluff tops. A Lexington observer dramatically reported: "The mangled remains of human beings were scattered over the wharf and on the bluff; and human blood, just warm from the heart, trickled down the banks and mingled with the water of the Missouri."[150]

Initial reports of casualties were exaggerated. One eyewitness claimed that two-thirds of the 175 people on board had been killed, but the losses were later determined to be 27 killed and many more injured. But newspaper readers at the time had no reason to doubt that the explosion had killed nearly 120 people.[151]

By the time the *Saluda* exploded, Congress was deeply involved with drafting a strong regulatory measure. During their lengthy consideration, the lawmakers were flooded with memorials from supporters and opponents. Appeals for regulation included those from the New Orleans Chamber of Commerce and many insurance companies, merchants, and bankers. The main opposition came from steamboat owners, who argued that further regulation was unnecessary and would add to their operating costs.[152]

Congressional proponents of more regulation easily prevailed, and the law establishing a federal Steamboat Inspection Service was approved on August 30, 1852. The measure, which was to go into effect on January 1, 1853, in the Mississippi River system and most other regions, specified that nine supervising district inspectors would administer steamboat inspection. They were to meet annually as a board to consider matters relating to the administration of the service. Within each district, the supervising inspector, together with the customs collector and the district judge, were to name a hull inspector and a boiler inspector. These two had to conduct annual inspections of all passenger steamers within their jurisdiction and certify that they met the act's requirements. The detailed law carefully prescribed that the hull and boiler inspectors had to have practical experience and be of good character. The supervising inspector and the hull and boiler inspectors were federal employees. To help defray the expenses of the service, the law provided that steamboat owners had to pay inspection fees.[153]

Congress's overriding concern with steamboat safety was evident from its specifications for boiler inspection and construction. All boilers had to be subjected to a hydrostatic pressure test, and their metal had to meet quality specifications. Further, each boiler had to be stamped to indicate that it met the standards. The act did not elaborate a method for hull inspection, but supervising inspectors later decided that the soundness of a vessel would be determined by drilling small holes in the bottom planking and other places.

Because Congress was convinced that the conduct of pilots and engineers was vital for steamboat safety, the law provided that they had to obtain annual licenses. To qualify, the pilots and engineers had to pass a written examination administered by the hull and boiler inspectors. Then each district supervisor had to maintain a list of qualified pilots and engineers. Although the Missouri and the Mississippi were in the same district, supervising inspectors decided that separate lists should be maintained for each stream. This meant that a pilot who qualified to guide a Mississippi River steamer would have to take a separate exam to qualify for the Missouri. Boat owners were prohibited from hiring unlicensed pilots or engineers. Violators were subject to a heavy fine.

The lengthy act, which ran to about ten thousand words, provided for a bevy of other safety measures. Pumps and lifeboats were required. The carrying of loose hemp, a fire hazard, was banned. All explosive or highly combustible materials, including gunpowder and oil of turpentine, had to be packed in clearly labeled metal containers and stored separately from like items and all other freight and at a specified distance from the boat's machinery.

The law had an immediate impact on western steamboating, whose packet operators were engaged in both the freight and passenger trade. The law did exempt ferries, because of their low accident rate, and boats that only carried freight. But these provisions meant nothing to operators of the regular Missouri River steamers. Although they expressed resentment about the act, some steamboatmen by the spring of 1853 saw an advantage in advertising that their boats had been retrofitted to meet "all the requirements of the new steamboat law."[154]

The law soon proved its worth. In its first eight years, despite more traffic, fatalities from steamboat accidents declined by a third of the total from 1845–52.[155]

Throughout the remainder of their days, steamboatmen had a dichotomous relationship with the federal government. They loved a government that was beneficent enough to improve rivers, but resented one that was so strong it could regulate them. Nonetheless, it is clear that the start of the Steamboat Inspection Service was prompted by a congressional response to public safety concerns rather than the arbitrary imposition of controls by bureaucrats.

By the time the Steamboat Inspection Act of 1852 went into effect, many Americans believed steamboats would soon be superseded by railroads. In Missouri the Hannibal and St. Joseph Railroad had been formed, and the Missouri Pacific Railroad was already under construction westward from St. Louis. Promoters of the Missouri Pacific hoped it would ultimately become a transcontinental line. Transcontinental railroad schemers nationwide stressed the urgency of linking distant California with eastern financial centers. But they realized that, with the exception of a portion of Utah, the vast region between Missouri and California had not been opened to white settlement, and a lack of paying customers along any railroad route would jeopardize its fiscal soundness.

Concern over building a central transcontinental route led to the opening of Kansas and Nebraska territories in 1854. Some "sooners" had illegally moved west of the Missouri before the Kansas-Nebraska Act was signed by President Franklin Pierce on May 30, 1854. The platting of new towns started shortly after the act's approval, and townsite promoters naturally sought locations on navigable streams. In Kansas, Atchison and Leavenworth were founded on the Missouri, and Lawrence and Topeka on the Kansas River. Iowans from Council Bluffs were instrumental in starting Omaha on the west side of the Missouri. From its start, Omaha was rivaled by Nebraska City, which became the main Nebraska steamboat port south of the Platte. The settlement of eastern Kansas and Nebraska not only led to the creation of new steamboat ports but also extended the trade of Missouri River merchants and steamboatmen.[156]

6

RAILROADS AND
NEW FRONTIERS, 1855–1860

In 1857, St. Louis steamboatmen were forced to begin sharing their city's western trade with railroads. During the initial advance of railroads westward from the Mississippi, St. Louis business benefited from the federal government's occupation of Utah, the Pikes Peak gold rush, army and settler expansion on the upper river, and the extension of steamboating to Fort Benton.

Dissatisfied with the inefficiency, seasonableness, and high costs of steamboating, Missourians developed an interest in railroads soon after their first use in the East. In 1836, only six years after the Baltimore and Ohio Railroad began operating 13 miles of the nation's first line, promoters assembled a railroad convention in St. Louis. It seemed that every Missouri community of note wanted a railroad. The conventioneers endorsed proposals for eighteen lines. Most of them were short, but two particularly ambitious plans were for St. Louis–Fayette and Louisiana-Columbia railroads. The state legislature chartered all of the proposed lines the next year, and a civil engineer surveyed an 85-mile route for the Louisiana to Columbia Railroad. His cost estimates of $626,950 were presented to the legislature, and promoters soon found that scheming was much easier than financing. The Panic of 1837, while not affecting Missouri as much as the eastern sections of the country, was severe enough to forestall railroad construction.[1]

In the fall of 1846, during the Mexican-American War, St. Joseph's business leaders started promoting a Hannibal to St. Joseph Railroad. They believed that such a line would give St. Joseph more direct contact with the East, lessen its dependence on steamboats, and reduce shipping costs. These advantages, in turn, would assure the emergence of their town as a serious rival of St. Louis in the western trade. The Missouri legislature obligingly incorporated the Hannibal and St. Joseph Railroad on February 16, 1847, but its first 10 miles of track were not completed until 1856.[2]

Although St. Louis lagged behind St. Joseph in promoting railroads, the steamboat city was jolted into the new age by national events. The acquisition of the

Southwest and California as a result of the Mexican-American War and the ensuing California gold rush stimulated demands for a transcontinental railroad. By the time St. Louis hosted a major national railroad convention in October 1849, its leaders recognized the importance of railroads as the most effective way of competing with the looming threat of Chicago's economic influence. The St. Louis Railroad Convention approved a proposal that St. Louis, Chicago, and Memphis would become starting points for feeder routes of a future transcontinental line to California. Calls for a transcontinental railroad were also issued by railroad conventions held at Memphis the week after the St. Louis convention and at Philadelphia in April 1850.[3]

Interest generated by the St. Louis convention led city promoters to persuade the legislature to charter the Missouri Pacific Railroad on March 12, 1850. With the aim of making it a portion of the transcontinental railroad, the incorporators authorized the company to construct a railroad from St. Louis to Missouri's western boundary, where it would join any line that had been extended eastward from the Pacific coast.[4]

St. Louisians looked north as well as west. On March 3, 1851, the legislature incorporated the North Missouri Railroad, the third line destined to have a direct effect on Missouri River steamboating. The North Missouri company was authorized to construct a line from St. Louis northwestwardly to the divide separating the Mississippi and Missouri watersheds. Then its route would lie along the divide to the state's northern boundary.[5]

The Missouri Pacific held an elaborate ground-breaking ceremony at St. Louis on July 4, 1851, but it did not finish constructing the 5-mile stretch to Cheltenham until the next year. In 1855 the line was completed to Hermann, 81 miles from St. Louis. Although Hermann was a Missouri River port, the arrival of the railroad did not alter the traditional pattern of St. Louis steamboating. But the completion of the road to Jefferson City in early 1856 had profound effects.[6]

Once the railroad reached a steamboat port in the central part of the state, it was able to challenge steamboats starting from St. Louis by offering through service to river points above Jefferson City by rail and cooperating steamboats. The Missouri Pacific detrimentally affected steamboating in general, but it made Jefferson City a short-lived major port. Initially, the construction of the Missouri Pacific westward from Jefferson City did not hurt the city's steamboat interests, because the company had decided to construct a rather direct line to Kansas City. This route, which ran well south of the Missouri, assured Jefferson City a rather exalted status as a steamboat port until the completion of the Hannibal and St. Joseph Railroad. But even after it lost some business to St. Joseph beginning in 1859, Jefferson City's port was significant until the Missouri Pacific was completed to Kansas City in 1865.

Although the Hannibal and St. Joseph Railroad lagged four years behind the Missouri Pacific in starting construction, it finished its line six years earlier. On February 23, 1859, the eastern and western divisions of the Hannibal and St. Joseph were merged at Chillicothe. The line's rapid construction, relative to that of the

Missouri Pacific, was facilitated by a more favorable federal land grant and greater proceeds from land sales.[7]

Only a week before the Hannibal and St. Joseph was completed, the North Missouri reached it at Macon, 169 miles from St. Louis. The North Missouri, which did not receive a federal land grant but was supported by state bonds, opened from St. Louis to St. Charles in 1855. In 1857 and 1858 it was built from St. Charles by way of Montgomery to Allen, near present Moberly. Ostensibly, the finishing of the line to Macon gave St. Louis direct rail connections with St. Joseph. But the debt-ridden North Missouri had to delay full operations until 1860 for lack of funds to purchase rolling stock. Furthermore, the managers of the Hannibal and St. Joseph and the North Missouri could not agree on a method of dividing the revenues from through freight and passengers. Their initial unwillingness to cooperate was complicated by the natural mutual distrust of the St. Louisians who dominated the North Missouri and the eastern capitalists who had invested heavily in the Hannibal and St. Joseph.[8]

In 1855, as the Missouri Pacific was being built from Hermann toward Jefferson City, its officers thought they would complete the line to the capital city before year's end. This feat would enable them to begin using a rail-steamboat combination to carry passengers and goods to western Missouri and points beyond with the opening of navigation. But their plan was ruined by a great disaster. On November 1, 1855, the train carrying the railroad's officers and guest dignitaries plunged to the bed of the Gasconade River when the bridge collapsed. Thirty-one persons, including the railroad's chief engineer, were killed and many more injured. This tragedy was not only a major public relations setback for the company but also meant that the Gasconade bridge had to be rebuilt before through service could be offered from St. Louis to Jefferson City.[9]

After hurriedly rebuilding the bridge and repairing a number of culverts and embankments that had been ruined by heavy rain, the line's first through locomotive from St. Louis entered Jefferson City on March 12, 1856. Soon thereafter, the *Jefferson Inquirer* announced "a new arrangement" for Missouri River trade and travel. Captains of the steamers *Henry Chouteau, Cataract,* and *F. X. Aubry* agreed with the Missouri Pacific to forward freight from Jefferson City to Weston. Shipping by the combined rail-river route from St. Louis was expected to take only 36 hours.[10]

But the combination did not actually launch service until June 20, when the *Cataract* left the Jefferson City levee. William M. McPherson, president of the Missouri Pacific, announced that the three steamboats chartered by his company were scheduled to offer regular service to the western boundary of the state. One of them would arrive and depart every Tuesday, Thursday, and Saturday. Apparently, the relaying from rail to steamer was delayed by the need to improve the city's wharf. Jefferson City gave the Missouri Pacific a three-block long stretch of waterfront property. The railroad then improved the landing and built a canopy-covered boardwalk from its depot to the docks. To further stimulate business, railroad officials arranged with Albert P. Richardson, owner of the Jefferson City steam ferry, to transport all freight free of charge. This move was intended to make the railroad competitive with steamboats for freight to and from the north side of the river.[11]

A private express service challenged both St. Louis–based steamboats and the Missouri Pacific's boats. In late March 1856, Joseph F. Ritcherdson of St. Louis announced that his daily express would run on the Missouri Pacific to Jefferson City, where it would connect with his river express. His steamboat component consisted of the *Polar Star, F. X. Aubry, Edinburgh,* and *James H. Lucas,* which offered semiweekly service to St. Joseph.[12]

The Missouri Pacific and Ritcherdson's Express combined used only seven of the estimated forty steamers on the Missouri in 1856. The others had to adjust to the new circumstance. One of their tactics was to try to match or beat the railroad's time. However, an attempt by the captain of the descending *New Lucy* took 20 hours longer than the six-hour railroad trip from Jefferson City to St. Louis. Matching railroad charges failed to attract passengers or shippers who wanted faster deliveries.[13]

Despite their new problems, St. Louis's steamboatmen had a definite advantage in exporting hemp and tobacco, both of which originated primarily in the area above Jefferson City. For bulky commodities in large units such as bales and hogsheads, there was no advantage to shippers in transferring them to the railroad at Jefferson City. The time consumed in unloading from the boats, transferring, and reloading on railroad cars would have negated any saving by the railroad's speed. Furthermore, drayage charges and increased manual labor would have made the railroad option costlier than using steamboats exclusively.

Trade statistics show the clear advantage of steamboats in shipping tobacco, hemp, and hemp products. In 1858, St. Louis tobacco receipts in hogsheads were 5,604 by river, 520 by railroad, and 50 by wagon. Tobacco shipments for previous years were all by river. In 1856, 53,636 bales of hemp reached St. Louis by river and only 192 by rail. The next year showed 78,957 by river and 1,137 by rail, and for 1858 the figures were 80,645 by river and 117 by rail. The same pattern prevailed in coils of rope. All of the 57,888 coils in 1856 were shipped by river. In 1857 the shipments were 44,251 by river and 2,233 by rail, and in 1858 there were 68,686 by river and 187 by rail.[14]

Although the Missouri Pacific did not greatly affect the hemp and tobacco trade, it did have some impact on Osage River steamboating. By the fall of 1856, quantities of lead mined in Newton and Jasper counties in southwestern Missouri were being hauled by wagon to the Jefferson City railhead. One miner estimated that a hundred wagonloads of lead would be delivered to the railroad depot by the end of the year. Conversely, Jefferson City became the starting point for wagons loaded with goods for southwestern Missouri and portions of northern Arkansas. Besides the wagon trade, Jefferson City received some steamboat freight from the Osage River.[15]

With a population of 1,924 in early 1857, Jefferson City was poised to continue its usual railroad-steamboat trade. But business exceeded expectations because of a sudden, dramatic action by the federal government. On or about May 20, President James Buchanan and his cabinet decided to send an army westward across the plains and mountains to occupy Utah. The affair, oftentimes called the Mormon War, resulted from long-standing mutual distrust between the government and the Mormons. By the time Brigham Young led his pioneer band to the Great Basin, Mormonism, in the minds of many Americans, was best known for its advocacy of polygamy. The plural-marriage issue was compounded by Mormon insistence that Deseret, their preferred name for Utah, would be a theocratic state where church and civil law would be indistinguishable. Relations became more strained after Franklin Pierce, Buchanan's predecessor, sent federal judges and other officials to Utah. After vying with church courts for jurisdiction, the federal appointees left Utah and reported the Mormon rejection of federal authority to their superiors. By the time Buchanan decided to dispatch troops, he was convinced that the United States was faced with the imminent threat of Utah's secession.[16]

Missouri, like the rest of the nation, had no premonition of Buchanan's decision. Since the president had not mentioned the Mormon question in his inaugural address of March 4, the rationale for the war was shrouded in mystery, and the campaign itself became very controversial.

However, despite any misgivings they may have had, army officials had to quickly organize and outfit an army at Fort Leavenworth, the traditional starting point for western campaigns. In June and July they assembled a 2,500-man Utah expedition and scrambled to purchase supplies and arrange wagon transportation for the approximately 1,200-mile march to Salt Lake City. By Independence Day, St. Louis quartermaster officers had purchased 302 horses, 234 mules, 325 wagons, 5,750 tons of quartermaster and commissary stores, 15,000 bushels of oats, and 70,000 bushels of corn. Although the giant overland freighting company of Russell, Majors, and Waddell was given the transportation contract, the army still had to haul some of its own goods.[17]

As usual, troops moving from east of the Mississippi to Fort Leavenworth were routed through St. Louis. In 1857, quartermaster officers discontinued their previous practice of using only steamboats. During that year they signed nineteen contracts with the Missouri Pacific to transport troops by rail and river from St. Louis to Fort Leavenworth. The transfers, which continued until late October, amounted to 79 officers and 2,859 enlisted men. The railroad had nearly three-fourths of the troop movement business. The eight contracts with individual steamboat captains called for transporting 38 officers and 1,093 men entirely by river. Steamboat rates at $12 per officer and $4.50 per enlisted man were slightly lower than the $13 and $5 charged by the railroad.[18]

Part of the 1857 movement consisted of reinforcements for the Utah-bound army. The expedition was plagued by logistical problems from its beginning. The first troops did not leave Fort Leavenworth until July 18, dooming any chance of reaching Utah before winter. Under increasing scrutiny by a critical press, the Buchanan administration was clearly disappointed when its 2,588-man expedition was forced to winter near Fort Bridger, some 200 miles short of Salt Lake City. The failure to fulfill the mission in 1857 proved to Buchanan and his advisers that they needed many more troops. By mid-January 1858, they decided to dispatch several thousand more men from Fort Leavenworth in the spring. The reinforcements, when assembled that spring, totaled 3,658 men. The combined 1857 and 1858 forces amounted to more than a third of the entire army's authorized size.[19]

The contract for carrying supplies for the massive army from the Missouri River to Utah was again awarded to Russell, Majors, and Waddell, which had to prepare for the contingency that the shipments might exceed 15 million pounds. On the allied matter of getting provisions to Missouri River ports, the army radically changed its procedure. Rather than negotiating many agreements with the Missouri Pacific and various steamboat owners, it decided to make a single contract with the railroad.

On March 1, 1858, Lieutenant Colonel George H. Crosman, deputy quartermaster general in St. Louis, signed a contract with William M. McPherson, president of the Missouri Pacific. They agreed the company would transport goods by rail and river from St. Louis to Missouri River ports as far upstream as Nebraska City. The selection of Nebraska City as a starting point for Utah-bound wagon trains was prompted by dissatisfaction with Fort Leavenworth and the adjacent town of Leavenworth. Alexander Majors, the manager of Russell, Majors, and Waddell's wagon trains, complained that it was impossible to find adequate grazing grounds for thousands of oxen if only one depot was used. The army, for its part, was attracted to Nebraska City because it was closer than Leavenworth to Fort Kearny, the convergence point for various feeder routes of the Oregon-California Trail. By using Nebraska City, 185 miles upstream from Leavenworth, the army shortened the overland distance and lengthened the steamboat route. Any decrease in overland travel would save time and money.[20]

McPherson obligated his company to transport supplies to Nebraska City throughout the navigation season. The rates were to be the same as those charged by "good steamers" at the same time, with the stipulation that freight to Leavenworth or Atchison could not exceed $1 per hundredweight. Express freight, of which 50,000 pounds were to be transported whenever required, commanded an additional 20 percent. Fares for officers and enlisted men were set at $12 and $6 respectively. McPherson agreed to transport 150 tons daily, except Sunday. No specific rates were included for Nebraska City, but the Missouri Pacific was to be paid "the regular current rates at the time."[21]

The contract transformed Nebraska City into an important steamboat port. Majors sent 34 wagon trains, totaling about 850 wagons, from the town.[22]

Although Nebraska City benefited the most from the 1858 army business, the effects of the Mormon War were felt throughout the Missouri River borderlands. The editor of the *Glasgow Weekly Times* observed that "but for the Government freight, for the Utah Rebellion, half of our boats would have been idle all the season."[23]

Obviously, those steamboatmen who forwarded freight and troops for the Missouri Pacific had the best season. Some of those who were excluded from the railroad's government contract business responded by launching a new cooperative arrangement. Once the Missouri Pacific's government contract became known, captains of twelve steamers organized the St. Louis and St. Joseph Union Packet Line. Their association consisted of some of the best-known Missouri River steam-boats—*A. B. Chambers, Ben Lewis, Colonel Crosman, D. A. January, Hesperian, Kate Howard, Minnehaha, Morning Star, Peerless, South Wester, Star of the West,* and *Twilight.* They offered regularly scheduled service, with one daily boat both ways six days of the week. In early July their freight charges from St. Louis to Glasgow and St. Joseph respectively were 25 and 50 cents per hundredweight.[24]

The economic boost to the Missouri River borderland towns from the Mormon War was short-lived. The bloodless conflict resulted in the peaceful entry of federal troops into Utah in the summer of 1858. One of the conditions of the peace arranged by Buchanan's emissaries and Mormon leaders was that troops were banned from occupying Salt Lake City. Military commanders established their main base at Camp Floyd (renamed Fort Crittenden in 1861), near present-day Fairfield, Utah, about 35 miles from the capital.[25]

The resolution of the Mormon issue was not popular in such Missouri River towns as Leavenworth, Atchison, St. Joseph, and Nebraska City. Steamboatmen, freighters, and town businessmen who knew the conflict had stimulated their local economies worried about their future, which was clouded by the lingering effects of the Panic of 1857. Tripped off in October 1857 by the failure of the Ohio Life Insurance Company of New York, the panic hit particularly hard in new frontier areas where overspeculation in land and wildcat banking were rife. By August 1858 the frequency of foreclosures and civil suits to attach property clearly indicated "an indebtedness on the part of many people, and a disposition on the part of whom the money is due, to get it."[26]

Given their dire prospects, it is not at all surprising that the river towns seized on the discovery of gold in the Pikes Peak region as their economic salvation. Long-standing rumors of gold in Colorado were confirmed by some prospectors in August 1858. Sensing the opportunity to launch a rush, the Kansas City *Journal of Commerce* boldly publicized "THE NEW EL DORADO."[27] Within days, journalists in rivaling Leavenworth, Atchison, St. Joseph, and Nebraska City assured erstwhile adventurers that their town had the best trail and merchandising facilities. Clark H. Green, editor of the *Glasgow Weekly Times,* hoping to encourage Pikes Peakers to outfit in his town, confidently told his readers that those who bought outfits in the border towns "from the sharpers who live in them, will get beautifully bit."[28]

Despite intense publicity, the fall migration to the new mining area was subdued. Only several hundred men moved to the region. They started Denver and Aurora and awaited the anticipated 1859 rush.[29]

For steamboatmen, the big question was how gold seekers would reach the starting points of the overland trails. By the opening of navigation, those traveling across Missouri had four main possibilities. They could move by steamboat from St. Louis, by the rail-river route through Jefferson City, by wagon, or on the recently completed Hannibal and St. Joseph Railroad. The Hannibal and St.

Joseph offered the fastest way for anyone starting from east of the Mississippi, but a number of emigrants apparently believed that outfitting in border towns would be too expensive. Others, who did not think that saving several days was important, chose to use steamboats. By March 10 the "tide of emigration . . . towards the new gold fields" was under way. All of the upward-bound boats that passed Glasgow were reported to be "more or less thronged with emigrants." Simultaneously, Glasgow merchants were busily outfitting emigrants moving by wagon.[30]

It is not possible to determine the number of emigrants who moved on the Hannibal and St. Joseph and Missouri River routes. But some contemporary statistics suggest that St. Joseph was the liveliest embarkation point for plains travel. In the week ending April 25 alone, its ferry carried 359 wagons, 1,428 horses and cattle, and 3,096 emigrants across the Missouri. The total extent of the movement to Colorado is likewise elusive. The 1860 federal census for Denver and the outlying gold mining areas showed 34,277 people. But this figure is probably considerably lower than the number who participated in the gold rush. Many of those who failed to find instant riches in 1859 became disillusioned and returned east.[31]

Once steamboat navigation was under way in 1859, it was clear that the Hannibal and St. Joseph Railroad and St. Joseph were the big winners. While the railroad was being completed, some St. Josephites formed the Hannibal and St. Joseph Railroad Packet Line. Their boats ran southward to Atchison, Leavenworth, and Kansas City and northward to Nebraska City, Council Bluffs, and Omaha. The business to Nebraska City, the sole starting point for Utah freight in 1859, was especially important. Although the Utah army was sharply reduced soon after the Mormon War, the Utah Department still had 3,164 men on June 30, 1859. The regular service of the Hannibal and St. Joseph Railroad Packet Line dominated the Nebraska City trade. From May through November, Nebraska City had 212 steamboat arrivals, which delivered 9,280 tons of freight. Voyages for the 128 miles from St. Joseph to Nebraska City usually took two days. But a record trip of the *William Campbell* was completed in only 22 hours and 50 minutes.[32]

Steamboat service south from St. Joseph soon had to adjust to the construction of the Platte County Railroad. In 1860 that line was completed from St. Joseph to Winthrop, opposite Atchison, and in April of the next year the remaining 16 miles to Weston was finished. The Weston railhead then became the connecting point for steamboats servicing Kansas City. Captain Samuel Burks, operator of the *Emilie*, made daily trips during the navigation season.[33]

The effect of the Hannibal and St. Joseph Railroad was evident in other ways. With rail connections to Chicago and points east, except for the gap from Quincy, Illinois, to Hannibal, St. Joseph could lessen its dependence on St. Louis and other Missouri points. The railroad's far-reaching impact was demonstrated in 1859 when the Leavenworth and Pikes Peak Express Company shipped 236 mules from Pennsylvania to St. Joseph. This and similar actions caused St. Louisians and some other Missourians to resent the Hannibal and St. Joseph, which they saw as being in league with hated Chicago.[34]

By 1860 the Hannibal and St. Joseph controlled most of the troop movements from St. Louis and Jefferson Barracks to Fort Leavenworth. After granting the Missouri Pacific a monopoly in 1858, the army reverted to its previous practice of making contracts for each consignment of troops. In 1860, St. Louis quartermaster officers signed six contracts with John H. Bowen, a railroad and steamboat agent, to transport troops and stores on the Hannibal and St. Joseph and connecting steamboats. The charge for officers was normally $10 and that for enlisted men, laundresses, and servants $3. The only contract devoted exclusively to freight specified a rate of 81 cents per hundredweight. But the army also used some steamboats all the way from St. Louis at rates about the same as those charged by the Hannibal and St. Joseph. The transportation of troops to and from points above St. Joseph, such as Omaha and Sioux City, followed the same pattern. Sometimes they moved in part over the Hannibal and St. Joseph, and in other instances they rode steamboats all the way to or from St. Louis.[35]

For the St. Louis business, the Hannibal and St. Joseph Railroad preferred to use its own steamboat connections rather than cooperate with the North Missouri Railroad. In 1860 the "Hannibal & St. Joseph Railroad & Steam Packet Lines" offered "the cheapest, quickest and most reliable route for Kansas City, Leavenworth City, St. Joseph, Nebraska City, Omaha, Council Bluffs, Sioux City, and the new gold mines." The company's steamers left St. Louis daily at 4:00 P.M. for Hannibal. At 10:30 the next morning a train left Hannibal for an 11-hour daily trip to St. Joseph. Thus travelers from St. Louis could reach St. Joseph in 29 hours and 30 minutes. Upstream and downstream packets were scheduled to leave St. Joseph "immediately on arrival of trains."[36]

St. Joseph's increased importance as a transportation center helped boom its population to 8,932 in 1860, about double that of Kansas City. At a time when there was considerable speculation about the emergence of a metropolis on Missouri's western border, the two cities were serious rivals. Kansas City was the mistress of the Santa Fe trade, but St. Joseph, in 1860, was designated as the starting point for the Pony Express and had the region's main cattle market.[37]

The effects of the North Missouri Railroad on steamboating were modest relative to those of the Hannibal and St. Joseph. Nonetheless, the North Missouri had an impact on some of the trade to St. Charles, and even before it reached Macon, it affected passenger and mail service. Its station at Allen, 6 miles east of Huntsville, was only about 25 miles northeast of Glasgow. By stagecoaches from Glasgow to Allen and rail to St. Louis, passengers and mail could be delivered in only 24 hours.[38]

In 1859 St. Louis steamboatmen created another organization to combat the railroad threat. Rather than attempting to revive the St. Louis and St. Joseph Union Packet Line, they formed the more-inclusive Missouri River Association to regulate all St. Louis–based packets that plied the Missouri. The organization was managed by a president and board of directors, who determined rates and schedules. Earnings were pooled and then divided according to the capacity of each boat. To provide regular service, the association started only one boat each day. Several captains tried to run their boats independently but found they could not match the association's through rates on passengers and freight, which at least matched railroad charges. While through passengers and shippers benefited from the new low rates, the association charged more for waypoints such as Glasgow, Brunswick, and Lexington, where there was no competing railroad.[39]

Probably because of resistance from shippers and some of its own members, the association was not renewed in 1860, a year of declining steamboat fortunes. Faced with a persistent drought and low water, steamboatmen raised their rates sharply. In the normally good navigation months of April and May, rates per hundred-weight from St. Louis to Weston and Council Bluffs peaked at $0.75 and $1.50 respectively. These high charges caused shippers of hemp and other articles to move large quantities of their commodities by rail from St. Joseph to Hannibal.[40]

In retrospect, the 1850s is regarded as the "golden age" of steamboating on most of the Mississippi River system. However, the label certainly is not apt for the upper Missouri, where most frontier development did not occur until after the Civil War. In terms of the number of steamboat landings, the lower Missouri trade peaked in the late 1850s.[41] In 1856 there were a reported 40 steamers on that portion of the river, and the next year the Kansas City wharfmaster recorded his city's combined number of arrivals and departures at 725. Glasgow's arrivals and departures in 1859 amounted to 715.[42]

The Glasgow landings were made by 57 different steamers. Several, including the *Chippewa* bound for Fort Benton, made only one stop. On the high side, the regular packets *Skylark* and *Emma* landed 34 and 26 times respectively.[43]

The author's study of 56 of the boats on which data could be obtained shows some interesting comparisons and contrasts to the steamboats registered at the St. Louis customhouse in 1848. Like the 1848 fleet, the 1859 boats, with 49 side-wheelers and 7 stern-wheelers, showed the continued dominance of side-wheeled rigs. Relative newness was another similarity. Less than one-fourth of the 1859 steamers were older than three years. The determination of building sites shows that Pittsburgh and environs had retained its prominence and St. Louis had suffered a relative decline. Of the 56 vessels, 19 were built in Pittsburgh and nearby Pennsylvania communities; 9 in Cincinnati; 9 in Jeffersonville, Indiana; 7 in St. Louis; 6 in Louisville; and 6 in other Ohio River sites.[44]

The major difference between the two fleets was that the 1859 boats were much larger than those of 1848. The median tonnage of the 1859 craft was 376 and only 173 for 1848. Average tonnages for 1848 and 1859 were 239 and 368 respectively. Part of the increased tonnage for the 1859 boats was accomplished by the continuing modification of steamboat hulls to increase the length-to-tonnage ratio. Some of the 1859 boats had a capacity of about 2 tons or more for every foot of length. The dimensions of the five longest 1859 steamboats illustrate this point (table 5).

During the late 1850s, social life on some Missouri River steamers was changed by the introduction of the calliope, or steam piano. Intended to entertain passen-

TABLE 5

LENGTH AND TONNAGE OF

THE FIVE LONGEST 1859 STEAMBOATS

Name	Length (feet)	Tonnage
Alonzo Child	236.0	493
B. W. Lewis	236.5	472
Kate Howard	235.0	504
Minnehaha	236.0	531
T. L. McGill	238.0	598

Source: See note 44 of chapter 6.

gers and spectators, the "steam pianer" of the *Twilight* disappointed the editor of the *Glasgow Weekly Times*. He complained that "it blowed 'Yankee Doodle' sky high and tore 'Susanna' wide open! It's an awful instrument, and we should guess a decided bore to passengers, however much it may amuse outsiders." However, about six weeks later when the calliope on the *Kate Howard* serenaded Glasgow, he was willing to concede that familiarity might make calliopes more acceptable, but he insisted that the instrument was "a very doubtful appendage, either for use or ornament."[45]

Calliopes were installed in only some of the packets, but they became regular and heavily used fixtures on the circus steamboats that toured Missouri River towns. In July 1858, "the Great Monkey Circus and Burlesque Dramatic Troupe," which was really the Spalding and Rogers Circus, advertised that the approach of its steamers *Banjo* and *James Raymond* would be signaled by "a new, enlarged, and improved CALLIOPE," which "in certain states of the atmosphere, will be distinctly audible for ten miles." In addition to its acting monkeys, dogs and goats, the circus featured a "SAX HORN BAND OF BEAUTIFUL YOUNG LADIES ... Donnetti's world renowned DIORAMIC DISSOLVING VIEWS ... AND BILLY BIRCH'S MINSTRELS."[46]

Rather than setting up onshore, the circus was performed on the two steamers, which were fitted up as showboats with stages and theater-like seating. The *Banjo*, which was considerably smaller than the *James Raymond*, had a seating capacity of two hundred. In their 1858 appearance at Glasgow, the animals and sax horn band performed first on the *Banjo*. Then spectators, who paid 50 cents for adults and a quarter for children under twelve, could shift to the *James Raymond* to hear the minstrels.[47]

G. R. Spalding, the circus's "managing proprietor," radically changed his troupe by 1859. When the *James Raymond* reappeared for performances at Glasgow, Brunswick, Cambridge, and other nearby towns, it had become a "European Circus," featuring gymnasts from France, Germany, England, Spain, and the United States. But Spalding also included minstrels and "the Museum of Living Wonders," which had a thirty-two-foot-boa constrictor and a fifteen-foot anaconda.[48] The *Banjo* failed to keep its later appointment because "some of the actors got into a mess while at Boonville; a pistol was used, and a woman shot in the difficulty, but not seriously hurt. The boat returned to St. Louis."[49] But the *Banjo* was back in 1860 with its "world-renowned" black minstrels who were to "pick the banjo, rattle the bones, sing songs and dance jigs."[50]

In the mid- to late 1850s the opportunities for Missouri River steamboatmen were expanded somewhat by Kansas River navigation. The operation of the first steamer on the Kansas was prompted by a change in the federal government's military frontier. Responding to an army recommendation, Congress in 1853 authorized the establishment of a new fort at a point near the juncture of the Republican and Smoky Hills rivers, the start of the Kansas River. Army officials believed that the site would not only provide the best protection for the Oregon and Santa Fe routes but would also enable them to phase out Fort Leavenworth, Fort Kearny, and several other posts.[51]

When Fort Riley was started in the summer of 1853, Edmund A. Ogden, its quartermaster officer, carried out his superiors' orders and arranged a survey of the Kansas River. Second Lieutenant Joseph L. Tidball, leader of the reconnaissance, concluded that he was "strongly impelled to the belief that there is a period of from two to four months of the year, dating from the first spring rise, during which boats can ascend"[52] to Fort Riley. Tidball's qualified observation was sufficient to cause some army officials to think there would be annual arrivals of steamboats at Fort Riley, 243 miles from Kansas City.

In 1854 Charles A. Perry and steamboat Captain Charles K. Baker seemingly proved that Fort Riley was indeed the head of navigation. Perry, of Weston, Missouri, was a part owner of the *Excel*, a 79-ton side-wheeler, and used it to ship 1,100 barrels of flour from Weston to Fort Riley in April 1854. The voyage, made during an unusually heavy rainy period, took only two days. On the boat's second trip that season, Perry fulfilled his contract to deliver 7,000 bushels of corn to the fort. His agreement also specified that he was to be paid $1.25 per hundred pounds for transporting "all such public stores as may be turned over to him" from Fort Leavenworth to Fort Riley.[53]

Any expectation that steamboat arrivals at the fort would be regular occurrences was subsequently dispelled. After the *Excel*, only two other steamers reached Fort Riley. The *Financier No. 2*, a 117-ton side-wheeler, not only reached the fort in 1855, but took a side trip about 40 miles up the Republican River to about present-day Clay Center, Kansas. Four years later, the *Colonel Gus Linn*, an 83-ton stern-wheeler, delivered freight to the post.[54]

Most of the Kansas River steamers were used to supply towns that started soon after the opening of the territory. Some townsite planners apparently chose riverside locations in the expectation that they would be supplied by steamboats. However, steamers usually could not be navigated above Topeka and oftentimes were forced to stop farther downstream, at Lawrence. Active settlement of the Kansas River valley attracted six steamboats in 1855 other than the *Financier No. 2*. Of these, the *Hartford* undertook the most ambitious voyage, to near Fort Riley.[55]

The Cincinnati and Kansas Land Company chartered the *Hartford*, a 143-ton stern-wheeler, for moving some of its members from Cincinnati to Manhattan. Crammed with perhaps as many as 150 passengers, a dozen or so houses, a steam sawmill, a gristmill, groceries, and personal belongings, the 146-foot-long steamer was easily navigated by Captain David Millard on the Ohio, Mississippi, and Missouri to Kansas City. The one- and two-story wooden Cincinnati houses it carried had been partially constructed in their namesake city and shipped in parts. Such prefab buildings were appealing expedients on the frontier, where skilled carpenters and lumber were always in short supply.[56]

Low water stopped the *Hartford* a few miles above the Big Blue, a short distance from its goal. The colonists unloaded the cargo, but the boat was stuck at the site for a month. Freed by a rise, the boat was stalled again and accidentally destroyed by fire.

After 1855, three to five steamers made at least one trip on the Kansas each year until the Civil War. Their business was fed by Missouri River steamers, which delivered thousands of emigrants to Kansas City. On one trip in April 1856 the *Keystone* was crowded with more than 400 aspiring settlers from the South. The large migration of the next year featured movement by railroad to Jefferson City and heavily loaded steamboats, including a passage of about 400 emigrants on a single voyage of the *David Tatum*. But during the tumultuous rivalry between free and slave proponents in Kansas, many people quit the territory. In the fall of 1856 some short-term Kansans moved by steamers to Jefferson City before boarding Missouri Pacific cars.[57] Within a month, the *Jefferson Inquirer* reported that "the misguided emigrants who crowded to Kansas in the spring, continue to leave that Territory in all directions. Every descending steamboat brings some of them and others have gone overland through Iowa."[58]

For the period 1854–1866, a total of about 30 steamboats were used on the Kansas River. Generally, their operators adjusted to navigating the shallow, crooked, sandbar-infested stream by using the smallest craft available. Among the most successful boats were the 62-ton *Lewis Burnes* and the 83-ton *Colonel Gus Linn*. Larger regular Missouri River packets made an occasional voyage when conditions permitted. None of the Kansas River steamers could be regarded as regulars in the sense that they were navigated on the river for a period of time or for even several years. Rather, as traders on the connected waterway that included the Missouri, Mississippi, and Illinois rivers, they were sometimes booked for voyages up the Kansas.[59]

As steamboating was being pioneered on the Kansas, commerce on the upper Missouri was increased by the start of an army post, the founding of Sioux City, Iowa, the creation of Dakota Territory, and federal government activities that encouraged the extension of steamboating to Fort Benton.

Fort Randall, established in June 1856 on the right bank of the Missouri about 37 miles above the Niobrara's mouth, resulted from the army's first conflict with the Sioux. Tensions between some Lakota (i.e., Teton Sioux) bands and Oregon

Trail emigrants led to an outbreak of hostilities in August 1854 near Fort Laramie. The triggering event, which frontier whites remembered as the "Grattan Massacre," was an immediate outcome of an Indian's killing of an emigrant's stray cow. Acting on a complaint by the cow's owner and irked by some earlier killings of emigrant livestock, the Fort Laramie commander decided to make an example of the culprit. Brevet Second Lieutenant John L. Grattan, with twenty-nine men, rushed to a sprawling encampment of about 2,000 Lakotas, who had assembled along the trail to await the arrival of government annuities. Misunderstanding, compounded by talking through an interpreter and the foolhardiness of the vastly outnumbered troops in firing the first shots, led to the death of Grattan, all of his men, and Conquering Bear, a Brûlé Sioux chief.[60]

After the incident, some Lakotas, upset by the killing of their chief, lashed out at convenient targets, including traders and mail carriers. Believing that these raids imperiled safe passage on the Oregon-California Trail, army officials reinforced Fort Laramie in the fall. Then, over the winter, they developed a grand strategy, which was approved by Congress. It called for sending a large force, led by Brevet Brigadier General William S. Harney, on a punitive expedition and the addition of a fort on the Missouri in the general vicinity of Fort Pierre, some 200 miles north of the Oregon-California Trail. The new post, working in concert with Forts Kearny and Laramie, was intended to check movements of hostile Indians.[61]

The War Department began preparing for the new fort about four months before Harney's expedition left Fort Leavenworth. Quartermaster General Thomas S. Jesup's inclination was to buy Fort Pierre from Pierre Chouteau, Jr., and Company rather than erect a completely new post. The army's interest in the trading post dated from at least 1849, when Colonel Aeneas Mackay, deputy quartermaster at St. Louis, visited to assess its suitability for army use. Mackay was then on an inspection tour of western forts, which also included a visit to Fort Laramie.[62]

In a letter of March 23, 1855, Jesup instructed Major David H. Vinton, the St. Louis quartermaster, to solicit updated information on Fort Pierre. A week later, Vinton responded that he had talked with Chouteau company partner John B. Sarpy, who pointed out that the fort was not suitable for a large military force because it was too old and too small and lacked nearby forage and timber. Although he had an unfavorable opinion of Fort Pierre, Vinton nonetheless wrote that "it must be concluded there is no place on the Missouri more eligible in view of the communications to be kept up with Fort Laramie."[63] Jesup agreed. On April 14 he signed a purchase agreement with Charles Gratiot, agent for the Chouteau company. The government agreed to pay $45,000 for the Fort Pierre site "with the building appurtenances, and building materials on the island and mainland."[64]

To ready the post for Harney's force, the government sent troops, civilian workers, supplies, and provisions by steamboats from St. Louis. Vinton had recommended to Jesup that the army purchase one or more light-draft steamers to do this work, but the need to act quickly caused the Quartermaster Department to use private contractors. From late May to mid-June, Vinton signed contracts with J.

Cheever of the *Clara*, Barton Able of the *Australia*, Pierre Chouteau, Jr., and Company of the *Kate Swinney*, John Shaw of the *Arabia*, B. Johnson of the *Sonora*, and Joseph Throckmorton of the *Genoa*. The first five contracts had identical terms. The contractors agreed to transport officers for $35 each and enlisted men, laundresses, and servants for $15 each. The freight rate was graduated according to the river's navigability. If it was unsafe to carry more than 180 tons because of low water, the rate was $3.70 per hundred pounds. Loads of 200 to 249 tons were to be transported for $3.40 and those of 250 or more at $3. Captain Throckmorton agreed to those freight payments but accepted lower passenger rates of $30 per officer and $12 per enlisted man.[65] With the exception of the *Kate Swinney*, which Chouteau was sending to Fort Union, the steamers had Fort Pierre as their final destination.

Before the first vessel reached Fort Pierre, Vinton had to replace the *Australia* and the *Sonora* with the *Grey Cloud* and the *William Baird*. The upbound *Australia* was snagged and sank in shallow water. Although salvagers later retrieved it, the boat was not used to supply Fort Pierre. For some reason the *Sonora* did not make the trip.

As the steamboats arrived in July and August, the Fort Pierre workforce was enlarged to several hundred men. Captain Henry W. Wessels led the advance party of 275 officers and men, which traveled on the *Arabia*, *Grey Cloud*, and *William Baird*. This vanguard was bolstered in August by the arrivals of the *Clara* and *Genoa*, with 155 officers and men. Wessels also employed 61 civilians who performed a variety of tasks, including herding, woodcutting, and haying. Because traders had exhausted the nearby supplies of wood, hay, and pasturage, Wessels's workers had to range far afield to supply the post.[66]

The usual variety of quartermaster supplies and commissary goods delivered by the steamboats included some very novel housing. Portable cottages, precut to specifications and transported in parts, were designed by quartermaster Captain Parmenas T. Turnley, whose superiors thought they would prove their worth in the plains environment. Turnley had a number of cottages built by woodworking firms in Cincinnati (perhaps the same companies that built Cincinnati houses for Kansas) and shipped to Fort Pierre by way of St. Louis. Arriving at Fort Pierre on July 13, the steamers *Grey Cloud* and *William Baird* brought 37 cottages, which were subsequently assembled into barracks, officers' quarters, storehouses, and the post hospital.[67]

To resupply the burgeoning Fort Pierre complement, Vinton arranged to send another steamer relatively late in the navigation season. His agreement of August 25 with Captain Joseph La Barge of the *Saint Mary* reflected the usual higher rates of low-water periods. La Barge was to be paid $5 per hundredweight for freight from either St. Louis or Fort Leavenworth. Vinton also agreed to pay the cabin rate of $35 for civilian "mechanics" as well as officers.[68]

On August 4, when work on Fort Pierre was well under way, Harney led troops northwestward from Fort Leavenworth. After sixteen days of slogging along the oftentimes muddy trail, the expedition reached Fort Kearny. Thomas S. Twiss,

Indian agent at Fort Laramie, informed the tribesmen that Harney would be moving into their country and instructed all those who wanted to indicate their peaceful intentions to move south of the Platte. Agreeable to this policy, Harney, who had left Fort Kearny with a 600-man force, was determined to attack the first Indians he met north of the Platte. He got his opportunity on September 23 when he encountered a Brûlé encampment on Blue Water Creek, six miles north of the North Platte, and rejected Chief Little Thunder's willingness to parley. The ensuing battle, identified as either the Battle of Blue Water or the Battle of Ash Hollow, was a smashing victory for Harney's expedition, and Harney was apparently satisfied that he had demonstrated the government's authority, which he seemed set on doing.[69]

After the battle, Harney delivered his prisoners to Fort Laramie. Continuing to display his power, on September 29 he commenced his expedition's 325-mile march through Sioux lands over the well-established traders' trail to Fort Pierre. When he arrived on October 19, Harney's unified command—including some reinforcements led from Fort Ridgely, Minnesota, by Captain Alfred Sully—amounted to nearly 1,200 officers and men. Quartering, sheltering, and feeding this assemblage taxed the fort's inadequate facilities. The summertime work had failed to restore the dilapidated buildings, and Harney, like Wessels, was shocked by the exhaustion of forage and timber. To help solve the resource shortages, Harney had three cantonments, staffed by a total of 664 officers and men, established at points 7, 12, and 28 miles upstream. Harney, with 20 officers, 486 enlisted men, and a number of unreported civilian workers, wintered at Fort Pierre. Their portable, leaky cottages, which were not finished inside, were little more than windbreaks.[70]

One severe winter was enough to convince Harney that Fort Pierre had deteriorated so much that it could not be repaired. His solution was to establish a new post about 250 miles downstream. He selected the site of Fort Randall on June 3, 1856, and at about the same time sent part of his command to a camp near the remnants of Fort Lookout, a post established by the Columbia Fur Company in 1822. The camp, designated Fort Lookout, was intended to police potential Indian hostiles in the area, but it was phased out in about a year. In late July, when Harney started transferring his main body to Fort Randall, he left two companies at Fort Pierre to safeguard the installation and some provisions.[71]

To supply Fort Pierre, Fort Lookout, and Fort Randall and assist in the transference of men, equipment, ordnance, and provisions, Major Vinton in St. Louis contracted with several steamboat captains. On May 13, 1856, Jackson Ivers of the *A. C. Goddin* agreed to carry freight to Fort Pierre for $3 per hundredweight. Within four weeks, officers of the *Amazon* and the *Emma* accepted the same rate to Fort Pierre, with the stipulation that goods delivered to intermediate points would be prorated on the basis of an assumed 1,500 miles to Fort Pierre.[72]

Later in the summer Captain John Shaw of the steamer *Clara* contracted for a series of movements. He agreed to transport five civilian workers from Fort Lookout to Fort Randall for $5 each and parts of a sawmill from a temporary camp at the mouth of the White River to the new post for $1.50. For each officer he moved from Fort Pierre to either Fort Lookout or Fort Randall, he was to be paid $10. The single-largest item in the contract was for transporting a battalion of infantry with their personal baggage from Fort Pierre to St. Louis at $30 per officer, $11 per enlisted man, and $2.50 per hundred pounds of freight. Part of the reduction of men and provisions on the upper Missouri included shifting army property from Fort Randall to Fort Leavenworth. For this service, Shaw was to be reimbursed at $2 per hundred pounds. Use of the steamers was supplemented by rafting. Some of the pre-fab cottages at Fort Pierre's were dismantled and floated down to Fort Randall.[73]

Near the end of the 1856 navigation season, the Quartermaster Department decided to follow up on Vinton's idea of operating its own steamers on the Missouri. Lieutenant Colonel George H. Crosman, Vinton's successor, arranged to purchase the *D. H. Morton* and have the *Mink* built.

On September 13, 1856, in St. Louis, O. B. Tharp sold the *D. H. Morton* to the army for $20,000. The 173-ton side-wheeler had been completed at Cincinnati earlier in the year. Soon after purchasing it, Crosman sent the *D. H. Morton* to the upper Missouri for use in troop and supply movements in the Fort Pierre–Fort Randall area. It never returned to St. Louis that season. In February 1857, when the boat was stranded 80 miles below Fort Randall, Crosman hired Henry A. Dix in St. Louis to pilot her. Dix agreed to work for $500 a month, "the usual ration, and $100 to defray expenses in going to the steamer." On the same day, Crosman employed James A. Dobbins to serve as the boat's first engineer. Dobbins, who was given the same travel allowance as Dix, agreed to work for $160 monthly.[74]

Once the *D. H. Morton* was operative, Captain Turner had it steamed to Sioux City to obtain provisions. When it tied up at the Sioux City levee on April 6, it gained the distinction of being the year's first steamboat arrival. Even after this first trip, Crosman continued making arrangements. On May 7, 1857, he hired W. C. Chappell in St. Louis to serve as an engineer at $150 monthly and the "usual ration." Then on June 13, he signed an agreement with S. A. Turner to subsist the officers and steamer's crew for 60 cents per day each.[75]

In early June the *D. H. Morton* was used to move men and freight to Fort Randall from Fort Pierre and other camps and then made two trips from St. Louis with supplies for Fort Randall. In 1858 the *D. H. Morton* made its last trip to the upper Missouri with the delivery of 175 soldiers to Fort Randall. On March 11, 1859, the steamer caught fire and burned on the Arkansas River while being used to carry supplies to Fort Smith.[76]

At about the same time he purchased the *D. H. Morton,* Crosman arranged to have another steamer built in St. Louis. He contracted with George B. Boomer and Company to build the hull and cabin for the boat, which was to be 170 × 32 feet, with a 5.5-foot hold. Boomer, who also had to provide a pilothouse, two yawls, and four derricks agreed to do the work for $11,542. For $4,714.90, Edward Boyle agreed to construct the boat's two boilers and two chimneys. The firm of McCords and Beck contracted to remove the engines from the steamer *Elephant,* put them in working order, and install them in the new boat for $3,625. For superintending the construction, which was to be completed by March 1, 1857, A. R. McNair was paid $250 monthly.[77]

Once completed in 1857, the brown-painted boat was named the *Mink*. To subsist its crew, Crosman contracted with E. N. Tracy of St. Louis, who was to be paid 60 cents per man daily. In the *Mink*'s first season, she was used for a month above Sioux City in troop movements involving the consolidation of Fort Randall and the abandonment of Fort Pierre. In both 1858 and 1859 the *Mink* carried troops and supplies from St. Louis to Fort Randall. Its 1859 voyage to Fort Randall was very difficult. To adjust to shallow water, the boat's officers had 60 tons of freight off-loaded at Omaha. Somewhat lightened, the *Mink* was able to reach Fort Randall but had to double-trip the remainder of its initial cargo from Omaha.[78]

The *Mink* outlasted the *D. H. Morton* by some fifteen months. In late June or early July 1860, apparently while engaged in the St. Louis–Fort Leavenworth trade, the steamer sank near Brunswick. On July 3, A. D. Fleak of St. Louis agreed to repair it "in a substantial manner so as to enable it to reach St. Louis safely." Fleak's compensation was $1,500. Soon after this repair the army sold the *Mink* to private parties, who renamed it the *Alexander Majors* after the famous wagon freighter.[79]

The army's abandonment of Forts Pierre and Lookout in June 1857 and the consolidation of their garrisons at Fort Randall coincided with the urgent assembling of the Utah Expedition at Fort Leavenworth. While the *D. H.* Morton and the *Mink* were involved in the Fort Pierre–Fort Randall business, the army had to have hundreds of troops moved from Fort Randall to Fort Leavenworth. Under compulsion to act quickly, Captain Thomas L. Brent, Fort Leavenworth's quartermaster, chartered the 385-ton *Emma* from Captain James A. Yore for $10,000 to make the Fort Leavenworth–Fort Randall round-trip. At 211 feet long and 35 feet wide, the year-old steamer was one of the largest on the Missouri.[80]

After the reduction of Fort Randall's garrison in 1857, the army supplemented the use of the *D. H. Morton* and the *Mink* with several privately contracted steamers. In late October 1857, after some upbound Fort Randall freight had been deposited at Sioux City because of low water, the 147-ton side-wheeler *Omaha City* was sent to deliver it to the fort. The boat managed to reach the post but, while attempting to return, was stranded near the James River for the winter. In 1859 and 1860 Joseph Throckmorton, with his steamer *Florence*, was the main contractor. In 1860 he was paid $40 and $12 respectively to transport officers and enlisted men, laundresses, and servants from St. Louis to the fort. The freight rates were $2 per hundredweight from St. Louis and $1.50 from Fort Leavenworth. By that time Fort Randall was advertised as the *Florence*'s last stop on its regular service above Omaha.[81]

From 1857 to 1863, Fort Randall was the only army post on the upper Missouri. As such, its garrison was responsible for policing the northern plains extending to the Yellowstone River. Although the fort was serviced by steamboats during the navigation season, it was also connected to Sioux City by an overland stage and freight route. Dr. Elias J. Marsh, while ascending on the steamer *Spread Eagle* in

1859, reported that the fort, which then was garrisoned by nearly 400 men, was the last place from which letters could be posted. This extension of a regular government service gave Fort Randall a symbolic importance. It lay in the transition zone between the advancing agricultural frontier and the vast Indian country where the fur traders still held sway. To those who equated white settlement with civilization, Fort Randall was the gateway to an uncivilized land.[82]

Until 1856, with the exception of steamers used by traders and the army, Council Bluffs and Omaha were the last destinations of regular St. Louis packets. That pattern was changed by the advance of a farming frontier into northwestern Iowa and the start of Sioux City.

Dr. John K. Cook was attracted to the Sioux City site while surveying northwestern Iowa under a federal government contract in 1854. The following winter Cook platted the townsite on the stable left bank of the Missouri at the mouth of the Floyd River. He selected a good steamboat landing and strategically placed the town a few miles downstream from the mouth of the Big Sioux River, which marked part of Iowa's western boundary. From its start, Sioux City was intended to be the gateway to the lands across the Big Sioux, which were still claimed by the Yankton Sioux.

In the summer of 1855, Cook and some powerful associates—including Iowa's U.S. senators, Augustus C. Dodge and George E. Jones—formed the Sioux City Company to develop the townsite. Realizing the importance of government functions, they got a federal district land office with S. P. Yeomans, a state legislator and friend of Senator Jones, as its register. The land office, which opened in October 1855, was one of the town's first buildings. By Christmas of that year Sioux City consisted of only seven log buildings. The population reportedly swelled to 150 by the spring of 1856, when the town was made the county seat. On January 16, 1857, Sioux City was incorporated by the state legislature.[83]

The earliest Sioux Citians moved overland, but until such time as they had a railroad, they depended on St. Louis–based steamboats for supplies. James A. Jackson, the town's pioneer merchant, arranged for the first steamboat delivery. With his partner Milton Tootle, Jackson also had stores at Council Bluffs and Omaha and was well acquainted with St. Louis merchants and steamboatmen. When the *Omaha*, a 307-ton, 206-foot side-wheeler, arrived at Sioux City in June 1856, it was loaded with some $70,000 worth of goods, including a steam sawmill, furniture, dry goods, hardware, lumber, and groceries. Before the end of the season there were three more steamer landings.[84]

Because of Fort Randall activity and a modest boom in settlement, Sioux City steamboating increased sharply in 1857. By early July there were twenty-eight arrivals at the levee. The regular St. Louis packets, the *Omaha* and the *Asa Wilgus*, had each made three landings. Eight landings were made by boats involved with the Fort Randall business and three by traders on their way to the Fort Union region.[85]

Like other frontier villages on the Missouri, Sioux City initially had to import virtually everything. Its residents depended on St. Louis and an infrequent steamer direct from Cincinnati for iron, lumber, manufactured goods, liquor, groceries, and other items, including ready-made houses. In July 1857 the *Asa Wilgus* brought up eight prefab houses, which were soon erected.[86]

Living 825 miles from St. Louis, Sioux Citians paid higher rates than other Missouri River townspeople. During most of the 1857 season, the *Omaha* and *Asa Wills* transported hundreds of tons at $1.75 to $1.95 per hundredweight. By early October, when the *E. M. Ryland* arrived, the rate had advanced to $2.75, with the expectation that any deliveries later in the fall would cost at least $3 and probably $3.50. The rates were disproportionately higher than those to downstream ports. Because of less competition, boatmen who ventured above Council Bluffs and Omaha were able to charge more. In May 1858 the prevailing rate to Sioux City was $2, slightly more than three times the 0.65 charged to Council Bluffs.[87]

S. W. Swiggett, the editor of the *Sioux City Eagle* and the town's self-appointed rate arbiter, commended the captains of the *Asa Wilgus* and the *Omaha* for charging consistent, fair rates but condemned the officers of such transient steamers as the *Ben Bolt* and the *Emigrant* for price gouging. These "outside boats," as Swiggett labeled them, did not attempt to foster goodwill, as the regular packets did. When the going rate of the regular packets was under $2, the officers of the *Ben Bolt* charged $6 to deliver two boxes with a combined weight of 115 pounds. For larger consignments, the transients charged about two and half times as much as the regular packets. Swiggett suggested that Sioux Citians could avoid being swindled if they did not ship on such transients as the *Ben Bolt* and the *Emigrant* and relied only on the regular packets. Swiggett's attitude about the regular packets and transients was in keeping with the tradition of other river towns. Captains of the regular packets curried local favor by doing such things as holding community dances on their boats, calling on town dignitaries, and, perhaps most importantly, advertising in town newspapers. The transients seem to have dropped in unannounced and acted like they might never return. Officers of the transient *Dan Converse* refused to pay a supply bill at a Sioux City store and flouted a legal writ of attachment by fleeing downstream.[88]

Of all the steamers that visited Sioux City, the *Omaha* was clearly the community favorite. It was remembered as the first arrival, and for the three seasons—beginning in 1857, when it was commanded by Andrew Wineland—it was given special attention by the Sioux City press. Part of the reason may have been that the highly reputed Wineland became identified with the community. After his death in October 1859, the *Omaha* was obtained by the Hannibal and St. Joseph Railroad for its St. Joseph to Council Bluffs–Omaha trade. The 1860 coverage of the *Sioux City Register,* the *Eagle*'s successor, indicates that Sioux City's new favorites were Captain Joseph Throckmorton and his *Florence.*[89]

Feeling their remoteness from St. Louis, Sioux Citians thought the best steamers were the fastest ones. Steamboat operators, well aware of the public's speed mania, raced against the clock to establish their status. The *Asa Wilgus* set a record when it arrived in Sioux City on July 17, 1857, in 8 days and 18 hours. But two days later the *Omaha* bested the time by 2 hours. On another ascent several weeks later, Wineland raced the *Omaha* from St. Louis to Sioux City. As the vessel approached the Pearl Street levee, Wineland flew a painted streamer proclaiming:

ST. LOUIS AND SIOUX CITY UNITED!
SEVEN DAYS AND SIXTEEN HOURS!
HARD TO BEAT!

For an added flourish, Wineland fired a salute of seven cannon shots—one for each day of the trip—as the *Omaha* approached the cheering crowd on the levee. Before the season was done, the citizens of Omaha presented Wineland with a pair of elk horns for reaching them in six days from St. Louis. By prominently displaying the horns on the *Omaha*'s pilothouse, Wineland stood as the new speed king. Not to be outdone by Omahans, Swiggett pledged that the *Eagle* intended to present Wineland another pair.[90]

Other than playing their speed games, steamboatmen sometimes tried to prove their boat's superiority by pushing it up some previously unnavigated tributary. Bragging rights may have been one of their motivations, but such ventures were usually encouraged by land seekers and townsite promoters who realized the economic advantages of being located on a navigable stream. In those areas where steamboat navigation was the most modern form of transportation, people naturally tried to extend it into questionable waters. As part of their promotion of the Big Sioux River valley, boosters from Sioux City and elsewhere asserted that steamboats could ascend the river for 100 miles, or within about 10 miles of present Sioux Falls, South Dakota.

Such high expectations for the Big Sioux were never realized. But in the summers of both 1858 and 1859, Captain Robinson, the operator of the 62-ton ferryboat *Lewis Burnes*, took some excursionists up the stream. On the first trip, Robinson navigated the little boat some 30 miles upstream. In June 1859, with about 35 excursionists, half of whom were ladies, he took the *Lewis Burnes* on a two-day pleasure cruise up the Big Sioux.[91]

Another tributary, the Little Sioux River, emptied into the Missouri on the Iowa side about midway from Sioux City to Council Bluffs and attracted some commercial steamboating. The particular draw was the community of Little Sioux, about three miles above the mouth. In June 1858 the *William Baird*, returning from Sioux City to Cincinnati, reached Little Sioux. Some residents, delighted to find themselves at a head of navigation, presented the captain with a beef and twenty-five cords of wood. But they must have wondered about the feasibility of steamboat navigation. The steamer, which could not be turned about in the narrow stream, had to be backed down to the Missouri.[92]

In 1859 the *Omaha* reached Little Sioux twice. On his initial trip, Wineland was actually able to turn the boat around, a first for Little Sioux River steam navigation. Since the river at the town was only as wide as the steamer's length, Wineland had to run the *Omaha*'s bow into one bank while the stern brushed the willow stands on the opposite bank. The feat was evidently the day's highlight for towns-people who cheered, fired their guns, and threw their hats in the air. On the Fourth of July, the *Omaha* returned to pick up more than 3,000 sacks of corn. Wineland helped the town celebrate by firing the boat's cannons. Because of its load, the *Omaha* could not be turned and had to back out to the Missouri.[93]

Hauling corn from Little Sioux was part of an emerging export trade for the area between Council Bluffs and Omaha. During the 1859 navigation season, corn and other produce were hauled downstream by steamers from Sioux City and various other landings above Council Bluffs. For Sioux Citians, the first exports indicated their economy was evolving out of its subsistence phase. On April 14, 1859, the *Register* reported that the *Omaha* had taken "away quite a large amount of corn and potatoes, the first produce we have ever shipped down the river. May this evidence of prosperity rapidly increase." Three weeks later the *Omaha* departed with several hundred bushels of corn and potatoes. St. Louis and Fort Leavenworth were the main destinations for corn shipped from points above Council Bluffs.[94]

Sioux City's first newspapers, the *Eagle* and the *Register,* were the typical boosterish frontier sheets that had a knack for making their town sound like the world's next metropolis. As promoters of development, they offered little comment on the Panic of 1857, which was a drag on the regional economy until the Civil War. The federal census of 1860, which showed Sioux City's population as 767, indicates only modest growth during the town's first five years.[95]

Despite its smallness, Sioux City was the principal community in northwestern Iowa and the base for opportunists who wanted to extend settlement up the Missouri west of the Big Sioux. The region came to be popularly called Dakota as Minnesota's quest for statehood was pending. Minnesota Territory was bounded on the west by the Missouri and White Earth rivers. But the Minnesota Enabling Act, approved by Congress in February 1857, specified the state's western boundary would run from the international boundary to Iowa by way of the Red and Bois des Sioux rivers, Lake Traverse, Big Stone Lake, and a straight line. With the admission of Minnesota, the land between its western boundary and the Missouri and White Earth rivers would presumably revert to unorganized territory.[96]

Control of the area that was to be left outside Minnesota was contested by promoters of settlement at the falls of the Big Sioux (present Sioux Falls, South Dakota) and the Missouri River valley. The Big Sioux group included the merged interests of the Dakota Land Company of St. Paul, Minnesota, and the Western Town Company of Dubuque, Iowa. In late spring 1857 the companies started Sioux Falls and created several other paper towns nearby.

Sioux City's response was led by Frost, Todd, and Company. Its partners, Daniel Marsh Frost and John Blair Smith Todd, were former army officers who had graduated seven years apart from the U.S. Military Academy and fought at the Battle of Cerro Gordo during the Mexican-American War. After the war, they were both stationed at Jefferson Barracks. Frost resigned his commission in May 1853 and became a St. Louis merchant. Todd was then commanding Fort Ripley on the upper Mississippi above St. Paul. They were reacquainted during Harney's occupation of Fort Pierre when Marsh was the post sutler and Todd a captain.[97]

Alert to the changing economy of the upper Missouri, Todd resigned from the army in September 1856 and was appointed sutler at Fort Randall. Shortly thereafter Frost and Todd formed their partnership to engage in Sioux City merchandising and compete with Pierre Chouteau, Jr., and Company in the upper Missouri fur trade. In 1857 they advertised themselves in Sioux City as grocers and commission merchants. To complement that business and their trade above Fort Pierre, they established a trading post on the James River near later Yankton. In 1858 they added a post near the mouth of the Vermillion River.[98]

By the time they began trading with the Yankton Sioux, Frost and Todd had apparently developed a strategy to frustrate the Sioux Falls group and dominate the creation of Dakota Territory. Through their Sioux City store and their trading posts, they became allies of such men as Theophile Bruguier, a veteran French-Canadian trader, and Charles F. Picotte, a well-educated Yankton mixed-blood. Bruguier and Picotte were instrumental in convincing Yankton chiefs that they should sell their lands between the Big Sioux and Missouri. Accompanied by Bruguier and Picotte, who acted as interpreters and counselors, Todd led a delegation of chiefs to Washington in late 1857.[99]

While the chiefs were in the capital, Frost and Todd organized the Upper Missouri Land Company, which included such prominent Sioux Citians as Dr. John K. Cook and S. P. Yeomans. The company's aim was to develop townsites on the Missouri when the land was opened.[100]

In the treaty they signed on April 19, 1858, the chiefs ceded their claims in present South Dakota between the Big Sioux and Missouri rivers and south of a line running roughly from near Pierre to Watertown by way of Faulkton and Redfield. Charles E. Mix, commissioner of Indian Affairs, agreed to pay them $1.6 million (about 12 cents an acre) in annuities over a fifty-year period. The Yanktons were also granted a 400,000-acre reservation, with a 30-mile front on the Missouri. While Senate approval of the treaty was pending, some sooners invaded the Yankton lands but were evicted by troops from Fort Randall.[101]

Yankton Indian removal proceeded rather quickly after the Senate approved the treaty on February 16, 1859, and President James Buchanan proclaimed it to be in effect ten days later. Upper Missouri Indian agent Alexander H. Redfield, who had witnessed the signing of the treaty, was pro-settlement. In July, when he arrived on the steamboat *Carrier* with the first installment of annuities, he found that some 2,000 assembled Yanktons were reluctant to move from their main village a short distance above the James River. Redfield solved the problem by withholding annuities from the anxious Indians and ordering the *Carrier* to proceed slowly upstream to Greenwood, the agency for the Yankton Reservation. The Yankton throng followed the steamer on their 65-mile trek to Greenwood.

Once the Yanktons were on their reservation, there were no legal and physical barriers to settlement in the Vermillion-Yankton area. Frost, Todd, and their

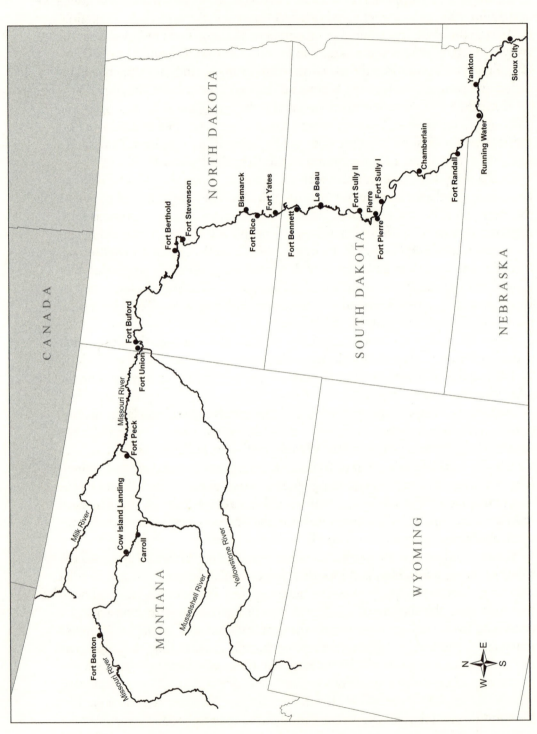

Major ports and destinations on the upper Missouri. (Current state and provincial boundaries are shown for reference.) *Prepared by James Worm.*

associates reorganized the Upper Missouri Land Company into the Yankton Land and Town Company, which platted the town of Yankton on the Missouri, about five miles above the James River. The site was chosen with an eye to steamboating. The deep channel of the Missouri ran along the foot of a gradually sloped natural levee. The Frost and Todd group was able to control Yankton, but other settlers started Vermillion and Elk Point.

Todd became the most important figure in agitating for the creation of Dakota Territory. After Minnesota was admitted as a state on May 11, 1858, there was considerable congressional interest in forming a new territory on its west. The aspirations of the Dakota Land Company at Sioux Falls were frustrated by its inability to attract settlers. Todd established himself as a Yankton resident, but Frost, who had been appointed a brigadier general in the Missouri militia, stayed mainly in St. Louis. Todd's lobbying in Washington was rewarded on March 2, 1861, when the lame-duck President Buchanan signed the act creating Dakota Territory. Congressmen were evidently unconcerned about its sparse population. The 1860 federal census showed only 2,576 whites and mixed-bloods within the proposed territory.[102]

The massive entity extended westward to the Continental Divide on the crest of the Rockies and northward to the international boundary. Hence, Fort Benton and all other upper Missouri trading posts were within the territory. The first territorial legislature, which began meeting in March 1862, selected Yankton as the territorial capital. With increased steamboating during the Civil War, Yankton and Fort Benton become more important as ports.

As the agricultural frontier was expanding in the Sioux City–Yankton area, steamboating was extended to Fort Benton, mainly because of federal government activities. The creation of Washington Territory and the passage of the Stevens Expedition from Fort Benton to Puget Sound in 1853 aroused interest in a northern line of communication. Until such time as a railroad would be completed, government officials assumed that movements to the Pacific Northwest would be by sea, overland from Fort Benton, or a combination thereof. Stevens's optimistic outlook about the prospects of steamboating to Fort Benton gave credibility to the northern route.

Since any trail from Fort Benton to western Washington would run through Indian lands, the situation on the northern route was similar to the earlier one on the Oregon Trail. The government had resolved the Oregon Trail question by the Fort Laramie Treaty of 1851, in which the Sioux and other signatory tribes agreed not only to trail rights for emigrants but also to tribal boundaries. The lands of the Blackfeet, who were not represented, were also described in the treaty. The Blackfeet, whose domain encompassed much of the upper Missouri, did not really seem to be an acute problem until the government wanted a Missouri River–Puget Sound connection.[103]

With the aim of getting concessions similar to those of the Fort Laramie Treaty, the government decided to negotiate with the Blackfeet in 1855. Alfred Cumming, head of the Central Superintendency based in St. Louis, and Isaac I. Stevens, were chosen as co-commissioners. Even though the government did not expect the Blackfeet to cede land, it nonetheless intended the treaty to be the characteristic show, replete with the distribution of gifts and other goods.

Cumming contracted with Pierre Chouteau, Jr., and Company to deliver the regular annuities for tribes in the Upper Missouri Agency and the treaty goods from St. Louis. The distribution points for the Upper Missouri Agency were Fort Pierre and Fort Union and undesignated stops between them. Chouteau was to be paid $4.75 per hundredweight for delivering annuities to Fort Union and points below. In the event Indians did not meet the steamer, the company was obligated to store the goods free of charge until distribution was possible—a standard provision in all Indian transportation contracts. Chouteau had stored some of the 1854 annuities for points above at Fort Pierre. For forwarding those in 1855, he was to be paid $2 per hundredweight. The rate for delivering the freight destined for the Blackfeet negotiation was $13.75 per hundredweight. From Fort Union, where it would be unloaded from the steamer, Chouteau agreed to forward it "in good Keel, Mackinac or other suitable and safe boats to Fort Benton in the Blackfoot Country."[104]

To deliver the Indian goods and ship its own freight, the Chouteau company arranged for the new steamer *Saint Mary*. The 295-ton side-wheeler, built at St. Louis under the supervision of Joseph La Barge, was half-owned by the company, with La Barge and St. Louis businessman John J. Roe each having a one-fourth interest. Even by the standards of the lower river, it was a large vessel, at 204 × 35 feet, with a 4.5-foot hold.[105]

La Barge steamed the *Saint Mary* away from the St. Louis levee on June 6. His passengers included Cumming; Alfred J. Vaughan, head of the Upper Missouri Agency; and Charles P. Chouteau, son of Pierre Chouteau, Jr. After a 36-day voyage, La Barge unloaded the Blackfeet goods at Fort Union and returned to St. Louis with a load of robes, furs, and antlers.[106]

Chouteau's men slowly moved the Blackfeet freight upstream on two large mackinaws. Aggravated by the delay and the lateness of the season, Cumming, who had moved ahead in a carriage, and Stevens decided to intercept the boats well below Fort Benton. Alexander Culbertson, Chouteau's manager in the region, arranged for the commissioners, the supplies, and some 2,000 Blackfeet to assemble on the left bank of the Missouri opposite the mouth of the Judith River.[107]

In less than two days of preliminaries, the commissioners and chiefs of all Blackfeet divisions signed an agreement on October 17. It placed boundaries on Blackfeet claims and defined the tribe's hunting rights in adjacent lands. The government agreed to pay the Blackfeet $20,000 worth of annuities for ten years and, for a like period, to spend $15,000 annually to instruct the tribe in "agricultural and mechanical pursuits" and educate their children.[108]

For its implications on steamboating, the most important outcome of the treaty was the establishment of a Blackfeet agency at Fort Benton. The agency provided another reason for the government and contractors to want faster, cheaper, and more efficient transportation on the upper Missouri.

Joseph La Barge, ca. 1875.
Working variously as a pilot, captain, and
steamboat owner during a half-century career,
La Barge was a Missouri River celebrity.
Photograph by J. A. Scholten.
Courtesy of the Missouri Historical Society, St. Louis.

La Barge, accompanied by Charles P. Chouteau, steamed the *Saint Mary* to Fort Union again in 1856, with the usual cargo of company goods and annuities from St. Louis and a small military group from Fort Pierre. On June 28, La Barge signed a contract with Captain Parmenas T. Turnley, the Fort Pierre quartermaster, to transport Second Lieutenant Gouverneur K. Warren and his 26-man party, consisting of troops and civilian specialists. La Barge agreed to carry Warren and his three assistants for $40 each and all others for $20 each. Warren's 7 tons of equipment and provisions was to be hauled at $3.50 per hundredweight. Warren, a topographical engineer who had surveyed the Fort Pierre site, was on his way to reconnoiter the lower Yellowstone valley to assess its military and scientific potential.[109]

After dropping Warren off at Fort Union, La Barge navigated the *Saint Mary* upstream to within ten miles of El Paso Point. Chouteau found the voyage instructive. He apparently concluded that in order to reach Fort Benton with a steamboat it would be necessary to forsake large side-wheelers in favor of relatively small stern-wheelers. Chouteau was one of the first to recognize that stern-wheelers would be advantageous in the debris-laden Missouri, because floating objects often damaged side-wheelers. But any plans Chouteau began formulating in 1856 had to be delayed three years by the threat of Frost, Todd, and Company, the new opposition firm.[110]

Frost, Todd, and Company was an amalgam of various anti-Chouteau elements.

It was partially financed by Robert Campbell, who in turn was associated with steamboat captain John Shaw. Probably through Campbell's influence, Frost and Todd formed an affiliation with Charles Primeau, who represented the remnants of Harvey, Primeau, and Company. In 1857, its first year of operating above Fort Pierre, Frost, Todd and Company used the old Harvey, Primeau, and Company posts.

Like its rival, Frost, Todd, and Company strove to augment its private trade with government Indian and military contracts. In 1857 it chartered the new steamer *Twilight*, commanded by John Shaw, to transport its trade goods and Indian annuities. Shaw had experience on the upper river in 1856 as commander of the *Clara*. The large side-wheeler *Twilight*, built at Jeffersonville, Indiana, had a capacity of 335 tons and a length of 215 feet. In part, because of heavy snows over the winter, Shaw was able to steam the *Twilight* above Fort Union to the mouth of the Poplar River. Company goods for Fort Campbell and the Blackfeet annuities had to be forwarded from there by other craft.[111]

During the year, Frost and Todd used their Sioux City store as a depot for the robes and furs shipped from their upriver posts. Mackinaws reportedly brought down "immense quantities." One consignment had 7,567 buffalo robes, 739 beaver pelts, 32 elk hides, 14 bear skins, 1 moose skin, and 34 packages of assorted deer, wolf, coon, and badger skins.[112]

Frost, Todd, and Company's upper river trade peaked in 1858. Captain Shaw and his *Twilight* again handled the company's business, which included transporting trade goods, annuities, excursionists, and a military escort. On Sunday, May 23, Shaw pulled the crowded boat, loaded with 120 tons of Indian annuities and 75 tons of trade goods, away from the St. Louis levee. The passengers included 125 Frost, Todd, and Company employees; Indian agents Alexander H. Redfield and Alfred J. Vaughan and 8 assistants; 2 Lutheran missionaries headed for the Crow Indians in the Yellowstone valley; and 15 pleasure seekers. The well-known St. Louis artist Carl Wimar was one of the excursionists, who paid $150 each for round-trip cabin passage. Perhaps influenced by the earlier excursions of George Catlin and Maximilian, a number of gentleman types by the late 1850s had decided that a steamboat trip up the Missouri would be a good outing. Charles P. Chouteau as well as Shaw tapped this tourist trade as another revenue source.[113]

At every stop, including the Indian villages above Sioux City, Shaw had one of his crewmen bang out tunes on the *Twilight*'s calliope. The offerings, which seem to have been limited to "Yankee Doodle" and "Oh! Susanna," evoked much the same reaction as that of the Glasgow newspaper editor. One of the passengers observed that the strains of the calliope convinced "me of the fallacy of the saying, 'music hath charms to soothe the savage beast,' and that it rather has a tendency to excite emotions of mirth."[114]

In only a week Shaw navigated the *Twilight* to Sioux City, where he took on 20 tons of Frost, Todd, and Company trade goods. But above there, the voyage was slowed by low water. Occasionally the boat, which had a six-foot-deep hold, had to be stopped and partially unloaded. Once the freight had been forwarded by mackinaws, it could proceed. Fortunately, Shaw was able to leave some of the annuities at the Yankton village, Fort Pierre, and Fort Atkinson, which helped lessen the draft. Some of the eyewitnesses assumed the Yankton distribution was in payment for the recently signed Yankton cession, but it was actually due from the Fort Laramie Treaty of 1851.[115]

Counting his crew, Shaw must have had about 180 men jammed on the *Twilight*. But at Fort Randall, he somehow found room for 40 more. Because the Sioux were becoming contentious at Fort William and Fort Union, the Indian Department had prevailed on the War Department to provide a military escort for Redfield and Vaughan. Under orders, First Lieutenant John D. O'Connell, Fort Randall's quartermaster, was in no position to negotiate effectively with Shaw, who charged $10,000 to transport Captain Henry W. Wessels and 40 troops to Fort Union and back. The men were given the worst possible deck passage. Replete with their arms, accouterments, baggage, camp equipage, and subsistence stores, they were crammed into a small deck space. The terms of the contract were extraordinary. The army was charged nearly $250 each for deck passage for a trip less than half as long as that taken by the excursionists for $150 with semiprivate cabins and meals provided. If nothing else, this deal helps explain why steamboatmen sought government contracts.[116]

Despite sandbars and the accidental breaking of a rudder and a wheel, the *Twilight* reached Fort William in the good time of 31 days and 2 hours. Redfield and Vaughan distributed annuities at several points, including Fort Atkinson, then being constructed by Frost, Todd, and Company for the Hidatsa and Mandan trade. As soon as the steamer reached Fort William, Atkinson, apparently acting on a pre-voyage company plan, vacated the post. The *Twilight* carried all of its goods, stores, and equipment, as well as Vaughan, the Blackfeet annuities, and some hundred men, upstream to about seven miles above the Big Muddy's mouth, where the company built Fort Stewart. The shift was prompted by the Sioux threats to Fort William and the desire to add a depot farther upstream to facilitate shipment of the Blackfeet annuities. At Fort Stewart, Edward G. Atkinson, a Frost, Todd, and Company partner, had mackinaws built to forward the Blackfeet annuities and Vaughan's party to Fort Campbell.[117]

Frost, Todd, and Company suffered a major setback when Pierre Chouteau, Jr., and Company was awarded the Indian transportation contract in 1859. But they used Captain Joseph Throckmorton and his steamer *Florence* to supply their posts as high as Fort Stewart and to ship robes and other products to St. Louis.[118]

In 1857 and 1858, when their only business on the upper Missouri was their own trade, the Chouteau company used the steamer *Spread Eagle*, captained by John La Barge (Joseph's brother). The new 389-ton side-wheeler was 210 feet long and 36 feet wide and had a 6-foot hold. In 1857 La Barge made a routine round-trip to Fort Union, but the next year, benefiting from high water, he was able to navigate the boat to within 50 miles of the Milk River. Charles Chouteau, who again made the trip, ordered company goods for Fort Benton forwarded by mackinaws and evidently concluded that the *Spread Eagle*, like the *Saint Mary*, could not be navigated to Fort Benton.[119]

Chouteau came out of the 1858 season with a renewed determination to get a steamer to Fort Benton. By then the government business was more important than it had ever been. Not only were the Indian Department and the War Department expanding their operations above Fort Union, but the fur trade was ailing. Because of mild weather over much of the United States and a glutted European market still suffering from the disruptions caused by the Crimean War, about 40,000 buffalo robes brought to St. Louis in 1857 remained unsold. These holdovers, when added to the 1858 receipts, further depressed the market. The value of the 1858 robes and furs was estimated at $300,000.[120]

Faced with uncertain prospects for the 1859 trade, Charles Chouteau realized the importance of government contracting. The immediate big prize was the transportation of Indian annuities to the upper Missouri, but Chouteau was also well aware that the War Department was planning to build a road from Fort Benton to Fort Walla Walla. The contemplated route, designed to promote national security, would obviously have great implications for commercial steamboating to Fort Benton. Chouteau and others—including Isaac I. Stevens, then Washington Territory's delegate to Congress, and War Department officials—envisioned a day when a combined river-land route by way of Fort Benton and Fort Walla Walla would be the great pathway to the Pacific Northwest.

To get the Indian transportation contract in 1859, Charles Chouteau had to outbid and out-lobby Frost, Todd, and Company and Captain Joseph Throckmorton. No bidder could be assured of winning of a government contract simply because he submitted the lowest bid, such as Chouteau did. Government officials were also permitted legally to consider such factors as the quality of the bidder's steamboats and his likely ability to carry out the contract. Obviously, this opened the way to allied considerations of the bidder's character and persuasiveness in presenting his case. Certainly there was some politicking involved in the 1859 upper Missouri Indian contract, but it is virtually impossible to find a competitive government contract that was negotiated without political considerations.[121]

In Washington, D.C., on March 15, 1859, Acting Commissioner of Indian Affairs Charles E. Mix signed a two-year contract with Pierre Chouteau, Jr., and Company to transport the annuities for the upper Missouri and Blackfeet agencies by steamboat or other craft. This entailed the delivery of goods to Fort Union and points below and to Fort Benton and Fort Sarpy, on the right bank of the Yellowstone about 25 miles below the mouth of the Bighorn. Fort Sarpy, a Chouteau post, was also the Upper Missouri Agency's contact point with the Crow Indians. The company was obligated to provide "a first class steamboat" approved by the superintendent of Indian Affairs at St. Louis. Chouteau also agreed to furnish free round-trip passage and subsistence for the two Indian agents and as many four assistants for each. The rates per hundredweight were $2.50 to Fort Union and from there $7.25 to both Fort Benton and Fort Sarpy.[122]

After signing the Indian contract, the Chouteau company also agreed to transport an army surveying party commanded by Captain William F. Raynolds, a topographical engineer. Raynolds was assigned to move up the Missouri by steamboat to Fort Pierre II and then proceed overland to Fort Sarpy. From that initial base, he was to generally examine the terrain between the Oregon Trail and the Missouri and, in particular, determine the best routes from near Fort Laramie to Fort Union, from the Fort Laramie vicinity to Fort Benton along the base of the Bighorn Mountains, and from South Pass to the Yellowstone.[123]

Raynolds's preparations were quite involved. Chouteau agreed to transport the expedition's ordnance from St. Louis to Fort Pierre II (nearly two miles above the site of the original Fort Pierre) at $2 per hundredweight. For carrying the provisions to Fort Sarpy, the company was to be paid $9 per hundredweight, consisting of $2 to the mouth of the Yellowstone and $7 from there to Fort Sarpy. En route, Chouteau agreed to pick up 100 mules, their forage, and 10 wagons at Fort Leavenworth. The rates for transporting them to Fort Pierre II were $20 per mule and $2 per hundred pounds for the forage and wagons. Lastly, Raynolds was to obtain a military escort at Fort Randall. For transporting it to Fort Pierre II, Chouteau was given $25 for the officer, $12 for each man, and $1.50 per hundred pounds of their provisions.[124]

With the addition of the mules and wagons, Chouteau could not rely only on the *Spread Eagle*. If he had been content just to reach Fort Union, he would have had more choice in obtaining a second steamer. But even before he embarked from St. Louis, Chouteau had evidently decided to try to steam to Fort Benton. He was able to charter the *Chippewa*, a 173-ton stern-wheeler that drew only 31 inches when loaded with 160 tons, from M. H. Crapster. With a length of 160 feet and a width of 30 feet, the *Chippewa* promised to be more manageable in shallow, narrow channels.[125]

Chouteau got his expedition under way in late May. The *Spread Eagle*, commanded by John La Barge, and the *Chippewa*, under Crapster, traveled separately until they joined near Omaha. Most of the annuities as well as the members of Raynolds's party were loaded on the *Spread Eagle*. Raynolds, who had gone ahead to make arrangements at Fort Leavenworth, boarded the *Spread Eagle* at St. Joseph. Above Sioux City, the boats had to make daily woodcutting stops. Raynolds's escort, consisting of First Lieutenant Caleb Smith and 30 men. joined the expedition at Fort Randall on June 13. After the Raynolds party left the steamers at Fort Pierre II on June 18, the steamers navigated without serious difficulty to Fort Union.[126]

Soon after the boats arrived at Fort Union on July 1, Chouteau had some difficulty with Crapster. Hiram Martin Chittenden, using information from Joseph La Barge, claimed that Crapster had defaulted on his agreement to navigate the *Chippewa* to Fort Benton. The matter was resolved by Chouteau's purchase of the *Chippewa* and Crapster's departure downstream in a mackinaw.[127]

Leaving the *Spread Eagle* at Fort Union, Chouteau set off for Fort Benton in the *Chippewa* on July 3. At 6:00 A.M. the next day, Chouteau's party observed

Charles P. Chouteau, ca. 1850.
As manager of Pierre Chouteau, Jr.,
and Company, Charles P. Chouteau was
principally responsible for extending
steamboating from Fort Union to
Fort Benton. *Courtesy of the Missouri
Historical Society, St. Louis.*

Independence Day by firing off thirteen rounds, one for each of the original states. The vessel—loaded with 160 tons of annuities, some provisions and equipment for Lieutenant John Mullan's road-building party, and the company's outfit— also had two mackinaw boats of 45-ton capacity each lashed to its sides.[128] Chouteau reported that he had the vessel staffed with a 95-man crew "composed chiefly of old voyageurs, so as to insure my overcoming all the difficulties represented to exist."[129] This extraordinarily large complement, about triple the size of usual steamboat crews, was needed to man the mackinaws and warp the steamer through rapids. Chouteau anticipated well. On four different occasions, the mackinaws had to be used as lighters to enable the *Chippewa* to be navigated through rapids. Two entire days were spent getting through Dauphin's Rapids, which Chouteau wrote was "by far the most formidable and dangerous on the river, and until cleared of the many boulders which are all loose, will ever be a serious barrier to Steam Boat Navigation."[130]

Above the mouth of the Judith River, Chouteau abandoned the mackinaws to reduce drag on the steamer. On July 17 the *Chippewa* reached the site of Old Fort McKenzie, 12 miles below Fort Benton. With his fuel supply exhausted and the river falling rapidly, Chouteau decided to unload the freight there. While making a skiff voyage to Fort Benton and back, he determined the channel was about three and half feet deep. Noting the well-timbered points and islands, he left instructions to have quantities of dry wood prepared for the next season. Chouteau, with little flair for the dramatic, simply reported that at 2:00 P.M. on July 18, "the Chippewa's prow was headed downstream." But Blackfeet agent Alfred J. Vaughan, who had accompanied the expedition from St. Joseph, observed that the departure was accompanied "with clamor and cheering and firing of cannon."[131]

The *Chippewa*'s accomplishment of nearly reaching Fort Benton was immediately recognized as marking the start of a new era. It was hailed in newspapers from Sioux City to St. Louis as the fulfillment of the dream to navigate the Missouri as far west as possible. Vaughan portrayed it as a heroic "fearless enterprise." In his report to Commissioner of Indian Affairs Alfred B. Greenwood, he lauded Chouteau and La Barge for their skill, energy, and good judgment. Like many people of his age, Vaughan thought the *Chippewa*'s technology was another indication of man's desirable conquest of the wilderness. In describing the steamer's approach to the Fort McKenzie site, he observed: "At length a shrill whistle pierced the sleeping solitude of the rugged mountains with the first joyous scream of civilization." In his own report to Secretary of Interior Jacob Thompson, Greenwood highlighted Vaughan's information that the *Chippewa* had gone 600 miles farther than any previous steamer and a total of 3,100 miles from the mouth of the Missouri. Greenwood's obvious implication was that henceforth Indian annuities would be delivered to Fort Benton by the latest technology.[132]

Charles Chouteau realized the *Chippewa*'s trip enhanced the importance of the northern route. On November 1, 1859, he sent a short report to Secretary of War John B. Floyd. After describing the *Chippewa*'s voyage from Fort Union in some detail, he concluded that "with suitable boats and the removal of boulders here and there" the navigation of the upper Missouri would be just as safe and easy as that of the upper Mississippi or Ohio. He had "no hesitation if affirming that the trip from Saint Louis to Fort Benton can be easily accomplished within thirty-five days."[133]

Chouteau's direct contact with Floyd was undoubtedly inspired by the War Department's project of constructing a wagon road from Fort Benton to Fort Walla Walla. The genesis for the work, which came to be called the Mullan Road, lay with Isaac I. Stevens. While engaged in his railroad survey, Stevens ordered Second Lieutenant John Mullan to survey much of the route during the winter of 1853–54. The War Department obtained some funding from Congress in 1855 to improve the road. But none of the appropriation was released until after some agitation by Isaac I. Stevens, when he was Washington Territory's delegate. Mullan did some work on the westernmost sector in 1858 and, after further congressional funding, started systematic surveying and improving from Fort Walla Walla on July 1, 1859. He and the various components of his surveying party reached Fort Benton, 624 miles from Fort Walla Walla, on August 1, 1860. Major George Blake and his 300-man force, who had ascended the Missouri on Chouteau steamers, were awaiting him.[134]

Apparently, a combination of the *Chippewa*'s success and Mullan's contention that use of the northern river-road route would be cheaper than ocean travel convinced Secretary of War John B. Floyd to send the troops. Pierre Chouteau, Jr., and Company's contract to move Blake's unit was signed in Washington, D.C., with Quartermaster General Thomas S. Jesup on March 31, 1860. The company agreed to transport "about 300 enlisted men, officers, servants, and laundresses with their military stores and supplies" from St. Louis to Fort Benton. Compensation was set at $100 per officer, $50 per man, servant, and laundress, and $10 per hundred pounds for "stores and supplies, including the subsistence of the men during the trip."[135]

Charles Chouteau prepared for moving the troops, annuities, and company outfit by readying three steamers—the *Chippewa*, the *Key West*, and the *Spread Eagle*. The three-year-old stern-wheeler *Key West* was only slightly larger than the *Chippewa*. The boats were loaded, and Chouteau got his small mountain fleet under way from St. Louis on May 3. On July 2 the *Chippewa*, commanded by Captain Robert Wright, and the *Key West*, commanded by John La Barge, reached Fort Benton. Their two-month passage proved to be less than the average time for later voyages from St. Louis.[136]

At the time, it seemed that Chouteau had proven the feasibility of the river portion of the new northern route to the Pacific Northwest. However, any expectation that Chouteau or War Department officials entertained that the Missouri–Mullan Road route would become a great military highway never materialized. Mullan helped Blake's force move to such destinations as Fort Colville and Fort Walla Walla. But after Blake, the army's use of the Mullan Road was minimal. Mullan did some additional work on the road in 1861 and 1862, but in timbered portions it was really nothing more than a pack animal trail. The road's greatest impact was to serve as a pathway for prospectors who entered Idaho and Montana from the west. After the Montana gold rush was under way, it was apparent that the Missouri River and the Mullan Road were not a continuous thoroughfare. Rather, the river and road segments each served to lead different groups of miners to the new El Dorado.[137]

7

THE WAR YEARS

During the Civil War, Missouri River steamboating had a mixed history. The trade from St. Louis to Kansas City declined sharply because of the disruption of Missouri's economy by military campaigns and harassment by guerrilla Confederate sympathizers. However, trade on the section of the river from Kansas City to Sioux City actually increased, because of the demands of the overland freighting towns, which were mostly supplied by the Hannibal and St. Joseph Railroad and its allied steamers. But the greatest expansion occurred above Sioux City because of the Montana gold rush and army campaigns against the Sioux Indians.

In the troubled spring of 1861, when the secession crisis led to the Confederate attack on Fort Sumter, South Carolina, Missourians were torn by conflicting Union and rebel sympathies. The ideological descendants of the planter elite that dominated the early Boon's Lick region naturally defended both slavery and states' rights. But mainly because of the influx of New Englanders and European immigrants during the four decades since the state's legalization of slavery, most Missourians were pro-Union.

Interestingly, their governor, Clairborne Jackson, was a secessionist. When President Abraham Lincoln called on each state to volunteer troops after the firing on Fort Sumter, Jackson not only pointedly refused but also attempted to take Missouri out of the Union and into the Confederate States of America. As commander in chief of the Missouri State Guard, Jackson insisted its members were subject to his authority. Influenced by Lieutenant Governor Thomas C. Reynolds, Jackson appointed Sterling Price, former Mexican-American War army officer and governor, as commander of the state guard.

Much of the resistance to Jackson's scheming came from pro-Union leaders in St. Louis. Within weeks a pro-Lincoln convention replaced Jackson with Hamilton R. Gamble, a staunch Unionist. Throughout the war, Missouri's state government supported the Union, and Sterling Price was one of the South's main military leaders in the area west of the Mississippi.[1]

In Missouri as elsewhere, the South's greatest successes occurred early in the war. On August 10, 1861, a Confederate force that included Price's militiamen defeated Union regulars in the Battle of Wilson's Creek, 10 miles southwest of Springfield. Emboldened by this success, Price led a fifteen-thousand man force northward to the Missouri River. In the Battle of Lexington, fought on September 18–21, his Missouri State Guard army overwhelmed a much smaller group of defenders. As Union reinforcements were rushed west, Price withdrew to the south. By the end of the year, Union troops controlled all of Missouri except the southwest. The Union position in the west was improved by its somewhat surprising victory at the Battle of Pea Ridge, near Bentonville, Arkansas, on March 6–8, 1862.

Price, who was prominently involved at Pea Ridge, tried to replenish his Missouri force after the battle by sending recruiters into northern Missouri. One of the most significant, Colonel Joseph O. Porter, raised a number of men before being routed in the Battle of Kirksville on August 6, 1862. Within days another newly formed Confederate unit was defeated by Union troops near Glasgow. These engagements solidified Union control of most of the area north of the Missouri River.

But throughout the war, pro-Confederate guerrillas raided steamboats, stage lines, and railroads. Using hit-and-run tactics, they were especially effective in disrupting transportation, killing Unionists in the countryside, and devastating the economy. The persistent guerrilla activity encouraged Price to think that Missouri was still vulnerable.

Late in the summer of 1864, he coordinated a resurgence of guerrilla raids north of the Missouri with his invasion into the southeastern part of the state. Believing the guerrillas would divert thousands of Union troops, Price thought his army could seize St. Louis, control the rest of the state, and establish a Confederate government. On September 19, 1864, when he was serving as the Confederate commander of the District of Arkansas, Price invaded with some twelve thousand mounted men. Stout Union resistance at Pilot Knob helped save St. Louis.

Frustrated by the Pilot Knob setback, Price abandoned his drive toward St. Louis. Instead, he led a month-long march across the state. He first moved northwestward from Pilot Knob to near Jefferson City. From just south of the capital, his army marched to Boonville. While his main force struck overland toward Waverly, two of his contingents attacked, seized, and briefly held Glasgow to the north and Sedalia to the south. From Waverly, Price's army followed along the south side of the river through Lexington and Independence. Meanwhile, Union troops, reinforced by Kansas and Colorado volunteers, readied to challenge the invaders near Independence. Price's campaign was ended by the Battle of Westport on October 23. Defeated within a few miles of Kansas City, Price began marching southward to Arkansas. His foray was the last Confederate show of strength in Missouri. But guerrilla bands continued intermittent raids for several months after Confederate commander Robert E. Lee surrendered to Ulysses S. Grant at Appomattox Courthouse, Virginia, on April 9, 1865.

Throughout the war, Union army officials and Missouri's government were determined to keep the state unified by safeguarding its key transportation lines. St. Louis's links with the western parts of the state were the Missouri River and the Hannibal and St. Joseph, North Missouri, and Missouri Pacific railroads. By the opening of hostilities, the Missouri Pacific was operating for 189 miles, from St. Louis to Sedalia. In southern Missouri the St. Louis and Iron Mountain Railroad was completed to Pilot Knob, and the Southwest Branch of the Missouri Pacific to Rolla.[2]

The railroads were heavily used in deploying Union troops from St. Louis. In June and July 1861, St. Louis quartermaster officers made twenty-five troop transportation contracts with the Missouri Pacific. Most of the agreements called for moving 5,400 troops to either Rolla or Hermann. For the nearly 400 men it transported to Jefferson City, the company was paid $3.35 each.[3]

Simultaneously, other troops were moved by steamboats on the Missouri. But Union navigation was contested for a time by Price's guardsmen. On July 4, the *Glasgow Weekly Times* reported, "The boats fell first into the hands of one party and then the other. They had to about-face, like a raw recruit on drill day." Other than troop transportation, Union forces used steamers in an effort to curtail rebel river crossings. Both before and after the Battle of Lexington, troops on the *Des Moines, White Cloud,* and *War Eagle* confiscated steam ferries and destroyed a number of flatboats that were used as ferries. They took the Brunswick ferry to the more staunchly Unionist Lexington and the Glasgow ferry to Boonville, which was fortified by pro-Union Home Guards. Ferry operators at the affected places were permitted to use only skiffs.[4]

Disrupting the ferry service may have inconvenienced some rebels but certainly did not control them. Days before the Battle of Lexington, a battery of three guns at Glasgow fired on the steamer *Sioux City,* which was carrying a detachment of Union troops. Another rebel battery at Brunswick blocked the passage of soldiers on the *Des Moines* and *White Cloud* while they were attempting to navigate from Jefferson City to Lexington.[5]

When Price withdrew after the Battle of Lexington, some towns, including Lexington and Osceola, were garrisoned by Union troops. Transporting and supplying them was sometimes done by steamboats. During the war, steamboating on the Osage was diminished, but on April 28, 1862, the *Silver Lake* delivered thirty thousand rations from St. Louis to the First Iowa Cavalry stationed at Osceola. The boat, a 70-ton stern-wheeler, was used on the Osage until it was accidentally burned on September 3, 1862.[6]

Although steamboats based at St. Louis were vital for Union army movements on the Missouri, Mississippi, Ohio, Tennessee, and Cumberland rivers, military authorities initially continued the prewar pattern of contracting with individual boat managers. But by late 1861 the shortage of steamers caused Brigadier General Samuel R. Curtis, commander of the Department of Missouri, to assert government control. As Curtis realized, St. Louis had to be the hub for river movements. New Orleans, the greatest port in the West, was then in Confederate hands, as were Vicksburg and even Island Number 10, only 55 miles below Cairo, Illinois. Furthermore, the government had purchased a number of steamers and converted them into gunboats, and the Confederacy had seized many others.

In his circular "Regulations for the River Commerce," issued on December 10, Curtis dictated that henceforth all St. Louis river commerce would be under military control. In order to take freight and passengers, any boat operator had to be authorized by either the commander of the Department of Missouri or the St. Louis District. Owners of all steamers and other craft were ordered to immediately register with the St. Louis quartermaster office. For every boat, they had to show all owners and the extent of their ownership.[7]

Not content with just controlling the boats, Curtis demanded patriotism. All boat officers, pilots, and other employees had to take a prescribed loyalty oath to the Union. Those who violated the circular's provisions would have to forfeit their vessel and be subject to court-martial. Those convicted could be sentenced to death or punished in other ways. Curtis, a former congressman from Keokuk, Iowa, evidently reacted to the widespread belief that many steamboat owners and operators favored the South. One claim was that all but two Missouri River pilots were Confederate sympathizers.[8]

The Union needed to control the St. Louis steamboats to carry out its grand strategy of reopening the lower Mississippi, thereby splitting the Confederacy. The lower Mississippi campaign was a three-pronged movement. One force, under Major General John Pope, moved against Island No. 10, which fell into Union hands on March 7, 1862, after a three-week assault. Another army, commanded by Ulysses S. Grant, moved up the Tennessee River. After taking Fort Donelson, Grant prevailed in the Battle of Shiloh on April 6 and 7. The Shiloh victory in Tennessee opened the way for Grant's movement into Mississippi, where his forces occupied Corinth. Confederate Major General Earl Van Doren, with some twenty thousand men, attacked Corinth, but its defenders, commanded by Major General William S. Rosecrans, repelled them in the battle of October 3 and 4. Meanwhile, a third Union force moving up the Mississippi from the Gulf of Mexico occupied New Orleans on April 26.[9]

The Island No. 10 and Tennessee river offensives involved a number of steamboats obtained by St. Louis quartermaster officers. About twenty steamers were used against Island No. 10, and an equal number were sent to support movements to Pittsburg Landing, Grant's supply depot on the Tennessee River near Shiloh and Corinth.

The Union victories at Island No. 10, Shiloh, Corinth, and New Orleans opened the way for the siege of Vicksburg, the main remaining impediment to controlling the Mississippi. By Christmas 1862, Major General William Tecumseh Sherman had assembled an impressive force for the movement against Vicksburg. With the assistance of St. Louis quartermaster officers, his army was based on sixty steamboats, including such familiar Missouri River traders as the *Emma, Iatan, Key West, Meteor, Omaha, Polar Star, Sam Gaty, Sioux City, Spread Eagle,* and *War Eagle.*[10]

After several months of preparation, Union forces began sieging Vicksburg on May 22. The city finally capitulated on July 4, five days before the Union seizure of nearby Port Hudson, Louisiana. The fall of Vicksburg, the turning point of the war in the West, not only divided the Confederacy but soon led to the revival of commercial steamboating on the lower Mississippi. Fortunately for St. Louis and Missouri River steamboating, the opening of the New Orleans route lessened the army's steamboat needs.

However, after the Vicksburg campaign, quartermaster officers of the Department of Missouri in St. Louis had to organize another large troop movement by steamboats. In early October 1864, when it became apparent that Sterling Price would take his invading army westward across Missouri, Major General William S. Rosecrans, recently named to head the Department of Missouri organized a pursuit. He ordered Captain Lyne S. Metcalf, assistant quartermaster, to "at once charter river transportation for 6,000 men for service on the Missouri River."[11] Steamboat transportation was vital because Jackson's troops had ruined much of the Missouri Pacific Railroad. Rosecrans's first objective was to protect Jefferson City. Anticipating Price's move, the Federals frantically rushed seven thousand men to the capital. Some moved overland from Rolla and others were transported by steamers. Once he reconnoitered this strong defense, Price dared not risk an assault and bypassed the city.[12]

Union army authorities were much more effective in dealing with regular units such as Price's army than with guerrillas. For steamboatmen, the most perilous stretch of the Missouri was between Glasgow and Kansas City, where the bushwhackers had considerable local support.

In late July 1862 a guerrilla band opposite Waverly completely riddled the *War Eagle* with small-arms fire. After the captain hoisted a surrender flag and pulled ashore, the gang took "whatever they wanted" and detained the boat for several hours. Robert H. Miller, publisher and editor of the *Liberty Tribune*, insisted that "such villainous outrages should be put down, and that too, in the most summary manner. The people can't afford to allow a few desperadoes to destroy the peace and business of the state."[13] Miller's outrage typified the reaction of those who expected their government to protect them from marauding thieves.

That fall the *Emilie,* captained by Joseph La Barge, was temporarily seized by a rebel gang at Portland, about 30 miles below Jefferson City. Its leader, John W. Shaddock, who was working with Joseph O. Porter, wanted free ferry service. He forced La Barge to unload part of his cargo to clear deck room for his men and horses. After the *Emilie* carried Shaddock's group to a point opposite Portland, he released the boat so La Barge could retrieve his off-loaded cargo and proceed.[14]

About the same time, a Jefferson City correspondent complained that rebel bushwhackers held sway in much of the region. The only safe places for Union people, he claimed, were the federal forts at Lexington and Sedalia. Stages running from the Sedalia railhead to Lexington were constantly harassed by rebel thieves.

A more disastrous raid was perpetrated on the *New Sam Gaty* in late March 1863 at Sibley Landing near Kansas City. About twenty-five guerrillas boarded the vessel when its captain was attempting to pull away from the landing. They robbed all the passengers and summarily executed three Union soldiers. The raiders threatened to burn the boat but were convinced to spare it by the captain, who agreed to throw all government freight, including a hundred sacks of flour and a number of wagons, into the river. As they withdrew, the assaulters took some twenty free blacks headed for Kansas as prisoners. One account relates that the guerrillas later killed all of them, but another version of the incident was that some survived.[15]

Two months later, bushwhackers fired on several upbound steamers between Lexington and Sibley. In a bit of an understatement, Miller of the *Liberty Tribune* observed that "boating is a rather hazardous business at this time."[16]

Since Union garrisons stationed in towns were incapable of stopping the surprise attacks, steamboat captains were left to their own devices. Their commonest method of protecting the pilothouse was to encase it in boiler iron, leaving only observation slits for the pilot. This device was used effectively on the *West Wind* when nearly a hundred shots fired by guerrillas near Camden hit its pilothouse. Another safety measure was to ignore anyone who attempted to flag a steamer. Captains were well aware that such a signal was likely to be a ruse, because gang members usually hid in the undergrowth until the steamer landed. Yet another practice was to keep up steam when docked for loading and unloadings. This precaution saved the *Live Oak* at Waverly when twenty or more mounted rebels suddenly rushed toward the boat. The captain was able to get under way promptly by cutting the mooring rope. Frustrated, the guerrillas fired two hundred balls into the boat. Despite this fusillade, they managed to kill only one horse and wound a man's hand.[17]

Captains sometimes tried to get assistance from Union troops. In March 1865, while stranded on a sandbar near Sibley Landing, the upbound *Sioux City* was raided by four or five men of the notorious William ("Bloody Bill") Anderson's gang. After capturing several crewmen who had gone ashore for wood, they boarded the boat and helped themselves to some whiskey and boots before fleeing. A detachment of Union troops pursued the renegades through parts of Jackson County but, as was often the case, failed to engage them.[18]

Fortunately for steamboat operators, guerrillas wanted only to harass, rob, and sometimes use their boats. There is no recorded instance of guerrillas ever destroying a steamer. Considering the high flammability of the wooden structures, it would have been relatively easy to set them on fire. Nevertheless, the constant threat of attacks had a disquieting effect on trade. In all likelihood, the St. Louis Board of Underwriters, which set maritime insurance rates, increased premiums on hull and cargo insurance because of guerrillas.[19]

Although steamboating was somewhat curtailed by guerrilla harassment and a depressed economy, it provided a vital service. Railroads by themselves were incapable of meeting all of the state's transportation needs. At various times the Missouri Pacific, North Missouri, and Hannibal and St. Joseph could not operate because of destruction by rebel commanders and guerrillas.

Clairborne Jackson himself, while still governor, had Missouri Pacific bridges over the Gasconade and Osage rivers destroyed, and he encouraged his supporters to ruin bridges and trestles on the North Missouri. His sabotage in June 1861 disrupted Missouri Pacific service for months. The entire line from St. Louis to Sedalia was not fully operative until late September 1862. By the time of Price's invasion in September 1864, the railroad had been completed to Warrensburg, 29 miles west of Sedalia. An estimated $1 million worth of damage to bridges, depots, and track by Price's troops required extensive repairs. St. Louis trains to Warrensburg did not run again until February 20, 1865.[20]

Most of the guerrilla damage to the North Missouri and the Hannibal and St. Joseph occurred during Price's move against Lexington in 1861 and his invasion three years later. On both occasions, he coordinated guerrilla strikes against the lines with his movements so that Union commanders were forced to commit thousands of troops north of the Missouri River to protect the railroads. Guerrilla attacks on the North Missouri in 1861 caught Union forces off guard. The raiders devastated a hundred miles of the line by burning bridges, tearing up track, and bending the rails by laying them atop piles of burning ties. Amazingly, after thousands of Union troops were rushed in, much of the razed portion was rebuilt in about three weeks. Guerrilla strikes against the North Missouri in 1864 were more random. Their most dramatic action was the seizure and destruction of a train at Centralia.

Bushwhackers lashed out at the Hannibal and St. Joseph at various points throughout its entire route. In September 1861 a rebel force of some 2,500 men tore up the track for 47 miles west of Hannibal. At about the same time, others sabotaged the 130-foot bridge over the Platte River, some 15 miles east of St. Joseph. When the next train passed over it, the partially burned timbers broke, plunging the locomotive, tender, and some passenger cars 30 feet to the streambed. Twenty people were crushed to death in the mangled wreckage, and some others were injured. The line was able to resume service from both east and west to opposite sides of the Platte several weeks before the bridge was replaced. Except for the inconvenience of having to haul passengers and freight across the river, the line could claim that it had resumed regular service. In response to the Platte River bridge incident, four thousand Union troops commanded by Brigadier General John Pope were dispatched to St. Joseph.[21]

The Hannibal and St. Joseph was the Union army's most vital connection of the Mississippi and Missouri valleys. By September 1864 the government had paid the line $2 million for carrying troops during the war. The importance of the road was not lost on Price and his cooperating guerrilla bands. When Price was moving across the state, small bands of bushwhackers attacked trains and on one occasion burned four coaches and ten freight cars between Hannibal and Monroe.[22]

Throughout the war, St. Louisans routinely complained that their river trade, other than that involving the military, was dull. Part of the difficulty, such as the Confederate blockading of their route to New Orleans for over two years, was war-related, but some of it was caused by the loss of steamboating opportunities

REGULAR MISSOURI RIVER PACKET.

For LEXINGTON, INDEPENDENCE, WESTON,
ST. JOSEPH AND COUNCIL BLUFFS.

THE NEW AND FAST RUNNING PASSENGER STEAMER

ROBERT CAMPBELL,

JOHN McCLOY, Master,
WILL LEAVE FOR ABOVE & INTERMEDIATE LANDINGS,

On _____ the ____ inst., at ____ o'clock, ____ M.

☞ FOR FREIGHT OR PASSAGE APPLY ON BOARD.
_1863_

(*this page and opposite*) *Robert Campbell* departure card.
Cards with accompanying tables of distance were a common form of St. Louis advertising.
Used by permission, State Historical Society of Missouri, Columbia.

due to recent railroad advances in the Ohio River valley, the upper Mississippi region, and Missouri. But despite its lagging trade, St. Louis continued—albeit on a greatly reduced scale—its prewar business of processing agricultural produce, including hemp, tobacco, pork, beef, wheat, and corn. Most of the hemp and tobacco and much of the meat and grain came from Missouri River towns.

In 1861 about twenty steamers engaged in the river trade from St. Louis to Kansas City. The *Florence*, which was sometimes steamed to Sioux City, and the *Mill Boy*, which went no farther than Glasgow, each made seven round-trips, four more than their nearest competitors. Thirteen other vessels made three round-trips, which suggests that they had long inactive periods between voyages. The author's tabulation of departures from the "Boats Leaving This Day" articles that were published regularly in the *Tri-Weekly Missouri Republican* shows that for the entire season there were only seventy-seven Missouri River departures from St. Louis.

To July 3, steamboats delivered to St. Louis, 13,662 rope coils, 15,958 bales of hemp, 2,745 hogsheads of tobacco, 30,999 barrels of whiskey, 2,951,134 bushels of corn, 953,626 bushels of wheat, 21,190,690 pounds of pork, 2,411,430 pounds of bacon, and 61,398 bushels of dried fruit. The amount of hemp, the bulkiest item, was only about 35 percent of that for the comparable period in 1860. All other items, except corn and dried fruit, which registered gains, had declined by from 20 to nearly 50 percent. The heavy reliance of hemp shippers on steamboats illus-

DISTANCES
From Saint Louis
TO
COUNCIL BLUFFS,

Mouth Missouri....		18	Miami.............	8	304
St. Charles	27	45	Hill's Landing	20	324
St. Auburn	30	75	Waverly	6	330
Augusta	5	80	Dover Landing.....	12	342
South Point........	7	87	Lexington	12	354
Washington........	3	90	Wellington	11	365
Pinckney	15	105	Camden	10	375
Hermann	15	120	Napoleon	8	383
Portland...........	20	140	Sibley	7	390
St. Aubert	10	150	Richfield...........	15	405
Bennet's Landing ..	10	160	Blue Mills Landing.	10	450
Mouth Osage.......	3	163	Liberty	10	425
Jefferson City......	10	173	Wayne City........	6	431
Claysville..........	7	180	Randolph	8	439
Marion	5	185	Kansas	5	444
Nashville..........	13	198	Parkville	15	4.9
Providence	2	200	Narrows Landing...	10	469
Rocheport	12	212	Fort Leavenworth ..	11	480
Boonville	10	222	Weston	6	486
Arrow Rock	15	237	Columbus Landing..	29	515
Glasgow	15	252	St. Josephs	33	548
Cambridge.........	8	260	Savannah..........	22	570
Keytesville Landing	7	267	Iowa Point	26	596
Brunswick.........	16	286	Council Bluffs......	204	800
Dewit	10	296			

trates the continuation of the prewar practice. Railroads in 1861 transported just 197 bales, only about 1.25 percent of the amount delivered by steamers.[23]

Lower Missouri River steamboating nearly maintained its approximate 1861 level for the next two years. In 1862 the *Mill Boy*, with nine round-trips from St. Louis to either Boonville or Glasgow, was the most active boat. The *New Sam Gaty* completed seven voyages to the same area, and nine other steamers made at least three trips each. The *Fanny Ogden* and the *Spread Eagle*, with five voyages each, were the 1863 leaders. Generally, the downstream cargoes consisted of some hemp, tobacco, rope coils, wheat, corn, bacon, and pork. The 1863 business was detrimentally affected by a persistent drought and ravaging guerrillas. In Saline County—a major producer of hemp, tobacco, corn, and wheat—chaos prevailed in midsummer. Many draft dodgers reportedly had "taken to the brush" and, in cooperation with guerrilla chieftain William C. Quantrill's gangs, were raiding stores and farms. Many farmers fled the countryside to the protection of Union forts. The Union was said to have only about a fourth of the men needed to safeguard the country. That October a rebel force, estimated at 1,500 men, plundered Boonville by robbing all its stores and completely stripping some of them.[24]

Steamboat traffic increased in 1864. At least forty-two different boats passed up the Missouri. Much of the business was due to army shipments to Leavenworth, the Montana gold rush, and General Alfred Sully's campaign in Dakota Territory. There is no reason to believe that the shipment of agricultural commodities within Missouri rose. The only substantial difference in the St. Louis–Kansas City trade resulted from the decision of the Missouri Pacific to complete its line by building from both ends. In June the company sent 1,700 tons of rails and iron as well as an engine and construction cars from St. Louis to Kansas City. Beyond Jefferson City at least, they were transported by steamers.[25]

Unlike such Missouri River communities as Glasgow, Brunswick, Lexington, and Waverly, whose economies were stagnant during the war, Kansas and Nebraska freighting towns prospered. Leavenworth was the main depot for the shipment of military supplies on both the Oregon-California and Santa Fe trails. At the start of the conflict, the Santa Fe Trail army business was based at Kansas City, but clashes between the town's Unionists and secessionists caused military authorities to transfer their depot to more secure Leavenworth. Atchison's business, which was mostly with private parties in Colorado and Utah, suffered from guerrilla harassment of the Hannibal and St. Joseph Railroad in 1861 but recovered sharply the next year. However, Nebraska City, which had the most direct route to Denver, was the mistress of the Colorado trade. Omaha was at a disadvantage in freighting to Colorado, because its freighters had to cross the troublesome Platte River at some point. However, the town became very significant in 1863, when the army decided to use it for shipping all supplies for installations on the Oregon-California Trail. Because of Indian hostilities along the trail, the military business expanded much more rapidly than the civilian trade. When Indian raids led to more general hostilities the next year, Omaha freighters expanded their operations to meet the army's needs in what Nebraskans remember as the Indian War of 1864. Freighters from a third Nebraska town, Brownville, also participated in private freighting to Colorado.[26]

Supplying the freighting towns was generally done by railroad-steamboat combinations. But they received some deliveries from St. Louis boats headed for the upper river, and, especially in 1864, Leavenworth was often serviced directly by boat from St. Louis.

Both the Hannibal and St. Joseph and the North Missouri ran trains to St. Joseph. The North Missouri was hampered somewhat by the lack of a bridge at its St. Charles crossing of the Missouri. Initially the company maintained separate sets of rolling stock on opposite sides of the river. Since the St. Charles ferry could accommodate nothing larger than wagons, all railroad freight had to be transferred to them from cars. After the wagons were crossed, their contents had to be reloaded in other freight cars. The service was greatly improved in May 1864, when an independently owned ferry company began running a specially constructed railroad ferry. By grading the banks and running inclined track to the water's edge, cars could be rolled onto tracks on the ferry's deck. The new ferry could handle as many as two hundred cars daily. Crossing the river without having to break bulk saved the railroad a day from St. Louis to St. Joseph. Because of this time gain, the North Missouri claimed it was able to offer through bills of lading from New York and Boston just as advantageously as the Hannibal and St. Joseph could via Chicago.[27]

To provide regular steamboat service from St. Joseph to Omaha–Council Bluffs and all waypoints—including Forest City, White Cloud, Rulo, Arago, Aspinwall, Brownville, Rockport, Sonora, Peru, Nebraska City, and Plattsmouth—the Hannibal and St. Joseph Railroad operated its own boats. The 1862 trade was done by the *Omaha*, the same vessel that had pioneered steamboating to Sioux City, and the *West Wind*, a 350-ton side-wheeler. The next year the railroad ran three steamers—the *Denver*, *Emilie*, and *West Wind*—in its Missouri River Packet Line. The *Denver*, a 225-foot-long side-wheeler, had been built at Madison, Indiana, over the preceding winter, and the *Emilie* was purchased from Joseph La Barge and his co-owners. Appealing to travelers bound for Colorado or Utah, the company advertised that its railroad-steamboat combination could get them from New York or Philadelphia to Nebraska City or Omaha in only 75 hours.[28]

Other than St. Louis–based steamboats, the Hannibal and St. Joseph's vessels faced some competition from Iowa railroads, which worked with the Western Stage Company in promoting passenger business from Chicago to Council Bluffs–Omaha. The route through Iowa was especially popular whenever guerrillas disrupted railroad operations in northern Missouri. In the fall of 1861, when the Hannibal and St. Joseph was forced to suspend operations temporarily, stages running from railheads at Eddyville and Marengo, Iowa, to Council Bluffs were reported to be crowded with passengers who were able to travel from Chicago to the Missouri in three days.[29]

Nebraska City, the main overland freighting depot throughout the war for Oregon-California Trail destinations, was the commonest destination for the Hannibal and St. Joseph Railroad's steamers. In 1862, over a four-week period, 632 wagons loaded with about two and a half tons each were sent from Nebraska City to Colorado and the numerous road ranches en route. By season's end nearly 4,000 tons of freight had been sent by wagon from Nebraska City. With the possible exception of some locally produced corn and other grain, the freight was delivered by steamboats. Comparable amounts were shipped the next year.[30]

Omaha was the starting point for Oregon-California Trail army posts only in 1863, but it and Nebraska City continued to benefit from the military buildup in 1864. Responding to numerous Indian raids, the army reinforced the garrisons at Fort Kearny and Fort Laramie and established new installations in Nebraska and Colorado. By the end of the year, slightly more than three thousand troops were stationed along the trail from the Missouri to Salt Lake City and the connecting South Platte route to Denver.[31]

Supplying the garrisons caused overland freighting and steamboating to surge. Nebraska City's wagon exports in 1864 totaled about 11,500 tons. In an effort to meet the new demand, the Hannibal and St. Joseph added two steamers to its line. But even with five boats shuttling between St. Joseph and Nebraska City, it could not handle all the military freight. The situation created openings for the Merchants Line, which ran six boats from St. Louis, and for several independent operators. By early May, Nebraska City's fifty-one steamboat arrivals had delivered more than 4,000 tons of freight. After that auspicious start, the trade accelerated yet more, with shipments reaching about 1,000 tons per week.[32]

Usually the railroad's steamers ran within the St. Joseph–Omaha section, but on occasion they were used to deliver passengers and freight to Sioux City and Yankton and even beyond Fort Randall. The *West Wind* navigated above Omaha with some regularity in 1863. It was one of the boats used to move Indians to the newly created reservation at Fort Thompson and was later employed to deliver commissary stores and grain to Sioux City and Fort Randall in support of the Sully Expedition. On at least one occasion, the *West Wind*'s sister boat *Emilie* delivered pork, sugar, and 2,000 boxes of hardtack to Sioux City for Sully's troops.[33]

Most of the river shipments were the ordinary items used by developing societies, such as groceries, hardware, iron, clothing, cloth, drugs, liquor, mining equipment, wagons, and livestock. But in July 1862 one of the Hannibal and St. Joseph's boats carried a most unusual cargo from St. Joseph to Nebraska City. Nebraska Citians were amazed when an enormous self-propelled steam wagon was run off a steamer under its own power.

The contraption, which weighed about 10 tons when its water tank was full, was massive. Its rear wheels stood 10 feet 2 inches, with rims a foot and half wide. The front wheels had a diameter of 6 feet. The machine and its owner, Joseph R. Brown of Henderson, Minnesota, soon became the toasts of Nebraska City. Brown was smitten with the notion of running a fleet of eight such vehicles from Nebraska City to Denver, a 535-mile trip that usually took ox-drawn wagons five weeks. He aimed to revolutionize overland freighting by moving goods much faster than the normal ox-drawn wagon rate of only two miles an hour. Having experimented with an earlier steam wagon in Minnesota, he was attracted to Nebraska City because of its lucrative trade with Colorado.[34]

Brown, with boundless faith in the novel technology, was not dissuaded by the breakdown of his first steam wagon on its first run in Minnesota. Convinced that shortcomings of the original wagon could be remedied, he had another one manufactured in New York City by an experienced ironworker. With a small accompanying party, including two experienced railroad engineers as the wagon's drivers, Brown escorted the behemoth from New York City to Nebraska City. It was moved by rail to Quincy, Illinois, then ferried to Hannibal, Missouri, and brought to St. Joseph by the Hannibal and St. Joseph Railroad.

Brown's finest hours were when he demonstrated the seeming prowess of the "prairie motor" by steaming it around Nebraska City while giving free rides to towns-

people. In a carnival-like atmosphere, he was hailed by local boosters as unimpeach-
able proof that Nebraska City's route across the plains was superior to all others.

Reality soon set it after the steam wagon started for Denver. Four miles from
downtown an engine crank broke, and the vehicle was stalled 531 miles short of
its goal. After promising to have the part repaired in New York and then return
to launch his steam wagon fleet, Brown left town. But he never returned. Because
of an outbreak of Indian hostilities near his home, he rushed to Minnesota, where
he was preoccupied with Indian affairs for the next several years. The steam wagon
he had abandoned rusted over the years and was ultimately dismantled. Good-
humored Nebraska Citians made sure the machine was remembered. In recognition of Brown's grand scheme, they named their overland freighting road to Fort
Kearny the Steam Wagon Road.

With each passing year of the war, steamboating increased on the upper river.
Its principal markets were the agricultural frontier about Sioux City, Vermillion,
and Yankton; the Indian trade; the Montana gold rush; and army campaigns in
Dakota Territory.

Sioux City was the main market in the recently settled country that extended
upstream to between Yankton and Fort Randall. Most of the town's service was
provided by the *Florence*, a 399-ton side-wheeler captained by Joseph Throckmorton. In both 1861 and 1862 the boat made five voyages from St. Louis to Sioux City
and was the only vessel that could be regarded as a regular trader. The *Omaha*
landed at Sioux City twice in 1861, and the *Isabella* once the next year.[35]

For the first time in its history, Sioux City's exports in 1861 exceeded its imports.
In May, when the *Florence* steamed away toward St. Louis loaded with large
amounts of corn, potatoes, furs, and dry hides, the *Register* proclaimed the dawn
of a new day: "The fact that every steam boat which leaves the Upper Missouri
country carries away more freight than she brings in is a cheering indication of the
advancement of this country in agricultural and other industrial pursuits, and is
conclusive evidence that the days when we had to buy everything and had nothing to sell are passed."[36] Two weeks later the *Omaha* arrived with a number of
passengers and a small amount of freight but returned to St. Louis loaded with
corn. Sioux City achieved its favorable balance of trade in part because its production of such essential items as flour and pork was sufficient to meet local demands.
Also, Sioux City general merchants, while evolving into suppliers of small independent traders upriver, became dealers in buffalo robes, furs, and peltries. Their
trade in furs was bolstered by the replacement of the traditional Indian gathering
system with more intensive trapping by white farmers. Though not fur traders per
se, Sioux City's merchants nonetheless offered new competition to the Chouteau
company.[37]

Approximately half of the steamers that traded with Sioux City went on to
Yankton and Fort Randall. But that stretch of the river was often challenging. In
April 1861 the *Omaha*, after discharging freight at Sioux City, was sent to Fort Ran-
dall to pick up three companies of troops who were being transferred protect

Washington, D.C. Its round-trip, which normally should have taken no more than three days, was extended to two weeks because of low water and high winds.[38]

In late fall, when regular St. Louis boats were scarce on the upper Missouri, Sioux City's steam ferry *Lewis Burnes* forwarded goods to Yankton and Fort Randall. In early November 1861 the vessel was loaded with corn for the fort on what should have been a routine run. But the trip took all winter. After unloading the grain, Captain Howard, faced with low water and icing up, decided to winter his boat at the fort. When the ice broke up the next spring, its pressure tore the steamer from its moorings. It floated about a hundred miles before stalling on a sandbar near St. Helena, Nebraska Territory. After making extensive repairs, Howard was able to navigate the boat to Sioux City.[39]

Above Fort Randall, the 1861 steamboat trade was dominated by Pierre Chouteau, Jr., and Company. To carry Indian annuities, some freight for a merchant at Hellgate (near later Missoula, Montana), and its own goods, the firm used the *Chippewa*, commanded by Captain William H. Humphreys, and the *Spread Eagle*, captained by John La Barge. Charles Chouteau, determined to personally direct company affairs on the upper Missouri, again accompanied the expedition. Other than several stops to distribute annuities and a long delay caused by low water, the passage to Fort Union was routine.

At the fort, Chouteau consolidated the freight and tourists bound for Fort Benton on the *Chippewa*. The much larger *Spread Eagle* was loaded with some 18,000 buffalo robes, and La Barge was able to rush down on the June rise. He sped the steamer to St. Louis in a record 9 days and 8 hours.

Meanwhile, disaster struck the *Chippewa*. When the boat left Fort Union for Fort Benton, it was crowded with its crew, company employees, and about 50 tourists and loaded with perhaps as much as 250 tons of freight. Goods stashed in the hold included gunpowder and liquor. If Chouteau had adhered to the Steamboat Inspection Act of 1852, the gunpowder would have been stored apart from other goods. And if he had complied with the federal ban on selling liquor to Indians, the beverage would not have been on board. Chouteau was smuggling the liquor, but the deckhands who helped load the boat obviously knew about it and apparently helped themselves to free drinks on several occasions. Considering the rather confined boat environment, this tippling should have been obvious to someone in authority. Perhaps Chouteau and Humphreys knew and simply assumed that gratis liquor was an employee benefit.[40]

About suppertime on June 23, when the *Chippewa* was a few miles below the mouth of the Poplar River, a deckhand replete with container and lighted candle went into the dark hold to get refreshments. Apparently he dropped the candle, which ignited the alcohol, located close to about a ton and half of gunpowder. As the man, clothes ablaze, emerged from the hold, the first engineer immediately ran the boat to shore. After everyone was hurriedly evacuated, the securing hawser was cut so the flaming vessel would drift downstream. The *Chippewa* floated a mile or so downstream, became lodged, burned for about an hour, and exploded. The boat was a total loss, but some of its widely scattered contents were salvaged by passengers and nearby Crow Indians.

Chouteau immediately sent Andrew Dawson, one of his supervisors, to Fort Benton to obtain ox-drawn wagons, while he escorted the stranded crew and passengers to Fort Union. Six weeks after the explosion, Dawson's twenty-vehicle train reached Fort Union. Subsequently, he hauled freight to Fort Benton and provided an escort for some of the tourists, who apparently hiked all the way.

Through 1861 the Chouteau company managed to control river transportation to the changing country above Fort Union. Charles Chouteau found that working with the government in delivering Indian annuities and assisting explorers was not incompatible with the fur trade. But as he no doubt anticipated, such activity was usually a prelude to advances by hordes of whites, who would hasten the end of the trade. As Chouteau tried to recover from the loss of the *Chippewa*, bands of argonauts were prospecting in western Montana. Their gold discoveries rapidly propelled Montana into a new age where mining, rather than fur trading, dominated its economy.

In Montana, as elsewhere, knowledge of gold alone was insufficient to ignite a rush. The first men to find gold in western Montana were not interested in developing mining. In 1852 one Francois Finlay, familiarly known as Benetsee, discovered small amounts of gold. Benetsee, probably a Métis, had been in California during the 1849 rush, but he returned to Montana to trade furs with the Hudson's Bay Company. The company factor at Fort Connah, near Flathead Lake, assayed Benetsee's gold and relayed the news to his superiors. But the company, fearful of the effects of a gold rush on their traditional business, kept silent.

Benetsee, however, told an acquaintance, who in turn informed members of the Stevens Expedition in 1853. On the basis of this story and reports from local Indians, some of Stevens's party assumed there were potentially rich mines in the general vicinity of later Missoula.

The next year, mountaineer John Silverthorne brought some gold dust from an unspecified location to Fort Benton. He convinced post bourgeois Alexander Culbertson to accept the dust in exchange for a $1,000 worth of goods. Culbertson, who realized a 50 percent profit when he sold the gold, kept the affair quiet at the time. Like his superiors in Pierre Chouteau, Jr., and Company, he knew fur traders could not control a gold rush.[41]

By the late 1850s circumstances in California created a climate for systematic searches for new El Dorados in the West. As California was passing out of its placer stage, when amateurs could get gold by washing gravel from streambeds, scores of experienced prospectors were forced to go elsewhere. The "Old Californians" drifted into Colorado, British Columbia, Idaho, and Montana. All carried with them the hope of striking the next great bonanza.

The persistent search for gold in western Montana began with brothers Granville and James Stuart, who had gone with their father from eastern Iowa to participate in the California gold rush. Their father went home first, but the brothers stayed in the Golden State until 1857. When their overland trek to Iowa was disrupted by Granville's "mountain fever," they decided to join some traders who wintered in the Beaverhead valley. The next spring, they moved northward into the Deer Lodge valley, where they found small amounts of gold on Gold Creek. Since they were the first dedicated miners to find gold in the region, Granville Stuart claimed that he and his brother were the "real" discoverers of gold in Montana. The Stuarts, who sorely needed mining equipment, were unable to begin expanding their operations until the rush began in 1862.

Meanwhile, Missouri River newspapers heavily publicized the Pikes Peak gold rush, which would be of the most benefit to their towns. The failure of the Colorado mines to live up to expectations diverted some attention to strikes along the Clearwater and Salmon rivers in Washington Territory, whose eastern boundary was the Continental Divide. Generally, prospectors in the region that became part of the newly formed Idaho Territory in 1863 came from the west by way of the Columbia River and Fort Walla Walla. Farther inland, Lewiston, established at the juncture of the Clearwater and Snake rivers, became the main depot for prospectors headed for the lower reaches of both the Clearwater and the Salmon. The Idaho finds, which also attracted a number of Willamette valley farmers, were first publicized in Oregon and California. News of Clearwater and Salmon mining, which soon spread nationwide, coincided with St. Louis and Sioux City promotion of the Missouri River route and the Mullan Road as the best way of reaching the Pacific Northwest. Some St. Louisians naturally assumed that any trade they could develop to the mines across the Continental Divide would also flow through Fort Benton.[42]

On March 22, 1862, a small group of St. Louisians, including H. M. Thompson, Josiah Fogg, and Nicholas Wall, organized the American Exploring and Mining Company. They had lofty aspirations. With Fogg as president and Wall, a veteran steamboat captain and agent, as expedition leader, the company announced plans to run a regular line of packets to Fort Benton. But with a capitalization of only $10,000, it barely had enough resources to outfit Wall with some goods. For steamboat transportation, Wall and his associates turned to the newly formed La Barge, Harkness, and Company.[43]

La Barge, Harkness, and Company was the most serious challenge to Pierre Chouteau, Jr., and Company since the demise of Frost and Todd. But other than competing with Chouteau for the Indian business along the Missouri, the new firm intended to trade with mining camps. It was well financed. Each of the partners—Joseph La Barge, John La Barge, James Harkness, Eugene Jaccard, and Charles E. Galpin—invested $10,000. Their talents seemed to complement each other well. The La Barge brothers were to command the steamboats; Harkness was to sell merchandise to miners; Galpin, a former partner in Pierre Chouteau, Jr., and Company, was to supervise the Indian trade; and Jaccard, a St. Louis merchant, was to manage affairs there. Robert Campbell, the old Chouteau nemesis, agreed to buy the company's furs.[44]

Seizing on the fever about what the press usually called the "Salmon River mines," the company readied two steamers—the *Emilie* and the *Shreveport*. Both were side-wheelers, but the plan was obviously to use the light-draft 145-ton *Shreveport*, whose dimensions were 155 × 28 × 4.4 feet, as a lighter for the *Emilie*, which was 225 × 32 feet, with a capacity of 388 tons. However, the main challenge above Cow Island proved to be a high, rapid current rather than low water.[45]

John La Barge had the *Shreveport* pulled away from the St. Louis levee on April 30. Joseph with the *Emilie* started two weeks later. Between the two vessels, they carried about 500 tons of freight, 160 cabin passengers, who paid $100 each for Fort Benton tickets, and about 140 deck passengers. Except for some health seekers who were intrigued by the notion that dry western air would alleviate their ailments, the passengers were headed for the mines on the west side of the Continental Divide.[46]

Although anxious to reach Fort Benton, the La Barges took time to curry favor with the pro-development elite of Sioux City and Yankton. The arrival of the *Shreveport* at Yankton prompted a celebration of the season's first boat. At the cry of "Steamboat! Steamboat!" the citizenry thronged to the levee, and the territorial legislature adjourned. The lawmakers—accompanied by Governor William Jayne, other territorial officers, and the federal court justices—boarded the vessel, where Captain John La Barge entertained them with champagne. After the obligatory round of toasts, the local editor observed that if "the host of good wishes . . . could all be granted, the Shreveport would soon return straining with golden treasure, and Dakota would speedily be overflowing with population and prosperity." Wanting to get under way quickly, La Barge declined invitations to spend time in town. As the boat cast off, "three hearty cheers were given" by the townspeople, and "she soon swung out into the stream and steamed away amid renewed cheers, clouds of smoke, and visions of gold."[47]

Joseph La Barge stopped the *Emilie* at Sioux City to promote his company's "Miners Line" of steamers. La Barge advertised that travelers on the company's two boats, by using connecting stagecoaches at Fort Benton, could get to the Bitterroot valley mines in only thirty to thirty-five days from St. Louis. Furthermore, he assured readers, that citizens of Oregon and Washington could reach "their friends in the states" in only one-fourth the time and expense of any other route.[48] Sioux City's schemers, who were then promoting a trans-Iowa stage line from Dubuque to Sioux City for argonauts, knew that any increased steamboating on the upper Missouri would bolster their trade.[49]

To face the challenge of La Barge, Harkness, and Company, Charles Chouteau sent the *Key West* and *Spread Eagle* to Fort Benton. With Chouteau again going upriver, the boats got under way after the *Shreveport* but before the *Emilie*. Competition between the companies was tinged with resentment, if not outright hostility. Chouteau, who had never tolerated rivals, had every reason to be bitter toward former employees Joseph and John La Barge and his onetime partner Galpin. Conversely, Joseph La Barge had been carrying a grudge since ending his service with the Chouteau company over a disagreement about his authority.

Mutual harsh feelings may account for Joseph La Barge's determination to overtake the Chouteau boats.

Tension erupted soon after the *Emilie* overtook the *Spread Eagle* above Fort Berthold near the mouth of the White Earth River. Robert E. Bailey, pilot of the *Spread Eagle,* challenged the more powerful *Emilie.* James Harkness, a passenger on the *Emilie,* noted: "The Spread Eagle is just alongside us, and we are having a race, (probably) the first ever run on the upper Missouri. She passed us and then we passed her, when she ran into us, breaking our guards and doing some other damage. There was a good deal of angry talk."[50] La Barge, convinced that Bailey had deliberately rammed him, filed a complaint with the steamboat inspector at St. Louis, who temporarily revoked Bailey's pilot's license.[51]

After the *Emilie* caught up with the *Shreveport,* the boats proceeded together to Fort Benton. The Missouri through the rapids was extraordinarily high and fast. At the fort the flooded stream was lapping at the front gate. The La Barges had the satisfaction of getting their boats to the head of navigation on June 17, three days before Chouteau's.[52]

As part of its trading plan, La Barge, Harkness, and Company built a rival post, Fort La Barge, a mile and a half above Fort Benton. Initially, the station was just a dumping place for the cargoes of the two steamers. But Harkness soon erected a warehouse and a set of cabins. Unlike traditional Missouri River trading posts, the buildings were not enclosed within palisades. Anticipating the need for lumber, Harkness had brought a steam sawmill, the first in Montana, up on the steamers.

By the end of 1862, La Barge, Harkness, and Company seemed to be a formidable challenge to Pierre Chouteau, Jr., and Company, and Montana gold mining was expanding rapidly. After his Fort Benton trip, Joseph La Barge returned to St. Louis with the *Emilie* and carried a consignment of trade goods to Sioux City. The *Shreveport,* better suited to late-season low water, forwarded the freight to Fort Galpin, the company's new trading post near the mouth of the Milk River. The firm also started Fort La Framboise near Fort Pierre II, as well as other stations near Fort Berthold and close to the Big Muddy near old Fort Stewart.[53]

In Montana, Harkness found that there was no need to ship goods as far as the Salmon River region. Some prospectors made their way to Fort La Barge, and there was a concentration of miners on Gold Creek in the Deer Lodge valley. When sales at the fort slowed, Harkness outfitted a wagon train and made his way to Gold Creek. There may have been a good market there, but Harkness seemed to lack the energy and zeal of a successful merchant. Furthermore, he did not deal well with life's daily torments, such as swarms of mosquitoes and temperatures that sometimes topped 100 degrees. By the time he reached Gold Creek, he was too homesick to pursue the trade. Rather than establish a store among the prospectors, he sold some of the goods to Nicholas Wall of the American Exploring and Mining Company and left the remainder for Wall to sell on consignment.[54]

The Gold Creek production of 1862, while not great, lured more prospectors to Montana. Any exports of gold were enough to convince hopeful seekers that much more awaited discovery. There was considerable excitement over a newspaper report that the *Shreveport* brought down $100,000 worth of gold dust to St. Louis. Presumably, this ore was from the Gold Creek region.[55]

One of the main characteristics of placer mining frontiers was for prospectors to rove into new areas in the hope of finding the great bonanza. Such was the case in Montana when strikes were made at Bannack (near present Dillon) in July 1862. By October the mines, where Bannack City was started the next year, had attracted four hundred people.[56]

Because of these new finds, everyone interested in Montana's gold—including the Chouteau company; La Barge, Harkness, and Company; hundreds of potential argonauts; and federal government officials—assumed that mining would boom the next year. But by the time Missouri River navigation opened in 1863, reaching Montana was greatly complicated by the aftermath of Minnesota's Indian War of 1862.

The Minnesota conflict, traditionally called the Sioux Uprising but more recently labeled the Dakota Conflict, began in August 1862. At the time, some 7,000 Dakotas (commonly called Santee or Eastern Sioux) were confined to two long, narrow reservations that together stretched from near New Ulm northwestward to Big Stone Lake. An aggressive assimilation policy pursued by federal agents had polarized the Dakotas into traditional and pro-white factions. The traditionalists railed against the treaties that had stripped them of their lands. Their long-standing discontent was compounded by food shortages, late annuity payments, bureaucratic red tape, and encroaching white settlement. When Indian militants lashed out at nearby farmers, their supporters amounted to a strong minority.[57]

In a ten-day offensive the hostiles, led by Little Crow, raided numerous farms, sieged Fort Ridgely (near later Fairfax, Minnesota), and attacked New Ulm. Four to five hundred whites were killed, and hundreds of others fled eastward. Alexander Ramsey, Minnesota's governor, responded by naming Henry Hastings Sibley, his predecessor and a veteran fur trader, to lead state forces against Little Crow. Early in Sibley's campaign, Ramsey persuaded the Lincoln administration to provide military support by creating the Department of the Northwest, commanded by Major General John Pope. Sibley's large force of some 1,600 men prevailed in two skirmishes, captured about 2,000 Dakotas, and forced the remainder to flee into Dakota Territory or Canada.

Most of the captives were peaceful women and children who were confined to a camp near Fort Snelling over the winter. But about 400 of those apprehended were accused of war crimes. More than 300 of them were convicted by a court-martial board. Of these, 38 were adjudged guilty of rape or murder and were executed by hanging at Mankato on December 26, 1862.

Widespread fear, fired by the Minnesota press, that hostiles would attack the state from Dakota led to calls that all Dakota Indians be evicted from Minnesota. The state's congressional delegation easily persuaded Congress to abrogate the treaties that had created the Dakota reservations and to provide for the removal of the Dakota beyond the limits of any state. The unfortunate Winnebagos, some 2,000-

strong, who had been recently moved to a reservation near Mankato, were likewise victimized by the anti-Indian sentiment. They had stayed neutral during the conflict, but angry whites insisted that all Indians in southern Minnesota be removed.[58]

Removal may have soothed some white anxiety, but the greatest security threat came from hostiles who had fled into Dakota Territory, where they were welcomed by their kinsmen. The Yanktonais, whose range extended through much of Dakota Territory east of the Missouri, and various bands of the Teton Sioux, or Lakotas, spoke essentially the same language as the Dakotas. Their ancestors had once been part of the Dakotas before moving out onto the plains. Such recent changes as the establishment of Fort Randall, the Yankton cession of 1858, increased army exploration, the movement of miners to Montana, and a declining fur trade led many Yanktonais and Tetons to believe that the Minnesota war was a preview of their fate. Threatening whites and sympathy for the Dakota refugees caused the indigenous Sioux of Dakota Territory to become more warlike.

The joining of Dakota refugees and their western kin created near panic in Minnesota and Dakota Territory. Still shocked by the violence of August 1862 and propagandized by fear-mongering newspapers, Minnesotans were generally convinced that a horde of Sioux would sweep into the state in the summer of 1863. Governor William Jayne warned that Dakota Territory, which was struggling to attract settlers, was indefensible without strong federal forces. Presuming that hostilities were inevitable, La Barge, Harkness, and Company worried about the security of its Missouri River posts. In their letter of January 14, 1863, to Commissioner of Indian Affairs William P. Dole, company officers claimed that all river installations between Fort Randall and Fort Benton were vulnerable. Their opinion was buttressed by Samuel N. Latta, head of the Upper Missouri Agency, who believed the Sioux would attack anyone who tried to move through their lands.[59]

Faced with a regional crisis, the Lincoln administration decided that the salvation of Minnesota and Dakota and the safeguarding of Missouri River navigation could be achieved only by crushing the Sioux. From his Milwaukee headquarters, Pope developed a grand strategy of trapping the Sioux in a giant double envelopment. One army would march overland from Minnesota toward Devils Lake, where Pope thought the hostiles were concentrated. It would drive the Indians westward to the Missouri, where another force that had steamboated up the river from Sioux City would intercept them. While the expeditions were being readied, Bureau of Indian Affairs officials supervised the removal of the Dakotas from St. Paul and the Winnebagos from Mankato.[60]

Commissioner Dole and his boss, Secretary of the Interior John P. Usher, decided that the Minnesota Indians should be relocated to a Dakota Territory site on the Missouri River near Fort Randall. Fearing that some might escape on a march across the plains, they opted for steamboat transportation provided by Pierre Chouteau, Jr., and Company. Since its own two steamers were committed to the Fort Benton trade, the Chouteau company chartered various Minnesota, Mississippi, and Missouri steamboats. To deport the 1,318 Dakotas from St. Paul, they used the *Davenport* and the *Northerner* of the Northern Line Packet Company. Before the *Davenport*, traveling a day ahead of the *Northerner*, reached Hannibal, its captain was notified that the *Florence*, which was to transport the Indians from St. Joseph to their new home, was still delayed in St. Louis. So rather than pay railroad fare, he took the cheaper course and delivered the Indians to St. Louis, where they were hastily transferred to the comparably sized *Florence*. When the already crowded *Florence* reached St. Joseph, the *Northerner*'s 547 passengers, who had arrived on railroad freight cars, were crammed on board. Neither the contractor nor the government seemed to be concerned about honoring the contract stipulation that the Indians were to be given "ample space for comfort, health, and safety."[61]

Clark W. Thompson, superintendent of Indian affairs for the Northern Superintendency, had traveled ahead of the Dakotas to select their Missouri River reservation. After engaging the steamer *Isabella*, provisions, and workmen in St. Louis, he hastened upstream to prepare for the arrival of the Indians. He selected a site for the new combined Dakota-Winnebago Agency at the mouth of Crow Creek, about 110 miles upstream from Fort Randall. When the *Florence*, with its sickly, hungry exiles, arrived only two days behind him, he had not had time to do anything more than unload the *Isabella*.

On its 13-day, 600-mile voyage from St. Joseph, the *Florence* was plagued by low water, sandbars, and high winds. The boat's officers once worked for two days getting the vessel over a bar. To lessen the draft at stoppages, the Indians were unloaded, made to walk across the sandbars, and await the steamer. On one occasion they stood at the head of a bar for almost a day without food while being pelted for a time by drenching rain.

Moving the Winnebagos from Mankato to Crow Creek was somewhat more complicated because it involved Minnesota River steamboating. The small regular Minnesota River packets *Favorite* and *Eolian* were used to St. Paul, and the *Canada* and *Davenport* downstream to Hannibal. After the railroad leg, the Winnebagos were delayed in St. Joseph before being carried to Crow Creek on the Hannibal and St. Joseph Railroad packet *West Wind* and the *Florence*. The arrival of the *Florence* at Crow Creek on June 24 completed the movement of 1,306 Dakotas and 1,945 Winnebagos. Thompson initially called the new agency Usher's Landing, but it was soon known as Fort Thompson, the name it retained.

Eight days before the last of the Winnebagos arrived at Fort Thompson, the army from Minnesota had started its northwest march. Led by Brigadier General Henry Hastings Sibley, the impressive force of 3,300 men and about 200 wagons made a five-mile-long column when it left Camp Pope near present Redwood Falls.[62]

Over the course of six weeks, Sibley led his troops to near Devils Lake and then westward to the Missouri near present Bismarck. After establishing a base, Camp Atchison, for his supply train and some 300 guards southeast of Devils Lake, Sibley's main force engaged Sioux warriors three times before reaching the river. Although the Sioux chiefs had from 1,000 to 1,500 warriors, they retreated strategically rather than fight a pitched battle. In the skirmishes of Big Mound, Dead

Buffalo Lake, and Stony Lake, fought in a five-day period in late July, Sibley easily routed the Sioux, forcing them to abandon much of their food and equipment and flee across the Missouri. Hoping to rendezvous with the Missouri River army of Brigadier General Alfred Sully, Sibley waited on the river for two days before turning homeward on August 1.

He made a wise decision. Sully's force, overdependent on steamboats, was still encamped on the Missouri's left bank about 10 miles above present Pierre. The expedition was delayed by record low water, complications in assembling steamboats and troops, and a change of command.

Near the end of March, when there was still good reason to believe the Missouri would rise, Pope announced that he intended to have more than 2,000 men at Sioux City and Fort Randall by April 15. He planned for the force to be in the field by May 10 or as soon as the grass was long enough for grazing animals.[63]

Logistically, the army's first step was to move equipment and stores from St. Louis to Sioux City, headquarters of its District of Iowa. By early April, quartermaster officers in St. Louis had chartered the *Isabella* and *Robert Campbell, Jr.* When the *Isabella*, loaded mostly with government freight, reached Sioux City on April 9 and the *Robert Campbell, Jr.*, carrying 25 wagons, 4 howitzers, and a supply of ammunition, landed nine days later, Pope's schedule seemed attainable. But there was a long delay before the steamers that were to accompany the expedition reached Sioux City. Finally, on June 7, the chartered *Belle Peoria, Glasgow, Sam Gaty,* and *War Eagle* delivered 480 mules, 123 horses, 100 wagons, and miscellaneous stores. Low water contributed to their tardiness, but because of the needs of the Vicksburg campaign, quartermaster officers in St. Louis also had difficulty procuring boats.[64]

Meanwhile, Nebraska officials were slow in releasing their territory's component of the expedition, and Sully had replaced Brigadier General John Cook. Pope had named Cook to command the District of Iowa soon after the Department of the Northwest was formed. But as the launching of the expedition became imminent, War Department officials decided that the command should be given to someone with experience in frontier warfare. Sully, an 1841 West Point graduate, had served in Florida's Seminole War, in Oregon's Rogue River War, with Harney's expedition at Fort Pierre, and against the Cheyenne. During the Civil War he had fought in several battles in Virginia and was promoted to brigadier general after distinguishing himself at the Battle of Antietam.[65]

The transfer of the Department of Iowa command from Cook to Sully did not occur until early June. Sully, slowed by the tardiness of troops and supplies, did not leave Sioux City until about June 20. His entire force, including some advance units that had been sent to Fort Randall, amounted to about 2,500 men. It was accompanied by the *Belle Peoria, Glasgow, Sam Gaty,* and *War Eagle,* each of which carried a one-company security guard and supplies. But the main body moved overland by way of the road through Elk Point, Vermillion, Yankton, and Fort Randall. Other than the 2,118 horses of the Iowa and Nebraska cavalry units and field batteries, the army had 234 wagons, 1,200 mules, 200 civilian employees, and

400 beef cattle. "Logroller," a Yankton correspondent whose report was published in the *Sioux City Register* of July 4, thought that it was "by all odds the most formidable expedition ever sent against the Indians on this continent." After conferring with Dakota Territory officials in Yankton, Sully decided to assign some 600 men to patrol duty in the area from Yankton to the Big Sioux River. Except for a few small raids, there had been no Indian presence in this section, but Sully evidently felt obliged to placate settlers' fears.[66]

Sully's first goal was to establish a base camp near Fort Pierre II and stay there until the supply-laden steamers reached him. He had no way of knowing that 1863 would be one of the severest drought years. He realized that the spring had been dry throughout the plains and that the Missouri was low, but those familiar with the river expected a June rise from melting mountain snow and accompanying rain in the usual wettest month on the plains. Neither occurred. In retrospect, it was obvious the drought period included the previous winter when there was a dearth of snow in the Rockies and a fifty-day rainless period on the plains.[67]

None of the chartered steamers, all side-wheelers, coped well with the shallow river. With the exception of the 263-ton *Belle Peoria*, which was 180 × 32 feet, they were large. The 340-ton *Glasgow*, which had a 5-foot hold, was 208 feet long and 34.5 feet wide. The 294-ton *Sam Gaty* was 210 × 36 feet, and the 446-ton *War Eagle* was 223 × 35 × 6 feet.[68] In even a normal year, such boats would have had difficulty on the upper Missouri. In procuring them, St. Louis quartermaster officers of the Western River Transportation Office probably had little choice, because of previous commitments to the Vicksburg campaign and other Mississippi River needs. They were also victimized by circumstances. If the river had been as high as in 1862, their choices would have been fine.

Dissatisfied with his steamboat escort, Sully impressed the *Alone* from Pierre Chouteau, Jr., and Company and the *Shreveport* from La Barge, Harkness, and Company while the boats were descending. Both the *Alone,* which the Chouteau Company had chartered from John G. Copelin, and the *Shreveport* were light-drafted.

The army's reimbursement for impressed boats was comparable to the voluntary agreements it made when chartering vessels.. Copelin was paid $170 per day for the use of the *Alone*. Daily rates for the *Belle Peoria, Glasgow,* and *War Eagle* were respectively $180, $215, and $225. Usually the boat's owners covered all expenses except fuel. Thus the somewhat higher reimbursement for larger boats was probably because of their labor and meal costs for larger crews.[69]

Pope knew the river was low, but he faulted Sully for continuing to rely on steamers. On August 5 he admonished: "I never had the slightest idea you could delay thus along the river, nor do I realize the necessity of such delay." Asserting that he "never dreamed you would consider yourself tied to the boats if they were obstacles in going up the river," Pope insisted that Sully should have used wagons.[70]

By the time Sully received Pope's missive, at least the first steamers had arrived at the base camp. Of the boats acquired in St. Louis, the *Belle Peoria* performed the best. It was used to forward supplies from the *West Wind,* which could not even reach Fort Randall. On August 1, the *Belle Peoria* and the *Shreveport* reached the camp. Sully, particularly impressed with the *Belle Peoria,* named his headquarters Camp Peoria in recognition of the boat's services. After extensive double-tripping, the other steamers reached Camp Peoria by August 12.[71]

While preparing to move out from Camp Peoria for his presumed rendezvous with Sibley, Sully used the *Alone* and *Shreveport* to establish a supply base about a hundred miles upstream. During the course of a four-week campaign from Camp Peoria, Sully's men moved along the Missouri to near present Bismarck, where they found evidence of Sibley's arrival and departure. They also determined that a large body of Sioux had recrossed the river after Sibley's departure. Assuming the Indians had gone to their traditional hunting grounds on tributaries of the James River, Sully led his force southeastward. After marching nearly a hundred miles, his scouts found a village of an estimated 1,500 Indians about 20 miles northwest of present Ellendale. In his victorious attack of September 3—the Battle of White Stone Hill—Sully reported 150 Indians had been killed, at the loss of 20 troops killed and 38 wounded.[72]

On September 14 the expedition completed its overland trek to Camp Peoria. Sully soon established a new base, Fort Sully, on the Missouri's left bank, about five miles below present Pierre. Sully, who was very familiar with the area because of his service with Harney, probably was influenced by long-standing Indian trade with Fort Pierre. A highly visible nearby military post would symbolize the government's determination to extend its control up the Missouri.

It was obvious to Pope, Sully, and virtually everyone else that the 1863 campaigns had not achieved their aim of controlling the Sioux. Captain Joseph La Barge of the *Robert Campbell* thought the future of the upper Missouri was at stake. He warned that failure to punish the Indians and fortify the region would mean "the government will be obliged to abandon the navigation of the Upper Missouri until the Indians see fit to lift their blockade."[73]

After arranging for the construction of log buildings at Fort Sully, the general and his staff moved to their winter quarters in Sioux City. On October 7 the *Alone* and *Belle Peoria,* the last two boats above Fort Randall, delivered sixty to seventy sick and wounded of Sully's command to the Sioux City hospital. During that month, the *Shreveport* and the new steamer *Calypso* brought supplies up the river, but they could not be navigated above Sioux City. For conveying supplies to Fort Sully during the fall and winter, the army relied on the Sioux City merchandising firm of H. D. Booge and Company and other contractors. The freighters, who used ox-drawn wagons, were paid $6 per hundredweight.[74]

Poor navigation frustrated the army on the upper Missouri in 1863, but it was disastrous for La Barge, Harkness, and Company and Pierre Chouteau, Jr., and Company, the contenders for the Fort Benton trade. The expanding Bannack mines promised a lively business in freight and passengers, and both firms had a chain of trading posts along the river upstream from Fort Pierre II and Fort La

Framboise to Fort Benton. But the prized contract for delivering Indian annuities had been granted to Joseph La Barge.

La Barge's contract of April 1 with Commissioner of Indian Affairs William P. Dole was made in his name, not that of La Barge, Harkness, and Company. Specified reimbursement rates per hundredweight from St. Louis were $0.75 to Omaha, $1.25 to the mouth of the Niobrara River, $1.50 to Yankton Agency, $2 to Fort Pierre, $2.25 to Fort Berthold, $2.50 to Fort Union or vicinity, $6 to Fort Benton or vicinity, and $5 to either Fort Sarpy or the mouth of the Milk River. La Barge, Eugene Jaccard, and Robert Campbell posted a $15,000 bond.[75]

To forward the mining goods, annuities, army supplies, and freight for Sioux City and Yankton merchants, La Barge, Harkness, and Company used the *Shreveport* and the *Robert Campbell, Jr.* Ideally the boats would have traveled together, but when the annuities were delayed in reaching St. Louis, the company sent the *Shreveport*, commanded by John La Barge, ahead. Its slow eighteen-day passage to Sioux City did not augur well for future navigation. But it was the most successful of the four Fort Benton bound steamers. On June 20 the *Shreveport* reached Snake Point near Cow Island. Faced with extraordinarily low water and no prospect of a rise, La Barge unloaded 85 passengers and 250 tons of freight about 130 miles short of Fort La Barge and about 400 miles from the Bannack mines. The stranded passengers, who had paid $125 and $50 respectively for cabin and deck passage, apparently had no recourse against the company. Boat captains usually carried only small amounts of petty cash, and after the ruinous season, the company would not have had the resources to honor its obligations.[76]

Before heading the *Shreveport* downstream, La Barge arranged for mackinaws to forward the freight and passengers. But when they could ascend only to the Judith River, Robert Lemon, Fort La Barge's manager, arranged with King and Gillette, pioneer Montana freighters, to haul goods to the Bannack mines. Their charge of $25 per hundredweight was one of the main reasons for the demise of La Barge, Harkness, and Company.

Nicholas Wall of the American Exploring and Mining Company was the principal consignee of the Bannack freight. He and his principal investor, John J. Roe, a St. Louis meat-packer, forwarding agent, and steamboat owner, challenged the added cost and demanded compensation from La Barge, Harkness, and Company. When the La Barge brothers and their partners did not pay, Roe and Wall brought suit against them in Montana, soon after the territory was organized in 1864. Roe and Wall prevailed. To satisfy its creditors, La Barge, Harkness, and Company had to relinquish its oxen to Roe and Wall and dispose of Fort La Barge and all its property, as well as the company's downstream holdings along the Missouri.[77]

The annuity contract proved to be another serious complication for the La Barges and their partners. Joseph La Barge, who was obligated to receive the Indian goods at St. Louis, naturally wanted to get under way as early as possible. But assembling annuities, which involved a complex of contractors and subcontractors, was usually slow. La Barge was not able to get under way with the *Robert*

Campbell, Jr. until May 13. The large 421-ton side-wheeler, at 226 × 41 × 6 feet, would have been challenged at a normal river stage when loaded only to capacity. But when it pulled away from the St. Louis levee, it was grossly overloaded with 650 tons and an army escort. Its passage to Sioux City took nearly a month, with numerous groundings, sparring over sandbars, and warping. Discharging 150 tons of freight at Sioux City and 200 at Fort Randall helped, but the worst part of the river was above Fort Pierre.

La Barge could not even manage to get the boat to Fort Union. A short distance below the Yellowstone, he was relieved by the descending *Shreveport,* which made five relays to Fort Union. Obviously, La Barge could not fulfill his obligation to deliver the Blackfeet and Flathead annuities to Fort Benton. He had no choice other than to arrange for storing most of them at Fort Union until the next season.

The Chouteau company was positioned better than La Barge, Harkness, and Company to withstand a really bad year. Charles Chouteau, who once again went to the upper river, was apparently convinced that only small, light-draft stern-wheelers were suitable. He obtained the services of the *Alone* and the new 249-ton *Nellie Rogers,* which was 178 × 32 × 4.6 feet. With company outfits, supplies for the Bannack mines, and passengers, the boats got under way from St. Louis on May 9. Their eighteen-day passage to Sioux City was the easiest part. In July the *Alone* was halted a few miles below the Poplar River, but the *Nellie Rogers* was navigated above to the Milk River.[78]

Combined, the Chouteau boats transported 500 tons of freight and perhaps as many as 300 passengers upstream. Charles Chouteau, who was traveling on the *Nellie Rogers,* arranged to have Joseph A. Slade forward part of the cargo to the Bannack mines by freight wagon. The poor performances by the La Barge, Harkness, and Chouteau boats stimulated Montana's overland freighting and led many miners and suppliers to think that steamboating to Fort Benton was impractical. It seemed to them that establishing a freighting depot below Fort Benton was desirable, if not necessary.[79]

Both the *Robert Campbell, Jr.* and the *Nellie Rogers* had freight and passengers on their return voyages. The La Barge boat delivered a large consignment of buffalo robes to H. D. Booge and Company at Sioux City. The *Nellie Rogers* transported 17,000 buffalo robes to St. Louis. An estimated 200 passengers from Fort Benton and the Bannack mines came down on the steamers. Charles Chouteau was disappointed with the season's returns. He said that because of low water and menacing Indians, the year was the worst in his quarter century of Missouri River navigation.

The drought drove up costs for the La Barge and Chouteau interests, but hostile Indians threatened to end navigation. All posts above Fort Pierre II were fired upon or menaced, but the greatest troubles occurred at and near Fort Union. When the *Robert Campbell, Jr.* and the *Shreveport* rendezvoused below the fort, a party of Indians killed three of the *Campbell*'s men. Both boats were barricaded with buffalo robes and boxes. The *Nellie Rogers* was spared from attack because of Father De Smet's intervention, and the *Alone* was fired into while temporarily stranded. Passengers on the descending boats reported that much of the already parched prairie had been burned by Indians. A 600-mile stretch on both sides of the river above Fort Berthold was said to have been blackened because the Indians were determined to deny subsistence to the animals of any invading army.[80]

Indian attacks on steamboats helped convince Pope that his greatest priority in 1864 was keeping the Missouri River open. He was also influenced by the growing importance of Montana's gold mining. In May 1863, prospectors made a rich strike in Alder Gulch, where Virginia City was soon established. By the end of the year about six thousand miners were working the gulch. Since the Missouri River was the main route to Montana, it was obvious that the need to supply miners would increase steamboating.[81]

Anticipating an 1864 rush to the mines by way of the Missouri and overland trails from Minnesota, Pope devised a new plan. He proposed to establish four new army posts—at Devils Lake, on the upper reaches of the James River west of the head of the Coteau des Prairies, on the Missouri near Long Lake, and on the Yellowstone. Pope thought the Yellowstone post should not be above the head of navigation, which he assumed would be from near the Powder River to as high as the Bighorn River.[82]

To secure the adjoining country, Pope ordered Sully to lead another expedition up the Missouri. Sully, who was to stay close to the stream to prevent Indians from molesting travelers, once again had to rely on steamers.

In contrast to his 1863 assignment to a nearly completed expedition, this time Sully had more control of preparations. After his first year's experience, he was worried about relying on steamboats when he arrived in St. Louis on March 10 or 11 to engage boats himself. Sully first turned to the aged Pierre Chouteau, Jr., and his son Charles. The Chouteaus easily persuaded Sully that he should use small light-draft stern-wheelers under their management. They were willing to transport all army freight from St. Louis to the Yellowstone for $4 a hundredweight.[83]

But Sully did not have authority to act on his own. Quartermaster officers in the Western River Transportation Office made all final decisions about the army's use of steamers. When commercial steamboating from St. Louis to New Orleans resumed soon after the Union's seizure of Vicksburg, it was somewhat easier for the quartermaster officers to acquire vessels. Apparently they believed it would be cheaper to obtain boats from a number of private owners rather than give the Chouteaus a monopoly.

In selecting specific boats, the quartermaster officers were influenced by the poor results of 1863 and Sully's lobbying for shallow-drafted vessels. They preferred small stern-wheelers but were unable to find enough to accompany the expedition. During April and May they obtained the *Alone* (211-ton stern-wheeler), *Calypso* (side-wheeler, 193 × 30 × 5 feet), *General Grant* (172-ton stern-wheeler), *Isabella* (361-ton side-wheeler, 211 × 32 feet), *Island City* (139-ton stern-wheeler, 140 × 30 feet), *Marcella* (300-ton side-wheeler, 180 × 32 × 8 feet), *Sam Gaty* (294-ton side-wheeler, 210 × 36 feet), and *Tempest* (stern-wheeler, 162 × 32.8 × 5.8 feet).[84]

Evidently, boat owners were generally not eager to participate in the Sully Expedition, which forced quartermaster officers to seize boats. At least four of the boats—*Island City, Isabella, Sam Gaty*, and *Tempest*—were impressed. Boat owners who resisted had no recourse. When John Dozier, captain and part owner of the *Isabella*, refused to accompany the expedition, quartermaster officers notified him that the boat would be taken anyway. After a short stalemate, F. W. Dozier, another part owner, agreed to command the vessel and raise a crew. Once a vessel was impressed, quartermaster officers negotiated a written "chartering" contract with its owners. Daily reimbursements for the *Island City, Sam Gaty*, and *Tempest* were $198, $322, and $290 respectively and an uncommonly low $116 for the *Isabella*.[85]

When the *Isabella*, the lead boat, reached Sioux City in late May, Sully and his superiors were very concerned about low water. Throughout the spring it appeared that navigation would be no better than that of 1863. But in early June the Missouri, fed by runoff from the Rockies, rose four feet in one day at Sioux City. This surge and subsequent timely rains in Dakota Territory provided reasonably good navigation throughout most of the summer.[86]

All eight of the steamers obtained in St. Louis arrived at Sioux City by mid-June. But Sully meanwhile had misgivings about his fleet. He wanted an additional steamer that was best suited for low water. Sully knew that two small stern-wheelers of the Idaho Steam Packet Company (also called the La Crosse Line) were moving up the Missouri for Fort Benton. The 93-ton *Chippewa Falls* and the comparably sized *Cutter* had started from near La Crosse, Wisconsin. At St. Louis they were loaded with about 300 tons of freight and 250 passengers for the mines. When the boats reached Sioux City in mid-May, quartermaster officers notified Captain Abe Hutchinson of the *Chippewa Falls* that they were impressing his boat. Captain Frank Moore of the *Cutter* somehow crammed the displaced freight and passengers onto his boat.[87]

Besides the nine steamers that were to accompany Sully upstream from Fort Sully, the army used eight others—*A. Majors, Effie Deans, J. H. Lacy, Kansas Valley, Louisville, Omaha, War Eagle*, and *West Wind*—to forward supplies to Sioux City, Fort Randall, Fort Sully, and Farm Island, near Fort Sully. The loss of the *Louisville* complicated the boat shortage. In late May, after delivering army goods to Sioux City, the boat was sent to St. Louis for another load. Sixty-five miles below the city, it was snagged and sank. Its loss made it even harder for Sioux City's merchants to import goods. Because the army had priority, they could not depend on obtaining steamer space. Throughout the season their commonest resupply method was to ship by wagons from the railhead at Marshalltown in central Iowa.[88]

Sully's campaign, which Pope, Sully, and Sibley had planned over the winter, called for the organization of two brigades that would join at the outlet of Swan Lake, on the east bank of the Missouri opposite and slightly downstream from the Moreau River's mouth. Sully organized the First Brigade, consisting of about 1,800 Wisconsin, Iowa, Nebraska, and Dakota troops at Fort Sully. The Second

Brigade of 1,551 mounted Minnesota troops (including 40 scouts) was readied at Fort Ridgely, 322 miles east of the Swan Lake outlet.[89]

When the Second Brigade, commanded by Colonel Minor T. Thomas, left Fort Ridgely on June 6, it was accompanied by a civilian wagon train headed for the Montana mines. The Holmes Train, named for its leader, Thomas A. Holmes, had 200 to 300 people and 113 to 175 wagons. Consisting mainly of Minnesotans, with some members from Connecticut, New York, and other states, it had been organized at Shakopee, Minnesota, and was one of eight trains sent from Minnesota to Montana during 1862–67. Sully and other military officials understandably resented having to allocate resources to escort civilians. But the Lincoln administration wanted to encourage gold mining to help finance the Union's war effort. As part of the drive to develop the mining region, Congress approved the creation of Montana Territory when the Holmes Train was being organized.[90]

After Sully and Thomas rendezvoused at Swan Lake Creek on June 30, Sully moved upstream with the steamers. On July 7 he selected the Fort Rice site, on the west side of the Missouri opposite and slightly above the mouth of Long Lake Creek. En route he used scouts to communicate with his command, which was marching up the east side of the river. After the boats were unloaded, Sully used seven of them to ferry the troops and emigrants across the Missouri. The movement took several days, with the Holmes Train crossing last on July 12. Quartermaster officers, who were obligated to pay the boats' fuel costs, charged the emigrants a cord of wood for each wagon. Producing their fee was relatively easy, because of extensive wooded areas near the fort.[91]

Sully left about a thousand troops behind when he led the expedition out of Fort Rice on July 19. Most of them were assigned to work on constructing the post, and smaller attachments were detailed to be security guards on the steamers.[92]

In coordination with his movement west by northwest toward the Badlands and the Yellowstone River, Sully ordered three of the smallest steamers—*Alone, Chippewa Falls,* and *Island City*—to carry corn and other supplies to a rendezvous area on the Yellowstone. He had planned to send more boats but could not spare them, because of a supply crisis. Sully assumed that some of the St. Louis steamers engaged in transportation to Sioux City, Fort Randall, and Fort Sully would make deliveries to Fort Rice. But none did. Instead some thousand tons of cargo, whose nature was unknown to him, were left at Fort Sully. This situation forced him to use two-thirds of his small fleet in forwarding this freight to Fort Rice.[93]

Much of the corn was lost when the *Island City,* owned by Adam Hine of Keokuk, Iowa, snagged and sank in shallow water on July 25 near the mouth of the Yellowstone. There were no casualties, and the boat's machinery was salvaged by the *Chippewa Falls* and the *Belle Peoria.* The *Belle Peoria,* which had made a private trip to Fort Union, transported the machinery to St. Louis. There it was sold for $3,800, which was given to Hine as partial compensation for his lost steamer.[94]

At about the same time as the *Island City*'s destruction, the *Isabella,* one of the six steamers being used to forward supplies from Farm Island to Fort Rice, was snagged and badly damaged near the Swan Lake outlet. Because it was leaking, Captain Dozier was allowed to return it to St. Louis, which was reached on August 18. An examination by James L. Bellas, an inspector selected by the Western River Transportation Office, revealed it had 93 broken timbers, about 300 square feet of broken plank, and extensive damage to its larboard wheelhouse and wheel.[95]

As Sully's expedition moved along the Cannonball and Heart rivers, his scouts found numerous signs of large Indian groups. Anticipating a fight, Sully ordered the emigrant train to camp at the Heart River with a military escort and await his return. When he defeated the Sioux in the Battle of Killdeer Mountain on July 28, Sully had about 2,200 men. He estimated the Indian strength at 5,000 to 6,000.

Anxious to reach the steamers on the Yellowstone before his supplies were exhausted, Sully, with the emigrant train in tow, decided to strike across the southern part of the Little Missouri Badlands. During the difficult 20-mile crossing, a short distance south of the present interstate highway I-94, troops struggled to get wagons through the sometimes steep terrain. To complicate matters, some marauding Indians who had trailed the expedition after the Battle of Killdeer Mountain, attacked the expedition's flanks. Before the force reached the Yellowstone, lack of grass, aggravated by a severe grasshopper infestation and alkali water, caused the death of many horses, mules, and oxen.[96]

On August 11, when the expedition was laboriously wending its way through the sharply eroded hills about 10 miles below present Glendive, Montana, troops heard the whistles of the *Alone* and *Chippewa Falls*. After the sinking of the *Island City*, the captains of the *Alone* and *Chippewa Falls* worried about ascending the shallow Yellowstone. Rather than risk both boats, Abe Hutchinson used the smaller *Chippewa Falls* to reconnoiter 40 to 50 miles upstream. His boat gained the distinction of being the first steamer on the Yellowstone. When he returned to Fort Union, Hutchinson was convinced that the *Cutter* and *Alone* could be taken even farther upstream if their loads were lightened. Accordingly, before the boats left Fort Union together their cargo was reduced to about 50 tons each. When they rendezvoused with Sully, they were about 90 miles from the river's mouth.[97]

After the rendezvous, Sully abandoned his original plan of campaigning north of the Yellowstone, because of poor grazing and the loss of the *Island City*'s corn. Instead he had the *Alone* and *Chippewa Falls* ferry his troops and the emigrants across the river preparatory to moving downstream to Fort Union. To save time, the livestock and some of the wagons were forded, with the loss of some animals and several men.[98]

Because the Yellowstone was falling, the *Alone* and *Chippewa Falls* had to be lightened. After Sully had much of their cargo transferred to wagons, the two boats were able to reach Fort Union. This experience reinforced Sully's misgivings about creating a post dependent on Yellowstone River steamboat navigation. After the troops and emigrants reached to opposite Fort Union, the two steamers completed ferrying them across the Missouri on August 20. To cram more men

Fort Berthold, shown in 1868, was established as a fur trading post but
became the base for a contingent of federal army troops in 1864.
Courtesy of the State Historical Society of North Dakota.

and equipment on the crowded boats, the wagons were disassembled. Once again,
the draft animals and cavalry horses were forded.[99]

During his short stay at Fort Union, Sully sent the *Alone* and *Chippewa Falls*
down with the sick and wounded troops and made an important decision about
starting a new fort. Rather than locate a post up the Yellowstone, which he thought
could not be supplied dependably by steamboat, he selected the site of future Fort
Buford, on the Missouri three miles below Fort Union. But, he concluded, low
water would prevent steamboats from bringing up construction supplies that fall.
So he opted to store military supplies at Fort Union and leave a company of troops
there to safeguard them. While marching his command to Fort Rice, Sully stopped
at Fort Berthold, where he stationed another company . He believed this action
was necessary to protect the Arikaras, Hidatsas, and Mandans, all supportive of
the government and traditional enemies of the Sioux. The Fort Union and Fort
Berthold garrisons completed the year's additions to the fortification of the northern plains. While Sully was in the field, Minnesota troops started Fort Wadsworth
(renamed Fort Sisseton in 1876) on the Coteau des Prairies near present Eden,
South Dakota. That site was substituted for a James River location when a reconnaissance determined that a river location near timber could not be found. Fort
Wadsworth was intended to protect the overland route of Minnesota emigrants
headed for Montana and to encourage settlement east of the James River. No

action was taken to found the Devils Lake post. By the time Sully left Fort Rice, Pope had decided it was too late in the season to start the post, which would have to be supplied by wagon from the Missouri River.

By September 9, when Sully's command reached Fort Rice, all of the steamers except the *Alone* and *Chippewa Falls* had been released. The *Calypso, Marcella,* and *Tempest* left Fort Rice for St. Louis on August 15. They were soon followed by the *General Grant* and *Sam Gaty,* which were released after transporting the last supplies from Farm Island to Fort Rice. By the time the boats descended, the Missouri was reported to be "exceedingly low." The *Calypso,* which drew only twenty-two inches light, frequently had to be sparred over sandbars.[100]

The river remained low all fall, but in September the *Effie Deans, J. H. Lacey,* and *Kansas Valley* brought up supplies and troops for Fort Randall, Fort Sully, and Fort Rice. The *Effie Deans* was loaded with a large contingent of troops enlisted from Confederate prisoners and deserters. These "Galvanized Yankees" were warmly greeted by Sioux Citians. Because of low water the steamer, loaded with troops for Fort Rice, had to stop 30 miles below the Crow Creek Agency. The men had to march from there.[101]

In reviewing his season's accomplishments, Sully insisted his force had proven its superiority to the Sioux. But he lamented what might have been. He attributed his failure to establish the Yellowstone post to a series of misfortunes, including the late rise of the Missouri, the loss of the *Isabella* and *Island City,* and the late-summer drought that made navigation difficult.[102]

Claims arising from the sinking of the *Island City* and the damaging of the *Isabella* took years to resolve. Quartermaster officers paid Adam Hine $13,191.75 for the use of the *Island City* from May 24, the date of its impressment, to its destruction on July 25. They also acknowledged that he was entitled to just compensation. But they and Hine disagreed over the boat's value. Hine produced documentation that he had been offered $28,000 for the boat shortly before she was impressed. But quartermaster officers thought that assessment was much too high. Their disagreement was carried through government channels to the Office of the Second Comptroller in the Treasury Department. In February 1868 the second comptroller ruled that Hine should be paid $20,300 for the boat and another $1,000 for personal services during its operation on the Sully Expedition. Since Hine had already received $10,000 from the boat's insurer and $3,800 from the sale of its salvaged machinery, the comptroller authorized the payment of $7,500. It seemed that this settlement resolved the matter, but in 1872 Hine had a Washington, D.C., law firm submit a claim for an additional $10,000 to Secretary of War William Worth Belknap. Hine evidently hoped to exploit his acquaintanceship with Belknap, formerly a fellow Keokukian. After investigating the history of the claim, Belknap confirmed the second comptroller's judgment.[103]

In the case of the *Isabella,* quartermaster officers acknowledged that the army was responsible for returning the boat to its owners in the same condition it had when impressed. Adhering to Bellas's initial estimate, they had $3,450 worth of repairs done.

But during a reinspection while the boat was being fixed, Bellas estimated that an additional $1,300 worth of repairs were needed. When the army refused to pay on the grounds that these damages did not occur during the boat's government service, John Dozier on behalf of himself and the other owners brought suit in the U.S. Court of Claims. In May 1874, nearly six years after the *Isabella* had been snagged and lost on the lower Missouri, the court awarded him and his partners $1,445.[104]

Over the winter of 1863–64, as Pope and Sully were planning the Sioux campaign, Montana gold stimulated great excitement in St. Louis and elsewhere. In 1863 about $8 million worth of gold was produced in the Bannack City and Virginia City vicinities. With good prospects for more finds in those and other areas, the entire region seemed ready to boom. As John G. Copelin and his father-in-law, John J. Roe, recognized, this new circumstance created a need for more steamboat shipments to Fort Benton. Unlike such competitors as the Chouteau company and the La Barge brothers, Copelin and Roe could devote themselves almost exclusively to the transportation of passengers and goods for the mining camps. They were unencumbered by such traditional businesses as the fur trade and shipping Indian annuities. Furthermore, Roe had established a position in the mining regions through his sponsorship of Nicholas Wall and the American Exploring and Mining Company.[105]

By early March, Copelin and Roe were advertising their St. Louis and Fort Benton Transportation Line. They intended to use four steamers—the new light-draft *Benton*, which would be operated as a shuttle above Fort Union, and the *Florence, Fanny Ogden,* and *Welcome.* But the upbound *Florence,* which was snagged and sunk at Atchison, was not replaced. Fares from St. Louis to Fort Benton for cabin and deck passengers were $150 and $75 respectively. The baggage allowance for each passenger was 100 pounds, and the freight charge to Fort Benton $10 per hundredweight.[106]

Copelin and Roe's plans for an early start were threatened by Pope, who wanted civilian boats to wait until Sully had quelled Indian opposition on the upper river. Pope also requested that the various operators travel together and bulletproof the vulnerable parts of their boats. But when Sully's negotiations in St. Louis were delayed, the army had to accommodate Fort Benton shippers. Copelin was in a position to be quite persuasive. He and three other well-financed St. Louis boat owners—Barton Able, John N. Bofinger, and George Peagram—had been awarded the army transportation contract between St. Louis and New Orleans. To conduct this large business, they had twenty steamboats at their disposal.[107]

The new 246-ton stern-wheeler *Benton,* which measured 197 × 33 × 5 feet, was the season's first steamboat to go above Sioux City, which it reached on April 15 after a nearly month-long voyage from St. Louis. Captain Thomas W. Rea got the boat to Fort Benton on June 10, with 200 tons of freight. Within days the trailing *Fanny Ogden* and *Welcome* were forced to stop near the Milk River, where they off-loaded goods at Fort Galpin. Their cargoes were forwarded by the *Benton,* which reached Fort Benton again on June 27 and the Marias River on July 9.[108]

Following their company's plan, Captain John P. Keiser of the *Fanny Ogden* and Thomas Townsend of the *Welcome* promptly started for St. Louis. Fearing his boat might be impressed, Keiser attempted to run it by Fort Sully by steaming full speed ahead on the far side of the channel. Sully, who was interested in gaining information from boat captains even if he did not intend to take their boats, was not about to be ignored. Keiser should have gotten the message when a cannonball landed in front of the bow, but he kept the boat moving until another, closer round caused him to land and talk.

In addition to the *Benton,* the *Cutter* reached Fort Benton in 1864. Slowed by low water, Moore finally got the boat to the port on July 17, nearly a month after leaving Fort Union. He had to leave a third of his cargo at Milk River (probably Fort Galpin). Moore never returned to retrieve it. In Fort Benton he became involved in a scheme to promote Ophir, a townsite at the mouth of the Marias, and wintered the *Cutter* there. He probably hired the *Benton* to forward his Milk River freight.

Both the La Barge brothers and Charles Chouteau were interested in the mining trade but had to devote resources to the delivery of Indian annuities. After its setbacks of 1863, La Barge, Harkness, and Company broke up. But Joseph La Barge hoped to recoup some of his personal losses by delivering the Indian annuities that he had stored at Fort Union. Indian Department officials had advised him that he could not be paid until the Fort Benton goods were delivered. To fulfill his contract and to do business in the mining camps, La Barge bought a controlling interest in the new stern-wheel *Effie Deans*. Assuming that he would be picking up the stored annuities at Fort Union, La Barge only partially loaded the boat with mining supplies at St. Louis.[109]

When he arrived at Fort Union, his already strained relations with Pierre Chouteau, Jr., and Company worsened. Chouteau's agent, who could not produce the stored annuities, insisted that he had distributed them to the tribesmen. Although he thought the Fort Union men had actually traded them as company goods, La Barge had no recourse. He set out for Fort Benton, but the *Effie Deans* was unable to proceed above Fort Galpin. Joseph La Barge turned the boat over to his brother, John, and arranged to have his goods forwarded by freight wagons. He sold some of them in Fort Benton and the remainder during a two-month stay at Virginia City. Carrying nearly $100,000 worth of gold dust, he made a long odyssey that took him by stage to Salt Lake City, then by wagon to Nebraska City, and thence on the season's last steamer to St. Louis, which he reached about December 1.

Mainly because of Joseph La Barge's failure to deliver the 1863 annuities, the 1864 Indian contract for the delivery of annuities to Fort Benton and waypoints was again awarded to Pierre Chouteau, Jr., and Company. Indian Department officials, who tended to be militant Republicans, generally resented the company, a long-standing favorite of Democratic administrations, which was widely rumored to have Confederate sympathies. But after the 1863 fiasco the Chouteau company was their best choice.

Perhaps because of the navigation problems in 1863 and the shortage of boats in 1864, the Chouteau company was paid considerably more than the La Barge rates. The greatest increases were for the Fort Union and Fort Benton goods. Chouteau's Fort Union rate of $4.50 per hundredweight was a $2 increase, and the Fort Benton charge of $10 was a $4 raise. A week after this agreement of March 18, Dole and the Chouteau company signed a contract calling for the delivery of the annuities from Fort Benton to Flathead Indian Agency, near present Dixon, Montana. Compensation for this wagon freighting was $9 per 100 pounds.[110]

To transport the annuities, supplies for the company's posts, goods destined for the mines, and some passengers, Charles Chouteau purchased the newly built *Yellowstone* for $70,000. In light of Chouteau's extensive experience on the upper Missouri, the rather large 378-ton side-wheeler, which measured 206 × 30 × 5.5 feet, was a surprising choice. As the man chiefly responsible for pioneering steamboat navigation to Fort Benton, Chouteau had been a strong advocate of small, light-draft stern-wheelers.

The *Yellowstone,* captained by William R. Massie and with Charles P. Chouteau on board, got away from St. Louis in mid-April. It was loaded with about 400 tons of freight, including the annuities, 200 barrels of whiskey and other company supplies, 300 passengers, and a 30-man army escort, which had two cannons. The passengers included the veteran missionary Father De Smet and John Buchanan, who was on his way to Virginia City with a printing press. Soon after reaching the bonanza community, Buchanan started publishing the *Montana Post,* the territory's first newspaper.[111]

Long before the boat completed its two-month passage to Fort Union, passengers were complaining about its inadequate engines and slowness. By the time the *Yellowstone* reached Cow Island, it was obvious to Chouteau and Massie that it could not be navigated over the upstream rapids. They anticipated a quick turn-about, but when the vessel was stranded for a week and half on a sandbar they had plenty of time to unload. Chouteau arranged for Joseph La Barge to move the passengers on the *Effie Deans.* Some of the annuities were distributed at Cow Island and the remainder and other provisions sent to Fort Benton by freight wagons and pack animals.

To add to Chouteau's dismay, fur receipts for the year were light. The returning *Yellowstone* bore only 1,700 bales of buffalo robes, some miscellaneous furs and peltries, some buffalo calves, two bald eagles and a number of other curiosities. Chouteau, who delighted himself by collecting mementos of the "Old West" certainly realized that it was being replaced by miners, townsite promoters, merchants, farmers and soldiers. The future of Missouri River steamboating seemed to lay with John G. Copelin and his like.

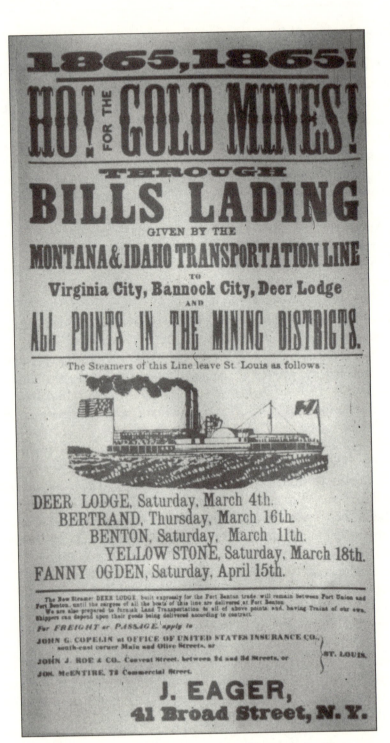

Advertisement of the Montana and Idaho Transportation Line.
The line, owned mainly by St. Louis business magnate John J. Roe and
his son-in-law John J. Copelin, heavily promoted the Montana gold rush.
*Courtesy of the U.S. Fish and Wildlife Service, Steamboat Bertrand Museum,
Missouri Valley, Iowa.*

8

Ho! For the Mountains

D uring the last half of the 1860s, St. Louis's trade with Fort Benton was the most lucrative aspect of Missouri River steamboating. To assure successful commerce by the river route, the federal government sharply increased its fortification of the upper Missouri, which in turn accelerated steamboat deliveries to army posts. The fur trade had lost its primacy in the regional economy during the Civil War but was still important enough that the successors of Pierre Chouteau, Jr., and Company regularly supplied their river outposts by steamboats. Because steamboating was the most efficient way of delivering annuities to upper Missouri tribes, the government located new Indian agencies along the river. Steamboat commerce to the agencies became more significant as buffalo herds diminished, making Indians more dependent on the government.

As the upper river trade was boomed by the gold rush and government expansion, there was a sharp revival of steamboating below Sioux City. Despite additional railroad construction in Missouri, the river commerce in hemp, tobacco, wheat, corn, and other produce was a key element in Missouri's economy. The construction of the Union Pacific Railroad west from Omaha stimulated the city's steamboat deliveries of railroad ties and army supplies. Although Fort Leavenworth had been bypassed by the advancing frontier and affected by nearby railroads, it continued to be an active steamboat port.

New discoveries by prospectors who fanned out from the Bannack and Virginia City mining regions fed Montana's gold rush. In July 1864 four prospectors made a rich strike in Last Chance Gulch. As word of their find spread, other miners rushed into the place, which was named Helena on October 30, 1864. Late in the year, prospectors found gold in the Big Belt Mountains about 35 miles east of Helena. Since the discoverers were from the South, their find was called Confederate Gulch. Diamond City was its main community. Reports of its incredible yields spread quickly—one section of the gulch was said to be producing $1,000 worth of gold per pan. As its placer mining boomed, Confederate Gulch was reported to be the home of some 10,000 people. The richness of these two gulches spurred widespread prospecting into some of the territory's remotest sections. Although they found nothing to match the 1864 strikes, prospectors in the next five years discovered some gold on the upper Yellowstone, at the headwaters of the Clark's Fork tributary of the Yellowstone, and in the Missoula vicinity.[1] For 1862–68, Montana's total gold yield from placer and quartz mining was an estimated $94 million. Placer mining alone produced $18 million in 1866 and at least $10 million annually for the next several years.[2]

Wherever they went, placer miners soon exhausted the ore that could be washed out by such simple devices as pans and sluice boxes. But they could not cope with deep deposits embedded in quartz—gold's mother rock. Like all mining frontiers, Montana moved rather quickly from placer to quartz mining, which required organized businesses, extensive capital, knowledge of deep mining techniques, and machinery for crushing quartz. The advent of quartz mining helps account for the scattering of placer miners and sharp population declines in boom areas. As quartz mining became more common, Montana Territory's population dropped from an estimated peak of about 28,000 in 1866 to the official 20,595 reported in the 1870 federal census, including only about 3,000 placer miners. During the decline in placering, increasing numbers of Montanans turned to agriculture and ranching.[3]

But during the flowering of the Montana gold rush, it promised to be the salvation of St. Louis steamboatmen. Squeezed by railroads in Missouri, they saw the Fort Benton trade as a golden opportunity to instant richness. Their mentality was quite like that of placer miners who hoped to find the fabled giant nugget. The voyage to Fort Benton was long, slow, and risky, but boatmen thought that in one fortunate trip they could easily recoup the cost of building their vessels.

As news of the Last Chance Gulch and Confederate Gulch strikes circulated, St. Louis boat owners readied for the 1865 season. In February, John G. Copelin and John J. Roe began advertising their Montana and Idaho Transportation Line, which offered steamboat service to Fort Benton and through bills of lading to all mining communities.[4]

During the season, Copelin and Roe and their competitors made six steamboat arrivals at Fort Benton. But only four of them were direct from St. Louis. The *Deer Lodge*, a new stern-wheeler measuring 165 × 35 × 5 feet and owned by Copelin and several associates, arrived thrice within several weeks. Its second and third arrivals were from Fort Copelin, a new depot on the north side of the Missouri 10 miles above the mouth of the Milk River. Troubled by low water on their initial ascent, the officers of the *Deer Lodge* had to off-load much of the cargo a short distance below Fort Galpin. When they forged ahead with the *Deer Lodge*, they left some men at the site, where they soon built Fort Copelin, a small wooden stockade. Copelin and his partners evidently thought that double-tripping from Fort Copelin would be a regular feature of Fort Benton steamboating.[5]

Other than the *Deer Lodge*'s three arrivals, Fort Benton was reached by three other steamers. Chouteau's *Yellowstone* brought up 250 tons of goods and 50 soldiers and

The *Deer Lodge,* a shallow-drafted 165-foot-long stern-wheeler,
made the most St. Louis–Fort Benton round voyages.
Courtesy of the State Historical Society of North Dakota.

took $400,000 worth of gold down. The *Twilight* delivered 200 tons. The *Cutter*, which had wintered in the vicinity, was not significant in the year's commerce.

The small number of arrivals at Fort Benton belied the extent of the mountain trade. Thirteen other St. Louis–based steamers stopped short of their goal. Eight of them reached the Marias with an aggregate 1,700 tons of goods for the mining camps. Two others, including the *Deer Lodge*'s second trip from St. Louis, were stopped at Dauphin's Rapids, and three others reached only the Fort Copelin vicinity. The *Bertrand*, laden with mining and farming goods, sank near present Blair, Nebraska.[6]

Three successive years of good navigation assured a lively Fort Benton trade. The number of arrivals for 1866, 1867, and 1868 were respectively 31, 41, and 36. During this boom, the *Deer Lodge*, earned an unmatched reputation by completing five round-trips (two each in 1866 and 1868 and one in 1867) from St. Louis.

But boatmen, merchants, miners, and government officials complained about the hazardous navigation through the rapids portion above Cow Island, despite the unprecedented number of arrivals. Gigantic boulders were a constant threat to the thin-hulled boats, and oftentimes captains had to gradually warp their way through the most rapid currents. One popular proposed solution was to avoid the entire Rocky River stretch by establishing a depot near the mouth of the Musselshell and freighting goods overland to Helena and other mining sites.

In 1866 the Rocky Mountain Wagon Road Company, whose partners included some Montanans and steamboat captain F. B. Kercheval, started Kercheval City at the mouth of the Musselshell. Like many other frontier promoters, their generous use of "City" denoted hope, not actuality. Granville Stuart, who passed the nascent site soon after its beginning, found that Kercheval City was only "two seven-by-nine log cabins with a little stockade around them."[7] The return of high water doomed the settlement, which never became a significant entrepôt during its two-year existence.[8]

Much of the appeal of the trade in Montana was that unlike raw agricultural frontiers, it had a valuable export. So steamboatmen often profited on both their up and down trips.

With the exception of some agricultural produce raised in the Gallatin River valley, Montanans had to import virtually everything else. Steamboats carried groceries, hardware, clothing, dry goods, drugs, liquor, quartz mills, wagons and other vehicles, bar iron, animals, and a variety of sundries. In addition, the passenger business was very important to boatmen. Their extensive advertising in St. Louis newspapers was designed to convince travelers that their boats were the fastest, newest, safest, and most commodious.[9]

Anyone moving to Montana knew that steamboats, with the exception of express stagecoaches, offered the fastest passage. But the opportunity for booking was relatively short. Most boats left St. Louis in late March or April with the expectation of arriving at Fort Benton in late May or June. Captains generally scheduled their departures to coincide with the ice breakups on the upper river and the spring and June rises of the Missouri.[10] When the steamers reached Fort Benton, some downstream passengers were always waiting. But most of the returning miners usually used mackinaws in the late summer or early fall.

The St. Louis–Fort Benton trade peaked in 1867. Army engineer Brevet Major Charles W. Howell, who compiled statistics during his examination of the river, reported that steamboats delivered 8,061 tons of freight to Fort Benton and the rapids portion above Cow Island. About three-fourths of it was for private parties, and the remainder for the federal government. Although Howell did not report a downstream tonnage, he observed: "It is safe to say that five-sixths of the mining products of Montana reach the east by way of the Missouri." A recent study by Joel Overholser placed the 1867 import and export tonnage at 9,219 and 600 respectively.[11] There is a sharper disparity in the number of passengers reported by Howell and Overholser. Howell estimated a total of 10,000 up and down passengers, but Overholser concluded there were only 2,200 up and 2,600 down.

Because of steamboating's riskiness, high demand, and lack of viable competition, freight and passenger rates for the St. Louis–Fort Benton business ran high. A St. Louis agent appraised the average value of a ton of merchandise destined for Fort Benton at $1,000. Steamboat transportation alone, to say nothing of wagon freighting from Fort Benton to the mining communities, sometimes added as much as 36 percent to the St. Louis value. Some freight charges in 1865 were 18 cents per pound and others in the 10- to 12-cent range. The increasing numbers of steamers and competition from overland suppliers forced rates down. In 1866 the prevailing rate was 11 cents per pound. The season-long average the next year was 9 cents, with highs and lows of 10 and 6 cents.[12]

Passenger fare was correspondingly high. Cabin fare was sometimes as much as $200 one-way and deck passage about half that. Howell reported the 1867 average was $150, which is consistent with John Mullan's report of $100 to $200. Robert E. Strahorn, author of another emigrant guide, stated that one-way steamboat passage cost $150 to $200. Obviously, rates fluctuated somewhat, depending on the availability of boats. In September 1867 the captain of the *Imperial,* which was tied up at Cow Island after failing to reach Fort Benton, charged $130 for deck passage to St. Louis.[13]

As a way of promoting the Montana gold rush, St. Louis newspapers often reported the value of gold brought down by steamers. Some individual shipments seemed to fulfill the claim that Montana was the new El Dorado. In 1866 the *Guidon* carried $1 million worth, and the *Only Chance* and *Gallatin* $500,000 each. Chouteau's *Yellowstone* in 1865 exported $250,000 worth of gold dust.[14]

Presumably, the publicized amounts were only for gold sent by express companies. Passengers tended to be tight-lipped about their valuables. The charge for transporting gold was based on its worth rather than its weight. The usual fee from mining towns to St. Louis by wagons and steamers was five percent.[15]

By emphasizing gold, St. Louis newspapers ignored the considerable worth of upstream cargoes. For example, in 1866 the largest single cargo delivered to Fort

With a capacity of 503 tons, the *Wm. J. Lewis* of the St. Louis and Omaha Packet Line was one of the largest steamers to reach Fort Benton during the Montana gold rush.
Courtesy of the State Historical Society of North Dakota.

Benton was 400 tons by the *Peter Balen*.[16] At the $1,000 per ton value reported by the St. Louis trade organ, the cargo was worth $400,000. Since unknown quantities of gold were brought down by mackinaws, it is quite likely that the total value of steamboat imports exceeded that of exports.

Profits made by individual steamers make the lure of the Montana mines more understandable. In 1866 the *Peter Balen* was said to have cleared $60,000 on its one Fort Benton trip. The combined profit of the *Peter Balen* and two other M. S. Mepham and Brother boats—the *Goldfinch* and *Iron City*—was $100,000. Two of the Montana and Idaho Transportation Line's steamboats—the *Deer Lodge* and *Wm. J. Lewis*—reported making $70,000 and $40,000 respectively.[17]

The profits were especially impressive in light of the high cost of running a boat. For example, the monthly expenses of the *Miner* in 1867 totaled $6,770: $3,640 for wages, $2,240 for feeding the crew (reckoned at $2 per day for each man), and $890 for fuel, depreciation, and miscellaneous expenses.[18]

Mainly because of profits from the Fort Benton trade, compensation for Missouri River boat officers was very rewarding. In the spring of 1866, captains were paid $400 monthly, first clerks $250, and pilots $725. Their Ohio River counterparts received only $150, $150, and $175. In 1867 Howell reported that Alpheus F. Hawley's compensation for commanding the *Miner* was $300. Each of Hawley's two pilots received $550, and the first clerk $150.

Montana gold rush steamboating attracted a number of companies and independent operators. The Montana and Idaho Transportation Line was probably the richest. John J. Roe, its principal financier, owned one of the nation's major pork-packing businesses and among his many other activities organized banks and insurance companies. Since Roe and his partner, John G. Copelin, also owned a Montana wagon freighting line, they could assure shippers of through deliveries to the mining towns. Their main competitor was the St. Louis and Omaha Packet Line. Led by Joseph Nanson of St. Louis, it was famous on the lower river as the "O Line." Its main purpose was to run triweekly packets from St. Louis to Omaha. But on occasion, Nanson sent some of his firm's steamers to points above Sioux City, including Fort Benton. With such celebrated captains as James A. Yore and Joseph Kinney, the line's best-known boats were the *Wm. J. Lewis, Kate Kinney, Glasgow,* and *Henry Turner.* M. S. Mepham and Brother ran at least three boats in 1866, and John P. and C. W. Keiser, prominent St. Louis merchants and steamboatmen, sent two or three steamers to Fort Benton annually.[19]

After the failure of La Barge, Harkness, and Company, Joseph and John La Barge worked as independent steamboat operators. They concentrated on the Fort Benton business but also delivered supplies to army posts and towns along the course of the lower river. Joab Lawrence, who had steamboated on the Alabama River, and Fred Dozier, whose family had a long career in steamboating, ran at least one boat to Fort Benton.[20]

In 1868, by which time it was evident that St. Louis's domination of the upper Missouri would soon end, two famous Pennsylvanians—James Rees and William J. Kountz—turned to upper Missouri steamboating. Of Allegheny City, near Pittsburgh, Rees was best known as a manufacturer of steamboat engines and other machinery. His first five steamers sent to Fort Benton, all described as "Splendid Light Draught Steamers," were the *Argosy, Ida Rees, Importer, Silver Cloud,* and *Silver Lake No. 4.*[21]

Before the Civil War, Kountz, originally from Allegheny City, had captained such renowned vessels as the *Crystal Palace* and the *City of Memphis* in the St. Louis–New Orleans business. During the first two years of the war, he was employed by Major General George McClellan to coordinate Union steamboat movements on the Ohio River. In this capacity he was deferentially called Commodore Kountz, a title he retained for the remainder of his steamboat career. Wherever he went, the cantankerous Kountz made enemies. In 1864, when he announced his candidacy for Congress from a Pennsylvania district, the editor of the St. Louis *Democrat* observed: "He is so well known here that he would get very few votes in this vicinity even among the boatmen. We understand he is making speeches. We can imagine how stupid and fulsome they must be."[22]

In March 1868, Kountz, in partnership with his brother-in-law Hiram K. Hazlett, offered service from St. Louis to Fort Benton by steamers that were "of the lightest draught and staunchest ever constructed."[23] Their fleet included the *Andrew Ackley, Arabian, Carrie, Ida Stockdale, Peninah, Leni Leoti,* and *Urilda.* They combined their gold rush trade with supplying army posts on the upper Missouri.[24]

During the Montana gold rush, steamboatmen showed an increasing preference for stern-wheelers. Of the thirty-six different steamers that reached Fort Benton in 1867, twenty-two were stern-wheelers and fourteen side-wheelers.[25]

Until the outbreak of the Civil War, about 90 percent of Missouri River steamers were side-wheelers. Because their wheels could be operated independently, they were highly maneuverable. Moreover, they were easier to build than stern-wheelers. With wheels placed along the sides, boat makers were better able to achieve an even keel and uniform draft from bow to stern. However, side-wheelers did not cope well with shallow water, and the wheels were subject to damage by floating objects such as logs, ice chunks, and buffalo carcasses.[26]

These difficulties prompted more experimentation with stern-wheelers. The single paddle wheel was lighter than two wheels and was shielded by the boat's hull. By reducing the weight, boat makers were able to lessen drafts, and by protecting the wheel, they could decrease the number of repair stops. Designers also found that with a single wheel outside the line of the hull, stern-wheelers could be widened and thus achieve more capacity than side-wheelers of the same length. Since the placement of a single paddle wheel at the rear of the boat complicated the problem of having an even draft, stern-wheel builders had to make adjustments in the placement of the engines and boilers. They also added to the boat's rigidity by a system of hog chains (actually iron rods) connecting the various boat sections.

By the time of the Montana gold rush, steamboat operators knew that stern-wheelers were better suited to the upper Missouri than side-wheelers. But in some instances, owners who had a major investment in boats that were normally used on the lower portions of the Missouri or the Mississippi were quite willing to assume the added risk of running them to Fort Benton.

The rewards were potentially great, but steamboating to Fort Benton required a major commitment in capital and time. Although steamboats were the most advanced technology in the vast realm above Omaha, they were agonizingly slow. The average and median times of the thirty-six ascents from St. Louis to Fort Benton in 1867 were respectively 70.6 and 70 days. The fastest passages were the *Octavia* in 41 days and the *Gallatin* in 50. The slowest were the *Nymph No. 2* and the *Viola Belle*, which needed 100 days and 92 days respectively. Direct returns to St. Louis were ordinarily made in 16 to 20 days.[27]

The long voyage to Fort Benton often irked passengers. Granville Stuart thought the Missouri was the "longest, crookedest, muddiest, coldest and most monotonous river in the world."[28] His boring 55-day ascent to Fort Benton in 1866 was mainly broken by wood stops and above Fort Sully by shooting at wild animals. The boat's assemblage must have been as well armed as any military force. They shot at any creature in the water or within sight on land. Some of the hunting was to supply the steamer *Walter B. Chance* with fresh meat, but much of the shooting evidently was to relieve the tedium. Near the Cheyenne River, where the first large antelope herd was spotted, Stuart observed: "The Captain and passengers fired many long-range shots at them; none hurt visibly."[29]

Fort Benton levee.
Stockpiled steamboat freight was moved inland by freight wagons.
Sometimes as many as 150 wagons were required to handle a single cargo.
Courtesy of the Montana Historical Society, Helena.

Swimming buffalo always provided sport for passengers and crew. Sometimes a steamer spent an entire day picking its way through immense herds. Hiram D. Upham, who went up on the *Twilight* in 1865, estimated that he saw fifty thousand of the beasts in a two-week period. He observed "they are continually swimming across the River in droves and very often they get caught in the current and carried right down by the boat so close that they are often struck by the wheels." At such short range the animals could easily be killed, even with revolvers.[30] Oftentimes calves were lassoed and hoisted aboard with a derrick. They were stabled on deck and taken downstream for private zoos or sold to breeders. One captain, who captured some two dozen calves on a single voyage, was able to sell all of them at Leavenworth.[31]

The acerbic E. W. Carpenter found his 1865 ascent to be "two months of life on a 'mountain steamer' with cracked roofs and warped decks, especially adapted to the broiling of passengers in fair weather and drenching them in foul; two months of life between a double wall of muddy bluffs bounding the river on either side and cutting off whatever scenery might lie beyond."[32] Carpenter was even more frustrated when low water stopped the boat at Dauphin's Rapids. A short-fall of mountain snow the preceding winter was the standard explanation for the poor navigation, but one of the boat's waggish passengers thought the barkeeper was to blame, because of his excessive dilution of drinks with river water.

Descents, which had the advantage of being much faster than ascents, were sometimes anything but routine. In the fall of 1867 the *Imperial*, a 286-ton stern-wheeler needed eight weeks to go from Cow Island to Bon Homme Island, a short distance above Yankton. Under the management of a Captain McComas, the boat left St. Louis on May 17. She was navigated to Sioux City in two and a half weeks and eventually stalled at Cow Island. With no prospect of a return cargo from Cow Island, McComas decided to wait until miners went down in the late summer and fall. His Fort Benton agents solicited a number of passengers, including John Napton and his cousin Lewis Miller, who had decided to go down to Boonville, Missouri, after mining for over a year.[33]

After paying $130 each for down passage on the *Imperial*, Napton and Miller were taken to Cow Island by mackinaw. There they found the managers had booked about 275 passengers, twice the boat's capacity. Napton complained that "at night the whole cabin was filled with men rolled up in their blankets as thick as sardines in a box."[34]

The slow-moving *Imperial* was constantly delayed by sandbars. McComas ordered sparring and warping and on occasion resorted to a novel way of loosening sand with a chain. He called for volunteers from the crew and passengers to work a heavy chain back and forth under the hull to start the sand moving. The method worked but had to be abandoned because the water was too cold for the men to bear.

By the time they reached Fort Buford, it was obvious to the passengers that the *Imperial* was being navigated without a pilot. McComas attempted to hire one from the passing *Benton* but would not meet the man's salary demands. So Napton and the *Imperial* parted ways. Napton and a dozen other passengers went to Yankton by mackinaw, and the pilotless steamer managed to reach Bon Homme Island after sparring 132 times from Cow Island. During the winter the abandoned boat was sold for $2,205 at a public auction. Apparently its purchasers were only interested in salvaging the machinery.[35]

Though not as wearing as the Fort Benton trips, shorter voyages could be miserable adventures. Brevet Brigadier General Philippe Régis de Trobriand, who in 1867 traveled from Omaha to Fort Stevenson on the *Deer Lodge*, found nothing to his liking. Soon after sunset "millions of mosquitoes invaded the boat, and nothing could protect us from them. They were everywhere—on the deck, in the salon, in the cabins. No matter what was done, they slipped in under the mosquito netting. Impossible to sleep a wink. We spent most of the night walking back and forth with our heads and necks covered by a handkerchief or napkin under our hats, hands gloved, armed with green boughs with which we defended our faces."[36]

Steamers always carried ice to preserve fresh meat. In the Missouri valley's settled portions they could depend on acquiring it from vendors who cut river ice and preserved it in small buildings insulated with sawdust. But above the agricultural frontier, the only source of ice was the widely scattered trading posts. Oftentimes steamers depleted their supply before reaching the next post. When the *Deer Lodge* was out of ice, the beef cattle that had been brought along for fresh meat could not be butchered. So De Trobriand and his fellow passengers suffered through meals of fried ham, potatoes, and corn cakes. The general complained that even the "yellow, dirty, unpurified, and tepid water of the Missouri" was better than the wine sold on the *Deer Lodge*.[37]

During the gold rush, hundreds of temporary Montanans went down the Missouri on mackinaws and other floating craft. Most started from Fort Benton, but others embarked on the Yellowstone at Emigrant, about midway from present Gardiner to Livingston. Fort Benton virtually monopolized the migration from Helena and Confederate Gulch, which were respectively about 140 and 170 miles from the port. But some Virginia Citians, when faced with the 270-mile route to Fort Benton, decided to go eastward across the valleys of the Madison and Gallatin rivers to the Yellowstone. They saved about 150 miles of overland travel, but Emigrant could not match Fort Benton's outfitting facilities, and their travel to the river's mouth was potentially more hazardous because the traffic was comparatively light, making, opportunities for assistance from fellow travelers more limited.[38]

There was some floating traffic whenever the river was open, but the great rush occurred in September. Returning miners and others who worked in mining communities chose to labor through most of the summer. But they wanted to reach their downstream destinations before the onset of cold weather. By the time they were ready to leave, most steamboats had been gone for two to three months. Captains, except for such unusual cases as McComas and his *Imperial*, did not linger on the upper river. They hurriedly unloaded their boats and rushed downstream in order to make other voyages from St. Louis to various points on the Mississippi and Missouri.

Some of the travelers who crowded into Fort Benton built their own boats. But others bought craft from local makers or booked passage on large commercial mackinaws. When John S. Collins and his party went down in 1866, they purchased two 30-by-6-foot mackinaws. The boats, dubbed the *Cora Bray* and *The Hulk*, carried twelve passengers each. Other mackinaws were more than twice as large. Zina French of Fort Benton, who owned and commanded a 75-foot mackinaw, was said to have cleared $5,000 for transporting eighty-two passengers to Yankton.[39]

Naming mackinaws was the usual practice. J. Allen Hosmer, who went down the Yellowstone and the Missouri, noted that the boats in his fleet bore such names as *Jeannie Dean, Montana, Antelope, Lady Pike, Helena City, St. Louis, Lady Jane, Otter,* and *Autocrat*. Obviously there was no formal registry of mackinaw names, so common names like "Montana" were probably used many times even during the same season. Nonetheless, the names helped facilitate communicating within fleets and conveying news about them.[40]

When migrants were preparing to leave, Fort Benton was a lively place. James H. Bradley reported that "scores of rough boats sprung into existence and day after day they would push off with a crew of from half a dozen to thirty and forty souls—sometimes singly—sometimes in flotillas." He estimated Fort Benton's annual departures at about 200 boats and 1,200 passengers. Most of the vessels were mackinaws, but some men used skiffs that accommodated only several men, and others went on flatboats. Some enterprising men, who had apparently seen horse ferries, tried to rig a large boat with a horse-propelled stern wheel. But their trial failed when the added weight of the horse threatened to break off the stern. Finally, they redesigned the craft and went down sans wheel and horse.[41]

Generally, those who floated down wanted to reach a railroad or a town that had stage and wagon connections to railroads. Council Bluffs, Sioux City, and Yankton were the commonest destinations. Council Bluffs and Sioux City had rail connections to the east by the time of the 1867 and 1868 migrations respectively. Although it was not a railhead, Yankton was often used by travelers who were forced off the river by cold weather. Some abandoned their boats when they encountered the first steamer that would take them down. From Fort Buford downstream, the army and Indian agency contractors always ran some steamboats until the river froze.

Mackinaw speed varied considerably. Those that avoided sandbars and other obstructions could move a hundred miles a day, but others made only 30 to 40. When a boat was grounded, all aboard would jump into the water and push it out toward the current. In the deepest channel, fear of capsizing was the greatest worry. The men usually stored their gold in a heavy wooden box tied to a buoy, which would mark the treasure's site if the box sank. Since most parties tried to live off the land, they had to make numerous stops to hunt. The food needs of migrants led several professional hunters to become meat suppliers to mackinaw fleets. In 1866 three hunters in a skiff, who kept apace with mackinaw fleets, supplied the migrants with fresh elk, deer, and sometimes buffalo and mountain sheep for some distance below Fort Benton. Sometimes food was purchased from steamers and from trading and army posts. From Yankton downstream, miners were good customers of town merchants. Whenever they bought, the miners paid in gold. With that expectation, sellers, be they traders, steamboat clerks, or town merchants invariably had gold scales.[42]

During the late fall, the mackinaw trade was more important than steamboating to Yankton and Sioux City. Rich miners who flooded into town needed supplies and, if cold weather had set in, transportation. On November 17, 1864, a fleet of seventeen mackinaws carrying 180 men stopped in Yankton. Their aggregate wealth in gold dust and nuggets was estimated at something over a half million dollars. One man, who had his gold belted around his body and supported by leather shoulder straps, reportedly could only move awkwardly because of its weight. The miners sold their boats for the value of their lumber, bought supplies, and hired every available vehicle to transport them to railheads in central Iowa.

Their experience became the pattern for all subsequent late-fall returnees. The boost in town sales was followed by opportunities for townspeople and farmers to temporarily become commercial transporters.[43]

The heaviest mackinaw trade was in the period 1864–68. The decline of placer mining detrimentally affected river commerce, and the completion of the Union Pacific Railroad made the overland route from Utah to Montana much more popular.

Throughout their Fort Benton trade, St. Louis steamboatmen faced competition from overland wagon freighters, packers, and stagecoach lines. The steamers that reached Fort Benton within a relatively short period could not fulfill Montana's year-round needs. Overland transportation, although greatly curtailed during the winter, could sometimes operate throughout the year. But many freighters were on the road during the peak navigation period, because mining town merchants found their charges were no higher than the river-overland route through Fort Benton. The river route per se was less expensive than any overland trail. But most of the goods delivered to Fort Benton had to be shipped to Virginia City, Helena, and other mining locales by wagon. When those charges were added to steamboat rates, the Fort Benton way was not necessarily cheaper than other routes. As for speed, certain goods, such as flour from Utah, could be delivered faster by wagon than by steamer and wagon through Fort Benton. Furthermore, if time was not really important to Montana buyers, even slow delivery from Kansas and Nebraska freighting towns was not an issue.

Overland deliveries to Montana came primarily from Kansas, Nebraska, Utah, and Oregon. There was some intermittent freighting from San Francisco and Los Angeles, which generally passed through Salt Lake City. But California was never an important supplier of Montana-bound goods.[44]

Freighters from Omaha, Plattsmouth, Nebraska City, and Atchison were attracted to Montana as an outgrowth of their Utah business. For years they had made regular deliveries to Salt Lake City, approximately 1,200 miles from the Missouri River. The Montana gold strikes gave them an opportunity to extend their trade. By the time of the rush, Utah had a surplus of some locally produced agricultural commodities such as flour, but still depended on Missouri River freighters for most other items. Consequently, Kansas and Nebraska freighters found they could deliver one cargo to Salt Lake City and another from there to Montana. For those who went by way of Salt Lake City, the distance to Virginia City was approximately 1,600 miles. Such a passage could take four to five months.[45]

Those who did not have Utah deliveries saved some distance and time by striking the Utah-Montana Trail near Fort Hall after going over the Continental Divide in South Pass. Before reaching their Montana destinations, they had to go over Monida Pass, their second crossing of the Continental Divide. In 1864 some wagon trains from Omaha, Nebraska City, and Atchison made direct trips to Montana. They continued the business into midsummer 1866, by which time the extension of the Union Pacific Railroad ended the long hauls. These three traditional freighting towns were challenged by Plattsmouth in 1865 and 1866. Plattsmouth suddenly became a major outfitting point when the army started some of its shipments there and many people were persuaded that the Indian threat was more severe on the north side of the Platte. Until the emergence of Plattsmouth, Omaha had an advantage in the Montana trade because its freighters did not have to cross the Platte.

Missouri River freighting to Montana was mainly a one-way business. Westward-bound wagons commonly carried quartz mills, groceries, hardware, cloth, clothing, drugs, and liquor. Some freighters sold vehicles and livestock in Montana, and most bullwhackers and mule skinners did not make the return trip. As with their earlier experience in the Colorado gold rush, freighting entrepreneurs recruited drivers whose main aim was to reach the gold fields. Many would-be miners found the cheapest way to reach the mining areas was to work their way west. Unlike the argonauts who paid steamboat passage, they not only traveled free but also collected their accumulated wages at their destination. The system worked well, because even if owners wanted to return all their vehicles to the Missouri, they could do so with fewer men and animals by lashing the nearly empty wagons together.

Although returning wagons did not transport cargo, many of them carried miners who chose to go overland rather than use mackinaws. The noted Omaha freighter Edward Creighton once brought back 200 passage-paying miners with a wagon train. Presumably some of them were carrying their own gold, but overland gold shipments by merchants were ordinarily sent on stagecoaches.

Freight charges from the Missouri River towns to Montana averaged about 25 cents per pound. Even at that rate they often at least matched the river-overland costs by way of Fort Benton. In 1865, when steamboat charges to Fort Benton ran as high as 18 cents per pound, freighters were charging as much as 10 cents per pound to haul goods to Helena. Over the course of the gold rush, river and overland charges declined. The proliferation of wagons, oxen, and mules in Montana and the rapid extension of the Union Pacific Railroad lowered overland shipping costs. The rate from Fort Benton to Helena was forced down to 1.25 cents per pound and, on occasion, even less. In 1866 an estimated 600 wagons and thousands of oxen and mules were used in Fort Benton–Helena freighting.[46]

Stagecoaches offered the fastest passenger, mail, and express freight service from the river towns in eastern Nebraska and Kansas to Montana. An "express" stage—one that operated round the clock—could sometimes make the trip in 16 days. Passengers had to pay $350 and a dollar or two for each meal at a stage station. Express freight, which consisted of relatively light packages, was $2 a pound. While offering an alternative to steamboat passage, stagecoaches did not allay Montanans' complaints about their isolation and costly transportation.[47]

An improvement—championed by Sidney Edgerton, Montana Territory's first governor, and the territorial legislature—was to open a more direct route east of the Bighorn Mountains. This path, which came to be known as the Bozeman Trail, was pioneered by John M. Bozeman in the winter of 1862–63. Bozeman, a Georgian who had prospected in Montana for three years, in working his way from Bannack City to the North Platte saved four to five hundred miles relative to the Monida Pass–South Pass route. During the summers of 1863 and 1864, Bozeman led groups to Montana by his new way. For Montanans, who bore the cost of overland freighting, the route promised to reduce freighting trips by about four to five weeks and to lower costs.[48]

Congress and the Lincoln-Johnson administration responded quickly to the Montana legislature's petition to open the road. During the summer of 1865, Brevet Major General Patrick Edward Connor led a three-pronged offensive into the Powder River country to assert control over buffalo hunting lands prized by the Sioux. Connor's expedition, like Sully's earlier campaigns, was another step in the federal government's policy of quashing any Indian resistance to whites' use of routes to Montana. Connor's poorly coordinated movement of almost three thousand men failed to engage the Sioux in a decisive battle. After several skirmishes, the general established Fort Connor, a temporary post near present Sussex, Wyoming.[49]

Because of Connor's wagon shortage, his quartermaster officers pressed overland freighters into service during the campaign. Other freighters followed in the wake of the expedition by taking the new route from the North Platte to Virginia City. Freighters coming from the east followed the Oregon-California Trail to a point eighty-two miles northwest of Fort Laramie before embarking on the Bozeman Trail. The road lay east of the Bighorns and swung around the northern end of the range and then through the town of Bozeman on the way to Virginia City. Nebraska City's freighters placed their distance to Virginia City at about 1,150 miles.

In 1866 the government completed its fortification of the Bozeman Trail. Colonel Henry B. Carrington, who led troops from Fort Kearny, first expanded Fort Connor, which had been renamed Fort Reno in the fall of 1865. Moving northward, he founded two other posts—Fort Phil Kearny, about twenty miles south of present Sheridan, Wyoming, and Fort C. F. Smith, some thirty-five miles southwest of present Hardin, Montana.

The freighters who used the trail came mainly from Omaha, Plattsmouth, Nebraska City, and, as the summer of 1866 progressed, the terminus of the Union Pacific. But another feeder route started from Sioux City, Iowa, whose promoters thought its more northward location gave them an advantage in Montana freighting. Sioux City's boosters contended that Montana shippers would save time and money if they used steamboats as far upstream as possible. Since Sioux City was the uppermost point that had both good steamboat service and adequate overland freighters, they insisted it was the best route to Montana. Actually, Sioux City was only about a hundred miles closer to Virginia City than Omaha, which would save approximately a week of overland travel. However, steamboats normally took a day or two to ascend from Omaha to Sioux City, so the net saving would be five or six days. But promoters dealt in hyperbole, not detail.

In 1864, when there was widespread dissatisfaction with the South Pass route, Sioux Citians began agitating for federal assistance to open a more northern route. Their request, presented to Congress by Representative Asahel W. Hubbard,

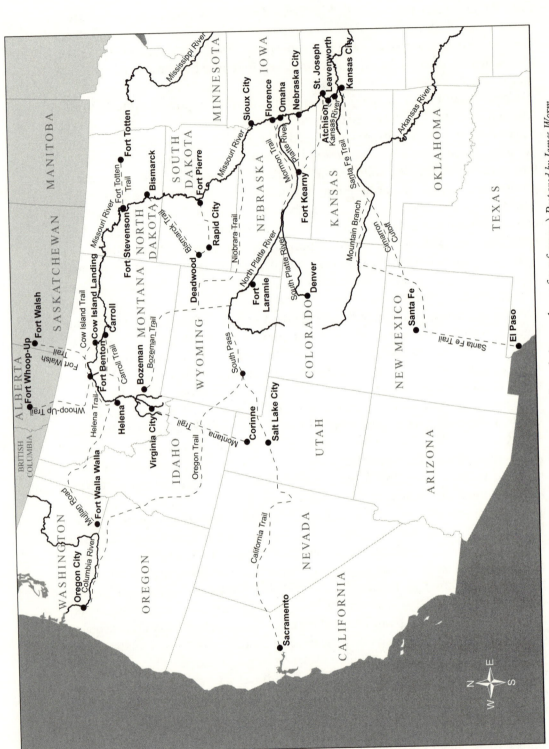

Missouri River and western overland trails. (Current state boundaries are shown for reference.) *Prepared by James Worm.*

coincided with Montana's Bozeman Trail plea. Easily convinced that Montana needed better communications across the plains, Congress appropriated $50,000 for surveying and improving a road from the mouth of the Niobrara, near Fort Randall, to Virginia City. The Niobrara Road, as it came to be called, was to have connections with both Sioux City and Omaha. Although Omaha was named as a starting point, Sioux Citians promoted it as their road, and Omahans feared it as a threat to their Platte River trail.[50]

James A. Sawyers, a Sioux City frontier army veteran and ferry operator, was named superintendent of the Niobrara Road. During the summer of 1865 his expedition, accompanied by a military escort and thirty-six freight wagons owned by a Sioux City merchant, located the route from the mouth of the Niobrara to the Bozeman Trail. Sawyers's party followed up the Niobrara for about three hundred miles before crossing northward to the Cheyenne River valley. From the headwaters of the Cheyenne the group struck westward to the Powder River and the Bozeman Trail. After four hard months the surveyors reached Virginia City. In the Powder River country, the Sioux harassed the party and killed several of its men.

Sawyers improved the Niobrara Trail with a small party in 1866. But even as he worked, the route was being rendered obsolete by the rapidly advancing Union Pacific Railroad. In 1865 the Union Pacific began laying track west of Omaha, its starting point. By the end of the year it had completed only forty miles. This slow pace disappointed railroad management and buoyed the hopes of overland freighters, who thought it might take years for the railroad to replace them. In 1866, however, construction greatly exceeded expectations. A point on the north side of the Platte opposite Fort Kearny, the year's goal, was reached in August. By year's end the road was completed 305 miles from Omaha, or slightly west of the new town of North Platte, Nebraska.[51]

Freighters from the river towns adjusted accordingly. In June 1866, Herman Kountze, an Omaha banker and businessman who was the contractor for the Bozeman Trail army posts, was starting his wagon trains from Columbus, ninety miles from Omaha. The next month Kountze and all other freighters, including those headed for Montana, were departing from Lone Tree (present Central City, Nebraska). By late August the freighters were working out of Kearney, the new depot started near Fort Kearny.

The Union Pacific was able to continue its rapid construction until the line met the Central Pacific at Promontory, Utah Territory, on May 10, 1869. The railroad reached Cheyenne on November 13, 1867, and Laramie the following May. By August 1868, end of track was 225 miles west of Cheyenne.[52]

During 1867 and 1868, Montana's overland imports from the East generally came by way of the Union Pacific as far as possible and then by wagon to the intersection of the trail from Salt Lake City. The Bozeman Trail never lived up to its promise. Although it was protected by three forts, the trail was under almost continual harassment by Lakota, Cheyenne, and Arapaho war parties. Red Cloud's War—highlighted by the killing of Captain William J. Fetterman and eighty-one other men on December 21, 1866, and two sharp skirmishes the following August—was a factor in leading the federal government to negotiate with the tribesmen. By the Fort Laramie Treaty of April 29, 1868, the government agreed to abandon the trail and leave the Powder River country as unceded Indian territory. When the troops were withdrawn in July and August 1868, it seemed to some that the closure of the Bozeman Trail was a great setback. But in actuality government negotiators realized they were not surrendering anything of great value. They knew that within months the Bozeman Trail, even if it had been kept open, could not compete with the Union Pacific–Corinne route. Under the circumstances, the government could not justify the costly safeguarding of the lightly used route.[53]

Although most of the overland freight to Montana came from the East, both Oregon and Utah delivered significant amounts. Merchants in Portland, Oregon, who obtained some of their goods from San Francisco, were the main suppliers of Idaho's gold miners. Generally, freight was shipped up the Columbia by steamboats to Wallula, the head of navigation, and then freighted overland through Lewiston, the jumping-off point for the mines. When gold was discovered on the east side of the Bitterroot Mountains, Portland suppliers extended their trade into Montana. But lacking a wagon road, they had to depend on Mullan Trail mule-pack trains. In 1865 an estimated 6,000 mules, carrying 200 to 300 pounds each, moved goods to Montana from the Columbia River. The season's total was reported to be 750 tons. The next year a reported 10,000 mules were used.[54]

An improved service was offered in 1866 by the Oregon and Montana Transportation Company, a subsidiary of the Oregon Steam Navigation Company, which controlled steamboating on the Columbia River. Freight from Columbia River steamers was unloaded at White Bluffs, a short distance above the mouth of the Snake River near present-day Pasco, Washington. Then it was freighted overland nearly 200 miles northeastward to the south shore of Lake Pend Oreille, in northern Idaho. The company's lake steamer carried freight, pack animals, and passengers up the Clark Fork River. After a portage around Cataract Rapids, another steamboat was navigated to Thompson's Rapids, which had to be portaged. Then a third steamboat was able to reach a Clark Fork landing about 125 miles from Fort Benton. Freight wagons ran from this head of navigation to Helena and other mining towns by way of Missoula. The service, which was abandoned in 1869, never posed a major challenge to Missouri River steamboating to Fort Benton.[55]

The wagon route from Salt Lake City to Montana communities was used by some of Montana's earliest prospectors, including James and Granville Stuart. Some goods were hauled over it before the first major discoveries, but by the time of the Bannack and Virginia City strikes, Utahans were well positioned to become commercial freighters. In 1861, when troops were desperately needed in the East with the advent of the Civil War, the army sold surplus wagons, oxen, and mules at Camp Floyd at bargain prices. With the acquisition of this property, Utahans were not only able to lessen their dependence on Kansas and Nebraska freighters but to become suppliers of the Montana gold rush as well.[56]

In terms of distance, Salt Lake City and other communities in northern Utah had a clear advantage over Oregon shippers. Salt Lake Citians who used the Montana Trail, which ran up the Malad River valley, then by way of Fort Hall and Monida Pass, moved about 350 miles to reach Bannack City, 385 to Virginia City, and 475 to Helena. But Utah freighters could not dominate the Montana business, because they lacked the variety of consumer goods. The main item shipped from Salt Lake City was Utah-produced flour, which was sometimes delivered in the winter. Until 1869, when Montana became a significant flour producer, Utah freighters dominated the flour market.

It is impossible to determine the relative importance of Missouri River steamboating and the competing overland routes to Montana precisely. Piecemeal statistics for each route are suggestive, not definitive. Obviously, the percentage transported on each Montana access would have varied from year to year. An estimate of the 1865 business by the journalist Albert D. Richardson during his tour of the West was that "about one-fifth of the supplies come overland from California and Oregon; one-fifth overland from Kansas and Nebraska; and three-fifths up the Missouri from St. Louis to Fort Benton."[57] In failing to make any distinction between Utah-originated shipments and the random ones from California, Richardson diminished the significance of Utah and elevated California's status.

During the Montana gold rush, army posts on or near the Missouri River in Dakota and Montana territories were important destinations for St. Louis steamboaters. The military presence above Fort Randall was increased because of the government's determination to assure safe navigation.

At the end of the Civil War, the army posts on the Missouri above Fort Randall were Fort Sully and Fort Rice, with some troops stationed at the Fort Berthold and Fort Union trading posts. Then, on May 1, 1865, Fort Dakota was established at present Sioux Falls, South Dakota. Intended to protect settlers, this inland post was supplied by way of a road from Yankton, the closest steamboat port. Within two years, a number of changes greatly expanded the military frontier. In 1866 the original Fort Sully was abandoned, and a fort of the same name, which is usually retrospectively identified as Fort Sully II, was established on the east side of the Missouri about twenty-eight miles above present Pierre. During the same summer, Fort Buford was started near Fort Union, which the army had completely evacuated by the end of August 1865. In August the army built Camp Cooke, Montana's first military fort, on the right bank of the Missouri just above the mouth of the Judith River.[58]

The 1866 changes were in keeping with the army's mission of safeguarding the Missouri River route. But the next year the army's role was expanded to include protecting an overland Minnesota-to-Helena mail route and providing security for the farming section in the Gallatin River valley.

Montanans, like virtually everyone else who ever lived on the frontier, complained frequently and loudly about their slow mail service. The government's solution was to establish a mail route from Fort Abercrombie to Helena. Optimistic newspaper editors, anticipating speedy service, dubbed the new system the Northern Pony Express.[59]

When the route was proposed, there was no army post between Fort Abercrombie, on the Dakota side of the Red River, and the Missouri River. Brigadier General Alfred H. Terry, who reconnoitered the area, recommended the establishment of two news forts—Totten, just south of Devils Lake, and Ransom, on the Sheyenne River about twenty miles west-northwest of present Lisbon, North Dakota. Fort Totten, which was to be a mail route station, was also to police the Devils Lake Indian Reservation, newly created for refugee Dakotas from Minnesota. Fort Ransom was intended to provide added protection for Minnesota-to-Montana emigrants. Since the old fur-trading post of Fort Berthold was inadequate to serve as the Missouri River base for the mail service, it was replaced by Fort Stevenson. About twelve miles below Fort Berthold, the new fort was also intended to protect river traffic and the Fort Berthold Indian Agency.[60]

Near the western end of the mail route, the army started Fort Shaw on the Sun River, about twenty-five miles above its confluence with the Missouri. It was strategically situated to safeguard the Fort Benton–Helena route. Late in the summer, Fort Ellis was established near Bozeman to protect nearby settlers and keep main roads open.[61]

Aside from the permanent posts, the army, as local situations required, sometimes manned temporary outposts. In the Fort Randall vicinity there was an outpost at the Ponca Agency and another at Fort Thompson.[62]

This reinforcement of the military frontier increased government steamboat shipments, which had implications for overland transportation as well. Freight destined for Fort Totten was unloaded at Fort Stevenson and then freighted over a 150-mile trail. Supplies for both Fort Shaw and Fort Ellis were carried by wagons from Fort Benton.

Despite the additions to the network of army posts, the northern mail service failed. During the summer of 1867 Charles A. Ruffee, who had been granted a three-year contract, laid out a route from Fort Abercrombie to Helena by way of Fort Totten, Fort Stevenson, Fort Buford, and Fort Benton. But from the start his riders were harassed by Sioux parties. Many attacks in the unfortified area west of Fort Buford prevented the men from getting through. When no mail had been delivered to Helena by late September, Ruffee drastically altered the western portion of the route, which was to cross the Missouri, pass through Fort Hawley, and follow the Musselshell River westward toward Helena. Fort Hawley, a new post of the Northwest Fur Company, was on the Missouri's right bank about fifteen miles above the mouth of the Musselshell. The new route did not help. Ruffee, doomed by a severe winter, Sioux raids, and mounting debts, discontinued his service in March 1868.[63]

Other than wood and hay supplied by civilian contractors near the forts and beef cattle driven overland from Iowa and Minnesota, all imports during the navigation season were delivered by steamboats. Freight was the most important to boatmen, but the army also depended on them to transport troops, dependents, and support personnel to and from and within the upper Missouri region. Post-to-post transfers were usually arranged by special contracts between quartermaster officers and steamboat captains.

Supplying the forts was a major component of the economies of Dakota and Montana territories. In 1868 there were 1,682 officers and men at the river posts. About 300 more—the combined strength of Fort Dakota, Fort Totten, Fort Shaw, and Fort Ellis—depended on steamboat transportation.[64]

In 1867, steamboats delivered more than 5,000 tons of military freight to Yankton and forts above. Seventeen different vessels unloaded 1,358.7 tons at Fort Sully, the greatest amount for any single army fort. Fort Buford and Fort Rice also received over 1,000 tons each. Seventeen of the steamers bound for Fort Benton deposited nearly 1,000 tons at Camp Cooke. The 1,828 tons of government freight delivered to Fort Berthold included both army and Indian service supplies. The same is true of the 1,101 tons unloaded at Fort Benton—the port for Fort Shaw, Fort Ellis, and the Blackfeet and Flathead Indian agencies. The St. Louis harbormaster, who kept a record of steamboat shipments, listed only "government freight," with no distinction between army and Indian goods.[65]

Given the great distances of the forts from major supply points, costly transportation was a key concern of army officials. In contemplating ways of increasing speed and reducing expenses, they regularly evaluated both the river and overland routes. The Missouri's greatest limitation was its relatively short navigation season, which varied greatly from the rapids portion above Cow Island to Yankton. Steamboat deliveries of army supplies to Camp Cooke and Fort Benton was generally restricted to May and June. After that, navigation of the rapids was difficult, if not impossible. Major General Winfield Scott Hancock, commander of the army's Department of Dakota, related his experience in descending through Dauphin's Rapids on July 9, 1869. When the officers of the steamer *Last Chance* found only seventeen inches of water over the rapids, they lightened the boat by unloading all freight and passengers. This action reduced the draft to seventeen inches. With its bottom scraping the rocky riverbed, the vessel was able to make a slow, hazardous passage. Hancock, obviously exasperated over the situation, ordered his chief quartermaster officer to prepare a recommendation for improving the rapids.[66]

Below the rapids, the navigation period was considerably longer. Although the river was sometimes closed by low water rather than ice, deliveries to Fort Buford and points downstream were often made in September and October and sometimes even later. Since the army feared any wintertime shortage of supplies, quartermaster officers tended to tempt fate by trying to rush in freight before the river froze. Realizing the increased risk of late-season navigation, steamboat owners regularly charged more for fall deliveries.

The need for this precaution was obvious by the experience of 1868, when five steamers were frozen in for the winter between Fort Sully and Fort Randall. The

Union and Dakotaian of November 18, 1868, reported that "the early cold weather this month, has raised the deuce with the steamboats." The *Ida Stockdale, Nile, Benton, Urilda,* and *Hiram Wood* were all trapped by the sudden freeze. Crews and passengers walked to either Fort Randall or Yankton, where they hired "every conceivable conveyance" to transport them to the railroad at Sioux City. In all likelihood, they left a watchman or two with each of the boats. George W. Kingsbury told of a Mr. Brown, a boat steward who, with a young cabin boy, spent a winter on an abandoned steamer. Their principal wintertime diversion was visits by nearby reservation Indians.[67]

During the gold rush, when there was a great demand for steamers, the army used several contracting methods. Some agreements were for the delivery of a specified amount of goods to a particular destination. On other occasions, quartermaster officers chartered boats at a daily rate for a period or a voyage. A third procedure, intended to reduce time in making arrangements and cost, was to grant a season-long contract to one person or company. Such an agreement gave the contractor a monopoly right to all goods originating at St. Louis, but he was free to use subcontractors. Even after the general contracting system was initiated in 1867, some post quartermaster officers chartered boats for particular missions unrelated to the shipment of supplies from St. Louis.

In the spring of 1866, when the demand for Fort Benton steamboats was high, the St. Louis quartermaster chartered at least six vessels to supply the upper river posts. Five of the boats commanded $550 per day, and one $600. Later in the season the quartermaster officer made a number of special contracts. On August 4, Lieutenant Colonel George P. Webster contracted with Frederick Dozier to transport 40 tons to Fort Randall, 90 to Fort Sully, and 80 to Fort Rice. For all three the rate was $2.48 per hundredweight. A month later Dozier agreed to take 100 tons each to Fort Sully and Fort Rice at $3.48 and $4.48 per 100 pounds respectively.[68]

In 1867 and thereafter the army relied on season-long contracts, supplemented by some chartering. William McPherson and John Copelin held the 1867 contract. But outside of the agreement, Second Lieutenant Robert A. Gibson, Fort Randall's quartermaster officer, chartered the steamer *Marcella* at $600 per day to make a round-trip with troops and supplies to Fort Rice. The next year Hiram K. Hazlett, acting in the interest of William J. Kountz, submitted the successful bid. Hazlett had the distinction of being the last St. Louis contractor to have an exclusive hold on the army's upper Missouri business. In 1869, contracts were let to route supplies from both St. Louis and Sioux City. John N. Bofinger, a longtime steamboat entrepreneur and sometime associate of John Copelin, gained the St. Louis contract and Joab Lawrence, president of the Northwest Transportation Company, was the contractor for the Sioux City freight.[69]

The general contracts contained very detailed tabular statements. They showed the rates for transporting officers, enlisted men, freight, horses, mules, cattle, wagons, ambulances, and carts from St. Louis and from point to point along the route to Fort Benton. Hazlett, for example, was paid, for each officer, $62 to Fort Benton, $55 to Camp Cooke, $42 to Fort Buford, $30 to Fort Stevenson, $27 to Fort Rice, $18 to Fort Sully, and $12 to Fort Randall. The cost for transporting an officer for any segment was the difference in the charge from St. Louis. For example, Hazlett would be paid $30 for each officer carried from Fort Randall to Fort Buford. The rate for enlisted men was approximately two-thirds less than that for officers, and the rate for cattle, horses, and mules was about the same as for officers. Freight rates per hundredweight were $6.50 to Fort Benton, $6.17 to Camp Cooke, $2.67 to Fort Buford, and $0.97 to Fort Randall.

The rates listed in the tabular statement were for the normal highest-water months—March, April, and May. But increases were provided in the expectation that boats starting after May would encounter lower water. The Fort Buford rates were 20 percent higher for June, July, and August and 90 percent above the spring rates for September and October. The Fort Benton adjustment for the summer months was the same as Fort Buford's, but the September and October advances were 75 and 125 percent respectively.[70]

Supplying river forts by steamboats was a bargain relative to inland posts that depended on boat-wagon combinations. In 1867 Michael Wall was paid $1.78 per 100 pounds to haul supplies the 60 miles from Fort Benton to Fort Shaw. The next year, partners James C. Burbank, Henry Clay Burbank, John L. Merriam, and Amherst H. Wilder of St. Paul contracted to freight supplies from either St. Cloud or Fort Stevenson to the forts in Dakota Territory east of the Missouri. They transported much of the Fort Totten freight from Fort Stevenson over the 150-mile trail. Their compensation for carrying 100 pounds for 100 miles was $1.80 for April, $1.45 for May, $1.14 for June through September, and $1.80 for October through March, 1869.[71]

Contractors, like all other shippers on the upper river, prepared their vessels for possible Indian attacks. The Sully expeditions only temporarily forced warriors away from the river, and the new forts, which were defensive bulwarks, did not have much impact beyond their immediate vicinity. Indeed, hostilities around Fort Buford increased soon after the army opened the post.

Fear of Indians, rather than actual attacks, was the usual condition. To protect his pilothouse, the most vulnerable part of a steamer, any captain had it sheathed with either boiler iron or heavy planks. Another precaution, encouraged by the army, was to arm the crew. Boat officers could borrow weapons and ammunition from quartermaster officers at St. Louis or any fort. Boats could usually also depend on their well-armed passengers.

Boats were most likely to be attacked where the navigable channel ran close to an overhanging bank or during wood stops. But despite the constant threat of shooting from shore, attacks were relatively scarce and, even if the fire was heavy, ineffective. In 1867 the *Antelope* was riddled with bullets but was not disabled. Frontier newspapers, whose editors always wanted more troops on the upper Missouri, never missed an opportunity to publicize a casualty such as the killing of George Merrick, the mate of the *St. John,* in 1865.[72]

Although eclipsed by the gold rush and supplying army posts, the fur trade was continued by the Northwest Fur Company—the immediate successor of Pierre Chouteau, Jr., and Company—and the firm of Durfee and Peck. The Chouteau company, which had usually controlled the licensed Indian trade of the upper Missouri, ran afoul of the Lincoln-Johnson administration in 1865. Officials in the nation's first Republican administration sharply criticized the company, which had long-standing ties to Democratic administrations and was thought to have pro-Confederate sympathies. But until near the end of the Civil War, the Indian service had no viable alternative to the Chouteaus.

However, that situation changed in 1865, when James Boyd Hubbell and Alpheus Fenn Hawley, two young men from Mankato, Minnesota, decided to apply for licenses to trade with the Sioux on the upper Missouri. Ardent Republicans, Hubbell and Hawley were favorites of Morton S. Wilkinson, Minnesota's first Republican U.S. senator. When Charles P. Chouteau went to Washington in March 1865 to solicit licenses from the Bureau of Indian Affairs, he found Hubbell was there for the same purpose. Recognizing that Commissioner of Indian Affairs William P. Dole favored Hubbell, Chouteau decided to sell out to his rival.

Despite its loss of licenses, the Chouteau company's sale to Hubbell and Hawley was somewhat qualified. It included all goods and posts on the upper Missouri except Fort Benton, Chouteau's richest site. Because Chouteau wanted to reap pending returns from Fort Benton, he and Hubbell agreed that its sale would be delayed until 1866.

While very ambitious, Hubbell and Hawley did not have enough capital to buy goods, staff posts, and provide steamboat transportation. Consequently, they soon formed a partnership with James A. Smith and Company of Chicago, which had some upper Missouri trading experience, and Caleb Francis Bates of New York City. Bates, along with his brother Martin, was a major buyer and exporter of buffalo robes, furs, and peltries. The partners named their firm the Northwest Fur Company.

Throughout its five-year existence, the Northwest Fur Company traded for robes and furs, operated several army post sutlerships, and for most of the time ran its own steamboat from St. Louis. When the company was formed, the partners assumed they would be able to buy the steamer *Yellowstone* from Chouteau. They were quite shocked when he did not even offer it to them but instead sold it to parties who removed it from the Missouri. Thus, during their first year of operation, Hubbell and Hawley, who directed field operations, had to have their goods and men transported by various steamers. Despite this complicated arrangement, the company made a profit on its first outfit. However, the partners decided they would improve business by operating their own steamboat.

Before the opening of navigation in 1866, Hubbell and Hawley arranged for the construction of a 539-ton stern-wheeler at New Albany, Indiana. Recognizing Bates's role as company financier, they named the $50,000 boat the *Frank Bates*. The new vessel had a very short history. On April 7, when it was nearly ready to embark on its first Missouri River voyage, the boat was burned with four other steamers on the St. Louis levee. Undaunted, the partners promptly bought the *Miner,* a new 299-ton stern-wheeler.

By the time the *Miner* was sent upstream, the Northwest Fur Company had purchased Fort Benton and its property, which included a variety of trading goods, 175 oxen, and 20 freight wagons. Fort Benton and Fort Union became its trading hubs, with other stations at Fort Sully, Fort Rice, and Fort Berthold. During the summer of 1866, it added Fort Hawley. Located near a major buffalo herd, the fort was intended to control the Crow Indian trade. Continually readjusting to nuances in the army-Indian trade, the company sold Fort Union in 1867 to the army, which used some of its materials in the building of Fort Buford. The company shifted its base in that area to Fort Buford, where it also held the post sutlership.

After the purchase of the *Miner,* Hawley became its captain. While working with the company, Hawley made eight trips from St. Louis to the upper Missouri, for which the firm netted $37,682.

Although they collected and marketed thousands of buffalo robes and numerous furs and peltries and had excellent returns to the goods advanced in 1865, 1866, and 1867, the partners agreed to dissolve the Northwest Fur Company in 1869. Despite their profits, they were convinced that each partner would fare better in separate enterprises. They sold all their holdings, except Fort Benton, their Fort Totten trade, and the *Miner* to Durfee and Peck, which had been a friendly rival ever since it opened business in 1867.[73]

Durfee and Peck was a partnership of Elias H. Durfee of Leavenworth, Kansas, and his brother-in-law Campbell K. Peck of Keokuk, Iowa. Like the Northwest Fur Company partners, they obtained Indian trading licenses because they were loyal Republicans.

Durfee and Peck entered the upper Missouri fur trade in 1867, when they built a store at Fort Union. Within weeks, they switched their operations to Fort Berthold. To ship their goods, robes, and furs, they bought and operated the steamer *Jennie Brown,* a 146-ton side-wheeler, whose dimensions were 137 × 23.6 × 4.5 feet.

Durfee and Peck both cooperated and competed with the Northwest Fur Company. At such places as Fort Berthold, where they both had traderships, they shared expenses for post maintenance and equally divided robe and fur proceeds. But Durfee and Peck tried to counter Fort Hawley's influence by building Fort Peck about a hundred miles upstream. On the north side of the Missouri about nine miles above the mouth of the Milk River, Fort Peck became the firm's main buffalo robe collection point.

Unlike the Northwest Fur Company partners, who were factionalized, Durfee and Peck worked well together. When the Northwest Fur Company decided to sell out, the Durfee and Peck firm was well positioned to expand its trade, which was on the upswing due to recent changes in federal Indian policy.[74]

The genesis of concentrating Sioux Indians on the upper Missouri River lay in a peace program initiated late in the Civil War. Newton Edmunds, Dakota Territory's governor and ex officio superintendent of Indian affairs, was one of its early advocates. Believing that negotiations were preferable to military action, Edmunds suggested to President Lincoln that peace agreements be made with the various bands of Teton Sioux and the Yanktonais. Lincoln approved and helped get a congressional appropriation for what came to be called the Northwestern Indian Commission. But the commission did not get organized until five months after Lincoln's assassination, when Edmunds was chosen to be its chairman.

After proceeding upstream from Yankton by steamboat, the commissioners signed nine treaties with tribal representatives at Fort Sully in October 1865. They made separate agreements with each of the seven bands of the Teton Sioux and the two Yanktonai divisions. The treaties had a common aim and in many instances the same language. The overall intention of the pacts was to wean the Indians away from their hunting lifestyle toward reservation life. In eight of the agreements the government agreed to support any voluntary Indian settlements for the purpose of pursuing agriculture. But in the case of the Lower Brûlé, the band agreed to locate on a reservation at and near the mouth of the White River between Fort Randall and Fort Sully. All of the treaties called for annual payments in exchange for Indian withdrawal from any established or future routes through their lands. The Senate approved the nine treaties on March 5, 1866.[75]

The following summer the reconvened commission went by steamer to Fort Rice, where it negotiated similar agreements with other Sioux bands and the Cheyennes. But these were never ratified, because the government turned its attention to a general conclave, in keeping with its proclaimed "Peace Policy." In June 1867, Congress authorized the creation of the Peace Commission, whose assignment was to end Indian opposition to frontier expansion.[76]

Among its other accomplishments, the commission negotiated the Fort Laramie Treaty of April 29, 1868, which affected the Powder River country, present west-river South Dakota, and the Missouri River agencies. In their conference with various Sioux bands and the Arapahos, the commissioners, who included Lieutenant General William T. Sherman and Brevet Major General William S. Harney, agreed to abandon the Bozeman Trail within three months, to leave the Powder River region as unceded Indian land, and to create the Great Sioux Reservation. The vast reservation was bounded by Nebraska's northern boundary on the south, the 104th meridian on the west (very near the present South Dakota–Wyoming boundary), the 46th parallel on the north (slightly south of the present North Dakota–South Dakota boundary), and the Missouri River on the east.[77]

These provisions made it appear that the government was retreating from its long-range goal of occupying the West. But the commissioners were wily enough to recognize that as long as the buffalo roamed, it would be impossible to entice all of the Sioux to agencies. However, knowing that some of the easternmost Sioux were more likely to accept reservation life, they agreed to create new Missouri River agencies.

Within several months after the treaty's signing and lengthy parleying with tribal leaders, Harney located three new agencies on the Missouri, at the mouths of the Grand and Cheyenne rivers and about thirty miles above Fort Randall at Whetstone Creek. As he worked to establish the agencies, replete with living quarters, warehouses, steam sawmills and blacksmith shops, Harney found that his $200,000 allocation was insufficient. Ultimately, he exceeded it by $485,784.21. As a harbinger of things to come on the upper Missouri, the greatest beneficiaries from outfitting the agencies were traders. Harney appointed James A. Smith and Campbell K. Peck, both operating independently of their respective companies, as his purchasing agents. Under their contract with Harney, Smith and Peck were paid $205,000 for the provisions they bought in St. Louis and elsewhere and another $113,000 for delivering them by steamboat.[78]

The addition of the agencies increased the government's dependence on steamboating. Other than such private traders as the Northwest Fur Company and Durfee and Peck, the economy of the entire region from near Yankton to near Fort Benton depended heavily on army and Indian service contractors.

While St. Louis steamboatmen were expanding their operations in Dakota and Montana, they were losing more of their Missouri market to railroads. The Missouri Pacific completed the second railroad across the state on September 18, 1865. Its crews, building from both east and west, met at the Little Blue River, 76 miles east of Kansas City and 207 west of St. Louis. This route not only directly affected steamboat deliveries to Kansas City but also established a basis for north-south branch lines. In 1868 the Osage Valley and Southern Kansas Railroad completed a 25-mile line from Tipton on the Missouri Pacific to the port of Boonville.[79]

The Missouri Pacific was soon paralleled on the north side of the river by the West Branch of the North Missouri from Moberly to its junction with the Kansas City and Cameron Railroad at Birmingham near Kansas City. Steamboating to Brunswick, which was first shocked by the Hannibal and St. Joseph, suffered another sharp reversal when the West Branch reached it on December 15, 1867. When the line was completed to Birmingham in 1868, it was routed through Carrollton and Lexington Station, only four miles north of Lexington. Meanwhile, in 1867 the North Missouri opened a twenty-two-mile branch line connecting Centralia on its main line and Columbia, which had traditionally been supplied by steamboats through the port of Providence.

Steamboating to Kansas City was also challenged by the completion of the Kansas City and Cameron Railroad in 1868. This line, which gave Kansas City a direct connection with the Hannibal and St. Joseph, was intended to improve transportation from Chicago to Kansas City by way of Quincy, Illinois. Its planners wanted to both supplant steamboating and transform Kansas City into a railroad center rival of St. Louis.

Relative to the depressed Civil War trade, steamboating increased, but because of the railheads at Jefferson City, Boonville, and Kansas City, it became more segmented. The number of steamboat arrivals and departures (which of course included all those to and from Dakota and Montana) was impressive, but most of the hauls had become shorter. In 1867, St. Louis's Missouri River steamboat commerce consisted of 318 departures and 318 arrivals. The numbers increased the next year to 361 and 356.[80]

A report by George H. Morgan, secretary of the St. Louis Mercantile Exchange, showed that the nature of the 1867 Missouri River trade, with the exception of railroad iron, was the same as it had been in the antebellum years. The main items sent upstream from St. Louis included 18,149 bars of railroad iron, 31,082 kegs of nails, 388,000 packages of sundries, 20,860 barrels of flour, and 129,875 packages of groceries. In March the prevailing rate for St. Louis to Lexington shipments was 50 cents per hundredweight. The principal St. Louis receipts of Missouri River freight for the entire year were 25,025 bales of hemp. Through September, 391,734 bushels of wheat, 325,660 bushels of corn, 8,487 hogs, 3,522 cattle, and 2,756 sheep were also delivered to St. Louis from Missouri River landings.

In addition, sixteen different steamers on the lower river in 1867 carried 1,632 tons of army freight to Fort Leavenworth. The *Wm. J. Lewis* alone made nine deliveries to the post. The boats supplying Fort Leavenworth were in direct competition with the Union Pacific, Eastern Division Railroad, which had completed a branch line from Lawrence on its main route to Leavenworth in May 1866.[81]

Once construction of the Union Pacific Railroad was started, steamboating from St. Louis to Omaha increased sharply. Much of the growth was related to Omaha's situation vis-à-vis other railroads. Initially, as the eastern terminus of the Union Pacific, Omaha did not have direct railroad connections with Chicago and points east. However, by November 1866, the westward-advancing Chicago and North Western Railroad was opened to about forty miles northeast of Omaha. To fill this gap between the railhead and Omaha, some prominent Omaha freighters and financiers formed the Western Transportation Company. They ran wagons and stages from the end of the Chicago and North Western to Omaha and from the terminus of the Union Pacific to western destinations. The company closed its Iowa phase when the Chicago and North Western reached Council Bluffs in the spring of 1867. But even then the unbridged Missouri was a major break in railroad service.[82]

Under the circumstances, some shippers, including the army, found it advantageous to use steamboats to Omaha, the gateway to many western forts. To protect the Union Pacific route and branch trails to Denver and Montana, the army maintained four posts in Nebraska (Fort Kearny, Fort McPherson, North Platte Station, and Sidney Barracks), eight forts in Wyoming (Bridger, Caspar [replaced by Fetterman in 1867], D. A. Russell, Halleck, Laramie, Phil Kearny, Reno, and Sanders), and three in Colorado (Collins, Morgan, and Sedgwick). In 1867 forty-seven steamboat arrivals from St. Louis delivered 3,912 tons of military freight to Omaha.[83]

The private trade to Omaha from St. Louis did not match the military's. However, in 1867 the *Evening Star,* one of the best-known boats on the lower river, delivered a variety of groceries, hardware, and furniture. The usual rates from St. Louis were $1 to $1.25 per hundredweight.[84]

As the Union Pacific was being built, railroad construction in Kansas ended steamboating on the Kansas River. There were no steamers on the Kansas from 1860 until 1864, when both the *Emma* and *Tom Morgan*, a 97-ton stern-wheeler, divided their time between the Kansas and the Missouri. The 1865 trade, which included some runs from Kansas City to Lawrence, was dominated by the *E. Hensley* and *Jacob Sass*, two small side-wheelers whose hulls were built at Wyandotte, with the final touches completed at Leavenworth. The *A. Majors*, which made some runs to Lawrence in 1866, was the last steamer on the river. The boat was chartered by the railroad company after its shipments were delayed because a flood ruined its Kansas River bridge.[85]

The Union Pacific, Eastern Division (renamed Kansas Pacific in 1869) made good progress in 1865. The line reached Topeka on January 1, 1866, and Junction City in November. This gave one of the most heavily settled areas in Kansas direct railroad ties with St. Louis. Over the winter of 1865–66, the 1.75-mile gap between the Missouri Pacific depot in Kansas City and the start of the eastern terminus of the Union Pacific, Eastern Division was closed.[86]

As steamboating was adjusting to advancing railroads, its long-standing reputation as a high-risk business continued. A Treasury Department study showed that 96 of the 1,042 steamers plying waters flowing into the Gulf of Mexico in 1868 were lost. Fifty-one of them sank (mostly by snagging), 29 were burned, 9 exploded, and 7 were wrecked by collisions. The 1869 loss was 86 of 995 inspected vessels. In 1868, of the 62 boats headed from St. Louis to Fort Randall and points above, 4 (*Amelia Poe, Arabian, Carrie, and Princess*) were snagged and totally lost.[87]

Boatmen reacted with the same argument they had always had: Snagging was the single greatest cause of accidents. Removing snags would make navigation safer and reduce costs for the government and private shippers. The navigable rivers were public highways. Improving them would enhance national security and benefit the citizenry. Therefore the government was obligated to improve rivers.

River improvement advocates found that Republican-dominated congresses had shed concern about the constitutionality of river and harbor improvement. They readily assumed that the central government, whose power had been greatly expanded as a result of the Civil War, naturally had the authority to aid any means of improving transportation. In its appropriations act of June 23, 1866, for "repair, preservation and completion of certain public works," Congress granted $550,000 for the construction of snagboats and other apparatus for clearing western rivers and an equal amount for improving the Mississippi, Missouri, Arkansas, and Ohio rivers. To administer these programs, the Army Corps of Engineers established an Office of Western River Improvements in Cincinnati, headed by John N. Macomb.[88]

In 1867 Macomb named Major Charles W. Howell to examine the Missouri and make appropriate recommendations. In the course of two and half months,

Howell traveled on the *Miner*, the Northwest Fur Company's steamer, from Sioux City to near Dauphin's Rapids and from there to St. Louis. He personally studied the river from Cow Island to Dauphin's Rapids and gathered information about the rapids above from steamboatmen. While descending, he compiled a partial list of snags from Fort Randall to the river's mouth.[89]

Believing that the commerce more than justified the cost, Howell recommended improvement of the rapids and systematic snag removal, starting at the river's mouth. He thought a good, navigable channel could be created through the rapids by using dams to force water into a main channel and by removing boulders in a number of places. The cost of this work, he concluded, would be repaid in a single season through reduced shipping costs to the army. Noting that some bends in the lower river had as many as forty snags, he held that commerce would be greatly enhanced by their removal.

The Corps of Engineers gave priority to snag removal on the Missouri, Mississippi, Ohio, and Arkansas by having three snagboats built. The boats—*J. J. Abert*, *S. H. Long*, and *R. E. De Russy*—were launched in December 1867. All were of a new design, with the machinery for pulling snags operated independently of the paddle wheels.[90]

The *R. E. De Russy* was used to remove snags on the lower river in 1868. High water forced the crew to start twenty miles upstream, abandoning the original plan to start at the mouth. From March to the end of June the boat removed 222 snags over a 100-mile stretch to slightly below Hermann. Excluding their roots, the total weight of the snags was 2,486 tons. The count did not include snags that could be cut off without hauling them aboard. This work was the start of a long-range snag removal program that gradually extended upstream.

During the Montana gold rush, government officials, railroaders, and steamboaters recognized that railroads were changing the pattern of Missouri River navigation from year to year. It was obvious that it was just a matter of time before some upstream site replaced St. Louis as the starting point for the upper river trade. In 1867 Howell observed: "Sioux City will probably soon become the rendezvous of the mountain fleet, since from that point the trip will be much shortened, the dangers of the lower river avoided, and two round trips to Benton assured. Rates of freight and insurance will be greatly reduced, and the commercial interests of Chicago will come in direct competition with those of St. Louis, cheapening the value of goods to the consumer in Montana."[91]

Other than failing to comprehend the impact of the Union Pacific and the abrupt end of the placer gold rush, Howell was a veritable seer.

9

NEW RAILHEADS
ON THE UPPER MISSOURI

From 1868 to 1873, rapidly advancing railroads drastically changed the pattern of Missouri River steamboating and the scope of the St. Louis hinterland. The new age became evident in 1868, when the Chicago and North Western Railroad was completed to Sioux City. Once it had a railroad tie with Chicago, Sioux City was positioned to challenge St. Louis for the Fort Benton steamboat trade. The rise of Sioux City reflected the broader competition between St. Louis and Chicago to control western commerce. But Sioux City soon faced sharp competition within Chicago's sphere of influence. The completion of the transcontinental Union Pacific in 1869 immediately made the railroad town of Corinne, Utah Territory, the depot for overland trade to Montana.

Sioux City's status as the mistress of the upper river trade was short-lived. In 1873 it was seriously affected by the completion of the Dakota Southern Railroad to Yankton and the Northern Pacific to Bismarck. The railroad extensions did not entirely end St. Louis steamboating to the upper river, but they nonetheless reoriented northern plains commerce. Before the railroads, St. Louis used its natural highway to dominate the business to distant Fort Benton. But its river route was supplanted by east-west railroad lines whose business flowed to and through Chicago. So rather than continue looking southward to St. Louis, most Dakota and Montana business interests were drawn eastward to Chicago.

As railheads, Sioux City, Yankton, and Bismarck became the key points on the upper Missouri. They enjoyed their unique roles as long as the regional economy depended on railroad-steamboat combinations.

In bold headlines, the *Sioux City Journal* of March 14, 1868, exulted in the arrival of the city's first train: "saved at last, it has come, All Hail Chicago! All Hail New York!" and "hail! all creation!!" City promoters, who aimed to make their town the next "gateway to the West" were finally rewarded for their twelve-year campaign to get a railroad.[1]

Planned and constructed by John I. Blair of New Jersey, the 75-mile-long Sioux City and Pacific Railroad was built northward from Missouri Valley, Iowa, about 20 miles north of Council Bluffs on the main route of the Chicago and North Western. Blair, well known throughout Iowa as an aggressive railroad promoter, specialized in taking over underfunded local lines. Continuing his practice of working closely with the Chicago and North Western, Blair leased the Sioux City and Pacific to it.[2]

At the opening of 1868 the Sioux City and Pacific was completed to within 20 miles of Sioux City, prompting the *Sioux City Register* of January 4 to observe that "we are almost 'out of the wilderness.'" Favorable weather in January and February enabled the contractors to lay track practically every day.[3] As the line approached Sioux City, it was hailed as a "radical change in transportation" from Chicago to Montana that would avoid about a thousand miles of "difficult navigation." The *Register* also reported that the *Helena Herald,* representing the hopes of Montanans, welcomed the new connection, which promised to speed up shipments to Fort Benton.[4]

The Chicago and North Western's monopoly of railroading to Sioux City was brief. By mid-August 1868, with the completion of the Council Bluffs and St. Joseph Railroad, Sioux City had direct rail connections to St. Louis. This development, which facilitated some trade up the Missouri valley, did not greatly affect the freight business of the Chicago and North Western. But Sioux City's pioneer railroad was sharply challenged by the completion of the Iowa Falls and Sioux City Railroad in July 1870. This line, which became part of the Illinois Central system, was built from both ends. Running by way of Fort Dodge, it gave Sioux City a more northern link to Chicago. Through competition with the Chicago and North Western, the Illinois Central caused a reduction in shipping costs from Chicago and points east, which in turn worked to the detriment of St. Louis steamboaters.[5]

As the Sioux City and Pacific was being constructed, the Chicago and North Western made arrangements with Joab Lawrence to forward goods by steamboat from Sioux City. Lawrence, whose experience included government contracting on the Alabama River, the management of a forwarding and commission business in Mobile, and captaining steamboats to Fort Benton, was president and superintendent of the newly formed Northwest Transportation Company. With an authorized capitalization of $150,000, the company was incorporated by the State of Iowa on November 11, 1867.[6] Cooperating with the Chicago and North Western and other railroads, Lawrence offered through bills of lading from company offices in Boston, New York, and Chicago. He claimed this through service to the upper river would save "1000 miles, 20 days and cut insurance costs by one-third."[7]

Despite the boasting, Lawrence and the Chicago and North Western recognized that Sioux City could not instantly become the great port for the upper river trade. In order to supplant St. Louis, Sioux City needed to have extensive warehouses, be a designated starting point for the government's Indian and military contracts, and have facilities for wintering its own home fleet. As the opening of navigation approached, Lawrence was constructing a large warehouse, but all of the steamers bound for Fort Benton and forts and agencies were scheduled to start from St. Louis.

Lawrence readied the Northwest Transportation Company's five steamers in St. Louis. Anticipating difficult passage to Fort Benton, he lightened the draft of the *Bertha, Deer Lodge, Fanny Barker, Nile,* and *North Alabama* by removing numerous planks and boards. The "extensively razed" craft were partially loaded in St. Louis and took on additional cargo at Sioux City. As an added precaution, none of them was loaded to capacity. To repel likely Indian attacks, each of them was outfitted with a howitzer that fired a twelve-pound ball, twenty stands of arms, and two thousand rounds of ammunition.[8]

With the *Deer Lodge* leading the way, Lawrence's boats arrived at Fort Benton in late May and June. After the vessesl returned to Sioux City, Lawrence sent it to Fort Benton again. He was so pleased with its twenty-two-and-a-half-day upstream voyage that he thought perhaps each of his boats could make three Sioux City–Fort Benton round-trips annually. After their Fort Benton trips, the boats transported annuities from Sioux City. As water levels dropped in late summer and fall, the Bureau of Indian Affairs began routing its supplies purchased in New York or Chicago to Sioux City on the Chicago and North Western.

Although accounting for only seven of the thirty-six steamboat arrivals at Fort Benton in 1868 (the *Deer Lodge* double-tripped on its first voyage), the Northwest Transportation Company and the Chicago and North Western were pleased with their season's work. Montana sales by Chicago suppliers were reported to have increased by $4 million because of routing on the Chicago and North Western. Furthermore, shipping through Sioux City lowered transportation costs for Montana buyers. The steamboat company charged, on average, 5 cents a pound for freight from Sioux City to Fort Benton. Through rates 8 cents from New York City and 6 cents from Chicago. Shippers, who were charged a 6.4 percent cargo insurance rate for St. Louis goods, paid only 3 percent for consignments starting at Sioux City. The boards of insurance underwriters, who weighed various risk factors before setting rates, were convinced that the avoidance of the snag-infested river below Sioux City increased steamboat safety.[9] Unlike shippers, however, passengers did not benefit by starting for Fort Benton from Sioux City. The Northwest Transportation Company charged $150 and $25 respectively for cabin and deck passage.[10]

To save time and money, Lawrence decided to winter his boats at Sioux City. Simply mooring them was not an option, because of the likely ice damage during the spring breakup. To assure that the vessels would be left "high and dry," the Northwest Transportation Company built ways on the Sioux City levee. Ways, sometimes called dry docks, consisted of long, heavy timbers lying perpendicular to the river on a gradually inclined bank. Before the wooden supports could be installed, the bank had to be graded by horse-drawn scrapers. Then deeply set posts, to which the timbers were secured, were dug into the bank. Boats were drawn up sideways by horse-powered capstans. Depending on the length of the ways, as many as five or six steamers could literally be stacked on them, with the lowermost boat placed somewhat above the high-water mark. Other than safeguarding the boats, the ways enabled boatmen to easily repair and caulk the vessels.

By mid-November, the Northwest Transportation Company had some forty to fifty carpenters working on the ways, the first on the Missouri above St. Louis. The $12,000 project was continued through some wintry spells for the next two months. Lawrence's steamers, with the exception of the *Nile,* which had been frozen in near Grand River, were drawn up on the ways by January 23, 1869.[11]

Over the winter, Lawrence announced that he intended to double the company's fleet to ten boats for the 1869 trade. He apparently fell somewhat short of this goal but was able to make a working arrangement with Alpheus F. Hawley for the services of the *Miner.* Hawley, one of the four principal partners of the Northwest Fur Company, had refused to relinquish control of the boat when the company was dissolved. Lawrence also obtained the stern-wheeler *Tennessee* in St. Louis, but it was snagged and lost on April 25 near Decatur, Nebraska, while ascending.[12]

Mainly because of its 1869 government contracts, the Northwest Transportation Company advanced Sioux City's cause at the expense of St. Louis. G. T. Nutter, the firm's New York agent, signed a transportation contract with Commissioner of Indian Affairs Ely S. Parker on May 13. The agreement, covering only May 13–July 12, specified that the company would receive all goods in New York City and route them through Sioux City to destinations from Yankton to Fort Benton. Rather than attempt to calculate distances to each delivery site, Parker and Nutter agreed on rates for rather long river sections. The $7.72 per hundredweight through rate for Yankton to Fort Sully was increased in dollar increments to $11.72 for freight delivered to Fort Benton and all other points above the Musselshell. The other three sectors were Fort Sully to Fort Rice, Fort Rice to Fort Buford, and Fort Buford to the Musselshell. Delivering Indian annuities was the most important aspect of the Northwest Transportation Company's 1869 business.[13]

Lawrence had to share the transportation of military freight with John N. Bofinger of St. Louis. The army, perhaps because of the political influence of certain St. Louisians, chose to make St. Louis and Sioux City each a starting point for steamboat shipments to the upper river. Consequently, it contracted with both Bofinger and Lawrence.[14]

Quartermaster officers, like every other steamboat shipper, were always concerned about accidental losses. A spate of 1869 accidents involving St. Louis–based steamers did nothing to allay their fears. On the evening of March 19, when many boats were preparing to start up the Missouri, seven steamers were destroyed by fire on the St. Louis levee. The blaze, which started near the boilers of the *Ben Johnson,* soon enveloped the *Armenia, Carrie V. Kountz, G. R. Allen, Fanny Scott, Henry Adkins,* and *Jennie Lewis.* Because of prompt, valiant action by the officers and crews, no lives were lost. But the property loss of the heavily loaded boats, of which six were scheduled for the upper Missouri, was estimated at half a million dollars. Fortunately for the city, the fire did not spread onto the levee.[15]

Other losses occurred as St. Louis boats struggled to navigate the Missouri, which remained low throughout the season. The greatly anticipated June rise, which was expected to provide relief, was very modest. Within several weeks in May and June, the *Antelope* and *Colossal* burned, the *Urilda* exploded, and the *Nick Wall* was snagged. While ascending, the *Antelope* was destroyed about 12 miles above Yankton, and the *Colossal* near Bon Homme Island between Yankton and Fort Randall. The boilers of the *Urilda,* one of the boats frozen in over the winter above Fort Randall, blew up about 20 miles above Sioux City while the boat was descending. The injured, including a number of soldiers, were rescued by Sioux City's steam ferry, *Undine.* Most of the *Nick Wall*'s cargo was lost when the vessel was snagged near Brownville, Nebraska, but the boat was repaired and reached Fort Benton later in the season.[16]

The *Peter Balen,* one of nineteen steamers that had to double-trip from Cow Island to Fort Benton, was burned to the water's edge when it was trapped by low water just above Dauphin's Rapids. This costly and slow double-tripping caused army authorities to question the wisdom of continuing to use the long supply route from St. Louis.

Partially because of his own experience in descending through the Rocky River, Major General Winfield Scott Hancock recommended a new strategy for staffing and supplying Dakota and Montana posts. All troops and freight, he thought, should be sent from Sioux City by steamboats for only two or three months after the opening of navigation, the river's normal high-water period. Since they saved about a thousand miles relative to St. Louis boats, Sioux City–based steamers could reach Fort Benton sooner and be off the Rocky River before water levels dropped. Later deliveries for the Montana posts should be by the Union Pacific to Corinne and the Montana Trail. The impact of this railroad-overland route was evident when the army sent 365 recruits over it from Omaha to Fort Ellis in the fall of 1869. Significantly, Hancock also reported that henceforth Montana would be able to furnish all the beef, flour, and forage required by troops stationed there. Not only would this local production reduce costs, but it would lessen the territory's dependence on both the Missouri River and the Union Pacific.[17]

Perhaps because of the declining Fort Benton trade, in March 1871 Lawrence and his associates sold the Northwest Transportation Company, including the Sioux City ways and freight depot, to Durfee and Peck, which retained the original name. Having expanded sharply with its purchase of the Northwest Fur Company, Durfee and Peck was well positioned to operate a steamboat company above Sioux City. As the holder of Indian trading licenses and post sutlerships and the region's largest fur dealer, it was the dominant firm in the mainly unsettled region from Sioux City to Fort Benton.[18]

The new Northwest Transportation Company was headed by Elias H. Durfee, who kept his home office in Leavenworth. His junior partner, Campbell K. Peck, who commuted to the Missouri from his Keokuk, Iowa, home, was named company secretary. Sanford B. Coulson, originally from Allegheny City, Pennsylvania, moved to Sioux City to carry out his duties as general superintendent. Durfee, Peck, Coulson, O. B. Taylor of Leavenworth, and William S. Evans, a close Allegheny City associate of Coulson's, constituted the firm's board of directors.

Continuing Lawrence's practice of cooperating with railroads, the company established agencies in New York, Pittsburgh, Chicago, and St. Louis to facilitate the routing of freight and passengers to Sioux City, its general depot. Isaac G. Baker represented the firm at Fort Benton. Baker, a St. Louisian who had served as the last agent of Pierre Chouteau, Jr., and Company at Fort Benton, had entered the general merchandise business after the demise of his employer.

The main business of the Northwest Transportation Company under both Lawrence and Durfee and Peck was supplying Indian agencies and army posts. The implementation of the Fort Laramie Treaty caused an increase in both agencies and military forts. During the summer and fall of 1868, Brevet Major General William S. Harney established new agencies on the west side of the Missouri near the mouths of Whetstone Creek, Cheyenne River, and Grand River. The Whetstone Agency for the Brûlé Sioux soon failed. Unable to attract large numbers of Indians, it was removed in 1870 to a White River location in northwestern Nebraska, 225 miles west of the Missouri. However, the original site continued as the steamboat landing for the wagon road to the new agency.[19]

Unlike Whetstone, the Cheyenne River and Grand River agencies boomed. Cheyenne River had about 1,500 permanent residents and as many as 7,000 soon after the summer buffalo hunt ended. The Grand River Agency reported a maximum population of 5,725 in 1871. The older Fort Berthold Agency to the north had a resident population of 2,700.[20]

The importance of supplying agencies is evidenced by Dakota Territory's sparse white population. The federal census of 1870 showed that the slow-growing territory had only 12,887 white residents and as many as 30,000 Indians. Elk Point, near Sioux City, was the largest town, with 775 inhabitants. Territorial capital Yankton had only 737. Thus, by far the territory's greatest population centers were Indian agencies.

The circumstances in Montana Territory were similar. In 1872 it had an estimated 30,412 Indians. The single largest concentration was 8,000 Teton Sioux at or near Fort Peck, which was named a joint Sioux-Assiniboine Agency in 1873. According to the census of 1870, the territory's non-Indian population was 20,595. Helena, the largest community, which replaced Virginia City as territorial capital in 1875, had 3,106 residents.[21]

Policing the new agencies was the major reason for an expanded army presence on the upper river. In 1870, posts were established on the Lower Brûlé, an outcome of the Edmunds Commission treaties, and on the Cheyenne River and Grand River agencies. The Lower Brûlé installation, built west across the Missouri from the mouth of Crow Creek, was formally named Fort Hale in 1878. The Cheyenne River post, which was called Fort Bennett beginning in 1878, was situated on the right bank of the Missouri just below the Cheyenne's mouth. The

Grand River Agency fort was moved about 30 miles upstream to Standing Rock in 1874, the year after the agency was moved there. Known initially as the Standing Rock post, it was named Fort Yates in late 1878.[22]

Unrelated to the agencies, the army made changes in its fortification plan. Fort Dakota at Sioux Falls was abandoned in 1869, and the next year Camp Cooke was closed and demolished. Fort Dakota's equipment and supplies were taken by wagon to Yankton and then forwarded by steamers to upriver posts. After an 1868 inspection tour, Major General Hancock wanted to close Camp Cooke in favor of a new post at the mouth of the Musselshell. He insisted that a Musselshell fort, roughly midway between Fort Buford and Fort Benton, would be an important link in adding security to the northern route to Montana. But rather than build a full-fledged fort there, the army in 1868 built Camp Reeve, a small temporary stockade near Kercheval City. It was staffed by a company of troops from Camp Cooke.[23] In 1872 the army added Fort Abraham Lincoln near present Mandan, North Dakota. Situated at the point selected by the Northern Pacific Railroad for its Missouri River crossing, the post was intended to protect railroad engineers and other workers.[24]

The annual transportation contracts for the agencies and forts were the great prizes for steamboatmen. Both the Indian and army contracts were negotiated through competitive bidding, but government agencies were not required to accept the lowest bids. They could consider such factors as the condition of the bidder's vessels and experience. Because the lettings of the army and Indian transportation contracts were separate processes, it was possible for one carrier to be awarded both.

The first carrier to gain that distinction was the Northwest Transportation Company in 1872. The company was awarded the Indian contract during Lawrence's three years but was challenged by St. Louis boatmen for transportation to the army posts. In 1869 Lawrence shared the army transportation with John N. Bofinger, because both Sioux City and St. Louis were designated starting points. But in 1870 the quartermaster general decided to let only one contract with St. Louis as the starting point. Hiram K. Hazlett, representing William J. Kountz, was the successful bidder. St. Louis's status as the starting point was not too meaningful. On their first trip, all of the Kountz boats were loaded at St. Louis, but thereafter the quartermaster department routed its supplies and men to Sioux City by rail.[25] Probably due to the pending sale of the Northwest Transportation Company, neither Lawrence nor Durfee and Peck was able to prepare a successful bid to the 1871 army contract. So once again, the business went to Kountz.

After Hazlett signed the army agreement on March 17, he and Kountz bid on the Indian contract. Following weeks of anticipation in Sioux City, Commissioner of Indian Affairs Ely S. Parker signed an agreement with Peck in Washington on May 23, 1871. Kountz greeted the development with his usual poor grace by denouncing Parker in his newspaper, the *Allegheny Mail*. The agreement, which extended to July 12, 1872, obligated the company to provide free storage in Sioux City for all annuities awaiting shipment. Reimbursement per hundred pounds

William J. Kountz, a steamboat
entrepreneur from Allegheny City,
Pennsylvania, was well known
throughout the course of the Missouri.
*Courtesy of the National Mississippi River
Museum and Aquarium, Dubuque, Iowa.*

from Sioux City was scheduled at 18 cents to the Yankton Agency, 80 cents to the
Cheyenne River Agency, $1.05 to Grand River, $1.48 to Fort Berthold, $2.75 to
Fort Peck, and $3.36 to Fort Benton.[26]

The Indian annuities, which had to be delivered to destinations ranging from
the Yankton Agency to Fort Benton amounted to about 8,000 tons. Most of the
goods originated in Baltimore, Philadelphia, and Chicago. But St. Louis merchants supplied an estimated 400 tons each of bacon and sugar. To forward the
St. Louis freight, the Northwest Transportation Company used three steamers.
Recognizing the epic change in the upper river trade, the *St. Louis Times* ruefully
observed that all of other annuities would be sent by rail to Sioux City.[27]

At the opening of navigation, the Northwest Transportation Company intended
to conduct the agency deliveries and Durfee and Peck's private business with seven
steamers. Three of its vessels—the *E. H. Durfee, Esperanza,* and *Nellie Peck* (named
for Campbell K. Peck's twelve-year-old daughter)—were new light-draft stern-
wheelers. The *E. H. Durfee* and *Esperanza* were built at Pittsburgh, and the *Nellie Peck* at nearby Brownsville. All featured a spoonbill-shaped bow, intended to
add stability to the hull, ease passage over sandbars, and turn aside floating debris.
Like the *Far West*, which had been constructed at Pittsburgh in 1870 under Sanford B. Coulson's supervision, they were hailed as "mountain boats." The four,
ranging in length from 177 feet for the *Esperanza* to 206 feet for the *E. H. Durfee,*

became the models for most of the boats subsequently built for the upper river trade. The company also used the *Silver Lake No. 4*, a small eight-year-old stern-wheeler; the *Ida Rees No. 2*, a six-year-old stern-wheeler, and the *Viola Belle*, a five-year-old side-wheeler.[28]

Finding that its seven vessels were inadequate during the spring and early summer rush, the Northwest Transportation Company contracted with Hawley to make deliveries with the *Miner*. By midsummer, when most of the annuities had been delivered or shipped, the company decided to reduce its fleet. The *E. H. Durfee* and the *Viola Belle* were sent down to engage in the grain trade on the lower river. The *E. H. Durfee* returned to Sioux City the next spring, but on August 21 the *Viola Belle* was snagged and lost near Doniphan, Kansas.[29]

The boats remaining at Sioux City were used until late fall. The company naturally wanted all supplies to reach Sioux City before water levels dropped, but that depended on a complex of suppliers. As railroad deliveries straggled in, navigation became increasingly difficult. By August 25, when the river was extremely low, about 1,500 tons of annuities were stored in the company's Sioux City warehouse. But they were not the season's final receipts. Not until October 12 could the *Sioux City Weekly Journal* report that the "last ton" of government freight had arrived by railroad. By then, navigation was torturously slow. The *Peninah*, a Kountz boat, needed 21 days to descend from Fort Buford. Several other boats still upstream were reportedly "sparring and sounding over half the time." While struggling to get back to Sioux City, the *Silver Lake No. 4* was frozen in below Fort Sully on November 20. Its officers and crew, including Captain Grant Marsh and Joe Todd, a pilot, managed to reach Sioux City by wagons and sleighs, although they were snowbound several times and suffering from frostbite.[30]

The Kountz Line's 1871 army contract was potentially richer than the Indian contract, because it included the transportation of personnel, equipment, and livestock as well as supplies. Significantly, its rates for personnel, freight, animals, and equipment were considerably lower than those of the previous year. For example, the 1870 pre-September hundredweight rate of $5 for freight from Sioux City to Fort Benton was reduced to $3.38. Furthermore, the army discontinued its practice of paying more for fall deliveries. In 1870 Kountz's September reimbursement was double those of the preceding months. Colonel Daniel H. Rucker, the quartermaster officer who negotiated both the 1870 and 1871 contracts with Hazlett, was able to force lower rates because he knew Kountz could not find other work for his boats.[31]

The 1871 contract gave Kountz a monopoly on all upper river army transportation from Sioux City. But the army reserved the right to engage other boatmen for any shipments from Fort Leavenworth, Omaha, or other lower river ports. The detailed agreement prescribed conditions for carrying officers, men, and animals. Officers, whose baggage allowance was 100 pounds each, were to be provided cabin passage. Each enlisted man could have 80 pounds of free baggage. The deck passage rate for the troops included a kitchen room, cooking stoves, and bunks. For feeding and transporting horses, mules, and cattle, the contractor had to provide water troughs and other "proper conveniences."

Rucker tried to reduce failures by restricting Kountz to boats that passed two inspections. The first was by the inspector of the St. Louis Board of Underwriters, whose report would be the basis of setting insurance rates, and the second by the resident Sioux City quartermaster officer. As an added safeguard for the government, Kountz agreed that if his line could not make steamboat deliveries, it would transport all affected freight overland at regular contract rates.

During the season, Kountz used eight steamers for supplying army posts and some private freighting from St. Louis to Sioux City, Yankton, and Fort Benton. Six of the vessels—the *Andrew Ackley, Carrie V. Kountz, Ida Stockdale, Katie P. Kountz, Mollie Moore,* and *Peninah*—were stern-wheelers built originally in Pittsburgh, Elizabeth, and McKeesport, Pennsylvania. The *Carrie V. Kountz* was rebuilt at St. Louis after the great fire of March 19, 1869. Kountz, who liked to honor family members, named the *Peninah* after his wife. The *Flirt* and *May Lowery* were probably owned by other parties who rented or leased the boats to Kountz.[32]

The Kountz boats carried some private freight when they left St. Louis for Sioux City and points beyond. In all likelihood, St. Louis shippers got greatly reduced rates from Kountz, who obviously did not want to run empty vessels. The private goods at least assured him of some income while he was positioning his boats for the army business. On its maiden trip, the *Ida Stockdale* carried 210 tons of freight for Fort Benton, including 700 stoves and a quantity of bar iron. The *Peninah* transported 600 barrels of salt and some miscellaneous goods to H. D. Booge and Company, one of Sioux City's principal merchants. The officers of the *Nellie Peck* augmented its St. Louis–Fort Benton consignments with 25 tons at Leavenworth and 15 at Sioux City. The Fort Benton cargoes of the Kountz boats, like those of the Northwest Transportation Company, usually consisted of both government and private goods.[33]

Kountz's 1871 practice of carrying some St. Louis merchandise became the pattern for the city's trade to the upper river. Despite being outflanked by the railroads to Sioux City and later to Yankton and Bismarck, St. Louis continued to be the source of some steamboating. New boats, usually built at Pittsburgh and environs, invariably picked up some cargo at St. Louis when they first navigated to Sioux City and above. Sometimes owners of upper river steamers sent them below for the winter to engage in the St. Louis–New Orleans cotton trade. Also, St. Louis was the nearest point where upper river boatmen could find facilities for major repairs and remodeling, such as lengthening a boat.

By late April the railroad had delivered "immense amounts" of army goods to Sioux City. Two large government warehouses and their surrounding platforms were reported to be "chuck full." The freight awaiting steamboat shipment included some 4,000 sacks of corn; 400 barrels and 1,000 sacks of flour; a large amount of medical stores; 400 bales of clothing; about 200 cases of hats, caps, belts, and knapsacks; lumber for warehouses at various posts; wagons, wheels, and spokes;

1,000 muskets with ammunition; tents; kegs of nails; and "a host of articles too numerous to detail."[34]

To facilitate his Sioux City shipments, Kountz had his own riverside warehouse built. Hazlett, who managed the line's day-to-day operations, moved his family to Sioux City for the summer.

Despite his careful preparations, Hazlett was continually frustrated throughout the long season. After the spring rush of goods to Sioux City, the army sent only intermittent shipments during the summer and fall. Without a continual flow of railroad freight to Sioux City, Hazlett could not keep his fleet busy. In early July when the *Peninah, Katie P. Kountz,* and *Andrew Ackley* were idled in Sioux City, Hazlett sent the *Carrie V. Kountz* to St. Louis with the intention of entering it in the Mississippi River trade.[35]

The inconstant supply of railroad freight was compounded by very low water in the fall. In early October, when there were only twenty-eight inches of "steamboat water" above Yankton, the officers of the *Andrew Ackley* had to discharge much of its freight for the Cheyenne River Agency at Bon Homme Island and Fort Randall. Greatly lightened, the boat still needed several weeks to complete the normal ten-day voyage to the agency. To make matters worse, during the low-water stage, Hazlett could not recruit enough deckhands in Sioux City. Such labor shortages were quite common in the sparsely populated upper river region.[36]

The Kountz Line did not complete the military contract until late October. When the last deliveries were being made, Hazlett planned to winter the *Andrew Ackley* at Sioux City and send all others to St. Louis.

Despite his frustrations in fulfilling the 1871 army contract, Kountz bid on both the military and Indian transportation contracts the following year. But the Northwest Transportation Company was awarded the army contract, and Durfee and Peck the Indian contract, thereby forcing Kountz to compete only in the private trade.

When the army contract was let in Chicago, Captain Grant Marsh submitted the Northwest Transportation Company's bid and a Mr. Spiker of Pittsburgh represented the Kountz Line. Spiker tried the unusual tactic of submitting two bids—one high and one low. But he erred by failing to post the required $10,000 bond for each bid. Contending that Spiker violated the rules by attempting to cover two bids with one bond, the Northwest Transportation Company appealed directly to Brevet Major General Montgomery C. Meigs, the army's quartermaster general. Meigs decided that Spiker's bids were invalid and awarded the contract to the Northwest Transportation Company. Spiker's blunder was costly to both Kountz and the government. His low bid was 15 percent less than the 1871 rates, and Marsh's bid was about 30 percent higher than Spiker's.[37]

The army contract was signed on February 28, well before the opening of navigation. But the Indian contract was not finalized until June 14. Probably because of its late completion, it was to remain in effect until July 1, 1873.[38]

Durfee and Peck agreed to accept supplies at Sioux City, St. Louis, Kansas City, and Omaha. Rates to Sioux City were set at 40 cents per hundred pounds from St.

Louis, 35 cents from Kansas City, and 18 cents from Omaha. For deliveries above Sioux City they accepted rates that were approximately one-third to one-half lower than the 1871 reimbursement. For example, for Sioux City–Fort Benton goods, they were to be paid $1.75 for June and August, $3 for September and October, and $2.25 for May and June 1873, whereas the 1871 season-long rate was $3.36.

Anticipating heavy business with the government, the Northwest Transportation Company added two steamers—the *Western* and the *Sioux City*. Sanford B. Coulson oversaw the construction of the *Western* at Allegheny City, and the company purchased the *Sioux City* from the Arkansas River Packet Company. Because they also had the contract to deliver Indian supplies from the Old Whetstone Agency to the agency on the White River, Durfee and Peck added an overland freighting component. In July some of their men drove forty yoke of oxen from Sioux City to the old agency. The wagons and supplies for the new agency were sent by steamers.[39]

The two government contracts and increased amounts of private freighting assured Sioux City a long, bountiful navigation season. A very early opening of the Missouri enabled the Northwest Transportation Company to dispatch the *Nellie Peck,* its first boat, on March 21. Commanded by Grant Marsh, it was bound for the Whetstone Agency landing and intermediate points with 300 tons of mostly government supplies.[40]

Army steamboat shipments upstream from Sioux City for April, May, and June amounted to 4,000 tons.[41] Indian supplies and private shipments increased the city's grand total to 6,688 tons, prompting the *Sioux City Weekly Journal* to boast: "River men claim that Sioux City is the sixth place in point of importance in river business in the United States, being exceeded only by St. Louis, Cincinnati, Louisville, Pittsburgh and New Orleans."[42]

By Independence Day, the freight demands on the Northwest Transportation Company were so heavy that the line radically remodeled its *Silver Lake No. 4.* By removing its passenger cabins and leaving only a small, partial deck for officers and crew, the firm refitted the boat for freighting only.

Above-normal rainfall in late summer and fall assured good water levels and timely deliveries. In September alone more than 1,500 tons of freight were carried upstream from Sioux City. Veteran rivermen were said to be astonished when the Missouri rose two feet at Sioux City in early October. By that time the Northwest Transportation Company had only about 325 tons of army provisions, or two relatively light steamboat loads, to deliver to forts in Dakota Territory.[43]

The year's navigation was highly gratifying for Sioux City and its boatmen. Remarkably, the record upriver shipments were accident-free. The *Sioux City Weekly Journal* observed: "It speaks well for the transportation management and for the class of boats employed that not a pound of freight has been lost, none damaged worth mentioning, and that not a single disaster involving loss of life or property has occurred."

The most striking feature of Sioux City's brief reign as the steamboat capital of the upper Missouri was the precipitous decline in the Fort Benton trade. Eight steamers reached the head of navigation in 1870 and only six the next year. There were thirteen arrivals in 1872, including the *Sioux City*'s double trip from Fort Buford.[44]

Some of Fort Benton's decline was caused by the demise of Montana's placer mining. But most of the port's ill fortune was due to competition from the Union Pacific and the Montana Trail from Corinne, Utah Territory. The railroad's completion on May 10, 1869, did not affect steamboating immediately. By then, most of the steamers that started from St. Louis were en route and in some instances were within days of reaching Fort Benton. But by close of the navigation season, private and government shippers to Montana were using the Union Pacific and the Montana Trail.

Soon after the railroad's completion, the army established a depot at Corinne. About 28 miles northwest of Ogden, on the railroad angle that passed north of Great Salt Lake, Corinne was the best location for shipping supplies to both Montana and Idaho. During their short 1869 season, overland freighters transported a modest 560 tons of goods to Montana. But the amount swelled to about 3,500 tons in 1870 and increased about 7 percent the following year. Fort Benton's steamboat imports for those years were 1,599 and 1,403 tons respectively.[45]

One of the main advantages of the Corinne route was that freighters had a much longer season than rivermen. Freighters could operate for months after the last steamer had left Fort Benton. Most of them did not stop their trains until Monida Pass and other places were snow-clogged. In the dry fall of 1872 Edgar G. Maclay did not close his Diamond R warehouse at Corinne until December 10. Sometimes the freighters were even able to make wintertime deliveries.[46]

Although far more freight was imported over the Montana Trail from Corinne than by steamboats, Montana's economy benefited by being supplied from both the Union Pacific and the Missouri. Because of its vastness, different sections of the territory fell within the pale of the railroad-overland and steamboat-overland transportation systems. Steamboatmen had an obvious advantage in transporting freight to Fort Benton and nearby places, but Corinne's freighters easily dominated shipments to more southern locales such as Bannack and Virginia City. Helena, which had emerged as the territory's principal city, provided an opportunity for more direct competition. It was 465 miles from Corinne, but only 140 from Fort Benton. Freighters using ox-drawn wagons, which usually moved at about 12 to 15 miles daily, spent about three to four weeks more on the trail from Corinne than from Fort Benton.[47]

Recognizing that time was money, two major freighters tried to obliterate Fort Benton's advantage by introducing express freight service from Corinne in 1871. Modeling themselves after express stagecoaches, Edgar G. Maclay organized the Diamond R Overland Express, and Hugh Kirkendall the Montana Fast Freight and Express Line. To gain speed they used mules rather than oxen, changed teams after short runs, and ran round the clock. On their first race to Helena the Diamond R won, with the spectacular time of seven days. Though speedy, the express service was relatively expensive. The two companies charged 10 cents per pound; more than twice the rate for regular deliveries.[48]

The express service was obviously designed for certain items that were needed quickly. But most overland freight continued to be shipped by slow-moving ox teams, which enabled boatmen to compete. Shipping costs to Montana were well analyzed by Thomas P. Roberts, a Northern Pacific Railroad Company engineer. In 1872 when the contemplated transcontinental line was being built west from the Red River, Roberts investigated a possible Northern Pacific–steamboat combination to control trade along the upper Missouri. In the course of assessing the impact of the Union Pacific, he noted that its completion had forced steamboatmen to keep their Fort Benton rates below the rail and wagon rates. Every time the railroad reduced rates, boatmen responded in kind.[49]

The prevailing rates in the spring of 1872 illustrated his point. Some of the river freight from St. Louis to Fort Benton had been transported for only 3 cents a pound. Freighting it to Helena added another 1.5 cents. The combined river-overland route charge compared favorably with the 6 cents a pound for Omaha-to-Helena freight by way of Corinne.

Other than dropping rates, boatmen tried to reduce the speed advantage of the Union Pacific by hurrying up their voyages to Fort Benton. The quest for speed, of course, predated railroads, but their technology, which threatened to make steamboating appear antiquated, presented a new challenge. Love of speed was an ingrained cultural characteristic regardless of the conveyance. People who were awed by the fastest man or the fastest horse naturally equated the fastest boat with the "best boat." Aside from the obvious economic advantage of saving time, a fast boat proved the superiority of its design, machinery and personnel.

Long accustomed to racing against time, cementing their bragging rights with the ceremonial awarding of elk horns, and gambling on outcomes, boatmen naturally transferred their traditions to Sioux City. Racing was encouraged by newspapers, boatmen, and public zeal. In the course of trying to set speed records for every conceivable route, be it upstream from Sioux City to Yankton or downstream from Fort Buford to Sioux City, individual boats soon gained reputations. The Northwest Transportation Company's *Far West* and *Nellie Peck* were known as the speediest. But no one would bet on such ridiculed "slow tubs" as the *Silver Lake No. 4* and *Katie P. Kountz*.[50]

Upper river towns, whose economies depended heavily on steamboating, resented any implication that the Union Pacific–Montana Trail route was the best way of shipping to Montana. Some Montanans, including a reporter for the *Helena Herald*, thought that the railroad-overland route would cause the decline of steamboating. But Yankton's *Union and Dakotaian* responded sharply: "Our great water route from the Mountains to the sea is more than a match for the railroad, and from this [day] forward the importance of the Big Muddy as a commercial route will send forth its own praise by its thousands of steamers and cheap freight." Obviously, the writer's vehemence was better than his steamboat count.[51]

The 1872 race between the *Far West*, commanded by Martin Coulson, and the *Nellie Peck*, captained by Grant Marsh, provided the best opportunity to promote the river route. In June, when the boats were being loaded for their second Sioux City–Fort Benton trips of the season, there was a good deal of levee banter about which steamer would reach the head of navigation first. Relishing a contest, Coulson and Marsh appealed to their fans, who eagerly bet considerable sums on the outcome. Since the *Nellie Peck* pulled out first, the race was only against the clock, with time to be measured in days and hours from departure to arrival rather than actual running time. Under the circumstances, it behooved both captains to exhort their crews to move quickly when unloading at numerous waypoints and refueling.[52]

Taking advantage of a high June rise, the boats were sped upstream out of each other's sight until just below Cow Island. Finally the *Far West* overtook and passed the *Nellie Peck* at the island. With a somewhat lighter cargo, the *Far West* stayed ahead and docked at Fort Benton at 7:30 A.M., June 30, a few hours ahead of the *Nellie Peck*. The winner's amazing time of 17 days and 20 hours smashed the previous record by nearly 5 days. Although he lost, Marsh was thrilled with his time. Company president Elias H. Durfee thought the times proved his line's superiority. The race fascinated the public, but Durfee was probably more gratified by the more mundane consideration that each of the boats cleared $12,000 on its voyage.

Coulson telegraphed his good news to Sioux City, which at least joyed his supporters. But some of Marsh's fans grumbled about the seeming inequity of the *Nellie Peck*'s carrying more cargo. Fort Benton's telegraph connection to Corinne, which had been completed in mid-June 1869, revolutionized communication. Before then, downriver people had to depend on descending steamers for the latest information. But once the service was in place, steamboatmen used it routinely to inform their home offices about their arrivals and departures and to exchange information about such things as river stages, boat conditions, and return cargoes. When Fort Benton entered the telegraph age, there was no line in the Missouri River valley above Sioux City. Sometimes, if instructions were changed soon after boats left Sioux City, they were overtaken by mounted couriers. But in 1870 a Sioux City company built a line to Yankton and extended it to Fort Randall the next year. By late May 1872 it was completed to Fort Sully.[53]

Near the end of the navigation season, Coulson and the *Far West* were formally feted in Sioux City. Planners of the "grand supper" and dance prepared a "splendid pair of elk horns, bearing the inscription '17 days and 20 hours.'" As time passed and memory of his fast voyage to Fort Benton faded, Coulson probably took a delight in explaining the cryptic wording.[54]

Through the Northwest Transportation Company and the Kountz Line, Sioux City was the main Missouri River depot for Fort Benton shipments. Normally, upbound steamers carried both government and private freight. Much of the private goods was distributed northward by Fort Benton's merchants, who developed new markets north of the border. The Canadian trade was started in the winter of 1869–70 by John J. Healy and Alfred B. Hamilton. Hamilton, a nephew of Isaac G. Baker, reportedly netted $50,000 for only six months of Indian trading.

Importantly, the Canadian trade opened up another source of buffalo robes and other furs.[55]

Other than the Fort Benton trade, steamboat shipments of private freight were concerned with the fur trade, agricultural produce, and, beginning in 1872, railroad supplies. Durfee and Peck dominated the fur trade. With several hundred employees, an annual business of over $250,000 (including post sutlerships and Indian trading posts), and such important installations as Fort Peck, it was the region's leading firm. Every spring, upbound steamers carried supplies and men to its various posts. Sometimes boats brought immense cargoes downstream. On one of its 1871 trips the *Ida Rees* delivered 39,000 buffalo robes to Sioux City. A few weeks later the robe, fur, and hide cargo of the *Nellie Peck* filled 23 railroad cars. The company's returns for 1872 by late June included 10,000 buffalo robes valued at $6.50 each, 24,000 antelope hides, 8,000 deer skins, 500 elk hides, 2,000 wolf pelts, 600 beaver pelts, and 1,000 fox pelts, as well as some bear skins and wildcat, badger, muskrat, and mink pelts. Their total sales of these products was estimated at $85,000.[56]

With good connections to Chicago and New York fur buyers, a number of independent operators engaged in the fur trade. John Goewey of Sioux City, a partner in a small firm that had opposed the Northwest Fur Company, continued to make personal buying trips to the upper river. John H. Charles, who was engaged in a wholesaling and forwarding business with Milton Tootle, bought and sold robes, furs, and hides. Other fur dealers included W. A. Eliot and Company and C. Ambrecht, both of Sioux City, and Walter A. Burleigh of Yankton.[57]

By the early 1870s the economy of the Missouri River valley from Sioux City to between Yankton and Fort Randall had made the transition from subsistence to commercial agriculture. Farmers were producing a surplus of wheat, the region's dominant crop. Much of it was sent to Sioux City by steamers from Yankton and Vermillion, as well as St. Helena, Nebraska. Because of the wheat culture, flour was one of the river town's first manufactured products. Since production exceeded local demands, some of the flour was marketed to and through Sioux City. Sometimes, after it was inspected by quartermaster officers and Indian agency contractors, it was sent back upstream to the various posts and agencies.

After the harvest of 1872, Yankton's grain dealers had thousands of bushels of wheat that they wanted to send to Sioux City's millers and railroads. But they faced a transportation crisis because the region's steamboats were busy moving freight for the government and various parties at Edwinton, including the Northern Pacific. They solved their problem by buying, repairing, and running the steamer *Hiram Wood*, which had been abandoned by its Kansas owner on the Sioux City levee in 1871.[58]

Built at Wyandotte, Kansas, in 1865, the 100-foot-long side-wheeler, which had a capacity of only 75 to 80 tons, was one of the last boats navigated on the Kansas River. The boat was reported to present a "dilapidated appearance," but fortunately its machinery was in excellent condition. After extensive carpentry work and repainting was complete, the new owners began running the boat exclusively in the Yankton–Sioux City grain trade. On one trip, the small craft was overloaded with 8,500 bushels of wheat, which would have weighed about 250 tons. Reportedly, its bottom dragged on the riverbed all the way down.

Those Sioux Citians who were overjoyed to get their first railroad in 1868 realized that their end-of-track status would be temporary. Someday their port would be bypassed by advancing railroads and eclipsed by some upriver point. Although they recognized the inevitability of the change, Sioux Citians probably did not anticipate its suddenness. By 1872 they were threatened by both a short-line railroad in the southern part of Dakota Territory and a transcontinental line extension in the northern section of the territory. Completion of the Dakota Southern from Sioux City to Yankton and the Northern Pacific from Fargo on the Red River to the Missouri would create two new steamboat ports that would take business from Sioux City.

The Dakota Southern was a Yankton scheme. Perhaps because it was the territorial capital, Yankton may have had more schemers in proportion to its population than any other frontier town. Unabashed optimists, Yankton's boosters had grand dreams, whether their object was opening the Black Hills to gold mining or building a railroad.

Dakota's territorial legislature began investigating the possibility of getting a railroad in 1864. Three years later, when farmers were demanding improved transportation, the lawmakers chartered the Dakota and Northwestern Railroad with the aim of constructing a line from Sioux City to Yankton. Lacking funds, the company's incorporators tried to get a federal land grant. After their effort was rejected by Congress in 1871, Yanktonites took another tack. On March 17, 1871, they organized the Dakota Southern Railroad, which they proposed to build with local funds. Since Yankton merchants, the principal buyers of company stock, did not have enough capital to construct the road, they sought assistance from local governmental units. Raising capital through the sale of county bonds was a well-established fund-raising method in Missouri and other states.[59]

Yankton's planners were aware of this, but Dakota Territory did not have any legal provision for it. Therefore they persuaded the territorial secretary, in his role of acting governor, to call a special legislative session. The legislators obligingly approved an act authorizing counties and townships to aid railroad companies. With the law in place, the pro-railroad faction convinced Yankton County's voters to authorize the issuance of $200,000 worth of bonds. With some financial support from Elk Point, the railroad's managers were able to complete building plans.

In December 1871 they contracted with the Chicago firm of Wicker, Meckling, and Company to construct the 60-mile line. The builders got started early in 1872 and did most of their work over the ensuing navigation season. Like many other railroad projects, the Dakota Southern stimulated steamboating. Its construction prompted Walter A. Burleigh to buy the *Miner* from the Northwest Fur Company. Alpheus F. Hawley, who had been operating the boat, quit the river and moved to Chicago.[60]

Burleigh's entry into steamboating complemented his many business and political activities. A native Pennsylvanian and a medical doctor, he moved to Dakota Territory in 1861 as the Lincoln-appointed Yankton Indian agent. With no aversion to mixing politics and personal business, he treated the agency as a private fiefdom. His administration was marked by alleged corruption, including a call by a federal inspector to investigate his conduct.[61]

Because of his political connections, Burleigh was able to thwart any formal investigation of his agency conduct. As the leader of a territorial Republican Party faction, in 1864 he was elected territorial delegate to Congress. His influence over Dakota's affairs was so great that he managed to get his father-in-law, Andrew J. Faulk, appointed territorial governor. In 1870 he and Faulk started the village of Bon Homme, near Bon Homme Island. Burleigh set up a sawmill there to produce oak railroad ties for the Dakota Southern. In July 1872 he was employing about fifty men and teams at his "tie camp" to cut trees, haul logs, saw ties, and stockpile them at the steamboat landing.

When he was supplying ties for the Dakota Southern, Burleigh also held a Northern Pacific grading contract. The Northern Pacific route was part of Jefferson Davis's 1853 transcontinental railroad plans. But after the Stevens survey, nothing was done until the company was chartered by Congress in 1864 to build a line from Duluth on Lake Superior to Puget Sound. The company was given a lavish land grant, which was really a deferred payment. Like other land grant railroads, it did not receive land until it completed a specified amount of track. The Northern Pacific was able to start construction only after the Philadelphia banking house of Jay Cooke and Company sold its bonds. On February 15, 1870, company officials broke ground at a railroad junction near Duluth. By the end of the next year the line was completed across Minnesota to the Red River, where the Puget Sound Land Company, the railroad's townsite subsidiary, started the twin towns of Moorhead, Minnesota, and Fargo, Dakota Territory.[62]

In 1872, when its rails were being extended westward from Fargo, the Northern Pacific decided also to prepare a roadbed eastward from the point selected for its Missouri River crossing. Burleigh's contract called for grading a 50-mile section. Like everyone else associated with the place, he moved all of his equipment, provisions, and men by steamboats from Sioux City to "The Crossing," as the site was dubbed by Sioux City journalists. In May 1872 the Puget Sound Land Company named the place Edwinton, in honor of Edwin Ferry Johnson, the Northern Pacific's longtime consulting engineer. Edwinton, which attracted some sooners who saw an economic advantage in being the town's pioneers, had thirty buildings by the end of the year.[63]

Edwinton and nearby sites were popular steamboat destinations. Even the boats whose primary destinations were Fort Benton or Fort Buford stopped because of the freight and passenger trade. Much of the activity was due to the building of Fort McKean (renamed to Fort Abraham Lincoln in November 1872) across the Missouri from the planned railroad terminus. Under its military contract, the

Northwest Transportation Company moved great quantities of bricks and lumber, as well as carpenters and masons, from Sioux City.[64]

The anticipated railroad arrival also attracted a number of migrants from Sioux City and other places who hoped either to find jobs or to speculate in land. By July an assemblage of two hundred teamsters, woodcutters, and others was encamped near Edwinton. Their community, which did not have a permanent location, was variously known as Carlton or Burleigh City. Although Burleigh City did not last, Burleigh's surname was perpetuated by the territorial legislature, which in July 1873 named its newly created county for the Crossing area after him.[65]

To forward lumber and other provisions from Sioux City to Edwinton, the Northern Pacific relied mostly on the Kountz Line. Since Kountz had been excluded from government contracting, he always had steamers available. The Northern Pacific supplemented the Kountz shipments by operating its own steamer. After buying the *Ida Stockdale* from Kountz, the company staffed it with its own crew to make voyages between Sioux City and Edwinton. The railroad was intrigued by the possibility of using a railroad-steamboat combination to send freight up the Missouri from Edwinton. Its projected route from Edwinton almost due west to the Yellowstone River would leave a long section of the Missouri dependent on steamboats. Through its experience with the *Ida Stockdale*, the Northern Pacific gained insight into how it should conduct its business after reaching the Missouri.[66]

At the opening of navigation in 1873, the Northern Pacific's track-laying crews were approaching Edwinton. Chronically short of capital, the Northern Pacific's officers and directors decided they needed to lure more European investors. As they well knew, much American railroad construction was financed with money raised by private bankers from venture capitalists in Great Britain, France, the Netherlands, and Germany. Hoping to attract the attention of German financiers, they renamed Edwinton to Bismarck, in recognition of the international fame of Otto von Bismarck, who had become chancellor of the newly created German Empire in 1871.[67]

Though enterprising, the name change did not cause an influx of German or any other foreign capital. Bismarck's first train arrived on June 5, 1873. Its freight included the printing press of the *Bismarck Tribune*, which soon became the promotional organ of the new railroad terminus–steamboat port. Rather than being the temporary end-of-track that company officials envisaged, Bismarck was given a unique status by a long delay in railroad construction. The disastrous Panic of 1873 temporarily ruined that attractiveness of American railroad investments. Because of the panic and ensuing depression, the Northern Pacific was stalled at Bismarck for six years, enabling the town to become a major depot for steamboating to Fort Benton and waypoints.[68]

Meanwhile, because of the completion of the Dakota Southern, Yankton had become Bismarck's main rival. By the time the line was opened to traffic on February 3, 1873, Yankton's leaders had made arrangements with Sanford B. Coulson to base his new steamboat company there. When Coulson broke with the Northwest Transportation Company, he took many of its key personnel with him.[69]

Railroad construction on the northern plains and the accompanying rise of Sioux City, Yankton, and Bismarck as steamboat ports ended St. Louis's reign as the metropolis of the entire Missouri. St. Louis–based steamboatmen adjusted by concentrating on the trade within the state of Missouri. Thus their business was characterized by direct competition with the intrastate railroads on both sides of the Missouri and numerous relatively short hauls of bulky farm products. By matching or undercutting railroad rates, the boatmen could oftentimes obtain freight shipments, but the passenger trade to points that had railroad service became insignificant. Travelers, unlike some freight shippers, invariably wanted to reach their destinations quickly, and they swarmed to the railroads. However, some travelers to small riverside towns that lacked railroads continued to use steamboats for short local runs rather than depend on stagecoaches.

The conversion of steamboating from a freight-passenger business to an almost exclusive cargo trade sharply changed the profession's nature. The boats became more Spartan in appearance and accommodations. Freight shipments did not require ornately furnished lounges, cabins furnished with comfortable mattresses, lavish meals, and calliope entertainment. Captains and clerks could curtail or even eliminate their chambermaid, steward, and kitchen services. Loss of passengers also changed promotional advertising. Commodious facilities and hospitable officers were not very meaningful to grain shippers, who were primarily attracted by low rates.

The overall effect of the changes was to make steamboating less visible to the public. Since few were concerned with how long it took to move a cargo of wheat from Glasgow to St. Louis, newspaper coverage became more sporadic. Once steamboating became secondary to railroads and lost its exalted status as the most technologically advanced form of transportation, its status diminished in the public view. After railroads, it no longer permeated every aspect of Missouri's life, but was only an auxiliary service for selected shippers. When riding on steamers became a remembrance rather than a continuing experience, the freight boats, for most people, were only reminders of a bygone age.

St. Louis's steamboating to Missouri River destinations declined sharply in the early 1870s. Boatmen compiled rather impressive statistics in 1870, when St. Louis had 321 departures for the Missouri and 329 arrivals from it. The business was dominated by the Omaha Packet Company, the Missouri River Packet Company, and the Miami Packet Company. All three were better-known by their colloquial names of O Line, K Line, and Star Line. The O Line ran six steamers, the K Line two, and the Star Line five. Three independent operators each managed one boat, which brought the total operating on the lower river to sixteen. Their season-long tendency was to make many short, quick voyages. The Star Line's *St. Luke* made 41 round-trips, and its *Alice* completed 29.[70]

By 1872 the numbers had dropped dramatically to 124 departures and 123 arrivals. Downriver shipments for 1872 were 26,895 tons but had been 72,579 for the pre-

Sanford B. Coulson became the
dominant figure in upper Missouri
steamboating after a railroad reached
Yankton, Dakota Territory, in 1873.
*Courtesy of Terry Coulson, Yankton,
South Dakota.*

ceding year. Upbound freight for 1871 and 1872 was 44,438 and 27,536 tons respectively. Statisticians for the St. Louis Board of Trade did not attempt to compile passenger statistics, because that business was reported to have "virtually ceased."[71]

St. Louis departures and arrivals did not account for all Missouri River steamboat business. In 1871 and 1872 the *Washington* operated in the Augusta-Bluffton-Portland area as a forwarder and deliverer for the Missouri Pacific Railroad. It was used to tap the trade of villages that did not have railroad service. Among other farm products, it carried great quantities of butter and eggs to the railroad. It is quite likely that its operators were being subsidized by the railroad, because on most of their trips their freight income was slightly less than their expenses.[72] But perhaps the *Washington*'s experience was typical of most other steamers. Blaming low water, a writer for the annual *Trade and Commerce of St. Louis* pronounced 1871 as "not a propitious one for steamboatmen."[73]

However, St. Louisians also acknowledged that railroads were mainly responsible for steamboating's decline. In 1871 the Missouri Pacific alone received 207,185 tons of freight and sent 204,926. Its receipts were matched by those of the North Missouri's route to Kansas City. So the combined railroad receipts were nearly seven times greater those of the steamboats.[74]

The speed and efficiency of North Missouri traffic between St. Louis and

Kansas City had been improved by the completion of Missouri River bridges at Kansas City and St. Charles. The Kansas City bridge, built one and a half miles below the mouth of the Kansas River, was dedicated and opened to traffic on July 3, 1869. The first to span the Missouri, it took two and half years to build. Its construction was a great economic and political coup for Kansas City, which had been rivaled by St. Joseph and Leavenworth in the prebridge era. Authorized by a congressional act of July 25, 1866, the bridge resulted from scheming by Kansas City's promoters to transform their city into the metropolis for the southern Great Plains. The bridge, which eliminated costly ferrying, was part of a grand plan, which included bridging the Mississippi River at Quincy, Illinois. Combined, the two bridges gave Kansas City uninterrupted railroad connections to Chicago by way of the Hannibal and St. Joseph and the Kansas City and Cameron railroads. The North Missouri benefited because of its connection with the Cameron line. The bridge worked wonders for Kansas City, which boomed as a railroad center soon after its completion. In the longer range, the bridge spurred construction of railroads south and southwestward from Kansas City.[75]

The St. Charles bridge, finished and opened to traffic on May 29, 1871, was promoted by the North Missouri Railroad. Most of the St. Charles Bridge Company's stock was owned by investors in the North Missouri. As with the Kansas City bridge, the one at St. Charles speeded service and permitted the railroad to be more competitive, because it no longer had to be concerned about ferry charges.[76]

Farther upstream, the Union Pacific completed its Council Bluffs–Omaha bridge, the third to cross the Missouri, in early 1872. The nearly four-year construction project cost $1.75 million.[77]

Reaction from steamboatmen was understandably anti-bridge. As they realized, the bridges not only decreased ferry services but also diminished the prospects of packet deliveries to the bridge towns. Being somewhat politically astute, however, boatmen chose not to contend that bridges gave railroads an economic advantage. Rather, they insisted the bridges were navigation hazards, which imperiled their way of life. While the Kansas City bridge was being erected, eighty-one steamboat pilots, captains, and owners signed a petition in which they claimed that it "endangers navigation at all times, but especially during high water, when it is impassable with any degree of safety. And we hereby pledge our best endeavors to effect its removal."[78] Interestingly, army engineer Captain Charles R. Suter, then in charge of Missouri River improvement, gave them some qualified support. He pointed out that because the main channel at the bridge followed the right bank, steamboats descending during high water would have difficulty avoiding bridge piers.[79]

Other than stone piers in the river, the height of bridges could be a problem. Soon after the completion of the Union Pacific bridge, officers of the *Mary McDonald*, en route from St. Louis to Fort Benton, found that the boat's chimneys would not clear the bridge. So they cut off two feet in order to pass under it. On their return trip weeks later the water level at Omaha had not changed, but the lightly loaded boat was riding much higher. So once again they had to saw two feet off the chimneys.[80]

As steamboating was declining on the lower river, the federal government intensified its river improvement program. The justification for snag removal and dredging projects was that, with hazards eliminated, boats could move faster and safer, which in turn would lead to reduced freight rates and insurance premiums. In 1871 Lieutenant Colonel William F. Raynolds, commander of the Office of Western River Improvement of the army's Corps of Engineers, claimed that river improvement saved boatmen $1,000 on a St. Louis–St. Joseph round-trip. This enabled them to become more competitive, which forced railroads to lower their rates. Thus the effects of river improvement permeated all aspects of the region's transportation system. Furthermore, Raynolds believed river improvement was relatively inexpensive. He placed the monthly operating cost of each snagboat at $5,000.[81]

During the early 1870s, army engineers operated several snagboats on the lower river. In 1871 the *J. J. Abert*, *S. H. Long*, and *S. Thayer*, as well as the dredge boat *Octavia*, were all used on the Missouri below St. Joseph. The next year, a fourth snagboat—the *R. E. DeRussy*—was added. Each of the snagboats was assigned to a section, bounded by St. Louis to Eureka, Eureka to Lexington, Lexington to St. Joseph, and St. Joseph to Omaha. For the entire season, the four snagboats, combined, ran 3,906 miles, removed 2,226 snags and 72 rock heaps, and cut 12,101 trees from the banks. Tree removal was intended to curtail the creation of new snags by the cutting channel. But nature never stopped working. Each year there was a new batch of snags. Consequently, the engineers found it was necessary to go over the same areas year after year. In 1873 the *R. E. DeRussy* and *S. H. Long*, combined, removed 841 snags and cut 1,408 trees from the mouth to Kansas City.[82]

As Congress liberalized funding for river and harbor improvement, army engineers were able to undertake Osage River improvement. The act of March 3, 1871, contained a $25,000 appropriation for the Osage. Approval of the allocation was influenced by an army engineer-sponsored reconnaissance in July and August 1870. Traveling downstream by skiff, civilian contractor D. Fitzgerald identified all shoals between Papinsville and the mouth. On the basis of his report, the Corps of Engineers hired another civilian contractor, Alonzo Livermore, to start dredging channels at the lowermost shoals. Working upstream from the mouth, Livermore's crew used horse-drawn scrapers to remove 11,200 cubic yards of sand from seven shoals. The men also extracted a number of logs and stumps from the channel and repaired wing dams that had been erected by the State of Missouri.[83]

With additional congressional funding, the engineers continued the Osage improvement project in 1872 and 1873. Shoals were dredged as high as Tuscumbia, and log and brush dams were built to prevent the dredged material from sliding back into the river. Army engineer W. S. Simpson, who filed a report after the 1873 work, was pessimistic about its long-range effects. "I have no faith in the permanency of the above works," he wrote.[84] He claimed that in meandering, silt-laden streams such as the Osage, improvements lasted only ten to fifteen years.

As proof of his observations, he noted that dams installed by the State of Missouri in the 1850s had caused new shoals to be formed below them. Hence navigation was worsened by the dam construction. The only solution for the Osage, he believed, was to install a system of locks and dams. But he thought that such a radical solution could not be justified by current and future steamboating.

Federal officials who encouraged river improvement also believed that steamboat safety would be enhanced by making some changes in the steamboat inspection service. Over the years, there had been complaints that the 1852 law, which provided for the licensing of pilots and engineers, was not inclusive enough. Critics believed that captains and mates, who were instrumental in boat management, should also meet licensing requirements. In 1871, Congress, acting on a recommendation by Secretary of the Treasury George S. Boutwell, included captain and mate licensing in a new steamboat inspection law. In the same act, the legislators moved to make the Steamboat Inspection Service more administratively efficient. They mandated that it be headed by a supervising inspector general, who would report directly to the secretary of the treasury. In addition to his normal administrative duties, the new official would preside at the annual meetings of the ten district supervisors.[85]

Until 1884 the entire Missouri River region was in the fourth district, headquartered at St. Louis. Traditionally the inspectors did all their work in St. Louis. But the introduction of boat wintering at Sioux City complicated their assignment. Beginning in 1870, the hull and boiler inspectors traveled by rail to Sioux City to conduct the required annual inspections of the steamers based there.[86]

Their travel underscored the new nature of Missouri River steamboating. Railheads at Sioux City, Yankton, and Bismarck reoriented trade patterns. Instead of looking southward to St. Louis, people of the northern plains turned eastward to Chicago. Initially, railroads to the upper river did not detrimentally affect steamboating to the extent they did in Missouri. Part of the reason was the location of the river vis-à-vis the railroads in the two sections. In Missouri, where the river lay east-west, the first tracks paralleled it. But above Sioux City, where there was a long north-south stretch, the first railroads only touched the river at widely separated points. Consequently, upper river boating boomed for a time in combination with railroads. Between Kansas City and St. Louis, the most prosperous steamboat era preceded railroads.

10

THE UPPER RIVER BOOM, 1873–1879

As new railroad termini, Bismarck and Yankton became the most important steamboat ports on the upper river. During their seven-year rivalry, steamboating reached new heights in response to rapid, dramatic changes in one of the nation's last frontiers. The uneasy calm effected by the Fort Laramie Treaty of 1868 was upset by the discovery of gold in the Black Hills. As prospectors swarmed to this latest El Dorado, some Lakotas and their Northern Cheyenne allies sought refuge in the Yellowstone River valley, where it was still possible to live by buffalo hunting. The federal government responded by launching offensives during the Great Sioux War of 1876–77. Fortification of the Yellowstone country caused a sharp surge in steamboating on the Yellowstone River, the upper Missouri's only navigable tributary. For a short time, Yellowstone River steamboating surpassed that of any other portion of the upper Missouri system.

While the military frontier was being established in the Yellowstone valley, there was a resurgence of steamboating to Fort Benton, and Yankton-based boats were a vital link in a combined rail-river-overland route from the east to the Black Hills. Fort Benton's revival was fueled by an expanding Montana population and the fortification of the Canadian West.

During the boom times at Yankton and Bismarck, four companies dominated steamboating—the Coulson Line, the Kountz Line, the Peck Line, and the Power Line. Walter A. Burleigh of Yankton and I. G. Baker and Company of Fort Benton also organized small lines.

The Coulson Line, formally the Missouri River Transportation Company, established itself as the leading carrier soon after its formation in 1873. Sanford B. Coulson, the firm's principal organizer, and his associates basked in the lavish praise of the regional press. They were the first boatmen to become closely identified with Dakota and Montana territories. During the company's first five years, Coulson and his family lived in Yankton only during the navigation season. They wintered in Allegheny City, Pennsylvania, where Coulson was the part owner of a bank. But in 1878 Coulson became a permanent resident of Yankton. In keeping with his status as an honorary "commodore," he built a $10,000 mansion, the town's most luxurious home. Coulson's fame as the upper river's leading boatman led some to call him "The Napoleon of the Big Muddy."[1]

Coulson had a talent for attracting capable associates. His chief financiers—James C. McVay, John B. Dallas, James Rees, William S. Evans, and D. S. H. Gilmore—were all from the Allegheny City–Pittsburgh area. After moving to Yankton, McVay served as the Coulson Line's treasurer while managing the First National Bank. For several years he also served as the treasurer of Dakota Territory. Dallas was the head of the boat chandlery firm of Evans, Dallas, and Gilmore. Other than working with Coulson in procuring army transportation contracts, he did not participate in the line's routine operations. Rees, who had run boats from St. Louis to Fort Benton during the Montana gold rush, was a part owner of some of the Coulson boats. He may have been the line's wealthiest member, because of his long experience as a Pittsburgh steamboat builder. Gilmore's main business was boat chandlery, but like many others involved in steamboat construction, he invested in various steamers. Evans, a brother-in-law of the Coulson brothers, had commanded several steamers on the Ohio and lower Mississippi before joining the Coulson Line. On the upper Missouri he usually served as the first clerk on a Coulson vessel.[2]

Sanford B. Coulson, who was only thirty-three years old when he organized the Missouri River Transportation Company, brought his three older brothers—John, Martin, and William—into the firm. Martin, famed for his record-breaking voyage from Sioux City to Fort Benton, returned to Allegheny City, where he supervised the construction of new Coulson Line steamers and oversaw the family's interest in an Allegheny City bank. John and William were among the most active masters and pilots on the upper river.[3]

Besides his Allegheny City associates and his brothers, Coulson recruited three experienced captains—Nick Buesen, Josephus (better known as Joe) Todd, and Grant Marsh—with whom he had worked in the Northwest Transportation Company. Buesen, a German immigrant, and Todd had worked together as boat officers on the Ohio and Mississippi before joining the Northwest Transportation Company. In the Coulson Line they were masters and part owners of various steamers. Buesen also assisted in the building of Coulson Line steamers at Pittsburgh.[4]

Marsh, nearly thirty-nine years old when he joined the Coulson Line, had been involved in steamboating for twenty-seven years. He started as a twelve-year-old cabin boy near his hometown of Rochester, Pennsylvania. Working westward to St. Louis, he progressed from deckhand to first mate. He entered the upper Missouri in 1864 as an officer on the *Marcella*, one of the boats providing support for the Sully Expedition. After the war, he worked as a pilot and master in the Fort Benton trade before joining the Northwest Transportation Company.

As the Coulson Line expanded its operations to the Yellowstone River, San-

Daniel W. Maratta left the Kountz Line
to serve as the Coulson Line's general
manager and the right-hand man of
Sanford B. Coulson. *Courtesy of the State
Historical Society of North Dakota.*

ford B. Coulson found he could not manage affairs from Yankton alone. Since most
of the freight and passengers for the Yellowstone and the upper reaches of the Missouri were moved by the Northern Pacific to Bismarck, it became necessary to station a manager there. In 1875 Coulson engaged Daniel Webster Maratta, who, next
to the commodore, became the most prestigious Coulson Line figure.

A native of the Ohio River port of Bridgewater, Pennsylvania, Maratta entered
steamboating as a cabin boy, where he became acquainted with Grant Marsh. By
1856 he was an assistant clerk on a Mississippi River boat. During the Civil War
he served as the master of a Union army steamer in the Vicksburg campaign. After
the war he joined the Kountz Line. In 1873 he entered the upper Missouri business as the captain of Kountz's *May Lowery*. The next year he captained the Kountz
Line's *Fontenelle* in the Bismarck–Fort Benton trade.

Before the opening of navigation in 1875, Maratta left Kountz to become Coulson's Bismarck manager. The move was not too surprising. The irascible Kountz
had difficulty maintaining long-term associations. Like Coulson, Maratta seems
to have been embittered about his experience with Kountz.[5]

Maratta, who was promoted to general manager in 1877, was the Coulson Line's
most effective promoter. He convinced many people that the company was, as he
was fond of advertising it, "the Old Reliable Line." Well known for his cordiality, Maratta moved easily in social circles—be they the frontier people of Bis-

marck, senior army officers, or congressmen. His usual demeanor was that of a fast-talking salesman, which caused a number of people to distrust him. Even some of the people who liked him called him "Slippery Dan."

Aside from his normal administrative duties, Maratta became a Coulson intimate. He was the commodore's right-hand man in contract negotiations and the company's principal congressional lobbyist. He spent part of every winter away from his Beaver, Pennsylvania, home in Washington, D.C., so that he could influence key congressmen to support the Coulson Line's bids for army transportation contracts.

Despite his wintertime absences, Maratta was accepted as a local boy by Bismarckians. Some of his popularity can be attributed to his politicking. As one of the territory's most prominent Democrats, he promoted his party through speaking at local rallies and otherwise helping in campaigns. Perhaps because of his political activities, he preferred to be identified as D. W. rather than Daniel Webster. His parents, who named their progeny after the famous Whig politician, certainly could not have realized the potential embarrassment of the name to an ardent Democrat.

In the Coulson Line's early years its principal rival was the Kountz Line. After hauling quantities of Northern Pacific freight in 1872, Kountz shifted most of his operations from Sioux City to Bismarck. At the new port, his steamers in 1873 and 1874 were the main forwarders of Northern Pacific deliveries destined for Fort Benton and waypoints. Unable to win army transportation contracts, Kountz concentrated on moving private freight for Montana merchants. By offering through bills of lading from Chicago and other starting points, Kountz became so closely identified with the Northern Pacific that his fleet was sometimes called the Northern Pacific Line.[6]

A permanent Allegheny City resident who spent part of the navigation season at Bismarck and an occasional winter in New Orleans, Kountz was apparently unconcerned about being accepted as a Dakotan. Unlike Coulson and Maratta, who curried public favor, Kountz continued to perpetuate his reputation as a crank. Through articles in his newspaper—the *Allegheny Mail*—he attacked such rivals as the Coulson Line and the St. Louis–based Anchor Line. Some of his resentment of the Coulson Line was caused by continuing contention over army contracts, but the acrimony may have started in Pennsylvania, where Kountz and the Coulson brothers were major stockholders in an Allegheny City bank.

Habitually uncompromising, Kountz extended his enmity for Sanford B. Coulson to include those who associated with him. John H. Charles, a Sioux City merchant, forwarding agent, steamboat investor, and government contractor with no particular personal loyalties, offended Kountz by having the effrontery to sometimes make arrangements with Coulson. In a private letter, Kountz bluntly admonished him: "Now Charles, I have known men to select very singular bedfellows, but I never in my life have known a man that I have always regarded as a man of high sense of honor, to get right into bed with such a dirty dog as you have."[7]

The Northwest Transportation Company, often called the Peck Line, also competed with the Coulson Line. Soon after Coulson broke with the Northwest Transportation Company, its parent organization—Durfee and Peck—failed. Elias H. Durfee and Campbell K. Peck had gained prominence as licensed Indian traders and post sutlers. Ardent Republicans, they benefited from the prevailing patronage system by the support of Secretary of War William W. Belknap (like Peck, a Keokukian) and other officials in the Grant administration. But during the summer of 1874, when Durfee was terminally ill with Bright's disease, federal officials rejected the Durfee and Peck bids for license renewals. The Indian agency business went to associates of Orville Grant, the president's brother, and the post sutlerships to various Belknap associates, including John M. Hedrick of Ottumwa, Iowa.[8]

After Durfee's death on September 13, 1874, Peck—in association with Durfee's brother George of Leavenworth, Kansas, and A. F. Brownell, a Keokuk banker—reorganized the Northwest Transportation Company. As company president, Peck continued to live in Keokuk, where he had a hardware business. Most of the line's business was done from Bismarck, where Henry C. Akin served as its resident agent. Because it owned the Sioux City ways, the company wintered most of its vessels there and especially during a season's maiden voyages carried freight and passengers upstream. Its ties to the town became yet more important in 1877, when Dr. A. F. Terry of Sioux City was awarded the army transportation contract for points below Bismarck. Lacking his own vessels, Terry formed a short-lived partnership with Peck. Technically, the boats Terry used were in the Contract Transportation Company, but it and the Peck Line both used Akin as their Bismarck manager and otherwise acted in concert.

Because of Peck's financial problems, the Peck Line was a struggling concern. When Peck's hardware business was failing, he was engaged in various suits against the U.S. government growing out of Durfee and Peck contracts. He filed for bankruptcy shortly before his death on December 2, 1879.

While the fortunes of the Peck Line were declining, those of the Power Line were increasing. The Power Line, formally organized as the Fort Benton Transportation Company, was a latecomer to steamboating. Thomas C. Power, the firm's key man, first visited Fort Benton as a civil engineer with a surveying party in 1864. Three years later he returned to establish a merchandising business. His first store was in a tent that Isaac G. Baker loaned him.[9]

A native of Dubuque, Iowa, Power was twenty-eight years old when he started his Fort Benton business. After he was joined by his younger brother, John, the two formed T. C. Power and Brother, which expanded from merchandising into ranching, mining, banking, and overland freighting.

By the time they entered steamboating, the Power brothers and their friendly rival, Isaac G. Baker, correctly sensed the revival of Fort Benton steamboating. The Helena market was expanding along with the buffalo robe trade and the supplying of Canadian outposts. The Powers and Baker believed there was a financial advantage in transporting some of their own freight from Bismarck to Fort Benton. They never aspired to control all of their steamboat business and continued to rely on the Coulson Line and other transporters.

Thomas C. Power, a Fort Benton merchant
who later became a U.S. senator from
Montana, was the main figure in the
Fort Benton Transportation Company.
Courtesy of the Montana Historical Society, Helena.

In mid-November 1874 the Power and Baker firms announced that they had jointly ordered the construction of a steamboat at Pittsburgh. Modeled along the lines of recently built mountain boats, the *Benton* was launched the next spring. Completing its maiden voyage to Fort Benton on May 27, 1875, the *Benton* was operated by Captain James McGarry as a Power-Baker boat in 1875 and 1876.[10]

Management of the Power-Baker steamboat interests was assigned to George A. Baker, the first secretary of the Fort Benton Transportation Company. The brother of Isaac G., George moved to Fort Benton in 1866 where he became a partner in I. G. Baker and Brother. By the time they began steamboating with the Powers, the Baker brothers had reestablished themselves in St. Louis. Isaac G., favoring the accommodations of city life, returned to the Missouri metropolis with his family in the fall of 1869. George soon followed and worked as a commission and forwarding agent, who among other things, bought and sold steamers and sold insurance. Year-round management of I. G. Baker and Company was left to the Conrad brothers—Charles E. and William G., who had become partners in the firm. Although he spent most of his time in St. Louis, Isaac G. Baker usually lived in Fort Benton during the summers and falls.[11]

Because the company served as a forwarder of freight and passengers from the Northern Pacific, it had to have a resident agent in Bismarck. James A. Emmons, a former steamboat captain, was its first. Emmons, well known in Sioux City for his steamboating exploits, was among Bismarck's earliest pioneers. In 1872, while operating a steamboat in the Sioux City–Edwinton trade, he decided to relocate to the new community, where he soon became well known as a land investor, liquor vendor, and local politician. In 1876, when he was the Power Line agent, he also operated the Bismarck–Fort Abraham Lincoln ferry.[12]

In 1877 Emmons was replaced by John Christie Barr, who first came to the upper Missouri as a clerk on a Power Line steamer. For four years beginning in 1877, Barr, as the director of the company's Bismarck office, was involved in all administrative aspects, including attempts to obtain government transportation contracts.

Until his death in Bismarck on July 11, 1879, James McGarry was the Power brothers most important partner. He supervised the construction of the company's steamers at Pittsburgh and commanded the *Benton* on its initial voyage to Fort Benton. At the time of his death from mountain fever, he was the master of the *Butte*. A man of some means, he was a part owner of various Power Line vessels, including the *Benton, Butte,* and *Helena*.[13]

By 1877, I. G. Baker and Company concluded that its cooperative arrangement with the Power Line was inadequate to meet its expanding market. The partners sold their interest in the *Benton* and created the Baker Line by buying the *Red Cloud* for $25,000 and leasing the *Fannie Tatum*. The four-year-old stern-wheeler *Red Cloud,* which had been operated by the Evansville and Tennessee River Packet Company, became the line's main vessel. In 1877 the *Fannie Tatum* made one landing at Fort Benton.[14]

Walter A. Burleigh and his son, Timothy B., had one or two steamers on the river at any given time. They had the nine-year-old *Miner* disassembled at Pittsburgh and used parts of it to have the 185-foot-long stern-wheeler *Carroll* built. With Timothy B. in command, the *Carroll* completed its first voyage—from Pittsburgh to Fort Benton—on May 28, 1875. Later in the season it made a Bismarck–Fort Benton round-trip. The next year, with three arrivals at Fort Benton and two at Cow Island, it was one of Montana's principal suppliers.[15]

By 1877 the Burleighs had organized the Yankton and Black Hills Line, which offered service to Fort Pierre. They planned to make regular runs with the *Carroll* and the new *Black Hills,* which was completed at Pittsburgh after its hull had been built at nearby California. Apparently the Burleighs did not have enough capital to fund their line's expansion. Timothy B. owned half of the *Black Hills,* and Thomas M. Rees and James C. McVay each held a one-fourth interest. After the *Carroll* was burned above Fort Randall on April 16, 1877, the Burleighs acquired a half interest in the *E. H. Durfee* and chartered another boat. Despite their modest boat holdings, the Burleighs consistently bid on the major government transportation contracts. Walter A. was awarded the army contract for destinations above Bismarck in 1876 but had to arrange with others, including the Coulson and Peck Lines, to fulfill his obligations.[16]

Outside of the organized lines, upper river steamboating was affected by such investors as John H. Charles of Sioux City and Amherst H. Wilder of St. Paul,

Minnesota. Charles was thirty years old when he moved from his native Pennsylvania to the new town of Sioux City in 1856. Over the years his many ventures included real estate, banking, wholesaling groceries, and working as a commission and forwarding agent. A strong civic booster, he encouraged Sioux City's aspirations to become the gateway to the upper Missouri region. After the official discovery of gold in the Black Hills, he gave financial support to the first group that trespassed on Indian land in a futile attempt to open the Hills. In 1876 he was elected mayor of Sioux City.[17]

Charles's interest in steamboating stemmed from his government contract business. Each year, the army and the Indian service advertised for sealed bids to transport and furnish supplies for posts and agencies. Although he failed to obtain the lucrative transportation contracts, Charles was quite successful in winning supply contracts. Typically, quartermaster officers or Indian agents would seek civilian contractors to deliver specified amounts of grain, hay, wood, flour, and other supplies. The contractor would agree to deliver the goods at a unit price. Hay and wood contractors usually worked in the vicinity of their destinations, but most of the grain and flour came out of the Sioux City market. Sometimes Charles sublet contracts and realized a profit from merely selling his rights. But when he filled grain and flour contracts, he had to make his own purchases and provide steamboat transportation. Therefore it behooved him to invest in steamboats. He first became a fractional owner of four steamers in the cash-stricken Peck Line and by about 1880 was a part owner of several Power Line vessels.

Amherst H. Wilder was one of Minnesota's wealthiest men. After moving to St. Paul from his native New York, he participated in banking, railroading, insuring, and government contracting. In association with several other St. Paulites, he was granted transportation contracts to supply northern plains army posts in the late 1860s. This experience helped draw him into Missouri River ventures. He probably became well acquainted with Charles during the construction of the St. Paul and Sioux City Railroad, which was completed in 1872. As the line's vice president, Wilder worked to create a southwestern outlet for Minnesota's bountiful supply of pine lumber and to ship wheat from the plains to Minneapolis, which was emerging as the nation's flour-milling capital. Ranging farther afield, Wilder helped finance the opening of the Yellowstone River valley. After acquiring an interest in the Diamond R Freighting Company, he was the principal investor in the Broadwater-Hubbell store in Miles City.[18]

Like Charles, Wilder obtained a variety of government contracts that involved steamboats. In 1873 alone, he held the Indian transportation contract for all agencies above Yankton, a contract for the overland delivery of annuities for the Brule Agency in northwestern Nebraska from Fort Randall, and three beef contracts for the delivery of some ten thousand head of Texas cattle to the upper river agencies. He managed these and other contracts by subletting with numerous other parties. Through part ownership of several Peck Line steamers, including a controlling interest in the *Silver Lake No. 4*, he was able to influence steamboat rates.

Most of the steamers used in the trade emanating from Bismarck and Yankton were "mountain boats"—shallow-drafted stern-wheelers with spoonbill-shaped bows. With only a few exceptions, they were built at Pittsburgh and nearby towns. Following a fairly common practice, owners would have the hulls built at such Monongahela River ports as Brownsville, California, and Elizabeth and then have them towed downstream to Pittsburgh, where the machinery was installed and all interior design work completed. With its local steel mills, forges, and specialized workforce, Pittsburgh dominated most of the boat-finishing business.[19]

The boats constructed for the upper Missouri were a culmination of design evolution that dated to steamboating's first decade. Like their predecessors, some of the mountain boats had three decks—main, boiler, and hurricane. The floor of the main deck covered the hold. Designers in the 1830s and 1840s found they could lighten drafts by broadening the hulls, reducing the depth of the holds, and adding a tiered superstructure to the main deck. Decreasing hold depths forced boatmen to store much of the cargo on the main deck, which had to be enlarged. Consequently, by midcentury, the height of the main decks on vessels in the 350- to 400-ton range had increased to 11 to 12 feet. Other than providing cargo space, the main deck was the location for the boat's machinery, fuel, crewmen other than boat officers, and deck passengers.[20]

The boiler deck, the second level above the waterline, was so-called even though it was above the boilers and engines. It included rooms for cabin passengers, lounges, and the dining saloon. Cabin passengers could thus be segregated from deck passengers throughout a voyage.

The boiler deck was topped by the mostly open hurricane deck, which was used as a cabin passenger promenade. By about 1845 some builders were adding a box-like structure in the center of the hurricane deck. These additions became known as texas decks, because, like the state of Texas, they were annexed. The texas deck, which provided sleeping quarters for the boat officers, was topped by the pilothouse.

The degree of variation from the above design by the Bismarck-Yankton boats depended on their intended use. Such steamers as the *Helena* and the *Red Cloud*, which were designed for both freight and passengers, were not greatly modified for upper river conditions. They had four levels—main deck, boiler deck, and hurricane deck with texas deck and pilothouse. Their main decks, which had to allow space for the bow spars, were approximately 25 feet longer than the boiler and hurricane decks. Their boiler decks were entirely devoted to cabin passenger accommodations. Their texas decks were rectangular structures about 40 × 20 × 9 feet. Any adaptation to shallow water was accomplished by broadening the hull and using lightweight woods such as pine in the construction of everything above the floor of the main deck.[21]

The greatest uniqueness was shown in such freight boats as the *E. H. Durfee*, *Far West*, and *Western*, which had only three levels—main deck, boiler deck, and pilothouse. Their texas decks, which provided accommodations for only the boat's officers and about a dozen cabin passengers, were placed on the boiler decks. Thus

Dining saloons such as this one of the *Far West,* which served only cabin
passengers, were usually the most luxurious steamboat feature.
Courtesy of the State Historical Society of North Dakota.

most of their boiler deck areas had nothing above them. By using only part of the boiler deck surface and eliminating the hurricane decks designers not only lightened the vessels but also lowered their profiles. They were obviously designed to operate efficiently in shallow water and high winds.[22]

Boatmen also adapted to shallow currents by transporting only partial loads. The *Far West*, which was 189 × 33.5 × 5 feet, had a carrying capacity of 397.81 tons. But its tonnage when drawing 2 and 3 feet was respectively 60 and 187.8 tons.[23]

Whether any given line relied on dual-purpose or freight boats depended on the nature of its business. The Baker and Power lines, which ran primarily in the Bismarck–Fort Benton trade, favored dual-purpose boats. But the Coulson Line, which was the most successful army contractor, usually ran freight boats. However, in 1879 Sanford B. Coulson supplemented his freight boat practice with the completion of the large, dual-purpose *Dacotah*, *Montana*, and *Wyoming*. The vessels, the last built for the Coulson Line, continued the firm's practice of using only seven-letter names for its craft. The frequency of seven-letter-named boats in the Coulson Line was attributed to the superstitious William S. Evans, who thought such names were good-luck omens.[24]

By the standards of the upper Missouri, the *Dacotah*, *Montana*, and *Wyoming* were behemoths. The *Dacotah* and *Montana* were built to the same specifications—252 feet long and 48 feet 8 inches wide. For some reason, the *Montana*, at 959 tons, had 2 feet more capacity than the *Dacotah*. The 257-foot *Wyoming* had a capacity of 1,034 tons.[25]

The Coulson Line advertised the elaborately furnished stern-wheelers as luxury boats. Each featured custom-made upholstered furniture, expensive silverware, a piano, and accommodations for about a hundred passengers. Their average construction cost was about $48,000.[26]

The vessels had four levels—main deck, boiler deck, and hurricane deck with texas deck topped by a pilothouse. Approximately 28 feet of the bows were left open so the spars could be operated. Both the boiler and hurricane decks were about 224 feet long. The texas deck, located just behind the chimneys, covered about one-fifth of the hurricane deck's surface.[27]

The boats, which had 6-foot-deep holds, were never loaded to capacity on the upper river. On its maiden trip the *Dacotah* was carrying 700 tons when it stopped for two hours at Sioux City en route to Fort Benton.[28]

The large vessels had short careers on the upper river. The *Dacotah* was the most successful. It was navigated to Fort Benton twice in its first year. But later in the summer the *Dacotah* incurred $3,500 worth of damages when it struck the Kansas City railroad bridge. The boat was back on the upper river in 1881, with two trips to Fort Benton and another to perhaps as high as the Poplar River. It reached Fort Benton once in 1882 and twice in 1883, its final year in the Bismarck–Fort Benton trade. On its second Fort Benton trip in 1883 it delivered 700 tons of freight, the all-time Fort Benton record for one boat. The Coulson Line, which was then rapidly reducing its operations, sold the boat to parties based in St. Louis. In 1884 it was snagged at Providence, Missouri, but later raised and run on the lower Missouri and lower Mississippi.[29]

The ill-fated *Montana* reached Fort Benton twice in 1879—once directly from Pittsburgh and then from Bismarck. After its second voyage, it was heavily damaged by a tornado while docked at Bismarck. The Coulson Line spent $2,000 to $3,000 to get it to St. Louis, where extensive repairs were made. Subsequently, the new owners used the *Montana* on the Mississippi and lower parts of the Missouri. In 1884 the boat sank at St. Charles after hitting a railroad bridge pier.[30]

The *Wyoming* completed its lone trip to Fort Benton on June 25, 1882. Soon thereafter the Coulson Line sold it to the Southern Transportation Company, which subsequently operated it in the Cincinnati–New Orleans trade.[31]

Probably only the *Dacotah* proved to be profitable for the Coulson Line. It is puzzling that the partners of the well-managed firm chose to launch three extraordinarily large boats in 1879. By then it was obvious that the Yankton–Fort Pierre trade would soon be curtailed by railroad advances. The Yellowstone River business, which was then booming, was suitable only for the smallest, lightest-draft vessels. So apparently the *Dacotah, Montana,* and *Wyoming* were intended for the increasing Bismarck–Fort Benton business. Because of river improvement at Cow Island and nearby trouble spots, Coulson and Maratta may have counted on transporting most of the Fort Benton freight. But they obviously did not reckon with the rapid expansion of the Fort Benton Transportation Company.

During the Bismarck-Yankton rivalry a rather complicated trade pattern prevailed on the upper Missouri. To a degree, each town had its own sphere of influence. Yankton's Coulson Line dominated the trade between the two communities, and boats based at Bismarck did most of the hauling for points above there. Part of the reason for this practice lay in the nature of the army transportation contracts under which both Bismarck and Yankton were starting points. Military freight shipped to Yankton by railroad was forwarded by steamers to the forts downstream from Bismarck, and that sent by the Northern Pacific to Bismarck was shipped to the upstream forts, including those that were serviced by way of either Fort Benton or Carroll. Bismarck interests questioned the wisdom of this policy with regard to nearby Fort Yates. The *Bismarck Tribune* insisted that the government would save money by sending the Fort Yates supplies to Bismarck and then steamboating them the short downstream distance. The paper's editor assumed that it was always cheaper to ship downstream than upstream. But the transportation contracts usually did not make a distinction between upstream and downstream rates. Even in those contracts where the specified downstream rates were 10 percent less than the upstream ones, shipping to Fort Yates via Bismarck was not necessarily an economy. Steamboat transportation was only one factor. Army quartermaster officers had to consider the combined rail-steamboat cost. Freight rates from Chicago to Bismarck were much higher than those to Yankton. In 1877 the rates per hundredweight were $1 to Bismarck, or nearly double the 52.5 cents to Yankton.[32]

The 957-ton stern-wheeler *Dacotah* was built by the Coulson Line in 1879 for use on the upper Missouri. *From the collection of the Public Library of Cincinnati and Hamilton County.*

This rail freight differential also helped Yankton boatmen get some deliveries to Fort Benton and other Montana destinations. It is also quite likely that the Coulson Line made its rates from Yankton to Montana points competitive.

Because it held most of the army transportation contracts and had the largest fleet, the Coulson Line was best situated to transcend community differences. Unlike the Baker and Kountz lines, which were closely identified with Bismarck, the Coulson Line operated boats out of both ports. By 1879, when the Power Line had been expanded to three steamers, it shifted part of its activities to Yankton. John Christie Barr, its general agent, divided his time between Bismarck and Yankton.[33]

In the transportation of private goods and civilian passengers, Bismarck had a great advantage in the Montana market. But Yankton–based steamers, the second link in the rail-water-overland route to the Black Hills, controlled the gold rush trade.

Naturally, there were some variables. The Peck Line, headquartered in Sioux City but operated out of Bismarck, would sometimes obtain freight in Sioux City and Yankton, and its boats would occasionally deliver buffalo robes, cattle hides, and other Montana products to Sioux City buyers.[34]

Although Bismarck-Yankton steamboating was conducted as a northern plains business, it had some contact with Pittsburgh and St. Louis. The new boats built at or near Pittsburgh invariably carried some freight on their maiden voyages. Since their owners were primarily concerned with getting them to the upper Missouri, they could afford to offer very competitive rates on any freight they could book at Pittsburgh, St. Louis, and other waypoints.

For example, the Power Line's *Butte* on its maiden voyage in 1879 booked freight at Pittsburgh and a number of other ports. At Pittsburgh on April 23–26 it obtained 181,500 pounds, including 85,407 pounds of refined oil shipped by the Standard Oil Company, 66,000 pounds of glassware, and 240 pounds of Hostetter's Stomach Bitters for Fort Benton. The charge for all goods was $1.35 per 100 pounds. The *Butte* added 1,965 pounds at Cincinnati on April 29 and 119,084 pounds at St. Louis on May 3–5. The St. Louis–Fort Benton rate was $1.25 per hundredweight on a variety of goods—soda, lye, window glass, paint, plaster, putty, red and white lead, linseed oil, aluminum, hardware, marble, one easy chair, tents, and pitch. On May 10 the boat obtained 7,241 pounds of hardware at Leavenworth, Kansas, and 4,203 pounds of wine in kegs at Doniphan, Kansas. Interestingly, the Fort Benton rates for the Leavenworth and Doniphan shipments were 20 percent higher than those from St. Louis. This higher charge for a shorter distance showed a reality that boatmen never advertised. In public, they wanted to leave the impression that they charged uniform rates. But in actual practice, such as this instance, they were influenced by bargaining. In all likelihood, the *Butte* had competition at St. Louis and none at Leavenworth and Doniphan.[35]

Somewhere along the line, the *Butte* picked up some freight for Sioux City. When the boat arrived on May 17 with 22 cabin and 18 deck passengers, its crew unloaded 75 tons of goods for Sioux City merchants. The only Sioux City cargo for Fort Benton was 1,000 pounds of bacon for the Blackfeet Agency in Montana. Its shipper was charged $1.25 per hundredweight. The *Butte* completed its six-week voyage to Fort Benton on June 9.

Most of the boats were wintered at Bismarck, Sioux City, and Yankton, but some made their season's first voyage to the upper river from St. Louis. Kountz, especially, was prone to sending boats down in the fall to engage in the wintertime cotton trade on the lower Mississippi. When they returned the following spring, they usually booked some freight and passengers at St. Louis. In the spring of 1875, St. Louis experienced a modest revival in its upper river trade when five steamers carried a total of 1,430 tons of Fort Benton freight. The amount was reported to be in excess of all shipments for the previous three years combined.[36]

Some other boats were started from St. Louis because they had been sent there to be repaired or remodeled. Steamboat crews usually included a carpenter to do routine maintenance, but there were no facilities on the upper river for major overhauling. Thus, when the *Montana* was damaged, the Coulson Line's only recourse was to send it to St. Louis. Likewise, when I. G. Baker and Company decided to lengthen its *Red Cloud* by 50 feet, the closest professional expertise was in St. Louis.[37]

Despite the sharp increase in private freighting after the completion of railroads to Bismarck and Yankton, the strong economic impact of federal government spending persisted. Supplying army expeditions and posts and Indian agencies continued to infuse highly desired federal dollars into the undeveloped upper Missouri region.

Steamboatmen eagerly sought the government business with its assurances of large shipments and year-long contracted rates. With the exception of the Power and Baker lines, which concentrated on moving private freight from Bismarck to Fort Benton, the other steamboat companies made government shipments their first priority.

The contracts for transporting army personnel and supplies were the most coveted. They became increasingly important as the government expanded the army's presence on the northern plains. While the Northern Pacific Railroad was stalled at Bismarck, its engineers, with large military escorts, surveyed its future route into the Yellowstone River valley. Then, as a result of the Great Sioux War, the army in 1877 established Fort Keogh on the Yellowstone and Fort Custer on the tributary Bighorn. Two years later, professedly to block the return of renegade Sioux from Canada and to pacify the region, the army started Fort Assinniboine about seven miles southwest of present Havre, Montana.[38]

The Coulson Line dominated the army transportation business. For three successive years, beginning in 1873, it held the contracts for all deliveries above Yankton, with Bismarck and Yankton as the designated starting points. But the Quartermaster Department had the authority to let separate contracts from Bismarck and Yankton. When it did that in 1876, the Coulson Line got the business from Yankton, and the Burleigh Line that started at Bismarck. The outcome did not seriously affect the Coulson Line's fortunes, because the contracts did not grant monopoly rights. If a contractor could not keep pace with the army's demands, local quartermaster officers could hire other transporters. When the two-boat Burleigh Line proved to be grossly inadequate to supply the troops campaigning in the Yellowstone valley, the business went to the Coulson Line.[39]

The same thing happened in 1877, the only year the Coulson Line failed to win at least one contract. Because of unusually heavy activity in the Yellowstone valley owing to fort construction, the army decided to let a special contract for the Yellowstone River. It went to the Yellowstone Transportation Company of St. Paul, Minnesota. The contract for Missouri River freight from Bismarck and Yankton was awarded to Dr. A. F. Terry of Sioux City, who submitted the lowest bid. Despite its failure to obtain any contracts, the Coulson Line actually did most of the army's hauling on both the Missouri and Yellowstone, because neither the Contract Line nor the Yellowstone Transportation Company had the wherewithal to meet the army's heavy demands.[40]

In 1878 the Coulson Line won the Missouri River transportation contract, and the next year was awarded it and the Yellowstone contract as well. Kountz, who invariably bid on both the army and Indian transportation contracts, finally obtained one in 1878 when he got the Yellowstone business starting from Fort Buford.[41]

Each of the contracts specified rates for five categories—officers, enlisted men (same rate for laundresses and servants), freight per hundredweight, animals (cattle, horses, and mules) per head, and vehicles (wagons, carts, and ambulances). In

TABLE 6

COULSON LINE FREIGHT SCHEDULE FOR
JUNE AND JULY 1874 FROM YANKTON TO FORT BENTON

From Yankton to . . .	Charge ($ per hundredweight)
Fort Randall	0.25
Whetstone Agency	0.25
Lower Brule Agency	0.25
Crow Creek Agency	0.25
Fort Sully	0.50
Cheyenne Agency	0.60
Grand River Agency	0.60
Fort Abraham Lincoln or Bismarck	0.70
Fort Stevenson	0.95
Fort Buford	1.15
Fort Benton	2.40

Source: See note 42 of chapter 10.

keeping with well-established practice, the rates varied somewhat from anticipated high-water to low-water periods.

The 1874 Coulson contract was a typical document. It included schedules for
all five categories, showing rates from Yankton for all installations to Fort Benton as well as those starting from any point en route (table 6).

The rates from Yankton to Fort Benton for officers, enlisted men, animals,
and vehicles were respectively $40, $18, $40, and $40. Rates to waypoints were
roughly proportional to the freight charges. The freight rates for any shipments
after August 1 were about 40 percent more than the June–July rates, but the charges
for all other categories were not adjusted for late-season navigation.[42]

Because the Quartermaster Department wanted to be able to negotiate some
contracts on the basis of unit charges per hundred miles, it developed its own table
of distances. The official army distances were generally less than those used by boatmen. For example, a popular list of distances published by the St. Louis Chamber of Commerce specified that Fort Benton was 1,974 miles from Yankton, but
the Quartermaster Department calculated the distance as 1,808, or approximately
8.4 percent less. However, the rate of the disparity was not uniform. The army's
Yankton-to-Bismarck distance was 678 miles, only 17 less than that from the St.
Louis Chamber of Commerce.[43]

Since the steamboat transportation contracts typically stipulated that any freight
undeliverable by water had to be carried overland by the contractor at the river rates,
the army also developed a set of overland distances. The overland routes, which
did not follow the Missouri's numerous sinuosities, were usually about two-thirds

that of the waterway distances. Thus the overland mileage from Yankton to Fort Benton was set at 1,187 miles.[44]

Competition for the transportation of Indian annuities, which was a considerably smaller business than the army contracts, was intense. Bidding for the annual contracts always attracted the Coulson, Kountz, and Peck interests and such speculators as John H. Charles, Amherst H. Wilder, and Charles D. Woolworth.

Coulson Line rivals were more successful in obtaining Indian contracts than army ones. Wilder had the 1873 contract for all goods shipped from Yankton. However, the Northern Pacific Railroad, which had a contract for deliveries to Bismarck, used the Kountz Line to steamboat annuities to Fort Peck and Fort Benton. Charles D. Woolworth of Sioux City, a sometime associate of Charles and Wilder, was the contractor for the Yankton shipments in 1875. That year the Northern Pacific, which had become disenchanted with Kountz, had all of its shipments from Bismarck forwarded by Coulson boats. Campbell K. Peck and his temporary partner, C. M. Primeau, held the 1877 contracts, with Yankton as their main port.[45]

The Coulson Line was the main contractor in 1874, 1878, and 1879. With the exception of some Crow and Blackfeet annuities transported by the Northern Pacific and Kountz boats, it controlled the 1874 business. The line was awarded most of the deliveries for 1878, but for some reason the Indian Bureau granted that transportation to several agencies, including Crow Creek and Cheyenne River, to the Peck Line. The next year, the Coulson Line transported all goods to Dakota and Montana agencies from Yankton.[46]

Most of the annuities were shipped by way of Yankton, in part because of aggressive marketing by George Merchant, superintendent of the Dakota Southern Railroad. Merchant, who worked closely with the Coulson Line, was very successful in getting special contracts for his railroad and in arranging through bills of lading from such supply points as New York City and Philadelphia.[47]

Government transportation contractors moved impressive amounts of freight. In 1877 an estimated 8,000 tons of army supplies were shipped from Bismarck to Yellowstone River destinations by Yellowstone Transportation Company and Coulson Line steamers. The Coulson Line's 1878 army contract for the Missouri River called for carrying up to 10,000 tons of supplies delivered by rail to Bismarck and Yankton and consigned to it by quartermaster officers. Additionally, two of the Coulson Line partners, Maratta and McVay, were awarded grain contracts. In April the chief quartermaster officer of the Department of Dakota made contracts with various parties that called for the delivery of 4,231 tons of corn and 5,545.5 tons of oats. McVay got a contract for 500 tons of corn and 1,000 tons of oats. Maratta contracted for 1,221 tons of oats. The other grain contractors whose bid price included delivery to a specific fort had to arrange their own transportation. Considering all contracts, by mid-June 9,000 tons had been shipped from Yankton alone.[48]

Indian agencies were less dependent on steamboat transportation than army posts were. The government's encouragement of agency agriculture led to local production of some grains and vegetables, and beef cattle were usually driven overland under special contracts. Thus the annuities ordinarily included blankets, clothing, cloth, hardware, and such groceries as flour, sugar, and bacon. The annuities for the Dakota and Montana agencies under the Peck and Primeau contracts of 1877 amounted to 2,500 tons. In 1879 the Coulson Line delivered 3,000 tons of annuities for the agencies.[49]

Both the army and the Indian Bureau followed written procedures in awarding transportation contracts. They would print notices in regional newspapers, calling for sealed bids to be presented by a specified date. The notices clearly indicated that submitting the lowest bid was the most important factor. But they also stated that the appropriate government officials could additionally consider the ability of any bidder to conduct the work. Thus the lowest bidder could be rejected if the government had reservations about such things as the poor condition of his steamers or his control of sufficient vessels.

Because it might be necessary to interview potential contractors, all aspirants were invited to the opening of the bids. This practice had the unfortunate effect of turning erstwhile contractors into lobbyists, who routinely curried favor with quartermaster officers and Indian officials. The opening of the army bids at the St. Paul headquarters of the Department of Dakota invariably attracted small delegations from every bidder. Sanford B. Coulson and D. W. Maratta were usually accompanied by other partners and sometimes George Merchant of the Dakota Southern.[50]

Naturally, Coulson and other bidders jealously guarded the details of their submissions. But keeping secrets was not easy because such individuals as Charles, Wilder, and Woolworth consorted with various parties. When the Coulson Line lost the army contract to A. F. Terry in 1877, its partners suspected foul play. The boatless Terry obviously had to negotiate with such investors as Charles, Wilder, and Woolworth. But Charles and Wilder were also trying to work out an arrangement with the Coulson Line. After losing the contract, William S. Evans bitterly complained to Sanford B. Coulson: "The Wilder and Charles party have been bulldozing us and it has been my opinion all the time they was not acting square ever since the bidding in St. Paul in January. For just as sure as the sun rose this morning . . . he Charles the unprincipled scoundrel stole the copy of the bid made out by you for Coulson and Wilder and gave it to Woolworth and he shaded it."[51]

Since Evans could not prove any quartermaster officer was at fault, he had no grounds for appeal. But even when the Coulson Line was awarded the contract by the chief quartermaster officer of the Department of Dakota, its officers pursued the matter politically. Still smarting from their rejection the previous year, in 1878 Coulson Line officials, who had been granted the contract in St. Paul, pursued the matter politically up the chain of command. The departmental quartermaster's recommendation had to be approved by the quartermaster general of the Division of the Missouri and finally by the secretary of war. To influence Secretary of War George W. McCrary, Coulson and Maratta went to Washington to personally lobby selected congressmen. On February 4, Maratta triumphantly wrote to McVay that "Wallace of Pennsylvania, Matthews Thurmond of Ohio and several members of the house will render us assistance when called."[52] Five weeks later McCrary approved the contract.

Besides using political influence, Coulson and Maratta schemed to form a combine large enough to assure that they would always be able to submit the lowest bid. They proposed to pool their interests with the Fort Benton Transportation Company, with the Coulson Line handling all of the military freight and the Power Line the private freight. Thomas C. Power was receptive to the idea, but other than cooperating in the hauling of each other's freight, the companies never completed a formal agreement.[53]

Animosities arising from the Indian contract competition turned ugly in 1875 when William J. Kountz charged that Indian Bureau officials had fraudulently rejected his bid. Kountz complained that he, rather than Charles D. Woolworth, should have been awarded the 1875 contract because he had submitted the lowest bid. After Woolworth signed his contract with Commissioner of Indian Affairs Edward P. Smith, Kountz protested to Clinton B. Fisk, chairman of the Board of Indian Commissioners. Fisk responded that the board members had voted against Kountz's bid because veteran Indian Bureau officials informed them that Kountz had failed to deliver goods under previous contracts. Therefore, Fisk admonished, Kountz should attribute his failure to his own inefficiency rather than fraud by the board. Fisk suggested that if Kountz still had a grievance, he should demand an investigation rather than launching newspaper attacks against the Bureau of Indian Affairs.[54]

Accepting Fisk's challenge, Kountz appealed to the House of Representatives Committee on Indian Affairs, which opened hearings on possible malfeasance in the Indian Bureau in January 1876. Primarily concerned with investigating the Indian Ring—the supposed collusion of licensed traders and agents to defraud the government—the committee invited Kountz to testify under oath.

In his appearance before the committee, Kountz described the circumstances of the May 13, 1875, contract awarding in New York City and presented copies of his correspondence with Fisk. When faced with the irreconcilability of Kountz's fraud charge and Fisk's inefficiency countercharge, the committee decided to summon witnesses familiar with Kountz's steamboating.

Over the course of several weeks, a litany of expert witnesses—including Walter A. Burleigh; quartermaster officers Captain Charles W. Foster and Colonel Daniel H. Rucker; Charles W. Meade, general managing agent of the Northern Pacific Railroad; Colonel David S. Stanley; and Charles A. Broadwater, a partner of the Diamond R Freighting Company—condemned Kountz. Foster stated that the *Mollie Moore* and *Katie P. Kountz* were large boats that could not be relied on after August 1 and that the *May Lowery, Mary Kountz,* and *Fontenelle* were "worthless for the business."[55] Meade testified that the Northern Pacific ceased its association with Kountz because his steamboats "were broken down and out of order all the time."[56] Broadwater, embittered by long delays in Kountz's Bismarck-to-Carroll business, denounced the boats as "utterly useless."[57]

Kountz counterattacked by presenting sworn statements from various boat officers that his steamers were indeed seaworthy. But after the damning testimony by persons well acquainted with his fleet, he could not salvage his reputation. His charge of fraud was dismissed, and after his testimony, his only government contract was to transport army freight and personnel on the Yellowstone in 1878.[58]

Army operations were mainly responsible for a short-lived surge in Yellowstone River steamboating. After Sully's use of two boats in 1864, there were no steamers on the Yellowstone for nearly a decade. But in 1873 the planned extension of the Northern Pacific Railroad renewed interest in the Yellowstone River region. When railroad engineers extended their survey from the Heart River crossing west of Bismarck to near the mouth of the Powder River, the army furnished a massive escort. Colonel David S. Stanley was ordered to lead over 1,500 officers and men, more than 300 civilian employees, almost 300 wagons and ambulances, and 2,300 horses and mules westward from Fort Rice.

Lieutenant General Philip H. Sheridan, commander of the Division of the Missouri, planned to establish a supply base on the Yellowstone.[59] To determine a desirable base site, he turned to the Coulson Line for a steamboat reconnaissance. With Lieutenant Colonel George A. Forsyth on board, Captain Grant Marsh navigated the *Key West* up the stream until he was unable to get over Wolf Rapids, a short distance below the mouth of the Powder River. Forsyth, who preferred a depot at the mouth of the Powder, established one well downstream at Glendive Creek. But anticipating future operations, Sheridan and his subordinates still wanted to get steamboats above Wolf Rapids. Consequently, late in the summer, Coulson assigned Marsh to captain the light-draft *Josephine,* newly arrived from Pittsburgh. After Marsh easily navigated the *Josephine* through Wolf Rapids, Stanley enthused that the boat could have ascended "perhaps to the falls of the Yellowstone."[60]

In 1875, when Sheridan was contemplating establishing posts near the mouths of the Tongue and Bighorn rivers, he wanted to determine the Yellowstone's steamboat head of navigation. The Coulson Line again used Marsh and the *Josephine.* When Marsh headed the vessel into the Yellowstone on May 26, he carried a military escort of 7 officers, 100 enlisted men, and 4 mounted scouts led by Forsyth. Taking advantage of high water, Marsh steered the *Josephine* past the mouths of the Powder and Tongue to the Bighorn. Determined to investigate the feasibility of navigating the Bighorn, Marsh and Forsyth ascended it for 12 miles. Above the mouth of the Bighorn, the Yellowstone became narrower and swifter, but Marsh pushed the *Josephine* on by sparring and warping. After sometimes moving no more than a sixth of a mile per hour, Marsh tied the vessel up on the evening of June 6 at the eastern edge of present Billings, an estimated 485 miles from the river's mouth and about 250 miles farther than the high point reached in 1873. Recognizing the impracticability of trying to go farther, Marsh and Forsyth decided to turn about. Before leaving , Marsh carved "Josephine, June 7, 1875" into the trunk of a large cottonwood tree.[61]

Although Marsh was regaled by the press for reaching the "highest point,"

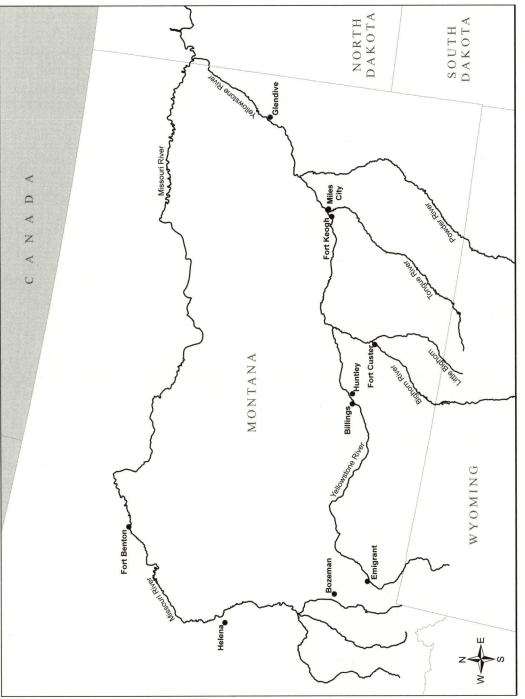

Yellowstone River. (Current state boundaries are shown for reference.) *Prepared by James Worm.*

Forsyth recognized that the *Josephine*'s feat would probably never be matched. He concluded that the Yellowstone's practical head of navigation was the mouth of the Bighorn. Army officials were heartened by the *Josephine*'s reconnaissance, but Bozeman's boosters saw it as the catalyst for revolutionizing Montana's transportation system. Bozeman, the principal community near the Gallatin valley agricultural settlement, was remotely situated relative to the territory's two main supply routes—the Missouri River to Fort Benton and the Montana Trail from Utah. Bozeman's *Avant Courier* championed replacing these "back door" routes with a "front door" passage up the Yellowstone. The *Josephine*'s success made this seem possible.

To promote Yellowstone River steamboating and Bozeman's growth, two of the town's businessmen, Achilles Lamme and Nelson Story, had the steamer *Yellowstone* built over the winter of 1875–76 at Jeffersonville, Indiana. The *Avant Courier* predicted that the boat's arrival on the Yellowstone and the opening of a wagon road from its landing spot to Bozeman would "be the dawn of a new era in Eastern Montana, bringing with it general prosperity to our people and making Bozeman the most important town in the Territory."[62]

But as the *Yellowstone* was steaming from Bismarck to Fort Buford in June 1876 with its principal owners, Lamme and Story, on board, they received alarming reports about impending war in the Yellowstone valley. Their plan to ascend the Yellowstone was aborted by military authorities at Fort Buford, who banned civilian travel on the stream. Lamme and Story's only option was to reroute their boat to Fort Benton. So the scheme to supply Bozeman by boats and wagons from the East had to be deferred. Pressed into service by the army, the *Yellowstone* was not used for private freighting on the Yellowstone until 1878. Its brief career was ended in the spring of 1879, when it was wrecked on Buffalo Rapids, 12 miles below Miles City.[63]

The underlying cause of the Great Sioux War was the Black Hills gold rush, which led the government to reverse its Fort Laramie Treaty assurance of a Great Sioux Reservation. Seeking refuge in one of the last buffalo-hunting grounds, hundreds of Lakotas, including many who had been living at or near agencies, migrated into the Powder and Bighorn basins. As the army prepared to move against them, its leaders planned to rely on steamboat-delivered supplies from Bismarck.

The army's strategy was to envelop the Sioux with three advancing columns from Fort Fetterman to the south, Fort Ellis to the west, and Fort Abraham Lincoln to the east. Brigadier General Alfred Terry's Fort Abraham Lincoln expedition was to be supplied by steamboats. But when quartermaster officers were establishing a supply depot at the mouth of Glendive Creek, they found that Walter A. Burleigh, who had been awarded the army transportation contract for the region above Bismarck, could not meet their demands. Burleigh, who then had only one steamer, probably anticipated making arrangements with other lines. But impatient quartermaster officers could not wait for him. They turned to the Coulson Line, which chartered some of its vessels to the government for $350 per diem and made special contracts to freight supplies from Bismarck.[64]

The Coulson Line's *Far West*, commanded by Grant Marsh, was used to transfer supplies from Glendive Creek to the Powder River. As Terry advanced beyond the Powder, he ordered Marsh to escort the troops up the Yellowstone and Bighorn to at least the mouth of the Little Bighorn. Because the accompanying army officer was confused about their rendezvous site, Marsh navigated the boat 15 miles upstream from its juncture with the Little Bighorn.

Marsh and the *Far West* were waiting at the mouth of the Little Bighorn on June 28 when word arrived that Custer's command had been annihilated three days earlier. He stayed there for five more days to load wounded Seventh Cavalry troops and on July 3 began racing toward Bismarck. Marsh's approximately 700-mile dash in 55 hours brought instant fame to both him and the *Far West*.[65]

Shocked by the Custer disaster, the army moved rapidly to quash Indian resistance in the Yellowstone valley. Colonel Nelson A. Miles and most of the Fifth Infantry were rushed upstream from Fort Leavenworth to establish a cantonment near the mouth of the Tongue River. But army officials soon decided that an offensive against the Sioux would be better served by building permanent posts at the Tongue's mouth and the confluence of the Bighorn and Little Bighorn. Congress quickly appropriated emergency funds, but construction had to be delayed until 1877 because of low water on the Yellowstone. Nonetheless, the Coulson Line's six steamers and six other chartered boats, including the *Yellowstone*, were used in the late summer to supply the Tongue River Cantonment.[66]

Anticipating unprecedented steamboating on the Yellowstone in 1877, the army let a special contract for that stream. Committed to their low-bid philosophy, quartermaster officers awarded the contract to John B. Davis of St. Paul and Peyton S. Davidson of La Crosse, Wisconsin, who were partners of William F. Davidson, principal owner of the Keokuk Northern Line. The Davidson brothers, Davis, and John H. Reaney, a St. Paulite, formed the Yellowstone Transportation Company.[67]

The firm relied on fourteen steamboats, some of which it leased in St. Louis. However, none of them had been built expressly for upper Missouri or Yellowstone waters. The partners compounded the problem of using questionable steamers by having some of the vessels tow barges as far as Fort Buford. Despite its relatively large fleet, the Yellowstone Transportation Company could not keep up with the army's demands. Consequently, quartermaster officers also arranged with the Coulson Line to transport freight and personnel to Post No. 1, later officially named Fort Keogh at the Yellowstone-Tongue confluence, and Post No. 2, which evolved into Fort Custer at the mouth of the Little Bighorn.[68]

Generally, Coulson Line steamers were more successful in passing through the rapids below the Bighorn, but both firms managed to get some of their boats to Fort Custer. Four Davidson boats, three Coulson boats, and the army's own *General Sherman* reached the post site. But they were exceptions to the general rule of having to unload at the Bighorn's mouth, where the supply depot Terry's Landing was established to ready wagon shipments to Fort Custer. Between June 27 and August 31, fourteen different steamers completed twenty-six voyages to Terry's Landing.

To supplement civilian contractors, the army had two small 266-ton stern-wheelers (145 × 28 × 4 feet) constructed at Jeffersonville, Indiana, in the spring of 1877. Built at a combined cost of $47,000, the *General Sherman* and the *J. Donald Cameron*, named after then Secretary of War James Donald Cameron, were designed for the Yellowstone. On their maiden voyages from Pittsburgh to the Tongue River post, they were loaded at Fort Leavenworth with the wives and children of Fifth Regiment officers, as well as servants, laundresses, a military escort, officers' personal property, and commissary and quartermaster supplies. While traveling upstream together, the *Cameron* was snagged and lost on May 18 in Fat Woman's Bend, about 40 miles below Sioux City. Because Captain John S. Ritchie was able to steer the boat into shallow water, all of the passengers and most of the personal baggage were saved. But the loss of the boat and cargo was estimated to be in the $100,000–$150,000 range. The *Cameron*'s passengers were crowded onto the *General Sherman*, which delivered them to the Tongue River cantonment. The army operated the *General Sherman* on the Yellowstone and on Bismarck–Fort Benton runs until 1881.[69]

Because of the fort construction, Yellowstone River steamboating in 1877 surpassed that of the Missouri above Fort Buford. Thousands of tons of building materials, as well as some 400 civilian carpenters, masons, and laborers, were shipped from Minneapolis and St. Paul by the Northern Pacific and Davidson and Coulson steamers. By the time the Yellowstone Transportation Company withdrew in early August, it had transported an estimated 9,000 tons of freight. The Coulson Line, which increased its fleet to eleven vessels, probably hauled as much. From July 23 to the end of August the line's boats delivered thirteen cargoes to Terry's Landing. Some of the Coulson steamers were very profitable. The *Big Horn* had a net gain of over $14,000 for a Pittsburgh–Little Bighorn–Bismarck trip. The *Far West*, which had a season-long net profit of $26,956.60, gained $8,000 for its two voyages from Fort Buford to Fort Keogh.[70]

Supplying Fort Keogh and Fort Custer by steamboats from Bismarck remained an important business until the construction of the Northern Pacific up the Yellowstone valley. But after 1877 the military trade declined relative to the total economy. The army's occupation attracted a number of aspiring settlers. Miles City, which was started on the eastern edge of the Fort Keogh reservation in 1877, became the valley's most important town. The same year, Perry W. McAdow, a Bozeman businessmen, became the principal founder of Coulson, at Marsh's highest point. Hoping to lure the Coulson Line to extend its services to them, McAdow and other settlers named their community after Sanford B. Coulson. Junction City, north across the Yellowstone from Terry's Landing, was the base for wagon freighters who supplied Fort Custer and an important station on the Yellowstone valley stage route. Huntley, a small community on the stage route, was started 10 miles below Coulson. Counting the scattered woodhawks, who were attracted by the steamboat trade, the Yellowstone valley had a population of about 1,300 civilians by 1880.[71]

Miles City was the most important steamboat port. In 1878, twenty upbound steamers landed there by July 12, which probably was about three-fourths of the season's business. Army engineers reported that steamboats in 1880 imported 6,000 tons of private and army freight, including more than 1,000 tons for the army posts. Steamboat exports the next year included 93,000 buffalo robes valued at $232,500, along with 263,000 pounds of hides said to be worth nearly $100,000 and many wolf skins and peltries.[72]

After the 1877 season the federal government decided that army engineers should make some improvements on the Yellowstone. Over the course of three years, beginning in 1878, the engineers surveyed the river from its mouth to Fort Keogh and dynamited rock ledges to open straight, deep channels through several rapids below the mouth of the Bighorn.[73]

Although Yellowstone River steamboating was vital to the army and the start of settlement in the valley, it never realized Bozeman's dream of supplanting the Fort Benton route. The Fort Benton trade, which suffered from competition with overland freighters from Utah and Carroll, not only persisted but boomed to unprecedented highs by the late 1870s. The underpinnings of Fort Benton's business were supplying Helena, the distribution point for much of Montana Territory, as well as area ranchers and farmers, army installations and Indian agencies, and an expanding Canadian market.

The Canadian business was stimulated by the Dominion of Canada's decision to fortify its western frontier. After gaining dominion status in 1867, Canadian officials, aspiring to create a transcontinental nation, bought the vast holdings of the Hudson's Bay Company, which had been granted much of central and western Canada when it was chartered in 1670. The first effect of the purchase was to create a political vacuum, which quickly attracted traders from Fort Benton. In 1869 John J. Healy and Isaac G. Baker's nephew Alfred B. Hamilton established a small trading post, Fort Hamilton, near present Lethbridge, Alberta. It was soon destroyed by Indians, but Healy and Hamilton constructed a more elaborate facility, which they named Fort Whoop-Up. The fort's name was given to the 240-mile trail that ran northwestward from Fort Benton, and a large contiguous area, including the Cypress Hills region of present southeastern Alberta and southwestern Saskatchewan, became known as the Whoop-Up Country.[74]

In Healy and Hamilton's vanguard, other traders supplied from Fort Benton established posts throughout the Whoop-Up Country. Although they obviously bartered a variety of goods to local Indians to obtain buffalo robes, they came to be best known by the disparaging label of "whiskey traders." The undesirable presence of the traders was well known when Sir John A. Macdonald, Canada's first premier, proposed to stabilize the Canadian West as a prelude to railroads and settlement.[75]

Wishing to avoid the lawlessness that characterized much of the American frontier, Macdonald suggested the formation of a national police force. Following his lead, the Canadian Parliament, by its Police Act of April 1873, created the North West Mounted Police. The first police contingent moved to the Whoop-

Up Country by marching overland across the plains of southern Canada. Recognizing that they could not feasibly be resupplied by this long overland route, Canadian government officials had planned to use I. G. Baker and Company as their supply contractor before the expedition began its trek.

Desperately short of supplies, leaders of the first police force sought aid from the Conrad brothers of the Baker firm while en route to Fort Whoop-Up. The Conrads, with an obvious eye to future good relations and trade, provided goods on credit. Soon after reaching the nearly deserted Fort Whoop-Up on October 9, 1874, the Mountie force started its own base, Fort Macleod, nearby on an island in the Oldman River.

The next year, another Mountie post, Fort Walsh, was established in the Cypress Hills. Situated about 150 miles northeast of Fort Benton and 37 miles southwest of present Maple Creek, Saskatchewan, Fort Walsh became an important market for I. G. Baker and Company. Trade with Fort Walsh and the nearby Baker store was sometimes called "Cypress shipments" by newspapers, which added to the confusion about the name "Cypress Hills." Since cypress trees are indigenous to swampy areas of the southeastern United States, they obviously did not grow in western Canada. "Cypress Hills" evolved out of a case of mistaken identity. French-speaking traders mistook the lodgepole pine, the commonest evergreen in the Cypress Hills, for the jack pine of eastern Canada, which they knew as *cypre*. In recording what they thought they were hearing, English-language users made the easy transition to "cypress."[76]

Fort Benton's trade with the Mountie posts helped revive the town's fortunes. With only seven steamboat arrivals in 1873, the head of navigation was challenged by a Northern Pacific Railroad–Helena scheme to bypass it. As the Northern Pacific prepared for its first full year of Bismarck operations, it moved to dominate the Helena trade to the detriment of both the Fort Benton and Utah routes by making agreements with the Kountz Line and the Diamond R. On September 2, 1873, railroad officials contracted with Edward G. Maclay of the Diamond R to open a wagon road from Helena to a steamboat landing at the mouth of the Musselshell River. The plan revived the old Helena dream of avoiding Fort Benton by a cutoff overland trail. Residents of Helena were intrigued by the idea, despite the failure of Kercheval City and its successor Musselshell to survive intermittent raids by Sioux Indians. After Musselshell was abandoned in 1870, the only remaining facility at the mouth of the Musselshell was Fort Sheridan, George Clendennin's trading post.[77]

Maclay agreed to have the new trail and port ready by the start of steamboat navigation and to transport all freight landed by Kountz Line steamers. For opening the route, the Northern Pacific promised to pay Maclay a $40,000 bonus. For his part, Maclay made the major concession of withdrawing Diamond R wagons from the Utah route. He also agreed to promote the Northern Pacific's interests. Judging by the subsequent heavy promotion of the trail by the *Helena Herald,* he certainly persuaded at least one newspaper editor.[78]

Maclay and his railroad and steamboat partners had high hopes for their new route. By avoiding the hazardous rapids above Cow Island, they believed steamboat navigation could be extended about two months. The prospect of steamboat deliveries into September, they thought, would compensate for the overland trail from Helena to the mouth of the Musselshell probably being about twice as long as the 140-mile Fort Benton–Helena route.

But when he had the trail reconnoitered, Maclay decided the best location for his new Missouri River port, which was named Carroll after Diamond R partner Matthew Carroll, was about midway between the Musselshell and Cow Island. By using a site about 40 miles above the Musselshell, he could reduce the freight wagon time from Helena by at least three days. He determined there was no advantage in building closer to Cow Island, because upstream from Carroll the river turned northwestward, which increased the distance from Helena.[79]

From Helena to present-day White Sulphur Springs there were two branches of the Carroll Trail. The northernmost and slightly longer variant went via Camp Baker, and the other route ran more directly eastward through the Big Belt Mountains. From the springs the trail traced eastward to the confluence of the northern and southern forks of the Musselshell (near modern Martinsdale). From that point it ran northeastward through Judith Gap, the wide opening between the Little Belt and Big Snowy mountain ranges. After crossing Big Spring Creek (present Lewistown), it skirted the western and northern flanks of the Judith Mountains before crossing Box Elder Creek and a stretch of badlands on its northeastward path to Carroll.[80]

Carroll, which William Ludlow reported was 243 miles from Helena by way of Camp Baker, was built by the Diamond R in the spring of 1874 with locally cut logs, lumber floated down from Fort Benton, and materials hauled from Helena. By the end of its first summer, it had developed into a community of about 150 permanent residents, with twenty log cabins, two stores, three restaurants, two blacksmith shops, and a hotel. Its founding prompted George Clendennin to abandon Fort Sheridan in favor of opening a store in Carroll.[81]

The army increased fortification of the Carroll Trail to safeguard it from marauding Sioux who roved northward from their Yellowstone valley camps. Camp Baker, a permanent post established in 1869, was 52 miles from Helena. Other than there, troops were on the trail only during the freighting and stagecoach season from April to late October. Three companies encamped at the forks of the Musselshell and two at Camp Lewis, 30 miles from Judith Gap. There were stage stations at both camps, and small consignments of men from the camps were assigned to guard the stage stations at Judith Gap and Box Elder Creek and to provide escort service. In 1874 some men from Camp Lewis were sent to Carroll, but the port was left unguarded the next year.[82]

Helena's Carroll Trail experiment lasted only two years. In 1874 four Kountz Line steamers—*Fontenelle*, *Katie P. Kountz*, *May Lowery*, and *Peninah*—made ten deliveries with an estimated total of 1,712 tons, only a few tons less than Fort Benton's total. The next year the Coulson Line's *Josephine*, *Key West*, and *Western*, combined, delivered about 1,500 tons in eleven trips, slightly over half of Fort Benton's receipts. Downstream cargoes, which consisted mainly of silver ore, buffalo robes, and cattle hides, amounted to 400 and 600 tons respectively in 1874 and 1875.[83]

The Kountz Line proved the touted advantage of the Carroll route of greatly lengthening the navigation season by making its last delivery on September 6. But despite this achievement Helena's shippers and the Diamond R were irate about the line's overall performance. They charged that the Kountz boats were slow, leaky, undependable, and greatly inferior to the Coulson Line steamers servicing Fort Benton. The most publicized failure of the Kountz Line was the mechanical breakdown of its *May Lowery* a short distance below Carroll. The boat was rescued by the Coulson's *Josephine*, which towed the disabled craft to Carroll for $1,250.[84]

The Diamond R's Charles A. Broadwater, who booked passage from Bismarck on the *Fontenelle*, claimed that the boat was idled one-third of time because of mechanical problems. He finally left it at Fort Peck, about 150 miles below Carroll, and went up on another steamer. Broadwater also asserted that all Kountz boats were old and leaky, which often caused water-damaged goods and damage claims from Helena's merchants. After the Diamond R's experience with Kountz, he insisted: "There would be no inducement in the world that would cause me to make a contract with the Kountz boats at any price."[85]

Echoing the opinions of the Diamond R partners and Helena's merchants, the *Helena Herald* concluded that the Carroll route's first season was a qualified success. It had lessened Helena's dependence on shipments from the Union Pacific, which had been Montana's main supplier since its completion in 1869. The Carroll trade, reasoned the *Herald*'s editors, returned most trade to its natural Missouri River path and boosted the territory's economy by using Montana rather than Utah freighters. But despite this salutary effect, the *Herald* conceded that Helena's merchants were unhappy with the slowness of Carroll deliveries. Declaring the Diamond R "blameless" for any delays, the *Herald* vilified the Kountz Line.[86]

In reviewing the Carroll Trail's first season, the *Helena Herald* concluded that the new route had succeeding in returning the bulk of Montana's imports to the Missouri River.[87] Nonetheless, shippers in Helena, Deer Lodge, Missoula, and Bozeman were unhappy with the tardiness of Carroll deliveries. The *Herald*'s editor believed that "a new deal on the river for the season of 1875 is absolutely requisite to restore the lost confidence of shippers in the efficacy and advantages of the route via Northern Pacific and Carroll."[88]

The "new deal" was to switch to Coulson Line boats. The Diamond R and the *Herald* praised the line's 1875 work. Coulson boats, led by the fast, light-draft *Josephine*, which made six of the eleven Carroll deliveries, extended navigation to five months with its earliest and latest arrivals on May 10 and October 10. The *Key West* had steamed from Bismarck to Carroll in a record 7 days and 6 hours, which bested the *Josephine* by 6 hours. Such speeds enabled passengers and light freight to move between Bismarck and Helena faster than ever. The weekly stagecoach once went from Carroll to Helena in less than two and a half days.[89]

To ready for its second season of Carroll freighting, the Diamond R expanded its facilities at the landing. The company hired George Clendennin to build a 100-by-45-foot warehouse with a capacity of over 800 tons of merchandise. The Diamond R, which devoted some 300 wagons and hundreds of mules and oxen to the Carroll business, strove to get its trains under way within two days after a steamboat arrival. If the trail was dry and firm, trains sometimes reached Helena in 13 days. But during the excessively wet spring of 1874 the first Diamond R train took about 50 days to make the round-trip from Helena. Despite this disappointing experience with a muddy road and flooded streams, the trail was never improved.[90]

In addition to sometimes poor road conditions, the freighters were challenged by wild animals and Sioux raiders. One train was delayed two weeks when stampeding buffalo, which ranged by the thousands in the eastern portion of the trail, ran off its oxen. The most serious incident with Sioux raiders occurred on July 7, 1875, when a war party killed three soldiers and drove off sixty horses near Camp Lewis. Twenty miles east of the camp some of the same force raided the Diamond R's mule herd and got away with nearly three dozen animals.[91]

It is impossible to determine if the Carroll Trail provided faster and cheaper transportation than the Fort Benton route. The *Helena Herald* insisted it did. But the *Benton Record,* which published its inaugural issue on February 1, 1875, pronounced the Carroll route a failure that could not match the traditional commercial way through Fort Benton.[92]

Over the winter of 1875–76 the *Herald* and Helena shippers reversed themselves. Near the end of the trail's second year, the *Herald* proclaimed that freight via Carroll "has not only been put through earlier, but quicker and cheaper than by any other route."[93] But the following spring the editor concluded: "Helena owes her growth, her wealth and permanent position more to her proximity, by good wagon road to Benton than to all other causes combined."[94] By omission, the editor consigned the Carroll Trail to the dustbin of history.

What caused the editor to change his opinion of the Carroll Trail so rapidly? The most plausible explanation is that he concluded that the Northern Pacific, the Diamond R, and Helena's merchants were not willing to risk using an unguarded trail. Over the winter, the War Department and Montana territorial officials decided that the territory's most pressing need was to remove the Sioux blockade of the Yellowstone River valley. In the spring, Fort Shaw commander General John Gibbon, with troops from Fort Shaw, Camp Baker, and Fort Ellis, led an expedition eastward into the Yellowstone valley. Given the urgency of the Sioux problem, troops could not be spared for the Carroll Trail. A review of the trail's brief history shows its strong dependence on army support. Freight trains and stages ran only when troops were posted along the trail. Any steamboat deposits that could not be delivered before the troops quit the trail in late fall were freighted by wagons routed through Fort Benton.[95]

The abandonment of the Carroll Trail helped stimulate Fort Benton's business, which in turn added to the importance of the Cow Island landing. Montana shippers aspired to be supplied via the Missouri about five months each year. But they were well aware that most Fort Benton steamboat deliveries were made during the high-water period in May and June. When the river became shallower, most boats could not be navigated through the rapids above Cow Island. Then freight had to be off-loaded at the Cow Island landing and forwarded by wagons to Fort Benton. The approximate 120-mile-long Cow Island Trail followed up Cow Creek before turning westward toward the northernmost bend of that portion of the Missouri. From the bend, it ran southwesterly near the river's left side to Fort Benton.

Cow Island's steamboat navigation season was much longer than Fort Benton's. In 1877, for example, the first of Fort Benton's arrivals occurred on May 7 and the last on August 14. But from August 24 to October 11, seven steamers delivered goods to Cow Island.[96]

Though useful, the Cow Island alternative was costly. Army engineer First Lieutenant Edward Maguire reported that the standard charge for wagon freighting from the island to Fort Benton was $2.50 per hundredweight, three times the steamboat rate. Maguire calculated that shippers, including the federal government, spent $25,000 annually to freight an estimated 500 tons from Cow Island to Fort Benton. This expense prompted Montana's newspapers and politicians to urge federal improvement of the rapids area.[97]

Pending completion of river improvements, I. G. Baker and Company started a steamboat forwarding service from Cow Island in 1878. Realizing that the steamers on the upper river were too heavy-drafted for the rapids during low water, the company had the small 110-ton stern-wheeler *Colonel Macleod* built at Cincinnati. After completing its maiden voyage to Fort Benton on August 29, the vessel made five more deliveries to the port and one to nearby Coal Banks. With its last arrival on October 19, the *Colonel Macleod* proved that Cow Island–Fort Benton steamboating was possible nearly until the river froze.[98]

The *Colonel Macleod*'s greatest impact in improving service from Cow Island was in its first year. In 1879 it was used mainly to make Bismarck-to-Benton voyages. Its latest arrival at Fort Benton on September 20 was bested by the *F. Y. Batchelor*, a conventionally built full-size mountain boat that reached the port on October 3. The *Batchelor*'s feat and eleven July arrivals, including the large *Dacotah* laden with 600 tons, represented an unprecedented degree of late-season navigation through the rapids. With the improvement of the most hazardous rapids by army engineers, more boats could get through, and the need for the *Colonel Macleod* as a forwarder from Cow Island diminished. Nonetheless, its owners planned to use the boat for a third season when they sent it to be wintered at Bismarck. But on November 18 it was crushed and sunk by the much larger *Butte*, which slid down the bank.

In 1877, Fort Benton steamboating began a remarkable run of seven consecutive years in which annual commerce sometimes exceeded the best gold rush year.

Twenty-five arrivals in 1877 delivered 5,283 tons and about 1,500 passengers. The next year, fifty-one arrivals had 9,653 tons, and the ten to Cow Island 686 tons. In 1879, forty arrivals unloaded 10,499 tons at the port. The increase in tonnage despite eleven fewer arrivals shows the impact of river improvement. With a better channel through the rapids, all steamers could be more heavily loaded. Even the large *Dacotah* was able to reach Fort Benton as late as July 13. For the season the *Dacotah* and *Montana*, with two arrivals each, accounted for more than one-fifth of Fort Benton's receipts.[99]

Bismarck was the commonest starting point for steamers that reached Fort Benton. Of the twenty-five arrivals in 1877, twelve were from Bismarck, seven from Yankton, five from St. Louis, and one from Pittsburgh. The following year a list compiled by the *Benton Record* of the first forty-five arrivals showed thirty from Bismarck, six from Yankton, four from Pittsburgh, two from St. Louis, two from Cow Island, and one from the Cheyenne Agency. The Bismarck–Fort Benton voyages usually took 12 to 15 days.[100]

During a navigation season, freight rates for shipments from Bismarck to Fort Benton ran from $1.25 to $2.50 per hundredweight. Rates were negotiated with each shipper. Daniel W. Maratta, general manager of the Coulson Line's Bismarck operations, gave the lowest rates to such large, regular shippers at T. C. Power and Brother and the Diamond R Freighting Company. Small consignments such as a single box were assessed the highest rates. Normally, all rates increased as water levels receded from June to fall. Any other increase in operating expenses such as wages and fuel prompted rate increases.[101]

The principal destinations for boat cargoes delivered to Fort Benton or Cow Island and intermediate points were Helena and towns connected to it by wagon roads, including Bozeman, Deer Lodge, and Missoula. Edward Maguire reported that about three-fourths of the freight delivered to Fort Benton in 1877 was destined for Helena and the other towns. The remainder was either freighted to the Mountie forts or sold locally. By including Fort Benton's local sales with that of the other Montana communities, the *Benton Record* concluded that the boats had delivered 4,648 tons of Montana freight at an average value of $300 a ton, which amounted to $1,394,400. The tonnage of the Canadian contract freight was 1,025, valued at $310,000.[102]

Fort Benton's main importers were the mercantile firms of I. G. Baker and Company, T. C. Power and Brother, Kleinschmidt and Brother, W. S. Wetzel and Company, and Murphy, Neel, and Company. Only Baker and Power supplied Mounties. In 1878 the Baker firm freighted at least 400 tons to Forts Macleod and Walsh, and the Power company hauled at least 100 tons to the forts. Power and Brother also received 2,750 tons of Montana freight and 800 tons of government supplies. The Montana receipts of Murphy, Neel, and Company and Kleinschmidt and Brother were 1,900 tons each, and those of W. S. Wetzel were 530 tons. Most of the Baker and Power deliveries were made by their own steamers, but the other firms relied mainly on the Coulson Line.[103]

The *Red Cloud* of the Baker Line was mostly navigated between Bismarck and Fort Benton. *From the collection of the Public Library of Cincinnati and Hamilton County.*

In 1879 the Coulson Line, with eighteen arrivals by nine different steamers, delivered 4,950 tons, nearly half of all Fort Benton's imports. The Power Line's three steamers—*Benton, Butte,* and *Helena*—made a total of eight arrivals at Fort Benton and five to Cow Island. With six arrivals by the *Colonel Macleod* and four by the *Red Cloud,* the Baker Line transported 2,160 tons to Fort Benton.

Most of the increase in steamboating in the late 1870s was due to the private business of Montana merchants. But the aftermath of the Great Sioux War and the unexpected Nez Percé campaign spurred military shipments as well. After his victory at the Battle of the Little Bighorn, Sitting Bull and hundreds of his followers fled across the international boundary. Most camped in the Cypress Hills near Fort Walsh, where they seemingly posed a major threat to Montana's northern frontier. To prevent their possible return and to ensure peace with large numbers of Sioux on the Fort Peck Indian Reservation, the U.S. Army started constructing Fort Assinniboine on May 9, 1879. When completed at a cost of nearly $1 million, the large, ten-company post, mostly built of brick, had fifty-nine buildings.[104]

To construct Fort Assinniboine, the army had to have great quantities of materials and supplies and several hundred civilian workers transported from St. Paul and Minneapolis. The combined rail-river-overland route went via Coal Banks, a landing about 42 miles by stream below Fort Benton. Located near the northernmost point of the great bend between the Judith River and Fort Benton, Coal Banks offered the shortest wagon route from the Missouri to Fort Assinniboine. Freighters starting from there saved about 22 miles, or approximately one-third of the Benton-to-Assinniboine distance. Occasionally, freight and passengers bound for Fort Walsh, which was north of Fort Assinniboine, were routed through Coal Banks.[105]

It is impossible to make a clear statistical distinction between Coal Banks and Fort Benton receipts. Many of the steamers that reached Fort Benton unloaded part of their cargoes at Coal Banks. In 1879 only one vessel, the *Rose Bud*, had Coal Banks as its uppermost destination. During the navigation season, when Coal Banks was a busy depot, it was guarded by a detachment of troops from Fort Assinniboine.[106]

While still shocked by Custer's defeat and fearful of further Sioux raids, Montanans were surprised by the invasion of some Nez Percés. After refusing to move to a reservation in their native northeastern Oregon, some nontreaty Nez Percés fled eastward in June 1877. Montanans became particularly alarmed after the Nez Percés defeated troops led by Colonel John Gibbon at the Battle of the Big Hole on August 9. The Nez Percés, led by Chief Joseph, tried to escape into Canada by a circuitous route through Yellowstone National Park and the Beartooth Mountains. The army pursued them with a force led by Brigadier General Oliver Otis Howard and tried to intercept them with troops from Fort Keogh under the command of Colonel Nelson A. Miles. Anticipating that the Nez Percés would try to cross the Missouri in the Cow Island vicinity, the army used steamboats from Bismarck to stockpile supplies and provisions in warehouses at the island.[107]

During the night of September 23, the Nez Percés destroyed some 50 tons of military and commercial goods at Cow Island, despite being challenged by the small guard of twelve infantrymen and four civilians. A week later, after an engagement with Miles's troops, Chief Joseph surrendered at the edge of the Bear Paw Mountains, only 40 miles from the Canadian boundary.

During the steamboating surge of the late 1870s, Montana's unfavorable balance of trade persisted. Nonetheless, there was a sharp increase in exports from the frontier region. In terms of both bulk and worth, the leading exports were ore and bullion (mostly silver, with some gold), buffalo robes, and wool. During the placer gold rush, silver was discovered in many of the same sites that had gold deposits. Silver, which could not be obtained by placer mining methods, required an extensive investment in mining and processing equipment. Nonetheless, led by returns from Butte, silver production doubled from 1874 and 1875. Generally, silver-bearing rock was concentrated into a high-quality product and then exported for refining. Some silver ore was freighted to Utah, and some was shipped over the Carroll Trail; after the trail's closure, it was transported to either Fort Benton or Cow Island.[108]

Steamboat exports in 1877 included 1,225 tons of ore and bullion with an average value of $750, or a total of $918,750, plus 50,512 buffalo robes and 104 tons of wool. With a value of $202,018, the robes were worth nearly ten times as much as all other wild animal pelts and skins, among them 68,530 pounds of antelope, deer, and elk skins. Aside from the wool, ranching products included some 15,000 cattle hides and 112 head of live cattle. The exports also included 595 and 350 tons respectively from Fort Macleod and the Cypress Hills. Buffalo robes and other wild animal hides and pelts were the main products of the Canadian prairies.[109]

The rapidly increasing importance of ranching was shown in the 1878 returns. Descending steamers transported 348 tons of wool, and one shipper, George Clendennin, exported 750 beef cattle. Six of the steamers were loaded with cattle. Shipments of buffalo robes, ore, and bullion remained high. T. C. Power and Brother alone sent 35,000 buffalo robes on steamers, and I. G. Baker and Company marketed 19,412. Without mentioning values, the *Benton Record* reported that Murphy, Neel, and Company sent 3,533 sacks of ore (apparently somewhat-processed silver) and 1,192 bars of bullion.[110]

Fort Benton's steamboat resurgence was generated mainly by market demands. But it was facilitated by federal government improvement of the Rocky River above Cow Island. Apparently influenced by Montana's pleas for river improvement, chief of engineers Brigadier General Andrew A. Humphreys on April 8, 1875, ordered Major Charles R. Suter of the St. Louis office to study the matter and make recommendations. After reviewing the 1868 report by Brevet Major Charles W. Howell and the 1872 report by Northern Pacific chief engineer Thomas P. Roberts, Suter concluded that the most imperative need was to deepen the channel and lower the gradient at Cow Island and Dauphin's Rapids. Subsequently, Humphreys requested and obtained a congressional appropriation of $20,000 in the Rivers and Harbors Improvement Act of 1876 to initiate the work.[111]

In 1877 First Lieutenant Edward Maguire was named project commander. Maguire's party of twenty-five men, organized at St. Paul, moved to the rapids by rail and steamboat. At Dauphin's Rapids, Maguire rendezvoused with an escort of one company of the Seventh Infantry. The infantrymen protected Maguire's group but could not prevent the Nez Percés from destroying the Cow Island river gauge records.

Maguire's primary mission was to open channels 100 yards wide and 4 feet deep at Cow Island and Dauphin's Rapids. But Maguire found the task too daunting to be completed in one season. In 1877 his men, using a scow-mounted derrick and dynamite, removed 2,400 rocks from Dauphin's Rapids, thereby creating a channel 100 feet wide and 1,800 feet long. At Cow Island they removed all rocks from the channel and, by closing the right chute with a wing dam, raised the water level, which in turn reduced the gradient. The dam, 419 feet long and 8 feet high, contained 710 cubic yards of stone. It created a channel depth of 2.5 to 5 feet around the island.[112]

The *Peninah* at Coal Banks Landing, Montana Territory, 1880.
About forty-five miles below Fort Benton, Coal Banks Landing was the start of the
main overland trail to Fort Assinniboine. *Courtesy of the Montana Historical Society, Helena.*

With increased appropriations and more workers, Maguire continued his
improvement work in 1878 and 1879 on the 40-mile stretch from Hammond Island
upstream to Dauphin's Rapids. At Dauphin's Rapids the 100-foot-wide channel
was lengthened to 3,400 feet, and a minimum depth of 2.5 feet was achieved.
Upper, middle, and lower wing dams were completed at Cow Island, which
achieved a navigable channel more than 3 feet deep. Additionally, Maguire's crews
opened a 100-foot-wide channel through the gravel bar at Bird's Rapids, removed
boulders at Cabin Rapids, and built wing dams at Hammond Island and Grand
Island.

Fort Benton's late 1870s boom coincided with increased steamboating due to
the Black Hills gold rush. Well before the official discovery of gold in the Black
Hills in July 1874, Yankton and Sioux City promoters believed the area held rich
mineral deposits. Some Yanktonites, who organized an exploring and mining
association in 1861, sponsored a private scientific reconnaissance of the Hills by Dr.
Ferdinand V. Hayden. Buoyed by Hayden's optimistic report, the association tried

to organize a more systematic reconnaissance in 1866 but was thwarted by military authorities, who refused to allow trespassing on unceded land.[113]

Schemes to open the Hills persisted after the Fort Laramie Treaty of 1868 created the Great Sioux Reservation. Led by newspaper editor Charles Collins, some Sioux Citians formed the Black Hills Exploring and Mining Association in 1872. But the army refused to permit their contemplated expedition to the Hills.

Federal officials were certainly aware of the schemes to open the Hills when Lieutenant General Philip H. Sheridan, commander of the Division of the Missouri, authorized a military reconnaissance. When Lieutenant Colonel George Armstrong Custer led a massive force of over a thousand men from Fort Abraham Lincoln, his expedition's ostensible purpose was to determine the site of a new post in the Black Hills vicinity. By 1874 the government recognized that the greatest concentration of potentially hostile Sioux was located between the Union Pacific and the planned Yellowstone River route of the Northern Pacific. The army wanted to restrict most of the Lakotas to reservations in northwestern Nebraska by a Black Hills fort rather than allowing them to range northwestward to the Powder River country, home of massive buffalo herds.[114]

The size and composition of the Custer expedition belied its stated mission of locating a fort site. It included scientists, journalists, an official photographer, and prospectors. Not surprisingly, some of the men found gold in French Creek near later Custer, South Dakota. When the returning expedition reached Fort Abraham Lincoln in August, telegraphic news of the strikes sparked headlines nationwide .

Like the Pikes Peak gold rush after the Panic of 1857, the apparent riches of the Black Hills seemingly offered relief from the disastrous Panic of 1873. As gold hysteria mounted, the government had neither the will nor the resources to maintain the Hills as part of a Sioux reservation. The first trespassers, the Gordon party from Sioux City, made their way along the old Niobrara Trail to the Hills in the fall of 1874 and held on through the winter before being evicted by troops. A rush of placer miners into the southern Hills in 1875 led to the inevitable political response of asking the Sioux to sell the Hills. The government's tactic of convening a grand conclave at the White River in northwestern Nebraska on September 20, 1875, backfired when Sioux chiefs adamantly refused to sell.[115]

Sioux alarm over the miners' invasion caused many reservation Indians to join their brethren along such Yellowstone tributaries as the Powder and the Bighorn. There on June 25, 1876, the Tetons and their allies shocked the nation by annihilating Custer's command. Though sensational as a military feat, the Little Bighorn battle proved to be a Pyrrhic victory for the Indians. Congress, completing abandoning diplomacy, decided that no further appropriations would be made for the Lakotas until they ceded the Black Hills. During September and October 1876, numerous chiefs and headmen agreed to the cession when federal agents traveled from reservation to reservation. By an act of February 28, 1877, Congress approved the cession terms. The Lakotas agreed to relinquish all claims west of the 103rd meridian and to the delta-shaped area east of the meridian between the Belle

Cow Island Landing, Montana Territory, 1880.
Because of the difficult rapids above it, Cow Island Landing was
an important depot for offloading Fort Benton–bound steamboat freight.
Courtesy of the Montana Historical Society, Helena.

Fourche and Cheyenne rivers. To facilitate access to the Hills from the east through unceded lands, the Sioux consented to the opening of three roads from the Missouri River. The Lakotas received no special compensation but were assured that the government would honor its financial obligations under the Fort Laramie Treaty.[116]

The legal opening of the Hills and the northern shift in placer mining benefited the Missouri River transportation hubs of Bismarck and Yankton. In 1875, when placer miners worked mainly in the southern Hills, the shortest and least expensive wagon and stagecoach routes were from the Union Pacific towns of Cheyenne, Wyoming, and Sidney, Nebraska. From either place the trail to Custer was about 170 miles long.[117]

Disappointing yields in the southern Hills spurred prospectors to range into the northern Hills, where significant finds were made in Deadwood Gulch. By July 1,

1876, an estimated 7,000 miners were in the Deadwood area and only 1,000 in all the rest of the Hills. Newspaper estimates in 1879 ranged from 15,000 to 25,000 for the Hills. However, the 1880 federal census reported only 16,487 in the three-county mining area, with approximately four-fifths of them in Lawrence, Deadwood's county.[118]

Despite its relatively sparse population, the Black Hills was an important market for supplies routed through Cheyenne, Sidney, Yankton, and Bismarck from Chicago, Omaha, California, and other places. Other than some locally produced lumber, hay, small grain, and vegetables, Black Hillers had to import virtually everything else.

When Deadwood replaced Custer as the main gold rush market, Yankton and Bismarck were advantageously located to challenge Cheyenne and Sidney freighters. The overland components of the Yankton and Bismarck routes to Deadwood were each about 200 miles long, or about 70 less than the most popular trail variants from Cheyenne and Sidney.[119]

Freight delivered to Yankton by the Dakota Southern Railroad was forwarded to Fort Pierre by steamers during the navigation season and then freighted westward. A Sioux City shipper advertised that goods and passengers could reach Yankton by the 61.5-mile-long Dakota Southern in 4 hours and be moved by steamboats the 290 miles from Yankton to Fort Pierre in only 60 hours.[120]

In 1876 George E. Merchant, superintendent of the Dakota Southern, and Sanford B. Coulson coordinated the shipping of Black Hills supplies to Fort Pierre. To avoid delays at the Yankton railroad terminus, Coulson agreed to have a steamboat awaiting arriving trains. To offer through bills of lading to the mining communities, Merchant and Coulson worked with two large wagon freighting firms—the Evans Line and the Merchants Line. Fred T. Evans of Sioux City was the principal owner of his namesake line. The Merchants Line was organized and owned by Downer T. Bramble and William Miner, who were engaged in Yankton merchandising, grain dealing, and flour milling.[121]

The Yankton–Fort Pierre service had a difficult first year. In 1876 the government closed the Fort Pierre Trail for a time because it ran through unceded land and was vulnerable to raids by marauding Lakotas. When Evans violated the ban, the army destroyed his first train. Even after the army relented and permitted transit, it refused to provide military escorts. Most shippers avoided the risky route in favor of either Cheyenne or Sidney. But the army's roundup of many Lakotas after the Custer defeat and the government's acquisition of the Black Hills led to a boom in the Yankton–Fort Pierre trade for three consecutive years, beginning in 1877.

Both Evans and Bramble and Miner depended on Coulson Line steamers, which ran on a semiweekly schedule. Evans's partner and fellow Sioux Citian John Hornick managed the Fort Pierre business in 1877. In early June he reported that the firm was "shipping immense amounts of freight every day. It looks like business to see fifty to sixty teams waiting to load up."[122] After Hornick left the firm in 1878, Evans supervised Fort Pierre shipments while his brother-in-law Edwin Loveland managed the company's Rapid City general merchandise store. Their consignment of nearly 50 tons shipped from Fort Pierre on July 6 was pronounced to be the largest one-day shipment made from any point to the Hills. In 1879 the Evans Line transported 5,000 tons, using about 200 wagons.[123]

During the 1879 navigation season, Evans quit using Coulson Line steamers from Yankton in favor of Peck Line boats from Sioux City. The move may have resulted from Campbell K. Peck's acquisition of Fort Meade's grain contracts. Fort Meade, established by the army in 1878 on the northeastern flank of the Hills near present-day Sturgis, South Dakota, soon became a major destination for Fort Pierre's freighters. Peck's contracts called for delivering about 650 tons of corn and a like amount of oats to the fort. He planned to obtain the corn at Sioux City and get it to the fort by his own line's boats and Evans wagons. He intended to have the oats raised near the fort.[124]

The Merchants Line of Bramble and Miner was nearly as large as the Evans Line. Bramble, Miner, and Company established a branch store at Fort Pierre and regularly ran mule and ox trains to the Hills. In 1880, when they had 2,000 animals and 300 men, their shipments amounted to 4,000 to 5,000 tons and may have included some wintertime hauling from Yankton.[125]

By 1878 far more supplies reached the Hills by way of Yankton and Fort Pierre than by any of the three rival routes. The *Black Hills Journal* of Rapid City reported that the Hills imported 23,000 tons of freight for the year. Evans claimed that two-thirds of it was moved through Fort Pierre. Some allowance has to be made for wintertime freighting, but it is clear that most of the freight was hauled by steamboats during the April–November navigation season. It is quite likely that more steamboat tonnage was received at Fort Pierre in 1878 than at any other Missouri River port. Since Fort Pierre did not have a newspaper or any other local recorder of steamboat arrivals, it is not possible to make a precise comparison with Fort Benton activity. But if the estimates of the *Black Hills Journal* and Evans are reliable, Fort Pierre would easily have surpassed Fort Benton's 9,653 tons. One 1878 prediction was that the next year's imports would increase to 35,000 tons.[126]

Further insight into Fort Pierre's business can be gauged by considering Yankton's steamboat arrivals and departures. In 1878 the port had 132 arrivals and 126 departures. The departures would have included vessels bound for Sioux City and other downstream points, as well as those that delivered cargo to such places as Fort Randall and Whetstone Landing. Nonetheless, probably at least two-thirds of the boats that left Yankton would have made Fort Pierre stops.[127]

The Yankton–Fort Pierre route became prominent because it offered the cheapest transportation. Evans advertised that Black Hills freight from Chicago through Yankton and Fort Pierre could be transported for 50 cents less per hundredweight than shipments through Bismarck, Cheyenne, and Sidney. Part of the reason for this was that the Chicago-Yankton rail segment was several hundred miles shorter than any other route. Information on steamboat charges from Yankton to Fort

Pierre is spotty. In 1876 Coulson charged 75 cents per hundredweight when navigation was good, but he doubled the rate in October and still later increased it to $2 because of low water, high wages, and a scarcity of wood.[128]

A saving of 50 cents per hundredweight was particularly meaningful to shippers of quartz mills, the bulkiest items sent to the Hills. By 1877 the Hills placer phase was superseded by hard rock mining. To extract gold particles from the quartz, it was necessary to crush the rock with giant metal wheels with numerous steel stamps. Such mills were powered by stationary steam engines. The complete outfit, including wheel, stamps, boiler, engine, and other equipment, sometimes weighed as much as 100 tons.[129]

The Yankton–Fort Pierre route also benefited from its proximity to the agricultural resources of southeastern Dakota Territory and Sioux City. With an economy geared to the harsh realities of supply and demand, the cost of flour and other products in the Black Hills was grossly inflated. The price of flour, the main food import, was the most meaningful economic indicator. Even when it was plentiful, flour usually cost $8 per 100 pounds. But shortages caused by high demand or impassable trails could easily double or triple that price. The high-priced market attracted merchants and farmers from the Yankton–Sioux City area, who sent flour, butter, honey, eggs, bacon, and poultry to the Hills. Some of this marketing was done by private freighters who transported their own goods all the way by wagon.[130]

Sometimes steamers returning to Yankton from Fort Pierre transported Black Hills exports. These shipments included gold ore, which was often destined for an Omaha smelter, along with buffalo robes and other hides and peltries.[131]

The Black Hills gold rush was the main reason Yankton was able to temporarily continue its rivalry with Bismarck. But 1879 was the town's last good year in the Black Hills trade. The 1880 extension of a railroad to Running Water, below Fort Randall, not only ended Yankton's brief reign as a significant port but also left Bismarck as the unchallenged mistress of upper river steamboating.

END OF LONG HAULS ON
THE UPPER RIVER, 1880–1887

L ike residents of all frontier territories, Dakotans and Montanans yearned
for a modern society replete with railroads, cities, and a vibrant economy
based on agriculture, ranching, mining, and manufacturing. As long as
their internal transportation depended heavily on steamboats and overland freighting, they could not realize those goals.

Population growth by 1880 indicated that the territories were losing some of their
image as isolated frontiers. Dakota, starting to benefit from the decade-long Great
Dakota Boom that began in 1878, had 133,147 white residents, a marked increase
over the 12,887 of 1870. With 3,777 inhabitants, Deadwood was the largest city, followed closely by Yankton, with 3,431. Bismarck had 1,758, and Fargo and Sioux
Falls, both growing as railroad centers, had 2,693 and 2,164 respectively. In 1880,
Montana's non-Indian population was 39,159, nearly double the 20,593 of 1870. Its
only three places with more than a thousand residents were Helena, with 3,624,
Butte, with 3,393 and Fort Benton, with 1,618.[1]

By 1887, when the Manitoba, St. Paul, and Minneapolis Railroad (renamed to
Great Northern in 1889) reached Fort Benton, both territories had been transformed by railroads. Yankton was the first port to succumb to railroad competition. Bismarck had to adjust to the loss of the Yellowstone River valley business
as the Northern Pacific advanced and to the end of the Fort Benton trade. But,
unlike Yankton, it was able to continue as a significant port, because sections of
the Missouri valley both above and below it were untouched by railroads for many
years.

Yankton's location in southeastern Dakota Territory, a potentially prime agricultural area, doomed its future as a steamboat port. As territorial promoters
extolled the region as the next Eden, railroad companies were quick to respond.
Before 1878 the southern part of Dakota Territory had only two short rail lines—
the Dakota Southern from Sioux City to Yankton, and the Chicago and North

Western Railway (hereinafter referred to as the North Western) from the Minnesota boundary to Watertown and nearby Lake Kampeska.[2]

But the opening of the land rush spurred rapid construction by the North Western and the rival Chicago, Milwaukee, Saint Paul, and Pacific Railway Company (i.e., the Milwaukee Road). The main routes for both lines ran east-west from the territory's eastern boundary to the Missouri River. After completing its track to Marion, about 20 miles southwest of Sioux Falls, in the fall of 1879, the Milwaukee Road constructed a branch line southwesterly to Running Water on the Missouri.

The completion of its main line from Marion to the Missouri was delayed until 1881. As its crews worked westward in 1880, the Milwaukee Road, through a subsidiary land company, started Chamberlain on the Missouri at the mouth of American Creek. Steamers, including the Peck Line's *C. K. Peck,* hauled building materials and other supplies from Running Water.[3] The company planned to finish laying track to Chamberlain soon after the town was platted, but a major snowstorm on October 15 halted construction 20 miles away. When flooding the next spring ruined bridges and roadbeds along its routes, the Milwaukee Road had to make repairs before resuming construction. As a result the track to Chamberlain was not completed until early September 1881.[4]

In the meantime the North Western had finished its line to Pierre in early November 1880. Thus, by the fall of 1881, Yankton was outflanked by railheads at Running Water, Chamberlain, and Pierre.

Although Running Water was only 40 miles above Yankton, the government and private shippers were convinced they could save time and money by using it as their Missouri River destination. The impact of Running Water was evident with the opening of navigation in 1880. Yankton had been designated as a starting point for government shipments, but the government essentially neutered that stipulation by contracting with the Milwaukee Road to deliver its goods to Running Water. The lack of warehouses and other facilities at Running Water did not deter the decision. Railroad deliveries were stockpiled on sandbars to await steamboats from Yankton and Sioux City, their winter bases. With the exception of grain and flour procured in the Yankton vicinity by Sanford B. Coulson and his associates, steamboats had no cargo from Yankton.[5]

The Coulson Line shifted most of its business to Bismarck, and the Peck Line quit operating from Sioux City and Yankton in favor of Running Water, which in 1880 was the main port for Black Hills business. Peck Line steamers dominated navigation from Running Water to Fort Pierre. During the course of the season, the *Fontenelle,* which was used as a regular shuttle on the 235-mile route, transported 3,696 tons of freight.[6]

In 1881, because of competition from Pierre, Running Water lost some business. Black Hills freight delivered by the North Western had only to be ferried across the river to Fort Pierre. The regular ferry was the *Jim Leighton,* owned by the Northwestern Express and Transportation Company of St. Paul, Minnesota. Built at Sioux City in 1880, the 57.29-ton stern-wheeler, whose dimensions were 119.5

× 30.1 × 3.6 feet, arrived in Pierre on October 27, 1880, only a few days before the railroad.[7]

Despite the more direct route of the North Western, the Milwaukee Road competed in the Black Hills trade. Until its main line reached Chamberlain, it sent freight through Running Water and then upstream by the Kountz Line's *General D. H. Rucker* and *Mollie Moore*. The two vessels were the only regulars in the 1881 Running Water–Chamberlain–Fort Pierre trade. As its Chamberlain line was being completed, the Milwaukee Road announced that these boats were forwarding the last 1,000 tons of Running Water freight for Chamberlain and points above.[8]

The *General D. H. Rucker* and *Mollie Moore* worked out of Chamberlain well into November 1881. To supplement them, the Milwaukee Road used its own steamer, the *Milwaukee*, which measured 136.5 × 30.3 × 5.3 feet. Initially commanded by a Captain Anderson, who was reported to be a twenty-year veteran of upper river boating, the *Milwaukee* had been built at Jeffersonville, Indiana, in 1880. Its principal owner was John H. Lawler of Prairie du Chien, Wisconsin. Lawler, an official in the Milwaukee Road, was also a key member of the townsite company that founded Chamberlain.[9]

The emergence of Pierre as a steamboat port coincided with the Great Flood of 1881, which inundated Missouri bottomlands throughout Dakota Territory and was particularly devastating in the Yankton-Vermillion area. The deluge resulted from a combination of natural occurrences. Heavy snows, which started in mid-October, persisted intermittently until spring, with an accumulation of several feet throughout much of the territory. The snowstorms were accompanied by severe cold, leaving the Missouri covered with thick ice. Then in late March, spring came with a rush. The river thawed near Fort Buford, as did its tributaries flowing eastward from the Black Hills area, while ice was still solid below Fort Randall. As torrents of water and ice floes were propelled downstream, the river rose sharply, causing ice jams in some bends and narrows. A jam several miles below Yankton and another a short distance below Vermillion dammed the stream for miles. Unfortunately, the blockages were accompanied by a cold spell, which delayed their breakups. Water collecting above the jams flooded the valley from bluff to bluff. Vermillion, which had been built on bottomland below the bluffs, was almost completely ruined when water and ice floes rushed through the town.[10]

Only the lower portion of Yankton was flooded, but the crashing ice destroyed two steamboats and damaged eleven others at Yankton and nearby locales. The first onslaught of ice ripped a twenty-foot-long gash in the Coulson Line's *Western*, which was tied up a short distance below the ways. Initially, there was some hope of saving it, because only the stern sank to the river's bottom. Crews frantically worked pumps and removed some deck furniture and other equipment. But the weight of the water-logged stern and more ice completely sank the boat. When workmen tried to salvage the boat's machinery after the flood subsided, they found that ice pressure had flattened the port boilers. The ferry *Livingston*, anchored near the *Western*, was pushed well up the riverbank. The Peck Line's *Far West, Nellie*

Peck, and *Peninah* were carried across the railroad tracks near the Dakota South-ern depot. Miraculously, the *Far West* was only lightly damaged and was the first boat to be put into service. But the *Peninah,* nearly half a mile from the river when the floodwaters ebbed, was not floated until July 27. The only three steamers on the ways, the Power Line's *Black Hills, Butte,* and *Helena,* were thrown together and heavily damaged.[11]

Several miles above Yankton, the Coulson Line's *Big Horn, Josephine,* and *Rose Bud,* which were moored on the Dakota bank, were pushed ashore and damaged. They fared much better than the Peck Line's *Fontenelle,* frozen in for the winter at a nearby island and reportedly reduced to "kindling" by the onslaught of gigan-tic ice floes. But the whims of nature saved the Peck Line's *General Meade,* which had spent the winter locked in ice above Fort Randall. Once the icy grip gave way, the boat floated downstream among the ice chunks. Its frantic watchman, the only person on board, called for help when he passed Fort Randall. Then he and the boat disappeared and were presumed lost. But they were saved when the *General Meade* was snared in a timber stand about 30 miles below the fort.

Although the flood was a setback for the Coulson and Power lines, it was not a fundamental cause for Yankton's rapid demise as a steamboat port. The bypassing of Yankton by upstream railheads to Running Water and Pierre occurred before the flood. By the time of the deluge, Yankton was living mainly on its reputation.

The completion of the Milwaukee Road to Chamberlain changed the pattern of post-Yankton steamboating somewhat. Railroad officials and town promoters, who worked in concert, tried to develop Chamberlain as a port and outfitting point for the Black Hills. These aims brought them into direct competition with the North Western and Pierre–Fort Pierre.

Milwaukee Road officials, with a keen interest in the Black Hills trade, had first reconnoitered a White River–Badlands trail from the vicinity of future Chamber-lain to Rapid City in 1879. But two years elapsed before a combination of Cham-berlain promoters, wagon freighters, and Rapid City business interests surveyed the road, which was intended to challenge the Fort Pierre route. In part because of the defection of freighters Fred T. Evans and Downer T. Bramble from Fort Pierre, Chamberlain and the Chamberlain Road did a lively Black Hills business in 1882. But the road had only one good year. Freighters could not cope with its disadvantages of being 40 miles longer than the Fort Pierre Trail and having sum-mertime water shortages in the Badlands section.[12]

Use of Chamberlain's Black Hills Trail diminished the need for steamboats. The *Milwaukee,* used primarily as a ferry, was the town's only season-long vessel. Kountz withdrew both the *General D. H. Rucker* and the *Mollie Moore.* He sent the *Rucker* to Sioux City to be repaired and abandoned the unserviceable *Mollie Moore* at the Chamberlain levee. In mid-July, Captain Henry J. King used the *Milwaukee* to tow the *Mollie Moore* a mile downstream to make more room at the landing.[13]

By the time King was hired as the *Milwaukee's* master in the spring of 1882, nearly three decades had passed since he had first navigated the upper river. His initial voyage to the Chamberlain vicinity was in 1855 on the *Genoa*, one of the vessels used to supply Harney's force. In 1866 he was one of the owners of the *Viola Belle*, which was engaged in the Fort Benton trade. He first appeared at the town of Chamberlain in 1881 as the captain of Kountz's *Mollie Moore*.[14]

In 1883, Milwaukee Road shipments for the Black Hills were hauled from Chamberlain to Fort Pierre by steamboats. Most of the freighting was performed by the *Milwaukee*, the only regular season-long Chamberlain–Fort Pierre packet.[15] Typically, the *Milwaukee*'s Black Hills freight included general merchandise, corn, and mining equipment. On one of its Pierre trips the boat was loaded (probably to capacity) with 75 tons of general merchandise and 75 tons of corn. Within a two-week period it transported 150 tons of corn.[16]

The freight never complained about Chamberlain's landing, but King's passengers apparently did. To reach the town from the river, they had to scale a steep hill, which, according to the *Democrat*, required a "Herculean effort." The editor insisted "a Rocky Mountain goat would shake his head in amazement and despair if required to make the ascent just subsequent to a heavy rain."[17]

Like other steamboat captains, King boasted about his speedy trips. He claimed to have broken the old record by half an hour when the *Milwaukee* made the 105-mile descent from Fort Pierre in eight and a half hours. On another occasion the *Milwaukee* completed a Chamberlain–Fort Pierre round-trip in two and a half days, the season's best time to late July.[18]

Between his Fort Pierre voyages, King often ferried passengers (including many reservation Indians), vehicles, and livestock across the river. In one particularly busy July evening the *Milwaukee* carried 600 head of Black Hills–destined cattle across and brought back 1,600 head of government cattle bound for the Crow Creek and Yankton agencies.[19]

Despite his busy schedule, King was unable to meet the Milwaukee Road's needs with his steamer. On August 24 the *Democrat* reported "freight for upriver and the Black Hills plenty, over 700 tons now here and still accumulating." To facilitate shipping, the railroad acquired the use of the *F. Y. Batchelor*, the most prominent Yellowstone River steamer during the last years of that trade. But even after the addition of the *F. Y. Batchelor*, railroad freight piled up at Chamberlain. Some of it was shipped by the transients *W. J. Behan* and *P. H. Kelley* and the Peck Line's *General Terry*.[20]

The *W. J. Behan* was a 165-×-33-foot stern-wheeler built at Jeffersonville, Indiana, in 1873. In February 1882, Grant Marsh bought the boat from the Red River Line and that spring navigated it up the Missouri to Bismarck. For a year Marsh operated the *W. J. Behan* as a transient, or "wild," boat, independent of any organized line. In May 1883 he sold it for $6,000 to Captain R. F. Woolfolk and his associates, including John Satterlund of Washburn and the McGrath Brothers of Stanton. The new owners wanted to concentrate on the trade from Bismarck upstream to Washburn and Stanton and downstream to Fort Yates.[21]

But Woolfolk, who commanded the boat, could not resist the opportunity to participate in the potentially more lucrative Chamberlain–Fort Pierre trade. He ran the *W. J. Behan* out of Chamberlain for about seven weeks prior to returning it to Bismarck in mid-October. On one of the trips to Fort Pierre, which were scheduled every ten days, the cargo amounted to 200 tons.[22]

After Grant Marsh sold the *W. J. Behan*, he had the *P. H. Kelley* built at Sioux City in 1883. He first ran the small 90-×-18-×-2.9-foot craft as a railroad transfer out of Running Water. Later in the season he shifted the Chamberlain trade, where the boat's longest trip was a voyage to Le Beau, at the mouth of Swan Creek near present-day Akaska, South Dakota. In 1884 and 1885 Marsh used the *P. H. Kelley* as a ferry at Memphis, Tennessee.[23]

The *General Terry*, the last steamer operated by the Peck Line, was used primarily to transport freight to such upstream destinations as the Cheyenne Agency, the fledgling community of Le Beau, and Fort Yates. From mid-July to mid-October, Captain Haley made at least five round-trips from Chamberlain with the vessel. Most of its freight consisted of supplies for the Cheyenne River and Standing Rock agencies and lumber and general merchandise for Le Beau. The boat's downstream freight included a Gatling gun, two caissons, and a quantity of condemned ammunition from Fort Hale en route to the federal arsenal at Rock Island, Illinois.[24]

While Yankton steamboating was being strangled by upstream railheads, opportunities for commercial navigation were further restricted by the extension of the Northern Pacific through the Yellowstone River valley. The reorganized and refinanced railroad, which had been stalled at Bismarck since 1873, resumed construction in 1879. On July 5, 1881, it was completed to Glendive, in the lower Yellowstone River valley. The "Gate City" immediately supplanted Bismarck as the starting point for Yellowstone River steamboats.[25]

Just before the railroad's arrival at Glendive, Yellowstone steamboating was dominated by Joseph Leighton and his partner and brother-in-law Walter B. Jordan. Leighton and Jordan, who were also post traders at Fort Buford, entered Yellowstone boating in 1878 with the new *F. Y. Batchelor*, measuring 180 × 30 × 3.5 feet. A classic mountain boat, the stern-wheeler was completed at Pittsburgh. From there, Grant Marsh, who had recently left the Coulson Line, navigated it to Fort Custer. Subsequently, the vessel became the most successful in navigating the Yellowstone and Bighorn. From 1878 to 1881 it made nine landings at Fort Custer, seven more than its closest rival. Leighton and Jordan doubled their Yellowstone Line early in 1881, when they were named army transportation contractors for the Yellowstone, by purchasing the *Eclipse*, a three-year-old vessel built at California, Pennsylvania. Other than having a slightly heavier draft, it had the same dimensions as the *F. Y. Batchelor*.[26]

Leighton and Jordan used the *Eclipse* in a massive deportation of Indians from the Yellowstone valley. In 1880, when several thousand Sioux returned to the United States from Canada, the army confined them at Forts Keogh and Buford. Over the winter, government officials decided that the Fort Keogh captives should be moved as one group by steamboats to the Standing Rock Agency. Since no sin-

The *F. Y. Batchelor*, built in 1878 for Joseph Leighton and Walter B. Jordan, was
the most successful freighter on the Yellowstone and its tributary Bighorn.
Courtesy of the State Historical Society of North Dakota.

gle line could provide enough facilities, quartermaster officers engaged the Yellowstone Line's *Eclipse*, the Coulson Line's *Josephine*, the Peck Line's *General
Terry*, and the government's *General Sherman*. Amid great apprehension about
possible Indian resistance, the steamers were crammed with 1,712 Sioux early in
the morning of June 13, 1881. The uneventful voyage to Fort Yates must have
seemed like the end of an era to both the Indians and steamboatmen.[27]

Later in the summer the *General Sherman* was used to transport the Lakota
chief Sitting Bull and 187 of his people from Fort Buford to Fort Yates. When Sitting Bull ended his Canadian exile, he formally surrendered to military authorities at Fort Buford. After a ten-day stay at the fort, the Lakotas boarded the *General Sherman* on July 29 for the three-day voyage to Fort Yates.

Soon after the Indian removal, Yellowstone River steamboating became the
handmaiden of the Northern Pacific. The railroad hastily constructed warehouses
at Glendive. In the first fifteen days after the railroad reached Glendive, 4,000 tons
of freight were shipped upstream. By season's end in early September, Glendive
had twenty-five upriver steamboat departures. Most of the voyages were made by
the *Eclipse* and the *F. Y. Batchelor*, which usually carried a mixture of military and
private freight to Miles City, Fort Keogh, and the mouth of the Bighorn.

After navigation was halted relatively early because of low water, the Northern
Pacific track layers continued working. By December 1881 they reached Miles City

and by the following May were within 60 miles of Coulson. The Northern Pacific doomed Coulson by locating its facilities two miles west in the new town of Billings.

As the "Magic City" boomed spectacularly, it became the main destination for railroad freight. Wanting their own steamer for the Billings trade, Northern Pacific officials bought the *F. Y. Batchelor* from Leighton and Jordan. They used it as well as Leighton and Jordan's *Eclipse* and the Peck Line's *General Terry* to forward cargoes from the ever-changing railhead. The boat operators hoped to reach Billings, which would have bettered Marsh's highest point, but they never made it. Huntley, 10 miles downstream from Billings, proved to be their head of navigation. The *Eclipse,* commanded by veteran Missouri River captain Thomas D. Mariner, performed the best. In June and early July, with cargoes averaging 110 tons, the *Eclipse* reached Huntley four times. Because of low water, the three steamers were taken off the river more than a month before the first locomotive pulled into Billings on August 22, 1882.[28]

The completion of the Northern Pacific to Billings ended frontier steamboating on the Yellowstone. But the railroad's officers wanted to be sure their monopoly would last. Before the opening of navigation in 1883, they signed an agreement with the Coulson and Power lines. In exchange for favorable railroad freight rates on shipments from Minnesota, the boat companies agreed to keep their vessels off the Yellowstone.

While the fortunes of Yellowstone River steamboating were plummeting, Fort Benton was booming. Its steamboat trade for 1880–82 surpassed that of the peak gold rush years. The port had 37 arrivals in 1880, 25 in 1881, and 46 in 1882. For those years, nearby Coal Banks was the destination of 7, 8, and 4 arrivals. As usual, Cow Island was the late-season high point, and an occasional boat had to turn about at the Marias and Judith rivers. Historian Joel Overholser, relying in part on estimates, concluded that the total imports of all Montana points on the Missouri were 12,460 tons in 1880, 12,928 in 1881, and 13,064 in 1882.[29]

A somewhat different perspective on Montana steamboat commerce was presented by army engineers. Captain Edward Maguire, while supervising river improvement in the rapids section, reported that the 1881 business set a new record. For all Montana destinations on the Missouri and Yellowstone, twenty-one steamers were used. They hauled slightly over 17,000 tons, valued at more than $5 million. Additionally, they transported 3,700 passengers (including 2,400 Indians), 1,800 head of horses and cattle, and 600 head of sheep. Among the exports were 23,000 buffalo hides, 180 tons of wool, and 127 tons of hides, furs, and wolf pelts.[30]

In reporting the 1882 trade, Maguire employed another method. Instead of using Montana imports, he reported Bismarck exports. During the season, Bismarck had 86 steamboat departures. For all Montana and Dakota destinations, the fleet carried slightly over 16,000 tons. The exports from Fort Benton alone were 58,000 buffalo hides and robes, 600 tons of wool, 1,000 cattle, 7,600 cattle hides, 1,250 bales of miscellaneous hides and peltries, and 22 tons of merchandise. Maguire noted that Fort Benton's exports amounted to 2,000 tons, worth an estimated $612,930.

Fort Benton's exports represented an economy in transition. As farmers and ranchers were extending their realms, the traditional extractive hunting and trapping activities lingered in some sections. Naturally, the encroachment of settlers and rising land values accelerated the killing of wild animals, which seemed to many frontier people to be nothing more than deterrents to progress. The overlapping of the hunting-trapping culture and the farmer-rancher lifestyle is reflected in the 1881 shipments of George Clendennin, Jr., one of Fort Benton's main exporters. His shipments, which amounted to about 521 tons, included 2,033 bales of wool (256 tons), 1,955 bales of sheep pelts (95 tons), 63 tons of cattle hides, and 161 beef cattle. His bulkiest wild animal export was about 4,000 buffalo hides and robes. But he also shipped 148 bales of antelope hides (12,437 pounds), 77 bales of deer hides (7,561 pounds), 24 bales of elk hides (2,839 pounds), 6 bales of beaver hides (620 pounds), 5 bales of wolf pelts (400 pounds),4 bales of mountain sheep skins, and 100 bales of mixed furs (8,562 pounds).[31]

The unprecedented business of Fort Benton and other Missouri River points below it was due to increased settlement, the founding of Fort Maginnis, the enlargement of Fort Walsh , the heavy demands of Fort Assinniboine and the Fort Belknap Indian Agency, and the expanding Whoop-Up Trail business.

Agricultural production in Fort Benton's trade area was spurred by rapid occupation of the Sun, Teton, Marias, Shonkin, Belt, Highwood, and Judith valleys. By 1881 newly settled farmers were producing grain, potatoes, and butter.[32] The farmers' frontier also expanded through the east side of the Judith Basin. In late 1881 a Fort Benton reporter observed that "almost every foot of arable land is taken up" in the area from present-day Lewistown to the Judith Mountains. Simultaneously, grazing lands in those sections had been claimed by sheep and cattle ranchers, who produced much of Fort Benton's exports.[33]

Fort Benton's merchants also benefited from silver strikes in the Barker District and the discovery of gold and silver in the Judith Mountains. The Barker strikes in the Big Belt Mountains, about 60 miles south of Fort Benton, were made in October 1879 by Buck Barker and his partner, P. H. Hughes. Within two years the Barker mines were one of the main sources of Montana silver. The rush of gold and silver miners to the Judith Mountains and the eastward expansion of farmers and ranchers led the federal government to establish Fort Maginnis.[34]

Founded in August 1880 about 20 miles northeast of present Lewistown on the east side and at the foot of the Judith Mountains, the fort was intended to encourage settlement of the Judith Basin and Musselshell valley. At the time, roving bands of buffalo-hunting Indians from the Fort Belknap Agency and elsewhere were regarded as a threat to settlers and transportation routes.[35]

Fort Benton's promoters desperately wanted a trade area vast enough to include Fort Maginnis. But the 150-mile-long stage and wagon route from the port to the fort by way of Judith Gap was a major deterrent. Fort Benton's *River Press,* especially, exhorted the Choteau County commissioners to improve roads from Fort Benton to keep the Judith Basin and Fort Maginnis markets from falling prey to

The *Josephine* at Fort Benton, May 3, 1882, photograph by Justus Fey.
This Coulson Line vessel was reputed to be one of the lightest-drafted, fastest steamers
on the upper Missouri. *Courtesy of the Overholser Historical Research Center, Fort Benton, Montana.*

competing sites. With vivid memories of Carroll, the editor warned that "unless the needed [road] work was done much trade that otherwise would come to Benton will go to Wilder's Landing or other points."[36]

Although the editor mentioned only the site known as Wilder Landing specifically, Rocky Point, across from it on the Missouri's south bank, was more of a threat to Fort Benton. Six miles above Carroll, Rocky Point by late 1881 controlled most of the trade that had previously gone to Carroll. Its rise was triggered mainly by the partnership of Charles A. Broadwater and the Minnesota entrepreneur Amherst H. Wilder, the supply contractors for Fort Maginnis. Carroll's prospects had been revived briefly in 1880 when construction supplies for Fort Maginnis were landed there and hauled over the Carroll Trail. But on December 28, 1881, the *River Press* gleefully reported that "Carroll has been washed away by the flood, only a few houses remaining." Rocky Point quickly emerged as the main jump-

ing-off place for Fort Maginnis and the Judith Mountain mines and as an important way station for steamers bound for Cow Island, Coal Banks, or Fort Benton.
The army stationed a quartermaster officer there to supervise the transshipment
of freight over the Carroll Trail to Fort Maginnis. Wilder Landing, connected to
Rocky Point by a ferry, was created as the supply base for a short-lived gold excitement in the Little Rocky Mountains some 40 miles to its north.[37]

Despite the advent of Rocky Point and Wilder Landing, the remnants of Carroll lingered for a time. On May 24, 1881, Isaac P. Baker, general superintendent of
the Fort Benton Transportation Company, quoted steamboat rates from Bismarck
to Carroll. Two years later his rate schedule included downstream charges from Fort
Benton to Carroll, and late in the summer of 1883 he specified passenger rates only
to Carroll, while listing both freight and passenger charges to Wilder Landing.[38]

Although Rocky Point and Wilder Landing were ordinarily regarded as rivals
of Fort Benton, they nonetheless depended somewhat on Fort Benton merchants.
Sometimes, after steamboat navigation ended, freight was shipped from Fort Benton to them by mackinaw. One such craft transported twelve and a half tons in
October 1882. Although mackinaw use had declined sharply from the gold rush
days, the boats were often used to transport passengers to steamers at Cow Island
or the Bismarck railhead.[39]

Shipping supplies and personnel by steamboats from Bismarck was vital to the
enlargement of Fort Walsh and the maintenance of Fort Assinniboine and the Fort
Belknap Agency. Generally, steamboat freight and personnel destined for Fort
Assinniboine and Fort Walsh were unloaded at Coal Banks Landing, the source
of the shortest overland route to the installations. But the logistical support for
Coal Banks commerce was supplied by Fort Benton's merchants. I. G. Baker and
Company, the main contractor for Fort Walsh, based part of its overland freight-
ing component at Coal Banks Landing. The company's managers, Charles E. and
William G. Conrad, usually had 100 three-wagon teams on the trails to Fort
Walsh and Fort Macleod during the freighting season. T. C. Power and Brother,
which also had a store at Fort Walsh, ran its own freight and stagecoach lines. Ordi-
narily, Mountie reinforcements for Fort Walsh entered the United States by Great
Lakes steamers at Duluth, Minnesota, and then moved by rail to Bismarck before
embarking up the Missouri.[40]

When steamers could not reach Coal Banks Landing, their cargoes for destinations north of the Missouri were usually unloaded at either Cow Island or
Broadwater Landing. Named for Charles A. Broadwater, Broadwater Landing was
on the river's left bank three and half miles above Wilder Landing and 32 miles
below Cow Island. Transferring government freight was its main business. Its
wagon trails led to the Fort Belknap Indian Agency and Fort Assinniboine. Because
of the fort business, the army stationed a quartermaster officer at the landing.
Like the Cow Island landing, Broadwater Landing depended on wagon freighters
from Fort Benton to forward goods. This business was conducted weeks after the
last steamboat had been unloaded. For example, in mid-November 1882, D. G.

Browne of Fort Benton sent twelve wagons and a number of mules to Broadwater Landing to deliver the last Fort Assinniboine freight.[41]

The very forces that fueled the resurgence of Bismarck–Fort Benton steamboating led to its undoing. Expanding markets both north and south of the international boundary stimulated rapid railroad construction. The completion of the Northern Pacific to Helena on June 12, 1883, greatly reduced Fort Benton's trade area. Meanwhile, Fort Benton's Canadian trade was being devastated by the Canadian Pacific Railroad, which reached Calgary on August 11. The Coal Banks–Fort Walsh business abruptly ended earlier in the summer when the line was being completed through western Saskatchewan and eastern Alberta.[42]

The combined effect of the Northern Pacific and Canadian Pacific was to remove the southern and northern parts of Fort Benton's trade zone. A year and a half before the Northern Pacific reached Helena, Fort Benton's commerce was detrimentally affected by the extension of the narrow-gauge Utah and Northern Railroad to Butte. Construction crews of the line, a branch of the Union Pacific, reached Montana's southern boundary in Monida Pass on March 9, 1880. As track was extended northward into the Beaverhead Valley, Union Pacific shipments to Montana rose. In 1880 the Utah and Northern and connecting wagon freighters delivered slightly over 16,000 tons of freight to Montana. The railroad began service to Dillon on October 8, 1881, and to Butte four days before Christmas. Butte, only 65 miles from Helena, remained the line's terminus for two years.[43]

Despite the Utah and Northern's incursion, Fort Benton steamboating expanded slightly in 1882. The region within 60 to 70 miles of Fort Benton, which was developing rapidly, was immune to influence by the Utah and Northern. Also, the Canadian trade was obviously unaffected by a Butte railroad terminus, and some of Fort Benton's leading merchants—including T. C. Power and Brother; Murphy, Neel, and Company; and the Kleinschmidt Brothers—operated stores in Helena and other Montana communities. T. C. Power and Brother opened its Helena branch store in 1870. Thomas C. Power made Helena his headquarters, and John W. Power managed the parent store in Fort Benton. In 1881 about one-fourth of the 6,000 tons delivered to Fort Benton by Power steamers was for T. C. Power and Brother. John T. Murphy and Samuel Neel established their general merchandise business at Helena in 1865 and started their Fort Benton branch in 1876 after removing from Carroll. Albert and R. H. Kleinschmidt started retailing and wholesaling at Fort Benton in 1878 and within three years had fifteen branch stores in Montana. All of these merchants continued relying on steamers and freight wagons to make Helena deliveries even after the Utah and Northern reached Butte.[44]

Fort Benton was able to adjust to the glancing blow of the Utah and Northern, but it could not withstand the direct thrusts of the Northern Pacific and Canadian Pacific. Because steamers were able to complete early-season runs to Fort Benton in 1883, the full impact of the railroads did not hit until the next year. Fort Benton had twenty-eight arrivals by nine different steamers in 1883. Imports from Bismarck amounted to 10,244 tons and exports to nearly 1,557 tons. Passenger business was light—only 965 people completed up and down voyages. In 1884 only five steamers were involved in the Bismarck–Fort Benton trade. With a total of fourteen arrivals, they delivered 3,821 tons of freight and took down 1,508 tons.[45]

Because of the curtailment of Yankton steamboating and the concentration of most commerce in the Bismarck–Fort Benton section, upper river commerce could be conducted by fewer boats. By the spring of 1885, the Fort Benton Transportation Company was the only surviving main line.

In 1880 at the start of the Fort Benton boom, the Coulson Line was the largest firm. Its partners owned and operated ten steamers—*Big Horn, Black Hills, Dacotah, Far West, Josephine, Key West, Montana, Rose Bud, Western,* and *Wyoming.* During the navigation season, its vessels made over a third of all Fort Benton arrivals. But the next year, the firm ran only four steamers—*Big Horn, Dacotah, Josephine,* and *Rose Bud*—from Bismarck to Fort Benton. It lost the *Western* during the Great Flood of 1881 and sold the *Black Hills* to the Power Line and the *Far West* to the Peck Line. The *Key West, Montana,* and *Wyoming* were run on the lower river and on the Mississippi below St. Louis.[46]

By the opening of navigation in 1882, the company had been reorganized and reduced. The net result of a series of transactions by the company's partners, each of whom was a fractional owner of most vessels, was to leave Joe Todd and Nick Buesen out. By trading their interests in the *Big Horn, Josephine,* and *Rose Bud,* Todd and Buesen each gained three-eighths ownership of the *Montana* and majority control of the *Key West.* Although several of their former Coulson Line partners remained as part owners, Todd and Buesen operated the two boats independently in the Bismarck–Fort Benton trade for one year. After 1882 they sold both vessels to parties on the lower river.[47]

The departure of Todd and Buesen left the remaining partners—Sanford B. Coulson, Martin Coulson, William S. Evans, James C. McVay, and D. W. Maratta—as part owners of the *Big Horn, Dacotah, Josephine, Rose Bud,* and *Wyoming.* As losses occurred, they simply reduced operations. They did not replace the *Western* or the *Big Horn,* which was snagged and totally lost on April 30, 1883, near the mouth of the Poplar River. After using the *Wyoming* for one Fort Benton voyage in 1882, they sold it. In 1883 it was run by the Southern Transportation Company in the Cincinnati–New Orleans trade.[48]

Despite its sharp decline, the Coulson Line outlasted the rival Peck Line. After Campbell K. Peck's death, the company continued as the upper river's second-largest line. A. F. Brownell of Keokuk served as president, Henry C. Akin—who lived variously at Bismarck, Yankton, and Sioux City—was superintendent, and Peck's widow, Helen, was part owner of some of the steamers. In 1880 the company's six boats were the *C. K. Peck, Fontenelle, General Meade, General Terry, Nellie Peck,* and *Peninah.* Having recently acquired the *Fontenelle* and *Peninah* from William J. Kountz, the firm was well positioned to bid on government transportation contracts and to engage in the Bismarck–Fort Benton trade.[49]

Perhaps because of their mutual fear of the Coulson Line's aggressiveness, the Peck and Power interests forged an alliance in 1880. They agreed that their vessels would run "in connection" with each other. Presumably this meant they would coordinate scheduling and share the hauling of freight from Bismarck to Montana destinations. By pooling their operations, the two lines aimed to reduce shipping costs in order to be more competitive with the Utah and Northern in the Montana market.

Concern about the expanding Utah and Northern led to a full-fledged pool in 1881 involving the Peck, Power, and Coulson lines. The partners of the three lines wanted to regularize rates and share the shipping of private freight. But their association was a matter of convenience. Mistrust permeated the arrangement.

As pool agent, Isaac P. Baker, the recently hired general manager of the Fort Benton Transportation Company, was usually at odds with both the Coulson and Peck interests. The twenty-six-year-old Baker, who moved to Bismarck from St. Louis, was the son of John F. Baker, general freight agent of the St. Louis and St. Paul Packet Line. He was also the nephew of Isaac G. Baker, the Fort Benton and St. Louis entrepreneur.[50]

The young Baker, who had attended Central College in Fayette, Missouri, and worked with his father in St. Louis, was decisive and sometimes arbitrary. Although he deferred to Thomas C. Power, he strictly bossed company employees. Baker was efficient in day-to-day management but was too loyal to his own company to work well within the pool. He compounded his estrangement from Coulson, Maratta, and Akin by agreeing to work also as the agent for I. G. Baker and Company's *Red Cloud*. When he shipped some of the pool's Fort Benton freight on the *Red Cloud*, his adversaries accused him of being unfair and lacking authority to make agreements outside the pool. Matters came to a head in August when Coulson, Maratta, Akin, and J. C. O'Conner, the Peck Line's Bismarck agent, invited Baker to attend a meeting to resolve the *Red Cloud* freight matter. The meeting only made matters worse. Baker responded to the attacks on his conduct by walking out, but not before proclaiming that he "declined to have anything more to do with the pool" unless instructed by Thomas C. Power.[51]

Baker was convinced that the "dirty underhand work" by Coulson, Maratta, and Akin dealt with issues far broader than the *Red Cloud* dispute. He confided to Power that "the Coulson and Peck Lines, Coulson, Maratta, Akin and O'Conner without exception would leave no stone unturned if they could underhandedly crush out this Co. [Fort Benton Transportation Company]."

Despite Baker's outrage, the Power Line had no choice but to continue its pool agreements for the remainder of the year. But any semblance of cordiality had disappeared after the August meeting. Baker, more determined to assert his authority, revoked Akin's power of attorney and informed John H. Charles, his company's superintendent, that no bills of lading "should fall into Akin's hands."[52]

After 1881, cooperation among the Coulson, Peck, and Power lines was greatly reduced. They did not renew the pool agreement but instead consigned freight to a competitor's vessel only when none of their own boats was available.[53]

The financially strapped Peck Line, unable to recover from Campbell K. Peck's bankruptcy and hounding creditors, soon succumbed. In 1882, Akin's upper river fleet was reduced to operating the *Far West, General Meade,* and *General Terry* in the Bismarck–Fort Benton trade. Because of a dispute with the Pittsburgh steamboat machinery manufacturers James Rees and Sons, Akin was barely able to retain rights to the *General Terry.* The vessel's machinery had been built in 1878 by the Rees firm for Walter A. Burleigh and John Todd, but its makers claimed they had not been paid for the cost of the engine, boilers, and other machinery. Burleigh and Todd were forced to give up the boat, which was sold by a U.S. marshal. The Peck Line purchased it at the auction, but the Rees Company claimed a lien on the engine, boilers, and other machinery. After a federal trial held in Yankton, the Peck Line was able to retain the boat, but only after compensating Rees and Sons.[54]

Akin sent the *C. K. Peck* and *Nellie Peck* to the lower river. He wanted to run the *Peninah,* but that unfortunate craft was immobilized by a dispute between the line and the federal government.

In 1881 the U.S. marshal for Montana Territory confiscated the *Peninah* because some of its crew illegally sold liquor at an Indian agency. The government wintered the vessel at Rock Haven, opposite and five miles above Bismarck, and moved it to Bismarck while its fate was pending in federal court. Helen A. Peck, who claimed part ownership, brought suit against the government on the grounds that the seizure was illegal. But while the matter was pending, the impatient Akin flouted the government. In early September 1882 some of his men distracted the *Peninah*'s watchman by plying him with liquor. While the watchman was being entertained, Captain David Campbell and other hands got up steam and attempted to escape downstream. Akin tried to foil federal deputy marshals by having the telegraph wires cut between Bismarck and Fort Yates. He should have realized the futility of trying to escape by river. After the telegraph was repaired a deputy federal marshal apprehended the *Peninah* a short distance below Pierre.[55]

Akin's caper ended the *Peninah*'s upper river career. The boat was sold and later operated on the Red River in Louisiana, where it was burned on November 7, 1887. To compound the Peck Line's problems, creditors had brought suits in federal courts against the *General Meade* and *Nellie Peck.* They were seized and sold by a federal marshal at Sioux City in November 1883.[56]

In 1883 the Peck Line operated only the *General Terry* out of Chamberlain and Pierre. Before the opening of navigation the next year, the line went out of business with the sale of the vessel to overland freighter Fred T. Evans, who had formed a partnership with R. F. Woolfolk. Woolfolk, who had run the *W. J. Behan* as a transient for two years, joined Evans after his boat was crushed by ice at Bismarck on March 28, 1884.[57] Evans and Woolfolk operated the "Evans Line" for two years out of Chamberlain, Pierre, and Bismarck. They expanded to two boats in the fall of 1884, when they purchased the *General D. H. Rucker* from Kountz.

Kountz had greatly curtailed his upper river operations after 1879. He sold the *Fontenelle* and *Peninah* to the Peck Line and from 1880 to 1884 operated only the *General D. H. Rucker* and the *General Chas. H. Tompkins* part of the time from Sioux

City, Chamberlain, and Bismarck. He was frozen out of the 1881 pool and did not participate in the Fort Benton trade. In 1883 he tried to win the army transportation contract through straw man Charles Wright. Initially, it appeared the Kountz won the business, but the army disallowed the bid because Wright, who was not of age, was not eligible to bid.[58]

Kountz sent the *General D. H. Rucker*, commanded by David Campbell, to Bismarck in 1884. Business was slow, and Kountz failed in his personal effort to organize a steamboat tour to Fort Yates. In September he had the boat steamed downstream, with the intention of taking it to St. Louis. But during his stop at Chamberlain, he sold the vessel for $9,000 to Evans and Woolfolk. Kountz temporarily retained the *General Chas. H. Tompkins*, but he soon also sold it to the Evans Line.[59]

By the time Kountz retired from the upper river, the Coulson Line was suffering through its last days. After its *Big Horn* was destroyed, it ran only the *Dacotah, Josephine,* and *Rose Bud* for the rest of the season. After sending the *Dacotah* to Fort Benton for the last time, Coulson and his partners sold it to men who initially ran it on the lower river.[60]

In 1884, when Fort Benton was ailing from the season-long impact of railroads for the first time, Maratta scrambled to keep the *Josephine* and *Rose Bud* busy. But after both vessels made one early-season Fort Benton voyage, Maratta had difficulty scheduling shipments.[61] Baker, who disliked both Maratta and Coulson, was hardly a gracious winner. On May 31, 1884, he gleefully wrote to John H. Charles: "Business dead dull on Upper End. . . . Coulson is played out on the Upper End—hope you will freeze him out below [at Sioux City]."[62]

The Coulson Line dissolved in April 1885 with the sale of the *Josephine* and *Rose Bud*. The federal government purchased the *Josephine* for use by the Army Corps of Engineers in its upper river improvement projects. The formal transfer occurred at Bismarck on April 9, with the ceremonial lowering of the Coulson flag and the hoisting of the engineer corps emblem. When Coulson and Maratta sold the *Rose Bud* to the Power Line, they arranged for Baker to close out their Bismarck affairs, including dealing with any prospective shippers who tried to contact the defunct Coulson Line.[63]

Meanwhile, Coulson and Maratta had decided to enter lower river steamboating. In February 1885, in association with St. Louis investors, they organized the Kansas City and St. Louis Electric Packet Line. With Coulson as president and Maratta as general agent, the company announced that it would start running steamers between St. Louis and Kansas City as early as March 15.[64] Maratta soon withdrew from the company because Democratic President Grover Cleveland appointed him U.S. marshal for Dakota Territory. He was, of course, removed after Cleveland was defeated by Republican Benjamin Harrison in 1888. But in 1893, when Cleveland again became president, Maratta was named U.S. consul to Melbourne, Australia.[65]

As the Peck, Kountz, and Coulson companies were failing, the Fort Benton

Bismarck steamboat landing, 1884.
After railroads bypassed Yankton, Bismarck became the mistress
of upper Missouri steamboating. *Courtesy of the State Historical Society of North Dakota.*

Transportation Company consolidated its position as the only major line on the upper river. From 1881, when it operated in the pool with the Coulson and Peck lines, to 1886, the firm (renamed the Benton Transportation Company in 1885) increased its fleet from four to nine steamers. Through Baker's efficient management and the accompanying difficulties of its rivals, the Benton Line established a near monopoly of upper river boating.

The Bismarck–Fort Benton trade was the line's main business, but Baker regularly sent boats downstream to Fort Yates and on occasion to Pierre and Chamberlain. The line's Fort Benton business benefited from the snagging and sinking of I. G. Baker and Company's *Red Cloud* about 60 miles below the mouth of the Musselshell on July 11, 1882. The loss ended the Baker Line; henceforth the trading company depended on vessels owned by others.[66]

Before expanding, the Benton Line lost two of its original steamers. The *Butte* was burned and totally destroyed on July 30, 1883, while en route from Bismarck to Fort Benton. When it caught fire at the third point above the Fort Peck Indian Agency, Captain Andy Johnson had its prow run into the bank so all passengers and crew could escape.[67] Baker was content to operate only the line's remaining three steamers—*Benton, Black Hills,* and *Helena*—the rest of the season. But he quickly replaced the *Black Hills* after it was crushed by ice at Bismarck on March 28, 1884.[68]

After the Great Flood of 1881, the Benton Line habitually wintered its vessels at Bismarck or nearby sites such as Rock Haven by simply tying them up to the bank and letting them freeze in for the winter. When the ice started thawing in the spring, workmen would chop the boats free. The practice worked most of the time. But very thick ice and a rapid thaw in 1884 caused ice floes to slam into the *Black Hills* and R. F. Woolfolk's nearby *W. J. Behan.* The hulls of both vessels

The *Rose Bud*, a classic mountain boat with spoonbill-shaped bow,
was used by both the Coulson Line and the Power Line.
Courtesy of the State Historical Society of North Dakota.

were smashed. Baker subsequently had the *Black Hills* dismantled and apparently salvaged its machinery. The destruction of the *Black Hills* and *W. J. Behan* spurred Baker and other Bismarck community leaders to launch a drive to build ways on the town's levee.[69]

Within several weeks after the *Black Hills* disaster, the Benton Line purchased the *F. Y. Batchelor* from the Northern Pacific. The line ran only three steamers—*Benton*, *F. Y. Batchelor*, and *Helena*—in 1884 but returned to its four-boat strength with the acquisition of the *Rose Bud* the next spring.[70]

With the exception of the government's *Josephine*, only Benton Line steamers reached Fort Benton in 1885. The firm had some competition above Bismarck from Leighton and Jordan's *Eclipse*, but with major stores at Fort Buford and Poplar River, the traders were primarily concerned with freighting their own goods.[71]

In the trade below Bismarck, Baker felt threatened by Evans's Missouri River Transportation Line. The partnership of Fred T. Evans and R. F. Woolfolk went into business with only the *General Terry* in the spring of 1884. They added the *General D. H. Rucker* that fall but replaced it in the summer of 1885 with the former Kountz steamer *General Chas. H. Tompkins*, which had been extensively repaired at Sioux City.[72]

Evans's main interest in steamboats was to operate them from the railroads at Bismarck and Chamberlain to Fort Pierre in conjunction with his overland freighting to the Black Hills. His scheme was undercut by the rapid construction of a branch line northward from Chadron, Nebraska, by the Fremont, Elkhorn, and Missouri Valley Railroad. In 1885 the railroad was completed from Chadron to Buffalo Gap, only about 45 miles south of Rapid City, the distribution point for Black Hills mining communities. In 1886 track was completed to Rapid City.[73]

The collapse of overland freighting from Fort Pierre forced Evans and Woolfolk to emphasize freighting to river sites below Bismarck, which brought them into direct competition with the Benton Transportation Company. Initially Baker, who seemed to like Woolfolk, cooperated with the Evans Line. In 1885 he engaged it as a subcontractor for the delivery of army and Indian goods from Bismarck and Pierre to all government installations between the two towns.[74]

But by the next March, Baker was determined to squelch Evans and any other possible opposition, including a rumored new line of steamers based at Sioux City. He and Charles in Sioux City advertised the Benton Line's expansion plans in regional newspapers and tried to locate agents in key river towns, including Chamberlain and Yankton. They had two goals in mind. They wanted to "scare Fred Evans" and to discourage any other would-be rivals, because, as Baker put it, "we want no new boats in the river."[75]

Actually, Baker and Charles had no reason to fear the Evans Line. Even as they were scheming to unnerve Evans, Woolfolk had come to the realization that he and Evans should consider selling out. He wrote to Baker: "Don't you think you had better buy half interest in our line and see if we cannot work in unison and make money for all interested? I think it could be arranged so you could buy out Evans."[76]

By the end of April 1886 the Benton Line acquired a half interest in the *General Terry* and *General Chas. H. Tompkins*. The half remaining with the Evans Line was covered by stock, which had a par value of $6,250. H. R. Lyon, a Mandan banker, bought over half of the stock. Even if Evans and Woolfolk owned the rest of the stock, which is unlikely, they would have retained less than a fourth interest in each boat. Regardless of the specific financial details, for all practical purposes the former Evans Line vessels were added to the Benton Line.[77]

Despite Baker's complaints about lack of freight and idle boats, he added three more steamers to the Benton Line after acquiring the *General Terry* and *General Chas. H. Tompkins*. The Benton Line purchased the *Eclipse* from Leighton and Jordan, the *Northern Pacific No. 2* from the Northern Pacific Railroad, and the *Missouri* from the federal government.[78] Joseph Leighton and Walter B. Jordan had been willing to sell the *Eclipse* on the condition that the Benton Line give them a reduced rate for transporting their goods from Bismarck to their Buford and Poplar River stores. Thomas C. Power, the Benton Line's main financier, concurred and signed an agreement to that effect with the traders on April 27, 1886.[79]

Northern Pacific No. 2, a stern-wheeler measuring 184.4 × 23.2 × 4.4 feet, was built at Mound City, Illinois, in 1881. The railroad used it and *Northern Pacific No. 1* as transfer boats at Bismarck before completing its Missouri River bridge in 1882. Subsequently, the company operated them on the Yellowstone to forward freight from the advancing railroad. After the Benton Line purchased the *Northern Pacific No. 2* in 1886, Baker had it rebuilt at Bismarck and reregistered it as the *Judith* with the federal customs service.[80] Describing the *Judith* as the "best equipped passenger boat on the Missouri River," Baker hoped the craft would help revive the line's lagging passenger business.[81]

The stern-wheeler *Missouri*, 133 × 25 × 3 feet, was built at Read's Landing, Minnesota, in 1880. Originally named the *Minnie H.*, it was renamed after the government bought it for river improvement work. In May 1886 the boat was laid up at Bismarck in need of major repairs, including replacing twenty broken oak floor timbers and twenty broken oak bottom planks, caulking, and painting. When Baker estimated that he would charge at least $1,675 to make the boat serviceable, the army engineers decided to dispose of it. The Benton Line purchased the *Missouri* sometime before February 1, 1887, and had it ready for the Fort Benton trade by the opening of navigation.[82]

By quickly acquiring the *General Terry, General Chas. H. Tompkins, Eclipse*, and *Missouri*, the Benton Line seemed assured of having a monopoly on upper river steamboating, with the exception of local ferries. But a new threat arose from an unexpected source—the Ohio Coal Company. In 1886 the company, based in St. Paul, had the contract for supplying coal to four army posts—Bennett, Randall, Sully, and Yates. After the completion of railroads to Running Water, Pierre, and Chamberlain, shipping coal to the forts from the railroads became a considerable business for steamboats. The 1886 contract called for the delivery of 2,100 tons.[83]

Baker informed J. E. McWilliams, general manager of the Ohio Coal Company, that the Benton Line could transport the coal from Bismarck, Pierre, Chamberlain, and Running Water to the forts. In addition to the steamboat charges, the company would have to pay for having the coal hauled from the landing to the post. For example, the Benton Line would freight the sacked coal from Pierre to Fort Sully for 25 cents per hundred pounds and charge 75 cents a ton for moving it from the landing to the post.

McWilliams evidently concluded that Baker's proposed charges were too high. So the coal company decided to send the steamer *Minnie Heerman* from the Mississippi to the upper Missouri. The small, 161-ton stern-wheeler, which measured 131 × 30 × 2.6 feet, was partially owned by a Mr. Worden, a stockholder in the Ohio Coal Company. Baker doubted that the vessel could complete the long voyage from the Mississippi and fulfill the coal contract in 1886. But he was disappointed when the boat delivered all the coal. The *Minnie Heerman*'s owners were so satisfied with the vessel's performance that they decided to leave it as a regular trader on the upper Missouri. However, it had a short career. It was snagged and lost three miles below Le Beau on August 23, 1887. Some of the deck freight, including 30 crates of bacon (averaging 450 pounds per crate) and 35 barrels of pork (averaging 356 pounds per barrel), was saved by the crew of the passing *General Chas. H. Tompkins*.[84]

The Benton Line was the only company that ran steamers above Bismarck in the last three years of the Fort Benton trade. In 1885 its *Benton, F. Y. Batchelor, Helena,* and *Rose Bud* made a total of thirteen arrivals at the head of navigation. For the season, the line transported from Bismarck 3,607 tons of freight to Fort Benton and 300 tons to Coal Banks and Poplar River combined. Its down freight, with wool as the main item, amounted to 1,000 tons.[85]

Army engineers did the only other steamboating to Fort Benton that year. Their *Josephine*, which made three arrivals, hauled all the lumber and other materials that were used to construct the steam dredge *City of Fort Benton* at the port. The *Josephine* and one trip by the *Missouri* brought up some 900 tons of freight.

The Benton Line's business declined somewhat in 1886. Five of its boats, with a combined eleven arrivals, delivered 3,045 tons of freight to Fort Benton. Their cargoes to the downstream destinations of Cow Island, Judith River, and Marias River amounted to 700 tons.

Primarily because of the rapidly advancing St. Paul, Minneapolis, and Manitoba Railroad (commonly known as the Manitoba Road), Fort Benton's steamboat business surged in 1887. The port had thirty steamer arrivals. With the exception of two by the government's *Josephine*, the others were all by eight different Benton Line boats. Only its *General Chas. H. Tompkins* was not run to Fort Benton. The amount of freight delivered—6,517 tons—was quite impressive. The most significant import was railroad construction supplies.

At the end of 1886, James J. Hill's projected transcontinental Manitoba Road had been constructed to Minot. Amazingly, in 1887 the line's remaining 550 miles to Great Falls was finished. Construction, which averaged 3.25 miles per day, was accomplished by an impressive workforce of 8,000 men, 3,300 teams for grading, and an additional 650 men and 225 teams for laying track and building bridges. The line was completed to the Fort Benton depot, 2 miles from the town, on September 28 and to Great Falls, emerging as the region's most significant locality, on October 15.[86]

As the Manitoba Road was being built between Minot and Great Falls, Hill and his Montana associate Charles A. Broadwater were building the Montana Central from Helena to Great Falls. This important branch line was completed a month after the Manitoba Road reached Great Falls.

Other than transporting railroad supplies in its various steamers, the Benton Line chartered the *F. Y. Batchelor* to Shepard, Winston, and Company for the entire season. The St. Paul firm, headed by David C. Shepard, was Hill's main contractor. At a monthly rate of $1,000, the contractor, who used the vessel only part of April, paid the Benton Line $6,700 for the April–October use. Mainly because of costly repairs to ready the vessel, the Benton Line's profit was limited to $3,009.20.[87]

Shepard, Winston, and Company also shipped supplies on the *General Terry* and *Eclipse* to Fort Benton and other landings from Williston westward to the Milk River, where the railroad generally ran close to the river. The records of the *General Terry* show how the railroad shortened steamboat runs as the season progressed. On its first trip to Fort Benton (May 12–June 6), the boat started at Bismarck. Its next voyage to Fort Benton began at the mouth of the Little Muddy River (present-day Williston), where the railroad first touched the Missouri. Subsequently, the boat started for Fort Benton from the mouth of the Big Muddy, a temporary railhead near present-day Culbertson, Montana.[88]

For the 1887 boating season, Benton Line steamers made twenty-five upstream trips from Bismarck and points above. Their freight total was 6,979 tons, nearly two-thirds of which was general merchandise for the Manitoba Road and Fort Benton merchants. Their business with Shepard, Winston, and Company alone amounted to slightly over 1,100 tons. Cargo of the twenty-five return trips amounted to nearly 1,262 tons. Wool, at 750 tons, was the main item, and domestic animal hides ranked next. The region's changing economy was indicated by the exportation of nearly 130 tons of grain. Something of its social life was shown by the deportation of 12.5 tons of beer cases.[89]

Steamers starting at points from Bismarck to Sioux City made thirty trips. They carried 6,064 tons and 1,020 passengers.

The passenger business, which was quite heavy for that time, was mainly due to troop movements. Most of the military passengers were carried on two short runs, when two regiments exchanged stations. The *Rose Bud* moved 235 troops, officers, and dependents from Bismarck to Fort Yates, and the same number from Fort Yates to Bismarck. A similar exchange took place downstream, where the *General Chas. H. Tompkins* transported 240 men and officers from Fort Bennett and Fort Sully to Fort Pierre, and an equal number from Fort Pierre to Fort Bennett and Fort Sully.[90]

Despite the extensive troop movements in 1887, the army's impact on upper

TABLE 7
BENTON LINE FREIGHT SCHEDULE FOR MAY 6–JUNE 30, 1887, FROM BISMARCK TO FORT BENTON

Type of freight	Charge ($ per hundredweight)
Heavy groceries, grain, flour, and lumber	1.00
Building material, hardware, and glass	1.10
Dry goods, drugs, and light freight	1.25
Oranges, lemons, and other fruit	1.25
Furniture	1.50
Buggies, carriages, and showcases	2.00
Machinery and harvesters	Special rates to be negotiated

Source: See note 92 of chapter 11.

river steamboating had declined during the 1880s. With the advance of railroads and settlers and the accompanying consignment of Indians to reservations, there was less need for fortifications. From 1878 to 1884, Forts Rice, Stevenson, and Hale in Dakota Territory were closed, as were Forts Logan and Benton in Montana Territory. Additionally, the construction of the Northern Pacific through the Yellowstone valley caused steamboats to lose the Fort Custer and Fort Keogh business. In 1887, shipment of army goods by steamboat from Bismarck to Fort Benton amounted to only about 7 percent of the total.[91]

Despite its monopoly on commercial steamboating above Bismarck, the Benton Line had to keep its rates low to meet competition from the Northern Pacific and connecting overland freighters. Baker's freight schedule for May 6–June 30, 1887, from Bismarck to Fort Benton enumerated varying charges based on type of cargo (table 7) and prescribed that higher rates would be charged before May 6 and after June 30. Thus the Benton Line's schedule followed the customary practices of adjusting rates to anticipated water conditions and determining the amount of space required for different types of goods.[92]

The Benton Line's passenger business was greatly reduced after the Northern Pacific reached Helena. Most passengers, even if their destination was Fort Benton, preferred to take the train to Billings or Helena and travel by stagecoach the rest of the way. In 1886 only 300 steamboat passengers arrived at or left Fort Benton, whereas 1,750 passengers had done so in 1882, the year before the Northern Pacific was completed to Helena. For both 1886 and 1887 the Benton Line passenger rate from Bismarck to Fort Benton was $35 for cabin and $20 for deck passage respectively.[93]

During the last two years of the Fort Benton trade, the Benton Line posted respectable profits. In 1886 its *Benton*, which reached the head of navigation twice and made other voyages, had receipts of $28,137.57 for freight and $1,500.90 for passengers. After deducting its expenses, which included $8,186.13 for wages, $5,014.06 for repairs, and $4,890.60 for fuel, the vessel's net gain was $7,295.12.[94]

In 1887 the line gained an average of $6,703 on its nine boats. But the returns included the sale of the *Benton, Judith,* and *General Chas. H. Tompkins,* the sinking and loss of the uninsured *Eclipse,* and a loss of $1,997.29 on the *Missouri* after deducting its purchase price. The *Rose Bud,* with a gain of $12,815 on its operations, was the most profitable.[95]

Part of the reason for the line's success was Baker's management style. He oversaw every operational detail and insisted that captains and clerks keep him informed of any expenses and labor problems. Holding money very dear, he consistently tried to suppress wages. He probably had more power than any other agent in the history of Missouri River steamboating. Traditionally, captains and clerks had been part owners of the vessels they operated, but Benton Line officers were hired employees. And Baker treated them as such. The monthly wages of the *General Terry*'s crew were $150 for the captain, $160 for the pilot, $100 for the clerk, $100 for the first engineer, $75 for the second engineer, $40 for the first cook, $20 for the second cook, $18 each for the cabin boy, pantryman, and chambermaid, and $30 each for three firemen and nineteen roustabouts.[96]

Realizing the impact the Manitoba Road to Fort Benton and beyond would have on future steamboating, Baker moved decisively before the end of the 1887 season. In July he started arranging for the sale of the *Benton, Eclipse,* and *Judith* in St. Louis by his father. In late August, John Baker sold the *Benton* to the St. Louis and Tennessee River Packet Company for $6,000. Subsequently, he sold the *Judith,* estimated to have an $11,000 value, for an unspecified sum. The *Eclipse,* which Isaac P. Baker thought was worth $7,000 to $8,000, was snagged and sank 15 miles below Sioux City on September 3 while heading for St. Louis.[97]

By fall, Baker had decided that the Benton Line's future business would require only five boats. He decided to send the *General Chas. H. Tompkins* to his father for sale in St. Louis. Aside from the lack of trade, Baker wanted to dispose of the boat to repay the loan he had obtained to buy a 7.5 percent stake in it. Most of the sales proceeds were paid to creditors, but the boat did show a profit of $1,262.93 for the year.[98]

The Manitoba Road changed the dynamics of upper river steamboating. Most importantly, it ended the Bismarck–Fort Benton long hauls. However, because it touched the river only at Williston and some points in Montana below the Milk River, some communities on the Missouri could be supplied only by boat. Realizing that river transportation was the best mode between the Northern Pacific at Bismarck and the Manitoba Road at Williston, Baker anticipated a long, profitable trade in that stretch. While he was reducing his fleet, he wrote to John Mercer of Fort Buford, "I have to say that steamboats will be running on the upper Missouri as far in the future as they have in the past."[99] Baker lived long enough to realize the fallacy of his prediction.

12

THE LAST YEARS

In the late nineteenth and early twentieth centuries, commercial steamboating on the Missouri and its navigable tributaries was severely challenged and ultimately ended by railroad expansion and new watercraft technology. Continuing railroad construction forced most boatmen into short-haul trade between railheads. Because this local trade did not require large vessels, some operators began using gasoline motorboats.

This short-haul mode was evident on the St. Louis–Sioux City section by the mid-1870s. Railroad extensions to Yankton, Bismarck, Running Water, Pierre, and Chamberlain caused a similar pattern in much of the upper valley. Finally, with the completion of a railroad to Fort Benton in 1887, short-haul navigation was the commonest method throughout the river's course. The most notable exception to this pattern was the St. Louis–Kansas City run, where various steamboat entrepreneurs engaged in head-to-head competition with the railroads.

The segmenting of the Missouri River trade into lower and upper regions and sections within them became more rigid as boatmen emphasized local markets. Beginning in 1882, for administrative convenience the Army Corps of Engineers used the southern edge of Sioux City as the demarcation between the lower the upper rivers.[1] Its compilations of trade statistics were invariably reported for each section. Further, it divided each of the broad areas into sections. The lower river was subdivided into two sections, with their demarcation at Kansas City. From Sioux City to Fort Benton there were three sections—Sioux City to Bismarck, Bismarck to Fort Buford, and Fort Buford to Fort Benton. The stream's uppermost navigation section lay above Fort Benton, from Great Falls to Stubbs Ferry, near Helena.

During steamboating's twilight years, the Missouri's heaviest commerce by far was below Kansas City. Sioux City–Fort Benton boating was locally significant at Running Water, Chamberlain, Pierre, and Bismarck. With the exception of ferry and sand businesses, there was only incidental commerce between Kansas City and Sioux City. The modest freight and passenger business above Great Falls required only several small steamers.

Army engineers categorized steamboating below Kansas City as short trade, long trade, ferriage, and excursion. Short-trade steamers, whose round-trips averaged less than 100 miles, usually ran in combination with railroads. Their major ports were Hermann and Jefferson City on the Missouri Pacific's main line and Boonville, which was connected to the Missouri Pacific in 1868 by a branch line from Tipton.[2]

Short-trade boatmen ordinarily served river communities and landings that had been bypassed by railroads. Numerous landings, which were the most convenient grain, produce, and livestock markets for farmers who relied on horse- or mule-drawn wagons, dotted the rural landscape. For example, there were nineteen landings, other than the town of Portland, in the 48 miles from Hermann upstream to Jefferson City.[3]

Typically, short-trade lines consisted of only one boat. In 1877 the Missouri River and Railway Fast Freight Line ran the small stern-wheeler *Morning Star* from Jefferson City. Its triweekly voyages extended only 31 miles upstream to Wolf Point. But it was the only regular freight packet offering service to Claysville, Marion, Providence, and other intermediate landings. It was scheduled to leave the Jefferson City railroad depot landing at 7:00 A.M. on Tuesday, Thursday, and Saturday and to return on Monday, Wednesday, and Friday in time for the St. Louis trains.[4]

The Missouri Pacific and the River and Railroad Transportation Company offered a comparable service out of Boonville in 1878 with the *Head Light*. Captained by W. C. Postal, the boat made daily round-trips from Boonville to Arrow Rock, 15 miles apart. In 1879 Postal, who then worked out of Boonville with both the Missouri Pacific and the Missouri, Kansas, and Texas railroads, switched to the Boonville–Jefferson City section. His triweekly service was coordinated with the Missouri Pacific's Jefferson City schedule, and he delivered upbound freight at Boonville for both railroads.[5]

The short trade out of Boonville and Jefferson City persisted for most of the 1880s. Various steamers, including the *Morning Star, Bright Light,* and *Aggie,* hauled railroad freight to river landings and usually returned with sacked wheat, produce, and livestock.[6]

Much of the short trade was ruined by new lines constructed by the Missouri Pacific and the Missouri, Kansas, and Texas. In July 1888 the Missouri Pacific completed its Boonville-to-Lexington branch. It ran along the Missouri's south bank for about 10 miles west of Boonville and then struck northwestward to Grand Pass. It again followed the river's south side from just east of Waverly to Lexington. Two years later the railroad was building a Boonville–Jefferson City line.[7]

In 1892 and 1893 the Missouri, Kansas, and Pacific built a competing line on the north side of the Missouri. Running from New Franklin on the west to the Bellefontaine bridge below St. Charles on the east, the road was reported to be doing a good business soon after it opened in the summer of 1893.[8] The Missouri River Commission observed that the railroad "has contributed not a little in diminishing the amount of freight carried by the short-line packets in the lower river."[9]

These new tracks forced boatmen into restricted sections where railroads did

The 92-feet long *Aggie* was used in the 1880s short-haul trade on the lower Missouri and Osage.
Used by permission, State Historical Society of Missouri, Columbia.

not flank streams. Their best possibilities were parts of the Missouri such as the section between New Franklin to slightly east of Waverly, and parts of the Osage and the Gasconade.

The popularization of short trading led boatmen to adjust the style of their craft to the new reality. Because their shuttle businesses did not require large carrying capacities and their passenger trade was ordinarily light, they generally switched to much smaller vessels. Not only did operators economize on construction costs and insurance, but they could reap additional savings by having smaller crews and using less fuel. In this last stage of steamboat evolution, boatmen only did what several generations of their predecessors had done. They adapted to prevailing conditions.

Many observers of the small steamers probably thought they were witnessing a devolution. As compared especially with the elegant passenger boats of the 1850s, the last-generation packets did not bear even a hint of luxury. Typically they were little, shallow-draft stern-wheelers with the machinery and most of the cargo crammed onto the main deck. Some of them also had a crew's compartment on that level. Features above the main deck varied from model to model. Some had only a pilothouse atop a short boiler deck. But others had both a crew's compartment and pilothouse on the boiler deck. Another fashion was three levels—main deck, boiler deck with compartment, and a short pilothouse atop the compartment.

Usually, they did not provide sleeping quarters or meals, except for the crew. The smallest packets had only one engine, one boiler, and one chimney.[10]

In 1887 fifteen of the nineteen Missouri River steamers in the customs district of St. Louis were small packets. Their capacities ranged from a minuscule 4 tons for the *A. W. Ewing* and *Troy* to 106.52 tons for the *Statie Fisher,* whose dimensions were 122 × 28.8 × 4.6 feet. Even at that size, the *Statie Fisher* had only one engine, one boiler, and one chimney.[11]

Unlike their large predecessors, which were ordinarily built at Pittsburgh and other traditional sites, the small packets were usually built close to their home base. Construction places of the 1887 boats included such communities as Osage City and Hermann on the Missouri and Linn Creek, Tuscumbia, and Warsaw on the Osage. It is quite likely that railroad transportation was an important factor in the decentralization of boat construction. With railroads, such highly specialized parts as engines and boilers, whose leading manufacturer was James Rees and Company of Pittsburgh, could be shipped conveniently to distant places.

In their quest to economize, some boatmen abandoned steamers in favor of gasoline packets powered by internal combustion engines. The use of the engines in watercraft coincided with their adaptation by pioneer automobile makers in the 1890s. Those navigators who turned to gasoline packets were apparently convinced that they saved time and money relative to steamers. Gasoline was lighter, cheaper, easier to handle, and much less space-consuming than wood, and refueling did not require long stops. Further, gasoline packets could be operated with Spartan crews. The captain usually doubled as the engineer, and there was no need for firemen. Thus, in addition to the captain-engineer, the crew usually included only a pilot, five or six deckhands, a cook, and a watchman.[12]

Gasoline packets generally resembled small steamers sans chimneys. They were light-draft stern-wheelers whose engines were 50 to 75 horsepower. About seven-eighths of the main deck space was used for cargo.[13]

The Missouri's first gasoline packet, the *Jumbo,* ran out of Hermann in 1891. Owned by the Honig brothers, the 25-ton craft measured 57.5 × 16 × 2.75 feet. In 1893, when the *Jumbo* was being operated on the Gasconade, six gasoline packets were engaged in short trade on the Missouri. The largest measured 78 × 14 feet, and their aggregate tonnage was about 182. They were credited with transporting 11,866 tons during the navigation season, about 4.5 percent of the total commerce downstream from Kansas City.[14]

More complete information about gasoline packets became available after they were brought under federal registration and inspection requirements in fiscal 1898. In 1897 eleven of them were operated between Hermann and Sioux City. Six ran from Missouri ports and four from Nebraska, with one based in Sioux City (table 8).[15]

Despite the increasing popularity of gas boats in the early twentieth century, some steamboat use persisted. The gas vessels were too small for moving quantities of grain over such long hauls as the St. Louis–Kansas City route. Furthermore,

TABLE 8

GASOLINE PACKETS OPERATING BETWEEN
HERMANN AND SIOUX CITY IN 1897

Name	Dimensions (feet)	Tonnage	Owner
RUNNING FROM MISSOURI PORTS			
Hermann	73.7 × 12.8 × 3.0	23.49	Hugo Kropp of Hermann
L. B.	63.2 × 10.3 × 3.2	13.32	Henry Strutmann of Jefferson City
Little Sam	60.0 × 13.0 × 2.5	13.53	J. T. Toomes of Rocheport
Romana	54.6 × 11.0 × 3.2	15.44	William L. Huber of Westphalia
Liberty	79.3 × 18.0 × 3.2	39.94	E. J. Held of Thornton
Sadie G.	Not reported	10	W. E. Garrett of Independence
RUNNING FROM NEBRASKA PORTS			
Ada, Queen of the West	55.0 × 16.1 × 3.0	25.21	A. Z. Martin of Brownville
Asa	74.0 × 12.5 × 2.4	21.44	W. F. Parker of Omaha
Mike Bauer	75.0 × 15.0 × 3.0	Not reported	Mike Bauer of Nebraska City
W. J. Bryan	Not reported	28.5 tons	Bellevue Transfer Company of Bellevue
RUNNING FROM SIOUX CITY			
Iowa	Not reported	48	B. H. Kingsbury

Source: See note 15 of chapter 12.

some short-trade steamboatmen chose to run their vessels as long as they were serviceable and in some instances replaced them with new steamers.

In contrast to short-trade operators, long-trade boatmen wanted the capability of moving sizable amounts of freight in a single trip. Consequently, they experimented with towboats and barges and continued to use large steamers. Since their vessels were not well adapted to the river, they wanted the river to be adapted to them. Unlike local traders, long traders tended to be controlled by major investors, who with the support of St. Louis and Kansas City business leaders, became powerful advocates of Missouri River improvement. Wanting something more than traditional snag removal, they ultimately sought the creation of a navigation channel established and maintained by the government. Also, rather than work with railroads, the long traders challenged them at all points along the lower river, including Kansas City.

On the lower river, the St. Louis–Kansas City run was the utmost long trade. The drive to reestablish and maintain its regular boat service grew out of the farmers' rebellion against railroads. As a way of forcing railroad rates down, shippers wanted reliable river service to New Orleans, the leading entrepôt for the international market. Conversely, they believed that upbound boats could save them more money by delivering consumer goods.

Kansas Citians started and led the long campaign to reestablish river trade with St. Louis. Their first impulse was to use barges. In late January 1878 a "large meeting" of Kansas City's "leading grain dealers and capitalists" called for organizing a barge line capable of moving 100,000 bushels per trip.[16] In response, the Mississippi Valley Transportation Company had the steam tug *Storm* tow three empty barges to Kansas City the following summer. Although they returned to St. Louis in early July with 83,450 bushels of corn, the company decided they were too large for the Missouri. The Babbage Transportation Company followed quickly with three small barges towed by the tug *Grand Lake*, which made three St. Louis–Kansas City round-trips in July and August. Outwardly, the voyages, on which they hauled a total of 208,516 bushels of corn and 44,198 of wheat, were successful, because the company made a 100 percent profit. But the tug and barges had to stop running because of low water. The annual coinciding of harvest time and low river stages was the principal deterrent to tug and barge traffic.[17]

Nonetheless, barge promoters thought they were witnessing the likely revival of steamboating in a new form. The 1882 report of the *Trade and Commerce of the City of St. Louis* observed that the recently introduced barge system "promises at no distant date to revolutionize the grain trade of the West."[18]

Such optimism was sobered by low water. In August 1882 the towboat *Fearless*, belonging to a Kansas City company, sank about 40 miles above the river's mouth while descending on its first trip. Its two barges, loaded with wheat and lumber, were not damaged. The boat's operators had intended to make a round-trip from St. Louis to Kansas City, but because of the shallow current had to pick up freight near Brunswick and turn about.[19]

A report in the 1882 *Trade and Commerce of the City of St. Louis* proclaimed that the attempt "to organize a barge line for handling bulk freight on the Missouri was a failure; and those who have given the matter thought, and looked at it from a practical standpoint, are of the opinion that until the river is improved there can be no success with barges on this stream."[20]

Nonetheless, later companies using large steamboats sometimes towed barges when the channel was deep enough.

The Kansas City Packet Company was the first to enter the field. In 1882 it ran the *David R. Powell*, a side-wheeler (258 × 38 × 7 feet) newly built at Cincinnati. The company, which provided the only regular St. Louis–Kansas City boat service, depended heavily on shipments of wheat, corn, flour, pork, and livestock from river towns that did not have rail connections. By charging less than railroads, the firm hoped to build a paying trade. But it soon failed financially.[21]

Sanford B. Coulson and his associates obviously thought they could succeed when they announced the formation of the Kansas City and St. Louis Electric Packet Line in February 1885.[22] Including "electric" in their name exuded a certain modernity, which was probably calculated to assure shippers that with electric light–equipped vessels, they would operate round the clock. But its boats were hardly unique. By then electric lights were quite common on steamers.

After Daniel W. Maratta withdrew as general superintendent, the line was managed by Hunter Ben Jenkins, one of Coulson's coinvestors, from his St. Louis office. In the first of its three seasons, the company ran the old Coulson Line's *Dacotah,* as well as the *General Meade,* a mountain boat that had been used for some years on the upper river, and the *C. C. Carroll.* The *C. C. Carroll's* 1,200-ton capacity nearly matched that of the *Dacotah,* but the large vessels were usually only partially loaded. For the 1885 season the three steamers, combined, made forty roundtrips from St. Louis to Kansas City, with three of them extended to St. Joseph. They transported an impressive 185,000 tons. In an attempt to explain the import of that statistic, army engineers observed: "Taking 20,000 pounds or 10 tons as a car load, and counting 30 cars to the train, we have 617 trains as necessary to move 185,000 tons of way freight, or one train each way for every day of the year excepting Sundays." The steamboats' rate for grain was 10 to 15 cents per hundredweight and shippers had to pay 2 percent cargo insurance.[23]

Its initial experience emboldened the company to expand. Captain James Kennedy of Kansas City, one of the line's officers, thought that: "with good crops of corn and wheat, there is plenty of business between Saint Joseph and Saint Louis still for three or four good boats, both up and down stream."[24] Part of the firm's expansion included purchasing the *Wyoming,* originally built by Coulson for the upper river. In February 1886, Coulson, Jenkins, and Captain George G. Keith paid over $20,000 for the vessel. Before the opening of navigation, they replaced the *General Meade* with the *David R. Powell.* With the *C. C. Carroll, Dacotah, David R. Powell,* and *Wyoming,* the Electric Line was the largest packet company on the lower river in 1886. Some competition was offered by the Portland Packet Company, which ran the *Dora No. 2* and *New Haven* from St. Louis to Portland, and the Augusta Packet Company, which operated the *General Meade* from St. Louis to Augusta.[25]

By 1887 the Electric Line was in serious financial straits. It operated the *Dacotah* for part of the year before selling it to parties for use on the lower Mississippi. Although the company failed, it did gain certain bragging rights when the *Dacotah* set a new Missouri River cargo record for a descending trip. On its 11-day, 17-hour round voyage the vessel hauled more than 16,000 sacks of wheat (135 pounds each), several hundred packages, and a number of hogs from Kansas City to St. Louis. Its Kansas City delivery consisted of 5,200 railroad ties (179 pounds each) and 450 tons of miscellaneous freight.[26]

Jenkins made sure that other boatmen were reminded of the *Dacotah's* record cargo and captain, George G. Keith. In his St. Louis office, he kept a manifest of the famous cargo as well as pair of elk horns that he promised to award any steamer that beat the record.[27]

The Electric Line could not compete effectively with railroads. Slower-moving steamboats could not attract enough high-class freight that commanded the best rates. Railroad freight was of five classes, with perishable goods being the

The *A. L. Mason* was the key vessel in the Kansas City and Missouri River Transportation Company's effort to revive St. Louis–Kansas City river commerce in the early 1890s. *Used by permission, State Historical Society of Missouri, Columbia.*

highest, and bulky items such as corn and wheat being the lowest. Because railroads could not transport all freight promptly during the harvest season, they left an opening for steamboats to secure part of the market. However, railroads naturally gave preference to high-class goods, which defaulted some of the grain trade to steamboats. The railroad preference for first-class freight is understandable, because its Kansas City–St. Louis rate was 55 cents per hundredweight, whereas its rate for grain was 15 to 20 cents[28]

Steamboat operators, when they could obtain first-class freight, usually transported it for 30 cents. Their charge for fifth class ranged from 9 to 12 cents. However, their lower rates were not necessarily advantageous to shippers who wanted fast deliveries. St. Louis wholesale merchants reported that retailers in river towns without rail service would usually order boat deliveries if the vessel could leave within a day of their requisition's receipt. Otherwise, they would ship by rail and connecting stage and wagon transportation rather than wait even two days for a boat.

The difficulty of matching railroad service was aggravated by continued high operating costs. Concerned about the traditional high-risk nature of Missouri

River steamboating, underwriters charged premiums as high as 12 to 13 percent on hull insurance for portions of the river in the mid-1880s.[29]

The one big lesson that was instructive to the Electric Line's immediate successor was that it had to obtain more high-class freight by actively soliciting the patronage of Kansas City merchants. The Kansas City and Missouri River Transportation Company, formed at Kansas City in November 1889, tried to make its venture a community effort. With A. L. Mason as president and Phil E. Chappell, a former Osage River steamboatman and Missouri state treasurer, as one of its directors, the company sold stock publicly. In its first few weeks over $50,000 was subscribed.[30] The company's formation was well publicized and enthusiastically greeted in Missouri River towns. The editor of the *Boonville Weekly Advertiser*, for example, thought the line would be "of great benefit to Boonville and all other intermediate points. . . . Hundreds of Kansas City people remember the old times and all of them earnestly wish for their return. Their wish seems almost on the eve of realization."[31]

The Kansas City and Missouri River Transportation Company started auspiciously by having three large steamers built at Madison, Indiana, in 1890. The *A. L. Mason*, *State of Kansas*, and *State of Missouri* were all stern-wheelers designed primarily for freight, but with some passenger accommodations. The *A. L. Mason* and *State of Kansas* had exactly the same dimensions (252 × 52.6 × 6 feet) and tonnage (1,130). But the *State of Missouri* was slightly larger (252 × 56 × 6.5, tonnage 1,220).[32]

The *A. L. Mason*, the first to be completed, left Madison in June for its inaugural voyage from St. Louis to Kansas City. To celebrate the occasion, Mason encouraged investors to meet the boat at Lexington or some other downstream point and ride triumphantly to Kansas City. Far more than investors were fascinated by the apparent revival of river transportation. When Captain A. K. Ruxton docked the boat at Kansas City on the night of July 8, a crowd of fifteen thousand spectators greeted them. The *State of Kansas* left St. Louis on its maiden run to Kansas City on August 28. Apparently, the novelty of a steamboat landing at Kansas City had not waned. Hundreds of people jammed the levee to welcome it.[33]

In its first season, the Kansas City and Missouri River Transportation Company made thirteen St. Louis–Kansas City round-trips, eleven by the *A. L. Mason* and two by the *State of Kansas*. Company officials decided there was not enough business to add the *State of Missouri*, which they entered in the St. Louis–New Orleans trade.[34]

A year-end report by the Commercial Club of Kansas City detailed the season's work of the *A. L. Mason*, which transported a total of 4,767 tons on ten of its round-trips (no details are available on the fourth trip). Its total freight revenues were $12,664.23, which was $8,862.69 less than the cost of shipping a comparable amount by rail. This saving to shippers was hailed as a great accomplishment, but the extent and nature of the cargoes obviously troubled the boats' owners. Since its twenty cargoes averaged only slightly more than 200 tons, the large vessel was usually lightly loaded. Furthermore, over three-fourths of its freight was fifth class and only about 4 percent of it first class.

But in its public utterances the company predicted better times lay at hand. In March 1891 it announced that all of its steamers would operate on the Missouri that year. It intended to run the *A. L. Mason* and the *State of Kansas* in the St. Louis–Kansas City trade and the *State of Missouri* on the St. Louis–Glasgow route. The plan was to alternate weekly departures from St. Louis of the Kansas City boats and to make weekly St. Louis–Glasgow voyages.[35]

But its performance did not live up to the advance notice. The *State of Missouri* was not put on the river, and the company withdrew the *A. L. Mason* and the *State of Kansas* in mid-September because of low water. Actually, it had been threatening "for some time" before then to remove the boats because of "parsimonious patronage" by Kansas City merchants.[36] For the season, the *A. L. Mason* and *State of Kansas*, combined, transported 4,774 tons, only 7 more than the *A. L. Mason* had done on ten of its round-trips in 1890.[37]

Prospects brightened in 1892, when company officials relished such newspaper articles as "The Mason Is Making Money" and "It Was A Good Season."[38] The combined upstream trade of the *A. L. Mason* and *State of Kansas* was 7,888 tons, even though low water ended navigation in September. The *A. L. Mason* hauled nearly twice as much as the *State of Kansas*, which was operated on other streams part of the year. On one of its trips, the *A. L. Mason* delivered 1,100 tons of freight to Kansas City, the largest cargo ever brought up the Missouri without using barges. The load consisted of canned goods and other groceries, glassware, hardware, buggy frames, and patent medicines.[39]

Citing the large freight increase over previous years, the company insisted that its 1892 trade had demonstrated the usefulness of steamboats. The *Boonville Weekly Advertiser* concluded, "In addition to carrying a considerable quantity of freight at a very low figure, the boats have materially assisted in keeping down freight rates by rail."[40]

Despite its improved performance, the Kansas City and Missouri River Transportation Company was still not satisfied with the degree of patronage from Kansas City businessmen. Before the opening of navigation in 1893, it issued a circular to retailers and wholesalers, asking for their guaranteed business. With such support, the company pledged it could have the *A. L. Mason* under way from St. Louis on March 21, with the *State of Kansas* leaving Cincinnati on April 2 and the *State of Missouri* departing from New Orleans on May 21. Actual launching of the trips would depend on the amount of assured freight.[41]

Aid from the merchants was not forthcoming. The threat of an imminent nationwide financial panic made businessmen wary of overextending themselves. Meanwhile, the boat company had internal problems. The A. L. Mason estate held a mortgage on the *State of Missouri* and the company was indebted to a St. Louis dock company. To help cover its obligations, the firm sold the *State of Kansas* for approximately $23,000 to Captain T. B. Simms of Memphis, Tennessee. But it still hoped to operate the *A. L. Mason* from St. Louis to Kansas City and to finally enter the *State of Missouri* in the Missouri River trade.[42]

But any hopes of recouping business were ruined by a full-fledged panic when the New York stock market collapsed in late June.[43] The lower Missouri River steamboat trade, which "suffered in the general depression of business, as did every other department of industry,"[44] declined by about a third in 1893. Challenged by reduced trade and a considerable debt, the company moved decisively. In October it sold the *State of Missouri* for $15,000 to the Cincinnati, Memphis, and New Orleans Packet Company and began running the *A. L. Mason* in the Anchor Line between St. Louis and New Orleans. It planned to return the *A. L. Mason* to the Missouri in 1894.[45] But the boat sank on the lower Mississippi in January 1894. The loss prompted the *Boonville Weekly Advertiser* to note pessimistically that many believed "she was the last freight steamer on the Missouri."[46]

In the wake of the *A. L. Mason*'s destruction, there was some wishful thinking about the possible revival of St. Louis–Kansas City steamboating. Captain James Kennedy, formerly of the Electric Line, hoped he could acquire one or two light-draft steamers from the lower Mississippi, and Captain Edward M. Baldwin, one of the pilots on the government snagboat *C. R. Suter*, thought that successful boating could be achieved only by using barges. He believed that a tug towing barges could carry freight for a third less than steamboats.[47] But these were only notions. A concerted effort to reestablish steamboat service between St. Louis and Kansas City did not occur until 1906.

The project grew out of a Kansas City campaign to have the federal government channelize the Missouri River as high as Kansas City. With a minimum-depth channel (8 and 12 feet were suggested as possibilities), Kansas City boosters thought they could have a significant barge trade.[48]

Congressman Edgar C. Ellis, Missouri's fifth district representative, spearheaded the channelization drive. Soon after his election in 1904, Ellis sought support from the National Rivers and Harbors Congress, a voluntary association, as well as from key members of Congress and President Theodore Roosevelt. Acting in his capacity as a member of the congressional Rivers and Harbors Committee, Ellis called a meeting of Kansas City businessmen on July 30, 1906, and encouraged them to form a Missouri Valley Improvement Association. Within a week and a half the association was organized, with Lawrence M. Jones, owner and operator of Jones Dry Goods Company, as president. Its principal aims were to prove the Missouri was navigable and to secure congressional appropriations for channelization.

Jones and the association's executive committee realized that in order to gain congressional support, they had to demonstrate that the Missouri was navigable. After the congressional abolition of the Missouri River Commission in 1902, most politicians assumed that boating had ended on the stream and was not likely to be revived. Jones knew that to dispel this notion, the association needed to organize a steamboat voyage, which, he believed, would have great symbolic value.

With funding from the Kansas City Commercial Club, Jones went to St. Louis, where he chartered the stern-wheeler *Lora* to make a September round-trip to

Kansas City. The boat was probably selected because of its relatively small size (150 × 30 × 4.5 feet). September was a low-water month, and Jones wanted a boat that would succeed.[49]

With Captain W. N. Mills in command and the veteran pilot William R. Massie as its most famous crewman, the well-loaded *Lora* left St. Louis on September 15, towing a 250-ton barge. Prominent passengers included Jones; A. G. Ellett, vice president of the Commercial Club's Freight Line Committee; W. P. Trickett, the club's transportation bureau commissioner; and reporters for the *Kansas City Star* and two St. Louis newspapers. Jones and his co-boosters obviously sought publicity. When the boat stopped at Boonville, Trickett made a point of talking to the local press. He said the steamer had engaged a full load of grain and grain products for the return trip and that it would undercut railroads by 40 percent.[50]

D. M. Bone, publicist for the venture, observed that "few things Kansas City has done have attracted such wide-spread attention to the city and given it such general and favorable advertising throughout the whole country as the remarkably successful voyage of the *Lora*." He reported that the vessel's ascent was celebrated at towns, villages, and landings from St. Louis to Kansas City because it "was rightly hailed as marking the resumption of navigation on the Missouri." At Kansas City a levee crowd of more than ten thousand people cheered the *Lora*'s landing.[51]

To prove that the *Lora*'s voyage was not a fluke, Jones and the Commercial Club arranged for trade by the *Thomas H. Benton*. The small seventeen-year-old sternwheeler (125 × 34.6 × 4.3 feet) had been used as a Quincy, Illinois, ferry for many years.[52]

Chartering the *Lora* and the *Thomas H. Benton* brought the desired instant publicity, but Jones and the Commercial Club decided their long-term needs could be met only by operating their own boats. They formed the Kansas City Transportation and Steamship Company, which was incorporated by the State of Missouri on April 29, 1907, with a capitalization of $200,000. Like the Kansas City and Missouri River Transportation Company of the early 1890s, it sold stock publicly. By May 1907 about $145,000 worth had been subscribed.[53]

The Kansas City Transportation and Steamship Company bought two sternwheelers—the *Cherokee* and the *Tennessee*. Officials renamed the nineteen-year-old *Cherokee*, for which they paid $30,000, the *Chester*. Measuring 216.4 × 33.9 × 6 feet, the boat was intended to be the company's main freighter. The considerably smaller *Tennessee* (170 × 32 × 5.5), for which they paid $10,000, had been built at Jeffersonville, Indiana, in 1897.[54]

The company offered sporadic St. Louis–Kansas City service with the *Chester* and *Tennessee* in 1907 and 1908. Its business was somewhat stultified by the Panic of 1907. In the spring of 1908, which officials hoped would be a better year than 1907, navigation was delayed. As late as early May, H. G. Wilson, the firm's transportation bureau commissioner, was still soliciting freight both ways. The amount of goods in St. Louis was insufficient to fully load even one of the boats. Prospective shippers were reluctant to use the vessels because underwriters would insure

The *Chester*, owned by the Kansas City Transportation and Steamship Company, was used in the St. Louis–Kansas City trade, 1907–1908. *Used by permission, State Historical Society of Missouri, Columbia.*

only for fire rather than issue general cargo insurance policies, which would also cover snagging, the Missouri's greatest risk.[55]

The underwriters' caution was well advised. On September 11 the 334-ton *Tennessee*, while ascending with a towed barge loaded with general merchandise, was snagged and sank a few miles below Kansas City. Although some goods were salvaged, the company suffered a $20,000 loss. Meanwhile, the *Chester*, which had sprung a leak several weeks before, was tied up at the St. Louis levee.[56]

The short-lived Kansas City Transportation and Steamship Company was a financial failure. But assessing it by that standard alone would overlook its value to the crusade by Kansas City shippers to win federal government support for a navigable channel to the sea. As early as the spring of 1909 there was talk about yet another possible revival of river commerce. Lauding the "Kansas City spirit," a boosterish article in the *Missouri and Kansas Farmer* told of a Kansas City businessman who said he had lost all the money he had invested in three previous boating ventures but "was ready to put money into another one."[57] He and men like him contributed to the formation of the last St. Louis–Kansas City steamboat line in 1911. But as D. M. Bone explained, forming an individual line was only a step in "this great movement [for river improvement] which means the commercial and industrial emancipation of the trans-Mississippi West from the thralldom of congested traffic conditions and paralyzing freight rates."[58]

Aside from the attempts to revive St. Louis–Kansas City commerce, there was some intermittent long trading from St. Louis to Osage River ports and to such

Missouri River destinations as Rocheport and waypoints. The principal steamers used in this business were old mountain boats from the upper river. When the railroad extensions to Running Water, Pierre, Chamberlain, Billings, and Fort Benton were devastating upper river commerce, boatmen there generally sold vessels to lower river parties. The lower river trade was poor in comparison with the antebellum decade, which many steamboatmen remembered as the "palmy days." Nonetheless, it was significantly larger than the business above Sioux City.

The amounts of steamboat freight reflected the sharp differences between the two regions. Missouri was relatively populous. In 1870 only four other states had more people. Dakota and Montana territories, which had vast tracts of unsettled land, were lightly settled. Not only was Missouri's population quite dense, but its communities had more of a river orientation that those of the upper Missouri region. In Missouri, where the establishment of river towns and landings had preceded railroads, there was a traditional market for steamboats. But on the upper river, most of the leading communities such as Bismarck, Chamberlain, Pierre, and Williston were railroad offsprings. Their livelihood depended on rail links with the East. Furthermore, the Missouri River counties between St. Louis and Kansas City were in a prime agricultural region. But above Sioux City many of the riverside counties were in semiarid lands with limited agricultural production.

To assess the potential steamboat market of both the St. Louis–Kansas City region and the upper Missouri, the Army Corps of Engineers analyzed census data to estimate the 1885 population and crop production of counties bordering the river. Its researchers determined that in round numbers the Missouri River counties in Missouri had a population of 700,000. From Sioux City to Fort Benton, only 93,500 people lived in counties adjacent to the river. Annual production of grains—barley, corn, oats, rye, and wheat— was about 95,500,000 bushels in the Missouri counties and about 8,224,000 for all the river counties in Dakota and Montana territories.[59]

Since the Missouri economy was much larger than that of the upper river area, it offered more opportunities for steamboatmen. In the fiscal year ending June 30, 1888, when Fort Benton was reached by rail, the steamboat commerce of the region above Sioux City totaled 12,895 tons. It remained relatively static for the next few years. The 1891 tonnage was 13,055. But the 1891 tonnage of only the long- and short-trade packets on the lower river (excluding sand boats, ferries, and rafts) amounted to slightly more than 105,000 tons.[60]

This great disparity, which continued a pattern that was evident by the early 1880s, created a certain shortage of steamers on the lower river and a surplus of them on the upper river. Thus, any lower river operators who needed a steamer found it was far more economical to buy an old mountain boat rather than build a new vessel. Longtime steamboatman William ("Steamboat Bill") L. Heckmann recalled that after railroads "cooked the goose" of upper river boatmen, "anybody wanting to buy a cheap steamboat could take 3 or 4 thousand dollars and go to the upper Missouri and buy himself a steamboat."[61]

THE LAST YEARS 361

Although Heckmann's purchase price was unrealistically low, his overall point was valid. In the 1880s many former upper river steamers, including the *Benton, Dacotah, General Meade, General Terry, Helena, Judith, Montana, Nellie Peck,* and *Wyoming,* were relocated to the lower Missouri or elsewhere.

Until the Missouri, Kansas, and Pacific Railroad completed its track north of the Missouri in 1893, there was usually at least one St. Louis–based steamer running as far upstream as Rocheport. The *Judith* and the *Helena,* both formerly of the Fort Benton Transportation Company, were used in that trade. Captain John L. Massengale and Augustus W. Black, the *Judith's* new owners, first used the boat on the Tennessee River. But in 1888, with Captain Charles B. Able in command, the *Judith* entered the St. Louis–Rocheport trade. Able was trying to complete his third trip when the vessel was snagged and sank 15 miles above St. Charles on July 30.[62]

The *Helena,* commanded by Archibald S. Bryan, was the principal freight packet for several years. Bryan, the nephew of Achilles Lamme, had worked on the Missouri for many years and had assisted his uncle in entering the *Yellowstone* in the Yellowstone River trade. His reputation and acquisition of the *Helena* helped revive hope in the successful future of lower river steamboating. Bryan kept the *Helena* busy. One season it delivered 167,000 sacks of wheat to St. Louis, and in 1891, its last year, it made thirty-two voyages from St. Louis.[63]

Bryan usually made weekly voyages to Rocheport and waypoints on the Missouri with occasional side trips up the Osage. Wheat was the main down cargo, with some lumber, hogs, cattle, lard, bacon, and hams. The up cargoes were a great variety of goods and products, including egg cases, wire, iron, stoves, plows, oil, lumber, shingles, furniture, seed, fish and other groceries, dry goods, clothing, liquor, binder twine, sewing machines, tinware, white lead, oakum, bricks, and saddlery. Freight charges from St. Louis to Warsaw were usually ranged from 15 to 25 cents per hundredweight. Passenger transport, which accounted for only about 3.4 percent of the *Helena's* business, was light. Cabin fares from St. Louis to St. Charles and Rocheport respectively were normally $1 and $2–$3.[64]

Despite their busy schedule, Bryan and his partners had a very disappointing season. With income of $26,377.59 and expenses of $26,630.70, they had a net loss of $253.11. Freight revenue of $24,970.05 accounted for nearly 95 percent of their income. Their only other income was passenger fares of $935.35, bar rent at $430.00, and $42.19 from the sale of sundries. Wages for the boat's officers were modest. Bryan was paid $100 monthly, or $25 more than the compensation for pilots. Nonetheless, over their nearly eight-month navigation season, wages for the entire crew amounted to over $11,500. Other major expenses included $3,377 for stores (provisions for crew), $3,614 for fuel, and $2,914 for repairs. To add to their frustration, they suffered an additional loss when the *Helena* was snagged and sank at the foot of Bonhomme Island, about 12 miles above St. Charles, on October 23.

Soon after the sinking of the *Helena,* long-trade steamboating on the lower river declined sharply. The failure of the Kansas City and Missouri River Transportation Company, the construction of a rail line through river towns and landings on the north side of the river, and the Panic of 1893 combined to dull both long- and short-trade boating.

However, ferrying continued to be significant. Ferry service was needed at a number of points. Even some places that had railroad bridges, such as Boonville and Kansas City, required ferries for local freight and passenger service. But at St. Charles, ferrying by the *John L. Ferguson* was discontinued in 1893 with the completion of a pontoon bridge suitable for wagons and pedestrians.[65]

A good sense of the ferry trade can be gleaned from the statistical record. In 1891 all steam ferries between the Missouri's mouth and Sioux City transported approximately 463,600 tons of freight and 635,600 passengers. Teams, including wagon loads and livestock, accounted for more than four-fifths of the tonnage. The short-run nature of the business is evident from the year's total of 504,161 ton-miles.[66]

While steam ferries were the commonest type, there was some use of cable and horse ferries, which transported 53,900 passengers and 31,709 tons of freight. The persistence of horse ferries is somewhat puzzling, because they were usually small and slow. But at least at Jefferson City in 1889, a four-horse ferry with a capacity of 1,000 sacks of wheat was competing with a steam ferry. Its captain insisted that when he used all four horses to turn the treadmill, the boat could move faster than a steamer.

Like all other steamboats, steam ferries had to be enrolled, licensed, and inspected by the federal government. Typically, their operating area was prescribed in the license. For example, the *Annie Cade,* owned by William A. Cade of Kansas City, Missouri, could run only on the Missouri five miles above or below Kansas City, and the *Joseph L. Stephens,* owned by Miss Mary E. "Birdie" Brent of Boonville, was restricted to crossing between Boonville and the opposite shore. But sometimes ferries were also permitted to engage in short-trade routes. The *Lois,* owned by J. D. Thomas of Waverly, could run 30 miles above or below the town.[67]

Ferries were usually smaller than vessels used as freight carriers up and down the river. The 178-ton *Annie Cade,* built at Leavenworth, Kansas, in 1879, measured 127 × 32 × 4.5 feet. Brent's *Joseph L. Stephens* was 103 × 29.4 × 4.2 feet, with a capacity of 86 tons. The 35-ton *Lois* (75 × 19 × 3) was one of the smallest steam ferries.[68]

Because of is longevity, the *Annie Cade* was probably the best-known ferry on the lower river. Captain Cade, who named the boat for his daughter, ran it from 1879 until 1901, and other boatmen operated the boat until it wore out in 1907. Much of its business was hauling farmers and their produce between Harlem (later North Kansas City) and Kansas City. The boat provided easier access for them than the Hannibal railroad bridge.[69]

In the February 16, 1900 issue, the editor of the *Boonville Weekly Advertiser* noted that the Missouri "has been almost abandoned" by steamboatmen because of its hazardous channel, the inability of shippers to get insurance, and railroads on both sides. The observation was particularly apt with respect to long-trade packets, but short traders had suffered as well.

Trade statistics show the precipitous decline during the 1890s. In 1891, long-trade vessels transported 31,458 tons of freight (6,437,472 ton-miles) and 6,000 passengers. The short-trade packet business was 73,890 tons (1,455,651 ton-miles) and 8,000 passengers. Trade remained at roughly those levels in 1892 but declined by over one-third in grain and livestock and over one-half in miscellaneous products the next year. Shipments of wheat, the single most important commodity, were down nearly 50 percent.[70]

The plight of boating worsened with each passing year. In 1895 the old mountain steamer *Benton* was the only regular long-trade packet on the lower river. It made twenty-three voyages from St. Louis, with four of them extending to Miami, 272 miles above the mouth. But its season was cut short when it hit an obstruction and sank at Arrow Rock on July 31. Although the boat was raised, its indebted owners did not reenter it in the lower river trade. In 1899 the 309-ton *Gus Fowler* was run in the lower river grain trade. But after completing only four voyages, it was snagged and sank.[71]

Only the *Gus Fowler*'s two longest voyages were categorized as long trade. The total long-trade tonnage for 1899 was a depressingly low 715 tons (98,193 ton-miles). Short-trade packets and miscellaneous boats, including ferries, transported over four times as many ton-miles, with an average round-trip of only 11 miles. Sand and wood steamers and barges recorded the highest tonnage. During the 1890s, sand dredging from the Missouri was started at many river communities. Usually the boats that hauled sand and fuelwood operated only in immediate locales. Sand and wood steamers and barges hauled 218,514 tons, and their total ton-miles of only 422,606 mean that their average round-trip was less than 2 miles.[72]

As trade declined, St. Louis lost much of its influence as the entrepôt for lower Missouri River steamboating. As a way of determining the extent of commerce, army engineers had river gauge observers record the number of boats that passed their stations. In 1891 Hermann was the most active point, with 179 steamer passings up and 181 down. St. Charles was next, with 110 up and 112 down. In 1897, when St. Louis had only five departures for the Missouri and nine arrivals from it, no tonnage was sent to the Missouri and only 250 tons were received from it. In 1899 there was a modest increase, with eleven arrivals and fourteen departures. But the receipts were a mere 565 tons, and no freight was sent. On the lower Missouri in 1899, Kansas City, with 193 and 192 up and down arrivals respectively, had the most active business. Coles Creek Landing, about midway from Hermann upstream to the mouth of the Gasconade, was a close second.[73]

The relatively high counts for Hermann and Coles Creek Landing undoubtedly were due to Gasconade River trade to the Missouri Pacific Railroad at Hermann. However, Kansas City's lead in 1899 stemmed from its lively excursion business.

As the number of steamers decreased and the population of the river counties became somewhat more urbanized, steamboat excursions became popular as family and group outings. Ferry operators oftentimes supplemented their usual business by hosting excursions. But in some places, such as Kansas City, there was

The *Libbie Conger*, formerly of the upper Mississippi's Diamond Jo Line,
was operated as an excursion boat at Kansas City in the early 1890s.
Courtesy of the National Mississippi River Museum and Aquarium, Dubuque, Iowa.

enough demand for leisure boating that selected boats were devoted entirely to excursions, and even long- and short-trade packet operators supplemented their trade with excursions.

The *Libbie Conger, Rob Roy, Alda,* and *Edna* were some of the best-known excursion boats. The *Libbie Conger,* originally built and used by Diamond Jo Line on the upper Mississippi, spent several years at Kansas City. When it passed down in August 1892, its managers took out excursionists at Jefferson City and other towns. The *Alda* and *Edna,* built by Joseph Walther of Boonville and named for his little daughters, were used as excursion boats and short traders in the Boonville-Rocheport area.[74]

Normally, excursions were routine affairs. Passengers would enjoy the scenery, listen to the band, and sometimes picnic at the turnabout point. But the *Rob Roy,* running out of Kansas City, once had a memorable adventure reminiscent of the chaotic Civil War days. When the boat was loaded with men, women, and children, six river pirates attempted to seize it. Captain Naff's response was to knock the pirate leader into the river. Then passengers helped throw the others in. Five were rescued, and one drowned.[75]

Excursionists made up most of the 1890s passenger business. Of the 41,823 passengers carried in 1892 by short-trade packets, ferries, and excursion boats, 34,693 were excursionists. In 1899, a very poor year for transporting freight, there were 225,485 excursionists out of a passenger total of 239,022.[76]

Late nineteenth-century steamboating on the lower river continued the tradition of mainly transporting agricultural products. However, in contrast to the hemp and tobacco emphasis of antebellum days, wheat was the principal article shipped on packets.

The change reflected the new face of Missouri agriculture. Wartime manpower shortages caused by military demands and the emancipation of slaves helped devastate the hemp culture—the most labor-intensive type of farming. Furthermore, for much of the war, Missouri was cut off from the South, the main market for its hemp products. The replacement of hemp sheathing with wire bindings for cotton bales soon after the war ruined the remaining market. In 1870, Missouri's hemp production, which had peaked a decade before, was only 2,816 tons. In 1879 and 1890 the state produced a mere 209 and 31 tons respectively. Tobacco production dropped precipitously, but there was some throughout the remainder of the century.[77]

With the declines in demand for hemp and tobacco, farmers, who benefited from the popularization of labor-saving machinery during the war, expanded their production of corn and the various small grains—wheat, oats, barley, and rye. Although its bushel production was second to corn's, wheat increased sharply during and after the war. Missouri's wheat production tripled during the 1860s. Its rank as a wheat-producing state rose from fifteenth on the eve of the Civil War to tenth in 1869 and seventh in 1889.[78]

Although corn was the dominant crop, wheat was the leading steamboat commodity. Wheat was in demand by millers in St. Louis and elsewhere, but most of the corn and oats was used as livestock food on farms.[79]

Part of the trade on the lower Missouri was linked to navigation of the Osage and Gasconade rivers. Commerce on those tributaries did not decline as rapidly as that of the Missouri, because they were less affected by railroads.

The Osage, historically the Missouri's most important commercial tributary, was never flanked by a railroad, but tracks were extended to it at several points. In November 1880 the Missouri Pacific completed a narrow-gauge line from Sedalia on its main track southward to Warsaw, 170 miles above the stream's mouth. During the same year, it also built a narrow-gauge connection from Jefferson City to a landing 70 miles above the mouth, where Bagnell was founded in 1882. These railheads effectively segmented commerce. Above Warsaw, rafters and sometimes a small steamer worked upstream in the 60-mile stretch to Osceola, with their imports and exports flowing through Warsaw. The Bagnell railhead had the same effect for upstream communities and landings toward Warsaw. Most of the packet operators who entered from the Missouri turned about at Tuscumbia, 10 miles below Bagnell.[80]

The two railheads caused a sharp drop in river commerce. In fiscal year 1881, when the branch lines were only partially operative, nine steamers were being used. Combined, they made 182 voyages upstream from the mouth, only 16 of which went above Tuscumbia. The largest boat, the 165 × 29 × 4.5 stern-wheeler *Phil E. Chappell*, made 18 trips, with 2 to Osceola, the head of navigation, and 2 to Warsaw. Three other vessels, combined, had 12 trips to Linn Creek, about 32 miles above future Bagnell. For the year, the total steamboat tonnage was 18,473, valued at approximately $475,000. However, the valley's most valuable commodities—railroad ties and logs— were rafted. Osage communities exported 1,143,000 railroad ties, valued at $457,216; 4 million cubic feet of oak logs, valued at $40,000; and 3 million cubic feet of walnut logs, valued at $75,000. The approximate tonnage of the ties and logs was 102,000 and 133,000 respectively, which, when added to the steamboat freight, brought the river's total commerce to over 253,000 tons.[81]

For the fiscal year July 1, 1885-June 30, 1886, the products shipped upstream by six steamers were valued at $45,960, and the estimated worth of their downstream cargoes was $225,223. The total value of all Osage commerce was $605,915, with 1 million railroad ties, valued at $333,333, the leading commodity. About half of the ties were floated to the Bagnell and Warsaw railheads, and the remainder to or just below Osage City. Tonnages were not compiled, but the ties and 170,000 cubic feet of oak and walnut logs would have amounted to over 93,000 tons.[82]

Throughout the 1890s, Osage commerce had much more stability than that of the lower Missouri. The tie business was strong, and the valley remained free of parallel railroad lines. Annual trade fluctuations were caused by varying demands for ties and logs and differences in agricultural production. The average annual tonnage for 1890–99 was slightly over 83,000 tons, with a high of 105,225 in 1894 and a low of 68,476 the preceding year. In any given year about 83 to 90 percent of the commodities was rafted. In 1894, for example, 73,361 tons of ties and 13,585 tons of wood and lumber were rafted downstream. The 18,299 tons that were moved by steam packets and miscellaneous boats (including an occasional flatboat) consisted of 8,100 of sand and gravel, 4,793 of grain (principally wheat), 2,140 of imported white pine lumber and exported wood, 1,356 of farm machinery and general merchandise, 1,076 of livestock, 440 of barite, 186 of produce, 128 of salt, and 80 of miscellaneous building material.[83]

Unfortunately, in their reports for most of the 1890s, army engineers did not separate export and import statistics, and they used more general categories such as "grain" rather than a specific cereal. However, their report for the fiscal year ending June 30, 1889, gave a more detailed picture of the commerce. For that time the exports consisted of 182,153 bushels of wheat, 4,250 bushels of corn, 200 bushels of clover seed, 1,620 bales of hay, 550 cases of eggs, 2,550 hogs, 520 cattle, 450 sheep, 1,500 sacks of flour, 500 cords of wood, 500 tons of barite, 1,100,000 railroad ties, 1,574,000 cubic feet of oak, ash, elm, sycamore, and walnut logs, 65,000 board feet of walnut lumber, and 846 tons of general merchandise. The imports were 132 sacks of flour, 1,130 barrels of salt, 627 kegs of nails, 382,000 board feet of white pine lumber, 1,800 bushels of coal, 37 tons of farm machinery, and 1,015 tons of general merchandise. With the exception of sand and gravel, which were first reported for 1894, there is no reason to believe the nature of the products changed during the 1890s.[84]

The commerce reflected the valley's economy, which was based on diversified farming, lumbering, and barite mining. Barite, a mineral with a variety of industrial applications, was found near the Osage in the Tuscumbia-Bagnell vicinity.

Some river shipment was reported from 1888 through 1894, with the heaviest exportation—2,775 tons—in 1891.[85]

Mainly because of the tie and log businesses, Osage commerce exceeded that of the Missouri in the late 1890s. For both 1898 and 1899, engineers computed the total ton-miles transported on the streams. In 1898 the Osage trade was over twice the Missouri's, and the following year was more than three times greater. But since approximately 90 percent of the Osage freight was rafted, Missouri River boating was greater than Osage boating.[86]

Most of the Osage steamers were relatively small stern-wheelers specifically designed for small rivers. Many of them were built in the Osage valley. Because the voyages were quite short, the annual fleet was small. In 1890 seven steamers were used, and there were some trips by ten in 1895. But in 1898 most of the trade below Tuscumbia, the most active area, was done by only two steamers.[87]

The heaviest used Osage steam packets in the 1890s were the *Black Diamond*, *Dan B. Hurlburt*, *Frederick*, and *J. R. Wells*. With a capacity of only 12.92 tons, the *Dan B. Hurlburt*, which measured 62.6 × 11 × 2.4, was the smallest. The *Black Diamond* had approximately 50 percent more capacity. The *J. R. Wells*, at 110.6 × 20.4, was the largest. Both the *Frederick* and *J. R. Wells* were built at Tuscumbia, and the *Dan B. Hurlburt* was built at Warsaw.[88]

Because of the slack trade on the lower Missouri, large steamers were sometimes run on the Osage. They included the old upper river mountain boats *Benton*, *General Meade*, and *Helena*. The *General Meade* was used for St. Louis–Tuscumbia runs in 1887, and in the early 1890s both the *Benton* and *Helena* made some voyages. Tuscumbia was their usual destination, but in 1890 Captain Archibald S. Bryan made a Jefferson City–Warsaw round-trip excursion voyage with the *Helena*. Passengers included Jefferson City agents of St. Louis grain buyers, who hoped to promote more business along the Osage.[89]

By 1898. Osage steamboat operators were facing some competition from gasoline packets. The *L. B.*, which was usually run on the Missouri, made five trips, including one as far as Linn Creek. Two other unnamed gasoline boats transported 70 tons in the lower part of the river.[90]

During that year there were only four steamers on the river. Most of the freight was transported by the *Frederick* and the *J. R. Wells*. Both ran in combination with railroads. The *Frederick* was used to connect with the Missouri Pacific at Osage City. The *J. R. Wells*, which the Anchor Milling Company of Tuscumbia owned and operated, worked with the Missouri, Kansas, and Texas Railroad. Its usual voyages were from Tuscumbia to Portland, on the Missouri's left bank 21 miles below the Osage's mouth. Combined, the two vessels made 122 trips, with 6 as high as Linn Creek and 33 to Tuscumbia.

Two very small stern-wheelers were used above Tuscumbia. The *Dauntless* (60.3 × 11.9 × 3.1, tonnage 26) provided shuttle service between Tuscumbia and Linn Creek. Much farther upstream the *Ranger* (36.2 × 10.3 × 3.1, tonnage 5) was run in the 54-mile section from Osceola up to Papinsville.[91]

The Gasconade, like the Osage, was an important commercial tributary of the lower Missouri. The stream, which flowed northward from its source in the Ozark Mountains, joined the Missouri 6.5 miles above Hermann. In the 61 miles from the mouth to Gascondy Landing it was about 400 feet wide with a gradient of 1.23 feet per mile. In that section the river consisted of a succession of pools and fifty-eight shoals. The pools, which were up to 2 miles long, were 4 to 15 feet deep at low water. On average the shoals were 800 feet wide. During favorable water stages, boats drawing from 12 to 15 inches could often reach Gascondy.[92]

But above there the stream was narrower, shallower, and steeper, with aggravatingly sharp bends. Steamboats could sometimes reach the landing for the town of Vienna, 78 miles from the mouth. The landing was the practical head of navigation. But army engineers regarded Arlington—107 miles above the mouth, about 10 miles west of present-day Rolla—as the actual head of navigation because it was once reached by a small steamer.

In comparison with activity on other streams, steamboating on the Gasconade was a relatively late development. There was some experimentation with several steamers on the lower Gasconade around 1870, but their operators soon withdrew. Henry Wohlt of Fredericksburg, a community about 9 miles from the Gasconade's mouth, was the best-known pioneer steamboatman. In 1872 he built the small *Stem*, but he soon replaced it with the *Light Western*. Wohlt's second steamer was used mainly as Hermann's ferry, but he operated it some on the Gasconade.[93]

Regular Gasconade packet trade began out of Hermann in 1880, when Wohlt merged his interests with those of William L. Heckmann (the father of Steamboat Bill). Although their alliance, later formalized as the Hermann Ferry and Packet Company, was sometimes broken for short periods, the Wohlt and Heckmann families dominated Gasconade steamboating well into the twentieth century.

By 1885 Wohlt and Heckmann were running four small stern-wheelers in the Gasconade trade, which they coordinated with the Missouri Pacific at Hermann. Their vessels—*Dora, Fawn, Royal,* and *Vienna*—typified those used subsequently on the river. They all measured about 90 × 20 × 3, with approximately 75-ton capacities and 14-inch drafts.[94]

The nature of Gasconade commerce as established in the 1880s persisted to the end of the stream's navigation. As on the Osage, the bulkiest commodities—ties, logs, and lumber—were rafted. In fiscal 1888 the three Gasconade steamers—*Fawn, Royal,* and *Vienna*—transported 2,817 tons, including 57,212 bushels of wheat (weighing about 1,600 tons), other grains, livestock, flour, salt, nails, and general merchandise. But rafts accounted for 44,750 tons of ties (500,000 ties) and 750 tons of yellow pine lumber.

For the 1890s the Gasconade's average annual commerce was 29,763 tons, with a low of 12,929 in 1892 and a high of 47,544 in 1895. Approximately 86 percent of it was rafted railroad ties, lumber, logs and wood. Steamboats sometimes reached Vienna but normally were operated in the lowest part of the river. In 1898, for example, only 9 percent of steamboat trips went beyond mile 53. Most of the steam-

The 110-foot-long *J. R. Wells* was one of the most popular Osage River steamers in the 1890s. *From the collection of the Public Library of Cincinnati and Hamilton County.*

boating that year was done by the 32-ton *Jack Rabbit* (73 × 16.2 × 3.3), which made forty-five trips, and the *Peerless,* which made twenty-one. Raft trips were generally longer, with the extreme starting point 97 miles up Big Piney Creek, which entered the Gasconade 122 miles above its mouth.[95]

The Missouri River Commission calculated ton-miles of commerce for the Gasconade and Osage after they were placed under its jurisdiction in 1894. The ton-miles for the Gasconade declined from 1894 to 1899. Nonetheless, in 1899 the Gasconade, with 1,387,129, bested the lower Missouri's 1,057,761.[96]

Although its business in the late nineteenth and early twentieth centuries was far below that of the lower river, upper Missouri steamboating remained significant at some sites. The leading port was Bismarck, home of the Benton Transportation Company, which was reorganized into the Benton Packet Company in 1904. Running Water's boating peaked in the late 1890s. Ferries at Chamberlain and Pierre also engaged in some short-haul trading. And during the late 1880s, steamboating was started in a section of the Missouri above Great Falls.

Like the trade on the lower river, the amounts of upper river boating fluctuated considerably. The extent of boating was closely linked to wheat yields, the region's main cash crop. In the quarter century after Fort Benton was reached by rail (1888–1912), waterborne commerce on the upper Missouri had an annual average of 24,729 tons. During 1905, the high year, 52,956 tons were transported, but during the lowest year, 1896, only 9,956 tons were moved. In 1904, the only year for which army engineers reported ton-miles, the 28,951 tons hauled amounted to 1,528,834 ton-miles.[97]

The Gasconade River steamboats *Pin Oak, Fawn,* and *Royal*
were typical of the small stern-wheelers operated as short-haul freighters.
Used by permission, State Historical Society of Missouri, Columbia.

Isaac P. Baker was the central figure in late upper river boating. He dominated the Benton Transportation Company, the region's largest line. When its charter expired in 1904, he and three associates—Thomas C. Power; Charles P. Power, Thomas's son; and Charles W. Blunt—organized the Benton Packet Company of North Dakota. The new firm, which was capitalized at $40,000, lasted until 1924, when two of Baker's sons formed the Benton Transportation Company under North Dakota law. Baker was its general manager, and Blunt its main captain. Blunt, who was only twenty years old when he moved to Bismarck from St. Louis in 1878, operated various boats independently until he became associated with Baker in the late 1890s. The Powers were content to be investors and did not participate in day-to-day company affairs.[98]

After Fort Benton steamboating ended, the Benton Transportation Company initially traded mostly below Bismarck. Its business was based heavily on private trade to such communities as Forest City (on the east side of the Missouri, opposite the Cheyenne River Indian Agency), Le Beau, and the railheads of Pierre and

Chamberlain. But it also did some government freighting as far downstream as Fort Randall. Baker's usual practice was to ship cargoes from Bismarck and then transport freight upstream from Chamberlain and Pierre.[99]

Because of competing operators, Baker periodically adjusted the range of his company's boats. In 1892, when the Benton Transportation Company's holdings were only the old mountain boats *F. Y. Batchelor* and *Rose Bud*, Baker announced that he would generally confine his operations to between Fort Berthold and Pierre. But four years later, in the face of stiff competition from Pierre boatmen, he decided to make Fort Yates, 77 miles below Bismarck, his southernmost destination.[100]

Baker's 1892 curtailment was caused by competition from the two-year-old Missouri River Transportation Company, directed by John M. Turner, and from boatmen from Pierre, Chamberlain, and Running Water. Turner, manager of the Mandan Roller Mills Company, went into steamboating with the acquisition of the *Abner O'Neal*, a six-year-old, 197-ton stern-wheeler. The boat, which had first been used on the Ohio and upper Mississippi, measured 150 × 28.4 × 3.8. In 1890, soon after it arrived on the upper Missouri, Turner used it in private and government freighting from Fort Sully to Sioux City. He wintered the *Abner O'Neal* at Sioux City before shifting it to the Bismarck area in 1891 to help supply his flour mill. While engaged in the wheat trade, the boat was snagged and lost near Painted Woods, 36 miles above Bismarck, on July 17, 1892.[101]

Shortly before the *Abner O'Neal* was destroyed, Daniel B. Weatherbee of Fort Yates began running the *Imelda*. The small stern-wheeler, measuring 90 × 17 × 2, had a capacity of only 30 tons. Weatherbee operated the steamer as an independent for a time before it was acquired by the Benton Transportation Company.

Once the Benton Transportation Company withdrew from freighting below Fort Yates, local operators at Pierre, Chamberlain, and Running Water became more important. Pierre's first resident steamer was the *Jim Leighton*, which started ferrying between Pierre and Fort Pierre in 1880. In 1887 the Northwestern Stage and Express Company, its first operator, sold the boat to the Chicago and North Western. However, B. F. Horn, who ultimately had seventeen years' experience as a Pierre boatman, continued as its captain.

After the *Jim Leighton* was wrecked by a windstorm in October 1894, the railroad salvaged its machinery for use in a stern-wheel steamer of the same name that was built at Pierre the following year. The second, *Jim Leighton,* was somewhat larger than the first. Since they could not be distinguished by their names, army engineers in their various reports showed a *Jim Leighton* built in 1880 and a *Jim Leighton* built in 1895. Horn left Pierre in 1897, but the Chicago and North Western kept running the *Jim Leighton* until a railroad bridge was completed between Pierre and Fort Pierre in 1907.[102]

Development of Pierre and Fort Pierre created opportunities for other boats by the mid-1890s. Pierre first benefited from the decision to make it the capital of the new state of South Dakota in 1889. As statehood was imminent, the federal government negotiated the acquisition of some nine million acres of Great Sioux

The *August Wohlt*, pictured in 1906, was run by
the Hermann Ferry and Packet Company on the Gasconade and
lower Missouri. *Used by permission, State Historical Society of Missouri, Columbia.*

Reservation lands west of the Missouri. The cession, which lay principally between the White and Cheyenne rivers, was legally opened to settlement in February 1890. Some homesteaders and ranchers were attracted to the choicest lands, but promoters failed to precipitate a big rush. Nonetheless, the number of newcomers was enough to enlarge Fort Pierre and enhance the Pierre railhead as a cattle and horse market.[103]

Expanding opportunities at Pierre–Fort Pierre attracted Edmond E. "Cap" Senechal, who moved from Chamberlain, where he had started boating in 1894. In 1895 he began running the small gasoline boat *Pearl* between Pierre and Fort Pierre. Two years later he built the gasoline packet *Peerless* for ferrying and freighting upstream to Le Beau and downstream to the Brule Agency near Chamberlain. After selling the *Peerless* to the Benton Transportation Company, he built the gasoline boat *Scotty Philip*, with the financial support of several partners. In 1904 he built another gasoline boat, the 80-ton stern-wheeler *City of Fort Pierre*. Senechal used the *City of Fort Pierre*, which measured 108.4 × 24 × 4, until the 1907 completion of the railroad bridge.[104]

A third Pierre–Fort Pierre ferry service was provided by Eli E. Lindsay of Fort Pierre, who began running a small gasoline packet in 1895. By 1904 he was operating five gasoline launches.[105]

In the 1880s and 1890s Captain Henry J. King and his son Martin were Cham-

The gasoline boat *Benton,* powered by an internal combustion engine, was used on the Missouri in North Dakota to transport grain and other freight. *Courtesy of the State Historical Society of North Dakota.*

berlain's leading boatmen. While commanding the Milwaukee Railroad's *Milwaukee,* King completed building his own boat, the *Josie L. K.,* at Chamberlain in May 1884. The 27-ton stern-wheeler measured 71.5 × 14.5 × 3.5. After two years of running it out of Chamberlain, King sold the *Josie L. K.* to Andy Larson of Sioux City, who among other things operated the Yankton ferry. The Kings replaced the *Josie L. K.* with the *Last Chance,* which they purchased at Lansing, Iowa, on the Mississippi in August 1886. After wintering it at St. Louis, they navigated the 50-ton stern-wheeler, which measured 98.2 × 17.8 × 3.0, to Chamberlain in the spring of 1887. Soon thereafter the Kings and Milwaukee Road officials decided they could manage their Chamberlain business with only the *Last Chance.* King steamed the *Milwaukee* to Prairie du Chien, where it was subsequently used on the upper Mississippi.[106]

When the Kings were operating the small *Josie L. K.,* they limited its navigation to a short stretch from Fort Thompson (Crow Creek Indian Agency), 20 miles above Chamberlain, to the Lower Brule Agency, 5 miles below and opposite Chamberlain. Their principal business was delivering supplies from the Milwaukee Road to the agencies. Oftentimes they booked excursionists, who were especially attracted by the slaughtering of beef cattle at the Lower Brule Agency every Saturday.[107]

With the larger *Last Chance,* Henry J. and Martin King in 1887 extended their trading range downstream 128 miles to Running Water and upstream 306 miles to Fort Yates, headquarters of the Standing Rock Agency. Transporting Indian supplies continued to be a significant part of their business, but their return freight to the Milwaukee Road included potatoes and wheat. In May 1888 the *Last Chance* was credited with delivering from below the first consignment of wheat that had ever reached Chamberlain by water.[108]

Most of the time, the Kings used the *Last Chance* for short runs to Fort Thompson, Lower Brule Agency, American Island, and Oacoma. The agencies and the large, heavily timbered American Island in front of Chamberlain attracted numerous excursionists for weekend and holiday outings. Sometimes the Chamberlain band entertained the parties. In June 1890 the Kings announced that the *Last Chance*'s round-trip fare for a July Fourth excursion to American Island would be 12.5 cents.[109]

Oacoma, across the river from Chamberlain, was established in the spring of 1890 when settlers began moving into the newly opened former reservation lands. In April the *Democrat* reported that the boat was kept busy in crossing settlers and their livestock and other belongings to the west bank. The Kings, who held the ferry franchise, were determined to control the business. They publicly warned that anyone who ferried with rowboats, skiffs, and other craft for pay, hire, or reward, could be charged with defrauding their franchise.

The Kings and their *Last Chance* were unchallenged at Chamberlain until 1897, when William Sims and J. W. Sanford began running boats there. Sims operated the *Capitola Butt,* a 57-ton stern-wheeler that had been repaired and put back into service after burning near Sioux City in May 1895. Sanford ran the 39-ton gasoline boat *Chamberlain* until it was destroyed by fire two miles below the town on April 27, 1899.[110]

Within a short time, Sanford had the field to himself. By 1898 he had acquired the *Capitola Butt,* and in the spring of 1899 the *Last Chance* was destroyed by ice. With the Kings out of the Chamberlain trade, Sanford expanded to two boats— the *Capitola Butt* and the 48-ton gasoline boat *Iowa.* Ferrying at Chamberlain was a vital part of the town's economy until the Milwaukee Road completed its line to Rapid City in 1907.

As the only point between Yankton and Chamberlain where a railroad reached the Missouri, Running Water was the leading port in its area. With the withdrawal of the Benton Transportation Company upstream, Running Water boating was dominated by Joseph Leach, Sr., and his four sons. Until 1899 their only boat was the *Little Maud,* a 59-ton stern-wheeler that had been built at Sioux City in 1882. The vessel, whose dimensions were 92 × 20 × 3.4, was federally licensed to run as a ferry the 2 miles between Running Water and Niobrara, Nebraska, and to engage in freighting to Fort Randall, 40 miles above Running Water.[111]

Leach was probably inspired to built a larger boat when James P. Boland proved there was enough trade for one. In 1897 Boland of St. Louis moved the old mountain boat *Benton* from the lower Missouri to Sioux City to engage in trade extending beyond Running Water. In June the *Benton* completed two voyages to Wheeler, a small community 17 miles above Fort Randall. But Boland's plans to establish a regular trade were dashed when the *Benton* was wrecked after colliding with a railroad bridge at Sioux City on July 18.

Taking advantage of the opportunity to freight above Fort Randall, Leach built the *South Dakota* at Running Water in 1899. With nearly 40 tons more capacity than the *Little Maud,* the 137.5 × 19.4 × 4.5 *South Dakota* became the most used freight packet above Niobrara. Oftentimes Leach used it in combination with the *Little Maud,* which ferried cargoes from Running Water to Niobrara.[112]

Much of Leach's steamboating arose from settlement near Fort Randall, which was prompted by the federal government's decision to make part of the military reservation land available to settlers. Furthermore, the opening of some Indian reservation land in 1890 resulted in the establishment of Fairfax about eight miles west of the post. By then the fort was no longer serving its frontier mission. It was vacated in December 1892, and within a few years the last portions of the tract were occupied by settlers.[113]

Unfortunately for Leach, the emerging agricultural economy was a magnet for railroad expansion. In 1902 the Fremont, Elkhorn, and Missouri Valley Rail Road was extended from Verdigre, Nebraska, through Fairfax to the new town of Bonesteel. The railroad extension coincided with the loss of the *South Dakota,* which was burned on May 10 between Running Water and Yankton.

For over a year after the loss of the *South Dakota,* Leach ran only the *Little Maud.* But sometime during the fiscal year starting July 1, 1903, with the acquisition of the *F. Y. Batchelor* from Isaac P. Baker and associates, he expanded from ferrying to promoting excursions below Running Water. In 1906 he purchased the *Josephine,* the last Coulson Line vessel, which had been owned and operated on the upper Missouri by army engineers for twenty-one years.

With these last two mountain boats, Leach toured the river with excursionists from Sioux City, Yankton, and other points. But this business soon ended disastrously. In March 1907 both vessels were destroyed by ice while being wintered at Running Water.[114]

After Isaac P. Baker decided to keep his boats above Fort Yates in 1896, he and his partners concentrated on the wheat trade above Bismarck. They established elevators at Mannhaven, Deapolis, Expansion, and other sites. Through their combined grain and boating businesses, they bought, stored, sold, and transported wheat to Bismarck for transshipment by the Northern Pacific to Duluth and Minneapolis markets. By dealing in bulk, they were able to negotiate favorable railroad rates.[115]

Because of the grain trade, Baker expanded the Benton Transportation Company's fleet. The *Rose Bud* was destroyed on June 16, 1896, when it dropped onto some submerged piling at Bismarck. But Baker acquired the *Imelda* and within the next few years added the gasoline packets *Bismarck* (nee *John H. Bloodgood*) and *Peerless.*[116]

Baker, who strove to monopolize Bismarck-area boating, was challenged when William D. Washburn of Minneapolis established a two-steamboat line in 1901.

Washburn had made a fortune in flour milling and railroading before serving a term (1889–95) in the U.S. Senate. After failing in his reelection bid, Washburn took a long tour of the Orient before resuming his business career. In 1898 he bought 115,000 acres of North Dakota land east of the Missouri and north of Bismarck from the Northern Pacific Railroad. To enhance its attractiveness to settlers, he decided to build a railroad from Bismarck. Washburn, who had served as the first president of the Minneapolis, St. Paul, and Sault Ste. Marie Railroad Company, formed the Bismarck, Washburn, and Great Falls Railway. The line reached Wilton in 1900, a year after construction began, and Washburn, the only point where it touched the Missouri River, the following year.[117]

Anticipating the completion of the railroad to the port of Washburn, William D. Washburn entered steamboating. He acquired the *Expansion* and had the *Washburn* built at Bismarck. The 78-ton stern-wheeler *Expansion,* measuring 123 × 26 × 3.5, was built at Bismarck in 1900 and first owned by the Mercer County Mercantile Company of New Salem, North Dakota. The stern-wheeler *Washburn,* completed in 1901, had a 57.4-ton capacity and dimensions of 98.7 × 24.8 × 3.1.[118]

Army engineers reported that the Bismarck, Washburn, and Great Falls Railroad Company was operating its boats a short distance above and below Bismarck in 1901. But Washburn soon decided that steamboating was unnecessary to his North Dakota business, which was expanding into lignite coal mining, and he traded the *Expansion* and *Washburn* to the Benton Transportation Company for some of its stock. By providing the Benton Transportation Company with another rail outlet, Washburn enabled Baker and his associates to expand to a fleet of four steamers and two gasoline packets.

As Baker was concentrating on the wheat trade near Bismarck and Washburn, there was a modest revival of boating on the lower Yellowstone, because of increasing settlement from the mouth 92 miles upstream to Glendive. The Charles Stevens Transportation Company of Mondak, Montana, 3 miles above the mouth, opened trade in the fall of 1905 with the steamer *O. K.* Originally named the *Burksville,* the 59-ton stern-wheeler, which measured 116.5 × 17.1 × 3.8, had been built at Cincinnati in 1899. When Oscar Knapp bought it in 1905 for contemplated use on the St. Croix, the Minnesota-Wisconsin border river, he renamed it with his monogram. But within days he sold it to the Stevens Transportation Company, which had it navigated from Dubuque, Iowa, on the Mississippi and Missouri.[119]

Captain George Stevens did some Yellowstone trading with the *O. K.* in 1906 and then, probably because of competition from the Benton Packet Company's *Expansion,* shifted the boat to Fort Benton. In 1907 and 1908 Stevens used the *O. K.* to deliver some supplies for farmers and ranchers as far downstream as the Milk River and to take excursionists upstream towards the Great Falls. While lying on the riverbank at Fort Benton, the boat was accidentally destroyed by fire on June 30, 1908.

Despite the *O. K.*'s checkered history, Charles Crepeau of Fort Benton thought steamboating at the place was still economically feasible. In 1909 he locally built the *Baby Rose,* a 71 × 18.2 × 2.5 stern-wheeler with one engine. He used it to carry

The *Baby Rose*, Fort Benton's last commercial steamboat, was built at Fort Benton in 1909.
Courtesy of the Overholser Historical Research Center, Fort Benton, Montana.

supplies to downstream settlers as far as the Judith River. But its use was limited to intermittent trips because the underpowered vessel could not move barges consistently. After two seasons, Crepeau abandoned the *Baby Rose* at the Fort Benton levee, where it was destroyed by ice during the winter of 1911–12.

Meanwhile, Isaac P. Baker decided to enter the Yellowstone trade. He sent the steamer *Expansion*, commanded by Grant Marsh, to the river in 1906. The vessel was used primarily to haul construction supplies and provisions from Mondak and Glendive to the U.S. Bureau of Reclamation water diversion dam that was under construction 18 miles below Glendive. But it also transported some private freight and passengers. Baker kept the *Expansion* in the Glendive-Mondak trade until the dam was completed during the 1909 navigation season. Army engineers reported that the boat hauled 7,700 tons of freight during its time on the river. Baker insisted that the dam ruined a potentially lively Yellowstone commerce. He urged army engineers to consider equipping the dam with a lock or removing it.[120]

The *Expansion* was the Yellowstone's last commercial steamer, but after the dam was finished, Edmond E. Senechal ran two gasoline packets from Mondak to just below it. Senechal and one of his sons, operating as the Missouri River Transportation Company, moved from Pierre–Fort Pierre to Williston in 1907. They used the gasoline boat *City of Fort Pierre* to haul wheat to the Great Northern Railroad at Williston. While continuing to operate out of Williston, the Senechals had another gasoline boat—the *City of Mondak*—built at Mondak in 1909.[121]

The steel-hulled *Rose* shown here at the Gates of the Mountains, ca. 1900, was used mainly as an excursion boat above Great Falls.
Courtesy of the Montana Historical Society, Helena.

They ran the *City of Fort Pierre* and the *City of Mondak* in 1909 and 1910 from Mondak and nearby Buford, North Dakota, to Intake, at the Bureau of Reclamation's diversionary structure. In each year their estimated commerce was 1,000 to 2,000 tons. But their business was short-lived. They were forced out of the Yellowstone by the completion of a branch railroad from Glendive to Mondak. However, they operated gas packets in the Williston area until 1921.

The last years of Missouri River steamboating included the first years of steamboating above the Great Falls. The idea of boating from the falls to near Helena was conceived during the gold rush of the late 1860s. Promoters thought boats above the falls would provide cheaper, faster transportation than Fort Benton–Helena overland transportation. The notion was kept alive, but no one attempted to operate a steamer on the upper-upper Missouri until territorial Governor J. Schuyler Crosby had the *Little Phil* delivered by the Northern Pacific to Townsend in 1883. Crosby intended to use the craft for private hunting parties. But during its trial run down to Stubbs Ferry, 12 miles northeast of Helena, he realized the underpowered vessel could not stem the current. Consequently, he abandoned it at Stubbs Ferry, where it subsequently broke up.[122]

The *Rose,* the next boat to be put above the falls, had a long career. Judge Nicholas Hilger had the steel-hulled stern-wheeler delivered by rail in two sections from Dubuque, Iowa, its building site, to Townsend in May 1886. Hilger, who had a ranch about 18 miles below Stubbs Ferry, planned to host excursionists. Because of rapids, sandbars, and shallow water, he recognized that only a very small boat could be operated. The *Rose,* with an estimated capacity of only 9 tons, measured 54 × 10 × 2.75. But with enough power to reach 12 miles per hour in calm water, the boat easily ascended the rapids.[123]

Since the Northern Pacific at Townsend provided the only railroad access, Hilger had to run the *Rose* through the most difficult section above the Great Falls. Army engineers considered the Missouri to be navigable for 131 miles from Stubbs Ferry to the falls. Over its 77-mile course from Stubbs Ferry down to the town of Cascade, the stream roared through canyons and plunged over rapids. Its average gradient was 3.73 feet per mile, but engineers reported: "In one stretch, 2 miles long, the total fall is 19 feet, and there are many places where for short distances the slope exceeds $9^1/_2$ feet to the mile."[124] The steepest spot was in Half Breed Rapids, 64 miles below Stubbs Ferry, where the stream dropped slightly more than 9 feet in half a mile. In fifteen places there was less than 2.5 feet of water, and the channel was often obstructed with large boulders.[125]

The 54-mile Long Pool from Cascade to the falls dropped gently, with an average gradient of only 0.52 feet per mile. The channel was generally more than 3 feet deep. Several sandy shoals were the most serious navigation hazards.

In 1886 Hilger had the *Rose* steamed from Townsend down to his ranch. He used it for some short local excursions and the next May ran it down to Great Falls.[126]

Meanwhile, a Montana-built steamer was being readied. In 1885 Asa L. Davison, a medical doctor in Twin Bridges on the Beaverhead River, built the hull of the *Fern.* The following year he floated the structure down the Beaverhead, Jefferson, and Missouri to Townsend. Davison had difficulty obtaining funding for the boat's machinery, but he finally launched the *Fern* in late September 1887. After six weeks of frequently difficult navigation, he managed to get the 88 × 20 × 2.5 stern-wheeler to Great Falls. Grossly underpowered with only a 26-horsepower engine, it was evident the *Fern* was incapable of ascending the rapids. The one voyage was enough to convince Davison that doctoring had more of a future than boating. He sold the *Fern* to some Great Falls businessmen and resumed his medical practice in Dillon. The boat's new owners, usually towing a 80 × 40 barge began freighting in the Long Pool in 1888. The next year, the *Fern* transported 4,500 cords of wood, 250 tons of hay, 79 tons of wool, and 5 tons of produce. But rafting accounted for much of the Long Pool trade. Two million board feet of lumber were floated to Great Falls in 1889, and the rafting business of 1890 to August 13 amounted to 3.5 million board feet of lumber and logs, 70,000 feet of linear piling, 12,000 railroad ties, and 4,500 telegraph poles.[127]

The Great Falls Chamber of Commerce and army engineers thought the river trade would force the Montana Central Railroad to lower its rates. The line, constructed by Charles A. Broadwater working in concert with James J. Hill, was completed from Helena to Great Falls in November 1887. The rapid growth of Great Falls and its upstream hinterland stimulated both the river and rail businesses. In 1890, Great Falls and its suburbs were reported to have 5,000 to 5,500 inhabitants, or double that of the preceding year. Some 2,000 to 3,000 lived in the valley along the Long Pool, and Cascade had a population of 500.[128]

The hopes of river enthusiasts were boosted with the expansion of steamboating above Great Falls. The *Fern* was not used after 1892, but by 1893 there were three other steamers—*Francis, Minnie,* and *J. J. Hill*—in addition to the *Rose.* The 29 × 7 × 3 *Francis* and the 50 × 10 × 4.5 *Minnie,* each with by a single screw propeller, were built at Great Falls in 1892. The *J. J. Hill,* the same size as the *Minnie* but powered by a double screw propeller, was built that year at Racine, Wisconsin. It was apparently delivered to Great Falls by the Great Northern Railroad. Because they were built like lake boats and drew considerable water, the three were operated only in the Long Pool, where they took excursionists out and hauled some hay and grain, Hilger's *Rose,* which was run above Cascade through scenic White Rock Canyon—better known as Gate of the Mountains—was heavily used by excursionists.[129]

Excursions dominated steamboating above Great Falls. The four steamers operating in 1897 and 1898 carried respectively 3,000 and an estimated 3,500 passengers. Freighting was light. Only in 1897, when 1,250 tons of packages and bulk freight were hauled, did the annual commerce exceed 1,000 tons. A scant 28 tons were transported in 1894, and none was hauled from 1898 through 1901. By 1900 only the *Rose* was still being operated. The boat was finally abandoned in 1906 after carrying an estimated 10,000 passengers during its Missouri River career.[130]

During the last years of Missouri River steamboating, the federal government sharply increased its river improvement work. This was inspired by a national trend to revive river commerce as a significant component of the nation's transportation system. Renewed interest in commercial boating was a natural outcome of the anti-railroad stances of the Populist and Progressive eras. River improvement was invariably justified on the grounds that it would benefit the public. Proponents insisted that with lowered risks and operating expenses, boating would force a natural reduction in railroad rates.

Congress provided the basis of an organizational framework for Missouri River improvement through rivers and harbors acts. In the 1882 act, it funded improvement from the mouth to Fort Benton. But the lawmakers stipulated separate allocations for two sections, with the southern edge of Sioux City as their dividing point. This in turn led army engineers to designate a lower Missouri and an upper Missouri.[131]

In 1884, Congress demonstrated its determination to further stimulate river improvement by creating the Missouri River Commission. The five-member commission was to be appointed by the president with the advice and consent of the Senate. Three of its members had to come from the Corps of Engineers. The two other positions had to be filled by civilians, of whom at least one had to be a civil engineer. The president was to appoint one of the army engineers as the commission's president. Specifically, the commission was charged with improving the river "sufficient for the purposes of commerce and navigation."[132]

Initially the commission had responsibility for improvement from the mouth to Fort Benton. But Congress reduced its jurisdiction to the lower division in 1890. The upper division reverted to the Engineer Department on November 30 of that year. In 1902, Congress, apparently convinced that the commission was an unnecessary appendage, abolished it effective June 30 of that year.[133]

The commission's greatest accomplishment was the completion of a survey from the mouth to Three Forks. Started in 1878, the survey had been extended upstream to Pierre by 1884, when the commission was designated to finish it. Most of the fieldwork was done by 1890, but the final triangulation rechecking was not completed until four year later. From 1892 through 1895, the commission published a set of eighty-four very detailed maps. Because of the survey, official distances were established for four sectors—mouth to Big Sioux River (810.6 miles), Big Sioux to Northern Pacific bridge at Bismarck (639.5 miles), Bismarck bridge to Fort Benton bridge (834.7 miles), and Fort Benton bridge to Three Forks (266.2 miles).[134]

When Congress abolished the Missouri River Commission, army engineers, strong improvement advocates, were convinced that this was the death knell for Missouri River commerce. In 1902 engineer Captain Hiram Martin Chittenden, who had worked on the Missouri, thought Congress intended "to abandon the river altogether in the near future."[135] But Chittenden underestimated the lobbying power of barge line proponents, the influence of local congressmen, and the attractiveness of the rivers and harbors acts as pork barrel measures. The voluminous acts, with line-item appropriations for several hundred projects, seemed to evidence the notion that every congressional district had a river or harbor deserving of improvement.

Congress not only continued Missouri River improvement but grandly expanded it by the 1912 Rivers and Harbors Act. The measure designated three discrete sections—mouth to Kansas City, Kansas City to Sioux City, and Sioux City to Fort Benton. Anticipating barge traffic between St. Louis and Kansas City, Congress appropriated $800,000 to further work on a six-foot navigable channel with the aim of finishing it in ten years at a total cost of $20 million. With the expectation that commercial boating above Kansas City would be continued, the law granted $75,000 and $150,000 respectively for the Kansas City–Sioux City and Sioux City–Fort Benton sections. The measure reinforced some long-standing notions about the future of Missouri River commerce. The 1890 Rivers and Harbors Act had called for the creation of the six-foot channel downstream from Jefferson City. But the project was erratically funded, and by 1912 the channel had been achieved in only a 45-mile section in the Jefferson City–Osage mouth vicinity. Above Kansas City, the prevailing belief was that commerce and riverside communities would be best served by snagging and bank revetment near towns and bridges.[136]

Because of their growing presence on the Missouri during the 1880s, army engineers decided to establish their own harbors. In 1892, Congress authorized a Missouri River Commission boatyard at the mouth of the Gasconade. This facility, which was transferred to the Corps of Engineers in 1902, was the base for improvement work from the mouth to Kansas City. It had ways for wintering and repairing vessels, as well as shops for building towboats, dredges, pile drivers, launches, skiffs, and barges for improvement projects.[137]

To serve the region above Kansas City, the Corps built ice harbors at Rock Haven near Bismarck and at the mouth of the Big Sioux. Rock Haven sans improvement had been used as a wintering site by Bismarck steamboatmen since the late 1870s. Construction of the Rock Haven harbor was started in the spring of 1894. Over the course of the next nineteen years it was enlarged to provide space for private as well as government boats, and its original wooden ways were replaced with concrete ones. Principally, Rock Haven was the base for a snagboat and other vessels used in river improvement extending to Fort Benton.[138]

The Sioux Ice Harbor, started within weeks of Rock Haven, was first used by engineer boats in June 1896. By 1900 it had been expanded enough to accommodate private craft. Usually it was the base for two snagboats, which worked downstream to Kansas City as well as upstream. Because of its relative proximity to bank revetment projects at Sioux City, Elk Point, Vermillion, and Yankton, the harbor had boatbuilding facilities. It was equipped with lumber storage warehouses and carpentry shops to enable its staff to build tugs, barges, and skiffs.

Improvement methods were dictated by Corps of Engineers goals for each of the three Missouri River sections and the tributary Osage, Gasconade, and Yellowstone. The commonest method, removal of snags and other obstructions, was done on the Missouri to Fort Benton as well as on the Osage and Gasconade. Bank stabilization at and near towns and cities and other landings was performed throughout the Missouri and the navigable portions of the Osage, Gasconade, and Yellowstone. Channelization, which entailed a combination of dredging, revetting, and diking, was confined to Kansas City to the mouth until 1927, when Congress authorized the extension of the minimum six-foot channel from Kansas City to Sioux City. The ultimate improvement method—a lock and dam—was built only on the Osage near its mouth.[139]

Since snagging was the foremost reason for boat losses, snag removal was a popular program. Boatmen and other advocates of river commerce championed it as the principal way of reducing risk and, consequently, insurance premiums. Over time, the use of government snagboats extended up the Missouri. They were first sent above Kansas City in 1868 and above Sioux City in 1891. Work by snagboats during the navigation season was sometimes supplemented by winter parties that traveled on the frozen river to blast snags and other obstructions and cut trees on overhanging banks. Snagging persisted through the decline and end of commercial steamboating. Snagboats were routinely used in the sections from the mouth to Kansas City and from Kansas City to Sioux City into the early 1930s. On the upper river, the snagboat *Mandan*, stationed at Rock Haven, worked upstream to Fort Benton as late as 1921. The *Mandan* was removed from the upper river in 1923, but during the late 1920s and early 1930s the removal of snags and other obstructions for long stretches above and below Bismarck was done by either winter parties or from the gas packet *Frayne*, which army engineers chartered

The elaborately equipped U. S. snagboat *Horatio G. Wright* was built
for the army's Corps of Engineers at St. Louis in 1880.
Used by permission, State Historical Society of Missouri, Columbia.

from the Benton Transportation Company. At the time, the company's two gas
packets were the only commercial vessels, exclusive of ferries, on the upper river.[140]

Bank stabilization, which featured stone revetting, brush mats, and wing dams,
was done within short boating distances of communities and landings. It was first
extended to the upper river in 1879 with a project at Vermillion. Much of the
rationale for the Sioux Ice Harbor was to have a convenient base for stabilization
projects both above and below Sioux City.[141]

Channelization aimed to force the current into a relatively narrow navigable
channel. The 1912 Rivers and Harbors Act did not specify a width for the six-
foot-deep channel, but in 1925 Congress required that it be at least 200 feet. To
achieve it, the channel was dredged, and water was forced into the excavation by
closing chutes with dikes and revetting banks to curtail the river's natural meandering. Channelization from the mouth to Kansas City proved to be much costlier and slower than Congress envisioned in 1912. By 1933, when the work was 97
percent completed, expenditures totaled nearly $69 million. By comparison, total
costs for the section prior to the channelization project were about $7.2 million.[142]

The most ambitious improvement plan on the tributaries was the Osage lock
and dam. Authorized by Congress in 1890, nineteen years after the first federal

improvement on the river, the project was chronically underfunded. Army engineers began operating the lock in March 1906, and the dam was completed five years later, although some refinements were not finished until 1914. Backwater from the dam enhanced navigation by raising levels for 21 miles.[143]

Federal improvement of the Gasconade, which was started in 1880, continued to the demise of commercial boating in 1928. It consisted principally of snag removal, dredging at shoals, and constructing wing dams to help create a good navigable channel.

The brief revival of Yellowstone River commerce in the first decade of the twentieth century caused business leaders of its main communities—Glendive, Miles City, and Billings—to lobby for river improvement. But when the Board of Engineers for Rivers and Harbors rejected their requests, Congress could not be convinced to authorize funding. Thus the last federal improvement on the stream was the revetment of the Glendive landing in 1896–97.[144]

As army engineers were channelizing from the mouth to Kansas City, commercial steamboating was ended on the Missouri. The section above Sioux City was the first to lose its last commercial steamboat. At the opening of navigation in 1918, the Benton Packet Company had only one steamer, the *Scarab*, and two motor vessels. In June, Isaac P. Baker had the *Scarab* steamed from Bismarck to St. Louis, where is was sold to a Mt. Vernon, Indiana, towboat company. Yankton's steam ferry, the *Josie L. K.*, lasted an amazing thirty-six years, until it was destroyed by an ice floe on April 20, 1920. Its owner, Joseph Giesler, replaced it with the steamer *B. A. Douglas*, which he operated until a privately built highway bridge opened at Yankton in October 1924.[145]

In 1918 only two steamers operated between Kansas City and Sioux City. One of them was destroyed during the season, and the other was removed from the Missouri. At season's end, army engineers reported that "commercial traffic on this section has been suspended."[146] But trade revived the next year when five privately owned towboats were working under contract with the Corps of Engineers to transport bank revetment materials.[147]

Hauling trees and brush for revetting and sand accounted for nearly all of the Kansas City–Sioux City commerce. The heavy products resulted in an impressive tonnage but did not contribute to an active up-down trade. In 1920, for example, the section's tonnage amounted to 149,255, valued at $185,040. But 119,600 tons were barged sand, and 29,550 tons were trees used in river improvement. The average haul of both was only 2 miles.

Transportation of any other items, including grain and animals, was infrequent and statistically insignificant. In the fall of 1924 the Western Barge Line, a Missouri corporation headquartered in Omaha, ran its 65-ton stern-wheeler *Decatur* (96.2 × 24.6 × 3.8) between Omaha and Sioux City. But the company withdrew the boat at the end of the season because their venture was losing money. Nearly two years later, Joseph Giesler, then of Sioux City, delivered the *B. A. Douglas* to its new Kansas City owner. The steamer transported only 25 tons of government machinery and lumber destined for an improvement project below Kansas City. But the voyage, reported to be the first trip from Sioux City to Kansas City by a steamer in twenty years, attracted public attention as a novelty.[148]

The final attempt to revive St. Louis–Kansas City steamboat trade was made by the Kansas City–Missouri River Navigation Company. The firm, organized in 1911 with a capitalization of about $1.2 million, sent its first steamers, the *Chester* and the *Unique,* from St. Louis to Kansas City in June. They were soon complemented by the *A. M. Scott,* and within two years the *Advance* was added to the line. The company also had several small barges, for which the federal Customs Service did not require registration. The 160-ton *A. M. Scott,* which measured 150.9 × 26 × 5.9, was equipped with screw propellers. The *Advance,* formerly the *Annie Russell,* had a capacity of 98 tons and dimensions of 120 × 23 × 4. After acquiring the *Chester,* which had been used in St. Louis–Kansas City steamboating in 1906–1908, the company replaced its stern wheel with propellers. The *Unique* was a 33-ton steam yacht, which was used primarily to reconnoiter the channel ahead of the larger vessels.[149]

Until its failure in 1918, the Kansas City–Missouri River Navigation Company was the Missouri's only long trader. Most of its business was transporting general merchandise and manufactured iron and steel from St. Louis to Kansas City, but it also had a modest passenger trade, including the conveying of prisoners and guards to the state penitentiary at Jefferson City. In any given year the company's shipments accounted for less than 10 percent of the total commerce on the section from the mouth to Kansas City. But they were far more valuable than the other commodities.[150]

During the navigation season, March 26–December 13, 1915, the section's total trade was 216,490 tons (12,234,843 ton-miles), valued at $7,516,372.80. The most valuable category—at $6,260,843.35—was 10,299 tons of general merchandise, transported an average distance of 376 miles. Other long-haul items—flour, feed, and manufactured iron and steel—had a value of $860,000. But the section's bulkiest commodities—167,371 tons of sand and gravel (127,234 cubic yards), which on average were moved only a mile—were valued at only $39,605.20. Typically, sand and gravel were taken from the river near their destinations and loaded on barges, which were towed to shore by steam tugboats.

Although it had no boat competition in the St. Louis–Kansas City river trade, the Kansas City–Missouri River Navigation Company was a losing proposition. In early September 1918 its steamers and barges were sold to the federal government, which transferred them to the lower Mississippi.[151]

Despite the failure of the Kansas City–Missouri River Navigation Company, Ed Heckmann of Hermann thought trade with St. Louis was still viable. Mainly by selling stock to his townspeople, he financed the construction of the steamer *John Heckmann.* The 163.6 × 30.5 × 4.2 craft, which drew only 16 inches light, featured twin stern wheels, said to be the first such design on the Missouri. Heckmann made his initial trip with the new vessel between Hermann and St. Louis in April 1919. Offering only freight service, he intended to make weekly Her-

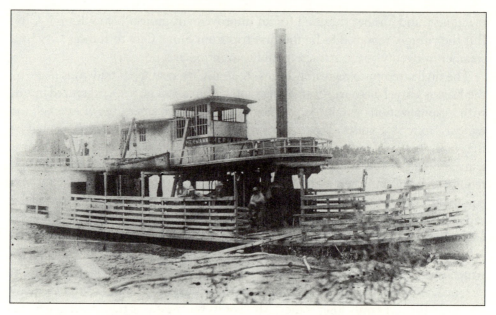

The *Hermann*, the Missouri's last commercial steamboat, was removed from the river in 1935.
Used by permission, State Historical Society of Missouri, Columbia.

mann–St. Louis round-trips. But the business was meager. In 1920, St. Louis had sixteen steamboat arrivals from the Missouri and the same number of departures to it. Tonnage received from the Missouri was 3,010, but a scant 200 tons were sent to it.[152]

Acknowledging that freight traffic was dead, Heckmann converted the *John Heckmann* into an excursion boat. As the Missouri River Excursion Company, he toured the Missouri as high as Omaha during the summers and used the vessel on the Cumberland and Tennessee rivers during the winters. The vessel was retired in 1929 and, while tied up near Hermann, was wrecked by ice the next year.[153]

As the *John Heckmann* was hosting excursionists, steamboating was phased out on the Gasconade and Osage. During the 1920s their boatmen were undercut by motor vehicles and improved roads. The rivers were used primarily to barge sand and raft railroad ties. In 1922, grain shipments on the Osage amounted to only 1,348 tons out of the total river freight of 58,553 tons. Gasconade tonnage for the season was 5,527, but only 594 tons, including 371 of grain, were items other than sand, gravel, and rafted ties.[154]

In 1927, when the last steamboat was engaged in Gasconade commerce, only 468 tons were freighted. The following year the entire Gasconade trade was 581 tons of rafted railroad ties. After that the only boats on the stream were gas-powered ferries. The Osage's steamboat era seemed to have ended at the end of the 1925 season. Only about 1,800 tons, excluding sand, gravel, and rafted ties, were carried by two gas packets in 1926. But in 1929 the stream's last steamer and a gas packet traded on the river, when shipments comprised 3,160 tons of logs, 1,596 tons of railroad ties, and a scant 22 tons of wheat.

The Hermann Ferry and Packet Company gained the distinction of operating the Missouri's last commercial steamboat. In 1925 its *Hermann,* built at Hermann in 1912, was the river's only steamer involved in trade. Army engineers did not regard sand company boats and vessels used by civilian contractors in river improvement as commercial boats. The *Hermann* was run only in the Hermann vicinity. In 1928 the company drastically remodeled the boat. As required by law, the Customs Service reenrolled the boat with a new official number.[155]

On December 31, 1935, the company, in its dissolution proceeding, sold the *Hermann.* The St. Louis purchaser removed it from the Missouri.

During the *Hermann's* last year, another milestone was reached in Missouri River navigation. In June 1935 the diesel towboat *Franklin D. Roosevelt,* equipped with screw propellers, pushed huge barges up to Kansas City through the recently completed six-foot navigation channel. A contemporary newspaper pronounced the event to have "ushered in a new commercial era in the history of Missouri River navigation."[156]

In retrospect, the old era of steamboats enjoyed its best days on the lower river in the two decades prior to the construction of the Missouri Pacific Railroad. Because the first railroads in the upper Missouri region generally reached or crossed the river rather than paralleling it, steamboating peaked as part of a combined rail-river transportation system. Even the Missouri's entire age of commercial steamboating, 1819–1935, is relatively brief in history's long scope. If nothing else, the advent, rise, decline, and death of Missouri River steamboating demonstrates the nation's persistent quest for the easiest and fastest ways of moving people and goods.

Appendix

VALUE OF THE U.S. DOLLAR FROM 1820 TO 1930 (IN 2006 DOLLARS)

Dollar of . . .	Value in 2006	Dollar of . . .	Value in 2006
1820	$14.44	1880	$20.91
1825	$17.84	1885	$22.46
1830	$18.95	1890	$22.46
1835	$19.56	1895	$24.26
1840	$20.22	1900	$24.26
1845	$21.66	1905	$22.46
1850	$24.26	1910	$21.66
1855	$21.66	1915	$19.95
1860	$22.46	1920	$10.11
1865	$13.18	1925	$11.55
1870	$15.96	1930	$12.13
1875	$18.38		

Source: "Consumer Price Index (Estimate) 1800–2006,"
http://woodrow.mpls.frb.fed.us/research/data/us/calc/hist1800.cfm

NOTES

CHAPTER 1

1. Moulton, *Journals*, vol. 3: *August 25, 1804–April 6, 1805*, 371, 374.
2. *Trade and Commerce, St. Louis, 1865*, 16.
3. Lobeck, *Geomorphology*, 224–29.
4. Hanson, *Conquest of the Missouri*, 205.
5. Missouri River Commission, *Map*, 1.
6. *Annual Report of the Chief of Engineers* (hereafter cited as *Annual Engineers Report*), *1887*, 2988.
7. Maximilian, *Travels*, 251, 264; U.S. Congress, House, *Improvement of Missouri River*, 4.
8. See, e.g., Giffen, *"Walks in Water,"* and Pope, "History of Steamboating."
9. Brackenridge, *Views of Louisiana*, 226; Sunder, *Fur Trade*, 19.
10. *Annual Engineers Report, 1915*, 1896.
11. U.S. House, *Improvement of Missouri River*, 5; *Annual Engineers Report, 1894*, 1739; Missouri River Commission, *Map*, 71–74.
12. Moulton, *Journals*, 4:228.
13. Missouri River Commission, *Map*, 74.
14. *Annual Engineers Report, 1894*, 1740.
15. Ibid., *1893*, 2304; *1913*, 929; *1915*, 1055; U.S. House, *Improvement of Missouri River*, 3; U.S. Congress, House, *Missouri River, from Sioux City to Fort Benton*, 15–16.
16. *Trade and Commerce, St. Louis, 1849*, 11; *Annual Engineers Report, 1883*, 1348.
17. Chittenden, *History of Early Steamboat Navigation*, 1:83; *Daily Tribune* (Jefferson City), 17 September 1891.
18. Here and below: *Annual Engineers Report, 1884*, 1539; *1915*, 1895; U.S. House, *Improvement of Missouri River*, 4; U.S. House, *Missouri River*, 16. "Below" as used here and hereafter refers to the text between the note number and the beginning of the next paragraph that has a note number.
19. Missouri River Commission, *Map*, 38; Bettis, *For Wood and Water*, 43.
20. Missouri River Commission, *Map*, 3, 7–9, 29.
21. U.S. House, *Improvement of Missouri River*, 5; Murray, *Travels*, 1:238.
22. Brackenridge, *Views of Louisiana*, 204, 208; Bradbury, *Travels*, 15, 22, 32.
23. Brackenridge, *Views of Louisiana*, 202, 214, 222–25, 231–35, 239, 244; Moulton, *Journals*, 3:11, 186, 200; 4:69, 110, 169.
24. Moulton, *Journals*, 4:124, 130, 133, 140; "C. J. Atkins' Logs," 354.
25. Lass, "Dakota Resources," 154, 166.
26. Ibid., 154.
27. Bettis, *For Wood and Water*, 17.
28. Ibid., 15; Moulton, *Journals*, 3:11; U.S. House, *Improvement of Missouri River*, 4; *Annual Engineers Report, 1893*, 2304.

29. Bradbury, *Travels*, 16; Moulton, *Journals*, 3:101.

30. Lass, "Dakota Resources," 168.

31. Fitzpatrick, *Nebraska Place-Names*, 171.

32. Moulton, *Journals*, 3:349.

33. James, *Account of an Expedition*, 219.

34. Ambler, *History of Transportation in the Ohio Valley*, 26; Chappell, "History of the Missouri River," 270; Chittenden, *Early Steamboat Navigation*, 1:91.

35. Chappell, "Missouri River," 271; Chittenden, *Early Steamboat Navigation*, 1:97–101; Brackenridge, *Views of Louisiana*, 231.

36. Chappell, "Missouri River," 271; Chittenden, *Early Steamboat Navigation*, 1:101–102; Brackenridge, *Views of Louisiana*, 245.

37. Baldwin, *Keelboat Age*, 41; Chappell, "Missouri River," 270; Chittenden, *Early Steamboat Navigation*, 1:92.

38. Nasatir, *Before Lewis and Clark*, 1:87, 97.

39. Moulton, *Journals*, 2:71n, 196, 215n; 4:24, 29, 108, 110–11, 152–56, 275, 305.

40. Here and below: Baldwin, *Keelboat Age*, 42; Chappell, "Missouri River," 270; Ambler, *Transportation in Ohio Valley*, 44.

41. Brackenridge, *Views of Louisiana*, 262; Bradbury, *Travels*, 111–12, 180; Luttig, *Journal of a Fur-Trading Expedition*, 33–34.

42. Here and below: Baldwin, *Keelboat Age*, 44.

43. Brackenridge, *Views of Louisiana*, 200; Bradbury, *Travels*, 46; Jensen and Hutchins, *Wheel Boats*, 45–67 passim.

44. Baldwin, *Keelboat Age*, 62–65; Brackenridge, *Views of Louisiana*, 205.

45. Chittenden, *Early Steamboat Navigation*, 1:107.

46. Ibid., 94–96; Bradbury, *Travels*, 180; Overholser, *Fort Benton*, 147.

47. Here and below: Chittenden, *Early Steamboat Navigation*, 1:94; Chittenden, *American Fur Trade*, 1:34; J. H. Bradley, "Bradley Manuscript—Book II," 103; Bradbury, *Travels*, 180.

48. Bettis, *For Wood and Water*, 126; *Jefferson City Inquirer*, 8 April 1848.

49. Here and below: Hunter, *Steamboats*, 85–100 passim; Lass, *History of Steamboating*, 108–10.

50. U.S. House, *Improvement of Missouri River*, 24.

51. Here and below: Hunter, *Steamboats*, 253–54.

52. U.S. House, *Improvement of Missouri River*, 23–24.

53. For Missouri River steamboat wrecks, see Chittenden, "Report of Steamboat Wrecks"; *Annual Engineers Report, 1897*, 3870–92; and McDonald, "The Missouri River and Its Victims," first–third articles. The McDonald list, which includes gasoline boats as well as steamboats, is more inclusive.

54. For the damming and channelization of the Missouri, see Hart, *Dark Missouri*, and Schneiders, *Unruly River*.

CHAPTER 2

1. For the background and nature of the War of 1812, see Horsman, *War of 1812*.

2. For detailed treatment on the Treaty of Ghent, see Engelman, *Peace of Christmas Eve;* and Bailey, *Diplomatic History of the American People*, 158–60.

3. Holmquist and Brookins, *Minnesota's Major Historic Sites*, 1.

4. Frazer, *Forts of the West*, 68–70; Gregg, "History of Fort Osage," 439–41, 444; McReynolds, *Missouri*, 54–57.

5. Frazer, *Forts of the West*, 75–76; Wesley, "A Still Larger View of the So-Called Yellowstone Expedition," 219.

6. A. E. Smith, *From Exploration to Statehood*, 87–90, 97.

7. L. M. Kane, Holmquist, and Gilman, *Northern Expeditions of Stephen H. Long*, 8–9.

8. [Calhoun], *Papers of John C. Calhoun* (hereafter cited as *Calhoun Papers*), 2:194.

9. Ibid.

10. Ibid., 195.

11. 9 May 1818, 14:192.

12. *Calhoun Papers*, 3:60.

13. L. M. Kane, Holmquist, and Gilman, *Northern Expeditions*, 3–5.

14. 16 February 1818, *Calhoun Papers*, 2:139.

15. Nichols and Halley, *Long*, 38, 58.

16. Ibid., 59.

17. Here and below: Thomas A. Smith to Calhoun, 26 June 1818; Calhoun to Joseph G. Swift, 1 September 1818; Swift to Calhoun, 10 October 1818; Calhoun to Long, 15 December 1818, *Calhoun Papers*, 2:350; 3:89, 199, 395. All dollar amounts used in the present book are of the times mentioned. For a guide to their relative value in 2006, see the appendix.

18. Long to Calhoun, 24 December 1818, *Calhoun Papers*, 3:423.

19. 10 July 1818.

20. Here and below: Tunstall Quarles to Calhoun, 27 August 1818; William Taylor Barry to Calhoun, 14 September 1818; Robert Wickliffe to Calhoun, 14 September 1818; Amos Kendall to Calhoun, 23 September 1818, *Calhoun Papers*, 3:72, 122, 129, 152.

21. James Johnson subsistence contract signed by Richard Johnson, 25 November 1818; Clay to Calhoun, 16 September 1818; Mason to Calhoun, 25 October 1818, *Calhoun Papers*, 3:300, 133, 233.

22. Jesup to Calhoun, 3 January 1820, *Calhoun Papers*, 4:621.

23. U.S. Congress, House, *Documents in Relation to the Claim of James Johnson*, 6.

24. Calhoun to Atkinson, 7 February 1820, *Calhoun Papers*, 4:646.

25. Here and below: Ambler, *Transportation in Ohio Valley*, 111–16.

26. Ibid., 122–24; Johnson, "Engineering the Ohio," 181.

27. Ambler, *Transportation in Ohio Valley*, 124–25.

28. Ibid., 127; Petersen, *Steamboating*, 73.

29. Ambler, *Transportation in Ohio Valley*, 126.

30. Thorp, "Beginnings of Steamboat Navigation," 378.

31. Ambler, *Transportation in Ohio Valley*, 126.

32. Lytle and Holdcamper, *Merchant Steam Vessels*, 173; Thorp, "Beginnings of Steamboat Navigation," 378; *Missouri Gazette* (St. Louis), 4 October 1817.

33. 24 April 1819, 15:144.

34. *Niles' Weekly Register*, 11 July 1818, 20:344.

35. Nichols, "Martin Cantonment," 4–6.

36. 17 October 1818, 15:117.

37. Long to Calhoun, 24 December 1818, 27 May 1819, *Calhoun Papers*, 3:422; 4:79.

38. Long to Calhoun, 30 December 1818, *Calhoun Papers*, 3:438; Nichols and Halley, *Long*, 66.

39. *Missouri Gazette and Public Advertiser* (St. Louis), 26 May 1819; Petersen, *Steamboating*, 84; Nichols and Halley, *Long*, 66.

40. Thorp, "Beginnings of Steamboat Navigation," 378.

41. Ibid.; *National Register* (Washington, D.C.), 10 July 1819, 8:32.

42. *National Register*, 10 July 1819, 8:32.

43. Nichols and Halley, *Long*, 77–79.

44. Here and below: Calhoun to Long, 8 March 1819, *Calhoun Papers*, 3:639–40.

45. "About the APS"; "History of the Academy"; Wood, *Stephen Harriman Long*, 65–72.

46. Simpson, "Baldwin, William"; Stroud, "Say, Thomas"; James, *Account of an Expedition*, 40n.

47. Long to Calhoun, 20 April 1819, 3 January 1820, *Calhoun Papers*, 4:31–33, 543; James, *Account of an Expedition*, 41n.

48. Lytle and Holdcamper, *Merchant Steam Vessels*, 116; James Johnson to Calhoun, 12 February 1819, and James Johnson to Thomas S. Jesup, 13 February 1819, *Calhoun Papers*, 3:570–71, 574–76.

49. Lytle and Holdcamper, *Merchant Steam Vessels*, 28, 68; Johnson to Calhoun, 30 March 1819, *Calhoun Papers*, 3:708; [Hubbell], "First Steamboats on the Missouri," 374.

50. Martin to Talbot Chambers, 15 January 1819, *Calhoun Papers*, 3:498.

51. Chambers to Calhoun, 7 February 1819, *Calhoun Papers*, 3:554.

52. Wesley, "Still Larger View," 224; Nichols, *General Henry Atkinson*, 55; Beers, *Western Military*

Frontier, 42; James, *Account of an Expedition*, 108; Atkinson to Calhoun, 7 June 1819, *Calhoun Papers*, 4:94.

53. The Council Bluff is the site near present-day Fort Calhoun, Nebraska (about ten miles north of Omaha) where Meriwether Lewis and William Clark met with Otoe and Missouri Indians on their 1804 ascent. It should not be confused with the nearby city of Council Bluffs, Iowa.

54. Calhoun to Jackson, 6 March 1819, *Calhoun Papers*, 3:633.

55. R. D. Hurt, *Agriculture and Slavery*, 2; Ridgway, "Howard County," 53.

56. Violette, "Early Settlements," 50; Voss, "Town Growth," 64–65.

57. As quoted in Voss, "Town Growth," 68.

58. Hurt, *Agriculture and Slavery*, 2; Kappler, *Indian Affairs*, 95–97.

59. H. M. Anderson, "Missouri, Land of Promise," 239.

60. [Peck], *Forty Years*, 135–37.

61. H. M. Anderson, "Missouri, Land of Promise," 229, 242.

62. Viles, "Old Franklin," 270; *History of Howard and Cooper Counties*, 127.

63. Viles, "Old Franklin," 270.

64. James, *Account of an Expedition*, 148.

65. Ibid., 158; [Peck], *Forty Years*, 143; *Missouri Intelligencer and Boon's Lick Advertiser* (Franklin and Fayette), 11 June 1819.

66. James, *Account of an Expedition*, 146.

67. Viles, "Old Franklin," 273.

68. Ridgway, "Howard County," 54; Moneyhon, "Rector, Henry Massey"; "Captain John Nelson," 509; Lytle and Holdcamper, *Merchant Steam Vessels*, 100; *Missouri Intelligencer*, 21 and 28 May 1819.

69. *Missouri Intelligencer*, 28 May 1819.

70. Ibid., 4 June 1819.

71. Ibid., 28 May 1819.

72. Ibid., 4 June 1819.

73. Viles, "Old Franklin," 279.

74. *Missouri Intelligencer*, 4 June 1819.

75. Here and below: ibid., 11 June 1819.

76. Atkinson to Calhoun, 7 June 1819, *Calhoun Papers*, 4:95.

77. [Hubbell], "First Steamboats," 374; Jesup to Calhoun, 2, 12 June 1819, *Calhoun Papers*, 4:86, 104–105; Johnson, "Engineering the Ohio," 185.

78. Atkinson to Calhoun, 22 May 1819, *Calhoun Papers*, 4:70.

79. Here and below: Long to Calhoun, 27 May 1819, *Calhoun Papers*, 4:79.

80. Nichols and Halley, *Long*, 86.

81. Schoolcraft, *View of the Lead Mines*, 242. On the estimated population of St. Louis, see Viles, "Missouri in 1820," 41.

82. *St. Louis Enquirer*, 26 May 1819.

83. Gardner, "Business Career of Moses Austin," 244; James Johnson to Richard Johnson, 23, 27 May 1819, *Calhoun Papers*, 4:72–74, 77–80.

84. Chambers to Bissell, 21 May 1819; James Johnson to Richard Johnson, 23 May 1819, *Calhoun Papers*, 4:68–70, 72–74.

85. Richard Johnson to Calhoun, 14 June 1819, *Calhoun Papers*, 4:107–109.

86. Jesup to Calhoun, 2 June 1819, *Calhoun Papers*, 4:86.

87. Chambers to Bissell, 21 May 1819, *Calhoun Papers*, 4:69.

88. 23 June 1819.

89. Chambers, *Old Bullion Benton*, 78–82.

90. Atkinson to Calhoun, 19 June, 11 July 1819, *Calhoun Papers*, 4:112, 143; *Missouri Gazette and Public Advertiser*, 30 June 1819.

91. Jesup to Calhoun, 26 June, 8 July 1819, *Calhoun Papers*, 4:119–21, 139.

92. Johnson to Jesup, 9 July 1819, *Calhoun Papers*, 4:141.

93. James, *Account of an Expedition*, 121.

94. 23 June 1819.

95. James, *Account of an Expedition*, 122.

96. Ibid., 124, 157.

97. Ibid., 173.

98. Ibid., 126–27; Long to Calhoun, 19 July 1819, *Calhoun Papers*, 4:160.

99. *Missouri Intelligencer*, 16, 23 July, 3 September 1819.

100. Calhoun to Long, 1 September 1819, *Calhoun Papers*, 4:292.

101. Long to Calhoun, 3 January 1820, *Calhoun Papers*, 4:160, 543; James, *Account of an Expedition*, 221.

102. Atkinson to Calhoun, 11 July 1819, *Calhoun Papers*, 4:143.

103. [Hubbell], "First Steamboats," 377.

104. Ibid., 374; *St. Louis Enquirer*, 21 July 1819.

105. *St. Louis Enquirer*, 21 July 1819.

106. [Hubbell], "First Steamboats," 377.

107. Johnson to Calhoun, 26 November 1819; Jesup to Calhoun, 8 July , 9 September 1819; Atkinson to Calhoun, 30 July, 13, 25 August 1819, *Calhoun Papers*, 4:434–45, 139, 311–12, 189, 237–39, 273–74.

108. [Hubbell], "First Steamboats," 380; *St. Louis Enquirer*, 15 April 1820; extract of letter from Uriel Sebree to James Johnson, 30 August 1819, *Calhoun Papers*, 4:446–47. On the wrecking of the *Jefferson*, see "First Steamboat Wreck on the Missouri," 188.

109. Atkinson to Calhoun, 3 October 1819, *Calhoun Papers*, 4:360; Sheldon, *Nebraska*, 1:192; Beers, *Western Military Frontier*, 44.

110. Long to Calhoun, 3 January 1820, *Calhoun Papers*, 4:546.

111. Memoranda from Jesup [December 1819]; Calhoun to Atkinson, 7 February 1820; Jesup to Atkinson, 22 February 1820; Atkinson to Calhoun, 10 March 1810, *Calhoun Papers*, 4:535–37, 645–47, 678, 708–10.

112. Richard Johnson to Calhoun, 26 July 1819; James Johnson to Calhoun, 27 November 1819, *Calhoun Papers*, 4:178–81, 452.

113. Richard Johnson to Calhoun, 5 July 1819; Monroe to Calhoun, 5 July 1819, *Calhoun Papers*, 4:134, 135.

114. U.S. Congress, *Annals of Congress*, 750.

115. *American State Papers: Military Affairs*, 2:68.

116. J. M. Jones, "When Expectations Exceed Reality," 261.

117. Wood, *Stephen Long*, 89–104; *St. Louis Enquirer*, 28 June 1820.

118. Jones, "When Expectations Exceed Reality," 262.

119. Apple, "Johnson, James"; McManus, "Johnson, Richard Mentor."

CHAPTER 3

1. Rafferty, *Historical Atlas of Missouri*, 34; Atherton, "Missouri's Society and Economy," 468; U.S. Bureau of the Census, *Fifth Census*, 23.

2. H. M. Anderson, "Frontier Economic Problems," 54, 60–62; D. B. Dorsey, "Panic of 1819," 80, 87–88.

3. Hurt, *Agriculture and Slavery*, 80–81, 103; *Missouri Intelligencer*, 11 November 1823.

4. *Missouri Intelligencer*, 30 October 1821; "Rope Walk," 190.

5. *Missouri Intelligencer*, 19 November 1822.

6. Ibid., 20 August 1822; Atherton, "Missouri's Society and Economy," 472.

7. *Missouri Intelligencer*, 7 May 1821.

8. Ibid., 11 December 1821.

9. Ibid.

10. Ibid., 21 May 1822.

11. Buley, *Old Northwest*, 1:446.

12. *Missouri Intelligencer*, 4 June 1822; Wetmore, *Gazeteer*, 269.

13. *Missouri Intelligencer*, 4 June 1822; 30 December 1823; 12 February, 12 June 1824.

14. Ibid., 16 September 1825.

15. H. M. Anderson, "Missouri, Land of Promise," 250; H. M. Anderson, "Missouri, 1804–1828," 172.

16. *Missouri Intelligencer*, 1 April 1823; Lytle and Holdcamper, *Merchant Steam Vessels*, 174; Voss, "Town Growth," 78. For extensive coverage of Howard County settlement, see Schroeder, "Spread of Settlement."

17. D. W. Eaton, "How Missouri Counties . . . Were Named," first article, 211, and second article, 278; Ford, *History of Jefferson City,* 11–13; Franklin, "Rocheport, Missouri," 3–4; Voss, "Town Growth," 75.

18. Van Zandt, *Boundaries,* 188; [Hubbell], "First Steamboats," 379; D. W. Eaton, "How Missouri Counties . . . Were Named," second article, 277; Kappler, *Indian Affairs,* 217–25; "Independence, Missouri," 31–32; Atherton, "James and Robert Aull," 3.

19. *Missouri Intelligencer,* 12 May 1826.

20. Ibid., 16 June 1826.

21. Ibid., 25 September 1829.

22. Ibid.

23. Ibid., 28 July 1832.

24. Ibid., 28 July 1832; 25 May 1833.

25. Ibid., 4 July 1835; Viles, "Old Franklin," 278; Voss, "Town Growth," 72.

26. James, *Account of an Expedition,* 14:149.

27. *Missouri Intelligencer,* 14 April 1826; 21 March, 25 April, 1 August 1828; *Missouri Republican* (St. Louis), 6 April 1826; 15 April 1828.

28. Walker, *Wagonmasters,* 18; Chittenden, *American Fur Trade,* 2:517.

29. McReynolds, *Missouri,* 93.

30. Walker, *Wagonmasters,* 19.

31. Gregg, "Fort Osage," 466; H. M. Anderson, "Frontier Economic Problems," 182–83.

32. McReynolds, *Missouri,* 96; Walker, *Wagonmasters,* 19.

33. Kappler, *Indian Affairs,* 246–50.

34. *Missouri Intelligencer,* 2 May 1828.

35. Ibid.

36. Ibid., 6 November 1829.

37. Frazer, *Forts of the West,* 84.

38. *Missouri Intelligencer,* 13, 27 May, 24 June 1820; *Missouri Gazette and Public Advertiser,* 6 June 1821; [Hubbell], "First Steamboats," 380.

39. F. L. Dorsey, *Master of the Mississippi,* 111; Lytle and Holdcamper, *Merchant Steam Vessels,* 226; Hunter, *Steamboats on the Western Rivers,* 76.

40. *Missouri Intelligencer,* 30 April 1821.

41. *St. Louis Enquirer,* 5 May, 16 June 1821.

42. *Missouri Intelligencer,* 7 May 1822.

43. Ibid., 4 November 1820; James, *Account of an Expedition,* frontispiece map, 286.

44. *Missouri Intelligencer,* 4 November 1820.

45. *St. Louis Enquirer,* 13 October 1821.

46. *Missouri Intelligencer,* 12, 19 November 1822; 6 May 1823.

47. *St. Louis Enquirer,* 1 March, 31 May 1824; *Missouri Intelligencer,* 3 April, 5 June 1824.

48. Here and below: Schell, *History of South Dakota,* 58; Sunder, *Joshua Pilcher,* 42–48; Olson and Naugle, *History of Nebraska,* 47.

49. The most detailed account of the Atkinson-O'Fallon Expedition is Jensen and Hutchins, *Wheel Boats on the Missouri.* For the development of horse boats, see Shomette, "Heyday of the Horse Ferry."

50. Beers, *Western Military Frontier,* 52; Olson, *History of Nebraska,* 49–60; Frazer, *Forts of the West,* 84.

51. Beers, *Western Military Frontier,* 94–95; Hunt, *History of Fort Leavenworth,* 12–23.

52. *Missouri Intelligencer,* 10 May 1827; Frazer, *Forts of the West,* 56.

53. *Missouri Republican,* 29 April 1828; 12 May 1829. This *Diana,* built in 1828 and lost in 1833, is not to be confused with the American Fur Company's *Diana,* built in 1834 (Lytle and Holdcamper, *Merchant Steam Vessels,* 54).

54. P. St. G. Cooke, *Scenes and Adventures,* 40.

55. Hunt, *Fort Leavenworth,* 26; *Missouri Intelligencer,* 16 September 1828.

56. Schusky, "Upper Missouri Indian Agency," 250; Hill, *Office of Indian Affairs,* 184; [Hubbell], "First Steamboats," 380.

57. Schusky, "Upper Missouri Indian Agency," 254; Hill, *Office of Indian Affairs,* 184.

58. Here and below: Gibson, *American Indian*, 312; Zornow, *Kansas*, 43ff.; Beers, *Western Military Frontier*, 94–96.

59. Kappler, *Indian Affairs*, 305–10; Beers, *Western Military Frontier*, 96.

60. *Missouri Republican*, 16, 23 June 1829; *St. Louis Beacon*, 4 July 1829; Lytle and Holdcamper, *Merchant Steam Vessels*, 230.

61. U.S. Bureau of the Census, *Fifth Census*, 150.

62. *Missouri Intelligencer*, 11 July 1835; Billington and Ridge, *Westward Expansion*, 296.

63. Taylor, *Transportation Revolution*, 32–36, 46; *Missouri Republican*, 19 August 1834; *Missouri Intelligencer*, 11 July 1835.

64. *Missouri Republican*, 19 August 1834; Wood, *Long*, 150.

65. Johnson, "Engineering the Ohio," 189; *Missouri Republican*, 31 March 1835.

66. *Missouri Republican*, 31 March 1835.

67. Ibid., 12 August 1834.

68. Ibid., 16 June 1835.

69. W. B. Stevens, *St. Louis*, 344.

70. *Missouri Republican*, 13 July 1830; 24 May 1831; 10 April 1832; 21 April 1834; 3 December 1835.

71. Ibid., 27 July, 7 December 1829; 10 April 1832.

72. Ibid., 23 July 1836.

73. Here and below: Registration of Vessels Act, (1789), 55–57 (1789); Schmeckebier, *Customs Service*, 65.

74. *Missouri Republican*, 23 July 1836.

75. Ibid., 12 August 1834.

76. Ibid., 14 May 1835.

77. Ibid., 23 July 1836.

78. Atherton, "James and Robert Aull," 3–8.

79. *Missouri Intelligencer*, 16 April 1831.

80. Atherton, "James and Robert Aull," 9–13.

81. Compiled by the author from numerous newspaper articles and data in Lytle and Holdcamper, *Merchant Steam Vessels*.

82. *Missouri Republican*, 22 September 1828; 7, 14 May 1836.

83. Haites, Mak, and Walton, *Western River Transportation*, 30, 137.

84. Hunter, *Steamboats*, 110.

85. W. B. Stevens, *St. Louis*, 262.

86. Johnson, "Engineering the Ohio," 187.

87. *St. Louis Enquirer*, 13 January 1824.

88. Hunter, *Steamboats*, 193; Johnson, "Engineering the Ohio," 188.

89. Here and below: F. I. Dorsey, *Master of the Mississippi*, 144–57 passim.

90. *Missouri Intelligencer*, 26 May, 18 August 1832.

91. Ibid., 7 July 1832.

92. Ibid., 21 July 1832.

93. Ibid., 29 September, 27 October 1832.

94. *Missouri Intelligencer*, 13 April 1833; *Missouri Argus* (St. Louis), 28 October 1836; *Missouri Republican*, 18 November 1834; 26 July, 30 November, 20 December 1836; McDonald, "Missouri River and Its Victims," first article, 233. Perhaps due to a typographical error, McDonald listed the *Chian* as the "*Chain*."

95. Barbour, *Fort Union*, 16, 39–40, 43.

96. Chittenden, *American Fur Trade*, 1:338.

97. D. Jackson, *Voyages of the Steamboat Yellow Stone*, 2.

98. 14 April 1831.

99. Jackson, *Steamboat Yellow Stone*, 1–2.

100. *Missouri Intelligencer*, 6 August 1831.

101. Jackson, *Steamboat Yellow Stone*, 29.

102. Quoted in Tolman, "Catlin, George."

103. Chittenden, *American Fur Trade*, 1:340.

104. *Missouri Intelligencer*, 28 July 1832.

105. Ibid.

106. Chittenden, *American Fur Trade*, 1:341.

107. Casler, *Steamboats*, 18; *Missouri Republican*, 19 March 1833.

108. Maximilian, *Travels*, 9–13, 234–37.

109. Ibid., 237, 327.

110. *Missouri Republican*, 16 July 1833.

111. Casler, *Steamboats*, 32; Chittenden, *American Fur Trade*, 1:350.

112. [Chardon], *Chardon's Journal*, 363, 371, 373; Michael M. Casler, Fort Union Trading Post National Historic Site, Williston, N.Dak., telephone interview by author, 25 February 2003.

113. [Chardon], *Journal*, 31, 33, 37, 381.

114. Chittenden, *American Fur Trade*, 364, 366.

115. *Missouri Republican*, 23 May, 16 July 1835; Casler, *Steamboats*, 22; [Chardon], *Journal*, 69–70, 380; McDonald, "Missouri River and Its Victims," first article, 239.

Chapter 4

1. Wetmore, *Gazeteer*, 267; *Daily Missouri Republican* (St. Louis), 21 December 1836; *Niles' National Register*, 25 January 1845, 323.

2. Kappler, *Indian Affairs*, 305–10; McKee, "Platte Purchase," 129–31.

3. McKee, "Platte Purchase," 132–40 passim.

4. *Missouri Republican*, 17 February 1835.

5. Ibid., 25 July 1835; Goodrich and Gentzler, *Marking Missouri History*, 4.

6. Western Boundary of Missouri Act (1836), 34.

7. Kappler, *Indian Affairs*, 466–73; Van Buren Proclamation (1837), 802.

8. *Daily Missouri Republican*, 26 June, 17 July 1837; McKee, "Platte Purchase," 143.

9. *Niles' Weekly Register*, 25 January 1845, 323; D. W. Eaton, "How Missouri Counties . . . Were Named," first article, 202, and fourth article, 336.

10. Willoughby, *Robidoux's Town*, 11, 16, 21.

11. Fitzgerald, "Town Booming," 11–12.

12. For full treatment of Francois Chouteau, see Marra, *Cher Oncle, Cher Papa*.

13. Here and below: *History of Jackson County*, 388, 395; "A History of Kansas City, Missouri," http://www.kcmo.org/kcmo.nsf/web/kchistory/.

14. Here and below: T. B. Smith and Gehrig, *History of Chariton and Howard Counties*, 236–38; "Brunswick Area History: Early History," http://jard.homeip.net/brunswick/history/earlyhist.html.

15. Wetmore, *Gazeteer*, 54; *Daily Missouri Republican*, 10 September 1839; *History of Howard and Cooper Counties*, 205–207.

16. Goodrich and Gentzler, *Marking Missouri History*, 150; *History of Franklin, Jefferson . . . Counties*, 302, 310.

17. *Jeffersonian Republican* (Jefferson City), 20 August 1842.

18. Ibid., 15 October 1842.

19. *Jefferson City Inquirer*, 22 November 1845.

20. *Daily Missouri Republican*, 14, 20, 21, 27 January; 1 February 1840; *Jeffersonian Republican*, 20 January 1844.

21. *Jeffersonian Republican*, 17 April 1841.

22. Ibid., 3 August 1839.

23. Here and below: *Jeffersonian Republican*, 3 August 1839; 11, 25, 30 June 1842; 18 May 1844.

24. Ibid., 8 May 1841.

25. Ibid., 26 March 1842.

26. Ibid., 31 July 1841.

27. Ibid., 12, 26 March, 23 April, 30 July 1842; 2 December 1843; 2 March 1844; *Jefferson City Inquirer*, 25 May, 3 August 1843; 29 February, 2 May 1844.

28. *Jeffersonian Republican*, 15 May 1841.

29. Ibid., 4 April 1840; 27 February 1841.

30. *Daily Missouri Republican,* 5 October 1839.

31. Wetmore, *Gazeteer,* 26; *Jeffersonian Republican,* 27 August 1842.

32. R. D. Hurt, *Agriculture and Slavery,* x–xiv; *Daily Missouri Republican,* 5 October 1839.

33. R. D. Hurt, *Agriculture and Slavery,* 100; *Daily Missouri Republican,* 5 October 1839.

34. *Daily Missouri Republican,* 5 October 1839; *Jeffersonian Republican,* 1 May 1841; *Niles' National Register,* 2 November 1844, 144.

35. *Jeffersonian Republican,* 22 May 1841; 23 April 1842.

36. M. W. Eaton, "Development and Later Decline of the Hemp Industry," 344–48.

37. Ibid., 349; Hurt, *Agriculture and Slavery,* 110.

38. *Jeffersonian Republican,* 26 January, 29 March 1839; 26 March 1842; 21 January 1843.

39. *Daily Missouri Republican,* 15 May 1838.

40. Ibid., 10 April 1839.

41. *Jefferson City Inquirer,* 29 May 1845.

42. Hunter, *Steamboats,* 394–96.

43. *Daily Missouri Republican,* 12 November 1839.

44. Johansen, *Empire of the Columbia,* 112.

45. Mattes, *Great Platte River Road,* 13.

46. Here and below: *Daily Missouri Republican,* 6 November 1838; 18, 25 March 1839; McReynolds, *Missouri,* 138–42.

47. Here and below: *Daily Missouri Republican,* 12, 16, 17, 19, 20, 22, 23 June 1840.

48. *Jeffersonian Republican,* 20 July 1844.

49. *Daily Missouri Republican,* 5 July 1839.

50. *Jeffersonian Republican,* 8 July 1843.

51. Ibid., 30 April, 7 May, 25 June 1842.

52. Murray, *Travels in North America,* 2:86.

53. *Daily Missouri Republican,* 9 June 1839.

54. Ibid., 20 June 1840.

55. *Jefferson City Inquirer,* 7 March 1844.

56. Ibid., 17 August 1843.

57. Olson and Naugle, *History of Nebraska,* 49.

58. Chittenden and Richardson, *Father Pierre-Jean de Smet,* 154.

59. Ibid.

60. *Daily Missouri Republican,* 6 May 1839; Bray and Bray, *Nicollet,* 141.

61. Casler, *Steamboats,* 18, 23–25, 31, 35; Bettis, *For Wood and Water,* x; Lytle and Holdcamper, *Merchant Steam Vessels,* 98.

62. Here and below: Bettis, *For Wood and Water,* x, 60, 73, 79; Casler, *Steamboats,* 18, 23–35, 31, 35

63. Bettis, *For Wood and Water,* 136ff.

64. Ibid., 144; *Daily Missouri Republican,* 17 July 1837; 17 July 1838; 1 July 1839.

65. Bray and Bray, *Nicollet,* 5–20 passim.

66. Ibid., 158.

67. Sterling, "Audubon, John James." For Harris's account, see [Edward Harris], *Up the Missouri with Audubon.*

68. Audubon, *Audubon and His Journals,* 1:455.

69. Ibid.

70. McDermott, *Audubon in the West,* 65.

71. Ibid., 176; Bettis, *For Wood and Water,* 77.

72. Here and below: Chittenden, *American Fur Trade,* 1:369–72; Sunder, *Fur Trade,* 54–87 passim; Casler, *Steamboats,* 23, 31; *Niles' National Register,* 27 July 1844, 352.

73. Dollar, "Smallpox Epidemic," 18–23.

74. R. W. Meyer, *Village Indians,* 91–97; Barbour, *Fort Union,* 118; Dollar, "Smallpox Epidemic," 24.

75. *Daily Missouri Republican,* 17 July 1838.

76. Here and below: Schultz, "Steamboat Navigation," 175; Rafferty, *Historical Atlas of Missouri,* 15, 22; "Osage River," 86–90.

77. *History of Henry and St. Clair Counties*, 981; Jenkins, *Through the Civil War*, 173–79; K. K. White and Miles, *History of Benton County*, 2:1219.

78. *Daily Missouri Republican*, 15 March, 22 April 1837; Lytle and Holdcamper, *Merchant Steam Vessels*, 9, 241.

79. *Daily Missouri Republican*, 29 March, 18 July, 1 August 1837; Lytle and Holdcamper, *Merchant Steam Vessels*, 159.

80. *Daily Missouri Republican*, 13, 21 April 1838; Lytle and Holdcamper, *Merchant Steam Vessels*, 3.

81. 11 May 1838; Lytle and Holdcamper, *Merchant Steam Vessels*, 183.

82. *Jeffersonian Republican*, 15 February 1840.

83. *Jefferson City Inquirer*, 20 May 1841; *Jeffersonian Republican*, 5, 12 November; Lytle and Holdcamper, *Merchant Steam Vessels*, 126, 134; Schultz, "Steamboat Navigation," 176.

84. Here and below: *Jefferson City Inquirer*, 15 February 1844; Schultz, "Steamboat Navigation," 176; Lytle and Holdcamper, *Merchant Steam Vessels*, 4, 98, 226; Goodrich and Gentzler, *Marking Missouri History*, 112; Jenkins, *Through the Civil War*, 174.

85. Verbatim copies of the laws, in *Daily Missouri Republican*, 15 May 1839.

86. Ibid., 3 September, 3 December 1839; *Jefferson City Inquirer*, 14 September 1843; *Jeffersonian Republican*, 27 January 1844.

87. Proceeds of the Sales of Public Lands Act (1841), 455.

88. *Jefferson City Inquirer*, 24 November 1842.

89. Here and below: *Jefferson City Inquirer*, 31 August, 14 September 1843; 11 January 1844; *Jeffersonian Republican*, 27 January, 2, 16 March 1844.

90. *Jefferson City Inquirer*, 4 September, 15 December 1845.

91. Giffen, *"Walks in Water,"* 84.

92. The Missouri River steamboats of 1841, as listed in the *Jeffersonian Republican* of 16 March 1842, were the *Amazon, Bowling Green, Colonel Woods, Emilie, General Brady, General Leavenworth, Glaucus, Gloster, Huntsville, Iatan, Lehigh, Little Red, Malta, Manhattan, Mary Tompkins, Oceana, Omega, Osage Valley, Platte, Preemption, Roebuck, Shawnee, Thames, Trapper,* and *Warsaw.* The summary of their nature and disposition, with the exception of the *Roebuck,* which was not listed, was calculated by the author from data in Lytle and Holdcamper, *Merchant Steam Vessels.* The *Colonel Woods,* which was sold to a foreign party in 1844, was used only in the determination of tonnage and construction site.

93. Bettis, *For Wood and Water,* x; Casler, *Steamboats,* 35. In comparing western steamboats of 1835, with an average tonnage of 159, to those of 1847, which averaged 168 tons, Hunter (*Steamboats,* 652) determined that the depth of holds on average decreased from 5.53 to 4.78 feet and that the 1847 boats were 6 feet longer and nearly 3 feet wider.

94. *Daily Missouri Republican,* 22, 25 April 1837; 4, 18 May, 13 July 1838; Chittenden, *Early Steamboat Navigation,* 1:56.

95. *Daily Missouri Republican,* 18 February 1837.

96. Ibid., 29 March 1837.

97. *Jeffersonian Republican,* 5 November 1842. According to the article "Boat Building in St. Louis" (47), Glenn built both the *North St. Louis* and the *Little Eagle* in St. Louis, but there is no record of the latter boat in Lytle and Holdcamper, *Merchant Steam Vessels.*

98. *Daily Missouri Republican,* 27 April 1839. Tonnage from Lytle and Holdcamper, *Merchant Steam Vessels.*

99. *Daily Missouri Republican,* 29 April 1839.

100. Ibid., 16 May 1839.

101. "Boat Building in St. Louis," 47–48.

102. Ibid.; Skillman, *Western Metropolis,* 105.

103. *Jefferson City Inquirer,* 2 October 1845; *Niles' National Register,* 2 March 1844, 4.

104. Rivers and Harbors Act (1838), 270; *Daily Missouri Republican,* 24 July 1838.

105. U.S. Congress, Senate, "Report of the Chief Military Engineer," in *Documents Accompanying the Report of the Secretary of War,* 203; *Jeffersonian Republican,* 13 April 1839; *Daily Missouri Republican,* 29 August 1839.

106. *Jeffersonian Republican,* 28 September 1839.

107. *Niles' National Register*, 21 January 1843, 333; *Jeffersonian Republican*, 12 August 1843.

108. Scharf, *St. Louis*, 2:1054.

109. *Daily Missouri Republican*, 7 August 1837; 23 July 1838.

110. Ibid., 13 September 1838.

111. *Annual Review, History of St. Louis*, 11; Scharf, *St. Louis*, 2:1055–60.

112. In 1838 to September 7, of the 80 steamboats lost on the Mississippi and its tributaries, 37 were snagged and 8 blown up. Seventeen were reported as "sunk." *Niles' National Register*, 7 September 1838, 32.

113. J. K. Brown, *Limbs on the Levee*, 10; Hunter, *Steamboats*, 123–27.

114. Brown, *Limbs on the Levee*, 114; Hunter, *Steamboats*, 523.

115. For graphic descriptions of the destruction of the three boats, see Lloyd, *Steamboat Directory*, 89–101, 105–107.

116. *Missouri Republican*, 25 May 1837.

117. U.S. Congress, Senate, *Report of the Commissioner of Patents, to the Senate*, 65; Lloyd, *Steamboat Directory*, 91; *Missouri Argus*, 17 May 1838.

118. *Missouri Argus*, 17 May 1838.

119. *Niles' National Register*, 29 February, 432; 8 August, 368.

120. Here and below: Security for Steam Passengers Act (1838), 304–306.

121. *Daily Missouri Republican*, 29 September 1838.

122. Ibid., 19 September 1838.

123. Ibid., 17 October 1838.

124. Ibid., 29 November 1838.

125. Act to Modify Security for Steam Passengers Act of 1838 (1843), 626.

126. U.S. Senate, *Report of the Commissioner of Patents, to the Senate*, 68–110 passim.

127. U.S. Congress, House, *Statement of Calvin Case*, 8.

128. Giffen, "Walks in Water," 82; McDonald, "Missouri River and Its Victims," first article, 241.

129. Here and below: *History of Vernon County*, 173; *Jeffersonian Republican*, 25 May, 22, 29 June, 6, 13 July 1844; *Jefferson City Inquirer*, 4 July 1844; *Niles' National Register*, 25 May, 1 June, 20 July 1844, 208, 224, 330.

130. Paxton, *Annals of Platte County*, 62.

131. "Statistics of Platte County," 326; Dixon, *Traffic History*, 23–24.

CHAPTER 5

1. J. D. Richardson, *Compilation of the Messages and Papers of the Presidents*, 4:442.

2. Clarke, *Stephen Watts Kearny*, 104; *Jefferson City Inquirer*, 27 May 1846.

3. McReynolds, *Missouri*, 145.

4. *Jefferson City Inquirer*, 10 June 1846.

5. Clarke, *Stephen Watts Kearny*, 111–13; Launius, *Alexander William Doniphan*, 90.

6. Clarke, *Stephen Watts Kearny*, 142, 161.

7. Launius, *Alexander William Doniphan*, 125.

8. *Jefferson City Inquirer*, 24 June, 1 September, 6 October 1846.

9. Here and below: Launius, *Alexander William Doniphan*, 146–90 passim.

10. *Jefferson City Inquirer*, 3 July 1847.

11. Ibid., 10 July 1847.

12. U.S. Congress, House, *Contracts Made by the War Department, 1847*, 81, 83.

13. Ibid.; U.S. Congress, Senate, *Contracts Made by the War Department, 1848*, 246–47.

14. Billington, *Far Western Frontier*, 194–95.

15. Sage, *History of Iowa*, 57.

16. Whittaker, "Kane, Thomas Leiper"; *Council Bluffs Chronotype*, 4 July 1855.

17. Billington, *Far Western Frontier*, 195–200; U.S. Bureau of the Census, *Seventh Census*, 575–76.

18. *Frontier Guardian* (Kanesville), 4 April 1849.

19. Ibid., 16 May 1849.

20. Ibid., 11 July 1851.

21. *Frontier Guardian and Iowa Sentinel* (Kanesville), 1 April 1852; *Western Bugle* (Kanesville), 2, 30 June 1852; Way, *Way's Packet Directory*, 263.

22. *Western Bugle*, 19 May 1852.

23. Ibid., 9 June 1852.

24. L. R. Cooke, "Letters," 217.

25. Ibid., 223–28.

26. *Frontier Guardian*, 22 August 1849; 29 May 1850; *Frontier Guardian and Iowa Sentinel*, 1 April 1852.

27. *Frontier Guardian*, 3 April 1850; *Frontier Guardian and Iowa Sentinel*, 6 May 1852.

28. *Frontier Guardian and Iowa Sentinel*, 1 April 1852.

29. Ibid., 28 May 1852.

30. *Western Bugle*, 19, 26 May 1852; *St. Joseph Gazette*, 9 June 1852.

31. Hafen and Young, *Fort Laramie*, 137–38.

32. Here and below: Mantor, "Fort Kearny," 175; Frazer, *Forts of the West*, 87.

33. Hafen and Young, *Fort Laramie*, 144.

34. Frazer, *Forts of the West*, 50, 56, 96–106; U.S. Congress, Senate, *Report of the Secretary of War, 1851*, 202.

35. U.S. Senate, *Report of the Secretary of War, 1851*, 289.

36. Ibid.

37. Here and below: U.S. Senate, *Contracts Made by the War Department, 1848*, 80; *1849*, 10, 18–21, 28–29; *1850*, 11, 15–16, 20–22; *1851*, 16–19, 23, 25, 28–29; *1852*, 10, 14, 19, 21; *1853*, 25, 28–29, 31, 33–35; *1854*, 9–10, 12–13, 14, 16, 19.

38. U.S. Senate, *Contracts Made by the War Department, 1849*, 24; *1850*, 22.

39. U.S. Senate, *Report of the Secretary of War, 1851*, 294–96.

40. Billington, *Far Western Frontier*, 218–20.

41. Ibid., 222; *Jefferson City Inquirer*, 9 December 1848.

42. Rohrbough, *Days of Gold*, 24–26.

43. Ibid., 55–61; Billington, *Far Western Frontier*, 225.

44. *Jefferson Inquirer*, 28 February 1852; *Brunswicker* (Brunswick, Mo.), 30 April 1853; *Glasgow Weekly Times*, 2 June 1853.

45. *St. Joseph Gazette*, 28 April 1852.

46. *St. Louis Republican*, as quoted in *Jefferson Inquirer*, 14 April 1849; *Liberty Tribune* (Liberty, Mo.), 13 April 1849.

47. Unruh, *Plains Across*, 119–20.

48. As quoted in *St. Joseph Gazette*, 5 May 1852.

49. *St. Joseph Gazette*, 30 June 1852.

50. Fitzgerald, "Town Booming," 31–63 passim; *Frontier Guardian*, 7 March 1849.

51. *Brunswicker*, 25 June 1853.

52. Dixon, *Traffic History*, 23; "Commercial Statistics," 373; *Trade and Commerce, St. Louis, 1849*, 11; "Statistics of Platte County," 326–27.

53. Here and below: *First Annual Report, Pacific Railroad*, 12–13, 61.

54. *Glasgow Weekly Times*, 3 March 1853; *Annual Review, Commerce of St. Louis*, 44.

55. *Jefferson City Inquirer*, 17 July 1847; *Glasgow Weekly Times*, 9 December 1852; *Annual Review, Commerce of St. Louis*, 44.

56. *Report of the Committee, Chamber of Commerce*, 18; *Glasgow Weekly Times*, 10 February 1853; *Brunswicker*, 19 February, 2, 23, 30 April, 11 June, 27 August 1853.

57. *Report of the Committee*, 15.

58. Ibid., 20; *Annual Review, History of St. Louis*, 21.

59. *Report of the Committee*, 18.

60. *Glasgow Weekly Times*, 25 March, 23 December 1852; *Report of the Committee*, 20; *Annual Review, Commerce of St. Louis*, 33.

61. Here and below: *Report of the Committee*, 14; D. W. Eaton, "Hemp Industry," 351.

62. Here and below: *Annual Review, Commerce of St. Louis*, 44–45, 49–50, 53.

63. *Annual Review, History of St. Louis*, 21, 16–28.

64. Here and below: *First Annual Report, Pacific Railroad*, 61, table N2; *Trade and Commerce, St. Louis, 1865*, 16.

65. *First Annual Report, Pacific Railroad*, table N2; Dixon, *Traffic History*, 26.

66. Here and below: "Statistics of Platte County," 366; *Trade and Commerce, St. Louis, 1849*, 11; *Jefferson City Inquirer*, 11 February 1846.

67. *Jefferson Inquirer*, 29 April 1854.

68. *Trade and Commerce, St. Louis, 1849*, 11.

69. Hattervig, "Jefferson Landing," 285; *Jefferson City Inquirer*, 10 April 1847.

70. Willoughby, *Robidoux's Town*, 49.

71. *Jefferson Inquirer*, 16 October 1852; *Glasgow Weekly Times*, 3 March, 5 May 1853.

72. *St. Joseph Gazette*, 25 May 1853.

73. Way, *She Takes the Horns*, 8–10; *Brunswicker*, 3 September 1853.

74. *Liberty Tribune*, 6 April 1849.

75. Here and below: *Glasgow Weekly Times*, 12 February 1852.

76. Ibid., 23 June, 14 July 1853.

77. Ibid., 10 February 1853; *St. Joseph Gazette*, 11 May 1853.

78. *Glasgow Weekly Times*, 7 April 1853; *St. Joseph Gazette*, 11 May 1853; Chittenden, *Early Steamboat Navigation*, 2:114; Way, *Packet Directory*, 232.

79. Here and below: *Glasgow Weekly Times*, 19 February 1852; *Brunswicker*, 18 June, 2 July 1853; *Trade and Commerce, St. Louis, 1865*, 16; Way, *Packet Directory*, 232.

80. *Jefferson Inquirer*, 22 March 1850; 14 June 1851; *Glasgow Weekly Times*, 18 March 1852; *St. Joseph Gazette*, 24 March 1852.

81. Finn, "Morse, Samuel Finley Breese"; *Jefferson City Inquirer*, 6 November 1847; Sunder, "St. Louis," 250.

82. *Jefferson City Inquirer*, 2 November 1850; 13 December 1851; *Glasgow Weekly Times*, 17 February, 26 May 1853; *Brunswicker*, 28 May, 18 June 1853; Hattervig, "Jefferson Landing," 288. For more information on the extension of telegraph service in rural Missouri, see Sunder, "Early Telegraph," 42–53.

83. *Brunswicker*, 11 June 1853.

84. Doherty, "Columbia-Providence Plank Road," 56.

85. Gentry, "Plank Roads in Missouri," 272.

86. Ibid., 273; Doherty, "Columbia-Providence Plank Road," 53.

87. *Glasgow Weekly Times*, 2 December 1852; Gentry, "Plank Roads," 280.

88. Here and below: Doherty, "Columbia-Providence Plank Road," 62–65; Gentry, "Plank Roads," 281–83.

89. Webb, "Independence, Missouri," 45.

90. Oliver, "Missouri's First Railroad," 12–18.

91. *History of Henry and St. Clair Counties*, 981.

92. "Improvement of the Osage River," 51; "Osage River," 88–89; *Jefferson City Inquirer*, 7 October 1848.

93. *Jefferson City Inquirer*, 7 October 1848.

94. Ibid., 2 October 1847.

95. Ibid., 7 October 1848.

96. Ibid., 26 February 1848.

97. Ibid., 20 May 1848.

98. Ibid., 7 October 1848.

99. Ibid., 22 April 1848; 31 March 1849; Schultz, "Steamboat Navigation," 179; Lytle and Holdcamper, *Merchant Steam Vessels*, 227.

100. Morrow, "Joseph Washington McClurg," 170–75.

101. Schultz, "Steamboat Navigation," 177–79.

102. Ibid., 178; *Annual Review, Commerce of St. Louis*, 52.

103. Here and below: Chittenden, *Early Steamboat Navigation*, 1:13, 22, 141, 154, 177, 184; Sunder, *Fur Trade*, 109.

104. Here and below: Casler, *Steamboats*, 22, 34; Sunder, *Fur Trade*, 125.

105. Miller and Cohen, *Military and Trading Posts*, 12: Lepley, *Birthplace of Montana*, 23.

106. Barry, *Beginning of the West,* 935; Merrill, *First One Hundred Years,* 276.

107. Here and below: "Navigation of the Upper Missouri," 416.

108. *Missouri Republican,* 8 July 1850; Barbour, *Fort Union,* 68.

109. Chittenden, *Early Steamboat Navigation,* 1:193; Carriker, *Father Peter John De Smet,* 131.

110. Russel, *Improvement of Communication,* 168–73.

111. Richards, *Isaac I. Stevens,* 93–98.

112. U.S. Senate, *Contracts Made by the War Department, 1853,* 28; Richards, "Mullan, John."

113. Richards, *Isaac I. Stevens,* 109; [Bancroft], *History of Washington, Idaho and Montana,* 609; J. H. Bradley, "Affairs at Fort Benton," 268.

114. [I. I. Stevens], *Report,* 14.

115. [Larpenteur], *Forty Years a Fur Trader,* 167. Here and below: Mattison, "Alexander Harvey"; Carter, "Robert Campbell."

116. *Jefferson City Inquirer,* 8 April 1848; Casler, *Steamboats,* 21.

117. Mattison, "Alexander Harvey," 123; Sunder, *Fur Trade,* 165.

118. Compiled by the author from data in Casler, *Steamboats;* Lytle and Holdcamper, *Merchant Steam Vessels;* and Way, *Packet Directory. Kate Swinney* is the correct name of the boat. However, the name often appeared in newspapers as *Kate Sweeney.* The misspelling was also given to Kate Sweeney Bend, where the vessel sank.

119. Scharf, *St. Louis,* 1017; *Niles' National Register,* 25 March 1843, 64; *Jefferson City Inquirer,* 11 September 1847.

120. *Jefferson City Inquirer,* 29 April 1848.

121. *St. Louis Business Directory for 1847,* 99.

122. Here and below: Lass, "Fate of Steamboats," 2–15.

123. "Great Fire in St. Louis," 347–48; A. B. Lampe, "St. Louis Volunteer Fire Department," 250, 257.

124. *Jefferson Inquirer,* 9 November 1850.

125. Ibid.; *Trade and Commerce, St. Louis, 1848,* 16–17.

126. *Annual Review, History of St. Louis,* 9.

127. *St. Louis Directory for the Years 1854–5,* 237; *St. Louis Business Directory for 1847,* 139–40.

128. "Commercial Regulations," 414–16.

129. *St. Louis Business Directory, 1854–5,* 57.

130. "Statement Showing Number and Class of Vessels Built," 685.

131. *Trade and Commerce, St. Louis, 1848,* 15.

132. Here and below: McLear, "St. Louis Cholera Epidemic," 176; Rosenberg, *Cholera Years,* 115–35 passim.

133. Taylor's statement as quoted in *Minnesota Pioneer* (St. Paul), 2 August 1849.

134. McLear, "St. Louis Cholera Epidemic," 179; "Cholera in Saint Louis," 209–10.

135. *Jefferson Inquirer,* 12 May 1849; *Frontier Guardian,* 16 May, 25 July 1849. For the effects of cholera on the overland routes, see Read, "Disease, Drugs, and Doctors," 260–76.

136. *Jefferson Inquirer,* 30 August, 6 September 1851.

137. Hattervig, "Jefferson Landing," 286.

138. *Jefferson Inquirer,* 17 July 1852.

139. 9 June 1852.

140. Hunter, *Steamboats,* 191.

141. J. D. Richardson, *Messages and Papers,* 4:461.

142. *Commerce and Navigation of the Valley of the Mississippi,* 7.

143. *Jefferson City Inquirer,* 17 July 1847.

144. Rivers and Harbors Act (1852), 56–60; Hunter, *Steamboats,* 192.

145. J. K. Brown, *Limbs on the Levee,* 53, 56.

146. U.S. Congress, Senate, *Report of the Commissioner of Patents: Documents;* U.S. Congress, Senate, *Report of the Secretary of the Treasury.*

147. *Report of the Commissioner of Patents: Documents,* 1, 55ff.

148. *Report of the Secretary of the Treasury,* 108.

149. *Report of the Commissioner of Patents: Documents,* 3.

150. *Lexington Express*, as quoted in *St. Joseph Gazette*, 14 April 1852.

151. Ibid.; Way, *Packet Directory*, 416; Lloyd, *Steamboat Directory*, 277. For detailed coverage of the *Saluda* disaster, see Hartley and Woods, *Explosion of the Steamboat Saluda*.

152. Brown, *Limbs on the Levee*, 61–64.

153. Here and below: Steamboat Safety Act (1852), 61–75; Short, *Steamboat-Inspection Service*, 3–4.

154. *St. Joseph Gazette*, 11 May 1853.

155. Brown, *Limbs on the Levee*, 71.

156. Connelley, *Standard History of Kansas*, 1:356ff.; Olson and Naugle, *History of Nebraska*, 78–82; Zornow, *Kansas*, 68–69.

Chapter 6

1. Taylor, *Transportation Revolution*, 77; Riegel, "Missouri Pacific," 3; *Missouri Republican*, 13 February, 21 December 1836.

2. Clevenger, "Building of the Hannibal and St. Joseph Railroad," 32, 41; Willoughby, *Robidoux's Town*, 54.

3. "Pacific Railway Convention at Saint Louis"; Russel, *Improvement of Communication*, 50.

4. Riegel, "Missouri Pacific," 7.

5. Fitzsimmons, "Railroad Development in Missouri," 159.

6. Here and below: Riegel, "Missouri Pacific," 9; Gates, "Railroads of Missouri," 134–39; Hattervig, "Jefferson Landing," 294–96.

7. Clevenger, "Building of the Hannibal," 41. For a detailed history of the economic impact of the Hannibal and St. Joseph, see Bennett, "Hannibal and St. Joseph Railroad." For the financing of the Missouri Pacific, the Hannibal and St. Joseph, and the North Missouri, see Templin, "Development of Railroads in Missouri."

8. Gates, "Railroads of Missouri," 136; Fitzsimmons, "Railroad Development," 160.

9. *Sixteenth Annual Report of the Board*, 7.

10. Ibid., 8; *Jefferson Inquirer*, 22 March 1856.

11. *Jefferson Inquirer*, 29 May, 14, 21 June 1856; Hattervig, "Jefferson Landing," 291.

12. *Jefferson Inquirer*, 29 March 1856.

13. Ibid., 5 July 1856.

14. *Trade and Commerce, St. Louis*, 10, 13.

15. *Jefferson Inquirer*, 4, 11, 18 October 1856; 14 February 1857.

16. For the background of the Mormon War, see Furniss, *Mormon Conflict*, 63ff.

17. Lass, *From the Missouri to the Great Salt Lake*, 57.

18. Compiled by the author from data in U.S. Congress, Senate, *Contracts Made by the War Department, 1857*.

19. Lass, *From the Missouri*, 57–58, 61.

20. U.S. Congress, House, *Contracts Made by the War Department, 1858*, 5; Lass, *From the Missouri*, 62–65.

21. U.S. House, *Contracts Made by the War Department, 1858*, 5.

22. Lass, *From the Missouri*, 68.

23. 16 August 1858.

24. *Glasgow Weekly Times*, 11 March, 8 July 1858.

25. Furniss, *Mormon Conflict*, 168–205 passim.

26. *Glasgow Weekly Times*, 26 August 1858.

27. Hafen, *Colorado Gold Rush*, 30.

28. 30 September 1858.

29. R. W. Paul, *Mining Frontiers*, 111; Hafen, *Colorado Gold Rush*, 155, 163, 177.

30. *Glasgow Weekly Times*, 10 March 1859.

31. *Leavenworth Daily Times*, 29 April 1859; U.S. Bureau of the Census, *Eighth Census*, 548.

32. U.S. Congress, Senate, *Report of the Secretary of War, 1859*, 608; *Nebraska News* (Nebraska City), 17 March 1860; *People's Press* (Nebraska City), 13 March, 23 August 1860.

33. Gates, "Railroads of Missouri," 138; Fitzgerald, "Town Booming," 204; Whitney, *Kansas City, Missouri*, 1:249.

34. *Glasgow Weekly Times*, 12 May 1859.

35. U.S. Congress, House, *Contracts Made by the War Department, 1860*, 6, 15–17, 21, 25, 30, 32, 35, 37, 40.

36. *St. Louis Directory, 1860*, [5].

37. Willoughby, *Robidoux's Town*, 45, 69; Poppewell, "St. Joseph, Missouri," 444–46.

38. *Glasgow Weekly Times*, 18 November, 23 December 1858.

39. Ibid., 24 March, 9 June 1859.

40. St. Louis Board of Trade, *Fifth Annual Report*, 10.

41. The most valid measurement of freight shipments is the ton-mile—the movement of one ton for one mile. For example, 100 tons moved 100 miles would equal 10,000 ton-miles. But this statistic is not available for the 1850s.

42. *Jefferson Inquirer*, 16 February 1856; Spalding, *Annals of the City of Kansas*, 72; "Port of Glasgow" articles in the *Glasgow Weekly Times* for 1859.

43. "Port of Glasgow" articles in the *Glasgow Weekly Times* for 1859. The steamers that stopped at Glasgow were the *A. B. Chambers, Adelia, Alonzo Child, Asa Wilgus, B. W. Lewis, Black Hawk, C. W. Sombart, Carrier, Chippewa, D. A. January, David Tatum, Duncan S. Carter, E. A. Ogden, E. M. Ryland, Emigrant, Emilie, Emma, Florence, Florilda, Hannibal, Henry Graff, Hesperian, Iatan, Isabella, James Raymond, John D. Perry, John Warner, Kate Howard, Messenger, Meteor, Michigan, Mink, Minnehaha, Morning Star, New Monongahela, Northerner, Omaha, Peerless, Platte Valley, Portsmouth, Prima Donna, Rowena, Saint Mary, Sioux City, Skylark, South Wester, Sovereign, Spread Eagle, Stephen Decatur, T. L. McGill, Thomas E. Tutt, Twilight, War Eagle, White Cloud, William Baird, William Campbell*, and *William H. Russell*.

44. Here and below: see entries for the steamers listed in note 43 in Lytle and Holdcamper, *Merchant Steam Vessels;* Way, *Packet Directory;* and Lass, "Fate of Steamboats," 3.

45. *Glasgow Weekly Times*, 29 April, 10 June 1858.

46. Ibid., 29 July 1858.

47. Ibid.; Way, *Packet Directory*, 37, 242.

48. *Glasgow Weekly Times*, 30 June 1859.

49. Ibid., 11 August 1859.

50. Ibid., 13 September 1860.

51. Dobak, *Fort Riley and Its Neighbors*, 26–31.

52. Langsdorf, "First Survey of the Kansas River," 156.

53. A. R. Greene, "Kansas River," 321–22; U.S. Senate, *Contracts Made by the War Department, 1854*, 7.

54. Greene, "Kansas River," 333; Lieber, "Ships That Have Passed in the Night," 6.

55. Greene, "Kansas River," 318.

56. Here and below: Lieber, *That Splendid Little Steamer Hartford*, 4–9; Greene, "Kansas River," 327–30.

57. *Jefferson Inquirer*, 26 April, 6 September 1856; 21 March 1857.

58. Ibid., 4 October 1856.

59. Greene, "Kansas River," 318–19, lists 34 steamboats. However, in his following narrative, he wrote that 2 of those listed—the *New Lucy* and the *Morning Star*—were only advertised for Kansas River trips. He did not present any evidence that they were actually navigated on the river. Likewise, there is some question about the *Adelia*'s being on the river. On Greene's contention that the *Lightfoot* was the first steamboat built on the Kansas River, see Langsdorf, "More about Kansas River Steamboats."

60. Hafen and Young, *Fort Laramie*, 222–30.

61. Ibid., 233–35; Schell, *History of South Dakota*, 66.

62. Sunder, *Fur Trade*, 118; Hafen and Young, *Fort Laramie*, 144.

63. "Official Correspondence Relating to Fort Pierre," 384.

64. U.S. Congress, Senate, *Contracts Made by the War Department, 1855*, 7.

65. "Official Correspondence Relating to Fort Pierre," 384; U.S. Senate, *Contracts Made by the War Department, 1855*, 12–13, 18.

66. "Official Correspondence Relating to Fort Pierre," 430–31; Schuler, *Fort Pierre Chouteau*, 134.

67. Nowak, "From Fort Pierre to Fort Randall," 102.

68. U.S. Senate, *Contracts Made by the War Department, 1855*, 18. As used in much of the nineteenth century, the term "mechanics" meant any skilled craftsmen. In all likelihood most of the mechanics at Fort Pierre were carpenters.

69. Hafen and Young, *Fort Laramie*, 237–42; Athearn, *Forts of the Upper Missouri*, 38; R. E. Paul, *Blue Water Creek*, 88-99.

70. "Official Correspondence Relating to Fort Pierre," 384; Schuler, *Fort Pierre Chouteau*, 135.

71. J. A. Greene, *Fort Randall*, 11; B. K. Jackson, "Holding Down the Fort," 3; Schuler, *Fort Pierre Chouteau*, 136.

72. U.S. Congress, Senate, *Contracts Made by the War Department, 1856*, 13, 14

73. Ibid., 22; Nowak, "From Fort Pierre to Fort Randall," 108.

74. U.S. Senate, *Contracts Made by the War Department, 1857*, 4.

75. Ibid., 6, 22; *Sioux City Eagle*, 4 July 1857.

76. *Sioux City Eagle*, 4 July 1857; *Sioux City Register*, 2 September 1858; Way, *Packet Directory*, 117.

77. U.S. Senate, *Contracts Made by the War Department, 1857*, 6, 21–22.

78. Ibid., 23; *Sioux City Eagle*, 4 July 1857; 24 July 1858; *Sioux City Register*, 19 May, 9 June 1859.

79. *Glasgow Weekly Times*, 5 July 1860; U.S. House, *Contracts Made by the War Department, 1860*, 22.

80. U.S. Senate, *Contracts Made by the War Department, 1857*, 19; *Sioux City Eagle*, 1 July 1857; Way, *Packet Directory*, 148.

81. *Sioux City Eagle*, 14 October 1857; 20 March 1858; U.S. Congress, House, *Contracts Made by the War Department, 1859*, 8; U.S. House, *Contracts Made by the War Department, 1860*, 13.

82. [Marsh], "Journal," 90.

83. *Sioux City Eagle*, 25 July, 8 August 1857; Marks. *Past and Present of Sioux City*, 802.

84. *Sioux City Eagle*, 18 July, 8 August 1857; Way, *Packet Directory*, 355.

85. *Sioux City Eagle*, 4 July 1857.

86. Ibid., 25 July 1857.

87. Ibid., 29 August, 12 September, 10 October 1857; 22 May 1858.

88. Ibid., 1, 15, 29 August, 12 September 1857.

89. Ibid., 15 August 1857; *Sioux City Register*, 14 April, 12 May 1859; *Glasgow Weekly Times*, 27 October 1859.

90. *Sioux City Eagle*, 25 July, 15, 29 August 1857.

91. *Sioux City Eagle*, 17 July 1858; 16 June 1859; Petersen, *Iowa*, 240.

92. *Sioux City Eagle*, 19 June 1858.

93. Ibid., 18 June, 23 July 1859.

94. Ibid., 7 May 1859.

95. U.S. Bureau of the Census, *Eighth Census*, 153.

96. Here and below: Lass, "First Attempt to Organize Dakota Territory," 144ff.

97. Heitman, *Historical Register*, 438, 964; Upham, *Minnesota Geographic Names*, 543; Lamar, *Dakota Territory*, 37.

98. Schell, *Dakota Territory*, 5; Sioux *City Eagle*, 1 August 1857; Schell, *History of Clay County*, 15.

99. Athearn, *Forts of the Upper Missouri*, 57.

100. Kingsbury, *History of Dakota Territory*, 1:118.

101. Here and below: Kappler, *Indian Affairs*, 776–80; Schell, *Dakota Territory*, 8.

102. Here and below: Lass, "First Attempt," 153–57; U.S. Bureau of the Census, *Eighth Census*, 551; Phillips, "Frost, Daniel Marsh"; Schell, *Dakota Territory*, 61; Van Zandt, *Boundaries*, 216.

103. Kappler, *Indian Affairs*, 594–96.

104. Contract between Pierre Chouteau, Jr., and Company and Alfred Cumming, superintendent of Indian Affairs, 29 May 1855.

105. Lytle and Holdcamper, *Merchant Steam Vessels*, 192, 295; Way, *Packet Directory*, 412; Chittenden, *Early Steamboat Navigation*, 1:201.

106. Sunder, *Fur Trade*, 166–67.

107. J. H. Bradley, "Affairs at Fort Benton," 272.

108. Kappler, *Indian Affairs*, 736–40; Burlingame, *Montana Frontier*, 35.

109. U.S. Senate, *Contracts Made by the War Department, 1857*, 3; Thompson, *Fort Union Trading Post*, 72–73.

110. Here and below: Sunder, *Fur Trade*, 173, 184.

111. Sunder, *Fur Trade*, 184; Lytle and Holdcamper, *Merchant Steam Vessels*, 216; *Sioux City Eagle*, 18 July 1857.

112. *Sioux City Eagle*, 18 July 1857.

113. Ibid., 31 July 1858.

114. *Sioux City Register*, 30 December 1858.

115. Ibid., *Sioux City Eagle*, 5 June 1858.

116. U.S. House, *Contracts Made by the War Department, 1858*, 15; *Sioux City Register*, 30 December 1858.

117. Ibid., 31 July 1858; *Sioux City Register*, 30 December 1858; Miller and Cohen, *Military and Trading Posts*, 84; Mattison, "Henry A. Boller," 49–53.

118. Sunder, *Fur Trade*, 207.

119. Ibid., 185, 189; Lytle and Holdcamper, *Merchant Steam Vessels*, 202, 298; Way, *Packet Directory*, 431.

120. *Trade and Commerce, St. Louis, 1858*, 39; Sunder, *Fur Trade*, 201.

121. Sunder, *Fur Trade*, 201.

122. Contract between Pierre Chouteau, Jr., and Company and Charles E. Mix, acting commissioner of Indian Affairs, 15 March 1859.

123. Raynolds, *Report on the Exploration of the Yellowstone River*, 4.

124. U.S. Congress, *Contracts Made by the War Department, 1859*, 9.

125. Sunder, *Fur Trade*, 202; Way, *Packet Directory*, 86.

126. Raynolds, *Report*, 18–19; [Marsh], "Journal," 85, 90.

127. Chittenden, *Early Steamboat Navigation*, 1:218; Sunder, *Fur Trade*, 205.

128. Chouteau, "Early Navigation," 253; W. T. Jackson, *Wagon Roads West*, 264.

129. Chouteau, "Early Navigation," 253.

130. Ibid., 255.

131. Chouteau, "Early Navigation," 256; U.S. Congress, Senate, *Report of the Commissioner of Indian Affairs for 1859*, 483.

132. U.S. Senate, *Report of the Commissioner of Indian Affairs*, 378, 483.

133. Chouteau, "Early Navigation," 256.

134. W. T. Jackson, *Wagon Roads West*, 258–66.

135. U.S. House, *Contracts Made by the War Department, 1860*, 5.

136. Overholser, *Fort Benton*, 39; Sunder, *Fur Trade*, 211–13; Way, *Packet Directory*, 271.

137. Burlingame, *Montana Frontier*, 131.

CHAPTER 7

1. Here and below: McReynolds, *Missouri*, 221ff.; Castel, *General Sterling Price*, 115ff.; March, *History of Missouri*, 2:915ff.; Monaghan, *Civil War*, 170ff.; and Parrish, *Turbulent Partnership*, 5ff.

2. Fitzsimmons, "Railroad Development," 20, 87, 232.

3. U.S. Congress, House, *Contracts Made by the War Department, 1861*, 13–14, 19–20.

4. *Glasgow Weekly Times*, 25 July, 22 August 1861; *Tri-Weekly Missouri Republican* (St. Louis), 24 September 1861.

5. *Tri-Weekly Missouri Republican*, 16, 25 September 1861.

6. U.S. War Dept., *War of the Rebellion*, ser. 1 (hereafter cited as *Rebellion Records*), 13:60; Way, *Packet Directory*, 426.

7. Here and below: verbatim copy of the circular, in *Tri-Weekly Missouri Republican*, 14 December 1861.

8. Chittenden, *Early Steamboat Navigation*, 2:249.

9. Here and below: Morris, *Encyclopedia of American History*, 234–36; *Tri-Weekly Missouri Republican*, 14 April 1862.

10. *Rebellion Records*, 17 (part 1): 614–15; *Liberty Tribune*, 13 March 1863.

11. *Rebellion Records*, 41 (part 3): 611.

12. Castel, *Price*, 224.

13. 1 August 1862.

14. Here and below: *Tri-Weekly Missouri Republican*, 20 October 1862.

15. *Liberty Tribune*, 3 April 1863; Chittenden, *Early Steamboat Navigation*, 2:251.

16. *Liberty Tribune*, 29 May 1863.

17. Ibid., 1, 15 July 1864.

18. Ibid., 3 March 1865.

19. Unrelated to guerrilla attacks, the steamer *West Wind* was burned at Glasgow on 16 October 1864 during the town's occupation by Price's men. Whether its destruction was deliberate or accidental cannot be determined (McDonald, "Missouri River and Its Victims," third article, 606).

20. Fitzsimmons, "Railroad Development," 35–36, 168–70.

21. Ibid, 133; *Tri-Weekly Missouri Republican*, 18 September 1861.

22. Fitzsimmons, "Railroad Development," 138.

23. *Tri-Weekly Missouri Republican*, 4 July 1861.

24. Ibid., 8 August, 16 October 1863.

25. Ibid., 6 June 1864.

26. Lass, *From the Missouri*, 114–43 *passim*.

27. *Tri-Weekly Missouri Republican*, 25 May 1864.

28. *Morning Herald* (St. Joseph), 21 April 1863.

29. *Nebraska Republican* (Omaha), 12 September 1861.

30. *People's Press*, 30 March 1863; *Weekly Commonwealth* (Denver), 10 September 1863.

31. Welty, "The Western Army Frontier," 385–90.

32. *Nebraska News*, 15 April, 6 May 1865.

33. *Sioux City Register*, 6, 27 June, 4, 11, 25 July, 8 August 1863.

34. Here and below: Lass, "Nebraska City's Steam Wagon," 24–33.

35. *Sioux City Register*, 20 April, 5, 25 May, 8 June, 13 July, 24 August, 9 November 1861; 17, 31 May, 5 July, 17 September, 4 October, 8 November 1862.

36. Ibid., 11 May 1861.

37. Ibid., 25 May 1861.

38. Ibid., 4 May 1861.

39. Ibid., 9 November 1861; 12, 19 April 1862.

40. Here and below: Overholser, *Fort Benton*, 39–40; Sunder, *Fur Trade*, 224–28; "Steamboat Arrivals at Fort Benton," 317.

41. Here and below: Burlingame, *Montana Frontier*, 79–81; R. W. Paul, *Mining Frontiers*, 43, 142; J. H. Bradley, "Affairs at Fort Benton," 3:277, 278.

42. Greever, *Bonanza West*, 257–60; Peterson, *Idaho*, 56–57.

43. *Hunt's Merchants' Magazine and Commercial Review* 42 (July–December 1862): 78.

44. [Harkness], "Diary, 343.

45. Casler, *Steamboats*, 22, 33.

46. Sunder, *Fur Trade*, 235–37.

47. *Dakotaian* (Yankton), 3 June 1862.

48. *Sioux City Register*, 24 May 1862.

49. Ibid., 31 May 1862.

50. [Harkness], "Diary," 347.

51. Chittenden, *Early Steamboat Navigation*, 2:289–91.

52. Overholser, *Fort Benton*, 41; Bradley, "Affairs at Fort Benton," 284.

53. Sunder, *Fur Trade*, 239.

54. [Harkness], "Diary," 355.

55. *Sioux City Register*, 13 September 1862.

56. Burlingame, *Montana Frontier*, 83–86.

57. Here and below: Carley, *Sioux Uprising*, 10–20, 40–62 passim.

58. Lass, "Removal from Minnesota," 353–54.

59. Here and below: R. H. Jones, *Civil War*, 60; Carley, *Sioux Uprising*, 45–52.

60. For detailed coverage of the removal, see Lass, "Removal from Minnesota," 357–64.

61. Contract between Pierre Chouteau, Jr., and Company and Clark W. Thompson, 16 April 1863.

62. Here and below: R. H. Jones, *Civil War*, 63–65; Carley, *Sioux Uprising*, 89–90; Gilman, *Henry Hastings Sibley*, 195–99.

63. R. H. Jones, *Civil War*, 62.

64. *Sioux City Register*, 11, 25 April, 13 June 1863.

65. R. H. Jones, *Civil War*, 61; Clow, "Sully, Alfred."

66. *Sioux City Register*, 6 June, 4 July 1863; R. H. Jones, *Civil War*, 67; Kingsbury, *Dakota Territory*, 1:288.

67. Kingsbury, *Dakota Territory*, 1:289.

68. Casler, *Steamboats*, 19, 24, 33, 36; Way, *Packet Directory*, 45, 188, 480.

69. U.S. Congress, House, *Lists of Vessels Bought, Sold and Chartered*, 162, 166, 184, 214.

70. *Rebellion Records*, 22 (part 2): 434.

71. Kingsbury, *Dakota Territory*, 1:289; Sneve, *South Dakota Geographic Names*, 515.

72. R. H. Jones, *Civil War*, 68–69; Schuler, *Fort Sully*, 26–29.

73. *Sioux City Register*, 1 August 1863.

74. Ibid., 10, 31 October 1863; 6 February 1864.

75. Contract between Joseph La Barge and William P. Dole, 1 April 1863.

76. Here and below: Overholser, *Fort Benton*, 42; *Sioux City Register*, 9 May 1863.

77. Here and below: Overholser, *Fort Benton*, 42–43; Chittenden, *Early Steamboat Navigation*, 2:327–28; *Sioux City Register*, 9, 30 May, 13 June 1863; *Dakotaian*, 16 June 1863.

78. Sunder, *Fur Trade*, 249; Casler, *Steamboats*, 31; *Sioux City Register*, 30 May 1863.

79. Here and below: Overholser, *Fort Benton*, 43; *Sioux City Register*, 1, 15 August 1863.

80. *Sioux City Register*, 1 August 1863.

81. Burlingame, *Montana Frontier*, 87.

82. *Rebellion Records*, 34 (part 2): 594, 622, 713, 806.

83. Ibid., 41 (part 2): 81.

84. Hanson, *Conquest of the Missouri*, 53; *Sioux City Register*, 14, 18 June, 13 August 1864; Casler, *Steamboats*, 17, 24, 26–27, 29, 33; Way, *Packet Directory*, 15, 69, 180, 227, 306, 416, 448.

85. U.S. House, *Lists of Vessels*, 188, 214, 220; Water Transportation Records, Isabella file, entry 1403.

86. *Sioux City Register*, 4 June, 13 August 1864.

87. Ibid., 13 August 1864; Overholser, *Fort Benton*, 47.

88. *Sioux City Register*, 14, 28 May, 4 June, 13, 27 August 1864.

89. R. H. Jones, *Civil War*, 2:524.

90. H. M White, *Ho! For the Gold Fields*, 108.

91. Ibid., 123–24; *Rebellion Records*, 41 (part 2): 80.

92. *Rebellion Records*, 41 (part 2): 228.

93. Ibid., 81.

94. Water Transportation Records, Island City file.

95. Ibid., Isabella file; Casler, *Steamboats*, 27.

96. Here and below: *Rebellion Records*, 41 (part 1): 142.

97. Lass, "Steamboats on the Yellowstone," 28.

98. *Rebellion Records*, 41 (part 1): 148; H. M. White, *Ho! For the Gold Fields*, 128; [Hilger], "General Alfred Sully's Expedition," 320.

99. Here and below: *Rebellion Records*, 41 (part 1): 148–50, (part 2): 628; *Minnesota in the Civil and Indian Wars*, 2:525.

100. *Tri-Weekly Missouri Republican*, 5 September 1864; *Sioux City Register*, 27 August, 3 September 1864.

101. *Sioux City Register*, 10, 17, 24 September 1864; *Rebellion Records*, 41 (part 1): 155.

102. *Rebellion Records*, 41 (part 1): 154.

103. Water Transportation Records, Island City file.

104. Ibid., Isabella file.

105. Overholser, *Fort Benton*, 45.

106. Ibid.; *Sioux City Register*, 5 March 1864.

107. *Democrat* (St. Louis), 17 March 1864; *Tri-Weekly Missouri Republican*, 18 March 1864.

108. Here and below: *Sioux City Register*, 23 April, 2 July 1864; Overholser, *Fort Benton*, 49–51.

109. Here and below: Chittenden, *Early Steamboat Navigation*, 2:322ff.; Sunder, *Fur Trade*, 256–57.

110. Contracts between Pierre Chouteau, Jr., and Company and William P. Dole, Commissioner of Indian Affairs, 18, 25 March 1864.

111. Here and below: Overholser, *Fort Benton*, 48; Sunder, *Fur Trade*, 255; *Sioux City Register*, 7 May, 23 July 1864; *Democrat*, 18 August 1864.

Chapter 8

1. Burlingame, *Montana Frontier*, 91–93.

2. Ibid, 94; Malone and Roeder, *Montana*, 53–55.

2. Malone and Roeder, *Montana*, 53–55.

4. *Democrat*, 22 February 1865.

5. Miller and Cohen, *Military and Trading Posts*, 26; Overholser, *Fort Benton*, 53; "Steamboat Arrivals at Fort Benton," 318; Stuart, *Diary and Sketchbook*, 39.

6. Here and below: Overholser, *Fort Benton*, 53–70. For the story of the *Bertrand* disaster, see Petsche, *The Steamboat Bertrand*.

7. Stuart, *Diary and Sketchbook*, 41.

8. J. H. Bradley, "Account of Attempts to Build a Town," 304.

9. For a sampling of ads, see *Democrat*, 10 March 1868.

10. For lists of departure dates from St. Louis, see *Trade and Commerce, St. Louis, 1866*, 26; *1867*, 21; and *1868*, 13. For dates of arrivals at Fort Benton for those years, see Overholser, *Fort Benton*, 59, 64–65, 69–70; and "Steamboat Arrivals at Fort Benton," 318–22.

11. Here and below: U.S. House, *Improvement of Missouri River*, 9; Overholser, *Fort Benton*, 64–65.

12. *Trade and Commerce, St. Louis, 1866*, 34; Mullan, *Miners and Travelers' Guide*, 7; *Union and Dakotaian* (Yankton), 1 February 1868; *Morning Herald*, 24 March, 7 April 1867.

13. U.S. House, *Improvement of Missouri River*, 9; Mullan, *Miners and Travelers' Guide*, 7; Strahorn, *Montana and Yellowstone National Park*, 19; Napton, "My Trip on the Imperial," 305.

14. Overholser, *Fort Benton*, 59; *Daily Dispatch* (St. Louis), 22 August 1866; *Democrat*, 20 June 1865.

15. Schwantes, *Long Day's Journey*, 150.

16. Overholser, *Fort Benton*, 59.

17. *Evening News* (St. Louis), 5 July 1866; *Democrat*, 7 July 1866, as quoted in *Union and Dakotaian*, 28 July 1866.

18. U.S. House, *Improvement of Missouri River*, 11–12; *Evening News*, 3 May 1866.

19. Here and below: Scharf, *St. Louis*, 1:616; *Democrat*, 22 February, 16 May 1865; *Daily Bulletin* (Leavenworth), 9 April 1868.

20. *Democrat*, 6 July 1865; 10 March 1868.

21. Ibid., 10 March 1868.

22. Ibid., 30 September 1864. For Kountz's wartime service, see Parker, "William J. Kountz," 237–54.

23. *Democrat*, 10 March 1868.

24. Ibid., 23 March 1868.

25. The thirty-six boats made a total of forty-one arrivals. The *Only Chance* made two trips from St. Louis, and four boats double-tripped from such places as Cow Island and Camp Cooke. The stern-wheelers were the *Agnes, Amaranth, Amelia Poe, Benton, Big Horn, Deer Lodge, G. A. Thompson, Gallatin, Guidon, Huntsville, Ida Fulton, Ida Stockdale, Lady Grace, Lilly, Little Rock, Luella, Miner, Nymph No. 2, Richmond, Saint John, Silver Lake No. 4,* and *Tom Stevens*. The side-wheelers were the *Abeona, Antelope, Ben Johnson, Cora, Jennie Brown, Mountaineer, Nile, Octavia, Only Chance, Tacony, Viola Belle, Walter B. Dance, Waverly,* and *Yorktown*. Overholser, *Fort Benton*, 64–65; "Steamboat Arrivals at Fort Benton," 319–20; information on steamboat rigs was calculated by the author from data in Casler, *Steamboats*; and Way, *Packet Directory*.

26. Here and below: Hunter, *Steamboats*, 85, 96, 99, 167ff.; U.S. House, *Improvement of Missouri River*, 27.

27. Calculated by the author from data in *Trade and Commerce, St. Louis, 1867*, 21; and *Sioux City Register*, 14 December 1867.

28. Stuart, *Diary and Sketchbook*, 14.

29. Ibid., 22.

30. P. C. Phillips, "Upham Letters," 312.

31. Ibid.; Kingsbury, *Dakota Territory*, 1:501.

32. Here and below: Carpenter, "Glimpse of Montana," 378. For a reminiscent account of an 1869 voyage from St. Louis to Fort Benton, see Haines, "A Voyage to Montana, Part I," 16–29; "Part II," 18–27.

33. *Trade and Commerce, St. Louis, 1867*, 21; *Sioux City Register*, 14 December 1867; Way, *Packet Directory*, 223.

34. Napton, "My Trip," 306.

35. Ibid., 307, 315; Way, *Packet Directory*, 223; *Union and Dakotaian*, 8 February 1868.

36. [De Trobriand], *Military Life in Dakota*, 36.

37. Ibid., 37.

38. *Trade and Commerce, St. Louis, 1865*, 17; Williams and Newell, "Yellowstone River Navigability Study," 12–14.

39. Collins, *Across the Plains*, 1:571.

40. [Hosmer], "Trip to the States," 152.

41. [J. H. Bradley], "Bradley Manuscript," 130; [Hosmer], "Trip to the States," 152.

42. Collins, *Across the Plains*, 47, 57; Kingsbury, *Dakota Territory*, 1:574.

43. Kingsbury, *Dakota Territory*, 1:570–75; *Union and Dakotaian*, 5 September, 27 October 1866.

44. Walker, *Wagonmasters*, 208.

45. Here and below: Lass, *From the Missouri*, 162, 165.

46. [J. H. Bradley], "Bradley Manuscript," 129; Schwantes, *Long Day's Journey*, 151.

47. Lass, *From the Missouri*, 163.

48. Here and below: Hebard and Brininstool, *Bozeman Trail*, 1:214–20, 237ff.

49. Here and below: ibid., 266–76; Lass, *From the Missouri*, 165.

50. For detailed coverage of the Niobrara road, see W. T. Jackson, *Wagon Roads West*, 281–95; and Holman, "Niobrara–Virginia City Wagon Road," 1–50.

51. Here and below: Lass, *From the Missouri*, 182–83.

52. Larson, *History of Wyoming*, 44, 46, 55.

53. Hebard and Brininstool, *Bozeman Trail*, 1:297ff.; Athearn, *Union Pacific Country*, 205.

54. Walker, *Wagonmasters*, 203–204; Schwantes, *Long Day's Journey*, 155.

55. B. E. Meyer, "Pend Oreille Routes," 81–83; Schwantes, *Long Day's Journey*, 173–75.

56. Here and below: Madsen and Madsen, *North to Montana!* 72, 75, 83, 91.

57. A. D. Richardson, *Beyond the Mississippi*, 482.

58. Thompson, *Fort Union Trading Post*, 87; Schuler, *Fort Sully*, 31; Miller and Cohen, *Military and Trading Posts*, 25; Frazer, *Forts of the West*, 134.

59. Gray, "Northern Overland Pony Express," 58–62.

60. Frazer, *Forts of the West*, 113–15.

61. Ibid., 80–83.

62. Welty, "Frontier Army on the Missouri," 94.

63. For detailed coverage of Ruffee's relationship with the Northwest Fur Company, see Lass, "History and Significance of the Northwest Fur Company," 34–35.

64. Welty, "Frontier Army on the Missouri," 94.

65. Fort totals compiled by the author from a list of government shipments in U.S. House, *Improvement of Missouri River*, 45–48.

66. U.S. Congress, House, *Report of the Secretary of War, 1869*, 53.

67. Kingsbury, *Dakota Territory*, 1:500. The essence of Kingsbury's story is probably true, but it contains errors. He identified the time as the winter of 1868–69 and the steamer as the *Nellie Peck*. But that vessel was not built until 1871. Furthermore, he stated the Indians were Santee Sioux from Crow Creek, but the Santees had been moved from Crow Creek to near the mouth of the Niobrara in 1866.

68. *Evening News*, 28 May, 18 June 1866; U.S. House, *Contracts by Quartermaster General*, 8, 13.

69. Water Transportation Records, Marcella file; U.S. House, *Report of the Secretary of War, 1869*, 212; *Press and Dakotaian* (Yankton), 28 June 1869.

70. Contract between Hiram K. Hazlett and Major General J. L. Donaldson, acting quartermaster general, 29 February 1868.

71. U.S. Congress, House, *Contracts by the Quartermaster Department*, 23; U.S. Congress, House, Quartermaster General's report, 20 October 1868, in *Report of the Secretary of War, 1868*, 830.

72. *Democrat*, 13 July 1865; *Union and Dakotaian*, 17 August 1867; Munson, "Pioneer Life," 204; *Morning Herald*, 29 March 1867.

73. Information on the Northwest Fur Company is from Lass, "Northwest Fur Company."

74. For complete coverage of Durfee and Peck, see Lass, "Elias H. Durfee and Campbell K. Peck," 9–19.

75. Kappler, *Indian Affairs*, 883ff.; Schell, *History of South Dakota*, 86–88.

76. Gibson, *American Indian*, 393.

77. Here and below: Kappler, *Indian Affairs*, 998–1007.

78. Lass, "Durfee and Peck," 12–13.

79. Here and below: Fitzsimmons, "Railroad Development," 39, 214–16; Gates, "Railroads of Missouri," 139–40.

80. Here and below: *Trade and Commerce, St. Louis, 1867*, 20, 63; *1868*, 12–13; U.S. House, *Improvement of Missouri River*, 44–45; Fink, Goldschmidt, and Co. bill of lading, 6 March 1867, in E. B. Trail Collection, folder 87.

81. U.S. House, *Improvement of Missouri River*, 45–48; "History of Railroad Building," 51.

82. Lass, *From the Missouri*, 184.

83. U.S. House, *Improvement of Missouri River*, 45–48.

84. Bills of lading in Trail Collection, folder 40.

85. A. R. Greene, "Kansas River," 319, 351–52.

86. Zornow, *Kansas*, 137; Fitzsimmons, "Railroad Development," 41.

87. U.S. Congress, House, *Steam-Vessels in the United States*, 16; *Trade and Commerce, St. Louis, 1868*, 13; Way, *Packet Directory*, 19, 26, 73, 378.

88. Appropriations for Public Works Act (1866), 70–74; *Annual Engineers Report, 1867*, 376.

89. Here and below: U.S. House, *Improvement of Missouri River*, 1, 6–7, 34ff.

90. Here and below: *Annual Engineers Report, 1868*, 58–59, 589–94, 613ff.

91. U.S. House, *Improvement of Missouri River*, 10.

CHAPTER 9

1. *Sioux City Journal*, 14 March 1868.

2. Casey and Douglas, *Pioneer Railroad*, 123–26.

3. *Sioux City Register*, 18, 25 January, 15, 29 February 1868.

4. Ibid., 1 February 1868.

5. Ibid., 15 August 1868; *History of the Counties of Woodbury and Plymouth*, 123.

6. *Democrat* (St. Louis), 6 July 1865; "Articles of Incorporation of the North West Transportation Company."

7. *Montana Post* (Virginia City), 18 January 1868.

8. Here and below: *Democrat*, 10 March 1868; *Montana Post* (Helena), 18 September 1868; *Union and Dakotaian*, 2 January 1869.

9. *Montana Post*, 18 September 1868.

10. *Union and Dakotaian*, 2 January 1869.

11. *Sioux City Register*, 14, 28 November 1868; 23 January 1869.

12. Lass, "Northwest Fur Company," 40; *Sioux City Register*, 1 May 1869; Way, *Packet Directory*, 448.

13. Contract between G. T. Nutter and Ely S. Parker, 13 May 1869.

14. U.S. House, *Report of the Secretary of War, 1869*, 212.

15. *Democrat*, 20 March 1869.

16. Here and below: *Sioux City Register*, 24 April, 8, 15 May, 21 August 1869.

17. U.S. House, *Report of the Secretary of War, 1869*, 56, 63.

18. Here and below: *Sioux City Weekly Journal*, 16 March 1871; Lass, "Durfee and Peck," 17.

19. Lass, "Durfee and Peck," 12; Schell, *History of South Dakota*, 91.

20. Here and below: H. H. Anderson, "History of the Cheyenne River Indian Agency, 423; *Report of the Commissioner of Indian Affairs, 1871*, U.S. Bureau of the Census, *Compendium of the Ninth Census*, 106.

21. Burlingame, *Montana Frontier*, 171; *Report of the Commissioner of Indian Affairs, 1872*, 47; Miller and Cohen, *Military and Trading Posts*, 11; U.S. Bureau of the Census, *Compendium of the Ninth Census*, 108, 251.

22. Mattison, "Military Frontier," 170–75; Schell, *History of South Dakota*, 91.

23. Miller and Cohen, *Military and Trading Posts*, 25, 74; *Report of the Secretary of War, 1869*, 60.

24. Frazer, *Forts of the West*, 111.

25. "Tabular Statement" from contract between Hiram K. Hazlett and Brevet Major General Daniel H. Rucker; *Sioux City Weekly Journal,* 7, 14 April, 5 May, 23 June 1870.

26. *Sioux City Daily Journal,* 21 June 1871; contract between Campbell K. Peck and Ely S. Parker.

27. *St. Louis Times,* 1 June 1871, as quoted in *Sioux City Weekly Journal,* 8 June 1871.

28. *Helena Daily Herald,* 12 June 1871; Way, *Packet Directory,* 135, 154, 162, 221, 342, 426, 470.

29. *Sioux City Weekly Journal,* 8, 22 June 1871; McDonald, "Missouri River and Its Victims," third article, 603.

30. *Sioux City Daily Journal,* 4, 5, 25 August 1871; *Sioux City Weekly Journal,* 12 October 1871; Way, *Packet Directory,* 426.

31. "Tabular Statement" from Hazlett-Rucker contract.

32. *Sioux City Weekly Journal,* 29 June 1871; Way, *Packet Directory,* 21, 74, 221, 268, 328, 366. Way used the spelling *"May Lowery,"* but Sioux City's newspapers (the *Journal* and the *Times*) always showed it as *"May Lowry."*

33. *Sioux City Weekly Journal,* 20, 27 April 1871.

34. Here and below: ibid., 27 April, 11 May 1871.

35. *Sioux City Daily Journal,* 8 July, 29 September 1871; *Yankton Press,* 23 August, 4, 11 October 1871.

36. Here and below: *Sioux City Weekly Journal,* 5, 19, 26 October 1871.

37. *Sioux City Daily Journal,* 6 February, 2 March 1872.

38. Here and below: ibid., 2 March 1872; contract between Durfee and Peck and F. A. Walker.

39. *Sioux City Daily Journal,* 29 March, 21 April 1872; *Sioux City Weekly Journal,* 18 July 1872.

40. *Yankton Press,* 10 April 1872; *Daily Journal,* 14 April 1872.

41. *Sioux City Weekly Journal,* 18 July 1872.

42. Here and below: ibid., 4 July 1872.

43. Here and below: ibid., 10 October 1872.

44. Overholser, *Fort Benton,* 77, 79, 81.

45. Ibid., 75.

46. Madsen and Madsen, *North to Montana,* 207.

47. Overholser, *Fort Benton,* 75.

48. Madsen and Madsen, *North to Montana,* 203, 210.

49. Here and below: Roberts, *Report of a Reconnaissance,* 27–28.

50. *Sioux City Weekly Journal,* 13 June 1872; Hanson, *Conquest of the Missouri,* 139.

51. *Union and Dakotaian,* 21 April 1870.

52. Here and below: *Sioux City Weekly Journal,* 13, 20 June, 11 July 1872; Hanson, *Conquest of the Missouri,* 139–41.

53. *Sioux City Weekly Journal,* 11 August 1870; 17 August, 5 October 1871; 11 July 1872; *Sioux City Weekly Times,* 8 April 1871; 30 May 1872.

54. *Sioux City Weekly Journal,* 19 September 1872.

55. Overholser, *Fort Benton,* 75.

56. *Sioux City Weekly Journal,* 27 June 1872; Lass, "Durfee and Peck," 15. A single steamboat cargo filling 23 railroad freight cars was not unusual at that time, because of each car's relatively small, 10-ton capacity (1,000 cubic feet) (J. H. White, *American Railroad Freight Car,* 136–37.)

57. *Sioux City Weekly Journal,* 22 June, 6 July 1871.

58. *Sioux City Weekly Journal,* 22 August, 5 September, 10 October 1872; Way, *Packet Directory,* 216.

59. Here and below: Schell, "Dakota Southern," 109–11.

60. *Sioux City Weekly Journal,* 8 February, 11 July 1872; Lass, "Northwest Fur Company."

61. Here and below: Schell, *Dakota Territory,* 78–80; Kingsbury, *Dakota Territory,* 1:630–33; *Sioux City Weekly Journal,* 16 May, 11, 25 July 1872.

62. Harnsberger, *Jay Cooke and Minnesota,* 70, 86–87.

63. Kingsbury, *Dakota Territory,* 1:694; Lounsberry, *Early History of North Dakota,* 335.

64. Frazer, *Forts of the West,* 111; *Sioux City Weekly Journal,* 13 June, 18 July 1872.

65. *Sioux City Weekly Journal,* 30 May, 27 June, 4, 18 July 1872; Kingsbury, *Dakota Territory,* 1:696.

66. *Sioux City Weekly Journal,* 11 April, 9, 30 May 1872.

67. Kingsbury, *Dakota Territory,* 1:691.

68. Robinson, *History of North Dakota*, 131.

69. Schell, "Dakota Southern," 99; Lass, *History of Steamboating*, 78.

70. *Trade and Commerce, St. Louis, 1870*, 37–41.

71. Ibid., *1871*, 18–19, 27; *1872*, 11.

72. Steamer Washington Account Book, 1871–72, in E. B. Trail Collection, vol. 51.

73. *Trade and Commerce, St. Louis, 1873*, 17.

74. Ibid., *1872*, 11.

75. Glaab, *Kansas City and the Railroads*, 2, 154.

76. Fitzsimmons, "Railroad Development," 210–11.

77. Morton, *Illustrated History of Nebraska*, 2:123.

78. *Annual Engineers Report, 1869*, 308.

79. Ibid., 304–308.

80. *Omaha Bee*, 24 August 1872, as quoted in *Sioux City Weekly Journal*, 29 August 1872.

81. *Annual Engineers Report, 1871*, 307.

82. Ibid., *1872*, 336; *1874*, 368.

83. Here and below: ibid., *1871*, 333; *1872*, 341; *1873*, 458.

84. Ibid., *1874*, 345.

85. *Proceedings of the Twentieth Annual Meeting*, 157.

86. *Proceedings of the Thirty-Second Annual Meeting*, 85; *Sioux City Weekly Journal*, 7 April 1870.

CHAPTER 10

1. *Press and Dakotaian*, 2 December 1878; 19 February 1881; *Yankton Press and Dakotan*, 27 May 1896.

2. *Daily Journal*, 10 November 1874; *Bismarck Tribune*, 26 April 1882.

3. Lass, *History of Steamboating*, 92.

4. *Press and Dakotaian*, 2 August 1879; *Daily Journal*, 27 August 1872; *Bismarck Tribune*, 11 December 1903; 4 January 1916; Hanson, *Conquest of the Missouri*, 35–61 passim.

5. Lass, *History of Steamboating*, 94–96.

6. Here and below: *Press and Dakotaian*, 2 July 1874; 10 June 1881.

7. John H. Charles to Sanford B. Coulson, 21 March 1877, in Isaac P. Baker Papers.

8. Lass, "Durfee and Peck," 9, 17.

9. Murphy, *Half Interest in a Silver Dollar*, 19.

10. *Helena Weekly Herald*, 19 November 1874; *Benton Record* (Fort Benton), 1 March, 1 June 1875.

11. Overholser, *Fort Benton*, 231, 234; *Bismarck Tribune*, 28 July 1875; Corbin, *Life and Times of the Steamboat Red Cloud*, 31–33; Murphy, *Half Interest in a Silver Dollar*, 20–23.

12. *Andreas' Historical Atlas of Dakota*, 238; *Bismarck Tribune*, 28 July 1875; Hoopes, *This Last West*, photo on plate 8 following p. 210.

13. *Bismarck Tribune*, 12 July 1879; *Benton Record*, 1 March 1875.

14. Corbin, *Steamboat Red Cloud*, 53; Way, *Packet Directory*, 389; Overholser, *Fort Benton*, 97.

15. *Helena Weekly Herald*, 3 June 1875; Way, *Packet Directory*, 74; Overholser, *Fort Benton*, 88, 92.

16. *Bismarck Tribune*, 21 June 1876; Hoopes, *This Last West*, 43; Way, *Packet Directory*, 54, 74.

17. Here and below: Marks, *Past and Present of Sioux City*, 32, 35; *History of the Counties of Woodbury and Plymouth*, 246; *Press and Dakotaian*, 24 February 1876.

18. *Bismarck Tribune*, 13 September 1876; Hoopes, *This Last West*, 35, 167, 369; Jarchow, *Amherst H. Wilder*, 100, 102–104, 141–42.

19. Entries for *Benton, Black Hills, E. H. Durfee, F. Y. Batchelor, Far West, Josephine, Katie P. Kountz, Key West,* and *Western,* in Way, *Packet Directory*, 50, 54, 135, 159, 163, 258, 268, 271, and 484.

20. Here and below: Hunter, *Steamboats*, 90.

21. Photograph of *Helena*, at State Historical Society of North Dakota, Bismarck; photograph of *Red Cloud*, in Frederick Way, Jr., Collection, Public Library of Cincinnati and Hamilton County.

22. Photographs of *E. H. Durfee* and *Western*, Way Collection; photograph of *Far West*, State Historical Society of North Dakota.

23. Lass, *History of Steamboating*, 108.

24. *Daily Journal*, 10 November 1874; *Bismarck Tribune*, 26 April 1882.

25. Way, *Packet Directory*, 118, 330, 492.

26. *Press and Dakotaian*, 26 February, 10 March, 29 April 1879.

27. Photographs of *Dacotah* and *Wyoming*, Way Collection.

28. *Sioux City Weekly Journal*, 22 May 1879.

29. Overholser, *Fort Benton*, 104, 113, 118, 122; Way, *Packet Directory*, 118.

30. *Bismarck Tribune*, 5 July 1879; 27 June 1884; Overholser, *Fort Benton*, 104; Way, *Packet Directory*, 330.

31. Overholser, *Fort Benton*, 118; Way, *Packet Directory*, 492.

32. *Press and Dakotaian*, 4 April 1877.

33. *Sioux City Weekly Journal*, 8 May 1879.

34. Ibid., 26 June, 10 July 1879.

35. Here and below: *Butte* bills of lading, 23 April–17 May 1879, Baker Papers; *Sioux City Weekly Journal*, 22 May 1879; Overholser, *Fort Benton*, 104.

36. *Benton Record*, 1 May 1875.

37. Corbin, *Steamboat Red Cloud*, 63; Way, *Packet Directory*, 389.

38. Miller and Cohen, *Military and Trading Posts*, 3, 26, 41.

39. Contract for Missouri River between Colonel Daniel H. Rucker, assistant quartermaster, and John B. Dallas; "Tabular Statement" from contract for Missouri River transportation from March 20 to October 31, 1874; "Schedule of Rates," from contract between Daniel H. Rucker and Sanford B. Coulson; "Tabular Statement" from contract between Lt. Col. S. B. Holabird, deputy quartermaster, and Sanford B. Coulson.

40. *Press and Dakotaian*, 13, 20 February, 30 March 1877; contract between John B. Davis and Peyton S. Davidson and B. C. Card.

41. Contract for Missouri River transportation, commencing March 20; contract for transportation on the Missouri and Yellowstone rivers; *Press and Dakotaian*, 12 October 1878.

42. "Tabular Statement" from contract for Missouri River transportation.

43. *Trade and Commerce, St. Louis, 1865*, 16; U.S. Army, Dept. of Dakota, *Table of Distances*, "Table of Distances on the Missouri River." (The *Trade and Commerce of St. Louis* showed the distance from Yankton to the Heart River, whose mouth is at present Mandan, North Dakota, opposite Bismarck.)

44. U.S. Army, *Table of Distances*, "Table of Distances on the Missouri River."

45. *Daily Journal*, 12, 14 June 1873; contract between W. Cass, president of the NPRR [Northern Pacific Railroad], and Edward Smith, commissioner of Indian Affairs; *Bismarck Tribune*, 11 August 1875; *Press and Dakotaian*, 4, 29 May 1877.

46. *Daily Journal*, 12 July 1874; *Press and Dakotaian*, 11 May, 19 June 1878; 25, 28 April 1879; *Bismarck Tribune*, 3 May 1879.

47. *Press and Dakotaian*, 4, 29 May 1877; 11 May, 19 June 1878.

48. Ibid., 8 April 1878; Lass, "Steamboats on the Yellowstone," 33.

49. *Press and Dakotaian*, 4, 29 May 1877; 25, 28 April 1879; *Bismarck Tribune*, 3 May 1879.

50. *Press and Dakotaian*, 30 March 1877.

51. William Evans to Sanford B. Coulson, 11 April 1877, Baker Papers.

52. Maratta to J. C. McVay, 4 February 1878, Baker Papers.

53. Maratta to Coulson, 10 December 1877, Baker Papers.

54. Here and below: U.S. Congress, House, *Testimony Taken before the Committee on Indian Affairs*, 1ff., 27, 29, 3.

55. Ibid., 29.

56. Ibid., 37.

57. Ibid., 212.

58. Ibid., 42–43.

59. Lass, "Steamboats on the Yellowstone," 29.

60. Stanley, *Report on the Yellowstone Expedition*, 13.

61. Here and below: Lass, "Steamboats on the Yellowstone," 27–28, 30.

62. *Avant Courier*, 5 November 1875.

63. Bryan, "Dr. Lamme's Gallant Sidewheeler 'Yellowstone,'" 31–34, 38, 41; Overholser, *Fort Benton*, 155.

64. Here and below: Lass, "Steamboats on the Yellowstone," 32.

65. Hanson, *Conquest of the Missouri*, 290ff.

66. Utley, "War Houses," 19, 24–25; Lass, "Steamboats on the Yellowstone," 33.

67. Contract between Davis and Davidson and Card.

68. Here and below: Lass, "Steamboats on the Yellowstone," 34–35.

69. *Sioux City Weekly Journal*, 24 May 1877; Lass, "Steamboats on the Yellowstone," 37, 39; Overholser, *Fort Benton*, 104, 108, 113.

70. Lass, "Steamboats on the Yellowstone," 34.

71. Ibid., 35–36; Van West, "Coulson," 43.

72. Lass, "Steamboats on the Yellowstone," 37.

73. Ibid., 39.

74. Sharp, *Whoop-Up Country*, 6–7, 48; Overholser, *Fort Benton*, 75.

75. Here and below: Corbin, *Steamboat Red Cloud*, 41.

76. Ibid., 38; *Benton Record*, 1 June 1875; Melody Nagel-Hisey, park area naturalist, Cypress Hills Interprovincial Park, Maple Creek, Saskatchewan, to William E. Lass, 29 April 2005.

77. Madsen and Madsen, *North to Montana*, 158; J. H. Bradley, "Account of Attempts to Build a Town," 305, 313.

78. Madsen and Madsen, *North to Montana*, 158; Hoopes, *This Last West*, 54.

79. Missouri River Commission, *Map*, 69–71; [Ludlow], *Exploring Nature's Sanctuary*, 53; Cheney, *Names on the Face of Montana*, 43.

80. Ludlow, *Exploring Nature's Sanctuary*, 13; Warner, *Montana Territory History*, frontispiece map.

81. Ludlow, *Exploring Nature's Sanctuary*, 13; *Helena Weekly Herald*, 11 June, 3 September 1874; J. H. Bradley, "Account of Attempts to Build a Town," 313.

82. Ludlow, *Exploring Nature's Sanctuary*, 13–15; *Helena Weekly Herald*, 22, 29 October 1874; 20 May 1875.

83. Overholser, *Fort Benton*, 85–89; *Helena Weekly Herald*, 21 October 1875.

84. Overholser, *Fort Benton*, 86.

85. U.S. House, *Testimony before Committee on Indian Affairs*, 213.

86. *Helena Weekly Herald*, 13 August 1874.

87. Ibid.

88. Ibid., 29 October 1874.

89. Ibid., 13 May, 8 July, 21 October 1875.

90. Ibid., 14 May, 4 June 1874; 13 May, 15 July 1875.

91. Ibid., 15 October 1874; 15 July 1875; Ludlow, *Exploring Nature's Sanctuary*, 11.

92. *Helena Weekly Herald*, 10 October 1875; *Benton Record*, 1 February, 15 May 1875.

93. *Helena Weekly Herald*, 21 October 1875.

94. Ibid., 13 April 1876.

95. Ibid., 26 November, 3 December 1874; 6, 17 April 1876.

96. *Benton Record*, 10 November 1877; Overholser, *Fort Benton*, 157.

97. *Annual Engineers Report, 1878*, part 1, 693.

98. Here and below: Corbin, *Steamboat Red Cloud*, 69; *Benton Record*, 10 November 1878; Overholser, *Fort Benton*, 104–105.

99. *Benton Record*, 10 November 1877; 4 October 1878; 2 January 1880; Overholser, *Fort Benton*, 104.

100. *Benton Record*, 10 November 1877; 4 October 1878.

101. Maratta to Coulson, 17 April, 10 May, 26 September 1877, Baker Papers.

102. *Annual Engineers Report, 1878*, part 1, 691; *Benton Record*, 10 November 1877.

103. Here and below: *Benton Record*, 22 November 1878; 2 January 1880.

104. Miller and Cohen, *Military and Trading Posts*, 3–5.

105. Corbin, *Steamboat Red Cloud*, 84, 86; Missouri River Commission, *Map*, 74.

106. Overholser, *Fort Benton*, 102, 105; Miller and Cohen, *Military and Trading Posts*, 5.

107. Here and below: Beal, *"I Will Fight No More Forever,"* 55ff., 202; M. H. Brown, *Flight of the Nez Perce*, 130ff., 371–74.; Zimmer, *Frontier Soldier*, 119.

108. Malone and Roeder, *Montana*, 142; *Benton Record*, 10 November 1877; 22 November 1878.

109. *Benton Record*, 10 November 1877; *Annual Engineers Report, 1878*, part 1, 693.

110. *Benton Record*, 4 October 1878; *Annual Engineers Report, 1879*, part 2, 1095–96.

111. Here and below: *Annual Engineers Report, 1875,* part 1, 517; *1877,* part 1, 520; *1878,* part 1, 695.

112. Here and below: ibid., *1878,* part 1, 695; *1879,* part 2, 1096; *1880,* part 2, 1472.

113. Briggs, *Frontiers of the Northwest,* 26–29; Schell, *Dakota Territory,* 42–43; Schell, *History of South Dakota,* 125–26.

114. Here and below: Schell, *History of South Dakota,* 126–29; Krause and Olson, *Prelude to Glory,* 1, 11.

115. Briggs, *Frontiers of the Northwest,* 34; Schell, *History of South Dakota,* 132.

116. Deloria and DeMallie, *Documents of American Indian Diplomacy,* 1:261–71.

117. Lass, *From the Missouri,* 197, 207.

118. *Black Hills Journal* (Rapid City), 22, 29 March 1879; U.S. Bureau of the Census, *Compendium of the Tenth Census,* 52–53.

119. *Black Hills Times* (Deadwood), 11 June 1878; *Black Hills Journal,* 12 April 1879.

120. *Sioux City Weekly Journal,* 15 February 1877.

121. Here and below: *Press and Dakotaian,* 20 May 1879; *Bismarck Tribune,* 7 May 1880; *Black Hills Journal,* 19 July 1879; *Black Hills Pioneer* (Deadwood), 26 April 1878.

122. *Sioux City Weekly Journal,* 7 June 1877.

123. *Daily Champion* (Deadwood), 2 June 1877; *Black Hills Journal,* 12 July 1879.

124. *Sioux City Weekly Journal,* 5 June 1879.

125. *Black Hills Pioneer,* 26 April 1878; *Black Hills Journal,* 19 July 1879.

126. *Black Hills Journal,* 22, 19 March 1879.

127. *Press and Dakotaian,* 1 January 1879.

128. Ibid., 17, 28 October 1876.

129. Lass, *From the Missouri,* 201.

130. Ibid., 193; Schell, *History of Clay County,* 48.

131. Lass, *History of Steamboating,* 134.

CHAPTER 11

1. U.S. Bureau of the Census, *Statistics, 1880,* 52, 70, 115–16, 250; *Compendium of the Ninth Census,* 160; *Compendium of the Tenth Census,* 333.

2. Here and below: Hamburg, "Railroads and Settlement," 167, 170.

3. Kingsbury, *Dakota Territory,* 2:1164; Way, *Packet Directory,* 66.

4. Here and below: Kingsbury, *Dakota Territory,* 2:1148; Schell, *History of South Dakota,* 162; *Dakota Register* (Chamberlain), 8 September 1881.

5. *Press and Dakotaian,* 30 April 1880.

6. Ibid., 28 December 1880.

7. Schuler, *Bridge Apart,* 57; *Annual Engineers Report, 1893,* part 3, 2302; Way, *Packet Directory,* 247.

8. *Dakota Register,* 4 August, 8 September 1881.

9. Ibid., 6 October, 10 November 1881; 17 May 1883; Way, *Packet Directory,* 322; *Andreas' Historical Atlas of Dakota,* 155.

10. Schell, *History of Clay County,* 57–59; Hoover, Rau, and Bruguier, "Gorging Ice and Flooding Rivers," 184–90; Kingsbury, *Dakota Territory,* 2:1148ff.

11. Here and below: *Dakota Herald* (Yankton), 2 April 1881; *Daily Press and Dakotaian,* 28, 30, 31 March, 28 July 1881; W. R. Hurt and Lass, *Frontier Photographer,* 120–23; Way, *Packet Directory,* 484.

12. P. S. Hall, "Ephemeral Chamberlain Road," 10–20 passim.

13. *Dakota Register,* 4, 18 May, 20 July 1882.

14. Bingham and Peters, "Short History of Brule County," 45; *Dakota Register,* 8 September 1881.

15. *Dakota Register,* 18 May 1882; *Democrat* (Chamberlain), 13, 20, 27 July, 3, 10, 17, 24 August, 7 September 1883.

16. *Democrat,* 24 August 1883.

17. Ibid., 27 July 1883.

18. Ibid., 13, 27 July 1883.

19. Ibid., 27 July 1883.

20. *Dakota Register,* 11, 18 October 1883.

21. *Bismarck Tribune,* 17 February 1882; 13 May 1883; Way, *Packet Directory,* 475; Hanson, *Conquest of the Missouri,* 414–20.

22. *Bismarck Tribune,* 1 November 1883; *Democrat,* 24 August, 12 October 1883.

23. Way, *Packet Directory,* 360; Hanson, *Conquest of the Missouri,* 421; *Dakota Register,* 2, 23 August, 11 October 1883.

24. *Democrat,* 27 July, 3, 10, 17, 24 August, 7 September, 12 October 1883; Sneve, *South Dakota Geographic Names,* 132.

25. Lass, "Steamboats on the Yellowstone," 39.

26. Ibid., 37–39; Way, *Packet Directory,* 140, 159.

27. Here and below: Lass, "Steamboats on the Yellowstone," 39; Hedren, "Sitting Bull's Surrender," 13.

28. Here and below: ibid., 40–41.

29. Overholser, *Fort Benton,* 108–109, 113, 118.

30. Here and below: *Annual Engineers Report, 1882,* part 2, 1782; *1883,* part 2, 1362.

31. *Benton Weekly Record,* 29 December 1881.

32. *River Press* (Fort Benton), 28 December 1881.

33. Ibid., 21 December 1881.

34. Ibid., 28 December 1881.

35. Ibid.; Frazer, *Forts of the West,* 83.

36. *River Press,* 30 November 1881.

37. Jarchow, *Amherst H. Wilder,* 87–91; Freedom, "Moving Men and Supplies," 121; Lepley, *Packets to Paradise,* 158, 160; Missouri River Commission, *Map,* 70.

38. Freight book of steamer *Helena,* Baker to Spratt, 24 May 1881, list of rates, 22 May 1881, and Baker to clerk of steamer *Benton,* 9 August 1883, all in Baker Papers.

39. *Benton Weekly Record,* 16 October 1882; 6, 20 October 1881.

40. *River Press,* 28 December 1881.

41. Freight book of steamer *Helena;* Missouri River Commission, *Map,* 70; *Benton Weekly Record,* 16 November 1882.

42. Overholser, *Fort Benton,* 119; MacGregor, *History of Alberta,* 132–34.

43. Madsen and Madsen, *North to Montana,* 238, 240–42, 246.

44. *River Press,* 28 December 1881.

45. Ibid., 2 January 1884; Overholser, *Fort Benton,* 122–23,126.

46. *Benton Weekly Record,* 18 June 1880; 2 June 1881; Overholser, *Fort Benton,* 113.

47. Here and below: *Benton Weekly Record,* 29 December 1881; *Bismarck Daily Tribune,* 21 February 1881.

48. Overholser, *Fort Benton,* 188; Way, *Packet Directory,* 492.

49. Here and below: *Benton Weekly Record,* 18 June 1880.

50. Lass, "Isaac P. Baker," 175; letterhead of St. Louis and St. Paul Packet Line, 1881, Baker Papers.

51. Here and below: Baker to Power, 23 August 1881, Letter Press Book, 21 April 1880– 19 January 1882, 31, Baker Papers.

52. Baker to Charles, 29 October 1881, Letter Press Book, 21 April 1881–19 January 1882, 204.

53. *Bismarck Tribune,* 8 June 1882.

54. Ibid., 17 May 1882; Way, *Packet Directory,* 183.

55. *Bismarck Tribune,* 5 May, 5, 16 September 1882.

56. Way, *Packet Directory,* 366; *Chamberlain Democrat,* 2 November 1883.

57. Ibid., 27 July 3, 10, 17, 24 August, 7 September, 12 October 1883; 17 April, 27 November 1884.

58. *Press and Dakotaian,* 6 March, 24 May 1883; *Bismarck Tribune,* 28 April 1883.

59. *Bismarck Daily Tribune,* 20, 26 June, 27 September 1884; *Chamberlain Democrat,* 2, 30 July 1885.

60. Way, *Packet Directory,* 53; Overholser, *Fort Benton,* 122; *Bismarck Tribune,* 14 November 1884.

61. Overholser, *Fort Benton,* 126.

62. In Baker Papers.

63. *Bismarck Tribune,* 10 April, 25 September 1885; *Chamberlain Democrat,* 21 May 1885; W. A. Wilson to Baker, 28 April 1885, in Letter Press Book, 9 April–15 November 1885, 47.

64. *Daily Tribune* (Jefferson City), 20 February 1885.

65. *Bismarck Daily Tribune,* 27 November, 11 December 1903.

66. Corbin, *Steamboat Red Cloud*, 3.

67. *Bismarck Tribune*, 2 August 1883.

68. Way, *Packet Directory*, 54.

69. Statement of wintering, repairs, labor, and dismantling, 2 March–1 May 1884, Baker Papers.

70. *Bismarck Tribune*, 26 April 1884.

71. Overholser, *Fort Benton*, 130.

72. *Chamberlain Democrat*, 27 November 1884; 30 July, 20 August 1885.

73. Hamburg, "Railroads and Settlement," 170; Casey and Douglas, *Pioneer Railroad*, 126.

74. Baker to Thomas C. Power, 25 April 1885, Letter Press Book, 4 April–15 November 1885, 41.

75. Charles to Baker, 19 March 1886, Baker Papers.

76. Woolfolk to Baker, 20 March 1886, Baker Papers.

77. Baker to John Farrington, collector of customs, St. Paul, 29 April 1886, in Letter Press Book, 9 April–24 May 1886, 36; H. R. Lyon to Thomas C. Power, 30 December 1886, Baker Papers.

78. Baker to Charles, 8 June 1886, and Baker to Thomas C. Power, 9 June 1886, both in Letter Press Book, 25 May–15 June 1886, 220, 229.

79. Baker to Power, 10 May 1886, and Baker to Jordan, 2 June 1886, both respectively in Letter Press Book, 9 April–24 May 1886, 148, and 25 May–15 June 1886, 94.

80. Way, *Packet Directory*, 260; Baker to A. Gernon, U.S. Collector of Customs, St. Vincent, Minn., 4 June 1886, Letter Press Book, 25 May–15 June 1886.

81. Baker to Power, 22 May 1886, Letter Press Book, 9 April–24 May 1886, 355.

82. Way, *Packet Directory*, 327; Baker to Lieutenant Bingham, U.S. Engineer and Secretary, Missouri River Commission, 26 May 1886, Letter Press Book, 25 May–15 June 1886, 41; Baker to N. E. Nelson, special deputy collector of customs, St. Vincent, Minn., 10 May 1887; C. B. Morton, Bureau of Navigation, Treasury Dept., 1 February 1887. The last two letters are in the chronological correspondence file, Baker Papers.

83. Here and below: Baker to Henry Smith, 24 July 1886, and Baker to J. E. McWilliams, 22 April 1886, respectively in Letter Press Book, 15 June–29 July 1886, 279, and 9 April–24 May 1886, 15.

84. Way, *Packet Directory*, 324; Baker to Charles, 8 June 1886, Baker to Henry Smith, 24 July 1886, and Baker to J. H. Hannaford, traffic manager, Northern Pacific Railroad, 14 October 1886, respectively in Letter Press Book, 25 May–18 June 1886, 229, 15 June–29 July 1886, 279, and 28 July 1886–18 March 1887, 280; memo of 24 August 1887 on sinking of *Minnie Heerman*, Baker Papers.

85. Here and below: Overholser, *Fort Benton*, 130, 133–34, 138–39.

86. Here and below: Malone and Roeder, *Montana*, 134; Robinson, *History of North Dakota*, 142; Overholser, *Fort Benton*, 137.

87. *Batchelor* Supplementary Statement: Charter to Shepard, Winston, and Co., Statement Book, 1887, 625, Baker Papers.

88. Shepard, Winston, and Company to Baker, 8 July, 8 August 1887, and *General Terry* Portage Book, 1887, all in Baker Papers.

89. Recapitulation of poundage carried to and from Bismarck during the boating season of 1887, Statement Book, 1887, 585, Baker Papers; *Annual Engineers Report, 1889*, part 4, 2761.

90. Baker to George Hays, 23 July 1887, in Letter Press Book, 27 June–7 September 1887, 171.

91. Frazer, *Forts of the West*, 79, 83, 113–14, 134; recapitulation of poundage carried above Bismarck, 1887.

92. Rates of freight between Bismarck and Fort Benton, Letter Press Book, 2 April–21 May 1887, 10.

93. Baker to clerk, Steamer *Helena*, 5 May 1886, and Baker to T.C. Power and Brother, 31 March 1887, respectively in Letter Press Book, 9 April–24 May 1886, 82, and 28 July 1886–18 March 1887, 544; Overholser, *Fort Benton*, 119, 134.

94. Steamboat *Benton* Ledger Book, 1886, Baker Papers.

95. Profit and loss statement for 1887, in Banton Transportation Company *Journal*, 1 March 1887–15 March 1888, 289, Baker Papers.

96. *General Terry* Portage Book, 1887, Baker Papers.

97. Baker to Thomas C. Power, 11 July 1887, Letter Press Book, 27 June–7 September 1887, 20; Baker to John H. Charles, 2 August, 4 September 1887, ibid., 217, 468; Baker to John F. Baker, 2 September 1887, ibid., 452; Way, *Packet Directory*, 140.

98. Isaac P. Baker to John Baker, 4 September 1887, Letter Press Book, 27 June–7 September 1887, 460; profit and loss statement for 1887, Baker Papers.

99. Baker to Mercer, 13 August 1887, in Letter Press Book, 27 June–7 September 1887, 305.

CHAPTER 12

1. *Annual Engineers Report, 1915,* 1891.

2. *Boonville Weekly Advertiser,* 23 July 1886.

3. Missouri River Commission, *Map,* index 1.

4. *Daily Tribune,* 5 August 1877.

5. *Boonville Weekly Advertiser,* 5 April 1878; *Daily Tribune,* 30 April 1879.

6. *Daily Tribune,* 22 October 1880; 15 July 1883; *Boonville Weekly Advertiser,* 23 July 1886.

7. *Daily Tribune,* 25 July 1888; *Boonville Weekly Advertiser,* 4 July 1890.

8. *Boonville Weekly Advertiser,* 16, 23 September, 16 December 1892; 4 August 1893.

9. *Annual Engineers Report, 1894,* 3117.

10. For illustrations, see Way, *Packet Directory,* plate 3 following p. 302; and Shrader, *Steamboat Legacy,* 51, 61, 65.

11. Here and below: *Annual Engineers Report, 1887,* 2994–95.

12. Morrissey, "Motor Packets," 2–3.

13. *Annual Engineers Report, 1912,* 834.

14. Ibid., *1891,* 3738; *1894,* 1620, 3117.

15. Ibid., *1898,* 3493.

16. *Boonville Weekly Advertiser,* 1 February 1878.

17. *Daily Tribune,* 26 June 1878; *Annual Engineers Report, 1887,* 2989.

18. 51.

19. *Daily Tribune,* 31 August 1882.

20. 56.

21. *Trade and Commerce, St. Louis, 1882,* 55; Way, *Packet Directory,* 121.

22. *Daily Tribune,* 20 February 1885.

23. *Annual Engineers Report, 1887,* 2988.

24. Ibid., 2989.

25. *Daily Tribune,* 18 February 1886; *Trade and Commerce, St. Louis, 1886,* 54.

26. Specific details of the downstream cargo vary somewhat in newspaper accounts. The *Daily Tribune* of 14 April 1891 reported 16,964 sacks of wheat, 584 packages of sundries, and 20 hogs. But the same paper on 19 July 1893 showed 16,131 sacks of wheat, 388 packages, and 199 hogs. For weights of ties and wheat, see *Annual Engineers Report, 1887,* 3041.

27. *Daily Tribune,* 30 April 1891; 19 July 1893.

28. Here and below: *Annual Engineers Report, 1887,* 2993; *Twelfth Annual Report of the Trade and Commerce of Kansas City,* 173.

29. *Annual Engineers Report, 1887,* 2991.

30. *Boonville Weekly Advertiser,* 22 November 1889; *Daily Tribune,* 22 February 1890.

31. 22 November 1889.

32. *Twelfth Annual Report, Kansas City,* 171; Way, *Packet Directory,* 2, 432.

33. *Boonville Weekly Advertiser,* 23 May, 29 August, 19 September 1890; *Daily Tribune,* 6, 10 July 1890.

34. Here and below: *Twelfth Annual Report, Kansas City,* 172–73.

35. *Daily Tribune,* 19 March 1891.

36. Ibid., 17 September 1891.

37. *Boonville Weekly Advertiser,* 16 December 1892.

38. Ibid., 24 June, 16 September 1892.

39. Ibid., 24 June, 16 December 1892.

40. Ibid., 16 September 18981.

41. *Daily Tribune,* 9 March 1893.

42. Ibid., 24 May 1893; *Annual Engineers Report, 1893,* 3934.

43. Morris, *Encyclopedia of American History,* 263; Somers, "Performance of the American Economy," 652.

44. *Annual Engineers Report, 1894,* 3117.

45. *Daily Tribune,* 21 October 1893.

46. 19 January 1894.

47. *Daily Tribune,* 28 January, 11 May 1894.

48. Here and below: Bone, *Annual Review of Greater Kansas City,* 57; Schneiders, *Unruly River,* 90–95; Whitney, *Kansas City,* 1:530–33.

49. Bone, *Annual Review,* 58; Way, *Packet Directory,* 292.

50. *Boonville Weekly Advertiser,* 21 September 1906.

51. Bone, *Annual Review,* 58.

52. Ibid., 56; Whitney, *Kansas City,* 1:533; Way, *Packet Directory,* 367, 450.

53. Whitney, *Kansas City,* 1:534; *Boonville Weekly Advertiser,* 24 May 1907.

54. *Daily Tribune,* 8 June 1907; *Boonville Weekly Advertiser,* 18 September 1908; Way, *Packet Directory,* 84, 448.

55. *Boonville Weekly Advertiser,* 1 May 1908.

56. Ibid., 18 September 1908; McDonald, "Missouri River and Its Victims," third article, 598.

57. As quoted in *Boonville Weekly Advertiser,* 7 May 1909.

58. Bone, *Annual Review,* 65.

59. *Annual Engineers Report, 1887,* 2990.

60. Ibid., *1891,* 2236; *1892,* 3263.

61. "W. L. H." [William L. Heckmann], "The Steamer Helena," handwritten manuscript, E. B. Trail Collection, folder 81.

62. *Daily Tribune,* 1 August 1888; McDonald, "Missouri River and Its Victims," second article, 471.

63. Here and below: Bryan, "Dr. Lamme's Gallant Sidewheeler," 27; *Daily Tribune,* 29 April, 26 July 1891; statement of 1891 freight for *Helena,* and Heckmann's sketch of *Helena,* both in Trail Collection, folder 81; *Helena* freight manifest for Trip No. 1, 1891, and *Helena* cabin register, 1891, vols. 43 and 46 respectively, Trail Collection.

64. Statement of *Helena*'s 1891 business and list of wages paid, Trail Collection, folder 81; McDonald, "Missouri River and Its Victims," second article, 464.

65. *Daily Tribune,* 29 August 1893.

66. Here and below: *Annual Engineers Report, 1892,* 3263; *Daily Tribune,* 23 July 1889.

67. *Annual Engineers Report, 1897,* 3865; *Boonville Weekly Advertiser,* 14 April 1905.

68. *Annual Engineers Report, 1897,* 3865.

69. "The Annie Cade," clipping from *Kansas City Star,* 28 May 1944, Missouri River Collection, Kansas City Public Library, Kansas City, Missouri.

70. *Annual Engineers Report, 1892,* 3263; *1894,* 3117.

71. Ibid., *1896,* 3786; *1900,* 4956.

72. Ibid., *1900,* 4956.

73. *Annual Engineers Report, 1892,* 3264; *1900,* 4957; *Trade and Commerce, St. Louis, 1897,* 108–109; *1899,* 114–15.

74. *Daily Tribune,* 2 August 1892; *Boonville Weekly Advertiser,* 12 August 1892; 24 June 1898.

75. *Boonville Weekly Advertiser,* 13 August 1886.

76. *Annual Engineers Report, 1894,* 3117; *1900,* 4957.

77. D. W. Eaton, "Hemp Industry," 358; Robert W. Frizzell, "Southern Identity," 253.

78. Frizzell, "Southern Identity," 254.

79. In 1885 the Missouri River counties in Missouri produced 72 million bushels of corn and 13 million of wheat, as well as 10.2 million bushels of oats, 200,000 of rye, and 100,000 of barley (*Annual Engineers Report, 1887,* 2990).

80. K. K. White and Miles, *History of Benton County,* 32j; *Annual Engineers Report, 1882,* 1660; D. W. Eaton, "How Missouri Counties . . . Were Named," third article, 194.

81. Way, *Packet Directory,* 370; *Daily Tribune,* 5 January 1878; *Annual Engineers Report, 1881,* 1592–93. This report did not include tonnage for the ties and logs. Those totals were computed by the author by using 179 pounds per tie and 38 pounds per cubic foot of the logs. In order to compare the 1881 trade with

that of any given year in the 1890s, it is necessary to include the tie and log tonnage, because it was included in the annual totals of the 1890s trade.

82. *Annual Engineers Report, 1887,* 1592.

83. Ibid., *1899,* 3686; *1895,* 3996.

84. Ibid., *1890,* 1998; *1898,* 3494.

85. Ibid., *1898,* 3494; Rafferty, *Historical Atlas of Missouri,* 81.

86. Statistics for 1898 illustrate the point. Only 349,955 ton-miles out of a total 4,175,054 for the Osage were moved by steam packets and other boats. The Missouri's commerce, which was almost entirely steamboats and gasoline packets, was 1,929,561 ton-miles. *Annual Engineers Report, 1899,* 3686; *1900,* 4938.

87. *Annual Engineers Report, 1890,* 1994; *1896,* 3794; *1899,* 3685.

88. Ibid., *1890,* 1994; *1894,* 1624; Way, *Packet Directory,* 119, 173, 236.

89. *Annual Engineers Report, 1888,* 1451; *Daily Tribune,* 25 March 1890.

90. *Annual Engineers Report, 1899,* 3685.

91. Ibid.; U.S. Congress, House, *Thirtieth Annual List of Merchant Vessels,* 224; U.S. House, *Thirty-First Annual List of Merchant Vessels,* 283.

92. Here and below: U.S. Congress, House, *Gasconade River, MO;* 42–43; *Annual Engineers Report, 1894,* 1619; *1895,* 3998; Shrader, *Steamboat Legacy,* 103.

93. Here and below: Shrader, *Steamboat Legacy,* 44–58 passim.

94. Here and below: ibid., 102, 264–65; *Annual Engineers Report, 1888,* 1449.

95. *Annual Engineers Report, 1897,* 3869; *1899,* 3683.

96. Ibid., *1897,* 3868; *1900,* 4938.

97. Ibid., *1912,* 845; *1905,* 1692.

98. "Articles of Incorporation of Benton Packet Company," 545; *Bismarck Tribune,* 21 June 1916; "Articles of Incorporation of the Benton Transportation Company," 515.

99. *Chamberlain Democrat,* 27 March 1890.

100. Baker to Charles W. Powell, 23 February 1892, and Baker to W. W. Pickens, 21 May 1896, both in Baker Papers.

101. Here and below: *Chamberlain Democrat,* 11 September, 2 October, 20 November 1890; *Annual Engineers Report, 1890,* 3272; *1893,* 2302; *1897,* 2188; Way, *Packet Directory,* 4; *Bismarck Daily Tribune,* 19, 26, 27 June, 10 December 1891; 13, 15 May, 27, 28 July, 2, 4, 12 August 1892.

102. Schuler, *Bridge Apart,* 58; *Annual Engineers Report, 1893,* 2302; *1902,* 1691.

103. Kingsbury, *Dakota Territory,* 2:1280ff; Schell, *History of South Dakota,* 247; Schuler, *Bridge Apart,* 45.

104. McDonald, "Missouri River and Its Victims," first article, 234; *Annual Engineers Report, 1898,* 1849; *1902,* 1691; B. L. Hall, *Roundup Years,* 482; "Much Goods Moved on River in Early 1900s," clipping from *Argus Leader* (Sioux Falls), 1 December 1942, in Senechal file, Biographical File, South Dakota State Historical Society, Pierre; Schuler, *Bridge Apart,* 58–59.

105. Schuler, *Bridge Apart,* 59–60. From 26 February 1885 to 3 March 1890, Fort Pierre was named Coulson in honor of Sanford B. Coulson. Local sentiment for the traditional name led to its reinstatement (Schuler, *Bridge Apart,* 29).

106. *Democrat,* 22 May 1884; 10 June, 5 August 1886; 28 April, 26 May, 17 November 1887; McDonald, "Missouri River and Its Victims," second article, 471; Way, *Packet Directory,* 259, 278.

107. *Democrat,* 31 July, 11 September 1884; 14 May, 18, 23 June 1885; 20 May 1886.

108. Ibid., 16 June, 14 July, 18 August, 8 September 1887; 10, 17 May 1888.

109. Here and below: ibid., 3, 10 April 1890.

110. Here and below: *Annual Engineers Report, 1892,* 3669; *1893,* 2302; *1894,* 1748; *1895,* 2237; *1896,* 1894; *1897,* 2189; *1898,* 1849; *1899,* 2225; *1900,* 2885; *1901,* 2394; *1902,* 1691; McDonald, "Missouri River and Its Victims," first article, 231, 233.

111. Here and below: *Annual Engineers Report, 1897,* 2188, *1898,* 1849; McDonald, "Missouri River and Its Victims," first article, 228.

112. *Annual Engineers Report, 1900,* 2885; Way, *Packet Directory,* 430.

113. Here and below: Casey and Douglas, *Pioneer Railroad,* 315; McDonald, "Missouri River and Its Victims," third article, 595; Sneve, *South Dakota Geographic Names,* 62; J. A. Greene, *Fort Randall,* 165, 172.

114. Way, *Packet Directory*, 159, 258; Nichol, "Steamboat Navigation," 210; U.S. House, *Thirty-Fifth Annual List of Merchant Vessels*, 229; *Thirty-Sixth Annual List*, 225; *Thirty-Seventh Annual List*, 431; *Thirty-Eighth Annual List*, 404; U.S. Dept. of Commerce and Labor, Bureau of Navigation, *Thirty-Ninth Annual List*, 236.

115. Lass, *Steamboating on the Upper Missouri*, 161.

116. Way, *Packet Directory*, 402; *Annual Engineers Report, 1901*, 2394.

117. Vyzralek, Grant, and Bohi, "North Dakota's Railroad Depots," 12; Lass, "Washburn, William Drew."

118. Here and below: *Annual Engineers Report, 1901*, 2394; *1902*, 1691; Way, *Packet Directory*, 157, 481; McDonald, "Missouri River and Its Victims," second article, 456; Frank E. Vyzralek to William E. Lass, 1 May 2006.

119. Here and below: *Waterways Journal* (St. Louis), 6 October 1962, 61; U.S. Dept. of Commerce and Labor, Bureau of Navigation, *Thirty-Ninth Annual List*, 267; Way, *Packet Directory*, 64, 351; U.S. Congress, House, *Reports on Examination and Survey of Yellowstone River*, 6; Lepley, *Packets to Paradise*, 174–76, 190, 227.

120. U.S. House, *Reports on Examination and Survey of Yellowstone*, 7, 17, 28.

121. Here and below: ibid., 18; McDonald, "Missouri River and Its Victims," first article, 234.

122. Davison, "White Hopes," 2–4, 15; *Annual Engineers Report, 1892*, 1906.

123. Davison, "White Hopes," 7; Way, *Packet Directory*, 402; *Annual Engineers Report, 1898*, 1849.

124. *Annual Engineers Report, 1895*, 2214.

125. Here and below: ibid.

126. Davison, "White Hopes," 10–11.

127. Ibid., 5, 14–15; *Annual Engineers Report, 1892*, 1906.

128. *Annual Engineers Report, 1892*, 1906–1907; Malone and Roeder, *Montana*, 134.

129. *Annual Engineers Report, 1895*, 2229.

130. Ibid., *1901*, 2394; *1902*, 1619; Way, *Packet Directory*, 402.

131. Rivers and Harbors Act (1882), 205; *Annual Engineers Report, 1887*, 2988–89.

132. Rivers and Harbors Act (1884), 145.

133. Ibid., 33 (part 1): 367; *Annual Engineers Report, 1891*, 3724.

134. *Annual Engineers Report, 1884*, 1538; Missouri River Commission, *Map*, title page.

135. *Annual Engineers Report, 1902*, 1689.

136. Rivers and Harbors Act (1912), 219; *Annual Engineers Report, 1892*, 3253; *1913*, 932–33.

137. Kishmar, "Facts and Events," 12–13.

138. Here and below: L. E. Bradley, "Government Ice Harbors," 32–34; Vyzralek to Lass, 1 May 2006.

139. *Annual Engineers Report, 1928*, part 1, 1152; *1913*, part 1, 946.

140. Way, *Packet Directory*, 306; *Annual Engineers Report, 1891*, 1876–77; *1918*, 2824; *1923*, part 1, 1146; *1927*, part 1, 1109; *1928*, part 1, 1157; *1929*, part 1, 1163, 1168; *1930*, part 1, 1244; *1931*, part 1, 1257; *1932*, part 1, 1162; *1933*, part 1, 716. The engineer reports contain statistics on the number of snags, rocks, and other obstructions removed, trees cut on overhanging banks, and miles of work.

141. *Annual Engineers Report, 1879*, 1080.

142. Ibid., *1928*, part 1, 1146; *1933*, part 1, 709–10; *1913*, 930.

143. Here and below: ibid., *1913*, 946; *1915*, 1072–73; *1888*, 1448; *1930*, part 2, 646.

144. Williams and Newell, "Yellowstone River Navigability Study," 9; U.S. House, *Reports on Examination and Survey of Yellowstone*, 30.

145. Vyzralek, "Down the Missouri in 1918," 502; Way, *Packet Directory*, 420, 474; McDonald, "Missouri River and Its Victims," second article, 471; clipping from *Kansas City Times*, 4 August 1926, Missouri River Collection, Kansas City Public Library; Schell, *History of South Dakota*, 358.

146. *Annual Engineers Report, 1919*, 2901.

147. Here and below: ibid., *1921*, part 1, 1260, 2929.

148. Ibid., *1927*, part 1, 1106; U.S. Dept. of Commerce, Bureau of Navigation, *Merchant Vessels of the United States, 1925*, 58; clipping from *Kansas City Times*, 4 August 1916.

149. *Annual Engineers Report, 1913*, 936; U.S. Dept. of Commerce and Labor, Bureau of Navigation, *Forty-Third Annual List*, 121, 151, 308; U.S. Dept. of Commerce, Bureau of Navigation, *Forty-Fifth Annual List, 1913*, 105; Way, *Packet Directory*, 84; *Boonville Weekly Advertiser*, 23 June 1911.

150. Here and below: *Boonville Weekly Advertiser*, 30 May 1913; *Annual Engineers Report, 1916*, 2668.

151. *Annual Engineers Report, 1919*, 2898.

152. *Boonville Weekly Advertiser*, 16 April 1919; Way, *Packet Directory*, 252; *Trade and Commerce, St. Louis, 1920*, 70, 80.

153. Shrader, *Steamboat Legacy*, 268.

154. Here and below: *Annual Engineers Report, 1923*, part 2, 899–900; *1927*, part 2, 591; *1928*, part 2, 631; *1929*, part 2, 617; *1930*, part 2, 645; *1931*, part 2, 670; U.S. House, *Gasconade River, MO*, 43–44.

155. Here and below: *Annual Engineers Report, 1927*, part 2, 589; Shrader, *Steamboat Legacy*, 267–68; Way, *Packet Directory*, 213; U.S. Dept. of Commerce, Bureau of Navigation, *Merchant Vessels of the United States, 1925*, 98; *1930*, 90. Because of the reenrollment, there is some question as to whether there was only one *Hermann* or two. Shrader ignores the 1928 reenrollment and describes the *Hermann* as operating on the Missouri in 1912–35. But the 1925 and 1930 annual reports of merchant vessels show a *Hermann* built in 1912 and another *Hermann* built in 1928. Both were stern-wheelers with 40 horsepower. The first *Hermann* (official number 210372) had a capacity of 35 tons and dimensions of 89 × 19.6 × 2.4. The second (official number 227908), with a 49-ton capacity, measured 86.8 × 18.7 × 2.7. Way, who often used the annual lists as his authority, reported two *Hermann*s with the 1912 and 1928 construction dates.

156. Clipping from *Kansas City Star*, 22 June 1935, Missouri River Collection, Kansas City Public Library.

BIBLIOGRAPHY

ARCHIVAL AND MANUSCRIPT COLLECTIONS

Baker, Isaac P., Papers. State Historical Society of North Dakota, Bismarck.

Kishmar, George. "Facts and Events on the Missouri River." Typed manuscript. State Historical Society of Missouri, Columbia.

Missouri River Collection. Kansas City Public Library, Kansas City, Mo.

Senechal file. Biographical file. South Dakota State Historical Society, Pierre.

Trail, E. B., Collection. Western Historical Manuscripts Center, Missouri Historical Society and University of Missouri, Columbia. The collection consists of steamboat records, clippings, photographs, and research notes collected and compiled by Dr. E. B. Trail, a dentist and steamboat aficionado from Berger, Mo.

Water Transportation Records, 1834–1900 (also known as Vessel Files). Record Group 92, NARA.

Way, Frederick, Jr., Collection. Public Library of Cincinnati and Hamilton County, Cincinnati.

Williams, Gary, and Alan Newell. "Yellowstone River Navigability Study." Manuscript prepared for U.S. Army Corps of Engineers Omaha District, August 12, 1974. Copy at Montana Historical Society, Helena.

GOVERNMENT DOCUMENTS

Act to Modify Security for Steam Passengers Act of 1838. *U.S. Statutes at Large* 5 (1843).

American State Papers: Military Affairs, vol. 2. Serial Set 017.

Annual Report of the Chief of Engineers. 1867–1931. (Published as separate reports by the Government Printing Office and also in the U.S. Congress Serial Set.)

Appropriations for Public Works Act. *U.S. Statutes at Large* 14 (1866).

"Articles of Incorporation of Benton Packet Company." Book of Corporations, no. 6. Office of the Secretary of State, State of North Dakota, Bismarck.

"Articles of Incorporation of Benton Transportation Company." Book of Corporations, no. 23. Office of the Secretary of State, State of North Dakota, Bismarck.

"Articles of Incorporation of the North West Transportation Company," 11 November 1867. Office of the Secretary of State, State of Iowa, Des Moines.

Contract between Campbell K. Peck and Ely S. Parker, 23 May 1871. Bureau of Indian

Affairs (BIA) Records, National Archives and Records Administration (NARA), Washington, D.C.

Contract between Durfee and Peck and F. A. Walker, commissioner of Indian affairs, 14 June 1872. BIA Records, NARA.

Contract between G. T. Nutter and Ely S. Parker, 13 May 1869. BIA Records, NARA.

Contract between Hiram K. Hazlett and Major General J. L. Donaldson, acting quartermaster general, 29 February 1868. Old Military and Civil Records Division, NARA.

Contract between John B. Davis and Peyton S. Davidson and B. C. Card, chief quartermaster, Department of Dakota, 20 March 1877. Old Army Records, NARA.

Contract between Joseph La Barge and William P. Dole, 1 April 1863. BIA Records, NARA.

Contract between Pierre Chouteau, Jr., and Company and Alfred Cumming, superintendent of Indian Affairs, 29 May 1855. BIA records, NARA.

Contract between Pierre Chouteau, Jr., and Company and Charles E. Mix, acting commissioner of Indian Affairs, 15 March 1859. BIA Records, NARA.

Contract between Pierre Chouteau, Jr., and Company and Clark W. Thompson, 16 April 1863. BIA Records, NARA.

Contract between Pierre Chouteau, Jr., and Company and William P. Dole, 18 March 1864. BIA Records, NARA.

Contract between Pierre Chouteau, Jr., and Company and William P. Dole, 25 March 1864. BIA Records, NARA.

Contract between W. Cass, president of the NPRR [Northern Pacific Railroad], and Edward Smith, commissioner of Indian Affairs, 13 May 1873. BIA records, NARA.

Contract for Missouri River between Colonel Daniel H. Rucker, assistant quartermaster, and John B. Dallas, 21 February 1873. Old Army Records, NARA.

Contract for Missouri River transportation, commencing March 20, and ending October 31, 1878, between Sanford B. Coulson and Chas. H. Tompkins, deputy quartermaster general, 12 March 1878. Old Army Records, NARA.

Contract for Missouri River transportation between Sanford B. Coulson and Chas. H. Tompkins, deputy quartermaster general, 13 March 1879. Old Army Records, NARA.

Contract for transportation on the Missouri and Yellowstone rivers between Sanford B. Coulson and Chas. H. Tompkins, 14 March 1879. Old Army Records, NARA.

Missouri River Commission. *Map of Missouri River.* 1892–95.

Proceedings of the Thirty-Second Annual Meeting of the Board of Supervising Inspectors of Steam Vessels, Held at Washington, D.C., January, 1884. Washington, D.C.: Government Printing Office, 1884.

Proceedings of the Twentieth Annual Meeting of the Board of Supervising Inspectors of Steam Vessels, Held at Washington, D.C., January, 1870. Washington, D.C.: Government Printing Office, 1872.

Proceeds of the Sales of Public Lands Act. *U.S. Statutes at Large* 5 (1841).

Registration of Vessels Act. *U.S. Statutes at Large* 1 (1789).

Report of the Commissioner of Indian Affairs, 1871. Washington, D.C.: Government Printing Office, 1872.

Report of the Commissioner of Indian Affairs, 1872. Washington, D.C.: Government Printing Office, 1872.

Rivers and Harbors Act. *U.S. Statutes at Large* 5 (1838).

Rivers and Harbors Act. *U.S. Statutes at Large* 10 (1852).

Rivers and Harbors Act. *U.S. Statutes at Large* 22, chap. 375 (1882).

Rivers and Harbors Act. *U.S. Statutes at Large* 23, chap. 229 (1884).

Rivers and Harbors Act. *U.S. Statutes at Large* 37, part 1, chap. 253 (1912).

"Schedule of Rates" from contract between Daniel H. Rucker and Sanford B. Coulson, 14 March 1875. Old Army records, NARA.

Security for Steam Passengers Act. *U.S. Statutes at Large* 5 (1838).

Steamboat Safety Act. *U.S. Statutes at Large* 10 (1852).

[Stevens, Isaac Ingalls]. *Report upon the Northern Pacific Railroad Exploration and Survey by Gov. I. I. Stevens.* 33d Cong., 1st sess. House Ex. Doc. 129, Serial Set 736 (1853-54).

"Tabular Statement" from contract between Hiram K. Hazlett and Brevet Major General Daniel H. Rucker, assistant quartermaster, 17 February 1870. Old Army Records, NARA.

"Tabular Statement" from contract between Lt. Col. S. B. Holabird, deputy quartermaster, and Sanford B. Coulson, 20 March 1876. Old Army Records, NARA.

"Tabular Statement" from contract for Missouri River transportation from March 20 to October 31, 1874, between Sanford B. Coulson and Daniel H. Rucker, 18 March 1874. Old Army Records, NARA.

U.S. Army. Department of Dakota. *Table of Distances in the Department of Dakota, Compiled under the Direction of the Chief Quartermaster of Dakota, St. Paul, Minn., January 18, 1875.* Washington, D.C.: Government Printing Office, 1875.

U.S. Bureau of the Census. *A Compendium of the Ninth Census, 1870.*

———. *Compendium of the Tenth Census, 1880.*

———. *Eighth Census, 1860: Population.*

———. *Fifth Census of the Inhabitants of the United States, 1830.*

———. *Seventh Census of the United States, 1850: Statistics.*

———. *Statistics of the Population of the United States, 1880.*

U.S. Congress. *Annals of Congress (Debates and Proceedings in the Congress of the United States).* 16th Cong., 1st sess., 1819–20.

U.S. Congress. House. *Contracts by the Quartermaster Department, 1867.* 40th Cong., 2d sess. H. Ex. Doc. 35, Serial Set 1330.

———. *Contracts by the Quartermaster General, July 1–December 1, 1866.* 39th Cong., 2d sess. H. Ex. Doc. 28, Serial Set 1289.

———. *Contracts Made by the War Department, 1847.* 30th Cong., 1st sess. H. Ex. Doc. 29, Serial Set 516.

———. *Contracts Made by the War Department, 1858.* 35th Cong., 2d sess. H. Ex. Doc. 50, Serial Set 1006.

———. *Contracts Made by the War Department, 1859.* 36th Cong., 1st sess. H. Ex. Doc. 22, Serial Set 1047.

———. *Contracts Made by the War Department, 1860.* 36th Cong., 2d sess. H. Ex. Doc. 47, Serial Set 1099.

———. *Contracts Made by the War Department, 1861.* 37th Cong., 2d sess. H. Ex. Doc. 101, Serial Set 1136.

———. *Documents in Relation to the Claim of James Johnson for Transportation on the Missouri and Mississippi Rivers.* 16th Cong., 2d sess., 1 March 1821. H. Doc. 110, Serial Set 55.

———. *Gasconade River, MO: Letter from the Secretary of War Transmitting Report from the Chief of Engineers on the Gasconade River, MO, Covering Navigation, Flood Control, Power Development, and Irrigation.* 72d Cong., 1st sess. H. Doc. 192. Washington, D.C.: Government Printing Office, 1932.

————. *Improvement of Missouri River.* 40th Cong., 2d sess., 1868. H. Ex. Doc. 136, Serial Set 1337.

————. *Lists of Vessels Bought, Sold and Chartered by the United States, 1861–68.* 40th Cong., 2d sess. H. Ex. Doc. 337, Serial Set 1346.

————. *Missouri River, from Sioux City, Iowa, to Fort Benton, Mont.* 62d Cong., 1st sess., 12 July 1911. H. Doc. 91, Serial Set 6116.

————. *Report of the Secretary of War, 1868.* 40th Cong., 3d sess. H. Ex. Doc. 1, Serial Set 1367.

————. *Report of the Secretary of War, 1869.* 41st Cong., 2d sess. H. Ex. Doc. 1, Serial Set 1412.

————. *Reports on Examination and Survey of Yellowstone River, from Its Mouth to Billlings.* . . . 62d Cong., 1st sess., 30 June 1911. H. Doc. 83, Serial Set 6116.

————. *Statement of Calvin Case, as to the Facts in Relation to the Loss of Boats on the Mississippi.* 27th Cong., 3d sess., 15 February 1843. H. Rep. 178, Serial Set 427.

————. *Steam-Vessels in the United States.* 42d Cong., 2d sess., 13 February 1872. H. Ex. Doc. 138, Serial Set 1513.

————. *Testimony Taken before the Committee on Indian Affairs Concerning the Management of the Indian Department.* 44th Cong., 1st sess., 1876. H. Misc. Doc. 167, Serial Set 1702.

————. *Thirtieth Annual List of Merchant Vessels of the United States, 1898.* 55th Cong., 3d sess. H. Doc. 100, Serial Set 3796.

————. *Thirty-First Annual List of Merchant Vessels of the United States, 1899.* 56th Cong., 1st sess. H. Doc. 18, Serial Set 3953.

————. *Thirty-Fifth Annual List of Merchant Vessels of the United States, 1903.* 58th Cong., 2d sess. H. Doc. 16, Serial Set 4669.

————. *Thirty-Sixth Annual List of Merchant Vessels of the United States, 1904.* 59th Cong., 3d sess. H. Doc. 16, Serial Set 4824.

————. *Thirty-Seventh Annual List of Merchant Vessels of the United States, 1905.* 59th Cong., 1st sess. H. Doc. 16, Serial Set 4978.

————. *Thirty-Eighth Annual List of Merchants Vessels of the United States, 1906.* 59th Cong., 2d sess. H. Doc. 16, Serial Set 5138.

U.S. Congress. Senate. *Contracts Made by the War Department, 1848.* 30th Cong., 2d sess. S. Ex. Doc. 17, Serial Set 529.

————. *Contracts Made by the War Department, 1849.* 31st Cong., 1st sess. S. Ex. Doc. 26, Serial Set 554.

————. *Contracts Made by the War Department, 1850.* 31st Cong., 2d sess. S. Ex. Doc. 11, Serial Set 589.

————. *Contracts Made by the War Department, 1851.* 32d Cong., 1st sess. S. Ex. Doc. 12, Serial Set 614.

————. *Contracts Made by the War Department, 1852.* 32d Cong., 1st sess. S. Ex. Doc. 18, Serial Set 660.

————. *Contracts Made by the War Department, 1853.* 33d Cong., 1st sess. S. Ex. Doc. 37, Serial Set 698.

————. *Contracts Made by the War Department, 1854.* 33d Cong., 2d sess. S. Ex. Doc. 46, Serial Set 752.

————. *Contracts Made by the War Department, 1855.* 34th Cong., 1st and 2nd sess. S. Ex. Doc. 7, Serial Set 815.

————. *Contracts Made by the War Department, 1856.* 34th Cong., 2d sess. S. Ex. Doc. 32, Serial Set 880.

———. *Contracts Made by the War Department, 1857.* 35th Cong., 1st sess. S. Ex. Doc. 31, Serial Set 924.

———. *Documents Accompanying the Report of the Secretary of War.* 26th Cong., 1st sess., 30 November 1839. S. Doc. 1, Serial Set 354.

———. *Report of the Commissioner of Indian Affairs for 1859.* 36th Cong., 1st sess. S. Ex. Doc. 2, Serial Set 1023.

———. *Report of the Commissioner of Patents: Documents Relating to the Preservation and Protection of Passengers from Injuries Resulting from Steamboat Accidents.* Sen. Doc. 4, 31 Cong., special sess., 1849, Serial Set 547.

———. *Report of the Commissioner of Patents, to the Senate of the United States, on the Subject of Steam Boiler Explosions.* 30th Cong., 2d sess., 30 December 1848. S. Ex. Doc. 18, Serial Set 529.

———. *Report of the Secretary of the Treasury on the Statistics and History of the Steam Marine of the United States Made in Compliance with a Resolution of the Senate.* 32d Cong., 1st sess., 21 January 1852. S. Ex. Doc. 42, Serial Set 619.

———. *Report of the Secretary of War, 1851.* 32d Cong., 1st sess. S. Ex. Doc. 1, Serial Set 611.

———. *Report of the Secretary of War, 1859.* 36th Cong., 1st sess. S. Ex. Doc. 2, Serial Set 1025.

U.S. Department of Commerce. Bureau of Navigation. *Forty-Fifth Annual List of Merchant Vessels of the United States.* Washington, D.C.: Government Printing Office, 1913.

———. *Merchant Vessels of the United States, 1925.* Washington, D.C.: Government Printing Office, 1926.

———. *Merchant Vessels of the United States, 1930.* Washington, D.C.: Government Printing Office, 1930.

U.S. Department of Commerce and Labor. Bureau of Navigation. *Forty-Third Annual List of Merchant Vessels of the United States, 1911.* Washington, D.C.: Government Printing Office, 1911.

———. *Thirty-Ninth Annual List of Merchant Vessels of the United States, 1907.* Washington, D.C.: Government Printing Office, 1907.

U.S. War Department. *The War of the Rebellion: Official Records of the Union and Confederate Armies.* 130 vols. Ed. Robert N. Scott et al. Washington, D.C.: Government Printing Office, 1880–1901.

Van Buren Proclamation. *U.S. Statutes at Large* 5 (1837).

Western Boundary of Missouri Act. *U.S. Statutes at Large* 5 (1836).

NEWSPAPERS

Avant Courier (Bozeman), 1875.

Benton Record (Fort Benton), 1875–82 (variously also named *Fort Benton Record* and *Benton Weekly Record*).

Bismarck Tribune, weekly, 1885.

Bismarck Weekly Tribune, 1881–1916.

Black Hills Journal (Rapid City), 1879.

Black Hills Pioneer (Deadwood), 1878.

Black Hills Times (Deadwood), 1878.

Boonville Weekly Advertiser, 1878–1919.

Brunswicker (Brunswick, Mo.), 1853.

Chamberlain Democrat, 1883–90.

Council Bluffs Chronotype, 1855.
Daily Bulletin (Leavenworth), 1868.
Daily Champion (Deadwood), 1877.
Daily Dispatch (St. Louis), 1866.
Daily Missouri Republican (St. Louis), 1836–40.
Daily Tribune (Jefferson City), 1877–1907.
Dakota Herald (Yankton), 1881.
Dakotaian (Yankton), 1862.
Dakota Register (Chamberlain), 1881–83.
Democrat (Chamberlain), 1883.
Democrat (St. Louis), 1864–69.
Evening News (St. Louis), 1866.
Frontier Guardian (Kanesville, Iowa), 1849–51.
Frontier Guardian and Iowa Sentinel (Kanesville), 1852.
Glasgow Weekly Times, 1853–61.
Helena Daily Herald, 1871.
Helena Weekly Herald, 1874–75.
Jefferson City Inquirer, 1843–57.
Jeffersonian Republican (Jefferson City), 1839–44
Leavenworth Daily Times, 1859.
Liberty Tribune (Liberty, Mo.), 1849–65.
Minnesota Pioneer (St. Paul), 1849.
Missouri Argus (St. Louis), 1836.
Missouri Gazette (St. Louis), 1817.
Missouri Gazette and Public Advertiser(St. Louis), 1819–21.
Missouri Intelligencer and Boon's Lick Advertiser (Franklin and Fayette), 1819–35.
Missouri Republican (St. Louis), weekly, 1826–50.
Montana Post (Virginia City and Helena), 1868.
Morning Herald (St. Joseph), 1863–67.
Nebraska News (Nebraska City), 1860–65.
Nebraska Republican (Omaha), 1861.
People's Press (Nebraska City), 1860–63.
Press and Dakotaian (Yankton), 1869–81.
River Press (Fort Benton), 1881–84.
St. Joseph Gazette, 1852–53.
St. Louis Beacon, 1829.
St. Louis Enquirer, 1819–24.
Sioux City Eagle, 1857–59.
Sioux City Journal, 1868–79.
Sioux City Register, 1859–69.
Sioux City Weekly Journal, 1870–79.
Sioux City Weekly Times, 1871–72.
Tri-Weekly Missouri Republican (St. Louis), 1861–64.
Union and Dakotaian (Yankton), 1866–69.
Weekly Commonwealth (Denver), 1863.
Western Bugle (Kanesville), 1852.
Yankton Press, 1871–72.
Yankton Press and Dakotan, 1896.

OTHER SOURCES

"A History of Kansas City, Missouri." http://www.kcmo.org/kcmo.nsf/web/kchistory?open document.

"About the APS" [American Philosophical Society]. http://www.amphilsoc.org.

Ambler, Charles Henry. *A History of Transportation in the Ohio Valley.* Cleveland: Arthur H. Clark, 1931; reprint, Westport, Conn.: Greenwood Press, 1970.

Anderson, Harry H. "A History of the Cheyenne River Indian Agency and Its Military Post, Fort Bennett, 1868–1891." *South Dakota Historical Collections,* vol. 28 (Pierre, 1957): 390–551.

Anderson, Hattie M. "Frontier Economic Problems in Missouri, 1815–1828, Part I." *Missouri Historical Review* 34 (October 1939): 38–70.

———. "Frontier Economic Problems in Missouri, 1815–1828, Part II." *Missouri Historical Review* 34 (January 1940): 182–203.

———. "Missouri, A Land of Promise." *Missouri Historical Review* 30 (April 1936): 227–53.

———. "Missouri, 1804–1828: Peopling a Frontier State." *Missouri Historical Review* 31 (January 1937): 150–80.

Andreas' Historical Atlas of Dakota. Chicago: A. T. Andreas, 1884.

Annual Review, History of St. Louis, Commercial Statistics, Improvements of the Year, and Account of Leading Manufactories, etc. From the *Missouri Republican,* 10 January 1854. St. Louis: Chambers and Knapp, 1854.

Annual Review of the Commerce of St. Louis, for the Year 1854. St. Louis: Chambers and Knapp, 1855.

Apple, Lindsey. "Johnson, James." *American National Biography.*

Athearn, Robert C. *Forts of the Upper Missouri.* Englewood Cliffs, N.J.: Prentice-Hall, 1967.

———. *Union Pacific Country.* Chicago: Rand McNally, 1971.

Atherton, Lewis E. "James and Robert Aull—A Frontier Missouri Mercantile Firm." *Missouri Historical Review* 30 (October 1935): 3–27.

———. "Missouri's Society and Economy in 1821." *Missouri Historical Review* 65 (July 1971): 450–77.

Audubon, Maria R. *Audubon and His Journals.* With zoological and other notes by Elliot Coues. 2 vols. New York: Charles Scribner's Sons, 1897.

Bailey, Thomas A. *A Diplomatic History of the American People.* 8th ed. New York: Appleton-Century-Crofts, 1969.

Baldwin, Leland D. *The Keelboat Age on Western Waters.* Pittsburgh: University of Pittsburgh Press, 1941.

[Bancroft, Hubert Howe]. *History of Washington, Idaho and Montana, 1845–1889.* Vol. 31 of *The Works of Hubert Howe Bancroft.* San Francisco: History Co., 1890.

Barbour, Barton H. *Fort Union and the Upper Missouri Fur Trade.* Norman: University of Oklahoma Press, 2001.

Barry, Louise. *The Beginning of the West: Annals of the Kansas Gateway to the American West, 1540–1854.* Topeka: Kansas State Historical Society, 1972.

Beal, Merrill D. *"I Will Fight No More Forever": Chief Joseph and the Nez Perce War.* Seattle: University of Washington Press, 1963.

Beers, Henry Putney. *The Western Military Frontier, 1815–1846.* Philadelphia: privately printed, 1935.

Bennett, Howard Franklin. "The Hannibal and St. Joseph Railroad and the Development of Northern Missouri 1847–1870: A Study of Land and Colonization Policies." PhD diss., Harvard University, 1950.

Bettis, Mark H. *For Wood and Water: Steamboating on the Missouri River from Saint Louis to Fort Union, Dakota Territory 1841–1846: A Collection of Journals by Captain Joseph A. Sire.* Villa Ridge, Mo.: Marhbet Productions, 2000.

Billington, Ray Allen. *The Far Western Frontier, 1830–1860.* New York: Harper and Brothers, 1956.

Billington, Ray Allen, and Martin Ridge. *Westward Expansion: A History of the American Frontier.* 5th ed. New York: Macmillan, 1982.

Bingham, John H., and Nora K. Peters. "A Short History of Brule County." *South Dakota Historical Collections,* vol. 23 (Pierre, 1947): 1–184.

"Boat Building in St. Louis." *Western Journal* 1 (January 1848): 46–50.

Bone, D. M., ed. *Annual Review of Greater Kansas City.* [Kansas City, Mo.]: by the editor, 1908.

Brackenridge, Henry Marie. *Views of Louisiana Together with a Journal of a Voyage up the Missouri River, in 1811.* 1814. Reprint, Chicago: Quadrangle, 1962.

Bradbury, John. *Travels in the Interior of America.* 1817. Reprint, Ann Arbor: University Microfilms, 1966.

Bradley, James H. "Account of Attempts to Build a Town at the Mouth of the Musselshell River." *Contributions to the Historical Society of Montana,* vol. 2 (Helena, 1896): 304–13.

———. "Affairs at Fort Benton from 1831 to 1869, from Lieut. Bradley's Journal." *Contributions to the Historical Society of Montana,* vol. 3 (Helena, 1900): 201–87.

———. "Bradley Manuscript—Book II." *Contributions to the Historical Society of Montana,* vol. 8 (Helena, 1917): 127–96.

Bradley, L. E. "Government Ice Harbors on the Upper Missouri." *North Dakota History* 60 (Summer 1993): 28–37.

Bray, Edmund C., and Martha Coleman Bray, eds. *Joseph N. Nicollet on the Plains and Prairies: The Expeditions of 1838–39, with Journals, Letters, and Notes on the Dakota Indians.* St. Paul: Minnesota Historical Society Press, 1976.

Briggs, Harold E. *Frontiers of the Northwest: A History of the Upper Missouri Valley.* New York: D. Appleton-Century, 1940.

Brown, John K. *Limbs on the Levee: Steamboat Explosions and the Origins of Federal Public Welfare Regulation, 1817–1852.* Middlebourne, W.Va.: International Steamboat Society, 1989.

Brown, Mark H. *The Flight of the Nez Perce.* New York: Putnam's Sons, 1967.

"Brunswick Area History: Early History." http://jard.homeip.net/brunswick/history/early hist.html.

Bryan, Charles W., Jr. "Dr. Lamme's Gallant Sidewheeler 'Yellowstone.'" *Montana the Magazine of Western History* 15 (July 1965): 24–43.

Buley, R. Carlyle. *Old Northwest: Pioneer Period, 1815–1840.* 2 vols. Bloomington: Indiana University Press, 1950.

Burlingame, Merrill G. *The Montana Frontier.* Reprint, Bozeman: Endowment and Research Foundation, Montana State University, 1980.

[Calhoun, John C.]. *The Papers of John C. Calhoun.* Vols. 2–4. Ed. W. Edwin Hemphill. Columbia: University of South Carolina Press, 1963–69.

"Captain John Nelson." *Missouri Historical Review* 21 (April 1927): 509.

Carley, Kenneth. *The Sioux Uprising of 1862.* St. Paul: Minnesota Historical Society, 1976.

Carpenter, E. W. "A Glimpse of Montana." *Overland Monthly* 2 (April 1869): 378–86.

Carriker, Robert C. *Father Peter John De Smet: Jesuit in the West.* Norman: University of Oklahoma Press, 1995.

Carter, Harvey L. "Robert Campbell." In *The Mountain Men and the Fur Trade of the Far West,* ed. LeRoy R. Hafen, 8:49–60. Glendale, Calif.: Arthur H. Clark, 1971.

Casey, Robert J., and W. A. S. Douglas. *Pioneer Railroad: The Story of the Chicago and North Western System.* New York: McGraw-Hill, 1948.

Casler, Michael M. *Steamboats of the Fort Union Fur Trade: An Illustrated Listing of Steamboats on the Upper Missouri River, 1831–1867.* Williston, N.Dak.: Fort Union Association, 1999.

Castel, Albert. *General Sterling Price and the Civil War in the West.* Baton Rouge: Louisiana State University Press, 1968.

Chambers, William Nisbet. *Old Bullion Benton: Senator from the New West.* Boston: Little, Brown, 1956.

Chappell, Phil. E. "A History of the Missouri River." *Transactions of the Kansas State Historical Society,* vol. 9 (Topeka, 1905–1906): 237–94.

[Chardon, Francis A.]. *Chardon's Journal at Fort Clark 1834–1839.* Ed. Annie Heloise Abel. Pierre, S.Dak.: South Dakota State Department of History, 1932.

Cheney, Roberta Carkeek. *Names on the Face of Montana: The Story of Montana Place Names.* Rev. ed. Missoula, Mont.: Mountain Press, 1983.

Chittenden, Hiram Martin. *The American Fur Trade of the Far West.* 2 vols. New York: Francis P. Harper, 1902; reprint, Stanford, Calif.: Academic Reprints, 1954.

———. *History of Early Steamboat Navigation on the Missouri River: Life and Adventures of Joseph La Barge.* 2 vols. New York: Francis P. Harper, 1903.

———. "Report of Steamboat Wrecks on Missouri River." In *Annual Report of the Chief of Engineers, 1897,* 3870–92.

Chittenden, Hiram Martin, and Alfred Talbot Richardson, eds. *Life, Letters and Travels of Father Pierre-Jean de Smet, S.J., 1801–1873.* New York: Francis P. Harper, 1905.

"Cholera in Saint Louis in 1849." *Western Journal* 3 (December 1849): 209–10.

Chouteau, Charles P. "Early Navigation of the Upper Missouri River." *Contributions to the Historical Society of Montana,* vol. 7 (Helena, 1910): 253–56.

"C. J. Atkins' Logs of Missouri River Steamboat Trips, 1863–1868 with Appendix." *Collections of the State Historical Society of North Dakota,* vol. 2 (Bismarck, 1908): 263–391.

Clarke, Dwight L. *Stephen Watts Kearny: Soldier of the West.* Norman: University of Oklahoma Press, 1961.

Clevenger, Homer. "The Building of the Hannibal and St. Joseph Railroad." *Missouri Historical Review* 36 (October 1941): 32–47.

Clow, Richmond L. "Sully, Alfred." *Encyclopedia of the American West.*

Collins, John S. *Across the Plains in '64.* Omaha: National Printing Co., 1904.

The Commerce and Navigation of the Valley of the Mississippi; And Also That Appertaining to the City of St. Louis: Considered With Reference to the Improvement, by the General Government, of the Mississippi River and Its Principal Tributaries. . . . St. Louis: Chambers and Knapp, 1847.

"Commercial Regulations: Tariff of Marine Insurance Premiums." *Western Journal* 3 (March 1850): 414–16.

"Commercial Statistics." *Western Journal* 3 (January 1850): 273–74.

Connelley, William E. *A Standard History of Kansas and Kansans.* 5 vols. Chicago: Lewis Publishing Co., 1918.

"Consumer Price Index (Estimate) 1800–2006." http://woodrow.mpls.frb.fed.us/research/data/us/calc/hist1800.cfm

Cooke, Lucy Rutledge. "Letters on the Way to California." In *Covered Wagon Women:*

Diaries and Letters from the Western Trails, 1840–1890, ed. and comp. Kenneth L. Holmes, vol. 4, 209–95. Spokane: Arthur H. Clark, 1991.

Cooke, P[hilip] St. G[eorge]. *Scenes and Adventures in the Army. . . .* Philadelphia: Lindsay and Blakiston, 1857.

Corbin, Annalies. *The Life and Times of the Steamboat Red Cloud, or, How Merchants, Mounties, and the Missouri Transformed the West.* College Station: Texas A&M University Press, 2006.

Davison, Stanley R. "White Hopes of the Big Muddy." *Montana the Magazine of Western History* 9 (April 1959): 2–15.

Deloria, Vine, Jr., and Raymond J. DeMallie, eds. *Documents of American Indian Diplomacy: Treaties, Agreements, and Conventions, 1775–1979.* 2 vols. Norman: University of Oklahoma Press, 1999.

[De Trobriand, Philippe Régis]. *Military Life in Dakota: The Journal of Philippe Régis de Trobriand.* Trans. and ed. Lucile M. Kane. St. Paul: Alvord Memorial Commission, 1951.

Dixon, Frank Haigh. *A Traffic History of the Mississippi River System.* National Waterways Commission Doc. 11. Washington, D.C.: Government Printing Office, 1909.

Dobak, William A. *Fort Riley and Its Neighbors: Military Money and Economic Growth, 1853–1895.* Norman: University of Oklahoma Press, 1998.

Doherty, Paul C. "The Columbia-Providence Plank Road." *Missouri Historical Review* 57 (October 1962): 53–69.

Dollar, Clyde D. "The High Plains Smallpox Epidemic of 1837." *Western Historical Quarterly* 8 (January 1977): 15–38.

Dorsey, Dorothy B. "The Panic of 1819 in Missouri." *Missouri Historical Review* 29 (January 1935): 79–91.

Dorsey, Florence L. *Master of the Mississippi.* Boston: Houghton Mifflin, 1941.

Eaton, David W. "How Missouri Counties, Towns and Streams Were Named, First Article." *Missouri Historical Review* 10 (April 1916): 197–213.

———. "How Missouri Counties, Towns and Streams Were Named, Second Article." *Missouri Historical Review* 10 (July 1916): 164–200.

———. "How Missouri Counties, Towns and Streams Were Named, Third Article." *Missouri Historical Review* 11 (January 1917): 263–87.

———. "How Missouri Counties, Towns and Streams Were Named, Fourth Article." *Missouri Historical Review* 11 (April–July 1917): 330–47.

Eaton, Miles W. "The Development and Later Decline of the Hemp Industry in Missouri." *Missouri Historical Review* 43 (July 1949): 344–59.

Engelman, Fred L. *The Peace of Christmas Eve.* New York: Harcourt, Brace and World, 1962.

Finn, Bernard S. "Morse, Samuel Finley Breese." *American National Biography.*

First Annual Report of the Board of Directors, of the Pacific Railroad; and the Report of the Chief Engineer upon the Preliminary Surveys. St. Louis: Republican Book and Job Office, Printer, 1851.

"First Steamboat Wreck on the Missouri." *Missouri Historical Review* 26 (January 1932): 188.

Fitzgerald, Daniel C. "Town Booming: An Economic History of Steamboat Towns along the Kansas-Missouri Border, 1840–1860." MA thesis, University of Kansas, 1981.

Fitzpatrick, Lilian. *Nebraska Place-Names.* Lincoln: University of Nebraska Press, 1960.

Fitzsimmons, Mary Louise. "Railroad Development in Missouri, 1860–1870." MA thesis, Washington University, 1931.

Ford, James E. *A History of Jefferson City*. Jefferson City, Mo.: New Day, 1938.

Franklin, Lillie. "Rocheport, Missouri: An Illustration of Economic Adjustment to Environment." *Missouri Historical Review* 19 (October 1924): 3–11.

Frazer, Robert W. *Forts of the West: Military Forts and Presidios and Posts Commonly Called Forts West of the Mississippi River to 1898*. Paperback ed. Norman: University of Oklahoma Press, 1972.

Freedom, Gary S. "Moving Men and Supplies: Military Transportation on the Northern Great Plains, 1866–1891." *South Dakota History* 14 (Summer 1984): 114–33.

Frizzell, Robert W. "Southern Identity in Nineteenth-Century Missouri: Little Dixie's Slave-Majority Areas and the Transition to Midwestern Farming." *Missouri Historical Review* 99 (April 2005): 238–60.

Furniss, Norman F. *The Mormon Conflict, 1850–1859*. New Haven, Conn.: Yale University Press, 1960.

Gardner, James A. "The Business Career of Moses Austin in Missouri, 1798–1821." *Missouri Historical Review* 50 (April 1956): 235–47.

Gates, Paul W. "The Railroads of Missouri, 1859–1870." *Missouri Historical Review* 26 (January 1932): 126–41.

Gentry, North Todd. "Plank Roads in Missouri." *Missouri Historical Review* 31 (April 1937): 272–87.

Gibson, Arrell Morgan. *The American Indian: Prehistory to the Present*. Lexington, Mass.: D. C. Heath, 1980.

Giffen, Lawrence Everett. *"Walks in Water": The Impact of Steamboating on the Lower Missouri River*. Jefferson City, Mo.: Giffen Enterprises, 2001.

Gilman, Rhoda R. *Henry Hastings Sibley: Divided Heart*. St. Paul: Minnesota Historical Society Press, 2004.

Glaab, Charles N. *Kansas City and the Railroads: Community Policy in the Growth of a Regional Metropolis*. Madison: State Historical Society of Wisconsin, 1962.

Goodrich, James W., and Lynn Wolf Gentzler. *Marking Missouri History*. Columbia: State Historical Society of Missouri, 1998.

Gray, John S. "The Northern Overland Pony Express." *Montana the Magazine of Western History* 16 (October 1966): 58–73.

"Great Fire in St. Louis." *Western Journal* 2 (May 1849): 347–48.

Greene, Albert R. "The Kansas River—Its Navigation." *Transactions of the Kansas State Historical Society*, vol. 9 (Topeka, 1905–1906): 317–58.

Greene, Jerome A. *Fort Randall on the Missouri, 1856–1892*. Pierre: South Dakota State Historical Society Press, 2005.

Greever, William S. *The Bonanza West: The Story of Western Mining Rushes, 1848–1900*. Norman: University of Oklahoma Press, 1963.

Gregg, Kate L. "The History of Fort Osage." *Missouri Historical Review* 34 (July 1940): 439–88.

Hafen, LeRoy R., ed. *Colorado Gold Rush: Contemporary Letters and Reports, 1858–1859*. Vol. 10 of *Southwest Historical Series*. Glendale, Calif.: Arthur H. Clark, 1941.

Hafen, LeRoy R., and Francis Marion Young. *Fort Laramie and the Pageant of the West*. Glendale: Arthur H. Clark, 1938.

Haines, Aubrey L. "A Voyage to Montana: Serena Washburn's Account of Her Trip up the Missouri River in 1869, Part I." *Montana the Magazine of Western History* 49 (Winter 1999): 16–29.

————. "A Voyage to Montana: Serena Washburn's Account of Her Trip up the Missouri River in 1869, Part II." *Montana the Magazine of Western History* 50 (Spring 2000): 18–27.

Haites, Erik F., James Mak, and Gary M. Walton. *Western River Transportation: The Era of Early Internal Development, 1810–1860.* Baltimore: Johns Hopkins University Press, 1975.

Hall, Bert L. *Roundup Years: Old Muddy to the Black Hills.* Reprint, Pierre, S.Dak.: Western South Dakota Buck-a-roos, 2000.

Hall, Philip S. "The Ephemeral Chamberlain Road: A Freight Trail to the Black Hills." *South Dakota History* 26 (Spring 1996): 1–23.

Hamburg, James F. "Railroads and the Settlement of South Dakota during the Great Dakota Boom, 1878–1887." *South Dakota History* 5 (Spring 1975): 165–78.

Hanson, Joseph Mills. *The Conquest of the Missouri: Being the Story of the Life and Exploits of Captain Grant Marsh.* Chicago: A. C. McClurg and Co., 1909.

[Harkness, James]. "Diary of James Harkness, of the Firm of La Barge, Harkness and Company." *Contributions to the Historical Society of Montana,* vol. 2 (Helena, 1896): 343–61.

Harnsberger, John L. *Jay Cooke and Minnesota: The Formative Years of the Northern Pacific Railroad, 1868–1873.* New York: Arno, 1981.

[Harris, Edward]. *Up the Missouri with Audubon: The Journal of Edward Harris.* Ed. and annotated by John Francis McDermott. Norman: University of Oklahoma Press, 1951.

Hart, Henry C. *The Dark Missouri.* Madison: University of Wisconsin Press, 1957.

Hartley, William G., and Fred E. Woods. *Explosion of the Steamboat Saluda: A Story of Disaster and Compassion Involving Mormon Emigrants and the Town of Lexington, Missouri, in April 1853.* Salt Lake City: Millennial Press, 2002.

Hattervig, Eldon. "Jefferson Landing: A Commercial Center of the Steamboat Era." *Missouri Historical Review* 74 (April 1980): 277–99.

Hawley, David. *The Treasures of the Steamboat Arabia.* Kansas City, Mo.: Arabia Steamboat Museum, 1995.

Hebard, Grace Raymond, and E. A. Brininstool. *The Bozeman Trail.* 2 vols. Reprint, Glendale, Calif.: Arthur H. Clark, 1960.

Hedren, Paul L. "Sitting Bull's Surrender at Fort Buford: An Episode in American History." *North Dakota History* 62 (Fall 1995): 2–15.

Heitman, Francis B. *Historical Register and Dictionary of the United States Army....* Washington, D.C.: Government Printing Office, 1903.

[Hilger, Nicholas]. "General Alfred Sully's Expedition of 1864." *Contributions to the Historical Society of Montana,* vol. 2 (Helena, 1896): 314–28.

Hill, Edward E. *The Office of Indian Affairs, 1824–1880: Historical Sketches.* New York: Clearwater, 1974.

History of Franklin, Jefferson, Washington, Crawford and Gasconade Counties, Missouri. Chicago: Goodspeed Publishing Co., 1888.

History of Henry and St. Clair Counties, Missouri.... St. Joseph, Mo.: National Historical Co., 1883.

History of Howard and Cooper Counties, Missouri. St. Louis: National Historical Co., 1883.

The History of Jackson County, Missouri. Kansas City, Mo.: Union Historical Co., 1881.

"The History of Railroad Building into and out of Kansas City." *Collections of the Kansas State Historical Society,* vol. 12 (Topeka, 1912): 47–52.

"History of the Academy." http://www.ansp.org/about/history.php.

History of the Counties of Woodbury and Plymouth, Iowa, Including an Extended Sketch of Sioux City. Chicago: A. Warner and Co., 1890–91.

History of Vernon County, Missouri.... St. Louis: Brown and Co., 1887.

Holman, Albert M. "Niobrara–Virginia City Wagon Road." In *Pioneering in the North-west*. Sioux City: Deitch and Lamar Co., 1924.

Holmquist, June Drenning, and Jean A. Brookins. *Minnesota's Major Historic Sites: A Guide*. 2d ed. rev. St. Paul: Minnesota Historical Society, 1972.

Hoopes, Lorman L. *This Last West: Miles City, Montana Territory, and Environs, 1876–1886.* . . . Miles City, Mont.: privately printed, 1990.

Hoover, Herbert T., John Rau, and Leonard R. Bruguier. "Gorging Ice and Flooding Rivers: Springtime Devastation in South Dakota." *South Dakota History* 17 (Fall/Winter 1987): 181–201.

Horsman, Reginald. *The War of 1812*. New York: Knopf, 1969.

[Hosmer, J. Allen]. "A Trip to the States in 1865." Ed. Edith M. Duncan. *Frontier* 12 (January 1932): 149–72.

[Hubbell, William David]. "The First Steamboats on the Missouri: Reminiscences of Captain W. D. Hubbell." Ed. Vivian K. McLarty. *Missouri Historical Review* 51 (July 1957): 373–81.

Hunt, Elvid. *History of Fort Leavenworth, 1827–1927*. Fort Leavenworth, Kans.: General Service Schools Press, 1926.

Hunter, Louis C. *Steamboats on the Western Rivers: An Economic and Technological History*. Cambridge, Mass.: Harvard University Press, 1949.

Hunt's Merchants' Magazine and Commercial Review, 1862.

Hurt, R. Douglas. *Agriculture and Slavery in Missouri's Little Dixie*. Columbia: University of Missouri Press, 1992.

Hurt, Wesley R., and William E. Lass. *Frontier Photographer: Stanley J. Morrow's Dakota Years*. Lincoln: University of Nebraska Press; Vermillion; University of South Dakota, 1956.

"Improvement of the Osage River." *Western Journal* 3 (October 1849): 51–53.

Jackson, Brenda K. "Holding Down the Fort: A History of Dakota Territory's Fort Randall." *South Dakota History* 32 (Spring 2002): 1–27.

Jackson, Donald. *Voyages of the Steamboat Yellow Stone*. New York: Ticknor and Fields, 1985.

Jackson, W. Turrentine. *Wagon Roads West: A Study of Federal Road Surveys and Construction in the Trans-Mississippi West, 1846–1869*. Berkeley: University of California Press, 1952.

James, Edwin. *Account of an Expedition from Pittsburgh to the Rocky Mountains*. Vol. 14 of *Early Western Travels*. Ed. Reuben Gold Thwaites. Cleveland: Arthur H. Clark, 1905; reprint, New York: AMS Press, 1966.

Jarchow, Merrill E. *Amherst H. Wilder and His Enduring Legacy to Saint Paul*. St. Paul: Amherst H. Wilder Foundation, 1981.

Jenkins, Clyde Lee. *Through the Civil War*. Vol. 1 of *Judge Jenkins' History of Miller County, Missouri*. Tuscumbia, Mo.: privately printed, 1971.

Jensen, Richard E., and James S. Hutchins, eds. *Wheel Boats on the Missouri: The Journals and Documents of the Atkinson-O'Fallon Expedition, 1824–26*. Helena: Montana Historical Society Press; Lincoln: Nebraska State Historical Society, 2001.

Johansen, Dorothy O. *Empire of the Columbia: A History of the Pacific Northwest*. 2d ed. New York: Harper and Row, 1967.

Johnson, Leland R. "Engineering the Ohio." In *Always a River: The Ohio River and the American Experience*, ed. Robert L. Reid, 180–209. Bloomington: Indiana University Press, 1991.

Jones, Jonathan M. "When Expectations Exceed Reality: The Missouri Expedition of 1819." *Missouri Historical Review* 94 (April 2000): 241–63.

Jones, Robert Huhn. *The Civil War in the Northwest: Nebraska, Wisconsin, Iowa, Minnesota and the Dakotas.* Norman: University of Oklahoma Press, 1960.

Kane, Adam I. *The Western River Steamboat.* College Station: Texas A&M University Press, 2004.

Kane, Lucile M., June D. Holmquist, and Carolyn Gilman, eds. *The Northern Expeditions of Stephen H. Long: The Journals of 1817 and 1823 and Related Documents.* St. Paul: Minnesota Historical Society Press, 1978.

Kappler, Charles J., comp. *Indian Affairs: Laws and Treaties.* Vol. 2. Washington, D.C.: Government Printing Office, 1904.

Kingsbury, George W. *History of Dakota Territory.* 2 vols. Chicago: S. J. Clarke Publishing Co, 1915.

Krause, Herbert, and Gary D. Olson. *Prelude to Glory: A Newspaper Accounting of Custer's Expedition to the Black Hills.* Sioux Falls, S.Dak.: Brevet, 1974.

Lamar, Howard Roberts. *Dakota Territory 1861–1889: A Study of Frontier Politics.* New Haven, Conn.: Yale University Press, 1956.

Lampe, A. B. "St. Louis Volunteer Fire Department, 1820–1850." *Missouri Historical Review* 62 (April 1968): 235–59.

Langsdorf, Edgar, ed. "The First Survey of the Kansas River." *Kansas Historical Quarterly* 18 (May 1950): 146–58.

———. "More about Kansas River Steamboats: The First Kansas-Built River Steamer." *Kansas Historical Quarterly* 18 (November 1950): 405–407.

[Larpenteur, Charles]. *Forty Years a Fur Trader on the Upper Missouri: The Personal Narrative of Charles Larpenteur, 1833–1872.* Ed. Elliot Coues. Reprint, Minneapolis: Ross and Haines, 1961.

Larson, T. A. *History of Wyoming.* 2d ed. rev. Lincoln: University of Nebraska Press, 1978.

Lass, William E. "Dakota Resources: Trader Edward T. Latta's 'List of Wood Sold to Boats,' 1866–1867." *South Dakota History* 35 (Summer 2005): 152–78.

———. "Elias H. Durfee and Campbell K. Peck: Indian Traders on the Upper Missouri Frontier." *Journal of the West* 43 (Spring 2004): 9–19.

———. "The Fate of Steamboats: A Case Study of the 1848 St. Louis Fleet." *Missouri Historical Review* 96 (October 2001): 2–15.

———. "The First Attempt to Organize Dakota Territory." In *Centennial West: Essays on the Northern Tier States,* ed. William L. Lang, 143–68. Seattle: University of Washington Press, 1991.–

———. *From the Missouri to the Great Salt Lake: An Account of Overland Freighting.* Lincoln: Nebraska State Historical Society, 1972.

———. "The History and Significance of the Northwest Fur Company, 1865–1869." *North Dakota History* 61 (Summer 1994): 21–40.

———. *A History of Steamboating on the Upper Missouri River.* Lincoln: University of Nebraska Press, 1962.

———. "Isaac P. Baker and the Baker Papers." *North Dakota History* 24 (October 1957): 174–79.

———. "Nebraska City's Steam Wagon." *Nebraska History* 79 (Spring 1998): 24–33.

———. "The Removal from Minnesota of the Sioux and Winnebago Indians." *Minnesota History* 38 (December 1963): 353–64.

———. "Steamboats on the Yellowstone." *Montana the Magazine of Western History* 35 (Autumn 1985): 26–41.

————. "Washburn, William Drew." *American National Biography.*

Launius, Roger D. *Alexander William Doniphan: Portrait of a Missouri Moderate.* Columbia: University of Missouri Press, 1997.

Lepley, John G. *Birthplace of Montana: A History of Fort Benton.* 2d ed. Missoula, Mont.: Pictorial Histories, 2001.

————. *Packets to Paradise: Steamboating to Fort Benton.* Missoula, Mont.: Pictorial Histories, 2001.

Lieber, Sonie. "Ships That Have Passed in the Night: Steamboating in Kansas." *Kansas Heritage* 6 (Autumn 1998): 4–8.

————. *That Splendid Little Steamer Hartford.* Manhattan, Kans.: privately printed, 1989.

Lloyd, James T. *Lloyd's Steamboat Directory and Disasters on the Western Rivers. . . .* Cincinnati: James T. Lloyd and Co., 1856.

Lobeck, A. K. *Geomorphology: An Introduction to the Study of Landscapes.* New York: McGraw-Hill, 1939.

Lounsberry, Clement A. *Early History of North Dakota.* Washington, D.C.: Liberty Press, 1919.

[Ludlow, William]. *Exploring Nature's Sanctuary: Captain William Ludlow's Report of a Reconnaissance from Carroll, Montana Territory, on the Upper Missouri to the Yellowstone National Park, and Return Made in the Summer of 1875.* With introduction by Paul K. Walker. Washington, D.C.: Government Printing Office, January, 1985.

Luttig, John C. *Journal of a Fur-Trading Expedition on the Upper Missouri, 1812–1813.* Ed. Stella M. Drumm. St. Louis: Missouri Historical Society, 1920.

Lytle, William M., and Forrest R. Holdcamper, comps. *Merchant Steam Vessels of the United States, 1790–1868: "The Lytle-Holdcamper List."* Rev. and ed. C. Bradford Mitchell. Staten Island, NY: Steamship Historical Society of America, 1975.

MacGregor, James G. *A History of Alberta.* Edmonton: Hurtig Publishers, 1972.

Madsen, Betty M., and Brigham D. Madsen. *North to Montana! Jehus, Bullwhackers, and Mule Skinners on the Montana Trail.* Salt Lake City: University of Utah Press, 1980.

Malone, Michael P., and Richard R. Roeder. *Montana: A History of Two Centuries.* Seattle: University of Washington Press, 1976.

Mantor, Lyle E. "Fort Kearny and the Westward Movement." *Nebraska History* 24 (September 1948): 175–207.

March, David D. *The History of Missouri.* 4 vols. New York: Lewis Historical. 1957.

Marks, Constant R., ed. *Past and Present of Sioux City and Woodbury County, Iowa.* Chicago: S. J. Clarke Publishing Co., 1904.

Marra, Dorothy Brandt. *Cher Oncle, Cher Papa: The Letters of Francois and Berenice Chouteau.* Trans. Marie-Laure Dionne Pal. Ed. David Boutros. Kansas City, Mo.: Western Historical Manuscript Center–Kansas City, 2001.

[Marsh, Elias J.]. "Journal of Elias J. Marsh: Account of a Steamboat Trip on the Missouri River, May–August, 1859." *South Dakota Historical Review* 1 (January 1936): 79–127.

Mattes, Merrill J. *The Great Platte River Road: The Covered Wagon Mainline via Fort Kearny to Fort Laramie.* Lincoln: Nebraska State Historical Society, 1969.

Mattison, Ray H. "Alexander Harvey." In *The Mountain Men and the Fur Trade of the Far West,* vol. 4, ed. LeRoy R. Hafen, 119–23. Glendale, Calif.: Arthur H. Clark, 1966.–

————. "Henry A. Boller." In *The Mountain Men and the Fur Trade of the Far West,* vol. 3, ed. LeRoy R. Hafen, 49–53. Glendale, Calif.: Arthur H. Clark, 1966.

————. "The Military Frontier on the Upper Missouri." *Nebraska History* 37 (September 1956): 159–82.

Maximilian. *Travels in the Interior of North America, 1832–1834*. Vol. 22 of *Early Western Travels*. Ed. Reuben Gold Thwaites. Cleveland: Arthur H. Clark, 1905; reprint, New York: AMS Press, 1966.

McDermott, John Francis, ed. *Audubon in the West*. Norman: University of Oklahoma Press, 1965.

McDonald, W. J. "The Missouri River and Its Victims: Vessels Wrecked from the Beginning of Navigation to 1925, First Article." *Missouri Historical Review* 21 (January 1927): 215–42.

———. "The Missouri River and Its Victims: Vessels Wrecked from the Beginning of Navigation to 1925, Second Article." *Missouri Historical Review* 21 (April 1927): 455–80.

———. "The Missouri River and Its Victims: Vessels Wrecked from the Beginning of Navigation to 1925, Third Article." *Missouri Historical Review* 21 (July 1927): 581–607.

McKee, Howard I. "The Platte Purchase." *Missouri Historical Review* 32 (January 1938): 129–47.

McLear, Patrick E. "The St. Louis Cholera Epidemic of 1849." *Missouri Historical Review* 63 (January 1969): 171–81.

McManus, Edgar J. "Johnson, Richard Mentor." *American National Biography*.

McReynolds, Edwin C. *Missouri: A History of the Crossroads State*. Paperback ed. Norman: University of Oklahoma Press, 1975.

Merrill, George P. *The First One Hundred Years of American Geology*. 1924; reprint, New York: Hafner, 1969.

Meyer, Bette E. "The Pend Oreille Routes to Montana, 1866–1870." *Pacific Northwest Quarterly* 72 (April 1981): 76–83.

Meyer, Roy W. *The Village Indians of the Upper Missouri: The Mandans, Hidatsas, and Arikaras*. Lincoln: University of Nebraska Press, 1977.

Miller, Don C., and Stan B. Cohen. *Military and Trading Posts of Montana*. Missoula: Pictorial Histories, 1978.

Minnesota in the Civil and Indian Wars. 2 vols. 2d ed. St. Paul: Pioneer Press Co., 1899.

Monaghan, Jay. *Civil War and the Western Border, 1854–1865*. Reprint, Lincoln: University of Nebraska Press, 1955.

Moneyhon, Carl H. "Rector, Henry Massey." *American National Biography*.

Morris, Richard B., ed. *Encyclopedia of American History*. Rev. ed. New York: Harper and Row, 1965.

Morrissey, Frank R. "Motor Packets of the Upper Missouri." *Motorboat* (January 25, 1913).

Morrow, Lynn. "Joseph Washington McClurg: Entrepreneur, Politician, Citizen." *Missouri Historical Review* 78 (January 1984): 168–201.

Morton, J. Sterling. *Illustrated History of Nebraska*. 5 vols. Lincoln: Jacob North and Co., 1906.

Moulton, Gary E., ed. *The Journals of the Lewis and Clark Expedition*. Vols. 2–4. Lincoln: University of Nebraska Press, 1986–87.

Mullan, John. *Miners and Travelers' Guide to Oregon, Washington, Idaho, Montana, Wyoming, and Colorado*. New York, 1865.

Munson, Lyman E. "Pioneer Life in Montana." *Contributions to the Historical Society of Montana*, vol. 5 (Helena, 1904): 200–234.

Murphy, James E. *Half Interest in a Silver Dollar: The Saga of Charles E. Conrad*. Missoula, Mont.: Mountain West, 1983.

Murray, Charles Augustus. *Travels in North America during the Years 1834, 1835 and 1836*. 2 vols. London, 1841.

Napton, John. "My Trip on the Imperial in 1867." *Contributions to the Historical Society of Montana*, vol. 8 (Helena, 1917): 305–15.

Nasatir, A. P. *Before Lewis and Clark: Documents Illustrating the History of the Missouri, 1785–1804*. 2 vols. St. Louis: St. Louis Historical Documents Foundation, 1952.

National Register (Washington, D.C.), 1819.

"Navigation of the Upper Missouri." *Western Journal* 4 (September 1850): 415–16.

Nichol, Ralph E. "Steamboat Navigation on the Missouri River with Special Reference to Yankton and Vicinity." *South Dakota Historical Collections*, vol. 26 (Pierre, 1952): 181–221.

Nichols, Roger L. *General Henry Atkinson: A Western Military Career*. Norman: University of Oklahoma Press, 1965.

———. "Martin Cantonment and American Expansion in the Missouri Valley." *Missouri Historical Review* 64 (October 1969): 1–17.

Nichols, Roger L., and Patrick L. Halley. *Stephen Long and American Frontier Exploration*. Newark: University of Delaware Press, 1980.

Niles' National Register, 1838-45.

Niles' Weekly Register, 1818-19.

Nowak, Timothy R. "From Fort Pierre to Fort Randall: The Army's First Use of Portable Cottages." *South Dakota History* 32 (Summer 2002): 95–116.

"Official Correspondence Relating to Fort Pierre." *South Dakota Historical Collections*, vol. 1 (Aberdeen, 1902): 381–440.

Oliver, R. B. "Missouri's First Railroad." *Missouri Historical Review* 26 (October 1931): 12–18.

Olson, James C. *History of Nebraska*. Lincoln: University of Nebraska Press, 1955.

Olson, James C., and Ronald C. Naugle. *History of Nebraska*. 3d ed. Lincoln: University of Nebraska Press, 1997.

"Osage River." *Western Journal* 1 (May 1850): 86–90.

Overholser, Joel. *Fort Benton: World's Innermost Port*. Fort Benton, Mont.: privately printed, 1987.

"Pacific Railway Convention at Saint Louis." *Western Journal* 3 (November 1849): 71–75.

Parker, Theodore R. "William J. Kountz, Superintendent of River Transportation under McClellan, 1861–62." *Western Pennsylvania Historical Magazine* 21 (December 1938): 237–54.

Parrish, William E. *Turbulent Partnership: Missouri and the Union, 1861–1865*. Columbia: University of Missouri Press, 1963.

Paul, R. Eli. *Blue Water Creek and the First Sioux War, 1854–1856*. Norman: University of Oklahoma Press, 2004.

Paul, Rodman Wilson. *Mining Frontiers of the Far West, 1848–1880*. New York: Holt, Rinehart and Winston, 1963.

Paxton, W. M. *Annals of Platte County, Missouri. . . .* Kansas City, Mo.: Hudson-Kimberly Publishing Co., 1897.

[Peck, John Mason]. *Forty Years of Pioneer Life: Memoir of John Mason Peck*. Ed. Rufus Babcock. Reprint, Carbondale: Southern Illinois University Press, 1965.

Petersen, William J. *Iowa: The Rivers of Her Valleys*. Iowa City: State Historical Society of Iowa, 1941.

———. *Steamboating on the Upper Mississippi*. Iowa City: State Historical Society of Iowa, 1968.

Peterson, F. Ross. *Idaho: A Bicentennial History*. New York: W. W. Norton, 1976.

Petsche, Jerome E. *The Steamboat Bertrand: History, Excavation, and Architecture.* Washington, D.C.: National Park Service, 1974.

Phillips, Christopher. "Frost, Daniel Marsh." *Encyclopedia of the Confederacy.*

Phillips, P[aul] C[risler], ed. "Upham Letters from the Upper Missouri, 1865." *Frontier* 13 (May 1933): 311–17.

Pope, James Sterling. "A History of Steamboating on the Lower Missouri, 1838–1849: Saint Louis to Council Bluffs, Iowa Territory." PhD diss., St. Louis University, 1984.

Poppewell, Frank S. "St. Joseph, Missouri, as a Center of the Cattle Trade." *Missouri Historical Review* 32 (July 1938): 443–57.

Pratt, Julius William. *Expansionists of 1812.* New York: Macmillan, 1925.

Rafferty, Milton D. *Historical Atlas of Missouri.* Norman: University of Oklahoma Press, 1982.

Raynolds, W[illiam] F. *Report on the Exploration of the Yellowstone River.* Washington, D.C.: Government Printing Office, 1868.

Read, Georgia Willis. "Disease, Drugs, and Doctors on the Oregon-California Trail in the Gold Rush Years." *Missouri Historical Review* 38 (April 1944): 260–76.

Report of the Committee Appointed by the Chamber of Commerce upon the Trade, Commerce and Manufactures of St. Louis Embracing a Period of Several Years. St. Louis: Missouri Republican Office, 1852.

Richards, Kent D. *Isaac I. Stevens: Young Man in a Hurry.* Provo, Utah: Brigham Young University Press, 1979. Reprint, Pullman: Washington State University Press, 1993.

———. "Mullan, John." *American National Biography.*

Richardson, Albert D. *Beyond the Mississippi.* Hartford, Conn.: American Publishing Co., 1967.

Richardson, James D., ed. *A Compilation of the Messages and Papers of the Presidents, 1789–1902.* 10 vols. [New York]: Bureau of National Literature and Art, 1904.

Ridgway, Walter. "Howard County Has Two Celebrations." *Missouri Historical Review* 11 (October 1916): 49–67.

Riegel, R[obert] E. "The Missouri Pacific Railroad to 1879." *Missouri Historical Review* 18: (October 1923): 3–26.

Roberts, Thomas P. *Report of a Reconnaissance of the Missouri River in 1872.* Washington, D.C.: Government Printing Office, 1875.

Robinson, Elwyn B. *History of North Dakota.* Lincoln: University of Nebraska Press, 1966.

Rohrbough, Malcolm J. *Days of Gold: The California Gold Rush and the American Nation.* Berkeley: University of California Press, 1997.

"Rope Walk." *Missouri Historical Review* 26 (January 1932): 190–91.

Rosenberg, Charles E. *The Cholera Years: The United States in 1832, 1849, and 1866.* Chicago: University of Chicago Press, 1962.

Russel, Robert R. *Improvement of Communication with the Pacific Coast as an Issue in American Politics, 1783–1864.* Cedar Rapids, Iowa: Torch Press, 1948.

Sage, Leland D. *A History of Iowa.* Ames: Iowa State University Press, 1974.

St. Louis Board of Trade. *Fifth Annual Report of the St. Louis Chamber of Commerce for 1860.* St. Louis, 1861.

St. Louis Business Directory for 1847. St. Louis, 1847.

St. Louis Directory, 1860. St. Louis: R. V. Kennedy and Co., 1860.

St. Louis Directory for the Years 1854–5. St. Louis: Chambers and Knapp, 1854.

Scharf, J. Thomas. *History of St. Louis City and County.* 2 vols. Philadelphia: Louis H. Everts and Co., 1883.

Schell, Herbert S. "The Dakota Southern: A Pioneer Railway Venture of Dakota Territory." *South Dakota Historical Review* 2 (April 1937): 99–125.

———. *Dakota Territory during the Eighteen Sixties.* Vermillion: Governmental Research Bureau, University of South Dakota, 1954.

———. *History of Clay County, South Dakota.* Vermillion: Clay County Historical Society, 1976.

———. *History of South Dakota.* Lincoln: University of Nebraska Press, 1961.

Schmeckebier, Laurence. *The Customs Service: Its History, Activities and Organization.* Baltimore: Johns Hopkins Press, 1924.

Schneiders, Robert Kelley. *Unruly River: Two Centuries of Change along the Missouri.* Lawrence: University Press of Kansas, 1999.

Schoolcraft, Henry R. *A View of the Lead Mines of Missouri.* . . . New York: Charles Wiley and Co., 1819.

Schroeder, Walter A. "Spread of Settlement in Howard County, Missouri 1810–1859." *Missouri Historical Review* 63 (October 1968): 1–37.

Schuler, Harold H. *A Bridge Apart: History of Early Pierre and Fort Pierre.* Pierre, S.Dak.: State Publishing Co., 1987.

———. *Fort Pierre Chouteau.* Vermillion: University of South Dakota Press, 1990.

———. *Fort Sully: Guns at Sunset.* Vermillion: University of South Dakota Press, 1992.

Schultz, Gerard. "Steamboat Navigation on the Osage River before the Civil War." *Missouri Historical Review* 29 (April 1935): 17–85.

Schusky, Ernest L. "The Upper Missouri Indian Agency, 1819–1868." *Missouri Historical Review* 65 (April 1971): 249–69.

Schwantes, Carlos Arnaldo. *Long Day's Journey: The Steamboat and Stagecoach Era in the Northern West.* Seattle: University of Washington Press, 1999.

Sharp, Paul F. *Whoop-Up Country: The Canadian-American West, 1865–1885.* Minneapolis: University of Minnesota Press, 1955.

Sheldon, Addison Erwin. *Nebraska: The Land and the People.* 3 vols. Chicago: Lewis Publishing Co., 1931.

Shomette, Donald G. "Heyday of the Horse Ferry." *National Geographic* 176 (October 1989): 548–56.

Short, Lloyd M. *The Steamboat-Inspection Service: Its History, Activities and Organization.* New York: D. Appleton and Co., 1922.

Shrader, Dorothy Heckman. *Steamboat Legacy: The Life and Times of a Steamboat Family.* Hermann, Mo.: Wein Press, 1993.

Simpson, Marcus B., Jr. "Baldwin, William." *American National Biography.*

Sixteenth Annual Report of the Board of Directors of the Pacific Railroad. St. Louis: George Knapp and Co., 1866.

Skillman, W[illiam] D., comp. *The Western Metropolis, or St. Louis in 1846.* St. Louis: privately printed, 1846.

Smith, Alice E. *From Exploration to Statehood.* Vol. 1 of *The History of Wisconsin.* Madison: State Historical Society of Wisconsin, 1973.

Smith, T. Berry, and Pearl Sims Gehrig. *History of Chariton and Howard Counties, Missouri.* Topeka: Historical Publishing Co., 1923.

Sneve, Virginia Driving Hawk, ed. *South Dakota Geographic Names.* Sioux Falls, S.Dak.: Brevet, 1973.

Somers, Harold M. "The Performance of the American Economy, 1866–1918." In *The Growth of the American Economy,* 2d ed., ed. Harold F. Williamson, 646–62. New York: Prentice-Hall, 1951.

Spalding, C[harles] C. *Annals of the City of Kansas*. Kansas City, Mo.: Van Horn and Abeel's Printing House, 1858.

Stanley, David S. *Report on the Yellowstone Expedition of 1873*. Washington, D.C.: Government Printing Office, 1874.

"Statement Showing the Number and Class of Vessels Built . . . for Year Ending 30th June, 1847." *Western Journal* 1 (December 1848): 685.

"Statistics of Platte County." *Western Journal* 5 (March 1851): 325–27.

"Steamboat Arrivals at Fort Benton, Montana, and Vicinity." *Contributions to the Historical Society of Montana*, vol. 1 (Helena, 1876): 317–25.

Sterling, Keir B. "Audubon, John James." *American National Biography*.

Stevens, Walter B. *St. Louis: The Fourth City, 1764–1909*. St. Louis: S. J. Clarke Publishing Co., 1909.

Strahorn, Robert E. *Montana and Yellowstone National Park*. Kansas City, Mo.: Ramsey, Millet and Hudson, 1881.

Stroud, Patricia Tyson. "Say, Thomas." *American National Biography*.

Stuart, Granville. *Diary and Sketchbook of a Journey to "America" in 1866 and Return Trip up the Missouri River to Fort Benton, Montana*. Los Angeles: Dawson's Book Shop, 1963.

Sunder, John E. "The Early Telegraph in Rural Missouri, 1847–1859." *Missouri Historical Review* 51 (October 1956): 42–53.

———. *The Fur Trade on the Upper Missouri, 1840–1865*. Norman: University of Oklahoma Press, 1965.

———. *Joshua Pilcher: Fur Trader and Indian Agent*. Norman: University of Oklahoma Press, 1968.

———. "St. Louis and the Early Telegraph." *Missouri Historical Review* 50 (April 1956): 248–58.

Taylor, George Rogers. *The Transportation Revolution, 1815–1860*. New York: Rinehart, 1951.

Templin, Lucinda de Leftwich. "The Development of Railroads in Missouri to 1860." MA thesis, University of Missouri, 1915.

Thompson, Erwin N. *Fort Union Trading Post: Fur Trade Empire on the Upper Missouri*. Medora, N.Dak.: Theodore Roosevelt Nature and History Association, 1986.

Thorp, Raymond W. "The Beginnings of Steamboat Navigation in the West." *Missouri Historical Review* 19 (January 1925): 377–78.

Tolman, R. P. "Catlin, George." *American National Biography*.

Trade and Commerce of the City of St. Louis. 1848–1920.

Twelfth Annual Report of the Trade and Commerce of Kansas City. Kansas City: Commercial Club of Kansas City, 1891.

Unruh, John D. *The Plains Across: The Overland Emigrants and the Trans-Mississippi West, 1840–60*. Urbana: University of Illinois Press, 1979.

Upham, Warren. *Minnesota Geographic Names: Their Origin and Historic Significance*. Reprint, with an introduction by James Taylor Dunn. St. Paul: Minnesota Historical Society, 1969.

Utley, Robert M. "War Houses in the Sioux Country." *Montana the Magazine of Western History* 35 (Autumn 1985): 18–25.

Van West, Carroll. "Coulson and the Clark's Fork Bottom." *Montana the Magazine of Western History* 35 (Autumn 1985): 42–55.

Van Zandt, Franklin K. *Boundaries of the United States and the Several States*. Geological Survey Bulletin 1212. Washington, D.C.: Government Printing Office, 1966.

Viles, Jonas. "Missouri in 1820." *Missouri Historical Review* 15 (October 1920): 36-52.

———. "Old Franklin: A Frontier Town of the Twenties." *Mississippi Valley Historical Review* 9 (March 1923): 269–82.

Violette, E[ugene] M[orrow]. "Early Settlements in Missouri." *Missouri Historical Review* 1 (October 1906): 38–52.

Voss, Stuart F. "Town Growth in Central Missouri, 1815–1880: An Urban Chaparral, Part I." *Missouri Historical Review* 64 (October 1969): 64–80.

Vyzralek, Frank E. "Down the Missouri in 1918: A Photographic Journey with Frank Fiske." *North Dakota History* 38 (Fall 1971): 502–17.

Vyzralek, Frank E., H. Roger Grant and Charles Bohi. "North Dakota's Railroad Depots: Standardization on the Soo Line." *North Dakota History* 42 (Winter 1975): 4–25.

Walker, Henry Pickering. *The Wagonmasters: High Plains Freighting from the Earliest Days of the Santa Fe Trail to 1880.* Norman: University of Oklahoma Press, 1966.

Warner, Frank W., comp. *Montana Territory History and Business Directory.* Helena: Fisk Brothers, 1879.

Way, Frederick, Jr. *She Takes the Horns: Steamboat Racing on the Western Waters.* St. Louis: privately printed, 1953.

———, comp. *Way's Packet Directory 1848–1983: Passenger Steamboats of the Mississippi River System since the Advent of Photography in Mid-Continent America.* Athens: Ohio University, 1983.

Webb, W[illiam] L[arkin]. "Independence, Missouri, A Century Old." *Missouri Historical Review* 22 (October 1927): 30–50.

Welty, Raymond L[eo]. "The Frontier Army on the Missouri River, 1860–1870." *North Dakota Historical Quarterly* 2 (January 1928): 85–99.

———. "The Western Army Frontier, 1860–1870." PhD diss., University of Iowa, 1924.

Wesley, Edgar B. "A Still Larger View of the So-Called Yellowstone Expedition." *North Dakota Historical Quarterly* 5 (July 1931): 219–38.

Wetmore, Alphonso. *Gazeteer of the State of Missouri.* St. Louis: C. Keemlf, 1837.

White, Helen McCann, ed. *Ho! For the Gold Fields: Northern Overland Wagon Trains in the 1860s.* St. Paul: Minnesota Historical Society, 1966.

White, John H., Jr. *The American Railroad Freight Car: From the Wood-Car Era to the Coming of Steel.* Baltimore: Johns Hopkins University Press, 1993.

White, Kathleen Kelly, and Kathleen White Miles. *The History of Benton County, Missouri.* 2 vols. Warsaw, Mo.: Printery, 1969.

Whitney, Carrie Westlake. *Kansas City, Missouri: Its History and Its People, 1808–1908.* 3 vols. Chicago: S. J. Clarke Publishing Co., 1908.

Whittaker, David J. "Kane, Thomas Leiper." *American National Biography.*

Willoughby, Robert J. *Robidoux's Town: A Nineteenth-Century History of St. Joseph, Missouri.* Westphalia, Mo.: Westphalia Publishing Co., 1997.

Wood, Richard G. *Stephen Harriman Long.* Glendale, Calif.: Arthur H. Clark, 1966.

Zimmer, William E. *Frontier Soldier: An Enlisted Man's Journal of the Sioux and Nez Perce Campaigns, 1877.* Ed. and annotated by Jerome A. Greene. Helena: Montana Historical Society Press, 1998.

Zornow, William Frank. *Kansas: A History of the Jayhawk State.* Norman: University of Oklahoma Press, 1957.

INDEX

References to maps and photographs are set in italic type.